THE INTERNATIONAL LAW OF BAYS

MITCHELL P. STROHL
Commander, U.S. Navy

THE INTERNATIONAL LAW OF BAYS

THE HAGUE
MARTINUS NIJHOFF
1963

ISBN 978-94-015-0381-5 ISBN 978-94-015-0967-1 (eBook)
DOI 10.1007/978-94-015-0967-1

Softcover reprint of the hardcover 1st edition 1963

PREFACE

The purpose of this book is to describe the problems posed in the formulation of international rules for bays at the present time, to investigate the history of the several interests that have influenced the development of such rules, to trace the efforts that have been made to codify the rules, and to suggest a further refinement of the rules.

This book seeks to combine the fruits of the writer's experience as a navigator with those of his studies in international law, geography, history and economics. Although, after study and thought upon the subject, there is likely to arise an initial desire to write a work that is truly definitive, one must resign himself to something of lesser scope. That being so, there is, if anything, an increased demand upon the writer to exercise careful judgment in his research, and in his exposition of the subject. This writer can only hope that he has discharged this responsibility to the degree that his efforts will have clarified some issues and that what he has set on paper may be of some assistance to others.

This writer has attempted to be as objective as possible in his interpretations, and he has made no attempt to defend the policy of any State. In so doing, he is well aware of the fact that for broader policy reasons, some of the views expressed herein cannot be officially accepted as bases for action.

Nothing contained in this writing shall be construed as reflecting the views of the United States Navy or of the United States government.

For assistance in obtaining materials that have been used in the writing of this book I am indebted to a great number of individuals. These persons are listed under a separate title. Above all, I am indebted to Professor Leo Gross in whose person are combined to a remarkable degree the traits of true scholarliness and confident leadership.

Mitchell P. Strohl
Commander, U. S. Navy.

Villennes-sur-Seine, France
1 February 1963.

ACKNOWLEDGEMENTS

Mr. G. A. Rau, Canadian Consul, Boston.
Rear Admiral Robert W. Knox, USC&GS (Ret), International Hydrographic Bureau.
Mr. Robert Miller, Russian Research Center, Harvard University.
Rear Admiral H. Arnold Karo, Director, U. S. Coast and Geographic Survey.
Commander A. B. de Vasconcellos, Brazilian Navy.
Captain S. T. Sun, Chinese Navy.
Captain Takaichi Itaya, Japanese Maritime Self Defense Force.
Professor Norman J. Padelford, Massachusetts Institute of Technology.
Mr. George S. Mitchell, Washington, D. C.
U. S. Naval Intelligence School.
Captain Ernest L. Schwab, Jr. USN, Office of the Chief of Naval Operations.
Dr. Ruth Schachter, African Studies Program, Boston University.
Raytheon Manufacturing Company, Boston, Massachusetts.
Weems & Plath, Inc., Annapolis, Maryland.
Sperry Rand Corporation
Insurance Company of North America
Mr. George Crossette, National Geographic Society.
Professor Keishiro Iriye, Tokyo, Japan.
Colonel A. S. Stewart, U.S.M.C., Military Staff Committee, United Nations.
Mr. Oscar Schachter, United Nations.
Mr. Chafik Malek, United Nations.
Commander H. Sucrow, Federal German Navy.
Professor Myres S. McDougall, Yale University Law School.
Professor Albert Feuerwerker, Center for East Asian Studies, Harvard University.
Lieutenant R. B. Bathurst, U.S.N., Office of the Chief of Naval Operations.

Mr. John DiNapoli, Librarian, U. S. Naval War College.
Mr. George Kirk, Center for Middle East Studies, Harvard University.
U. S. Navy Hydrographic Office.
Commander Myron L. Ogden, U.S.N., Boston Naval Shipyard.
Chief Draftsman John E. Andrews, U.S.N., Headquarters, U. S. European Command.

TABLE OF CONTENTS

LIST OF DIAGRAMS AND CHARTS

PART ONE

INTRODUCTION

CHAPTER ONE

THE PROBLEM OF BAYS IN THE LAW OF THE SEA

Section A NATIONAL SOVEREIGNTY VERSUS FREEDOM OF THE SEAS

The late Professor Brierly wrote:

The line from which territorial waters [1] are measured ceases to follow the sinuosities of the coast when it reaches a bay or other indentation in the coast, both shores of which belong to the same state, and it crosses the waters of the bay from shore to shore. So much is generally admitted, but two important questions remain: (i) what is the character of the waters on the landward side of this imaginary line drawn across the bay? and (ii) where is the line to be drawn? [2]

The foregoing quotation sets forth in its most elementary form the problem of the international law of bays. Although the juridical character of the waters on the landward side of the imaginary line will be discussed in detail, *infra*, we shall accept for the moment the seventeenth century opinion of Lord Hale [3] and the twentieth century

[1] In order to resolve ambiguity in terminology, this writer will substitute the words "marginal belt" for "territorial waters" when referring to a State's coastal waters which are to seaward of the base line and through which a right of innocent passage is normally accorded by International Law. In some instances writers have called these waters "territorial" waters, e.g., Brierly; some have called inland waters "territorial", while others have applied the term 'territorial waters' to both the marginal belt and to inland waters. Examples of the ambiguity: (1) Jessup writes: "There can be no question that such bays are included within the territorial waters of the State." *The Law of Territorial Waters and Maritime Jurisdiction*, p. 358. (2) Moore, in discussing the ten mile line, writes of "the transgression of an encroachment upon territorial waters," 13 *Annuaire de L'Institut de Droit International* (1894–95), p. 146. (3) Cressy writes: "The waters within this three mile limit from the coast are called by Dr. Twiss a State's Jurisdictional Waters; and the term is convenient as distinguishing them from the parts of the sea that are within its ports, havens, and landlocked gulfs, which may be quite correctly called its territorial waters," *First Platform of International Law*, p. 237. Hyde is careful to distinguish the terms, *International Law Chiefly as interpreted and applied by the United States*, 2nd Ed., p. 451, 468. A clearly phrased distinction is contained in Resolution I adopted by the Institute of International Law at its session of Amsterdam, 18–27 Sept. 1957, reprinted in 52 *American Journal of International Law* (Jan. 1958), at pp. 103–5.

[2] James L. Brierly, *The Law of Nations, An Introduction to the International Law of Peace*, 4th Ed., (1949), p. 166.

[3] Lord Chief Justice Hale, *A Treatise Relating to the Maritime Law of England*, p. 10.

opinion of Sir Cecil Hurst,[4] that these waters, hereinafter called "internal waters" [5] are entirely a part of the territory of the littoral state; a part of the national domain,[6] where claims are as complete and absolute as those concerning events upon the land base;[7] internal waters do not generally permit of a right of innocent passage.[8]

The question of where the line is to be drawn is one that has stirred great controversy over the years.[9] This question has been slightly obscured in the United Nations International Law Commission's debate concerning an arbitrary length of this line between low water

[4] Sir Cecil Hurst, "The Territoriality of Bays," *British Yearbook of International Law*, 1922–23, p. 42. See also: A. L. Shalowitz, U. S. Coast and Geodetic Survey, "The Concept of a Bay as Inland Waters," 13 *Surveying and Mapping* (Oct.-Dec. 1953), pp. 432–40.

[5] n1, *supra*. This term will be used by the writer when referring to those waters of a bay which are to landward of the closing line. This is the term used in the 1958 Geneva Convention on the Territorial Sea and Contiguous Zone. Care should be exercised not to confuse the term "internal waters" in the context of this book with the term "inland waters" as used by mariners entering United States coastal waters, where in certain localities they are required to operate under what are called Inland Rules of the Road. United States legislation uses the term "Inland Waters" in specifying where such rules apply. Public Law 232, 83rd Congress (67 Stat. 497). The boundary lines for "Inland Waters" within the meaning of United States Inland Rules of the Road do not necessarily coincide with the base lines delimiting the regime of internal waters as understood in general international law. *United States* v. *Newark Meadows Improvement Co.* 173 Fed. 426 (1909). Boundary lines delimiting U.S. inland waters for purposes of rules of the road are shown in CAPT Raymond F. Farwell USNR, *The Rules of the Nautical Road*, Rev. Ed. by LT Alfred Prunski USCG (1954), pp. 391–6. See also, A. L. Shalowitz, "Where are our Seaward Boundaries?" 83 *U. S. Naval Institute Proceedings* (June 1957), pp. 616–627). Certain French writers have applied the adjective "national" to describe these waters. e.g. Doctor Jean Mochot uses "la mer national" in *Le Régime des Baies et des Golfes en droit International* (1938). Doctor Romée de Villeneuve uses les eaux nationales', in *La Ligne séparative des Eaux nationales et de la Mer Territoriale* (1914). Professor Gidel uses the term "les eaux interieures" in *Le Droit International Public de la Mer* (1934).

[6] Hyde, *op. cit.*, p. 468.

[7] Myres S. McDougal and William T. Burke, "Crisis in the Law of the Sea: Community Perspectives versus National Egoism," 67 *Yale Law Journal* (Feb. 1958), p. 551.

[8] Provision for an exception to the general rule appears in Part I, Art. 5(2) of the Convention on the Territorial Sea and Contiguous Zone (Geneva, 1958) (Hereinafter referred to as the 1958 Geneva Convention) which reads: "Where the establishment of a straight baseline in accordance with Article 4 has the effect of enclosing as internal waters areas which previously had been considered as part of the territorial sea or of the high seas, a right of innocent passage, as provided in Articles 14 to 23, shall exist in those waters." 52 *American Journal of International Law* (1958), p. 835. This provision was recommended by the United Nations International Law Commission in its final draft on the law of the territorial sea. U.N. General Assembly, 11th Session, 6th Committee. *Reference Guide to the Articles concerning the Law of the Sea adopted by the International Law Commission as its Eight Session*, A/C.6/L.378 of 25 Oct. 1956. The Commentary on this recommended provision, contained in General Assembly, Official Records: Eleventh Session, Supplement No. 9 (A/3159), at p. 14, indicates that it was entered to safeguard the rights of foreign States to continued passage after a State has altered its system of baselines, which the commission seemed to conclude was permissible as a result of the decision in *United Kingdom* v. *Norway*. See *International Court of Justice Reports* 1951, pp. 129–130.

[9] *Infra*, Chapters 4 and 5.

marks: 10, 25, 15, or 24 miles.[10] But the length of the line has a great bearing on its position in a bay,[11] and the controversy is ultimately concerned with the position of the line, inasmuch as this will determine the area of internal waters coming under absolute control of the State. It is elementary, of course, to observe that the farther to seaward this line is drawn, the farther beyond will be the boundary between the marginal belt and the high seas.

The foregoing questions, when applied to a particular arm of the sea, assume that such body of water is a geographic bay. The next questions have to do with determining when a bay can be said to exist according to international law. An overview of the matter may be had by considering it as the final of two exceptions. (The so-called historic bay is the third exception – or an exception to the rules for determining the juridical existence of bays in general). Commencing with the marginal belt we observe that this belt is usually measured from what is called the normal base line, the line of the low water mark along the coast.[12] An exception to this normal base line is made where the coastline is deeply indented and cut into, or where there is a fringe of islands along the coast in its immediate vicinity. In such case, the method of straight base lines may be employed in drawing the baselines from

[10] *Infra*, Chapter 5. See also UN Doc. A/C.6/1.378, and Eric Suy, "Les Golfes et les Baies en Droit International Public," 54 *Friedens-Warte* (Nov. 2, 1957), pp. 108–111.

[11] *Infra*, Chapter 2.

[12] Art. 3 of the 1958 Geneva Convention on the Territorial Sea and Contiguous Zone reads: "Except where otherwise provided in these Articles, the normal baseline for measuring the breadth of the territorial sea is the low-water line along the coast as marked on large-scale charts officially recognized by the coastal state." It may be observed that differences in the range of tides and beach gradients in various parts of the world are, in the interest of establishing a general rule, necessarily ignored. Likewise ignored are differences in showing low-tide marks, or "reference planes," as among the several charting systems in use in the world today: Mean low water, mean lower low water, and mean low water springs. Hill, Utegaard and Riordan, *Dutton's Navigation and Piloting* (1958), p. 203. Detailed comments on this matter were received by the preparatory committee for the 1930 Hague Codification Conference, 24 *American Journal of International Law, Supplement* (1930), p. 30. The 1958 Geneva Conference, on the recommendation of the International Law Commission, considered that detailed provisions could be omitted inasmuch as it was not believed that such omission would induce governments to shift low-water lines on their charts unreasonably. UN Committee of Experts Report, A/CN.4/61/Add.1; UN Doc. A/3159, p. 13; UN Doc. A/C6/L.378, pp. 24–5; Gidel, in *Le Droit international public de la Mer* (1934), Tome III, discusses the matter of tidal differences in some detail at pages 517 to 521. At page 520 he includes a table showing the chart reference planes of various maritime States. In connection with the clause, "on large-scale charts officially recognized by the coastal state," Sub-Committee No. II of the 1930 Hague Conference reported: "Not every State, it is true, possesses official charts published by its own hydrographic services but every Coastal State has some chart adopted as official by the State authorities." The UN Committee of Experts recommended that, "if no detailed charts of the area have been drawn, which show the low-water line, the shore line (high-water line) should be used." It may fairly be conjectured that if a coastal State has any interest at all in its seaward boundary, it will take appropriate steps to measure the low-water mark and adopt an "Official" chart.

which the marginal belt is measured.[13] Waters to landward of such base lines are part of the internal waters of the State.[14] There exists no rule on the maximum length of base lines,[15] and the opinion of the International Court of Justice in *United Kingdom* v. *Norway* suggests that a universal rule for such base lines would be most difficult to establish. In that case, the court simply ruled that the base lines must follow the general direction of the coast.[16] The ruling finds subsequent expression in Article 4 (2) of the 1958 Geneva Convention on the Territorial Sea and Contiguous Zone which reads, *inter alia,*

The drawing of such base lines must not depart to any appreciable extent from the general direction of the coast....

The second exception is provided for in connection with those arms of the sea which are geographically classed as bays. Bays are indentations which also call for straight base lines, but international law now gives some precision to the configuration and area of the enclosed internal waters. Since the early half of the Nineteenth century, international conventions and judicial bodies have come to express in miles the maximum allowable width of a bay other than a "historic" bay.[17] It will be observed that the fixed-length base line for enclosing internal waters applies only to the case of bays. This raises the question as to what, juridically speaking, is a bay. Within the community of States there has arisen in the twentieth century the desire to seek agreement upon some mathematical criteria by which an arm of the sea, whatever given name it may bear, can be classified in International Law as a bay.[18]

[13] Art. 4 of 1958 Geneva Convention on the Territorial Sea and the Contiguous Zone.

[14] Art. 5 of 1958 Geneva Convention on the Territorial Sea and the Contiguous Zone.

[15] In the various Meetings of the United Nations International Law Commission, efforts were made – and then abandoned – to apply an arithmetic rule to the establishment of base lines. The Committee of Experts recommended a maximum length of ten miles. UN Doc. A/6N.4/61/Add. 1. For a discussion of the rationale (limit of vision) behind a 10-mile rule, see Chapter 5. *infra*. In its Third Meeting, the Commission adopted the recommendation and further agreed that every such line should be drawn within five miles of the coast. UN Doc. A/CN.4/77, p. 7. UN Doc. A/C.6/L.378, p. 30. Subsequently, the Commission recommended, and the Geneva Conference adopted, rules more in line with the opinion in *United Kingdom* v. *Norway.*

[16] *International Court of Justice Reports* 1951, pp. 129–130.

[17] See *infra*, Chapter 5, for a discussion of the development of this formula, and efforts at codification.

[18] *Ibid.* The apparent need for such criteria was evident in the North Atlantic Coast Fisheries Arbitration of 1910. In that case, the tribunal was directly confronted with the problem of defining a bay. The tribunal, in its opinion, said that it was "unable to understand the term 'bays' .... in other than its geographical sense, by which a bay is to be considered as an indentiation of a coast, bearing a configuration of a particular character easy to determine specifically, but difficult to describe generally." There followed in the opinion

Preoccupation with formulae for determining the extent of a State's internal waters should in no wise obscure what is really the fundamental problem of territorial waters in International Law: the constant and nearly universal contest between those who defend the principle of freedom of the seas and those who espouse enlarging the exclusive sovereignty of States over coastal waters.[19] This struggle is one of the oldest in recorded history.[20] The special situation of internal waters, and bays in particular, is really only a part of the overall problem. And the views which States may have upon the problem, and the special interests which generate such views, are subject to the dynamics of continuous change. But alongside this dynamism is the equally urgent demand for stability, stemming as it usually does from the desire on the part of at least one of the principals to preserve the *status quo* and from the desire of a host of "objects" of the law who simply want rules that are permanent, reliable, and understandable.

In the 1951 Fisheries case, (*United Kingdom* v. *Norway*), the British Government in its reply to the Norwegian counter-memorial said that there must be a certain degree of precision in the rules regulating the conflicting interests.[21] In subsequent comment on this case, Charles de Visscher, a former judge of the International Court of Justice, wrote that the problem of delimiting territorial sovereignty in bays is at present insoluble on the plane of international law.[22] Much on

descriptive language which can be interptered, not inaccurately, as saying that a bay is something shaped like a bay. One of the tribunal, Dr. Luis Drago, dissented vigorously, saying, in part, "But no rule is laid out or general principle evolved for the parties to know what the nature of such configuration is or by what methods the points should be ascertained from which the bay should lose the characteristics as such. There lies the whole contention, and the whole difficulty...." Vol. I, *Senate Document No. 870, 61st, Congress, 3rd Session*, pp. 93–112.

[19] Reply of the United Kingdom, *I.C.J. Reports*, 1951, Vol. II, p. 416.

[20] See Section B., *Origins*, *infra*, pp. 8–10,

[21] *I.C.J. Reports*, 1951, Vol. II, p. 416. The United Kingdom Government requested the Court to make certain precise pronouncements in its decision, including a 10-mile ruling on the closure line for bays. This the court declined to do. One can discuss at great length, and without much productive result, the likely motives behind this request and the long run value of making it at all. Superficially, a positive ruling by the court, has some merit. It has great appeal to those who seek neat, tidy, solutions: Dr. Rommée de Villeneuve wrote in his 1914 thesis: "On ne concevrait plus, de nos jours, un État qui ne soit pas fixé sur un territoire nettement délimité." *La Ligne séparative des Eaux nationales et de la Mer territoriale*, p. 9. From here, the argument on borders and the obsolescence of the system of nation state territorial sovereignty can proceed indefinitely. De Lapradelle wholly understated the situation when he wrote: "Le phénomène politique de la frontière n'est pas un phénomène simple." Paul G. de Lapradelle, *La Frontière* (1928 doctoral thesis, University of Paris) p. 14.

[22] Judge de Visscher wrote further: "Authors, who, like Professor Schücking, have taken a different position have been guided less by objective observation of the state of the law in force than by a spirit of generalization that pushed them to codify the matter." *Theory and Reality in Public International Law*, Tr. by P. E. Corbett (1957), p. 215. The Professor

both points of view will be discussed in this book. It is suggested at this early juncture, that all facets of the problem require examination and understanding. It has occasionally been the thought of this author that lawyers and policy makers have not attempted to understand maritime boundaries as they are seen through the eyes of mariners – the group of individual actors to whom the law on bays is ultimately addressed. But it would certainly be "unscientific" [23] to discuss the International Law of Bays solely as it seen by mariners; the issues and their myriad underlying forces are far too important to allow to be settled on the basis of what happens to be convenient to a few thousand professional seamen. On the other hand, the technical problems of the navigator must be understood if any projected rules on delimiting sovereignty at sea are to have feasibility. It is for this reason, that the author, a naval officer by profession, has undertaken to explain at some length the rudiments of these problems.

At its base, it is reiterated, the controversy on the law of bays involves the espousal of one or the other of two solidly established principles of International Law: freedom of the seas and territorial sovereignty. The main prize is the economic bounty to be extracted from the section of the earth's surface that happens to be in dispute.

Section B(i) Origins of the problem

A cursory glance at the literature on the law of the sea may suggest that the special branch having to do with bays is a comparatively recent field of consideration. Doctor Mochot indicated that early conventional law mentions bays only in a vague and incidental way, the first treaty known to have contained the word being that concluded between the Emperor Charles V and King Francis I on 2 August 1521.[1] This writer

Schücking, to whom Judge de Visscher refers, prepared the draft convention for the 1930 Codification Conference. UN *Memorandum on Historic Bays*, A/Conf.13/1, p. 44; *League Publication V*, Legal, 1927, V. 1, p. 58.

[23] When applied to the social field of law, the adjective, "scientific," appears to refer to a method of analysis combining precise observation and objective reasoning. Harriett Martineau, *The Positive Philosophy of Auguste Comte* (1853), Vol. I, p. 16; Will Durant, *The Story of Philosophy* (1926), p. 352; Julius Stone, *The Province and Function of Law*, (1946), pp. 401–2; Hans Kelsen, *General Theory of Law and State* (1949), p. 438. Obviously, the social fields seldom pose problems yielding solutions having the finality of euclidean geometry.

[1] Jean Mochot, *Le Régime des Baies et des Golfes en Droit international* (1938). Like Mochot, this writer has drawn his conclusions largely from a study of: du Mont, *Corps universel diplomatique du Droit des Gens contenant un Recueil des Traités* (1731) and (Un ancien) Diplomate, *Le Régime des Capitulations, son Histoire, son Application, ses Modifications* (1898). The conclusion is fortified by the comments of a number of authors cited hereinafter.

has been unable to arrive at any different conclusion through his own research.

But as suggested in the preceding section, the law on bays is in the nature of an exception to that having to do with internal waters in general.[2] Moreover, we are reminded by the recent fisheries case of *United Kingdom* v. *Norway* that there exists a difference of opinion as to whether the regime of territorial waters (and of internal waters) is a truncated relic of far greater pretentions to sovereingty over the seas, or whether such a regime represents an encroachment upon areas of the earth's surface which were always *res nullius*.[3] Sir Henry Maine writes that one of the most disputed of all questions at the birth of international law was the question of *mare clausum* and *mare liberum*.[4] The United Kingdom Reply in *United Kingdom* v. *Norway* maintains that the transition from ancient history to modern times took place in the sixteenth century when the regime of *mare clausum* commenced progressively to be superceded by the principle of *mare liberum*.[5] Review of the writings of Selden and Grotius,[6] the two seventeenth century protagonists in the question of *mare liberum* and *mare clausum* inspire some curiosity as to the more ancient roots of this controversy. There is the suggestion that the Grotius-Selden arguments represented a sort of crescendo which had been preceded by a lengthy period of gathering intensity during which States or Empires made, accommodated themselves to, or contested various claims to sovereignty over territorial seas. There lurks the thought-provoking social question whether dominion over sheets of sea water near the coast stems from man's use and need of these waters or from his avarice or uncompromising desire for exclusive owner ship.

Proceeding to the beginnings of civilization, we are struck by the suggestion of von Martens, writing in 1802:

> Originally everything, and consequently the sea, the rivers, etc., belonged to all the world in common.[7]

[2] pp. 5–6, *supra*.

[3] *International Court of Justice Reports* 1951, Vol. II, p. 309.

[4] Sir Henry Maine, *International Law* (1888), p. 75. This view seems to be shared by Professor Percy Corbett in a much more recent wotk. *Law in Diplomacy* (1959), Ch. IV.

[5] *I.C.J. Reports*, 1951, Vol. II, p. 312.

[6] Hugo Grotius, *The Freedom of the Seas*, first published in 1608. The version here is the Magoffin translation, published by the Carnegie Endowment for International Peace in 1916.

[7] G. F. Von Martens, *A Compendium of the Law of Nations*, Tr. William Cobbett (1802), p. 160.

Selden and Huet, by invoking the Holy Scriptures, argue that the change came after the great flood and its final abatement, at which time the sons of Noah divided the earth.[8]

Referring to the conclusions of other scholars of early social development, we are, in general, left with the impression that von Martens' suggestion of 1802 is a valid one. The sea seems to have been in some sense similar to a jungle: useful for some things, an area from which marauders sometimes appeared, but belonging to no one.[9] In fact, in tribal societies, it appears that territory, whether land or water, was not a ground of community in political functions; the sole ground was kinship in blood.[10] When we turn to the origins of the law of property, we are constrained to conclude that the conception of a possibility of dominion over any part of a water area was born at a period considerably later than the time when ownership of land or some sort of communal sovereignty came to be recognized and understood.[11] On the other hand, it appears that use of the water as a medium of transport is likely to be as pre-historic as the beginning of agriculture.[12]

It is this author's conclusion, after reflection upon the studies of a number of scholars and writers, that the origin of a communal proprietary attitude toward any part of the sea lies with the beginnings of commerce and the communal development of ports. The port of Patala in what is now modern Hyderabad existed seven thousand years before the Christian era. The port of Ur in Asia Minor is said to have been in existence in 2250 B.C.[13]

Contemporary with the most early use of waters for commerce and

[8] John Selden, *Mare Clausum; the Right and Dominion of the Sea*, Tr. by J. H., Gent, (1663). All page references hereinafter are to this edition of Selden's work; M. Huet, *Histoire du Commerce et de la Navigation des Anciens* (1773), pp. 7–11. These authors refer to the Book of Genesis, Chs. 8–10.

[9] LCDR John Forsyth Meigs USN (RET), *The Story of the Seaman*, (1912) pp. 3–10; Frank C. Bowen, *The Sea, Its History and Romance* (1924) Vol. I.; A. Du Sein, *Histoire de la Marine de Tous les Peuples* (1879) Vol. I. The Meigs work shows evidence of protracted and careful scholarship by a devoted American officer whose promising naval career was cut short by physical infirmity.

[10] Sir Henry Maine, *Early History of Institutions* (1888); pp. 378–382; B. Malinowski, *Crime and Custom in Early Society* (1926), pp. 50–59; E. Adamson Hoehl, *The Law of Primitive Man* (1954), pp. 121–3; I. Shapera, *Government and Politics in Tribal Societies* (1956), p. 2; Sir Henry Maine, *Ancient Law* (1888) Holt Edition, p. 124; Julius Stone, *The Province and Function of Law* (1946) pp. 451–7.

[11] Maine, *Ancient Law*, Ch. VIII; Maine, *Early History of Institutions*; Lauterpacht, *Private Law Sources and Analogies of International Law* (1927), pp. 91–106, concerning analogy between law of property and territorial sovereignty.

[12] Meigs, *op. cit.*, pp. 6–9. H. A. Calahan, *The Sky and the Sailor, A History of Celestial Navigation* (1952), Ch. I. The Calahan book is one written for the general reading public.

[13] Hewitt, *Ruling Races in Prehistoric Times* (1894–5), p. 140. Pariset, *Histoire de la Soie*, p. 121.

with the beginnings of ports was their use for piratical marauding against peaceful users of the sea and against peoples on shores. Historians of the antiquity indicate that such marauding and plunder were the ordinary practice of early communities.[14] As peoples learned to pool their strength, they also increased their vested interests in coastal communities and water borne commerce, and some saw the advantage of protecting their gains and living more or less peacefully. It was then that they united to defend themselves against piratical depradations and to make rules governing entrance to their ports in coastal indentations and estuaries. A port became a place of protection against man's predatory and encroaching fellow man as well as against the elements. It appears conclusive that pretensions toward possession of an arm of the sea sprang not from any rapacious ambitions of social groups or their rulers, but from the need for protection.[15] Thus, there was early recognized the possibility of a dominion over a port of the seas. Peoples of the Levant, well prior to the Greek and Roman eras, took the attitude that it was quite possible to create and maintain a dominion over a sea area comparable to that exercised on land.[16] But it is the extent and legal nature of such dominion that is of primary concern to us.

It can be observed that in the very ancient times, declarations pretending to the possession of vast areas of the seas came to be expressed concurrently with, or subsequent to, the general utilization of already developed techniques in the art of navigation. Ships sailed very long distances in open seas before the time when techniques of navigation are known to have existed. But even after such techniques had been perfected, most shipping did not willingly depart from the sight of land. There appear to be several reasons for this: First, the findings and theories of astronomers and other scholars were slow in

[14] James Reddie, *Researches Historical and Critical in Maritime International Law* (1844), pp. 23–4; Huet, *op. cit.*, pp. 12–18; Selden, *op. cit.*, pp. 17–42; Mauritius Müller-Jochmus, *Geschichte des Völkerrechts im Altertum* (1848), pp. 17–20; Domenico A. Azuni, *The Maritime Law of Europe* (1806), pp. 1–8; Voltaire, *A Philosophical Dictionary* (English Edition of London, 1824) Vol. V, pp. 240–2; Charles Malloy, *A Treatise of Affairs, Maritime and Commerce*, 3rd Ed. (1682), pp. 29–38. The writer is especially indebted to the work of Henry A. Ormerod, whose work, *Piracy in the Ancient World* (1924), is a scholary and thoroughly documented book indicating research that would be difficult to equal.

[15] Sir Henry Maine writes: "The closing of seas meant delivery from violent depradation at the cost of or by the exertion of some power or powers stronger than the rest." *International Law*, p. 77. This is an obvious conclusion to be drawn from Plutarch's life of Cimon, *Plutarch's Lives* (Modern Library Edition) pp. 577–592; Müller-Jochmus, *op. cit.*, pp. 236–8, citing Herodotus, Bk. VII, and Aristotle, Bk. II.

[16] Coleman Phillipson, *The International Law of Ancient Greece and Rome* (1911) Vol. II, p. 367; John Selden, *op. cit.*, Chs. 6, 10; Pitman B. Potter, *The Freedom of the Seas in History, Law and Politicus* (1924), p. 11.

coming to the attention of and finding acceptance by seamen, who were obviously members of a different segment of society. Second, ships were small, slow, and comparatively unseaworthy, and they often required shelter from the weather.[17] Third, there was an inherent and deep-seated fear by the land-animal, man, of the un-natural and unknown environment of the sea. It can fairly be concluded, after a review of the evidence, that for a long period after navigation techniques had been perfected and published, long sea voyages out of sight of land were the adventuresome exceptions to the older practices founded on caution and superstition. It is believed that, only after the writing of the *Almagest* and *Geographica* of Claudius Ptolemy about 150 A.D., the more advanced distribution and utilization of knowledge by the Romans, and the evolution of more generally seaworthy ships, sailing out of sight of land came into general practice.[18]

By the time such sailings were common for mariners, port construction and utilization were highly developed. Piracy also proceeded apace, and it became customary for some communities to prohibit all foreigners from entry to sheltered waters, however friendly the ingress might be or however compelling might be the conditions of *force majeur*. Here it becomes difficult to assess the evidence in order to determine whether continued and firm unilateral possession of ports and sheltered arms of the sea were for purposes of protection of the ports and coasts as against pirates, or for purposes of robbing and enslaving the mariners seeking trade or shelter. Perhaps both motives were equally at play, but one is relieved of any doubt concerning the possession of

[17] Naval architecture of the antiquity has been quite thoroughly studied as is evident by the plethora of carefully written books on the subject and by the number of reproductions of ancient ships that have been constructed. Homer describes the ships in some detail in the *Oddysey*. For comments on their lack of seaworthiness, see: LeRoy, *La Marine des Anciens Peuples* (1777), pp. 28–35; J. L. Torr, *Ancient Ships* (1894), p. 5 *et seq*; Arthur MacCartney Shepard, *Sea Power in Ancient History* (1924), p. 12.

[18] Levin Goldschmidt, "Universalgeschichte des Handelsrechts," Part I, Tr. John H. Wigmore, *Primitive and Ancient Legal Institutions* (1915), Albert Kocourek and John H. Wigmore, Eds., p. 411. Goldschmidt writes "... as the art of seamanship developed, and the observation of the heavens increased their knowledge of astronomy (amounting in Babylon to a veritable science), voyages on the high seas were made as early as the Phoenician period." Frederick J. Pohl and CAPT Leonard B. Loeb USNR (Ret) write that as early as 146 to 126 B. C., Hiparchos, the Greek astronomer on the island of Rhodes, established the geographical system of latitude and longitude, "Americo Vespucci, Pioneer Celo-Navigator and Geographer," 83 *U.S. Naval Institute Proceedings* (Apr. 1957), p. 399ff. But Meigds, *op. cit.*, Chs. 1–2; and Bowen, *op. cit.*, Vol. I, who have related their studies to the whole body of the maritime arts, lead one to the conclusion that high seas navigation and sailing were much slower to eventuate in general practice than some of the accomplishments of early astronomers and the recorded histories of some adventurers would suggest. See also: Per Collinder, *A History of Marine Navigation* (1954), Chs. I–III; Baron de Montesquieu, *The Spirit of Laws*, Tr. Thomas Nugent (1900), Vol. I, pp. 334–349; Bowditch, *American Practical Navigator*, 1958 Edition, pp. 15–29.

such water areas by the littoral communities and the general acceptance by all communities that such possession and control were matters of ownership and of right.[19]

In view of the above argument, it is the opinion of this writer that possession and control of what are now known as internal waters were established and accepted considerably before the advent of larger claims. We must now proceed to examine the scope, nature, and degree of acceptance of early claims to dominion over areas which we would consider the high seas.

It is generally agreed that the Kingdom of Minos in Crete first made claims to areas of the high seas. According to the studies of Doctor Phillipson, the Minoan sea empire existed during the fifteenth century before Christ. For a long period subsequent thereto, according to Eusebius, there was a succession of rulers who sought to preserve control of the waters over the eastern Mediterranean and the Levant. In general, it appears that historians and publicists have drawn their conclusions concerning such "dominion" from the writings of Herodotus, Eusebius, Indorus Sicubus, Seneca, and Aristotle. John Selden invoked these writings in his *Mare Clausum*, as did Huet, Azuni, Pardessus, and Justice.[20] Professor Potter, in his book *The Freedom of the Seas in History, Law, and Politics*, discussed these claims and concluded that they could not be evidence of a legal concept of maritime dominion, because, he says, the concept of interstate law itself had not yet emerged.[21] Mauritius Müller-Jochmus, on the other hand, argues that there was in the minds of the ancients a *rechtsansicht* (legal idea) of sea dominion.[22] John Selden argues at great length in an effort to demonstrate that legal dominon was grounded in a substantial body of state practice. He writes that arguments against such dominion by reason of the nature of the sea itself are without merit [23] and cites the Scriptural writings concerning Noah as initial evidence.[24] Cornelius van

[19] Ormerod, *op. cit.*, p. 154.

[20] Azuni, *op. cit.*, pp. 24–32; Selden, *op. cit.*, bk i, ch. 3. M. Huet, *Histoire du Commerce et de la Navigation des Anciens*, (1716), Ch. VII; Pardessus, *Us et Coutumes de la Mer* (1847) Ch. I; Justice, *A General Treatise of the Dominion of the Sea* (1710), pp. 16–24. Within these pages, Justice has prepared a sort of brief digest on sea sovereignty, complete with references to ancient writers.

[21] Professor Pitman B. Potter, *The Freedom of the Seas in History Law, and Politics* (1924), p. 15.

[22] Mauritius Müller-Jochmus, *Geschichte des Völkerrechts im Altertum* (1848), p. 237.

[23] John Selden, *op. cit.*, pp. 4–5, 127–135.

[24] He cites the Book of Genesis I : 2, 28 in which it is written that after the Great Flood, the Lord permitted Noah to divide the earth and the seas into dominions over which his sons were to rule. Apparently, this Divine guidance was, in the eyes of Selden, sufficient to quash any argument against possession of the sea by reason of its nature. Huet also uses this argument, commencing his historical analysis with the abatement of the Great Flood.

Bynkershoek, arguing chiefly on the basis of the Roman law of property, writes that "possession [of the sea] seems to extend out as far in the sea as the sea can be held in subjection to the land." [25]

Mindful of the truism that the Bible has the facility to substantiate either side of this question, as well as a wide variety of other controversies, it is of some interest to note that the Old Testament, in some passages concerning territory, clearly points out that possession terminates at the sea.[26] In passing, it might be worthy of mention that The Qur'an, appearing in the Seventh century of the Christian era and prescribing the law for the Muslim community, seemingly ignores the secular concept of territory altogether.[27]

When subjected to the standard of recognized right, the evidence of ancient practice and behavior would indicate considerable difference between possession of a port or sheltered arm of the sea and asserted domain over vast sea areas, although there appears no evidence of any effort to erect boundaries between them. Herodotus tells us of the great privileges granted to merchants by Naucratis, a city on the Nile delta. He writes that if anyone arrived at any other mouth of the Nile he was obliged to take an oath that he had come there against his will, and then sail in the same vessel to the Canupic Mouth; but if stress of weather prevented his doing so, he was compelled to unload his cargo and convey it in barges around the delta and land it at Naucratis, "which had an exclusive privilege." [28] In about 431 B.C. the towns of Aeantheia and Chalaum on the gulf of Crissa concluded a treaty securing the total discontinuance of seizures in ports and restricting the practice to the open sea.[29] During the Phoenician era, the harbors of Tyre and Sidon were subject to entrance and internal regulations

[25] Cornelius van Bynkershoek, "De Dominio Maris Dissertatis," Tr. R. V. Magoffin. *The Classics of International Law*, James B. Scott, Ed., p. 43.

[26] Numbers 34 : 10; Joshua 15–20; Psalm 95 : 15 reads, *inter alia*, "The sea is his, for He made it"; Psalm 115 : 16 reads, *inter alia*, "but the earth He has given to the sons of men." Of passing interest is the fact that the word bay is mentioned four times in the King James version of the Bible as follows: Joshua 15 : 2, 5: Joshua 18 : 19 and Acts 27 : 39. References in the Book of Joshua concern the termination of a land boundary at a bay in the Dead Sea. A reference in the Book of Acts concerns a bay used as shelter during a voyage of the apostle Paul; John W. Ellison, *Nelson's Complete Concordance of the Revised Standard Version Bible* (1952), p. 133.

[27] Abdullah Yosuf Ali, *The Holy Qur'an, Text, Translation and Commentary*, 2 vols (1946). According to Majid Khadduri, Muslim law defines the status of the territory with respect to the Muslim community, not the status of the Muslim in relation to territory. Since the allegiance of the dwellers in a community appears to be the basis of territorial sovereignty under Muslim law, it would appear illogical for Muslim law to provide for sovereignty over other than land areas. *War and Peace in the Law of Islam* (1955), pp. 154–8.

[28] "The History of Herodotus," Bk. II, Sect. 179. *Great Books of the Western World*, Vol. 6, p. 87.

[29] Phillipson, *op. cit.*, p. 70.

quite similar to those regulating today's shipping in ports throughout the world.[30] Caesar writes of the people of western Gaul who had but a few ports lying here and there "which are in their possession."[31] In Chapter XVI of his *Mare Clausum*, John Selden argues that private ownership of the seas was customary under the Romans and in the Eastern Empire. As usual, his citations and quotations provide rather rebuttable evidence for his contentions when they are subjected to the strong light of verification.[32] What this author's partial verification has disclosed is that the authorities had in mind small ports or arms of the sea: ports, bays, and estuaries, and that State possession of them was well understood and accepted.

It is believed that the first reported example of conventional law providing for dominion over a portion of the high seas is that mentioned in Plutarch's biography of the Greek naval commander, Cimon. This treaty, which John Selden describes as having "shut the Greek Seas to the Emperor," [of the Persians][33] is said by Plutarch to have been concluded after a naval battle between forces commanded by Cimon of Athens and Xerxes, King of the Persians. The passage in "Cimon" referred to by Selden reads (Dryden Translation):

> The success of Cimon so daunted the King of Persia that he presently made that celebrated peace by which he engaged that his armies should come no nearer the Grecian face than the length of a horse's course, and that none of his galleys or vessels of war should appear between the Cyanean and Chalidonean isles.[34]

Müller-Jochmus places the year of this treaty at 494 B.C., [35] while Professor Potter indicates that it was concluded in 478 B.C.[36] In any event, these dates are contemporaneous with those struggles of the Greek cities with the Persian invaders which reached their decisive battle at Salamis. Thereafter, the Persian strength receded and the Greeks were relieved of the threat from the east. But there hangs heavy doubt as to whether the treaty mentioned by Plutarch and cited by Selden was in fact ever concluded. The Greek wars with the Persians have been described in detail by a number of ancient and modern

30 Philip K. Hitti, *Lebanon in History* (1957), p. 99. citing *Strabo*, Bk. XVI, Ch. 23.

31 Julius Caesar, *Gallic Wars*, Bk. III, Ch. 8, cited by John Selden, *op. cit.*, p. 76.

32 Regretfully, the author does not have a reading knowledge of Latin or Greek, and was thus prevented from verifying all citations.

33 Selden, *op. cit.*, p. 93.

34 Plutarch, "Cimon," *Plutarch's Lives* (Modern Library Edition), p. 587. Instead of "galleys or vessels of war," Selden's own translation reads "a ship built long or beaked." According to LeRoy (*op. cit.*, p. 84) long or beaked vessels were, characteristically, warships.

35 Müller-Jochmus, *op. cit.*, p. 243.

36 Pitman Potter, *op. cit.*, p. 18.

historians,[37] but only in Plutarch's life of Cimon is it said that this treaty was actually made. Rudolph von Scala in his work, *Die Staatsverträge des Altertums* (1898), does not cite this treaty although his work contains a substantial number of treaties solemnized during and after the Persian War period. The student of international law or the navigator bent on drawing on a chart the maritime barrier suggested by Plutarch is likely to encounter disappointment if he envisions some line enclosing a portion of the Aegean Sea. Actually the Cyanean Isles were located in the Black Sea off the entrance to the Bosphorus,[38] and the Chalidonian Isles were off the southwest shore of Asia Minor, near the cape now known by the Turks as Gelidonya Burnu.[39] Instead of a "horse's course," Doctor Curtius called the distance one day's cavalry march; its significance is that the Persian armies were not to approach any nearer to the Aegean coast than that distance.[40] In his final comment on this purported treaty, Doctor Curtius writes:

> The contemporary historians offer no information, while in subsequent generations such a mass of unintelligible and contradictory traditions accumulated round this treaty that it is impossible to discover the true state of the case.[41]

Althought the treaty, even if it had been concluded, would not have seen a geographical closure or demarcation of a portion of the sea, it is of some interest to us that ouch a treaty was contemplated at all. Historians seem to agree that there was an Embassy of the Athenian Callias to the court of Artaxerxes for the purpose of negotiating the treaty.[42] Moreover, there is evidence that at the height of their power, the then independent Greek city states contemplated the establishment of a legal regime for the Aegean. A conference of ambassadors was convened for the purpose. The conference was a failure, we are told, by reason of the uncooperative position taken by Sparta.[43]

[37] e.g. Herodotus, VI,; Thycidides, VII; Shepard, *op. cit.*; Meigs *op. cit.*, G. Grote. *History of Greece* (1864), Vols. II, V; Dr. Ernest Curtius, *The History of Greece* (1883), Vols. II, III; George W. Cox, *The Tale of the Great Persian War* (1861); ADM Sir Reginald Custance, Royal Navy, *War at Sea, Modern Theory and Practice* (1919).

[38] Dr. William Smith, *A Dictionary of Greek and Roman Geography* (1878), Vol. I, pp. 424–606.

[39] National Geographic Society Plate 47 of Jan 1959; "Lands of the Eastern Mediterranean."

[40] Curtius, *op. cit.*, Vol. II, p. 454. Giuseppina Lombardo interpreted the Greek writing as meaning "three-days' journey" by road. See n.41, *infra*.

[41] Actually, the treaty was the objective of the Embassy of an Athenian citizen, Callias, to the court of Artaxerxes, King and heir of his father who commanded the Persian invading forces. Curtius writes that Artaxerxes would have felt no compulsion to sign the treaty and that it is highly unlikely that he would have so acceded to the wishes of the Greeks. Curtius, *op. cit.*, p. 455. In *Cimon, Ricostruzione della Biographica e Discussioni Storografiche* (1934), Signorina Giuseppina Lombardo attempts to unravel the strands of the treaty story, and concludes that it is unlikely that such a treaty was signed (pp. 128–138).

[42] Curtius, *op. cit.*, Vol. I, p. 454.

[43] *Plutarch's Lives*, "Pericles," p. 197.

The two events discussed above would suggest that the ancient Greeks had some notions concerning a positive international law of the sea. While one effort definitely ended in failure and the other probably met the same fate, the germ was certainly there. Moreover, there is certainly evidence that the waters immediately adjacent to and part of a port were considered to be under the absolute control of the community enjoying sovereignty over the land. We are therefore constrained to differ somewhat from the sweeping statement of Professor Potter in his conclusion that there is no evidence of the recognition of a law of nations.[44] We are more likely to accept the suggestion of M. Hautefeuille who wrote: "Quelques auteurs ont prétendu que le droit international avait été inconnu chez les anciens; je regarde cette opinion une erreur." [45]

Any lingering doubts in the premises are laid to rest by the more recent study of Professor Georges Ténékideş. He demonstrates convincingly that the ancient Greek city States developed and carried into practice a body of rules of inter-State law and orginazation the context of which bears striking resemblance to similar rules in the present era.[46]

We should now attempt to ascertain whether there was in this germinating maritime law of nations any conscious distinction between control over waters in port areas and such control over larger areas, that is to say, over the high seas. Historians have attributed wide maritime dominion to the Greeks and to earlier rulers in Crete and Tyre, but such dominion was never defined either in extent or in nature. Doctor Phillipson declares that the ancients' terms: "ruler of the sea," "lord and master of the sea" and "to have command of the sea" were used with varying meanings. It was his conclusion that they were seldom used in a sense of complete ownership and that they designated a "temporary supremacy or predominating influence."[47] Professor Potter writes that the Greeks regarded sea dominion as a matter of military power and that they did not lay down any formal rules of legal right.[48] Baron Malouet, writing in 1810, invites our attention to

[44] Pitman Potter, *op. cit.*, p. 15.

[45] L. B. Hautefeuille, *Histoire des Origines, des Progrès, et des Variations du Droit maritime international* (1858), p. 83.

[46] George Ténékideş, "Droit international et Communautés féderales dans la Grèce des Cités" 90 *Recueil des Cours de l'Académie de Droit international de la Haye* (1956), vol. II, pp. 475–636.

[47] Phillipson, *op. cit.*, vol. II, p. 376.

[48] Pitman Potter, *op. cit.*, p. 25.

the words of an Athenian orator enjoining his city to refrain from doing so:

On a eu l'occasion d'observer, dit Isocrate, que tous les peuples de laGrèce qui ont eu l'empire de la mer, ou qui ont seulement osé y aspirer, se sont précipités dans un abîme affreux de désastres et de calamités: cette domination, ajoute-t-il, n'est pas naturelle; c'est une chimère qui ennivre tellement les hommes qu'elle leur ôte le sens commun; et ils s'attirent tant d'ennemis, et des ennemis si redoutables, qu'il leur est impossible d'y résister à la longue.[49]

It is the conclusion of this writer that the dominion exercised over portions of the high seas by the ancient Greeks was either for purposes of police action against pirates, or for defense against invaders.[50] There is no evidence that dominion was recognized *de jure* by other states, Rather, it appears to this writer that the purported dominion over the sea finds its modern day counterpart in the geopolitical concept of sea power, or command of the sea.[51]

Thus, in the earliest origins of an international law of bays, we perceive the emergence of three ideas:

(a) That there was a halting, incomplete, but discernible move on the part of the ancient Greeks to enact into positive international law a regime for the Greek seas.

(b) That there was an earlier recognition of the right of the littoral state to the waters of a port, such port usually being in a sheltered arm of the sea, that is a bay. This recognized right can be said, not inaccurately, to have ripened into customary law.

(c) That there is in evidence a distinction between the attitude taken toward the waters of ports and the attitude toward dominion over greater areas of the seas. Although there is no evidence of a commonly understood line of demarcation between the inner seas and the high seas, there is considerable evidence that, starting with the Greeks, interested society clearly understood that two separate concepts of control were involved.

In view of the early conceptual separation between pretensions toward dominion over high seas, and the beginnings of a regime of internal waters, further consideration of the origins of the law of bays will be more confined to developments in the regime of internal waters.

[49] Baron Malouet, *Considérations historiques sur l'Empire de la Mer chez les Anciens et les Modernes* (1810), p. 7.

[50] Plutarch described Cimon's performance as a sea commander thus: "He made the Aegean a free sea." *Plutarch*, "Cimon" p. 587.

[51] Friedrich Ratzel, *Das Meer als Quelle der Völkergrösse. Eine Politisch-geographische Studie* (1900); RADM Alfred T. Mahan USN (RET), *The Interest of America in Sea Power, Present and Future* (1918); James A. Field, Jr., "Sea Power and Military Strategy Today," VIII *U.S. Naval War College Review* (Apr. 1956), pp. 21–39.

It is proposed that hereinafter discussion of the regime of the high seas or that of marginal belt be limited to those instances where obvious ambiguities emerge or where there is a distinct relationship between those regimes and the narrower matters of internal waters and bays.

Section B(ii) THE ROMAN PERIOD

The Romans entertained a strictly utilitarian attitude toward the sea and, as a great land power with many outlets to the sea, displayed no desire to exercise powers of sovereignty over the sea. Their interest was to keep the sea free for waterborne commerce, and especially the commerce with the granaries of Egypt and the North African littoral. As with the Greeks, the greatest continuing concern of the Romans was with pirates. For a time, although piracy was not totally stamped out even in the Mediterranean, its practice was rendered risky beyond the point of attractive profit. While Carthage was still a power, it was the Carthaginian practice to sink any foreign ships entering her coastal littoral.[52] Although this practice no doubt arose as a defense against pirates, the defenders themselves adopted most of the proclivities of the marauders.[53] In due course, there was said to have been concluded between Carthage and Rome a treaty providing for a boundary separating the waters of the two powers, and providing that the ships of one power could enter freely into the ports of the other.[54] Actually, Carthage and Rome were not great sea powers simultaneously, and the Punic wars terminated the very existence of the former. Thereafter, the Romans used the seas as avenues of conquest and to consolidate the empire which eventually included all of the then known civilized world.

It is not too surprising, therefore, that the Romans made no pretensions toward sovereignty over the seas. At its highest stage of development, the Roman Empire embraced nearly all of the Mediterranean littoral as well as the coasts of Britain and Gaul. It was not necessary to maintain sovereignty as against pirates and barbarians who had no legal rights in the eyes of the Romans. Thus the Institutes and the Digest declared the sea to be common and free for use of all

[52] Henry A. Ormerod, *Piracy in the Ancient World*, p. 140.

[53] *Ibid.*

[54] Reddie, *op. cit.*, pp. 27–9; Plybius, Bk. 3, Ch. 3; von Scala. *op. cit.*, p. 85; Azuni, *op. cit.*, p. 49.

men and susceptible of ownership by no one. Doctor Sereni maintains that the conception of even a territorial sea finds no basis in Roman sources of law, [55] and there is no evidence to suggest the contrary. The studies of Müller-Jochmus and Raestad, based on empirical data of a more practical sort, however, lead to the conclusion that in coastal areas and especially in the approaches to ports, Rome assumed special authority over such waters under the principle of public use, and in the collective interest.[56] This concept, which enjoyed general recognition, found expression in two articles of the Digest.[57]

In large measure, then, it appears that the practice of Rome, with respect to what are now classed as internal waters, differed little from the practices of older states: utility, order, and protection furnished the impetus for the establishment of a regime of absolute sovereignty and control in ports and the approaches thereto. Strictly speaking, the Roman jurisdiction was entirely a function of national law, since there really were no other States in the Western civilized community. For purposes of this study, the most that can be said for the Roman era is that it illustrates a continuum of State practice.[58]

Section C THE ECONOMIC INTEREST

In the proceding section we noted that from the earliest of times men inhabiting coastal lands settled and lived near small, protected indentations in the otherwise inhospitable coastal littoral. The land masses adjoining such indentations protected man to some extent from the elements while he endeavored to extract some benefit from the

[55] Angelo Piero Sereni, *The Italian Conception of International Law* (1943), p. 70.

[56] Müller-Jochmus, *op. cit.*, p. 252; Arnold Raestad, *La Mer Territoriale* (1913), pp. 8–9, 51–52.

[57] *Digest* XLIII, 3, 8.

[58] It is believed to be much beyond the scope of this study to discuss in further detail the question of the sea in Roman law, since, as Raestad explains, it has primarily to do with interpretations of what was understood and intended by the Romans in their written law and practice with respect to jurisdiction on the high seas. Raestad points out the use by the Roman jurisconsults of the terms *communia* and *publia*. One must agree with Raestad that the jurisconsults did not always distinguish the two terms with nicety. But it appears that *communia* was generally applied to the sea, in a manner *juris gentium*, while *publia* or a public thing, that is belonging to Roman people, was applied to rivers and ports. Raestad, *op. cit.*, pp. 1–10. But one must fairly conclude that the distinction here was one of degree rather than of legal concept. It is the considered opinion of this author that one puts a strain upon Roman history and law if one attempts to utilize them in arguments concerning freedom of the sea. It does not appear that in Roman times, freedom of the sea was a matter of formal International Law. Pitman Potter, *op. cit.*, pp. 33–5; Percy E. Corbett, *Law in Diplomacy* (1959), p. 116; See also, Arthur Nussbaum, *A Concise History of the Law of Nations* (1954), p. 10, on *Juris gentium*. See Azuni, *op. cit.*, pp. 54–76, for a concise account of Roman operations for control of the sea.

arm of the sea. The usefulness of the sea-arm, or bay, might arise from the fluid medium of the water itself wherein it was possible for man to move himself and his goods with greater ease than over the surrounding terrain. Or the bay might yield up some form of animal life which could contribute toward man's food supply. In certain areas of the world food from the sea could be obtained at considerably less effort and with greater certainty than from hunting land-bound animal life. Moreover, in certain areas characterized by rigorous climatic conditions, an abundance of fish counterbalanced an absence of agriculture and animal domestication, which were delayed by poor terrain conditions ashore. For many thousands of years, food obtained from the sea was thought to come from a perpetual stock. There was little reason to think otherwise inasmuch as the amount extracted by the relatively small human population could have no appreciable effect upon the reproductive cycle of marine life. Thus at the earliest time in human history the waters of the seacoast, and more especially the protected bay, contributed toward man's requirements for services and goods.

In the preceding section we also noted that from the earliest of times, men were either forced to protect their possessions from their fellow men, or they experienced the compulsion to increase their possessions or well-being at the uncompensated expense of others. Such reciprocal depredations were simply manifestations of man's craving for control of more of what nature provides, or other men possess, in order to improve his own position, as he conceives it, and with the minimum of effort and risk to himself. When economists say that their discipline has to do with the allocation of scarce things,[1] or with what, how and for whom commodities shall be produced,[2] they are referring to what is essentially a socio-biological process with directly traceable antecedents going back for milleniums. As man has become a more cooperative and social animal, as the nation state system has matured and developed, and as the world has become a closed geographical system, there has developed a sort of easily upset equilibrium in which social groups tend toward a reciprocal recognition and stabilization of their respective shares of nature's endowments. That there exists any such equilibrium, or the expectation of it, in the behavior of the members of the present day social groupings, known as the

[1] James R. Schlesinger, "The Perspective of Economics," *National Security Studies* 1957, U.S. Naval War College. Doctor Schlesinger cites the oft-quoted statement of the British Professor Lionel Robbins: "Economics is the science which studies human behavior as a relationship between ends and scarce means which have alternative uses."

[2] Paul A. Samuelson, *Economics*, 4th Ed. (1959), p. 16.

State system, does not appear to be the result of any fundamental change from man's basically acquisitive urge. It is rather the result of rational assessments by governing elites who determine that the fruits of success might not justify the means and efforts to obtain them. or that the risk of failure might be unacceptable. But the compulsion remains as does the urge to consolidate or simply to hold what a state conceives as belonging to itself.

This scource of international friction is exacerbated by improved communications, extraordinary and unprecedented population growth,[3] and by relative changes in the strength and well-being of nation states. It is further exacerbated by the fact that a part of the world, the sea, having an ever increasingly understood economic potential, is the subject of a legal concept which prescribes it as being in the possession of no state but for the common use of all. This concept is in fundamental contradiction to the concept that most [4] of the world's land surface and its resources should be divided into a number of parts, each of which is subject to the absolute sovereignty of a single nation state. It is no surprise, then, as the economic potential of the sea becomes more and more to be realized, that states should view this last unpossessed frontier area with envious eyes and should attempt various rationalizations for increasing their sovereign possession over neighboring parts of it. The endeavor to increase the size of the juridical bay is only one such rationalizing attempt.

The foregoing development is a breeding ground for international friction stemming from economic attitudes inherent in the nation state system and from the fact that a number of maritime states do in fact re- the seas as open to all. That they do so regard the seas is, of course, a function of the particular paths taken in their economic development. The economic attitude which has been inherent in the nation state system is that a State need not concern itself with the economic well-being of peoples outside its own boundaries, and that each State is free to determine what is necessary to maintain and advance its own economic well-being. Where such determination contemplates exploitation of

[3] World population is estimated currently at 2.6 billion persons. The rate of increase is estimated to be 1.3 percent annually. This will lead to an estimated world population of nearly 5 billion by 2000 A.D. and nearly 7 billion by 2050 A.D. United Nations Publication, *The Determinants and Consequences of Population Trends*, ST/SOA/Ser. A/17 (1953), pp. 10–14; Brown, Bonner and Weir, *The Next Hundred Years* (1937), Ch. 7; Sir E. John Russell, *World Population and World Food Supplies* (1954), pp. 17–23; UN *FAO Stat. Year Book*, 1951.

[4] The exceptation is Antarctica, and even here the United States is the principal great power refusing to recognize a number of claims to sovereignty over parcels of land in that barren continent.

marine resources, and there ensues a dispute between a State who considers that sovereignty over sea areas should be restricted to the barest minimum and a State who claims sovereign possession over some part of it, the controversy is highly difficult of settlement either on the basis of positive international law or on the basis of an equitable assessment of the relative economic positions of the two parties. The latter method, however, is certainly suggested in the opinion in *United Kingdom* v. *Norway*.[5] While two contending State parties may announce that fishing in a disputed area is essential to their respective economies, and while the contention of one can perhaps be discredited on economic grounds (usually a rather difficult feat), it has not normally been tenable for the government of a State to accept the adverse decision. Even in a single State under a dictatorship, the control of economic forces and their harnessing into a framework of decrees is an entangling multidimensional problem.[6] Within many other States, the re-allocation of factors of production to compensate for even small economic losses resulting from international disputes is likely to impose unpalatable political strains. But there is at present no countervailing or mediatory power in the international arena to defend on behalf of all the nations the concept that a portion of the earth's surface is open to all of the nations. In the absence of such power and in an atmosphere of distrust of solutions based on justice (the seed has not matured), international law at this time seems largely confined to prescribing some general parameters of action, and within these parameters, through *post facto* development, to confirming what has already taken

[5] See *infra*, Ch. 4. Professor Riesenfeld writes that legal solutions of economic controversies and legal adjustments of conflicting interests are seldom furnished by simple formulas. He stresses the difficulty in ascertaining the law. *Protection of Coastal Fisheries under International Law* (1942), p. 2. The North Atlantic Fisheries Arbitration case exemplifies the absence of then prevailing positive rules, although the tribunal's opinion does not reflect any consideration of relative economic interests; Scott, *Hague Reports*, p. 146ff. In 1933, Lauterpacht struggled to suggest some means of settling economic conflicts and suggested, in a not altogether satisfying fashion, that States might resort to conciliation, *The Function of Law in the International Community*, pp. 366–371. Stone concludes: "To seek to transfer notions of justice automatically from the municipal to the international sphere is to sow strange seeds in unprepared soil, and reap little harvest." *Legal Controls of International Conflict*, p. 56. While this is perhaps true, we have only the choices of growing unrest, politically inspired charity, or sowing the seed. It would appear that in the interim between 1910 and 1951, some of the seeds have been sown. It is to be observed, however, that if disputes in an increasingly complex world are to be settled on the basis of notions of justice rather than on abstract right resting in an insufficiently developed law, then basic understanding of the complex causes of issues must proceed apace.

[6] Excellent examples, among a vast wealth of materials, are explained in George N. Halm, *Economic Systems, A Comparative Analysis* (1951); Robert W. Davies, *Development of the Soviet Budgetary System* (1957), and Holland Hunter, *The Soviet Transportation System* (1956). The latter work is especially significant for its explanation of the 2-year rail transport crisis of 1930–2 in the Soviet Union.

place. For these reasons, it can resonably be predicted that States will make ever-widening claims to sovereignty over the high seas when it appears in their economic interest to do so, and under international law the most that can be done is for other States to seek a regularization and rationalization of the claims. Since sovereignty over a bay, where one can be juridically demonstrated to exist, has gradually come to have a quality more absolute than that of the marginal belt, an assertion of such sovereignty appears especially attractive. Moreover, since the closure line of a bay is recognized as part of the system of baselines, the nation State asserting sovereignty over a bay extends its marginal belt to seaward and thereby gains a qualified sovereignty over an additional area of what was previously high seas.[7]

Since the determination of economic necessity as grounds for an assertion of sovereignty is one which at present can only be made by a State and is thereafter challengeable only under a rather primitive legal system, there may be a growing suggestion that further discussion of the economic interest in the international law of bays is a fruitless exercise. But to accept such a suggestion is to ignore the careful reasoning in these premises of several judicial decisions. Moreover, to ignore the economic interest would be to retreat from one of the real causes of the issue in controversy.

Economic necessity, objectively assessed, and the politico-economic interest resultant therefrom are usually changeable qualities whose relative values, even in a single State, are dependable for only a short period of time.[8] Any particular economic factor is likely to be viewed through a filter of political pressures which tend to shroud to a marked degree its objective meaning in a country's overall economic structure.[9] In the international arena, the gain or loss of an economic resource may be quite insignificant to a State's overall economy, but the internal political problems engendered may compel the government to be far

[7] See pp. 3–4, *supra*, for distinction between internal waters and the marginal belt.

[8] What is involved here is the dynamics of economic change, the extreme variability and inefficiency of some markets and the oft-opposing pressures of dynamism and stability in a field where all factors are interrelated, but where the degree of relationship itself may not be clearly understood. Tibor Seitovsky, *Welfare and Competition* (1951), Ch. XXI; Lorie Tarshis, *Introduction to International Trade and Finance* (1935), pp. 8–14; Gottfried Haberler, *A Survey of International Trade Theory* (1955), pp. 17–25.

[9] The classic example is the domestic debate in the United States over commercial policy. On this, even American economists who are primarily academicians can differ rather fundamentally, e.g., Charles P. Kindleberger, "Statement on Imports, the Tariff, and the Need for Adjustment," *Compendium of Papers on U.S. Foreign Trade Policy*, U.S. House of representatives Committee on Ways and Means (1957), pp. 73–8; and Seymour Harris, *International and Interregional Economics* (1957), pp. 324–328. In the U.S. domestic field *per se*, the great and well-known example is the farm subsidy program.

more intractable in its foreign policy than can be justified by the net economic interest at stake. Thus, even if it can be statistically demonstrated that the closing of a large bay to foreign fishermen will greatly increase the gross national product of the littoral State, and that such closing will decrease very little the gross national product of another State whose flag vessels had previously fished in the area in question, it is the prerogative as well as the normal reaction of the second State to assert that the income heretofore derived from the fishing in question is absolutely essential to her economy. For these reasons, there should be certain guide lines for analyzing and cutting through the statistics and verbiage with which a State will defend its position, and for understanding the economic factors which bring about a State's position. It is believed that such an understanding was attained by the International Court of Justice in *United Kingdom* v. *Norway*; the following passages from the Court's opinion are significant in this respect:

> Along the coast are situated comparatively shallow banks, veritable under-water terraces which constitute fishing grounds where fish are particularly abundant; these grounds were known to Norwegian fishermen and exploited by them from time immemorial....
>
> In these barren regions the inhabitants of the coastal zone derive their livelihood essentially from fishing.
>
> Such [*inter alia*] are the realities which must be borne in mind in appraising the validity of the United Kingdom contention that the limits of the Norwegian fisheries zone laid down in the 1935 Decree are contrary to international law.
>
> Finally, there is one consideration not to be overlooked, the scope of which extends beyond the purely geographical factors: that of certain economic interests peculiar to a region, the reality and importance of which are clearly evidenced by long usage.[10]

Bays are important to a country's economy for two principal resons:

(a) The commerce entering and using the protected waters of the bay and the ports located therein, and

(b) The useable products that can be extracted from the marine life in the waters of the bay.[11]

[10] *ICJ Reports*, 1951, pp. 127, 128, 133.

[11] Excluded from this discussion, of course, is the continental shelf, the sea-bed, and the sub-soil except insofar as it is concerned with sedentary fisheries. It is of interest to note, however, that if a state exercises sovereignty over a large bay in which are located structures for the extraction of minerals from the sub-soil, such State would not appear bound to observe rules of international law such as are proposed in Artivle 5 of the 1958 Geneva Convention on the Continental Shelf. 52 *American Journal of International Law* (Oct. 1958), p. 859. In this connection one must observe that Article 15 of the 1958 Convention on the Territorial Waters and the Contiguous Zone requires the coastal State to give appropriate publicity to any dangers to navigation, of which it has knowledge, within its territorial sea. *ibid.*, p. 838. This provision does not extend to internal waters except under an appropriate interpretation of Article 5(2) of the latter Convention. *ibid.*, 835.

The economic interest centering upon waterborne commerce entering and moving within bays has not been a significant source of international dispute in recent times,[12] and expanding the size of the juridical bay, which is the the current desire of many countries, should encounter little opposition from foreign economic interests concerned with ocean shipping bound for ports within the bays.[13] A potential source of difficulty, however, is the situation in which a State claims sovereignty over a large bay through which foreign shipping had previously exercised the right of innocent passage. It is to be observed that Article 5(2) of the 1958 Geneva Convention on the territorial sea and contiguous zone is designed to overcome this difficulty.[14]

The primary source of economic concern, then, lies with the marine products found in coastal waters, and the matter is sufficiently complex so as not to permit the simple rationalization that to the coastal state should belong such of the adjoining natural bounty from ocean waters that its economy may require. The natural shelter provided by bays is important in the harvesting and processing of marine products for one or more of the following reasons:

(a) Fish or other marine products have a tendency to enter the relatively quieter waters of bays, especially to spawn.

(b) Fishing can be conducted from small boats and for long periods without interruption in bays because of the more favorable weather conditions.

(c) In former times, bays were especially important to fishermen in that they provided sheltered land upon which to process and preserve the newly harvested catch.

In his dissertation of 1938, William H. Dean, Jr., made the obser-

[12] Although both juridical bays and ports embrace internal waters, and the jurisdictional rights permitted the coastal state by International Law are substantially alike, they are handled separately by most publicists. e.g. Oppenheim and Hyde. While all except man-made harbors are located in some sort of bay or coastal indentation, it hardly follows that every bay has potential value as a harbor. For an excellent discussion of what characteristics are prerequisite for a commercial harbor, see Klimm, Starkey and Hall, *Introductory Economic Geography* (1937), pp. 278–283. While the legal status of a harbor as internal waters has seldom been doubted, the territoriality of bays has had a more mixed history (See Chapter 4). As late as 1955, Lauterpacht maintained that in bays, navigation must be open, *Oppenheim*, 8th Ed., p. 510, but this is a highly doubtful proposition not supported in the 1958 Geneva Conference. It appears that separate treatment of harbors and bays is something of an anachronism and as a practical matter the distinction is lost on the mariner.

[13] Since such bays would become internal waters, it is conceivable that the littoral State might seek to increase its revenues from harbor dues and pilotage charges for services which might be manifestly unnecessary in the view of the mariner. It is to be noted that International Law permits such charges without limit in internal waters.

[14] There appears to be a thorny problem of interpretation of this provision which will be commented upon (along with other drafting matters) in Chapter 5.

vation that the ultimate significance of a geographic region lies in its relation to human life; he noted that the region represents the material, physical, "given" to which economic life must adjust itself with some degree of efficiency.[15] Roxley, writing in 1908, described a natural region as an area throughout which a particular set of physical conditions prevail. He observed that a particular set of physical conditions will lead to a particular type of economic life.[16] The line of reasoning suggested by those students is further refined by others: A. Waerkof attempted a definition of regions on the basis of food resources and diets.[17] Aronsseau in 1921 and Usher in 1930 discussed the regional problem as related to population distribution and ultimately to food resources.[18] The findings of these studies suggest that a closer understanding of the economic interest in bays may result from a probing of certain other disciplines.

Turning to marine life itself and more particularly fish, we find that the type of marine life upon which fish feed, copecods, plankton and swimming snails, are found in the colder waters of the world. Although there is an abundance of marine life in warmer waters, it is in the waters of lower temperature that enormous numbers of a few species of these marine animals dwell. This is so because cold waters, having greater turbulence than warm waters, are richer in the minerals upon which these animals dwell. Where there is less turbulence, the minerals tend to sink to the ocean floor and remain there. The thriving marine life of cold waters attracts the fish to those waters, and especially to the shallower reaches of those waters. Of passing interest to our study is the fact that in the middle of the oceans life is scarce and there are very few surface breeding fishes.[19] It is to be noted, also, that in certain of the tropical regions, surface marine life is abundant; this happens where steeply rising currents bring up cold water and nourishing minerals from the deep sea. The Humboldt Current off the Pacific

[15] William H. Dean, Jr., *The Theory of Economic Activities, with Special Reference to Historical Change*, Unpublished PhD dissertation, Harvard University 1938, p. 103.

[16] Percy M. Roxley, "What is a natural region?", IV *Geographical Review* (1908). p, 127.

[17] A. Waerkof, "La Géographie de l'alimentation humaine," XX *La Géographie* (1909), pp. 225–240, 281–286.

[18] M. Aronsseau, "The Distribution of Population: A Constructive Problem," XI *Geographical Review* (1921), pp. 579–80; A. P. Usher, "The History of Population and Settlement in Eurasia," XX *Geographical Review* (1930), pp. 110–132.

[19] Rachel Carson, *The Sea Around Us* (1950), p. 25. Robert Morgan, *World Sea Fisheries* (1956), Chs. I, II. In the foreword to his work, Doctor Morgan says it is his intention to make a survey of the sea fisheries of the world as a whole and to isolate the most significant features and trends from the mass of detail in official statistics. Written on the assumption that not all of its readers are familiar with fishery matters, this book commends itself to those requiring a good general orientation.

Coast of South America is the best known example. In general, then, it appears that the ocean fisheries of greatest abundance occur in parts of the world where climatic conditions are likely to be too rigorous for more than marginal support of human life through agriculture and animal husbandry. In such areas, the soils near the coasts are often very thin and thus cannot support large forests commercially convertable to timber. The wood that is available is more likely to be used for dwelling construction in the immediate area and for fuel. In times past, the fishing industries in such parts of the world seem to have been limited in the extent of their catch by the size and construction of the fishing boats and by the vicissitudes of the weather. There appears, then, to have been something of a coincidence of factors operating to limit the size of human populations adjacent to the world fisheries, to make those populations economically dependent on the fisheries, and to keep such peoples in a condition of semi-isolation from the climatically more hospitable parts of the world.[20]

Finally, we must take note of another natural feature evident in many land masses adjacent to fishing areas. That feature is the highly irregular configuration of the coast line resultant from the peculiar pressures and movements of glaciers during the ice age.[21] In the colder parts of the world such broken up coast lines have tended to remain substantially unchanged. Rivers deposit comparatively little silt at their mouths because the valleys they drain have little loose soil to be washed away. The turbulence of the neighboring waters tends to dissipate any silt which might be drained down from the sea. The result of this particular geological condition is that numerous bays were formed millions of years ago and these arms of the sea have tended to retain their shape through the centuries, offering shelter to the land-dwelling inhabitants as well as a source of life supporting food.[22]

The foregoing brief discussion has sought to explain the natural

[20] One must hasten to add, however, that there are sea areas containing a super-abundance of fish upon which no significant neighboring population ashore is economically dependent. One such area is the Bristol Bay region off the Alaskan coast. In this area all major fishing has been done by American, Canadian or Japanese companies based in their home countries. L. Larry Leonard, *International Regulation of Fisheries* (1944), pp. 3–5; H. E. Gregory and K. Barnes, *North Pacific Fisheries* (1939), p. 11.

[21] W. Gordon East and A. E. Moodie, *The Changing World* (1956), p. 43; W. V. Blanchard and S. S. Visser, *Economic Geography of Europe* (1931), pp. 35–6.

[22] Encyclopedia Britannica World Atlas, Plates 19 through 32; Jean Braun, *Human Geography* (1920), Ch. I. Friedrich Ratzel, *Politische Geographie* (1908), pp. 122–7; Ellsworth Huntington, *Civilization and Climate* (1915), Ch. XIII; Eric Dardel, *L'Homme et la Terre* (1952), Ch. II. For some of the insight contributing to the few paragraphs immediately above, the author is especially indebted to the lectures of Dr. Saul Cohen, Professor of Geography at Boston University.

features which seem to coincide to form the fishing areas of the world into rather specialized regions having their own special economic characteristics and interests. The bays indenting the seacoats in such regions are a particular natural feature which contributes in a rather fundamental fashion toward making the regions humanly viable. We must now consider those economic interests which lie outside the fishing region but which have developed fishing industries of their own. It is here that the economic issue is joined. The controversy over the bay, its definition, and its juridical status is immediately related to and is symptomatic of this economic issue.[23]

Professor Whittlesey wrote: "Wherever nature's bounty can be reaped without replacement, man is prone to seize upon it, especially if it lies in an unclaimed area. This is particularly true of fishing." [24] He then states that before Columbus discovered America, Bretons and Basques appear to have fished along all the shores and on all the banks of the North Atlantic as far west as the Grand Bank of Newfoundland.[25]

Extracting food from the open seas at great distances from man's domicile has apparently always appeared attractive. With relative ease and aided by the naturally furnished power of wind propulsion, one could proceed to the harvesting areas. These areas could not easily be barred and defended by others because forts, fences and natural obstacles could not stand in the way of encroachers. It is but a short step between obtaining food for consumption by one's own people and harvesting for commercial enrichment. The economic virtues of these peculiar characteristics of the fishing industry have been rediscovered from time to time. A remarkable example of their explanation is that of the Scotsman, James Anderson, writing in 1775. Mr. Anderson, in a rather large book, laments the impoverished condition of Scotland and proceeds to outline in great detail a program for the country's economic development. A segment of this program is extension of the fishing industry into more distant waters whose bounty is available merely for the taking.[26]

[23] A concrete example is succinctly described on a single page of the record of *United Kingdom* v. *Norway*. See *International Court of Justice, Reports*, 1951, Vol. II, p. 309.

[24] Derwent Whittlesey, *The Earth and the State* (1944), War Department Education Manual (EM 234) Edition, p. 32.

[25] *Ibid.*

[26] James Anderson, *Observations on the Means of Exciting a Spirit of National Industry* (1775), pp. 466–498. When compared with the modern works of Mason, Nurkse and Kindleberger on economic development, Anderson has left little unsaid except reduction of the problems to a generalized theory. Edward S. Mason, *Economic Planning in Undeveloped Areas* (1958); Ragnar Nurkse, *Problems of Capital Formation in Undeveloped Countries* (1957); Charles P. Kindleberger, *Economic Development* (1958).

It appears that the fishing industry can be important to a State's economy for one or both of two reasons: To augment an otherwise insufficient diet within the State itself (or one that can be rendered sufficient by other foods only at much greater expense), or to increase the relative wealth of the State through sale of the food internationally. Both motivations play a part in the fishing industries of most countries, although one usually predominates.

Doctor Dean writes that it is estimated that to sustain a man on a meat diet requires eight times as much as it does to sustain him on a plant diet.[27] He does not reveal his authority, but his statement does invite our attention to the obvious fact that more land is required to graze animals than to plant crops. Ignored, of course, is the fact that climatic conditions in some countries require more meat to sustain human life than they do in others. When such is the case and little arable or grazing land is available and human life is to be sustained at all in the area, there must be importation of food or resort to fishing. In some parts of the world where there might have been sufficient land suitable to sustain the population, there were present other natural resources rendering it more profitable to turn men's efforts to industry and commerce, and to trade for food from external sources. In such cases, at least since about 1750 A.D., the populations of such areas grew at a rate making importation of food absolutely necessary. The relative cheapness of fish as a food made its importation highly desired. Such countries then *might* have the choice of trading for such food or obtaining it through their own fishing industries. In the fragmented condition of international society, the choice, if one could possibly be made, was obvious. While the 19th Century saw an increasing development of an international market economy and division of labor, the unsettled legal status of the sea and its fisheries prevented any clear adjustment via international comparative advantage and the price system. Grain from Argentina, coal from England and Wales, and iron ore from Lorraine came from land assuredly under the sovereignty of States. Fish from the high seas adjacent to coasts were still free for the taking. With the increase in populations, the demands for the sea products increased, the profits from fishing increased, and the competition for the available fish increased. Also, the techniques for catching and processing the product improved, and it became more apparent that this bounty of nature was not inexhaustible. The pressures thus engendered produced the inevitable conflicts and legal controversies,

[27] Dean, *op. cit.*, p. 106.

and new rules of International Law began to take shape. These rules, of course, were designed in one fashion or another to set up boundaries delimiting fishing areas: On one side, the fishing industry of a State could enjoy a monopoly. On the other, the "high seas," fishing was still free to all nations unless subsequently limited by international agreement. One of the several legal devices for setting up such boundaries was the law on bays. While, as we shall see, there were other influences at work on this law – influences powerful enough to cause the waters of bays to be classified as internal waters, there is little doubt that the economic interest exercised a major, if not a predominating influence. This section has sought to generalize upon the background and history of the economic interest. In subsequent chapters, the economic interest will be dealt with in more specific detail.

Section D THE NAVIGATION PROBLEM [1]

It is the purpose of this section to discuss some of the practical aspects of coastal navigation in order to illustrate the problem created for the mariner and the coastal state by the erection of jurisdictional boundaries along a State's maritime littoral. It is here that the practical implementation of the law of the sea must inevitably take place. While paying the most humble respect to the work of the many distinguished jurists who have concerned themselves with the international law of territorial waters, this writer feels constrained to question whether some of the grass-roots results of contemplated codification or changes in the law have generally been considered or understood.

From the point of view of the mariner, the bay and internal waters in general present the very fundamental problem of ascertaining when the border between one maritime regime and another has been reached. For the agencies of the littoral State, precise knowledge of the extent of jurisdiction must be known since its unwitting exercise beyond the boundary may very likely bring embarrassment upon the State and

[1] Technical reference books used by the author are: Hill, Utegaard and Riordan, *Dutton's Navigation and Piloting* (1958); CDR R. S. Crenshaw, Jr. USN, *Naval Shiphandling* (1955); Kells, Kern and Bland, *Piloting and Maneuvering of Ships* (1943), and Bowditch, *American Practical Navigator*, 1958 Edition. Although navigation principles are universally the same, methods vary widely with the equipment available, the professional acumen of the mariner, and the requirements of private and public institutions governing their activities. The author believes that in the United States, sea navigation practice can be divided into three broad classifcations: The U.S. Navy, merchant mariners and fishermen, and yachtsmen. Needless to say, much that is written in this section is founded upon the author's own experience as a seagoing naval officer in various waters of the world.

its agents and may well be the source of international friction.[2] For the mariners of other States, precise knowledge is essential in order that they may know by which legal regime their conduct is to be governed. Although it is by no means a universal truism, the facts of maritime life are such that it is the small and less well-equipped vessels, such as those manned by fishermen that are the most frequent violators of the laws of the littoral State and it is these vessels which although least well-equipped to know their exact positions at sea, are most in need of information with respect to the imaginary line that separates the high seas from the marginal belt,[3] or the imaginary line that separates the marginal belt from internal waters including bays.

One can perhaps illustrate this by noting that on the part of the captain of an ocean going freighter, liner, or friendly visiting naval ship, interest in these boundaries is largely confined to local navigating, pilotage and other rules. To a fisherman, these boundaries may have a direct bearing on the size of his fishing catch, hence on his economic livelihood. The divergence of interests is similar insofar as the littoral State is concerned. What makes the problem of the visiting foreign ship much more difficult is what in marine parlance is called the "landfall," or the first establishment of a ship's position with respect to the coast when coming from sea. While the littoral State's patrol vessels have been in constant contact with the coastal landmarks, the visiting foreign ship or fishing vessel has the problem of first identifying the coastal landmarks before he can ascertain his position. If he is without modern or long-distance aids to navigation, or if weather has prevented him from taking celestial observations, he may unwittingly find himself in a position not of his choosing. This situation calls for the best in the mariner's professional judgment and ability.[4] If the coastal State has established its base lines in such a manner as to cross wide expanses of the open sea, it must be prepared for some accidental encroachments of its marginal

[2] A term sometimes used for such friction in international case law is "Post-judicial Consequences," of which the Moray Firth case of 1906 in Scotland is perhaps the best known example in the law of bays. *Mortensen* v. *Peters*, 14 Scots Law Times Rep. 227; Fulton, *Sovereignty of the Sea* (1911), p. 717ff; Jessup, *The Law of Territorial Waters and Maritime Jurisdiction* (1927), pp. 430–6; Ralph H. Jones, *The Context of International Law* (unpublished U.S. Naval War College manuscript) contains the entire report of the court's opinion in this case, as well as the complete report of the ensuing debates in the House of Lords.

[3] LCDR Robert May USMS and LT Leland Pearson USMS "Landfall, The Navigator's Tensest Moment," 15 *Sperryscope* (2nd Qtr. 1959), pp. 12–16. This is an excellent article depicting the problem from the point of view of the mariner in a small vessel.

[4] *Ibid.*

belt and internal waters unless it has undertaken to provide adequate measures to warn approaching mariners.

It is elementary to note that a navigator of a large ship, having a trained assistant using a self-synchronous alidade[5], mounted upon a pelorus containing a gyroscopic compass repeater, should be able to obtain and record on a chart the bearing of a distant landmark far more accurately than can the captain of a small, unsteady fishing vessel. The latter probably uses the naked eye and a magnetic compass with no repeater. He must correct for ship's heading, variation, and deviation before he can use the bearing so obtained to calculate his position. It is also elementary that the greater the distance from a landmark, the greater the linear error in position resulting from an angular error in bearing observation.

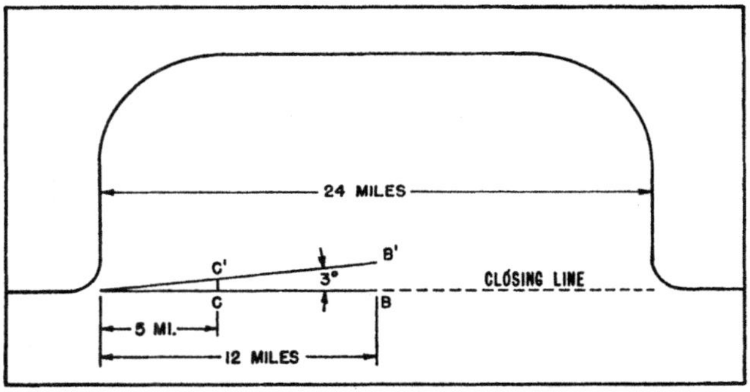

LINEAR ERROR DUE TO FAULTY OBSERVATION

Fig. 1.

Note: If we suppose an observation to be 3° in error, and the distance from the landmark is 12 miles, then the distance subtruded is BB[1] or 1200 yards. This is more than a half mile. If the observation is taken 5 miles from the landmark, then the linear error resultant from the faulty observation is about 500 yards.

[5] Definitions of technical equipment mentioned in this paragraph:

(a)*Self Synchronous Alidade:* A small motor driven telescope mounted over a gyroscope compass repeater pelorus. When set to any bearing or landmark on shore, this instrument will remain fixed in the true direction of that landmark until reset, despite any motion of the ship.

(b) *Pelorus:* A dumb compass set at a convenient point, such as the wing of the bridge, in order that the navigator may have a clear view in a number of directions, usually through about 180°.

(c) *Gyroscopic Compass Repeater:* Usually a ship contains only one gyroscopic compass, and for best maintenance and operation, this is located deep in the interior of the ship. This compass, called the master, runs on electric power and seeks to align its axis with that of the earth. The repeater (of which there may be a large number) operates to show direction by electrically transmitted indications from the master.

(d) *Magnetic Compass:* One of the oldest navigation instruments in the world. It depends for its directive force on the earth's magnetic field. Accuracy of readings depends upon corrections made in advance (called compensation or adjustment) and those made on the

While it is quite beyond the scope of this book to discuss in comprehensive detail the techniques of coastal piloting,[6] it is necessary to illustrate, albeit briefly, the problem that the mariner is called upon to solve.

A ship's position in marine parlance is called a fix. If we assume a clear day and accurate observations, establishing the position is accomplished by crossing on a chart, at least three lines of observed bearing of landmarks, thus:

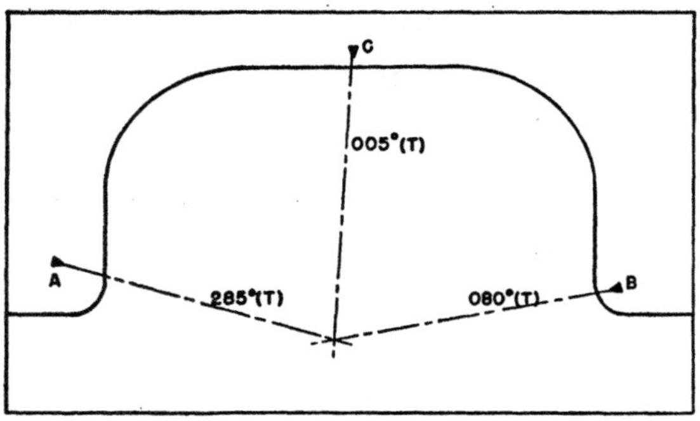

THREE BEARING FIX

Fig. 2

If one or more of these observations is in error, a small triangle will result, and the error is resolved by arbitrarily accepting the ship's position as being at the center of the triangle. See Fig. 3.

If only two landmarks are available, we have a two-bearing fix, and there is no way of knowing or resolving the error of an observation, if any, except by successive observations. See Fig. 4.

occasion of each reading. Corrections made upon reading are for Ship's heading, Deviation, and Variation. This has to be a rapid arithmetic computation, usually accomplished under awkward physical and psychological conditions. Of passing interest to the political science scholar is the formula for correction whose symbols are memorized by every American midshipman through the use of the phrase: *Can Dead Men Vote Twice?* Variation is the error brought about by the normal lack of coincidence between magnetic and geographical meridians. Deviation is the divergence between the axis of the magnetic compass card and a magnetic meridian and is brought about by the magnetic properties of the ship in which a magnetic compass is mounted. *Bowditch,* Chapter VI.

[6] Among mariners, navigation is usually divided into two classifications: celestial navigation and piloting. The former is concerned with finding the ship's position through observation of heavenly bodies and calculations based upon that branch of mathematics called spherical trigonometry. Piloting is concerned with finding the ship's position along coasts by means of observation of natural landmarks or man-made aids. The recent advent of such electronic aids as loran has somewhat blurred the distinction. Radar navigation is definitely a part of piloting.

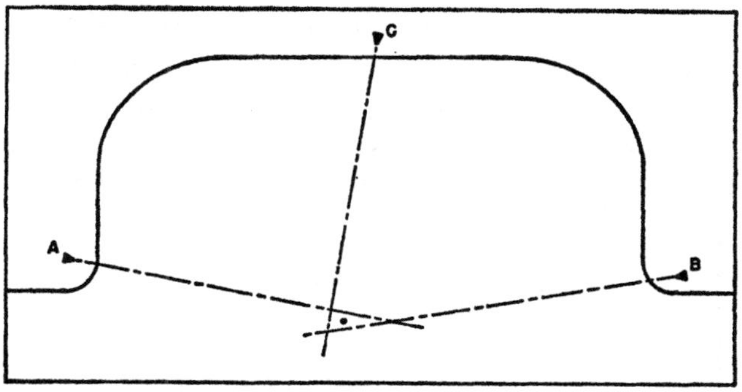

THREE BEARING FIX WITH ERROR

Fig. 3

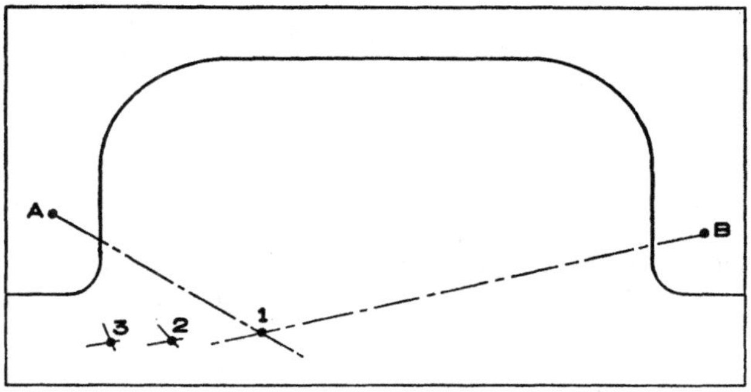

TWO BEARING FIX

Fig. 4

Note: If the ship is pursuing a straight course and there is no wind or tide, the error can be reduced by successive observations.

If only one landmark is available, the position is obtained through an approximation called a running fix. See Fig. 5.

It will be noted that the landmarks used are landmarks on the ground, and that the chart used represents an accurate survey of the position of the landmarks. In practice it is quite unusual anywhere in the world today for charts not to show with accuracy the man-made landmarks used by navigators. This is also true of such natural markings as peninsulas and islands. It is less true of mountain peaks and visible terrain characteristics inland.[7] Buoys are helpful as short range markings, but they are susceptible to changes in position in areas having substantial tidal changes.

[7] An outstanding example, in the author's experience is Mount Vesuvius which is useless for accurate navigation in the Bay of Naples. Such southeast coast of Spain.

Up to this point, the discussion has assumed that observations have been taken from the sea as a flat surface. In fact, of course, the curvature of the earth has much to do with the distance at which observations can be taken, and the distance at which objects at sea level can be observed are a direct function of the height of the observer's

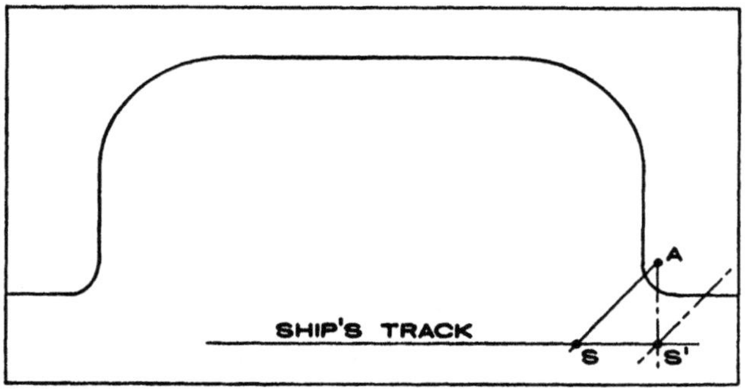

RUNNING FIX

Fig. 5

Note: the navigator makes observation at S, and then notes elapsed time to second observation at S[1]. He runs a line parallel to SA to cross at S[1]. The distance SS[1] is dependent upon the course and speed of the ship between the times of two observations. Assumed is some previous and presumably accurate fix from which the ship's track was drawn.

eye above the water line.[8] Thus the higher the observer is above the water line, the farther he can see an object, other things being equal. On a fishing vessel, the mariner's height of observation is unlikely to be very great, perhaps twenty feet at the most. In such a case, if his ship is exactly at the midpoint of the boundary between the marginal belt and the internal waters in a bay, he will be just able to make out the shore lines terminating the boundary on each side of the bay, if such bay is 10.2 nautical miles wide at the closure line.[9] If a bay is twenty four miles wide at the boundary or closure line, the observer's eye, if his ship is at the midpoint of the boundary must be 110 feet above the surface of the sea if he expects to see the shore line on both sides of his ship. Fortunately, lighthouses and other landmarks are usually positioned well above the surface of the sea. Also, ships seldom cross boundaries at the exact midpoint, and if navigation is otherwise accurate, there is no special advantage in being able to see the shore

[8] In mariners' parlance this is called "horizon dip." Hill, *et al*, p. 148. Bowditch, *The American Practical Navigator* (1958 Ed.), Table 8.

[9] See Chapter 2, for definitions of the nautical mile. The distance of the horizon for a twenty foor height of the observer's eye is 5.1 miles.

line termini of the boundary of a bay. What is important, however, is that for every increase in distance at which a mariner must determine his position with accuracy, there is an additional premium placed upon his professional skill, the size of his craft, and the capabilities of his navigating equipment. It should place no great exertion upon the imagination to appreciate that the farther out at sea a ship is located, the fewer are the identifiable landmarks available to the mariner and the greater is the difficulty in making accurate observations.

Heretofore, we have confined our comment to daytime navigation. At night, of course, the opportunities for accurate observation of landmarks are considerably reduced in number.[10] Use of lights depends upon their being seen and upon their positive identification by the mariner. While it is presupposed that if the mariner can see the light he can identify it,[11] the distance at which he can see the light is a function of the light's geographical position above the surface of the sea, the mariners height of eye, and the candlepower of the light. As a practical matter, the light's candlepower is the most important consideration, since, in general, the most powerful lights are so situated as to be at considerable heights above the surface of the sea. But the difficulty for the mariner who is concerned about his ship's position with respect to a water boundary separating different regimes of the sea is that lights do not appear to have been erected primarily for that purpose. In 1956, the U.S. Navy Hydrographic office made a survey of the seaboard navigational lights of the world and found that of the 30,302 such lights then known to exist, only 5,721 could be seen twelve miles or more at sea, or about nineteen per cent of the total.[12] Care, however, must be exercised in assessing the U.S. Navy's use of gross figures. It so happens that very often the areas in which observance of sea boundaries is rather strictly enforced for economic reasons are also areas of difficult and hazardous navigation. As a result, the lighting

[10] It should be noted, however, that where navigational lights are visible, accuracy in their identification and observation may actually be increased. While lighthouses have various paint schemes for daytime identification, the lights themselves are distinguished by their phase characteristics (on-off flashes and, in some cases, color variations) and their ranges of visibility. Also, at night, the observer does not have to contend with light diffusion, distortion etc., which in areas of high atmospheric temperatures can be quite pronounced.

[11] While failure to identify lights correctly is a frequent cause of ship's grounding, it is assumed that the navigator can do this. Failure is universally regarded as an indefensible professional shortcoming of the mariner. Publications called "Light Lists," contain complete and accurate information concerning lights.

[12] These figures are not known to have been published in any sources. They were disclosed to an *ad hoc* committee convened in August 1956 to study the effects of a possible 12-mile l imit of territorial waters. The author was a member of the committee.

systems in such areas usually have long range lights, efficiently spaced.[13]

Lighthouses and navigational lights are normally erected to warn the mariner of hazards to his ship and to mark the entrance channels to harbors. It has been the author's experience that navigational aids used to mark jurisdictional limits are of low power, wherever they do occur, and that they usually take the form of buoys or other low visibility beacons. Usually they mark the limits of harbors.

In view of the preceding discussion it should be apparent that the drawing of an imaginary line as a boundary between one regime of the sea and another (or more specifically for purposes of this book, between the marginal belt and the internal waters of a bay), does not warrant the foregone conclusion that reasonable and prudent men can thereafter be expected to observe this boundary unless its establishment is complemented by appropriate navigational aids and techniques. Through most of history, jurisdiction over internal waters and the possibility of accurate navigation through them were in balance. The areas of the sea claimed to be under the exclusive control of a State presented no great problem to the mariner equipped with even rather rudimentary instruments. In light of the political moves being made to expand the area of the marginal belt,[14] the recent decision of the International Court,[15] the moves being made to expand the waters enclosed in the juridical bay,[16] and the recent claims to large bays on the basis of historic title,[17] the possible disturbance of this balance must necessarily be explored. In the past, the balance between sovereignty over coastal waters and techniques in navigation was quite incidental and thought of only in a peripheral way; some theorists expressed the view that sovereignty should terminate at the limit of man's vision.[18] It appears, however, that the above mentioned developments must lead to a greater consciousness of the problems of the

[13] Study of navigational charts of Iceland, Norway, Newfoundland, Japan, Alaska and British Columbia will quite easily substantiate this conclusion. In view of the recent Anglo-Icelandic dispute concerning violations of the Icelandic marginal belt, the author has made a close study of the navigational aids of the Icelandic coast. He was compelled to conclude that mariners are unlikely to intrude unwittingly upon Iceland's marginal belt (12 miles, with many straight base lines) by reason of the paucity or inefficiency of the navigational aids ashore. Materials used are: MacChesney, *U.S. Naval War College International Law Situation and Documents* (1956), pp. 466–472; British Admiralty Chart No. 75; *Sailing Directions, East Greenland and Iceland*, U.S. Navy Hydrographic Office Publication No. 75 (1951), Chs. 5–8; and *List of Lights* Vol. 5, U.S. Navy Hydrographic Office Publication No. 34 (1954), pp. 486–512.

[14] *Infra*, Chapter 5.

[15] *United Kingdom* v. *Norway*, 1951 (Commonly referred to as the Anglo-Norwegian Fisheries Case).

[16] *Infra*, Chapter 5.

[17] Norway in the Fisheries Case, and the Soviet Union in the case of Peter the Great Bay. See Chapter 8, *infra*.

[18] *Infra*, Chapter 4.

navigator. Perhaps developments in the art of navigaton and international legislation having direct effects upon the mariner's equipment may minimize or vitiate the problems. Perhaps the members of the international society may wish to disregard the balance; perhaps many or most States are more concerned about expanding their coastal waters than about the mariners' problems so engendered. It may be noted that as the boundaries of the marginal belt and internal waters are moved to seaward, making it more difficult for the mariner to fix accurately his position by methods so far discussed, the mariner may find himself confronted with the choice of remaining even farther out at sea or of incurring greater risk of arrest (in the case of fishermen) by reason of imperfect navigation. It is this author's belief that proposals envisaging expanded sovereignty over coastal waters should not be isolated from technical problems thus engendered. It is with this thought that a number of technical developments will be discussed briefly below.

Lighthouses: As mentioned above, this type of navigational aid is not usually constructed for purposes of enabling the mariner to establish his position with respect to seaward boundaries, but rather to mark navigational hazards and to guide vessels into entrance channels. A review of the U.S. Navy Hydrographic Office *Lists of Lights* and corrections thereto published within the period 1949–1958 does not suggest that coastal States have erected new lights nor strengthened the candlepower of old ones with a view toward insuring that mariners will be able to fix their positions so as to remain outside some finite width of a marginal belt or outside some large bay containing internal waters. It is to be observed that the construction of lighthouses is very expensive as is the increasing of the candlepower of a light already in commission.[19] While many States might argue for sovereignty over greater areas of the seas, it is difficult for this author to envision the situation in which States would be willing to undertake the expense of erecting facilities to ensure that mariners could determine the positions of extended boundaries through observation of landmarks.[20]

[19] Discussion with officers, 1st Coast Guard District, Boston, Mass., 1959. Actual statistics for recent construction not available. Opinions appear confirmed by Frederick A. Talbot, *Lighthouses and Lightships* (1913), Chs. II, III; and, Thomas Stevenson, *Lighthouse Construction and Illumination* (1881).

[20] This is a conjecture on the part of the author whose research failed to disclose any instances in which the question was raised. In his own experience, the only observation of high-powered lights especially erected for warning purposes are those at the western entrance to the Dardanelles.

Radar Navigation: Radar is a term derived from the words *radio detection and ranging*. The principle of operation is that a narrow beam of high frequency electrical energy is directed toward some object and some of the energy rebounds to the instrument from which it was emitted. The range of the object is determined by a device which measures the time difference between the emission and the return and relates this time to distance. The time-distance relationship is constant for the machine in use. Direction of the beam, and thus the target-object, is related to a compass on the ship. This is done either directly on the machine by use of a gyroscopic compass repeater, or manually by noting the ship's true heading at the moment the beam is placed on the target. Radar employs a line of sight transmission which is adversely affected by the earth's curvature. It is a characteristic of the machine that the higher the frequency of emission, the greater the accuracy. But also, the higher the frequency, the greater is the power required for a given range capability. The expense of radar equipment rises very steeply as its range capability is increased.[21]

In other than military utilization, radar has the additional low-visibility use of detecting other ships at sea in order to prevent collisions and navigating in coastal waters.[22] In light of the notoriety to which radar has been exposed by reason of certain recent collisions such as that between the *Andrea Doria* and the *Stockholm*,[23] it is relevant to mention that ship detection by radar and navigation by radar are different functions requiring different techniques and skills. It would be difficult to say which requires the greater skill and experience, but by its very nature radar navigation appears to enlist a greater psychological readiness on the part of the mariner and he is far more in control of his situation since no problem of relative motion exists. Moreover, since he has his chart before him, he is usually in a position to make fairly accurate judgments as to whether his equipment is operating properly.[24]

[21] In the U.S. Navy, radar equipment capable of very long range detection (200 miles plus) and very high accuracy has been perfected. Such equipment is very costly to develop and to maintain; it is also quite heavy and bulky. It may be expected that as development proceeds and as longer range equipment is released for commercial production, costs of production and manufacturer's prices will drop significantly. Interview with officials of Raytheon Manufacturing Co., 10 September 1959.

[22] For a detailed discussion of radar and radar navigation, see: COMO Ralph S. Wentworth USN (Ret.) and CDR John V. Noel, Jr., USN, *Knight's Modern Seamanship*, 12th Ed., (1953), pp. 96–9; Hill, *et al, op cit.*, pp. 238–249; Orrin E. Dunlap, Jr., *Radar* (1948); John S. Hall, Jr., *Radar Aids to Navigation* (1947), Ch. 9; and J. Francis Reintjes and Godfrey T. Coate, *Principles of Radar* (1952).

[23] Alvin Moscow, *Collision Course*, (1959).

[24] There are testing procedures to determine proper operation of the equipment; such procedures may involve shutting off the equipment for varying periods.

When the equipment is operating satisfactorily and it is in the hands of a reasonably experienced navigator, it is the belief of this author that within the range limits of the machine, a ship's position can be obtained as accurately as one obtained through visual observations.[25]

Turning again to our sketches of a hypothetical bay, we shall observe how radar is used for position finding.

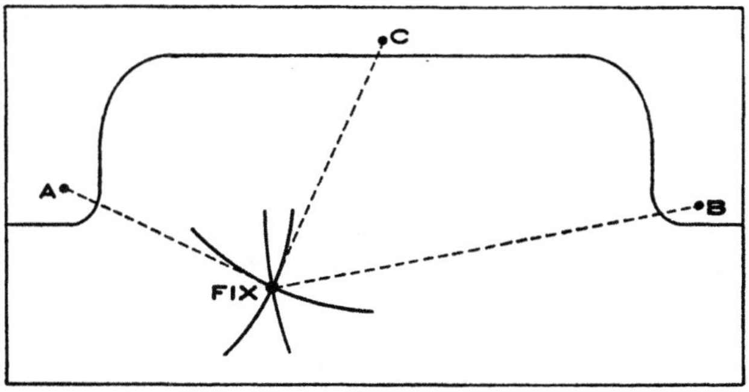

RADAR FIX, RANGES

Fig. 6

Note: The operator directs his beam toward landmark A, notes the range, and with his compass draws an arc whose radius is equal to that range as reduced to the exact scale of the chart being used. He repeats this at B and finally at C. Two men as a team can get a radar fix such as this one in less than 30 seconds.

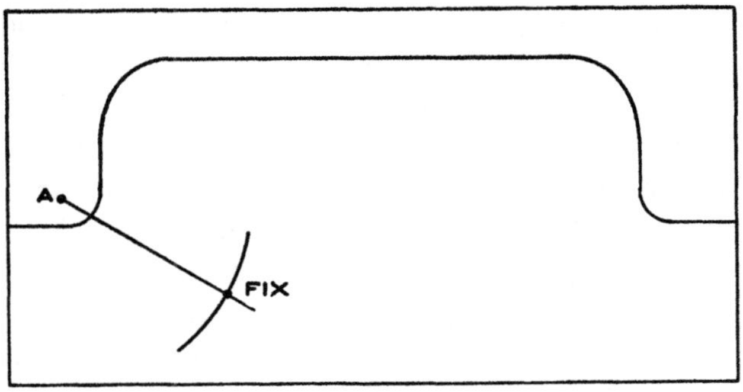

RADAR FIX, BEARING AND RANGE

Fig. 7

Note: Here the operator directs his beam at A, notes both bearing and range and plots them on the chart. Radar fixes using bearings are not recommended since the average ship-board radar used for navigation purposes has less "discrimination" (accuracy) in bearing than in range.

[25] To support his conclusions, this writer has had, among others, the following personal experiences as a ship's navigator using radar: Entering Attu, Alaska, harbor in a heavy snowstorm; entering Newport harbor in zero visibility fog; anchoring in the harbor of Kuwait in a sandstorm; and navigating in the vicinity of a World War II minefield in the northern part of the Aegean Sea.

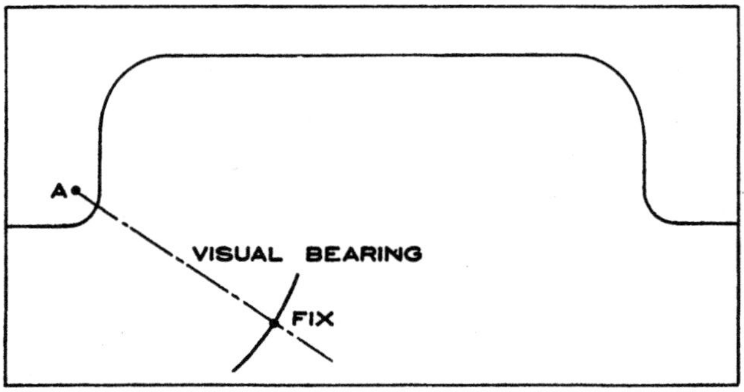

RADAR FIX, RANGE AND VISUAL BEARING

Fig. 8

Note: Here the navigator takes a visual bearing of the landmark, and simultaneously ascertains its range with the radar. He plots both on his chart. This can give a very accurate fix.

It may fairly be concluded that while line of sight limitations and shore target discrimination problems limit the usefulness of radar for fixing a ship's position with respect to the boundary between the high seas and the marginal belt, (especially if such belt is twelve miles in width), the situation is likely to be manageable even if the entrance to the bay is twenty-four miles wide. Unless the shorelines at the entrance are of very low elevation, the mariner using radar should experience little difficulty in fixing his position, even in a fishing vessel. In this connection, it is to be observed that there is little likelihood of a ship's entering a large bay directly at the midpoint of the boundary line. Should the littoral State consider it expedient to warn mariners of the approach to the internal waters of a bay, relatively inexpensive radar reflectors can be erected at the points of entrance.[26]

The present legal position of radar is uncertain and this is not to be unexpected in light of its comparatively recent technical development.[27] The more recent revision of the Rules of the Road do not speak of this important topic.[28] The case law in the United States appears thus far

[26] Radar reflectors are large metallic structures erected to increase the electronic reflecting properties of a target or landmark. Hall, *op. cit.*, p. 324ff, discusses in detail the construction of these reflectors. A more elaborate device is the radar beacon which transmits an identification signal when a radar beam strikes it. This signal will be observed on the radar equipment's visual indicator. Hall, *op. cit.*, pp. 322–3. See also, *Radar Beacons*, Vol. 3 of Massachusetts Institute of Technology Radiation Laboratory Series.

[27] RADM Ira H. Nunn USN, "Admiralty Law and its Relation to Command at Sea," VI *Naval War College Review* (Dec. 1953), pp. 1–29.

[28] These Rules were revised by the International Conference on Safety of Life at Sea, London 1948. *Treaties and Other International Acts Series* (TIAS) No. 2495. B4unson MacChesney, U.S. Naval War College *International Law Situation and Documents* 1956, p. 509. Another such conference is scheduled to convene in 1960.

to disclose no instances where possession of radar has been held to be required.[29] But there are collision cases in which ships having the equipment were held at fault for failure to use it,[30] or failure to use it properly. [31] It is difficult and perhaps imprudent to attempt to suggest the course of future legal development with respect to a possible requirement that ships have radar installed and in use. It appears, however, that radar is coming into ever more universal use on ships.[32] Such increase in use of radar is spurred by the attitudes of Marine Insurance underwriters as well as by the obvious safety advantages.[33] It is believed that in due course one can expect a court decision paralleling that of the *T. J. Hooper*, but with respect to radar.[34] In the *T. J. Hooper*, the court found the vessel at fault for failure to have installed a radio set with which to receive weather warning signals. Whether or not the 1960 International Conference on Safety of Life at Sea will adopt rules concerning radar is impossible to predict, but it is difficult to see how the subject can be avoided. In view of these developments, actual and potential, it may be expected that radar will come into ever more common use. Certainly the price is not beyond the realm of reason.[35] Eventually, it can be expected that radar alone will rob of their present validity most of the navigator's objections to greater widths of the marginal belt and the juridical bay.

Loran. This is a system of electronic navigation in which a shipboard

[29] Grant Gilmore and Charles L. Black, Jr., *The Law of Admiralty* (1957), p. 422; *Anglo-Saxon Petroleum Co.* v. *U.S.* 88 Fed. Supp. 158, 160, 1950 A.M.C. 631 (D. Mass. 1950).

[30] *The Medford*, 65 F. Supp. 622, 1946 A. M. C. 795 (E.D.N.1/. 1946) *U.S.* v. *The Australia Star* 172 F. 2nd 472, 1949 A.M.C. 423 (2nd Cir. 1949) *certiori* denied 338 U.S. 823.

[31] *Chesapeake and Ohio Ry. Co.* v. *Cleveland Tankers*, 121 F. Supp. 830, 1954 A.M.C. 1921 (E. D. Mich. 1954).

[32] The Marine Department of the Insurance Company of North America estimates that about 90% of all vessels operating in the northwest Atlantic are now equiped with radar and with loran receivers.

[33] It appears that the current attitude of Marine Insurance underwriters in the United States, as well as of Lloyd's, is not one of assessing lower rates for vessels equipped with radar and other electronic aids, but of refusal to insure vessels not so equipped. It is believed that this attitude is the single greatest factor militating toward shipowners' installing radar in their vessels. Author's interview with General Manager, Marine Department, Insurance Company of North America, 5 August 1959.

[34] CCA NY, 60 Fed (2nd) 737 (1931).

[35] A very simple radar can now be purchased for about $ 350.00, plus installation costs. One quite satisfactory for a medium-sized fishing vessel can be purchased for about $ 1,800 plus installation. A radar set with a bridge repeater suitable for use in an ocean merchant vessel can be purchased for $ 3,500 plus about $ 800 installation cost. Interview with Boston manager of Sperry Gyroscope Company Sales, 3 August 1959; Interview with Raytheon Manufacturing Company officials, 10 September 1959.
See also: *New York Times*, 6 November 1959, p. 38, cols. 7, 8. This article mentions that the Sperry Mk. 5 radar now sells for $ 1,495. Other equipment and prices mentioned: Sperry Loran D, $ 1,495; small transistor radio direction finder, $ 249; electrohydraulic automatic pilot, $ 1,289; and Mk. 22 Gyro Compass, $ 2,986.

receiver is tuned to signals emitted from a pair of land stations. The time difference between the two signals is electronically compared. Any given time difference will signify that the ship is on a hyperbolic line of position whose location on the earth's surface is a function of the geographical location of the pair of stations. The lines are drawn on special charts; and the frequency for each pair of stations is called a rate. When the navigator obtains the time-differences for two or more rates, he refers to the corresponding hyperbolic lines on his chart, and his position is where these lines cross. Fig. 9 shows one pair of stations and Fig. 10 shows two such pairs. Obviously, loran navigation is limited by the amount of coverage of the earth's surface being given by emissions from land bound stations, and by the range of signals which is a maximum of about 1500 miles. Reliability diminishes rapidly after about 800 miles especially during hours of daylight. On the other hand, loran can be excellent for coastal navigation in the

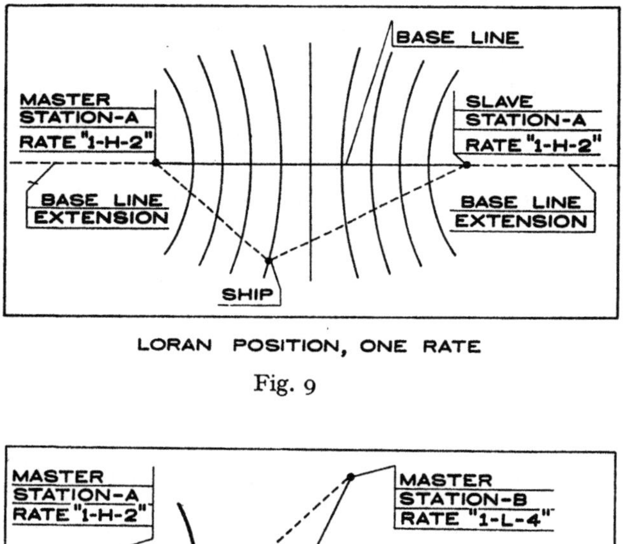

LORAN POSITION, ONE RATE

Fig. 9

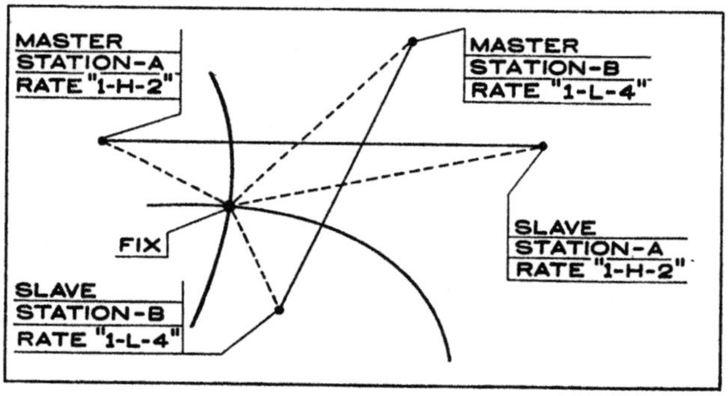

LORAN FIX, TWO RATES

Fig. 10 showing fix from two stations

areas covered. Shipboard equipment is inexpensive [36] and relatively easy to use. The shore stations for emitting loran signals can, however, be quiteexpensive to build and maintain.[37]

Currently, Loran coverage exists for the coastal United States, Japan, Philippines, and most of the coast of China. There is one pair of stations giving coverage for the south coast of Iceland, north coast of Scotland and the southeast coast of Norway. The Norwegian coast in controversy in *United Kingdom* v. *Norway* is not covered by reliable loran transmissions. Peter the Great Bay in Siberia is well blanketed by loran transmissions from Japan.[38]

Where good loran coverage exists, a mariner can obtain his position with great accuracy and he should have little difficulty in ascertaining when he has crossed a boundary into the marginal belt or into internal waters in most coastal areas having loran coverage.[39] Loran lines can be used in conjunction with other observations such as visual sights, celestial lines of position and sea depth measurements. Expansion of loran coverage, like expanded use of radar will assist in closing the gap between the navigation problems generated by States' extension of sea boundaries and the mariner's capabilities for solving them.

Other Electronic Navigational Aids

Decca. This is a system similar to Loran but with a somewhat different method of measuring transmissions. Range is limited, but within the limits of the range, position accuracy is extraordinary. The system is in operation on the coasts of Britain. Shipboard equipment is considerably more expensive than the loran receiver.[40]

Fathometer. This is a depth measuring machine that determines depth of of water by electronic timing of a sound impulse traveling to the bottom and returning. Navigation by this method (and in combination with others), can achieve great accuracy in the hands of a mariner who has had long practice in its use.[41]

[36] About $ 250. There is even a brisk second-hand market in loran equipment.

[37] Construction, maintenance and manning of U.S. Stations are a responsibility of the U.S. Coast Guard. A number are on isolated islands. They require about 12 men for each master and slave station. Construction costs have been as high as $ 4. million. Discussion with officers at Headquarters, 1st Coast Guard District, Boston, Mass., 10 September 1959.

[38] Hill *et al*, *op. cit.*, p. 254.

[39] The exceptation exists in bays surrounded by high landmasses. These tend to blank out loran signals.

[40] The decca fix is said to have a plus or minus accuracy of 10 yards. Decca is the finest electronic navigation equipment this author has ever seen. In a carefully controlled test, under ideal conditions, this author obtained a decca fix with zero error. Because of its cost and the monopoly position of the manufacturer, the equipment does not enjoy widespread use. The equipment is normally leased, not sold, by the Decca Company of London, Ltd. Lease of the equipment for two months' use in the ship commanded by the author cost £ 98 in 1956. Purchase and installation costs were about $ 5,000 per set in 1961.

[41] Usefulness of the fathometer for position finding depends on the contour of the ocean bed. A smooth bottom gradient reduces its value. Off the entrance to Chesapeake Bay, the author often navigated using the fathometer and one loran line of position.

Radio Direction Finder. Several decades ago, this was the only electronic aid to navigation.[42] A bearing line of position is obtained from a shore radio station transmitting a code signal identifying it. Radio direction finding is subject to great inaccuracies and much personal error. This system is no longer in use in the U.S. Navy. The system is of value because of the rather world wide existence of Marine Radio beacons.[43]

It is the belief of the author that international lawyers and diplomats who concern themselves with the law of the sea have more often than not ignored the technical problems of the mariner whose activities the law governs. Writing over thirty years ago in the *American Journal of International Law*, another American naval officer expressed the same conviction.[44] The record of the 1958 United Conference on the International Law of the Sea contains little mention of the practical ramifications of the propositions advanced and the provisions voted upon.

It is almost by coincidence, then, that the pretensions of a number of States toward widening their marginal belts and extending the limits of their internal waters are being paralleled by technical developments which aid the navigator in determining his position. There is no doubt that widening the marginal belt to twelve miles and increasing the lengths of lines enclosing the internal waters of bays could cause some measure of inconvenience to the navigator. It is equally clear that States most desirous of bringing new areas of the sea under their sovereignty have shown no special disposition to erect

[42] World War I saw the accelerated development of the Radio Direction Finder and the Radio Compass, a striking parallel to the accelerated development of radar and loran in World War II. In 1924, there were 48 radio direction finder stations on the coasts of the continental United States. CDR Charles W. Harrison, Jr., USN and James E. Blower, "Electronics – Your Future," 62 *Journal of the American Society of Naval Engineers* (Feb. 1950), pp. 99–137. Like the *Stockholm-Andrea Doria* collision and the evidently faulty use of radar, there was a major marine disaster resulting from human error in the use of radio direction finding equipment; nine U.S. destroyers ran aground on 8 September 1923 at Point Honda, California. LCDR Richard B. Hadaway USNR, "Course Zero Nine Five," 83 *U.S. Naval Institute Proceedings* (Jan. 1957), pp. 40–48.

[43] Hill, *et al*, *op. cit.*, pp. 234–8. See also, U.S. Navy Hydrographic Office Publication No. 205. *Radio Navigational Aids*.

[44] RADM William L. Rodgers USN, "What Parts of International Law may be codified?," 20 *American Journal of International Law* (1926), pp. 437–443. One cannot fail to be impressed with the pertinent remarks of a much more famous authority, S. Whittemore Boggs, in his article "Delimitation of Seaward Areas under National Jurisdiction," 45 *American Journal of International Law* (1951). At p. 243, he writes: "The writer never theorizes verbally in these water boundary matters but tries out hypotheses on actual coasts and therefore on hydrographic charts, because the real geographic situations are more varied than one can imagine." In a footnote, he adds: "While engaged in writing this article the writer spent several days on surveying ships off the coasts of New Jersey and New York, ... to be sure he had escaped the office-desk viewpoint, to observe the means used in obtaining positions with latitude and longitude shown on sailing charts and to objects visible on shore, and to get the criticism of the ships' commanders regarding the principles and techniques presented in this article, then in draft form."

aids to assist the mariner in honoring the projected new boundaries. But the mariners of the world are rapidly becoming equipped to meet the new problems. It is the internationally shared desire for improvement in maritime safety that spurs scientists, manufacturers and shipowners to design and install modern navigation equipment. The pressure of the insurance underwriters, the continuing work of the International Maritime Consultative Organization,[45] the increasing complexity and costliness of ships of all classes,[46] and the downward trend in the prices of electronic aids, all stimulate the safety consciousness of mariners and shipowners. It is again emphasized that the same instruments which improve a ship's safe navigating capabilities with respect to other ships also render it possible for the navigator to fix his position at increased distances from the coast without visual aids on the shore. It is in consideration of more stringent safety requirements that modern equipment is likely to achieve permanent stature before the law. As this development approaches its inevitable maturity, there appears little reason to doubt that positions ascertained by electronic aids to navigation will be considered in maritime jurisdiction cases. It is therefore suggested that if States persist in their claims to wider areas of what are now high seas, jurists and cognizant international organizations should become increasingly alive to the technical problems precipitated by the prospective realization of such claims. It is also suggested that jurists be prepared to assess arguments to the effect that new claims to greater sovereignty are, for technical reasons, unreasonable and undesirable. Technical shortcomings may not be as pronounced as the arguments might suggest.

Section E THE DEFENSE INTEREST

This section has to do with the interests of national defense in the International Law of Bays as the matter appears to this author at

[45] Henry Reiff, *The United States and the Treaty Law of the Sea*, (1959), Pp. 227–238.

[46] The increasing complexity, size, and costliness of all classes of commercial ships appears to be a post-World War II phenomenon of seemingly limitless proportions. Fishing Companies, shipping firms and petroleum companies appear to share the common conviction that larger, faster, and better equipped ships give a larger return on investment and operating costs. Obviously, loss or damage to any one ship represents a correspondingly greater loss of earnings to the owner. Insurance costs and safety requirements rise proportionately. CAPT E.B. Perry USN (RET), "The U.S. Merchant Marine and Obsolescence" 70 *Journal of the American Society of Naval Engineers*, (May 1958), pp. 354–8; Herbert Solow, "Those Resourceful Greek Shipping Men," 48 *Fortune* (Oct. 1953), p. 142ff.; Interview with General Manager, Marine Department, Insurance Company of North America, 6 August 1959.

the present time. Specific influences that the interests of national defense have exercised upon the development of the Law of Bays will be discussed in subsequent chapters.

From the military point of view, a bay in a country's littoral usually commands special attention for one or more of these reasons:

(a) It is usually in bays that ports are located. These and their facilities are at once important components in the country's military logistics system and prime targets for the enemy.

(b) Bays and their ports serve as sheltered areas for naval repair facilities and naval operating bases. Seaplanes nearly always operate from the sheltered waters of bays. Some large bays are even used for the conduct of naval training exercises.

(c) The geological fold or the river system that created a bay in the first place, usually created in the landmass adjacent to the bay some sort of physical depression or valley which tends to assist in the egress of communications from the water's edge to the hinterland of the country concerned. For this reason and up to the present, at least, bays and their port facilities, if any, have been prime military action looking toward invasion and occupation of the interior.

(d) Bays and the ports that may be located in them are likely to be frequented by visits of the warships of friendly powers in peace time. It is of some interest to note that while movements of troops and aircraft on to foreign soil in peace time were virtually unheard of until the current era, the tradition of friendly visits of foreign warships for ceremonial and courtesy reasons is a very old one. Of this, more will be said below.

In view of the somewhat special exception in International Law which results from the generally accepted tradition of friendly visits of warships we shall comment upon their legal status in foreign waters. While International Law may present the superficial appearance of permitting great jurisdictional freedon to the visiting warship, it does in fact allow the littoral state considerable latitude to regulate the behavior of such a ship while in her marginal belt or internal waters.[1]

[1] Although there is no multilateral convention directly defining a warship, Hague Convention VII (1907), by enumerating the conditions to be satisfied in order to convert a merchant vessel into a warship, indirectly defines the latter. Such a vessel must be under the direct authority, control and responsibility of the State whose flag it flies. It must bear the external

Although warships, like other ships enjoy the right of innocent passage through the marginal belt, Article 23 of the 1958 Geneva Convention on the Territorial Sea and the Contiguous Zone specifies:

If any warship does not comply with the regulations of the coastal state concerning passage through the territorial sea and disregards any request for compliance which is made to it, the coastal state may require the warship to leave the territorial sea.

This provision appears reasonable enough, and the legislative history of it, both at the Geneva Conference and in the International Law Commission, leaves no doubt that a number of States insist upon such an article because they want a clear understanding of their right to invoke appropriate regulations.[2]

Submarines are required to navigate on the surface in the marginal belt and to show their flags.[3] The right of innocent passage does not extend to the air above the marginal sea, and military aircraft may not fly over foreign territory without special authorization.[4] While a warship remains under the jurisdiction of her flag state during her stay in foreign internal waters and no legal procedings can be taken against her for any cause,[5] said foreign State is competent to exclude the warship from all or certain of her internal waters,[6] to impose what

marks distinguishing the warships of that State. (Some States have special national ensigns designed specifically for men of war, e.g. the United Kingdom White Ensign). (Commissioned vessels of the U.S. Navy and U.S. Coast Guard, fly what is called a "commission pennant"). The Commander of the vessel must be in the service of the State, duly commissioned, and listed among the officers of the fighting fleet (most of the world's Navies publish an annual Navy List (United Kingdom) or Register of Commissioned Officers (United States). The crew must be subject to naval discipline, and the vessel must observe in its operation the laws and customs of war. U.S. Navy Department, *The Law of Naval Warfare*, Art. 500c; Robert W. Tucker, *U.S. Naval War College International Law Studies* (1955), pp. 38–9; Higgins and Colombos, *International Law of the Sea*, 2nd Ed. by C. John Colombos (1951), p. 350. It will be observed that outward appearance above does not distinguish a warship, nor does size. Articles 21 and 22 of the Geneva 1958 Convention on the Territorial Sea and Contiguous Zone specify that government ships, whether operated for commercial or non-commercial purposes, shall be subject to the rules applicable to merchant ships, although nothing in such rules shall affect the immunities they enjoy under other rules of international law.

[2] United Nations. *Reference Guide to the Articles concerning the Law of the Sea adopted by the International Law Commission at its Eighth Session.* A/c.6/L.378 of 25 October 1956, pp. 86–92; United Nations, *Report of the International Law Commission Covering the work of its Eighth Session.* Supp. No. 9 (A/3159), 1956, pp. 22–3.

[3] Oct. 14 (6) of 1958 Geneva Convention on the Territorial Sea and Contiguous Zone.

[4] Convention for the Regulation of Aerial Navigation of 1919, Hudson, *Int. Legislation*, No. 9, p. 359ff; Lauterpacht, *Oppenheim's International Law*, Vol. I., 8th Ed., (1955), pp. 519–521.

[5] The doctrine in *The Schooner Exchange* v. *McFaddon*, 7 116, appears to be upheld, universally, on the position of State ships. Lauterpacht-Oppenheim, *op. cit.*, p. 852n.

[6] *Ibid.*, p. 853. Lauterpacht writes that this is controversial, citing Westlake, *International Law* Vol. I., p. 196 and Hall, *International Law*, 8th Ed., by Higgins. In this author's mind, there appears little controversy, if any. It appears that States at the present time consider it their absolute right to exclude foreign warships except under *force majeure*. It is believed that

conditions it considers necessary upon foreign warships,[7] or to require such ships to leave.[8]

Turning now to the law of bays and the relationship it may have with the defense interest, we first consider the matter in time of peace. Here, again it turns largely on the position of the closing line, that is to say, the extent of the littoral State's internal waters; the distance to seaward that the closing line is positioned, and thus the distance that the marginal belt has been moved to seaward. The law protects the State from unwanted visits of warships, and from the nearby presence of submerged submarines, and it grants the State competence to impose rules upon warships on innocent passage in the marginal belt. Bays and their closing lines serve to increase the area of such sovereign competence. One must hasten to add, however, that if a State contemplates positive measures with respect to this competence, an increase in the area of its marginal belt or internal waters will compound considerably its problems of patroling the seas.[9] From the standpoint of the speed of a foreign warship, the difference between a relatively large expanse of territorial sea and a small one is insignificant and the added protection which a State may enjoy because of it, is insignificant. Where there can be some advantage to the littoral State, however, is in the matter of photographic intelligence. The wider the area over which the littoral State enjoys sovereignty, the more difficult it is to photograph her coast from the surface of the sea. There have been some remarkable recent advances, however, in the photographic science and in the art of photography and photogrammetry.

For security reasons, in peacetime, the United States and several other States have closed certain bays to warships and merchant ships

naval powers accept this proposition and that it has crystallized into customary law. From the tenor of the writing in Westlake and Hall, it is the conjecture of this author, that Lauterpacht's statement that the matter is controversial results from the earlier authors' broadly classing all waters as territorial. For ships of the U.S. Navy, the manifestation of the right of the foreign State to exclude is in the elaborate procedure for obtaining "clearance" for a visit, the various classifications of visits: Operational, courtesy, or diplomatic, the "Naval Visit Agreements," and the prompt and unquestioned acquiescence when the foreign State suddenly declares a planned visit "inconvenient." Commander Burdick H. Brittin, U.S. Navy, *International Law for Seagoing Officers* (1956), pp. 86–7. Except under that old provision of International Law concerning protection of nationals, it is virtually inconceivable in this author's eyes that a warship of any State would enter the internal waters of another without prior permission. (Straits, canals, *force majeure* are exceptions.)

[7] Implied in Articles 16 (2) and 23 of the 1958 Geneva Convention on The Territorial Sea and Contiguous Zone.

[8] Provided for in Article 23 of the 1958 Geneva Convention on the Territorial Sea and Contiguous Zone.

[9] See, *infra*, Ch. 4 on the problems of neutrals.

of other states.[10] In the United States such areas are called Defensive Sea Areas, and they include appropriate neighboring sections of the marginal belt.[11]

Passing now, to the military interest in a Bay as a prime military target and as a convenient point of communications contact with the interior, we look at the bay as a direct element in the littoral State's scheme of defense. As an object of military consideration, a bay may very well have qualities which increase the State's overall vulnerability while at the same time offering other qualities which may enhance defense.

As an objective for amphibious attack, the bay may offer the advantage of relatively sheltered waters for maneuvering and operating of small landing boats. It may very well offer beaches with smoother gradients and less beset by breakers than those directly exposed to the open seas. Very important, too, is that on the bay there is greater likelihood of the existence of a roadnet for easy egress from the immediate beach area. If a port is located on the bay, a near-by beach provides the most direct avenue of approach for its capture.[12] Finally, a bay offers the ideal water area for required traffic after the amphibious assault has taken place.

But there are certain features of a bay which also aid the littoral State in its own defense. Well knowing that a particular bay is a prime target for the reasons noted above, the littoral State can concentrate its defenses in such an areas, and the same conditions that make the bay a desirable objective for direct military action lend themselves to the area's defense. It should be remembered that in World War II, the Allies elected to land on the Normandy beaches rather than in the vicinity of Cherbourg, Le Havre, Dunkerque or Ostend. The oldest method of defense from land, of course, is shore-mounted artillery.[13]

[10] A list of such areas and their limits is compiled in United Nations International Law Commission, *Second Report on the Regime of the Territorial Sea*, A/CN.4/61 at pp. 11–17.

[11] Bays currently so included by U.S. Executive order are: Pearl Harbor and Kaneohe Bay in Hawaii; Kodiak, and Whittier, in Alaska; Guantanamo Bay, Cuba; and all bays and harbors in the following areas: Kiska, Unalaska and Kodiak Islands, Alaska; Guam, Palmyra, Johnston and Midway Islands; Kingman Reef; and Culebra Island. MacChesney, *op. cit.*, pp. 603–4. There are various specific security reasons for closing these bays, and few would have any great commercial interest to other states. Culebra is closed primarily because most of the island serves as a target for practice gunfire from U.S. Navy ships.

[12] Direct assault upon a port area from the sea is likely to be more difficult and to result in more casualites than a beach assault with subsequent overland maneuver with the port as an objective of the troops ashore. Explanation of the reasons for this is needlessly involved for purposes of this book.

[13] The fact that the United States dismantled its Coast Artillery Installations and abolished the Coast Artillery Corps after World War II, does not necessarily invalidate this statement. The measure was a calculated one and some other States who evaluate their own

Properly located on a bay that lends itself to the purpose, the cross fire of such artillery can be particularly devastating, as can the fire of such newer weapons as short-range missiles and rockets. Secondly, the waters of a bay lend themselves to defense by mines and underwater obstacles. In the quieter waters of a bay, such weapons and measures are more likely to remain where placed than in the waters directly along open coasts. When an invading force undertakes mine-sweeping operations preparatory to amphibious assault, the mine-sweepers can be subjected to artillery fire and low level air attack. An ancient principle of war is that of concentation and it works two ways.

Another principle is defense in depth. Still another is timely planning and organization. It is now a well-worn statement that warfare with today's weapons is likely to be distinguished by the extraordinary swiftness and ease of weapons delivery, as well as by the tremendous lethality of such weapons. With its capability for stealthy operation, the submarine is peculiarly suited to modern war. But to combat it, defenses must be organized in peacetime and some of them must be put in place in peacetime. Some measures such as mines and nets tend to hamper innocent passage; moreover, traversing ships can damage some passive measures such as nets, heralds and moored mines.[14] For these reasons as well as for security controls and more positive measures of defense in depth, an increase in the extent of a State's internal waters is an obvious consideration. Whether this particular defense consideration will continue to have validity is at least questionable. Improvement in weapons and in guidance systems may eventually render it unnecessary for a submarine to enter a State's internal waters or marginal belt despite recent efforts toward increasing the breadth of those waters. Therefore the efforts at underwater defense of bays may well become unnecessary and useless.

As for amphibious assault and defense, it can be argued, too, that in an age of total war and high-yield weapons, this has become an outmoded tactic. Sensing no requirement in this paper to debate the possibilities of limited war (or lack of them) the author believes that should there be limited war, something similar to an amphibious operation is still likely. The water borne assault proper, with its

military situations differently continue to maintain such organizations. e.g. the Soviet Union, Sweden, Turkey and the Netherlands. It may be recalled that it was a Norwegian artillery battery that sank the German cruiser Blücher in World War II. VADM Friedrich Ruge, Federal German Navy, *Der Seekrieg*, Tr. CDR. M. G. Saunders, Royal Navy (1957), p. 90.

[14] The mine referred to here is the type whose explosion is controlled from shore. The herald is a type of underwater detection apparatus.

requirement for quiet seas, may well give way to vertical envelopment and helicopter assault. Should such tactics supplant older ones, the bay might be less prominent as a place of direct military action. That it would continue to be important for other military reasons mentioned herein appears probable.

As a peacetime military base, the bay and its port facilities will continue to be important for some time to come. Unlike commercial ships, naval vessels usually remain in ports and bases for long periods. Often they go to sea for a day or a few days of training and then return for logistic and personnel reasons.[15] Except when actually undertaking shore-assisted repairs or loading supplies, there is no reason for warships to take up the usually scarce and expensive space alongside piers in ports. Hence they anchor in bays in the vicinity of ports. Anchoring any appreciable number of ships requires a large amount of water area. Since waters in a bay are relatively quiet, anchorage in a bay is desired.[16] In this respect, a bay containing an expanded area of internal waters is very much a matter of a State's defense interest.

Bays are also of interest to a State's defense preparations for such reasons as: providing quiet waters for research and development of weapons and detection equipment, actual conduct of training exercises, calibration of equipment, and certain maintenance such as degaussing.

It is believed that the defense interest in bays will continue as long as there are navies and as long as the land-sea communications contact points lying within bays continue to be regarded as significant military objectives.

[15] In this context, the author is referring to peacetime navies in general. The protracted post-war sea operations of the U.S. Navy are an exception.

[16] It should perhaps be mentioned that, contrary to common belief, a bay is not necessarily the most desirable place to be during storms. Most bays do not protect from very high winds. Warships having powerful engines and of the size of a destroyer, or larger, will often go to sea in storms preferring to ride it out rather than run the risk of grounding. In bad weather, anchors may drag and mooring lines may part; in such event, maneuvering in a bay's restricted waters can be hazardous in the extreme.

CHAPTER TWO

TERMINOLOGY

Section A(i) Definition of a bay as formulated by the 1958 United Nations Law of the Sea Conference

The purpose of this Section is to quote the definition of a bay as formulated by the 1958 Geneva Law of the Sea Conference, to offer an interpretation of it, and to indicate how it may increase the number of juridical bays and increase the areas of internal waters in a number of other bays. It is not the purpose of this section to comment upon the process through which this definition was formulated or to express any views upon the merits of the definition.

The definition of a bay is contained in Article 7 of the 1958 Geneva Convention on the Territorial Sea and Contiguous Zone.[1] Article 7 is quoted, *in toto*, hereunder:

Article 7

1. This article relates only to bays the coast of which belong to a single state.

2. For the purposes of these articles, a bay is a well-marked indentation whose penetration is in such proportion to the width of its mouth as to contain land-locked waters and constitute more than a mere curvature of the coast. An indentation shall not, however, be regarded as a bay unless its area is as large as, or larger than, that of the semi-circle whose diameter is a line drawn across the mouth of that indentation.

3. For the purpose of measurement, the area of an indentation is that lying between the low water mark around the shore of the indentation and a line joining the low-water marks of its natural entrance points. Where, because of the presence of islands, an indentation has more than one mouth, the semi-circle shall be drawn on a line as long as the sum total of the lengths of the lines across the different mouths. Islands within an indentation shall be included as if they were part of the water area of the indentation.

[1] United Nations Document A/Conf. 13/L.52; reprinted in 38 *Department of State Bulletin* 1111 (1958); reprinted in 52 *American Journal of International Law* (Oct. 1958), at pp. 835–6.

4. If the distance between the low-water marks of the natural entrance points of a bay does not exceed twenty-four miles, a closing line may be drawn between these two low-water marks, and the waters enclosed thereby shall be considered as internal waters.

5. Where the distance between the low-water marks of the natural entrance points of a bay exceeds twenty-four miles, a straight base line of twenty-four miles shall be drawn within the bay in such a manner as to enclose the maximum area of water that is possible with a line of that length.

6. The foregoing provisions shall not apply to so-called "historic" bays, or in any case where the straight baseline system provided for in Article 4 is applied.

The Convnetion contains other articles which must occasionally be taken into consideration when applying the definition of article 7 to a particular body of water.

After considering several methods of interpreting Article 7 and applying this interpretation, the author has arbitrarily chosen to proceed through a step-by-step method which the authorities of a State might use to determine whether a given body of water is a bay within the meaning of the Article, and whether this bay shall contain internal waters.

(1) Paragraph 1 is self explanatory. The provisions of Article 7 are described as being intended to apply only to bays the coasts of which belong to a single state. While this statement is unequivocal, it should be noted that there exists no other development in conventional International Law to be applied to a bay in the littoral of two or more States. There are a number of such bays,[2] and it may be conjectured that should the States so concerned contemplate an international agreement concerning the legal regime for such a bay, they will be influenced by some or all of the provisions of Article 7. On the other hand they would not be bound to do so, and Paragraph 1 bars any other States from making legitimate protests on the grounds that the character of the regime so contemplated is significantly different from that provided for by Article 7.

(2) Paragraph 2. This specifies that the bay must be a well-marked indentation in such proportion to the width of its mouth as to contain land-locked waters and constitute more than a mere curvature of the coast. Explorers and others who have applied names to those parts of the earth's crust which are identifiable by some physical characteristic, have often applied the word "bay" to parts of coasts which are in fact merely gentle curvatures. Such an appellation may

[2] Bays in the littoral of two or more states will be discussed in Chapter Nine.

often have stemmed from the language native to the namer.[3] Or, the name may have been appended by one unfamiliar with the use of geographical terms.[4]

The specification that the bay must be of such proportion as to contain *land-locked* waters, is difficult to reconcile with the physical shape of most bays in the world which might otherwise qualify as juridical bays. If one takes the adjective "land-locked" in its literal meaning,[5] it is the opinion of this author that the bay would necessarily be required to have an entrance channel from the sea that is curved in such a manner as to enter upon a body of water that is truly landlocked. There are few such bays in the world: Purvis Bay, British Solomon Islands: The Gulf of Corinth in Greece; Trondheimfjord in Norway; Galveston Bay in Texas; The North Gulf of Evvoia in Greece; Port Philip Bay in Australia and Lake Maracaibo in Venezuela. Hudson Bay in Canada could no doubt be placed in this category. Since such a strict construction of the provision would seriously reduce the general applicability of Article 7 and is practically in conflict with paragraph 5 thereof (of the bays mentioned above as being truly landlocked, none has an entrance remotely approaching twenty-four miles in width, except Hudson Bay), the adjective "landlocked" must be given an extremely liberal interpretation. It cannot be ignored entirely because to do so would be to leave dangling, at least partially, the words "whose penetration is in proportion to the width of its mouth." It appears to the author that what would satisfy the probable intent of this rule and still permit the rule to enjoy some reasonably wide use, would be for the length of the bay, from a line across its mouth to the deepest point of penetration on the landward side, to be equal to or exceed the width of the mouth (See Fig. 11). Such a proportion would honor the requirement that the bay be more than a mere curvature of the coast and the body of water would be "locked" by land in three directions. Such a body of water would exceed the minimum mathematical qualification to be discussed hereunder. It is believed that application of any stricter interpretation of the term "land-locked" would operate to exclude as juridical bays a number of such bodies of water which are presently called bays and which enclose waters generally considered by States to

[3] See Section C, *infra*, for linguistic variations in terms.

[4] This was obviously the case in a number of instances reported by Keller, Lissitzyn, and Mann in *Creation of Rights through Symbolic Acts, 1400 to 1800* (1938).

[5] René de Kerchove, in his exhaustive work, *International Maritime Dictionary* (1948), writes at page 396, simply: "LANDLOCKED. Surrounded by land, said of harbors and anchorages."

be internal waters.[6] It can resonably be conjectured that an attempt to maintain a stricter interpretation would not enjoy the consent of a great many coastal States.

Assuming then that our body of water meets the above qualification, it must meet the second qualification specified in paragraph 2, a mathematical one: that the indentation shall not be regarded as a bay unless its area is as large as or larger than, that of the semi-circle whose diameter is a line drawn across the mouth of that indentation. It should be observed that if the body of water is truly "land locked" the need to apply the mathematical definition is removed entirely. If we were to apply the more liberal interpretation of the term "land locked", as proposed above, the use of the mathematical formula is still unnecessary.

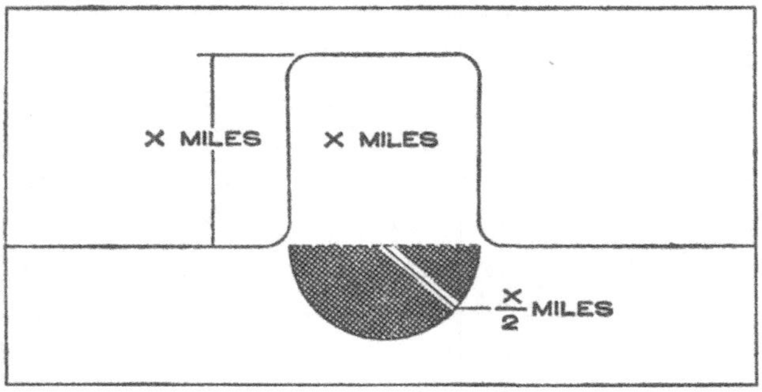

THE SEMI-CIRCLE RULE

Fig. 11

If, however, the adjective "land locked" is given an interpretation even more liberal than that proposed herein, or if it is tacitly ignored (which this author considers a likely possibility), then the mathematical formula would undoubtedly find some use. In the event of a dispute and submittal thereof to an international tribunal, it is conjectured that the tribunal would consider all parts of the rule in the course of arriving at its opinion. Measurement of large expanses of water areas, a contingency suggested by paragraph 2, is discussed in Section D of this chapter.

(3) Paragraph 3. The first sentence of this paragraph reads:

For the purpose of measurement, the area of an indentation is that lying between the low-water mark around the shore of the indentation and a line joining the low water marks of its natural entrance points.

[6] Bays that fulfill these qualifications include the vast majority of bays in the world as any good atlas will quickly indicate.

Section B, hereunder, discusses the reference planes of charts and the methods of marking charts to show low-water tidal conditions. At this juncture it is pertinent, however, to note Article 3 of the 1958 Convention which reads:

Except where otherwise provided in these articles, the normal baseline for measuring the breadth of the territorial sea *is the low-water line along the coasts as marked on large-scale charts officially recognized by the coastal State.* (Emphasis supplied).

There exists the possibility that more than one large scale chart has been made of a particular area. This may be the result of different surveys made at different times by different countries.[7] Moreover, charts may be drawn using several different types of projection.[8] On the large scale charts contemplated in Article 3 differences as between projections are unlikely to be noticeable [9] unless the chart is of a rather large bay such as Hudson Bay or the Gulf of Carpentaria in Australia. At this juncture the most important point to bear in mind is that the chart to be used is that which has been officially recognized by the coastal state. In Coastal States having hydrographic services, ascertaining the officially recognized chart of the area would probably involve no more than a determination of the chart being issued by the hydrographic service of that State. Among some of the less developed or smaller countries, identification of the officially recognized chart might present more of a problem.

It will be observed that paragraph three mentions the area lying between the *low-water mark around the shore of the indentation* and a line

[7] The customary system for design and use of navigation charts is that States having hydrographic services conduct their own coastal surveys, design their charts and then supply such charts to the Hydrographic services of interested countries. Information concerning new surveys and the availability of new charts is usually distributed through the International Hydrographic Bureau in Monaco. The U.S. Navy Hydrographic Office will seek permission to reproduce the charts for sale to interested mariners. During the 19th and 20th Centuries, the Royal Navy and the United States Navy have surveyed vast areas of the world for which accurate charts did not previously exist and in which the littoral States concerned were not prepared to undertake the necessary surveys. Hill, *et al, op. cit.*, pp. 16–28; Bowditch, *op. cit.*, Ch. V.; K. T. Adams, *Hydrographic Manual. Special Publication No. 143*, U.S. Coast and Geodetic Survey (1942), Ch. I. In passing, it should be noted that surveying and charting of coasts of the United States and possessions, including TRUST territories is, the responsibility of the United States Coast and Geodetic Survey, See Section B, below, for more detailed discussion of the low water mark.

[8] The most widely used projection is the cylindrical one, commonly called the Mercator projection, after its inventor. Other types of projections are: transverse Mercator, oblique Mercator, simple conic, Lambert conformal, polyconic, azimuthal, gnomonic, sterographic, and orthographic, and azimuthal equidistant. Hill, *et al, op. cit.*, p. 17. Description of these projections is considered beyond the scope of this text. An excellent layman's description is contained in Nicholas J. Spykman, *America's Strategy in World Politics* (1942).

[9] Hill, *et al, op. cit.*, p. 16.

joining the low-water marks of its natural entrance points. Absent from this provision is any mention of mouths of rivers flowing into bays or ports located within bays. For consideration of these, it would appear that inferences might be drawn from other articles of the Convention.

Article 13 provides that if a river flows directly into the sea, the base line shall be a straight line across the mouth of the river between points on the low-tide line of its banks. No provision is made for the situation where a river flows into a bay. In many cases, there is an identifiable natural entrance point to the river, such as at the mouth of the Seine in France, the River Foyle in Ireland, or the mouth of the Weser in Germany where it empties into the Jade. In other cases, where there is a gradual widening, the cut-off point for measuring may bring forth some doubt. Where the Delaware River becomes Delaware Bay; where the Severn becomes Bristol Channel in England; and the extent of the Para in Brazil are cases in point. Where the natural entrance points are obvious, it would be logical to draw a straight line connecting these points, but in such cases as well as those where the location of the mouth of the river is not so obvious, it would probably be necessary to take into account the practice of the State concerned, to take notice of any domestic decisions in the premises, or both. Lest one suggest that this involves unnesessary hair splitting, it should be observed that in doubtful cases, it is in the littoral State's interest to have the largest area possible in its "bay", and such area might be appreciably increased by considering the waters of a river (especially if there is a tidal flow in the river) as part of the bay.

Article 8 provides:

> For the purpose of delimiting the territorial sea, the outermost permanent harbour marks which form an integral part of the harbor system shall be regarded as forming part of the coast.

The initial clause makes it clear that this Article is for the purpose of delimiting the territorial sea. Article 1, paragraph 1, and more especially Article 5, paragraph 1, lay aside the possibility of any ambiguity as between the "territorial sea" (in this book, called the marginal belt) and the regime of internal waters. It is apparent that in the application of Article 8 to a specific situation, the benefit lies with the coastal State. Such seems to be the tenor of a number of other provisions, for example: Article 4, paragraph 1 and 4; Article 7, paragraph 4; and Article 13, to mention only three (as will be noted below, the case of islands within a bay operates to the benefit of the State). Now if the provision of Article 8 were to be applied to the measurement of a bay and the port were to be considered a part of the coast, it could not be reckoned as part of the bay's water area. From the point of view of what a State might consider to be to its advantage the effect would be opposite of the reckoning where a port lies directly on the coast. For these reasons, it is the opinion of this author that the waters of a port area within a bay are likely to be considered a part of the bay waters when an areal measurement is contemplated.[10]

The next sentence of Paragraph 3 reads:

> Where, because of the presence of islands, an indentation has more than one mouth, the semicircle shall be drawn on a line as long as the sum total of the lengths of the lines across the different mouths.

Superficially, this provision appears self-explanatory, but when applied to a specific chart, questions immediately arise, because nature has not seen fit to arrange islands in a convenient line across bays. Hence, the two or more mouths may not form a smooth, continuing whole, simply disconnected by islands. A glance at a chart to the entrance to Narragansett Bay, Rhose Island, will demonstrate this. Moreover, a bay may have one side partially enclosed by a string of closely spaced islands lying along a gentle curve, such as Buzzards Bay in Massachusetts. Is the closure line to be drawn across the bay at the main entrance or are the water distances between the fringe islands (which are also mouths) also to be considered in the sum total? How such lines are drawn can make a significant difference in the total numerical value of this closing line, with which the area of the bay is to be compared. Article 4, paragraph 1, in which provision is made to establish a base line along a fringe of islands, may be of some assistance, but it again seems to suggest that such islands will be in a neat, orderly row.[11] There is little more in the Convention to which one can appeal for guidance in the settling of any controversies turning on this fine point, other than Paragraph 4 of Article 4 and the rule of reason.[12]

[10] There is the possibility, of course, that the location of a port close to the entrance to a bay may bring about an opposite decision. If the port area is near the entrance to a bay, the littoral State may, of course, take a directly opposite view. By excluding such port area from being considered as part of the bay's waters, it might be possible to bring an otherwise larger indentiation within the twenty-four mile limit.

[11] If islands are the result of silting at the mouth of a bay, they are likely to be in some sort of orderly array. If they are the mountainous remnants of a submerged peninsula, this also may be true. On the other hand, if such islands are the result of independent volcanic action or some multiplicity of natural causes such as erosion from tidal currents, their positions may display no logical arrangement.

[12] Here, of course, we are presented with a minute and no doubt relatively unimportant example of one of the problems of codification. There is a limit to the process of advance formulation of general rules to be applied in particular cases involving particular circum-

The final sentence of paragraph 3 reads:

Islands within an indentation shall be included as if they were part of the water area of the indentation.

This is self explanatory and has but two features of interest in its implementation. First, the inclusion of the islands in the total area of the bay. Were they not to be so included, the littoral State would have to reckon upon a larger overall bay area to be compared with the semi-circle whose area is determined by the length of the closing line. This provision would appear to favor the littoral State in converting bay waters into internal waters. Where islands are present and the bays has more than one mouth, the provisions of the Convention lead to something of an oddity. An island is not a point in space, but a finite area of land. If the measurement line or a 24-mile closing line is split into additive segments as provided for by the second sentence, these segments will strike the islands at some point along the littoral. One part of such an island might then be within the bay – and its area counted as part of the waters of the bay, and the other part of the island might be outside of the bay. The low water mark of this latter part of the island, depending on the island's size and shape, might form part of the "normal" baseline of the territorial sea (marginal belt). States might find in their interest to invoke either paragraph 1 or paragraph 2 of Article 4 to resolve the difficulty. Again, this is something in the nature of hair splitting, but there are bays containing relatively large islands at the mouth and it is conceivable that hydrographic offices might become quite concerned about just how this rule should be applied.

(4) Paragraphs 4 and 5. These two paragraphs may perhaps be better understood if they are combined, thus:

If the distance between the low-water marks of the natural entrance points of a bay does not exceed twenty-four miles, a closing line may be drawn between these two water marks, and the waters enclosed thereby shall be considered as internal waters. Where the distance between the low water of the natural entrance points exceeds twenty-four miles, a straight base-line of twenty-four miles shall be drawn within the bay in such a manner as to enclose the maximum area of water that is possible with a line of that length.

It is the conjecture of this author that if paragraph 4 is read separately from paragraph 5, there *may* result a tendency in determining

stances. Further discussion at this juncture would involve a matrix of theoretical analysis at the expense of the objective of this section. For a brief view of codification as applied to the 1958 Geneva Conventions, see Max Sørenson, "Law of the Sea," 520 *International Conciliation* (Nov. 1958), p. 255.

the status of coastal waters (other than in cases of historic bays) to search for indentations, to measure their openings to ascertain whether they are more or less than twenty-four miles across, to compare them with the semi-circular area determined by the closing line, and then to decide whether there exist internal waters under the rules for bays. If the two paragraphs are read together, there appears greater likelihood that one will reconsider the matter in order to determine first whether a bay, under the provisions of paragraph 2 exists at all. The author's conjecture results from much reading of the literature where great stress is laid upon the 10-mile rule of bays, 24-rule of bays etc. It would seem that such stress can lead to a superficial conclusion on the part of some that if the distance between entrance points exceeds that prescribed by the rule, there can be no juridical bay.[13]

We now turn to the term, "natural entrance points," which are also mentioned in paragraph 3. If the indentation is one well marked, as provided in paragraph 2, and if the waters are land.locked at least to the extent suggested by the author above, and if the indentation is more than the mere curvature of the coast, as provided in paragraph 2, the bay will almost inevitably have natural entrance points, which are easily discernable. While there probably exist situations in which the indentation commences with a gentle curve *on each side* and then sharpens into a deep and well marked cut (Fig. 12), this author, after consulting numerous charts, has been unable to find one. A much

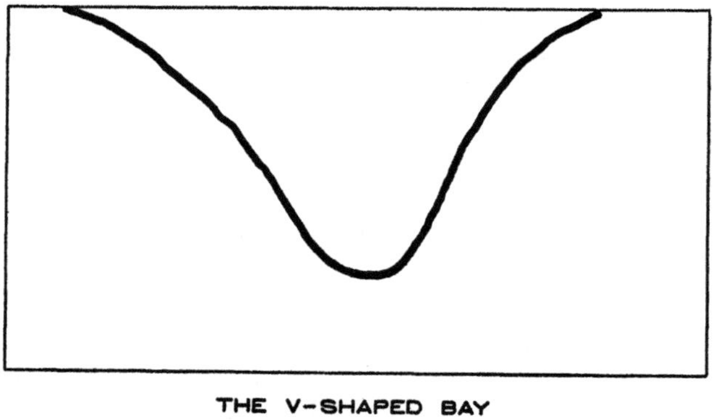

THE V-SHAPED BAY

Fig. 12

[13] It has been this author's experience that an appreciable number of busy decision makers, as well as some scholars, exhibit a tendency to fasten their thoughts upon what they conceive of as being the most important, rather than to proceed logically from the general to the particular. Stated another way, it can be said that for reasons and values not here specified a premature occlusion to inquiry takes place.

more frequent occurrence is that of a well marked entrance point on one side, and a gentle curve on the other. An example of this is the case of the Gulf of Cutch in India (Fig. 13).

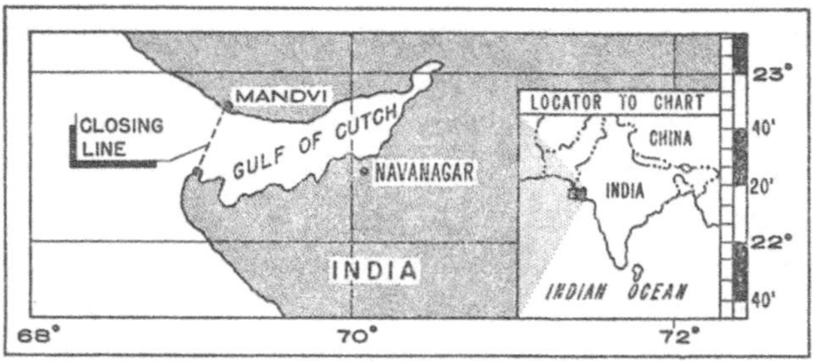

GULF OF CUTCH, INDIA

Fig. 13

The most logical method for drawing a closing line in such a situation would be to locate its origin on the side having the well marked entrance point and to locate its terminus at the closest point of land on the opposite side as shown in Figure 13. Any other line would, of course, be longer. If this shortest line is over twenty-four miles in length, then the littoral State will no doubt use it to determine the existence of a bay under the semi-circle rule. If the shortest possible line is under twenty-four miles in length, the littoral State may be expected to so locate the terminus of the closing line as to ensure a length of exactly twenty-four miles, on the seaward side. By so doing, the State acquires the greatest possible area of internal waters.

The "miles" referred to here are nautical miles of 6,076 feet or one-sixtieth of a degree of latitude.[14]

If the penetration we are considering meets the criteria for a bay and if the distance between the natural entrance points exceeds twenty-four miles, then a straight base line may be drawn in such a manner as to enclose the maximum area of water that is possible with a line of that length. Truly, a bay or indentation can be almost any size and meet most of the criteria of paragraph 2, except for the "land locked" provision,[15] which is dubious at least. Moray Firth is $73\frac{1}{2}$ miles

[14] For a more detailed discussion of the nautical mile, see Section B, below.

[15] Comment on the 24-mile maximum closing line is contained in Chapter 5. It might be pertinent to observe here, more perhaps in the role of a practicing mariner, than as a student of international law that generally speaking, a "land locked" bay having an entrance twenty-four miles across represents something of a contradiction in terms.

across between its natural entrance points.[16] This provision appears quite reasonable inasmuch as the extreme landward side is usually the most sheltered and most desired as internal waters. Also, because the interiors of bays have no uniformity or regularity of shape, the rule of so locating the 24-mile line as to enclose the maximum water area is the only general rule in the premises that is feasible and acceptable. But bays could be of such a shape and of such size as to make the choice of location of one 24-mile line rather difficult. The Gulf of Taranto in Italy (75 miles across) and the Gulf of Carpentaria in Australia (340 miles across) meet the semi-circle requirements for bays. But their interiors are of such a shape that more than one enclosure behind a 24-mile line is possible and the obvious choice for location of such a line in the Gulf of Taranto (enclosing the port of Taranto) is not the location at which there is yielded the maximum enclosed water area. Is there a solution in this situation? The rule appears to exclude more than one baseline by its use of the singular, and it uses the imperative "shall" rather than the permissive "may". For these two bays there appears no satisfactory solution under Article 7, if Australia or Italy, respectively, desire in these bays, areas of internal waters where such a maritime regime might best serve the interests of those States. The choice of these States would be:

(a) To enclose a segment of internal waters in accordance with the Article 7 rules, or

(b) Choose not to avail themselves of the Bay Rule at all with respect to these bays, or

(c) To make claims to complete sovereignty over these bays, involving Article 7, paragraph 6, and claiming these waters as "historic bays". [17]

(5) Paragraph 6. This paragraph reads:

The foregoing provisions shall not apply to so-called "historic" bays, or in any case where the straight base line system provided for in Article 4 is applied.

Historic bays are discussed in some detail in Part Three of this book. It is sufficient to point out that the wording of paragraph 6 is such that *no part* of the provisions of Article 7 shall be held to apply to the so-called "historic bays. While it provides that the bay

[16] See Chapter 4 for discussion of the Moray Firth case of 1906. This case is often known also as *Mortensen* v. *Peters*. See Section B, for chart of Moray Firth.

[17] This option is clearly conditional. The State making the claim has the onus of proving its right to do so. See Chapter 7, below.

rules shall not apply where the straight base line rules of Article 4 are used, it does not and cannot very well exclude from consideration and guidance the rules for Bays or some of the contents of Articles 4 and 5.

Section A(ii) IMPACT OF THE DEFINITION ON SOVEREIGNTY OVER THE WORLD'S BAYS

Hereunder are two lists of bays whose sovereignty status is believed to undergo the greatest change as a result of the 1958 Geneva Conventions, should it be finally adopted. The first list comprises those bays which might have been considered juridical bays prior to the advent of the 1958 Convention, but whose areas of internal waters would be increased by a factor of three or more as a result of the 1958 Definition. The second list comprises those bays which, by reason of their configuration, would not have been considered juridical bays before the 1958 Convention, but whose waters, in their entirety, would become internal waters as a result of the Convention.[18]

Bays whose areas of Internal Waters are increased by a factor of three or more [19]

1. Tasman Bay, New Zealand
*2. Spencer Gulf, Australia
**3. St. Vincent Gulf, Australia
4. Vansittart Bay, Australia
5. Maccluer Gulf, Dutch New Guinea
6. Labuk Bay, North Borneo
7. Darnel Bay, North Borneo
8. Rogay Bay, Philippines
9. Gulf of Martaban, Burma
***10. Skagafjiord, Iceland
11. Skjalfandi, Iceland
12. Pistilfjord, Iceland
13. Aarbus Bugt, Denmark
14. Bristol Channel, England
15. Thames Estuary, England
16. The Jade, Germany
17. Saronikos Kolpos, Greece
18. Lakonikos Kolpos, Greece
19. Golfo de Tadefoura, French Somaliland
20. Baie du Levier, French West Africa
21. Delagoa Bay, Mozambique
22. St. George's Bay, Newfoundland
23. Liverpool Bay, Northwest Territories, Canada.
24. Yakuta Bay, Alaska
25. Norton Bay, Alaska
26. Cook Inlet, Alaska
27. Baia do Marajo, Brazil
28. Golfo de Uraba, Colombia
29. Kara Bay, U.S.S.R.
30. Gulf of Cutch, India
31. Gulf of Cambay, India.

* Increase brought about by islands in mouth of bay.

** Increase due to islands in mouth of bay, but status in doubt in absence of careful measurement.

*** In mentioning Icelandic Bays, that State's recent domestic legislation on baselines is ignored. MacChesney, *U.S. Naval War College International Law Situation and Documents* 1956, pp. 466–72.

18 The author made a survey of all coastal areas in the world using *The Times Atlas*, *The Encyclopeadia Britannica Atlas* and appropriate charts of the U.S. Navy Hydrographic

Bays which become juridical Bays under the 1958 Convention and whose areas become internal waters in their entirety [20]

1. Huraki Gulf, New Zealand
2. Gulden Bay, New Zealand
3. Van Dieman Gulf, Australia
4. Exmouth Gulf, Australia
5. King Sound, Australia
6. Goodenough Bay, New Guinea
7. Wide Bay, New Britain
8. Astrolabe Bay, New Guinea
9. Brunei Bay, Borneo
10. Gulf Alaminos, Philippines
11. Lagonay Gulf, Philippines
12. Sibuguey Bay, Philippines
13. Suraga Wan, Japan
14. Uchiura Wan, Japan
15. Toyama Wan, Japan
16. Nemuro Wan, Japan
17. Tokchok Kundo, Korea (Inchon)
18. Kinchow Wan, Manchuria (Liaotung Peninsula)
19. Baie de Kompong Som, Cambodịa
20. Ao Ban Don, Thailand
21. The Wash, England
22. Lubecker Bucht, Germany
23. Baia de Setubal, Portugal
24. Golfo dell'Asinara, Sardinia
25. Golfo di Cagliari, Sardinia
26. Golfo di Napoli (Bay of Naples), Italy
27. Messinakos Kolpos, Greece
28. Corisco Bay, French Equatorial Africa
29. False Bay, Republic of South Africa
30. George Bay, Nova Scotia
31. Cape Cod Bay, Massachusetts, U.S.A.
32. Bahia de Banderas, Mexico
33. Ensenada de la Broa, Cuba
34. Bahia Camerones, Argentina (Doubtful)
35. Gulf of Iskenderum, Turkey
36. Sea of Azov, U.S.S.R.
37. Bay of Cancale, France
38. Bay of Chaleur, Canada
39. Conception Bay, Newfoundland
40. Miramichi Bay, Canada
41. Trinity Bay, Canada
42. Chesapeake Bay, U.S.A.
43. Delaware Bay, U.S.A.

Office. In a survey of such magnitude, it is quite conceivable that errors can occur. It is hoped that only a minimum of errors have been made. The few doubtful cases have been so labeled. In doubtful cases careful calculation using using on the spot surveys would be in order.

[19] In arriving at this list, the author adopted the assumption that there did, in fact, exist a 10-mile rule of bays and that the bays in this list were juridical bays. Thus the 'factor of three or more' difference in the area of internal waters results from a comparison of the area bounded by a 10-mile closing line with that bounded by a 24-mile closing line. Brief consideration will probably cause the reader to agree that this is not an unreasonalbe procedure. If a bay is of such a configuration as to permit a 10-mile closing line, there is great likelihood that the State will have considered its waters as internal waters; that such a statement is likely to reflect the reality of any given situation can be easily demonstrated by reference to appropriate large charts in the 1 : 1,000,000 scale category or larger.

[20] In compiling this list, it was first assumed that the bay in question had not been considered a juridical bay by its littoral State, except possibly as an historic bay. By reason of the configurations of most of these bays, this is a reasonable assumption because the majority of them are bowlshaped, or approximately so, having coast lines well open to the sea. Secondly, there are included only those bays which are twenty-four miles or less in breadth at the mouth. To select those bodies of water having entrances greater than 24-miles in breadth and then to establish by trial and error a 24-mile closing line yielding the greatest area of internal waters would, for a world survey, involve an extraordinarily lengthy series of calculations; this was considered impractical. All bays included in this list have been compared with the semi-circular area rule and they qualify as juridical bays. Those bays which are claimed now as historic bays but which also qualify for this list are included.

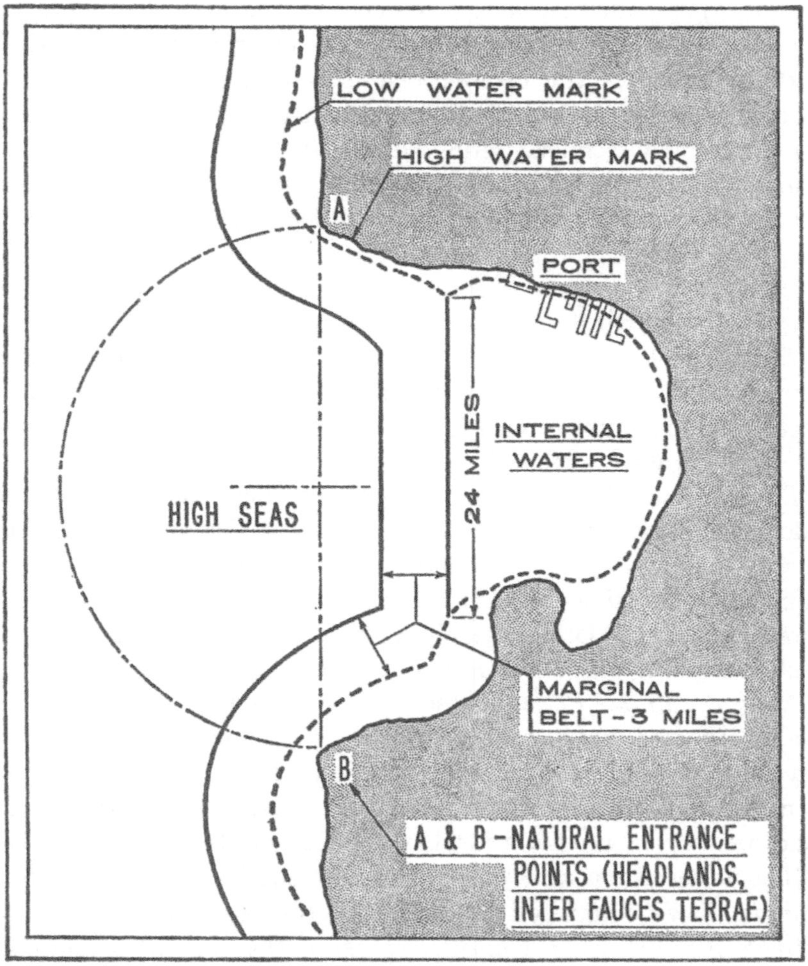

A HYPOTHETICAL BAY

Fig. 14

Section B GLOSSARY OF TERMS

The preceding Section discussed the definition of a Bay as formulated by the 1958 United Nations Conference on the Law of the Sea. It is the purpose of this Section to define the technical terms associated with the study of the International Law of Bays and to illustrate through sketches of hypothetical and actual bays the application of the terms. All technical terms contained in Article 7 of the 1958 Convention on the Territorial Sea and Contiguous Zone are defined herein, as are those terms appearing in other articles of the Convention which are pertinent to this study.

Figure 14 is a sketch representing a hypothetically "ideal" bay containing many of the terms defined herein.[1]

Coast, coast line: The coast is the edge of the terra firma in immediate contact with the sea. The coast line is a more less indefinite and irregular line resulting from meteorological or other conditions, along which the contact is made.[2]

Land-Locked Waters: In the preceding section this term was considered at some length. As applied to bays it has only a rhetorical quality tending to emphasize that, in accordance with Article 7 of the Convention, a juridical bay must constitute more than a mere curvature of the coast. Otherwise, the term when used generally in connection with bays is devoid of precise meaning.

Natural Entrance Points: These are the points at which the coastline can most reasonably be said to turn inward to form an indentation or bay. In the history of the law of bays and its codification, this is a new term. It appears to be about as accurately expressive of the natural conditions envisioned for a juridical bays as any that can be devised. Although never appearing in the Drafts of the United Nations International Law Commission on the law of the sea, it was used in the opinion of the Court in *United Kingdom* v. *Norway*. Other and older

[1] This particular sketch is similar to that often used by A. L. Shalowitz, U.S. Coast and Geodetic Survey, in the articles he has written for various technical journals in recent years. Examples are: Aaron L. Shalowitz, "Boundary Problems Raised by the Submerged Lands Act," 54 *Columbia Law Review* (Nov. 1954), pp. 1021–48; and A. L. Shalowitz, "Where Are Our Seaward Boundaries," 83 *U.S. Naval Institute Proceedings* (June 1957), pp. 616–627.

[2] Capitaine de Frégate (CDR) Henri Bencker, French Navy, "Maritime Geographical Terminology Relating to Various Hydrographic Subdivisions of the Globe," XIX *International Hydrographic Review* (Aug. 1942), pp. 60–74.

terms which have been used are mouth of the bay,[3] headlands,[4] or *inter fauces terrae* (sometimes called *inter fauces terrarum*).[5]

Island: Article 10, paragraph 1, of the 1958 Convention defines an island as a naturally formed area of land, surrounded by water, which is above water at high tide.[6]

Low Water Marks: Reference has been made to this expression in Section A, above, and further reference will be made in Section D of this chapter and in Chapter 6, CODIFICATION. Before proceeding with a definition, attention is again invited to Article 3 of the Convention where the normal base line is described as the low-water line along the coast as marked on the large scale charts officially recognized by the country.

Low Water mark is the intersection of the plane of mean low-water with the shore.[7] On nautical charts, the shore line shown is the boundary between land and water at *high tide.* Where the low-water line (or mark) differs considerably from the high-water line, the low-water line may be indicated by dots in the case of mud, sand, gravel, or stones (with the kind of material indicated) and by a characteristic symbol in the case of rock or gravel.[8] Such markings are more likely to appear on large scale charts then on small scale charts, hence the provision in Article 3 is well taken. The plane of mean low water is, specifically, the average of all low tides, and it serves as the average

[3] This is the term which was favored in the drafts of the International Law Commission. It is the author's belief, that practical application of this term can lead to some imprecision of expression. The U.S. Navy Hydrographic Office defines "mouth" as: "An opening such as that through which the water of a river is discharged, the entrance to a harbor, etc." *Navigation Dictionary*, U.S. Hydrographic Office Publication No. 220 (1956), p. 144. It appears to be used interchangeably with "natural entrance points" in rticle 7.

[4] This term is used by the Tribunal in its Award and Recommendation in the North Atlantic Coast Fisheries Arbitration, 7 September 1910. James B. Scott, *Hague Court Reports*, p. 146ff. Its name is applied to a particular doctrine or school of thought on the law of bays, Chs. 4 and 5, below. For purposes of present usage, the term "headland" is not satisfactory since to the mariner it connotes a precipitous cape or promontory. H. O. *Navigation Dictionary*, p. 100; René de Kerchove, *International Maritime Dictionary* (1948), p. 331.

[5] This is the term used rather consistently by the Court in *Mortensen* v. *Peters*, 1906, (Moray Firth Case), and in the ensuing debate in the House of Lords. 14 *Scots Law Times* (1906) Rep. 227; 169 Hansard, *Parliamentary Debates* (4th Series) Cols. 979, 983ff. Jessup, *The Law of Territorial Waters and Maritime Jurisdiction* (1927), pp. 430–6; Jones, Unpublished Naval War College Manuscript. In current codification studies, it appeared in the United Nations Committee of Experts Report, (A/CN.A/61/Add. 1 of 1953).

[6] Commander Bencker writes that the International Hydrographic Bureau formulated mathematical definitions for small islets (1 to 10 square kilometers), islets (10 to 100 square kilometers), and islands (100 to 5×10^6 square kilometers). While the marine parlance of some languages makes more continuous use of these distinct terms, they do not find common use in International Law.

[7] Kerchove, *op. cit.*, p. 435. See also: 24 *American Journal of International Law, Supplement* (1930), p. 248; and U.S. Naval War College, *International Law Situations*, 1937, p. 128.

[8] Bowditch, *American Practical Navigator*, p. 107.

or reference plane from which the depth of water is indicated on nautical charts. It is to be noted that the reference planes used for chart construction vary with the agency or country constructing the chart. For this reason, the modifying phrase "officially recognized by the coastal state" is necessary. Mean low water is the reference plane for nearly all charts prepared by the U.S. Navy Hydrographic office from its own surveys. Mean lower low water, the average of the lower of the two daily tides, is the plane used on the Pacific Coast of the United States, the Hawaiian Islands, the Philippines, and Alaska. Mean low water springs, the average of the low waters at spring tides,[9] is the reference plane for most British Admiralty Charts.[10] In areas of the world where there is a large tidal range, the reference plane can be quite significant.

Large Scale Chart: The scale of a chart is the ratio of a given distance on the chart to the actual distance on earth which it represents. A "natural" scale is a simple fraction or, say, one inch on the chart equals 80,000 inches on earth, and is usually expressed $\frac{1}{80,000}$. 80,000 inches equal 1.097 nautical miles. A "numerical" scale is a statement indicating usually the number of miles per inch. Scale varies with latitude on Mercator charts and most nautical charts are on the Mercator projection. Where one uses a large scale chart, the change due to differences in latitude is relatively insignificant. A chart covering a large area is called a small scale chart and one covering a relatively small area is called a large scale chart. Coast charts and harbor charts having scales of $\frac{1}{50,000}$ to $\frac{1}{100,000}$ are those generally referred to as large scale charts.[11]

Closing line: This is the line marking the boundary between the internal waters of a bay and the marginal belt. It is used where the boundary is drawn between the natural entrance points. By the terms of the 1958 Convention, the maximum length of this line is twenty-four miles. Paragraph 3 of Article 7 of the Convention points out that this line can be discontinuous if islands are situated in the mouth of the bay.

[9] Spring tides occur near the time of the full moon and new moon when the tidal effects of sun and moon are in phase. When the sun and moon are thus acting together, high tides are higher than average, and low tides are lower. When the moon is at quadrature, at first and last quarter, the tidal effects of the two bodies are opposing each other and the range of the tide is less than average. These are called *neap* tides.

[10] Hill, Utegaard and Riordan, *Dutton's Navigation and Piloting* (1958), pp. 201–203.

[11] *Bowditch*, pp. 103–4.

Mile: As used here and in general nautical parlance, the mile is a unit of measurement associated with the size of the earth. In 1929, the International Hydrographic Bureau recommended adoption of a standard nautical mile valued at 1852 international meters. This is 6,076.1033 U.S. feet. The United States adopted this value in 1954, and nearly all major maritime countries now use it.[12] A mile is approximately 1/60 of a degree of latitude.

Other Measures of Length

League: Older cases, texts and national laws make frequent use of the term league (French "lieu"). Captain Meyer of Norway who has done extensive research in this matter, writes that the league measurement has gone through many changes. Originally the geographical league was described as 1/15 of a degree at the equator and that a quarter of this was 1855.109 meters. The 18th Century German sea league of 1/15 of a degree of latitude was adopted by a Royal decree for the then kingdom of Denmark and Norway on 22 February 1812. Hence, today, the Norwegian Sea League (and the Norwegian Marginal belt) is 1/15 of a degree or four nautical miles. The English marine league, as well as the French "lieu" is 1/20 of a degree of latitude or 3 nautical miles.[13]

Fathom: An ancient measurement now used for measuring depths of water, cordage and anchor chains. It is equal to six feet. Charts constructed by countries using the metric system usually show depths in meters.[14]

Cable: This is a unit still favored in British maritime parlance. It is generally considered to be about 600 feet with 10 cables to the nautical mile. In the Royal Navy, it is reckoned as exactly 608 feet. In the U.S. Navy it is 720 feet.[15]

Straight Base Line: This line has the same boundary purpose as the closing line, but in Article 7 of the International Convention the term is used for bays to distinguish such a boundary when drawn within a juridical bay from the closing line which is drawn between the natural entrance points. Because of possible confusion with the base-line system provided for in Article 4, this author has chosen to use the term "base line" rather sparingly in connection with the law of bays.

Harbor, Port: This term is mentioned in Article 8 of the Convention and it should be considered in connection with the law of bays, as suggested in Section A, above. Kerchove's definitions for these terms is quoted:

Any place which affords good anchorage and a fairly safe station for ships, or in which ships can be sheltered by the land from wind and sea. Also called haven. It is not necessary that it be landlocked or absolutely safe for ships. It is enough that it affords a reasonably safe place of retreat from wind and storms. A place where ships are brought for commercial purposes to load and unload goods and

12 *Bowditch*, pp. 26–27.

13 CAPT Christopher B. V. Meyer, Royal Norwegian Navy, *The Extent of Jurisdiction in Coastal Waters* (1937), pp. 521–2.

14 *Bowditch*, p. 27.

15 *Navigation Dictionary* (H.0.220), p. 31.

passengers. The term "harbor" strictly speaking applies only to the area of water with the works necessary for its formation, protection, and maintenance, such as breakwaters, jetties, and so on. A port is made up of a harbor plus the freight and passenger structures such as docks, wharves, quays, and so forth, with their equipment.[16]

Having discussed in Section A the definition of a bay within the meaning of Article 7 of the 1958 Convention, and having defined, above, some of the more frequently used, but often not so well iunderstood terms, we shall proceed to illustrate through the use of part of a typical chart and several sketches, a representative number of bays. While many of the features of a bay can be shown on a sketch, only a large scale nautical chart will show all of them. The first illustration is that of a chart of Moray Firth. In this bay, the line between the natural entrance points is 73.5 miles long. Both the old 10 mile closing line and the twenty-four mile line are shown. Not illustrated is the semi-circle whose area must be compared with the area of the bay in order to determine if a juridical bay is present. Next is a sketch of Apalachee Bay in Florida which is truly, a mere curvature of the coast; the sketch shows the comparison between the area of this indentation and the area of a semi-circle. Next is a sketch of Galveston Bay which is truly land-locked and which contains several harbors. Next is a sketch of Saronikos Kolpos which shows the difference an island can make in establishing a 24 mile line. The final sketch is of Buzzard's Bay, Massachusetts, which illustrates how a fringe of islands can make up one side of a bay.

[16] Kerchove, *op. cit.*, p. 323.

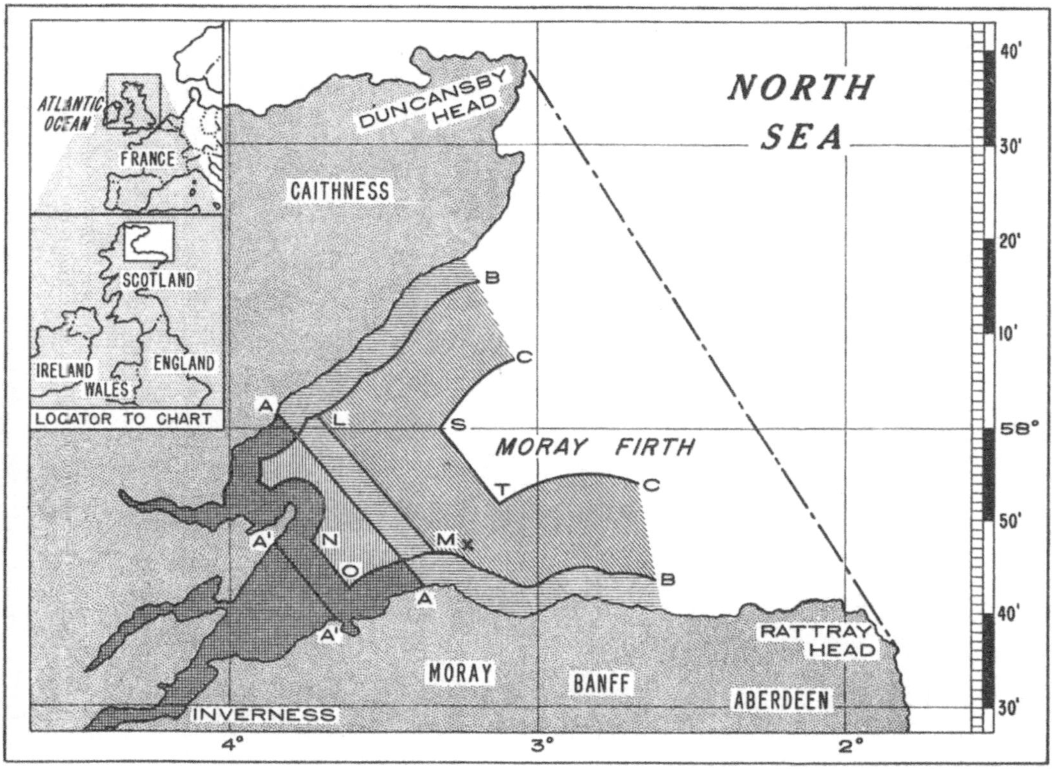

MORAY FIRTH, SCOTLAND

Fig. 15

LEGEND

AA – 24-mile closing line.
BLMB – Outer limit of 3-mile marginal belt using 24-mile closing line.
A'A' – 10-mile closing line.
BLNOMB – Outer limit of 3-mile marginal belt using 10-mile closing line.
CSTC – Outer limit of 12-mile marginal belt using 24-mile closing line.
-—- – Line *inter fauces terrae*, as described in Moray Firth Case of 1906.
X – Site of alleged offense of Emmanuel Mortenson in Moray Firth Case of 1906.

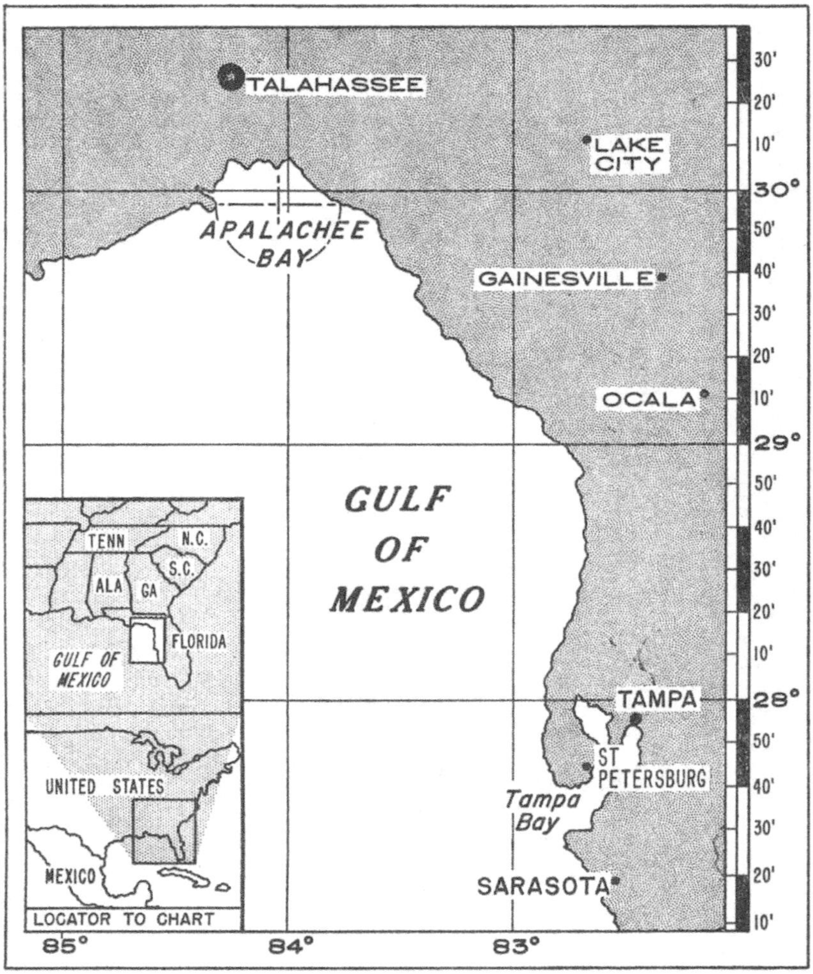

APALACHEE BAY

Fig. 16

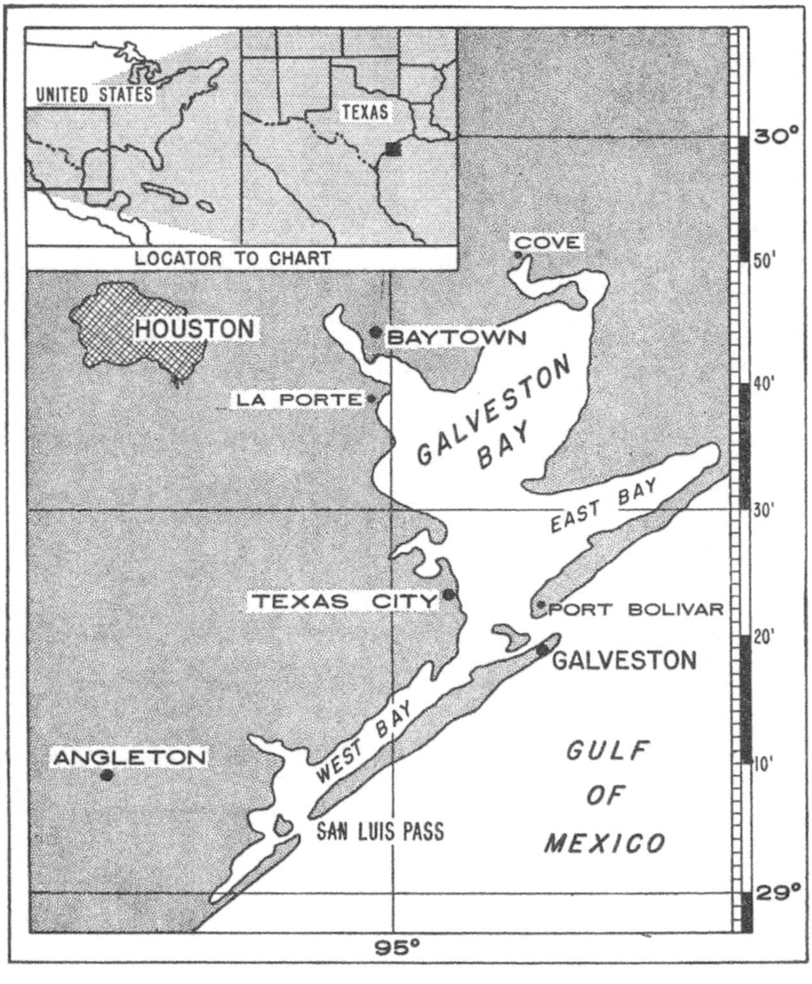
UNITED STATES
TEXAS
LOCATOR TO CHART
30°
50'
40'
30'
20'
10'
29°
95°
COVE
HOUSTON
BAYTOWN
LA PORTE
GALVESTON BAY
EAST BAY
TEXAS CITY
PORT BOLIVAR
GALVESTON
WEST BAY
ANGLETON
SAN LUIS PASS
GULF OF MEXICO

Fig. 17

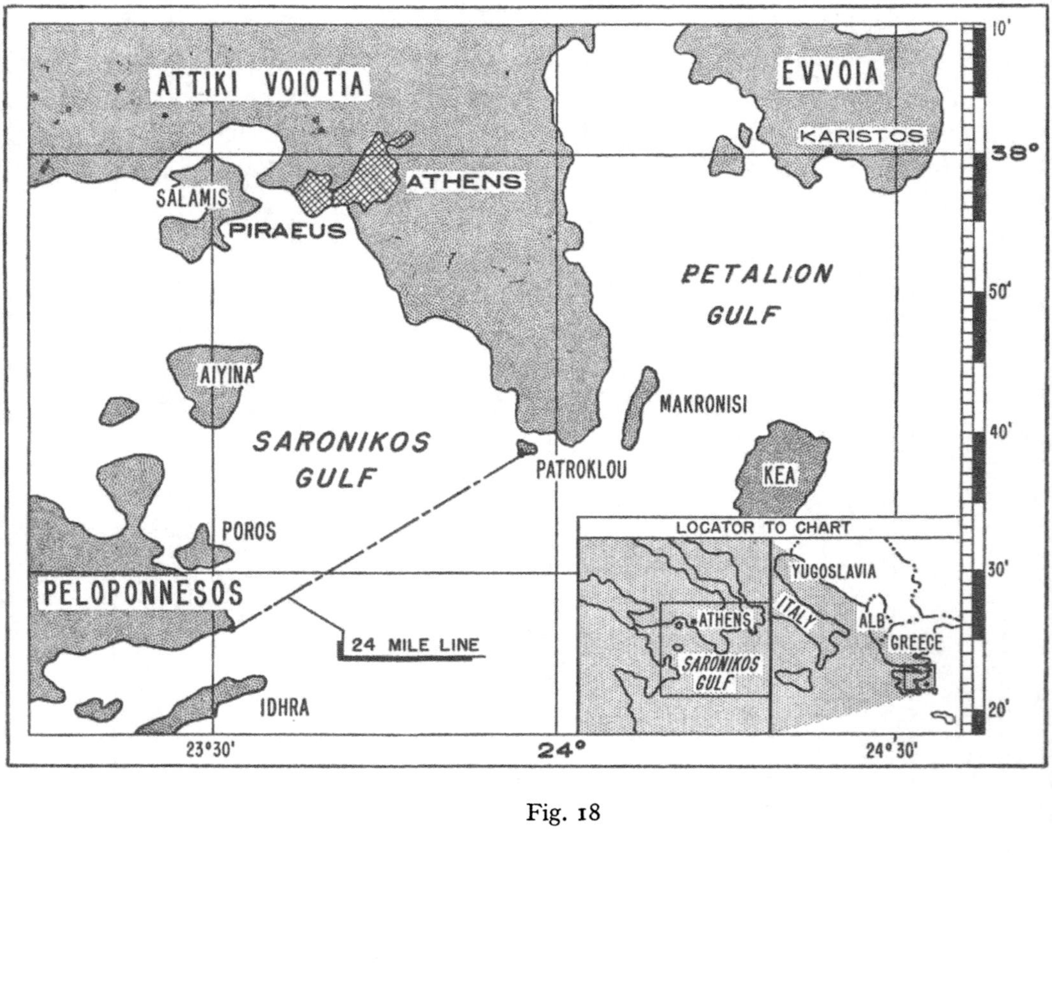
ATTIKI VOIOTIA
EVVOIA
KARISTOS
ATHENS
SALAMIS
PIRAEUS
PETALION
GULF
AIYINA
MAKRONISI
SARONIKOS
GULF
PATROKLOU
KEA
POROS
PELOPONNESOS
24 MILE LINE
IDHRA
LOCATOR TO CHART
YUGOSLAVIA
ITALY
ALB
GREECE
ATHENS
SARONIKOS
GULF
10'
38°
50'
40'
30'
20'
23°30'
24°
24°30'

Fig. 18

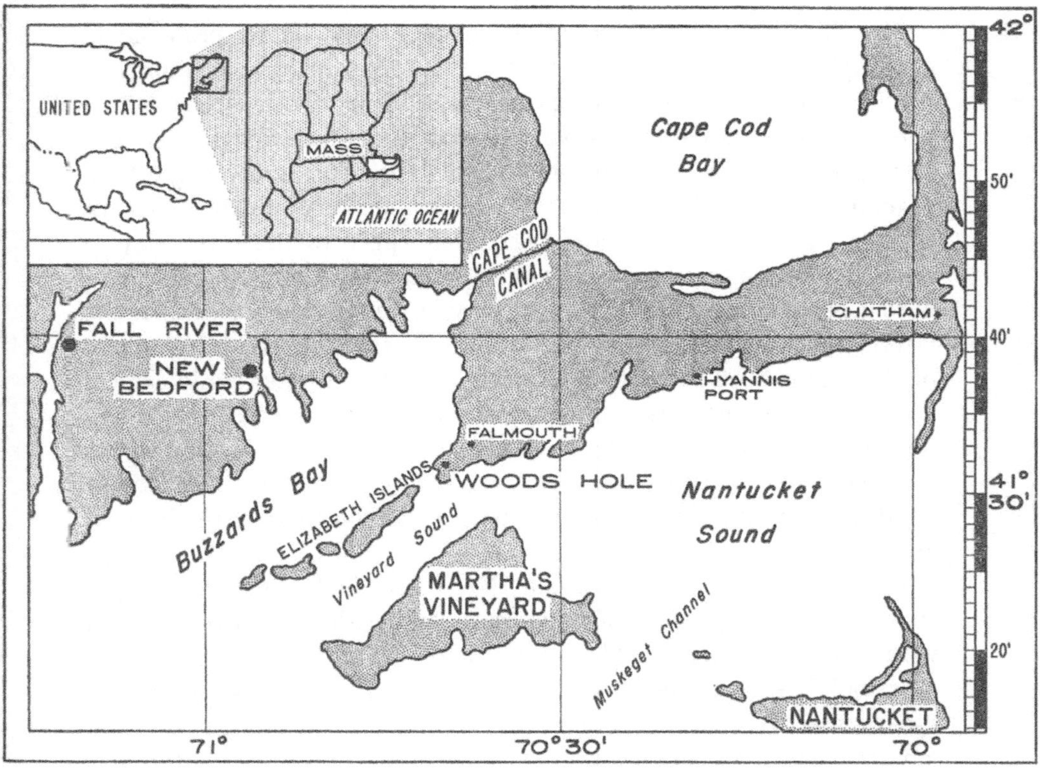

BUZZARDS BAY

Fig. 19

Section C Linguistic variations in terms

Sumner W. Cushing, in an article entitled "The Boundaries of the New England States," wrote this concerning bays:

Bays are usually used for harbors, and most harbors are places of concentrated activity where strict and prompt jurisdiction is required.[1]

Mr. Cushing was not an international lawyer but a professional geographer who specialized in economic geography and municipal problems. He was an academician and a student of a discipline whose subject matter is closely associated with that discussed herein. His statement, whether written peremptorily or after some cogitation, reminds us that others, who may not and probably do not concern themselves with the law, may very well apply to the term, bay, a nuance to which the lawyer may be understandably oblivious. Perhaps with a particular subject matter, it may be quite unnecessary that the lawyer have a knowledge of semantic variations in the terminology of that subject.[2] That is to say, it may eventuate that terminological variations in a particular subject matter are of such a nature that they do not materially affect the lawyer's consideration of it. But we do not really know until we investigate, and for the subject matter at hand this author is unwilling to dispose of the question on the basis of any intuitive conclusions.

A contemporary British author, Mr. F. N. Ball, says very simply that the main object of language was – and perhaps still is – to deal with material objects.[3] The contemporary Dutch Doctor Boasson describes law as a social phenomenon which makes use of words, spoken and written. He points out that there is no thought possible outside verbal discussive argument; that the imparting of thought is *a priori* tied down by the limits of communicative language; that to a great extent the thought *follows* the language while the writer (or speaker) pursues his ideas; and that here is an obvious impediment to international contact and international law.[4] But very long ago,

[1] Sumner W. Cushing, "The Boundaries of the New England States" X *Annals of the Association of American Geographers* (Jan. 1928), at p. 28.

[2] Semantics or semiotics, is the study of a general theory of signs which investigates the properties of all forms of linguistic expression. Hans Reichenbach, *The Rise of Scientific Philosophy* (1958), p. 226.

[3] F. N. Ball, *Intellectual Calculus* (1951), p. 77.

[4] Charles Boasson, *Sociological Aspects of Law and International Adjustment* (1950), p. 37. The ideas of Boasson and Ball appear to be shared by the late Oxford philosopher Ludwig Wittgenstein: "The Uses of Language," *The Age of Analysis*, Morton White, Ed., (1955), pp. 225–236. See also Quincy Wright, *The Study of International Relations* (1955), pp. 269–306.

Voltaire brought the matter into perspective by pointing out to us that while there is no complete language, all words in all languages are necessarily images of sensations; and while through long and ever more faulty usage, there are words which no longer signify what they ought, all languages have some natural or common words whose meanings vary hardly at all.[5] The question is, it seems to the author, is there a word or language problem in connection with the law of bays? Or, stated another way, is the legal definition of a bay *sufficiently* expressive of the image of a bay beheld by the objects of international law? This leads to the closely tied question: Do the objects of international law in different States, using different languages, entertain of the word "bay" images which are sufficiently similar to be expressed by a single legal definition? In short, does one definition for "bay" meet needs on a universal and polylingual basis? The word "bay" is perhaps not as simple as the word "horse" but it should not present such obstinate complexities as "democracy" or "agression"; it probably does permit reasonable analysis leading to reliable conclusions without exhaustive and completely definitive investigation and discussion. As the late Henry L. Mencken's work, *The American Language*, suggests, investigative pursuit of the origins and nuances of even a presumably simple word can be quite lengthy and, except for students of lexicography, not altogether fruitful. On the other hand, where disputes arise and their settlement appears to turn on the meaning applied to a word, a disinterested observer is likely to react by suggesting that if both parties really had the same thing in mind, the dispute would probably not have arisen.[6]

Commencing, first with the English language, we find a standard dictionary definition of the term to be:

An inlet of the sea, usually smaller than a gulf, but of the same general character. The name is often used for large tracts of water around which the land forms a curve, or for any recess or inlet between capes or headlands.[7]

Roget's Thesaurus does not classify "bay" as the leading word of a group, but reserves that to the word, gulf.[8] Turning from the lexico-

[5] Voltaire, *A Philosophical Dictionary*, English Translation of 1824, Vol. V, pp. 281–299.

[6] That the lexicographer's definition of a bay may play a part in the settlement of a dispute at law is illustrated in the opinion of the Supreme Court of California in *Ocean Industries* v. *Supreme Court of California* (1927) 200 Calif. 235; McNair and Lauterpacht, *Annual Digest of International Law Cases 1927–28* (1931), Case No. 89.

[7] *Webster's New International Dictionary*, 2nd Ed., (1935), p. 234.

[8] The passage is quoted in pertinent part:

393. "*Gulf.* – N. land covered with water, gulf, gulph, bay, inlet, bight, estuary, arm of the sea, fiord, armlet; frith, firth, ostiary, mouth; lagune, lagoon; indraught; cove, creek; natural harbor; roads; strait narrows; Euripus; sound, belt, gut, kyles."

grapher's view to that of the mariner, we may be somewhat surprised by the latter's definition. *The Sailor's Word Book* of 1867 offered the following:

An inlet of the sea formed by the curvature of the land between two capes or headlands, often used synonymously with gulf; though in strict accuracy, the term should be applied only to those large recesses which are wider from cape to cape than they are deep. Exposed to sea winds, a bay is most insecure. A bay has proportionally a wider entrance than either a gulf or haven; a creek has usually a small inlet, and is always much less than a bay.[9]

A few years later a Lieutenant F. S. Basset, U.S. Navy, writing for an American word book, had this to say:

An inlet of the sea, having a wide entrance, and usually smaller than a gulf, although many large sheets of water are named bays. Of the many names adapted to designate inlets from the seas, those of fiord and vuk may be properly included under the head of bay.[10]

A more contemporary work, that of de Kerchove, offers this definition:

The expanse of water between two capes or headlands. A comparatively slight indentation in the coastline, as distinguished from a gulf, lock, firth, and so on. The limit of maritime jurisdiction (called seaward limit) of a bay or estuary, the entrance to which does not exceed ten nautical miles in width, is a line drawn across the entrance. Where the entrance spreads ten nautical miles in width, the saward limit is a line drawn accross the bay or estuary where the width first narrows to ten nautical miles.[11]

From the above, it will be seen that the Anglo-American view stressed headlands or capes, the fact that the indentation is relatively broader than it is deep, and that shelter is not one of the prominent characteristics. What purported to be an international definition was, according to Commander Bencker, formulated by the International Hydrographic Bureau in 1940–41. The Bureau's definition of the bay was:

Penetration of the sea into the coast; wider in the middle than at the entrance.

By comparison, a gulf was defined as:

Vast expanse of the sea which penetrates into the interior of the land; in general the entrance is wider than its length.[12]

Subsequently, the U.S. Navy published its *Nagigation Dictionary* wherein bay is defined as:

A portion of the sea which penetrates into the interior of tha land. It is usually wider in the middle than at the entrance. It may be similar to a gulf but smaller.

[9] ADM. W. H. Smyth, Royal Navy, *The Sailor's Word Book*, Rev. by VADM E. Belcher, Royal Navy (1867), p. 87.

[10] *A Naval Encyclopedia* (1881), p. 70.

[11] René de Kerchove, *International Maritime Dictionary* (1947), p. 45.

[12] Bencker, "Maritime Geographical Terminology," *op. cit.*, at p. 69.

The definition given for gulf is identical with that of the International Hydrographic Bureau, as mentioned by Commander Bencker.[13]

It is apparent that, from a technical point of view, the definition has undergone some changes. Headlands and capes seem no longer to be mentioned and the proportions have changed. The bay seems bottle shaped rather than bowl shaped as it was before.[14]

Turning now to languages other than English, we shall first indicate a representative list of such languages, and the word for bay in each of them:

French	– Baie
German	– Bucht
Spanish	– Bahía
Portuguese	– Baía (Bahía also used in Brazil)
Italian	– Baia
Dutch	– Baai
Greek	– Ormos
Japanese	– Wan (Same word for gulf or inlet)
Finnish	– Lahti
Chinese	– Haiwan
Russian	– Bukhta
Turkish	– Koy
Danish	– Bugt
Norwegian	– Bukt
Swedish	– Bukt
Arabic	– Khaleez, or Sham min al bakr

The meanings actually applied to these terms are discussed below.

French. The brief definition from *Nouveau Petit Larousse Illustré* is:

rade, petit golfe.

In that work, golfe is defined:

Partie de mer qui s'enfonce dans les terres.[15]

[13] U.S. Navy Hydrographic Office, *Navigation Dictionary*, H. O. Publication No. 220 (1956), pp. 23, 96.

[14] A reversal of the trend appears, however, in the definition contained in the second (and latest) dictionary of the International Hydrographic Bureau. This definition reads: "A comparatively slight indentation in the coast line with a wide opening, in distinction to GULF, LOCH, FIRTH, etc." *Hydrographic Dictionary*, compiled by the International Hydrographic Bureau, 2nd Edition, (1951), p. 7. The reason, then, for pursuing the matter further than a simple resort to the word book of the International Bureau is obvious.

[15] This definition was submitted to the author, in the U.S. Naval Intelligence School Letter of 29 June 1959, hereinafter referred to as U.S. Naval Intelligence School letter.

Emile Littré in his *Dictionnaire de la Langue Française* of 1885 defined the term:

Petit golfe dont l'entrée est reserrée.[16]

Pierre Larousse in his *Grand Dictionnaire Universel du XIX Siècle* offers the following:

BAIE s.f. (bê-du v. fr. bayer ou beèr, être ouvert) Geogr. et mar. Petit enfoncement de la mer dans l'intérieur des terres, qui comme un port, peut servir d'abri aux vaisseaux.[17]

In *La Grande Encyclopédie Larousse*, the following is offered;

En Marine on désigne particulièrement sous le nom de baie une partie de mer s'enfoncant dans la terre, intermédiaire comme grandeur entre le golfe et l'anse, et largement ouverte du côté de la haute mer. Une baie ne peut donc servir de mouillage que lorsque'il n'y a pas à redouter de forts vents du large, et que la terre du fond y est très bonne.[18]

Dictionnaire Diplomatique offers the following:

La Baie est une échancrure dans une côté par où la mer pénètre. Baies, golfes et anses ne différent que par leur importance matérielle, la baie étant l'intermédiaire entre le golfe et l'anse, l'un vaste, l'autre miniscule. C'est parce que les baies ou golfes peuvent être d'une étendue différente que se pose alors la question de l'État riverain sur le territoire maritime.[19]

Summing up, then, the French version agree that a bay penetrate into the land, as a sort of gate; that it is likely to be something of a shelter, and that it is relatively large in area.[20]

German. Meyers *Konversationalexikon* has the following definitions:

BAI. Eine Einbiegung des Meeres in das Land. Die Bai ist kleiner als der Meerbusen, grösser als die Bucht, doch ist im allgemeinen der Gebrauch dieser Namen willkürlich.
BUCHT. Ein von einer Seite öffener Meereseinschnitt, kleiner als die Bai.
GOLF. Soviel wie Meerbusen (vom Griechischen Kolpos).
MEERBUSEN. Weit ins Land hinreichende Einbiegen des Meeres; vgl. Bai. Ist die Verbindung mit dem öffenen Meer nur schmal, so entsteht ein Binnenmeer.
BINNENMEER. Mit dem Ozean nur durch einen im Verhältnis zu ihrer Oberfläche sehr schmalen Kanal in Verbindung stehende Meeresteile, wie das Mittelländische und das Schwarze Meer, die Ostsee, das Rote Meer, u.s.w.

[16] Vol. I, p. 278. Included therewith is a discussion of the etymology of the word. The passage is quoted hereunder as Appendix A.
[17] Vol. II, p. 55.
[18] Vol. IV, p. 1171.
[19] Vol. I, p. 273.
[20] French also has the following more or less synonymous words: Anse – très petit golfe (inlet).
Estuaire – golfe formé par l'embouchure l'un fleuve.
Nouveau Petit Larousse Illustré.

German does not seem to have special words for inlet or estuary. The German words for sound, *Sund* and *Meerenge*, are really words for strait, the former having to do specifically with the channel between the Danish Seeland and the Swedish Schonen, the passage between the Kattegat and the Baltic.[21] There is a special word for a body of water that is virtually landlocked. No mention is made of shelter or headlands. It appears that the German definitions have much in comm on the French.

Russian.[22] The most frequently used and most widely accepted equivalent for the word, bay, is *bukhta* (sing.) or *bukty* (plu.) Definitions are:

BUKTY. More or less deeply indented (into land) sectors of seas, oceans or lakes of relatively complex outline. Being connected with the sea only with narrow passageways or inlets. BUKTY are sheltered from the direct effects of winds; consequently in the development of the shore line the effect of tides is much less than along the open sea shoreline.[23]
BUKHTA. A small gulf, more or less sheltered from storms and wave washing.[24]
BUKHTA. A small gulf protected from waves and winds by promontories jutting out into the sea.[25]
BUKHTA. Not large; protected naturally by rocks; where of sufficient depth, it provides a convenient anchorage for boats.[26]

The Russian equivalent of the word, gulf, is *zaliv*. This is a portion of the sea or lake jutting into the land with a wide open egress.[27]

It is the conclusion of Mr. George S. Mitchell that the word *bukhta* is generally used for bays and that *zaliv* is reserved for larger, deeper and more exposed bodies of water. The Russian translation for Bay of Biscay use the term *zaliv* and not *bukhta*. Other Russian terms are:

CUBA. Drowned River Mouth.[28]

[21] Naval Intelligence School letter.

[22] The author is much indebted to Mr. George S. Mitchell of Washington, D.C. who kindly sent appropriate excerpts from his unpublished thesis, ***Russian-English Dictionary-Glossary in Geomorphology and Related Sciences***. Other sources are the Russian Research Institute of Harvard University and the U.S. Naval Intelligence School.

[23] USSR. Vsesoivznyi naucho-issledovatel′ skii′ geologieheskii institut. *Geologicheskii slovaŕ*, Tom (Vol.) 1–2, Moskva, 1955, pp. 402; 445, hereinafter referred to as Geologicheskii slovar'.

[24] A. S. Barkov, *Slovaŕ Spravochnik po Fizicheskoi geografii*, (1954), p. 307, hereinafter referred to as Barkov.

[25] U.S. Naval Intelligence School, citing *Bolshaya Sovetskaya Entseklopeduja*.

[26] Russian Research Institute of Harvard University, citing the *Dictionary of Modern Russian Literary Usage*.

[27] Mitchell thesis citing *Geologicheskii Slovaŕ*, p. 289 and *Barkov*, pp. 90–91.

[28] Barkov, pp. 90–1, cited by Mitchell.

LAGOON. A borrowed Spanish word which, in Russian, means a shallow body of water enclosed in the shore zone, having water of varying salinity, and formed as a result of drowned estuaries of rivers, gulfs and bays being cut off from the sea by a spit or bar.[29]

The Russian term emphasizes the narrow passageway to the open sea and the quality of protection.

Portuguese. The U.S. Naval Intelligence School, citing *Pequeno Dicionario Brasileiro Da Lingua Portuguesa,* offers the following definitions:

Bay, *Baía.* A small gulf, with a narrow entrance. To this, Commander A. B. de Vasconcellos, Brazilian Navy, of the Brazilian Naval War College, adds:

BAÍA (or Bahía). A small gulf with a narrow entrance or a part of the sea between two points of land that penetrates into the sea leaving between them an opening.[30]

Gulf, *Golfo.* A portion of the ocean or sea extending into the land and whose entrance is very wide.[31]

Inlet, *Enseada* or *Angra.* A small bay or a curve in the coastline.

The Portuguese definitions appear to emphasize the narrow entrance and the distinction between a bay and a gulf.

Italian. From *Dizionario Enciclopedico Italiano* (1956), we are offered the following definition:

BAIA. Insentura della costa marina, nom molta estesa e alquanto prolungantesi nell'interno. L'equivalente ingl. bay, a volte, anche se meno propriamente, è usato per indicare dei bracci di mare di notevole estensione e alquanto operti (es.: la baia di Baffin, la baia di Hudson). Nell'uso comune baia è sinonimo di insentura: la baia di Pozzuoli.[32]

Short definitions follow:

Bay, *Baia.* Little Bay (*seno*) formed by the sea, larger at the center than at the entrance.

Gulf, *Golfo.* Portion of sea extending between two stretches of land

Inlet, *Insenatura.* Curved cavity on the shores of seas, lakes or rivers.

[29] *Geologicheskii Slovať*, Vol. I, p. 371, cited by Mitchell.
[30] Letter to the author of 2 December 1958.
[31] U.S. Naval Intelligence School letter.
[32] Vol. II, p. 22. The English translation is:
Inlet or creek from the seacoast, not very large and extending somewhat into the interior. The English equivalent, bay, is at times and less properly used to indicate arms of the sea which are of notable extension and somewhat open (such as Baffin Bay or Hudson Bay). In common usage, bay is synonymous with creek; for example, the Bay of Pozzuoli.

Estuary, *Estuario*. Large mouth forming a gulf in the sea.[33]

From the foregoing, it appears that in Italian usage, the emphasis is on proportional measurement, a constricted opening and a large center. One should pay attention to the final sentence of the definition from *Dizionario Enciclopedico Italiano* because therein is reflected the most accurate picture of Italian usage: The word *baia* is usually applied to a rather small arm of the sea, and *golfo* to the larger openings. In truth, *golfo* enjoys far more prevalent use.

Turkish. Here the definitions take a new turn from those previously discussed; concepts are obviously different and do not fit the previous pattern wherein there appears to have been much borrowing of meanings. These will be shown – directly as received from Mr. Dogan Horgan, Professor of Turkish at the U.S. Naval Intelligence School.[34]

Turkish: Koy. Denizin karaya doğru girmoş kismi.
English: *Bay*. The shallow part of the sea which enters the land.
Turkish: Korfez. Koy'un siğ olmayani ve büyüğü.
English: *Gulf*. The bigger size of the bay which is not shallow.
Turkish: Küçük Körfez. Veya Koy
English: Inlet. Small bay.
Turkish: Uzun ve dar körfez. Bir nehrin meddücezirli büyük ağzi.
English: *Estuary*. The large mouth of a river in a tide.

It would appear that in Turkish the gulf and the bay can be parts of the same body and that there is no emphasis whatever on proportional dimensions or on shelter.

Japanese.[35] The Japanese language appears to have one word which is generally used for Bay, Gulf and Inlet. This word is *Wan*, which is defined simply:

Water entering into the land in a manner appearing like a bow.

The word *Irie* is a word used for inlet, but never in conjunction with proper names. It is defined as:

Water entering into the land.

The word *gata* is a word used in the same way American English sometimes uses the word "sound". It is defined as:

Shallow water entering deeply into the land.

[33] From U.S. Naval Intelligence School letter citing G. Bartoli, *Il Nuovissimo Melzi* and *Dizionario Tecnico*. See also *Vocabulario e Dizionario dei Regutini e Fanfani*, which contains definitions substantially similar.

[34] In letter of 26 June 1959 to the author.

[35] The author is indebted to Captain Takaichi Itayo, Japanese Maritime Self Defense Force, for his letter of 1 December 1958, in which the Japanese usage was discussed at length.

Chinese (Mandarin). The U.S. Naval Intelligence School has furnished the author a set of definitions which are quoted hereunder:[36]

Chinese: Haiwan. Wei haishui shenju luti.
English: *Bay*. A part of the sea indenting the shore line.
Chinese: Haiwan. (same as Bay)
Engllsh: *Gulf*. (same as Bay)
Chinese: Haik'ou, P'u, Haiaowan. Tashui yu Hsiaok'ou.
English: *Inlet*. A small indentation into the land.
Chinese: Hok'ou, Chiangk'ou. (No definition available. Literally, mouth or entrance of a river)
English: *Estuary*.

Captain S. T. Sun, Chinese Navy, of the Taiwan Naval Command and Staff College, in his letter to the author of 12 December 1958, furnished the additional information.

Ao: (1) A small creek.
(2) A sheltered corner of small water area.
(3) A large area of water with a small inlet.
Kao: A bend in a coast forming an open bay always between distant headlands.
Hai-ko: A long narrow arm of the sea between headlands.
Hai-ku: A long arm of the sea partially landlocked.
Wan: A small sheltered creek or nook.
Kang: An open water area suitable for anchoring vessels, but without other facilities.

In evaluating the foregoing the author was impressed by the reference works cited by the U.S. Naval Intelligence School, as well as by the care with which Captain Sun submitted his information. It appears that although there exist the Chinese words to express the meanings of interest to our study, there is probably less regularity of usage than we observe in European languages.[37] Captain Sun advises that in official translations the word chosen is that which the bay in question resembles most. The Institute of East Asian Studies, Harvard University, advises that *wan* is used when the word, bay, is to be translated as a general word.[38]

Finnish. The Finnish word for bay is *lahti*, which *Nykysuomen Sanakir ja* (Modern Finnish Dictionary) describes as: "an extension of the water of a sea or a lake into the coast. It can be wide or narrow,

[36] The U.S. Naval Intelligence School cites the following authorities: *Comprehensive English-Chinese Dictionary*, *Tz'u Hai*, *Gwoyeu Tsyrdean*, and *English-Chinese Dictionary of Nautical Terms*.

[37] Discussion of 4 August 1959, The Institute of East Asian Studies, Harvard University.

[38] The legal department of United Nations Headquarters did not have a Chinese language copy of the 1958 Geneva Conventions and was unable to furnish the author with a translation of the word, bay, as used in those conventions.

deep or shallow." *Lahti* can mean any size of bay or gulf and diminutives are often added to denote a small bay, or a bay forming part of a lake, pond, or larger bay.[39]

Spanish. As noted above,[40] the Spanish word for bay is *bahia.* The word for gulf is *golfo.* Inasmuch as the general usage for these words and parallel Portuguese words [41] is identical, they will not be discussed further. The following discussion of *bahia,* taken from *Enciclopedia Universal Illustrada* (1912) is nevertheless pertinent.

Sinusosidad de la costa formando una entrada o seno donde el mar penetra. Es mayor que la ensanada ó caleta y comúnmente menor que la denominada golfo, si bien á algunos de estos, y anu á ciertos mares, se les da el nombro de bahía como la de Baffin, Australia y la de Hudson. Aunque menos abrigados que los puertos, en particular de las marejadas y vientos de fuera, suelen ser las bahías engares appropiados para fondear las embaraciones.[42]

Of special interest in this description is the emphasis placed upon shelter, and the distinction between bay and gulf.

Conclusions: Of the languages considered in this abbreviated survey, it appears that the Western European and Russian tongues have developed words that, when mutually translated, indicate closely approximate images of bays. That there have been some fairly recent changes in the meanings applied, there can be no doubt, but the trend appears to be narrowing toward a uniform image. Some definitions stress the aspect of shelter, some stress shape and shelter, and some stress a comparison with words for inlet or gulf. There does seem to be a trend toward stress of proportionality as between width at the entrance versus width at the center. With the Turkish language and the two oriental languages considered, there appears to be some slight doubt as to whether people in Turkey, Japan, and in Mandarin-speaking China are, in fact, thinking of the same type of body of water when the words for bay are used. There is evidence, although a bit sketchy, that they probably are thinking in similar terms. It is not evident that any of the users of these languages entertain images running

[39] This translation and information was furnished by Mr. Arvo Pietarinen of Helsinki, Finland, student at the Fletcher School of Law and Diplomacy, 1958–59.

[40] P 81, above.

[41] P 81, above.

[42] Tomo VII, pp. 192–3. A translation of this passage is: Sinuosity of the coastline forming an entrance or cavity into which the sea penetrates. It is larger than a creek or inlet and ordinarily smaller than that termed a gulf, although some of these (gulfs) and even some seas are called bays such as Baffin and Australia and Hudson Bay. Although less sheltered than harbors, especially from swells and outside winds, bays are often suitable for anchoring shipping.

directly counter to the majority. The most recent definition of the International Hydrographic Bureau appears to be an anomaly which is difficult to justify. Discounting that definition, it is concluded that it is possible to formulate a legal definition for the word "bay" which, on a polylingual basis, will probably meet the linguistically expressed requirements of a vast number of people.

Section D GEOGRAPHIC AND HYDROGRAPHIC MEASUREMENTS [1]

Mindful of the fact that Article 7 of the 1958 Geneva Convention is greatly dependent for its implementation upon accurate measurement of large areas of water, we will direct our inquiry toward some of the methods used to make such measurements, and to some of the technical terms employed.

Paragraph 2 of Article 7 specifies that for a juridical bay to exist, the area within the closing line drawn across its mouth must be equal to or larger than the area of a semi-circle drawn across its mouth. Paragraph 3 specifies that the necessary measurements must be made at the low water tidal level.[2] To implement these requirements, the followin quantities must be measured:

(a) Distance between the natural entrance points of the indentation.

(b) Area of the enclosed indentation.

The measurements must be taken at the low-water mark. It should be observed, of course, that where the land-mass around the indentation is steep-to, that is, without perceptible beach gradient, measurements at low-water mark and at any other tidal level will be equal or nearly so.

Paragraph 4 specifies that where the distance between the natural entrance points is twenty-four miles, all waters within a line drawn

[1] Nearly all material used in this section is derived from three sources:
(a) Bowditch, *American Practical Navigator*, 1958 Edition, U.S. Navy Hydrographic Office Publication No. 9.
(b) *Hydrographic and Geodetic Surveying Manual*, U.S. Navy Hydrographic Office Publication No. 215.
(c) *Hydrographic Manual*, U.S. Coast and Geodetic Survey Special Publication No. 143.
In addition, the author is indebted to RADM Karo, Director, U.S. Coast and Geodetic Survey and Rear Admiral Robert W. Knox, U.S. Coast and Geodetic Survey (Ret.), President of the Directing Committee, International Hydrographic Bureau, for supplementing information. RADM Karo's letter to the author is dated 8 December 1958. That of RADM Knox is dated 1 December 1958.

[2] See Sections A and B, above, for discussions of tidal levels.

between those points shall be considered as internal waters. Paragraph 5 specifies that where this distance exceeds 24 miles, there shall be a straight base line drawn within the bay in such a manner as to enclose the maximum amount of water area. To implement these requirements, which assume that the indentation has already been established as a juridical bay, the following must be done:

(a) A line 24 miles long must be drawn across the bay between low-water marks.

(b) The area within the line is measuerd.

(c) The line is shifted to other possible positions in which the opposite shores are 24 miles apart and area measurements made.

(d) The areas so calculated are compared; the largest area will determine the position of the closing line.

Bowditch's *American Practical Navigator* makes the following statement at page 848.[3]

> Nearly 71 per cent of the earth's surface is covered by water. Only a small part of this area has been adequately surveyed, and much of the land area has not been accurately measured. The changes caused by nature and man, and the continued increase in requirements of more precise and more nearly automatic systems and methods of navigation, render obsolete the charts and surveys once considered adequate. Consequently, the need for ever more accurate, more complete surveys continues, with no end in sight.[4]

Ignoring for a moment the warning implicit in the above quotation, we shall proceed to demonstrate the simplest method of measurement, which is by chart inspection. This is accomplished in the following steps:

(a) On the largest-scale chart of the area, determine the natural entrance points of the indentation, and join the low-water marks of the two points by a straight line. With this line as a diameter, construct a semi-circle, and determine its area.

(b) Determine the area within the low-water marks of the indentation, using one of these methods, depending on the accuracy required:

(1) Simple inspection. In many cases the differences in area will be quite obvious and further work is unnecessary.

[3] 1958 Edition.

[4] Often, as a practicing mariner, the author has had reason to doubt the accurary of the only charts available for a particular area. Such is usually the case in some of the less traveled areas of the world, or in areas which have more recently come into prominence.

(2) Use of squares or rectangles. By this method, one marks off the enclosed area into equal squares or convenient rectangles and obtains the total area by adding the areas of these figures. Irregularities at the perimeter are accounted for by drawing smaller regular figures, obtaining their areas and adding to the total.

(3) Use of a plainmeter which is an instrument for measuring irregular areas on a map or chart.[5]

(4) Measurement of the area by use of one or another method of mathematical approximation using Simpson's Rule or the Trapezoidal rule.[6]

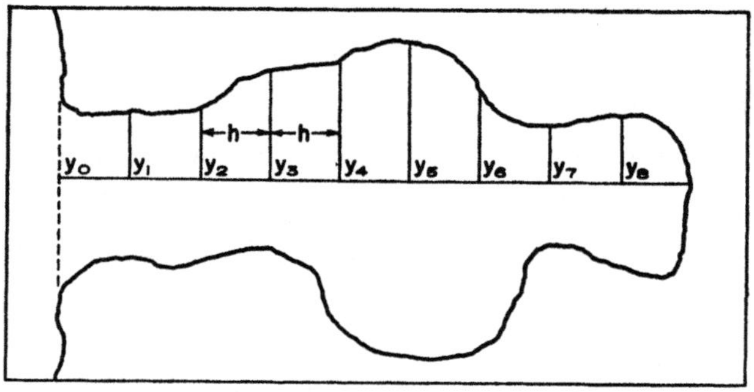

THE TRAPEZOIDAL RULE

Fig. 20 Measurement of the area of a bay by use of Simpson's rule or the trapezoidal rule.

(c) Compare the two areas.

[5] Letter of RADM Karo, USC&GS, to author dated 8 December 1958.

[6] These rules do manually what the plainmeter does by continuous integration. For use of either rule, a line is drawn down the center of the bay on the chart, and a series of perpendiculars, evenly spaced, are drawn from the center line to the low-water mark on the chart. The Simpson's rule formula is $A = \frac{h}{3}(1/o + 4y + 2y_2 + 4y_3 + 2y_4 + \ldots 4y_{u-1} + y_u)$, where u is even, y is the length of each perpendicular drawn from the center line to the perimeter, and h equals the distance between the equally spaced perpendicular. This rule can be stated: $A = \frac{h}{3} f(A)$. The Trapezoidal rule formula is $A = h(\frac{1}{2}yo + y. + y_2 \ldots y_{u+1} + y_u)$, where the values are similar to those for Simpson's rule. The Trapezoidal rule can be stated $A = h\, f(A)$. Manning and Schumacher, *Principles of Warship Construction and Damage Control* (1935), pp. 23–4. The method must be repeated until all parts of the indentation are measured. See Figure No. 20, above, for demonstration of this system.

(d) If the comparison qualifies the indentation as a juridical bay and the length of the closing line is 24 miles or less [7] the problem is finished, and all of the area inside the closing line may be considered as internal waters.

(e) If the 24-mile line must be moved inside the bay, it may be very simple to find the position where the maximum water area is enclosed. If a bay has a fairly regular shape, or has an internal throat or constriction (Fig. 21), the choice for positioning the line is an obvious one.

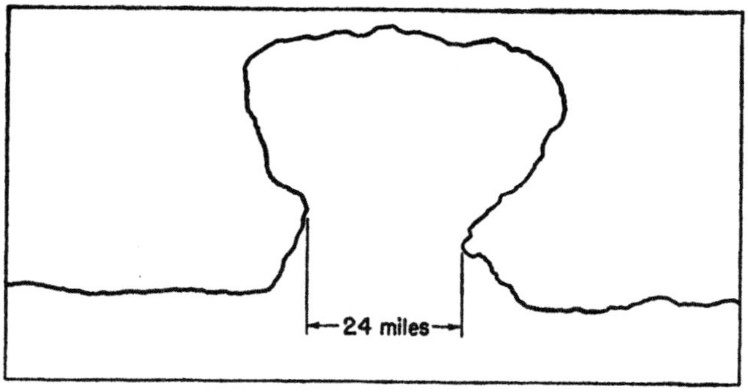

BAY WITH INTERNAL THROAT

Fig. 21

If the bay is irregularly shaped, the line may have to be positioned by trial and error and successive computations made until the maximum water area is ascertained. A plainmeter could solve the problem in a few minutes. Manual calculation might be very tedious and, of course susceptible of human error.

If the case at issue is a borderline one, or if the accuracy of the chart is in doubt, an accurate survey and measurement of the bay would be necessary. This would involve a ground survey and an accurate determination of the low-water line. It may well be in order here to distinguish two terms that are used:

(a) Geodetic Central Survey. A survey for precise determination and marking of positions on land, and accurate measurement of reference direction and distance, taking into account the earth's curvature.

[7] The twenty-four miles are nautical miles of 6,072 feet. If, for any reason, the scale of the chart is in English statute miles, then one should use 27.6 statute miles to equal 24 nautical miles, or multiply the number of statute miles by. 87 to get nautical miles. Table No. 20 at page 1276 of *Bowditch*, 1958 edition can also be used. It should be observed, too, that a nautical mile is 1,852 kilometers. To convert kilometers to nautical miles, multiply thenumber of convert kilometers by .54. 24 nautical miles equals 44.4 kilometers.

(b) Hydrographic Survey. Measurement of details of water areas and appropriate details of adjoining coastal areas.

Both of these are required, and in addition, photographs are taken by an aircraft flying at exactly low water. Obviously, the time of exact low water must first be ascertained.

It is believed to be beyond the scope of this thesis to engage in a discussion of the technical details of geodetic and hydrographic surveying. It is an involved process requiring highly trained and experienced personnel. It is also time consuming, although electronic measuring devices have appreciably reduced the time and effort involved; they have also increased the accuracy of such methods. Judging from the study made of the coasts of the world incident to the preparation of the lists of bays in Section A of this chapter, it is this author's opinion that there would be very few borderline situations which would require geodetic and hydrographic surveys to establish the juridical quality of the indentations or to establish exact the extent of internal waters in bays.

Appendix A ETYMOLOGY OF THE WORD 'BAY'

From: Emile Littré, *Dictionnaire de la Langue française,* (Paris: Librairie Hachette et Cie., 1885), Vol. I, p. 278.

BAIE (be) s.f. Petit golfe dont l'entrée est resserrée. Etyn. Espagne. bahía; ital. baia; angl. bay; du bas latin, port (portum veteres a bajulandis mercibus vocabant baias, dit Isidore). Mais bajulare ne peut donner baia. On a indique pour étymologie baie, "porte" parce que la baie est une ouverture dans une côte, et l'irlandais bâdh ou bâgh, petit golfe, mais baie, porte, ayant un radical bada, et le celtique bâdh ou bâgh ne sont pas conciliables avec le baia de Isidore; à une époque aussi reculée que le VIe siècle, la consonne aurait été conservée, et le mot eût été bada ou baya. On a indiqué aussi la ville de Bayonne, dont le nom se décomposerait en deux mots basques, baia, port, et ona, bon; mais ceci est un cercle hypothétique où Bayonne explique baie, et baie explique Bayonne. Il ne faut pas sortir du domaine latin: il y avait Bajai qui, signifie un lieu agréable; de là le sens roman de baie, qui est un refuge pour les marins. Une particularité vient à l'appui: le latin disait bajae, en deux syllables avec l'accent sur ba, d'où italien baia et le français baie; le grec disait Bata en trois syllables, avec l'accent sur t, d'où une double accentuation qui s'est conservée dans L'espagnol bahía.

PART TWO

THE BAYS WITHIN THE LITTORAL OF A SINGLE STATE

A. Development of the Law of Bays

CHAPTER THREE

DEVELOPMENT FROM THE FALL OF ROME TO 1800

Section A INTRODUCTION

The purpose of this chapter is to apply something of a functional approach to the development of the International Law of Bays during the period from the fall of Rome in 476 A.D.[1] to 1800. A number of scholars and advocates, using more or less the techniques of writing legal history,[2] have made studies of the development of the international law of the sea during this period. To adopt the same formula, narrowed to a study of the law of bays, would appear to travel over rather well-trodden ground, and would probably yield little satisfaction to the author or to the reader. It is for this reason that a functional or cause-and-effect approach has been adopted.[3] The his-

[1] The Fall of Rome is generally described as to have taken place in 476 A.D., the year in which the Roman Empire of the West ceased to exist. It is generally conceded to be the year marking a new era in history. Leslie Lipson, *The Great Issues in Politics* (1954), pp. 328–9; Lynn Thorndike, *The History of Medieval Europe* (1917), p. 86.

[2] CAPT Christopher Meyer, RNorN, *The Extent of Jurisdiction in Coastal Waters* (1937); James Reddie, *Maritime International Law* (1847); Thomas W. Fulton, *Sovereignty of the Sea* (1911); Henry G. Crocker, *The Extent of the Marginal Sea* (1919); Domenico A. Azuni, *The Maritime Law of Europe* (1806); Arnold Raestad, *La Mer Territoriale* (1913); Gilbert Gidel, *Le Droit international public de La Mer* (1934).

[3] It is believed that a functional approach offers a fruitful vehicle for clarifying some issues of International Law. Such an approach seems to address itself more readily than others to the purpose this author believes International Law – and all law – should serve: the widest possible satisfaction of human wants and needs with the least possible amount of waste and friction. Roscoe Pound describes this puropse as "efficacious social engineering." *An Introduction to the Philosophy of Law* (Yale Paper-bound), p. 47. Actually, analysis of the sort envisioned by Pound has obvious pitfalls and it is not without its thoughtful critics, e.g. Karl R. Popper (*The Poverty of Historicism*), because it *can* lend to empirical theorizing on the needs of a planned society (Karl Mannheim, *Man and Society*, p. 6). Perhaps, it leads to what Walter Lippmann called "piecemeal engineering." (*The Good Society*, pp. 203–240). Scholars, like most other human beings seem to have a predilection for erecting general theories seemingly *ab initio* or upon the basis of "objective" study. The author experiences a distinct feeling of discomfort when under exposure to most theories because of the human tendency to select such past or future events which will indicate the theories. On the other hand there must be a starting point with a well placed hunch for all study, since nothing is accomplished otherwise. This author believes that the best service the student can render

torical development is centered around three interdependent influences: Navigation, economics and defense. Other terms synonymous with these could as readily be used. For purposes of this book the term navigation embraces not only the art of navigating the earth's surface and its accompanying scientific developments, but also the developments in the building, handling, and manning of ships at sea. The term economics, in our context here, embraces a study of man's needs and desires for physical things as well as some of the natural and man-made barriers to satisfaction of such needs and desires. The term defense embraces physical conflicts between groups for control of nature's maritime bounty and the offensive as well as defensive measures that have been resorted to in connection with such conflicts. With ease, one can conjecture upon the likelihood of an interdependence among the three influences. Had there been no progress in the arts of ship construction, navigation, and seamanship, satisfaction of economic needs and desires would not have been sought through maritime exploitation and discovery. Likewise, there would have arisen little to comment upon in the matter of defense. But, had there been no quest for the satiscfaction of economic needs and desires, there would have been no incentive for development of the navigating arts and no reason for any preoccupation with defense. Finally, had groups of individuals not concerned themselves with collectively defending their acquisitions or, for that matter, if they had not endeavored to dispossess the weaker and more backward groups, human society would probably have remained fragmentized and at the subsistence level – with no incentive for progress within any framework.

Thomas Wemyss Fulton, on the first page of his incomparable work, *Sovereignty of the Sea*, expressed the following thought on the maritime life of early England:

> First and foremost was the necessity of securing the land from invasion; then came the duty of safeguarding shipping and commerce;[4]

But, ships had to transport the invaders, a matter of ship construction, seamanship, and navigation. And there had to exist an incentive for invasion: a matter of crude economics or the desire for something the invaders did not already possess.

himself is to operate from a thought-out hunch, readily admit his own uncertainties, and concede that he may ultimately be wrong. On that basis, the author has selected the functional approach. Admittedly, such a *modus operandi* may result in some untidiness and may be criticized for its absence of what is admiringly called "tightly reasoned" argument. But this author believes that often where such scholarly sophistication is not present, sophistry has also been excluded.

[4] *Sovereignty of the Sea* (1911), p. 1.

Section B NAVIGATION

In the Fifth Century, A.D., seagoing craft were of very limited carrying capacity, primarily dependent upon oars for propulsion, and quite unseaworthy by present standards. Ships were flat-bottomed, or nearly so, and the sails used were rectangular pieces of cloth. For this reason it was impossible to propel ships by wind unless the direction of the wind and the intended direction of the ship were approximately the same.[1] Even, however, had it been discovered that ships could be maneuvered close to the eye of the wind by sail alone, it would have been impractical to fit ships of the era with such sails, because the absence of compensating hull structure below the water line would have caused those ships to capsize in winds from directions other than astern. Lacking maneuverability and seaworthiness, early ships were dependent upon human oarsmen, fair weather, and favorable winds. The hull construction and the required oarsmen combined to minimize the cargo capacity of such ships, to keep ships within easy reach of sheltered bays, and to minimize their cruising radius. The required oarsmen were sometimes freedmen but usually prisoners or slaves (the terms here are virtually synonymous), and a continuous supply of these human machines was required since their mortality rate was high. By reason of these facts it is not surprising to note that the Roman ships in commercial traffic from the corners of the empire numbered in the thousands and that the number of ships with the accompanying slave oarsmen had continually to increase in order to support the growing needs of metropolitan Rome.[2]

Although oars were used for the propulsion of ocean going ships for some eleven hundred years after the fall of Rome,[3] their use became

[1] Briefly, the propulsion of a ship with sails involves problems of ship construction, sail design, and sail positioning. With winds from directions other than those within about twenty degrees of either side of a line drawn from the stern of the ship, the mechanical effect of a wind driving a ship in a chosen direction is the result of a highly complex resolution of forces. For a given ship with a given set of sails this effect is susceptible of precise mathematical description. Obviously, such description is beyond the scope of this text, and in any event serves little useful purpose because technological progress with sailing ships was the result of slow, trial-and-error evolution. It is sufficient for our purposes to note that ships' hull construction, sail design, and techniques of handling are all mutually dependent.

[2] From the viewpoint of navigation, the Roman era is of very little historical interest. Their methods of ship construction and propulsion were taken directly from the Greeks and Roman talents were not devoted to this field. Charnock, *History of Marine Architecture* (1800), Vol I., p. 141.

[3] Oars or "sweeps" were used on some ships of the Great Armada of 1588 as well as during the maritime wars between England and the United Provinces. Charnock writes that the

ever more confined to warships where they contributed to maneuverability and to speed during light breezes and calm weather. Oarsmen were expensive and relatively inefficient in rough weather.[4] After the fall of Rome, no one State or group had the resources either for a large navy or for the slaves to man it. The slow evolution that took place in ship construction in Europe from 500 A.D. to 1800 A.D. represenst a hybridization of ideas that were communicated among the seafaring communities through their coastal commerce and as well their piracies. The direction of progress was toward faster and more seaworthy ships that could be sailed in bad weather and could be defended against pirates. The melting pot of ideas was the Mediterranean. From Scandinavia came the Norsemen who ranged the west coast of Europe and the farthest reaches of the Mediterranean. Their ships were narrow, long, and smooth lined, and they rested deep in the water so that they were less likely to capsize in heavy seas. From the Levant came the lateen sails, which when adapted to a narrow, swift ship, could be so positioned to enable the ship to sail close to the eye of the wind.[5] At some early time it appears that if a ship were built with an enlarged wetted surface,[6] the ship could be built with a higher and heavier freeboard [7] and it could have taller masts and more sails. The result was better sea-keeping quality, better defensive qualities, more protection for cargo and crew and, and greater speed. Ships continued to bear the marks their own local builders, local peculiarities of weather, and the uses to which they were put. Until the Age of Discovery, however, there was a limit in size beyond which it was uneconomic to build ships. Aside from limitations in knowledge of the shipbuilding arts, there was no demand

first naval battle between fleets of oarless ships occured in 1342, during the war of Edward III. The last great naval battle in which oared ships were used almost exclusively was the battle of Lepanto, 7 October 1571. However, galleys were a part of the French Navy until 1748 and were used by the Italian States until the Wars of Napoleon I. VADM William L. Rodgers USN (Ret.), *Naval Warfare under Oars, 4th to 16th Century* (1939), pp. 233–4.

[4] An oar is most efficient when so extended from the propelled craft that it strikes the water at a slight angle with the surface. In a rolling sea, the use of oars becomes difficult and inefficient unless used with craft especially constructed for heavy weather. Examples of such craft are modern whale boats and the ships of the Norsemen.

[5] For his crusade, Louis IX in 1248 ordered several two masted ships which were the first large ships to use the rudder instead of the steering oar. At a somewhat later date, Portuguese ship-builders adopted lateen sails to two and three-masted ships. These could sail very well in contrary winds. Per Collender, *A History of Marine Navigation* (1954), p. 115.

[6] This is the naval architect's term for the portion of the ship below the surface of the water. LCDR G. C. Manning CC USN and LCDR T. L. Schumacher CC USN, *Principles of Warship Construction and Damage Control* (1935), p. 32.

[7] This is the vertical distance from the water to the weather deck at any point in the length of the ship. *ibid*, p. 17.

for ships above a relatively small size.[8] The normal risks of maritime life were such that they could not be offset by prospects of a very rich early return on the investment necessary for construction of a very large ship. Moreover, since the structural differences between war and merchant ships were very few, construction of a large, well-found ship for commercial use would have made it attractive for impressment into the service of the Prince for use in the endemic wars of the age. Better to spread the risk. Thus until the age of discovery, shipbuilding developed new techniques to increase efficiency and reduce costs but the size of ships reached an upper limit which for a protracted period was seldom exceeded.

Until the Age of Discovery and the era of mercantilism that followed, the influence of ship construction and maritime commerce upon notions of maritime sovereignty appears rather indirect.

Turning now to a review of the progress in the art of navigation. During the Middle Ages and the Age of Discovery we have what was undoubtedly a major influence in the development of international law. Ships and shipbuilding had improved, but it was the development of navigating instruments and techniques which gave the mariner some assurance that he could sail vast expanses of unknown seas and live to return home. The author believes that development in the art of navigation and in the companion sciences of astronomy and cartography should be more precisely understood, if we are to consider the evolution of the Law of the Sea in proper perspective. It is hardly satisfactory simply to note the writings of early publicists, or even to note the decrees of ruling Princes without attempting to ascertain whether the rules so made or suggested were susceptible of fulfilment. Moreover, it is necessary to distinguish between the conclusions of academicians of any given era and the actual practices of mariners.[9] It would appear that in some

[8] This is not to say that quite large ships were not built on some occasions. In 357 A.D., the Roman Emperor Justinian had constructed a ship to transport an obelisk from the Nile to the Tiber. The obelisk was 115 feet long and weighed about 1500 tons. No ship in existence in 1800 was considered capable of transporting such a load. In 1191 A.D., the ships of Richard the Lion-hearted captured a Saracen galley manned by 1300 men. It is recorded that the great crusader directed 1100 of the Saracens to be thrown overboard. Charnock, *History*, vol. I, pp. 156, 329.

[9] It is not the view of the author that such writings have no value if they fail to reflect the actual practices or capabilities which were known to exist as of the time of writing. The interrelationship between practice and juridical idea appears very unclear in the works of some writers on the Law of the sea, however, and this relationship is what the author hopes to establish, at least in part. Professor Alf Ross reminds us that "In the continental tradition the law is very largely an academic product, and therefore in a corresponding degree bears the stamp of academic thinking and its urge toward systematic analysis and rationality." *On Law and Justice* (1959), p. 89. On the other hand, we in the United States are reminded in the opinion of the U.S. Supreme Court in *The Pacquete Habana*, that "such works [of text

instances, the proposals of the publicists were virtually impossible of fulfilment by mariners of the same era.[10] In other instances, proposals were theoretically possible of fulfilment because scholars in astronomy and cartography had arrived at solutions to problems, but such work as they did was written in Latin and not communicated to mariners. It could be communicated to other scholars, working in law and writing in Latin, but its percolation to the mariner was a slower process.[11]

writers] are resorted to by juridical tribunals, not for the speculation of their authors concerning what the law ought to be but for trustworthy evidences of what the law really is." 175 U.S. 677 (1900). The late Professor Hyde wrote: "Whenever such writers do not evince a disposition to mirror the practice of their time, the views expressed lack evidential value." *International Law Chiefly as Interpreted and Applied by the United States* (1947), p. 12. It would appear that the work of a text writer, or a glossator, or an early writer in the service of a Prince might have a transcendent quality which grows in stature and importance to decision makers with the passage of time. Such work may reflect a reasoned conclusion as to the probable course of events. Ross writes: "With a firm foundation in the tradition of the law, and by way of rational thinking, an attempt is made to arrange the rules of law systematically in conformity with them." *op. cit.*, p. 89. Perhaps the author's own problem (fundamentally, one of assessing the worth of a publicist's work in differentiation to time), comes nearer to solution through a synthesis of these suggestions: "But inasmuch as a source of law is conceived as a factor influencing the judge in rendering his decision, the work of writers may continue to play a part in proportion to its intrinsic scientific value, its impartiality and its determination to scrutinize critically the practice of States by reference to a legal principle." Lauterpacht, *Oppenheim's International Law*, vol. I, 8th Ed., p. 33. "Indeed, it is not too much to say that the true and recognized course of this new department of English law [Conflicts of Law] – is a stream of foreign juristic writing beginning in the fourteenth century; and that when judges follow the precedents of our own courts in this domain, they are often really affirming principles enunciated by Continental Jurists of the 16th and 17th Centuries. ... What is true of Private is even more true of Public International Law." Carleton K. Allen, *Law in the Making*, 4th Ed. (1947), p. 239. "The views expressed by learned writers on International Law have done in the past and will do in the future valuable service in helping to create the opinion by which the range of the consensus of civillezed nations is enlarged." Lord Alverstone, C. J., in *West Rand Central Gold Mining Co., Ltd.*, v. *The King*, 2 K.B. 391 (1905).

[10] Bartolus, a fourteenth century Italian jurist and teacher of law laid down the proposition that a State had jurisdiction over a belt of the adjacent sea one hundred Italian miles in width. Angelo Sereni, *The Italian Conception of International Law* (1943), p. 71; C. Baldoni, *De Mare territoriale nel diritto internazionale commune* (1934), p. 54. An Italian mile of the time measured 5,000 English feet. J. B. Hewson, *A History of the Practice of Navigation* (1951), p. 156. Italy is situated in a generally north-south orientation. The north-south water boundary, must then have the same orientation. Knowing the position of a ship with respect to it involves a problem in calculating longitude. But a method of calculating longitude at sea was not perfected until the second half of the eighteenth century. Nathaniel Bowditch, *Americân Practical Navigator*, 1958 Edition, pp. 45–7. By reconstructing the methods used as of the time of Bartolus, the author doubts that a mariner approaching Italy from the west or southwest could ascertain his position with greater accuracy than plus or minus twenty miles with respect to such a line. Mindful, however, of the matters discussed in footnote 9, above, one should note that Bartolus has been credited with contributing directly to the formation of the modern conception of territorial waters. Arnold Raestad, *La Mer territoriale, Etudes Historiques et juridiques* (1913), pp. 15–18.

[11] Commander Hewson makes this comment: "Scientific Navigation was advancing beyond the resources of the individual trading ship-master. It was not he who brought about the great navigational developments that began in the Middle Ages. It was the wealthy patron, the learned geographer and the scientifically-minded navigator who rubbed shoulders

The accompanying table[12] contains an abbreviated survey of the development of navigational aids and techniques from prehistoric times to 1800 A.D. Most important, for our immediate purposes, is to note the dates when aids or techniques came into general use by mariners. It will be observed that by 476 A.D., there were well considered schemes of map-making and compendia for instructing mariners navigating strange coasts. But there was no compass, very few lighthouses, and the maps in existence were really intellectual curiosities. They had no relationship to sailing directions. It is to be noted, too, that the geographical concept of the State was something imprecise.[13] By the time of the crusades, fairly good charts of the Mediterranean were in existence, and discussion of their features was coordinated in the the Portolani sailing directions. By the Age of Discovery, the compass had come into being, as had accurate methods of finding latitude.[14] By then the world had the mercator projection and some reasonably accurate methods of map-making. It is to be noted that the techniques available to navigators were the same techniques available to explorers and statesmen who could not communicate the extent of their sovereignty claims with precision and, with certain limitations, expect foreign mariners to take due cognizance of the claims. With respect to bays, the age of discovery brought forth these features:

(a) Many new bays were to be discovered and claimed by explorers.

(b) There were available techniques which made it possible for States to expand their jurisdictional claims beyond some line-of-sight boundary between headlands.

Thus, with the advent of the age of discovery, which also saw the commencement of ths State system, we have the beginning of the

with the mathematician ashore, who brought about the development in charts as in every other branch of navigation. *A History of the Practice of Navigation* (1957), p. 6. The matter is made more difficult, from a research standpoint, by reason of the paucity of recorded information concerning early maritime practice. "... no group of people in the history of mankind has been more reluctant to keep records than professional sailors," Lloyd A. Brown, *The Story of Maps* (1949), p. 114. Mr Brown has exaggerated a bit, perhaps, but there is no doubt some truth in what he says. The well-kept descriptive log book is the exception and it occupies a fairly low priority in the average mariner's mind.

[12] The table is compiled from information to be found in the following works: Nathaniel Bowditch, *American Practical Navigator*, 1958 Edition; J. B. Hewson, *A History of the Practice of Navigation* (1951); Hill, Utegaard and Riordan, *Dutton's Navigation and Piloting* (1958); Per Collender, *A History of Marine Navigation* (1954); Lloyd A. Brown, *The Storu of Maps* (1949); and Leo Bagrow, *Die Geschichte der Kartographie* (1951).

[13] G. P. Gooch, *Nationalism* (1920), p. 5.

[14] Accurate means of determining longitude were not perfected until a much later date, as the table shows. Correspondingly, small scale (large area) charts became reasonably accurate, by present-day standards, in latitude orientation, but they were distorted in their longitude presentation.

Annex A

TABLE OF NAVIGATION

DEVELOPMENT TO 1800 A.D.

Aid or System	Development	Description	Probable Date and Originator	Approx. Date of General Use	Significance
A. Charts	1. Gnomonic projection	System of charting from, a single point on earth's surface showing distance as great circles on the earth.	Thales of Miletus, 600 B.C.	16th Century A.D.	Showed distances on earth viewed as a sphere, hence in true perspective. Great circle sailing first used by Cabot in 1498 and Verrazano in 1524.
	2. World Map	First charted latitudes and longitudes.	Claudius Ptolemy, 2nd Century A.D.	15th Century A.D.	First descriptive chart showing land locations. Fixed convention that top of map is north. Commenced direction orientation. Used by states during late Roman Empire.
	3. Portolan Charts	Showed distances and landmarks from surveys very accurately.	Venetians about 1000 A.D.	12th Century A.D.	First charts used to illustrate sailing directions. With these, mariners and states had two of three basic directional aids for position keeping and jurisdictional demarcation.
	4. Padron Real	First portfolio of charts corrected and kept up to date from mariners' reports.	Casa de Contratacion, Seville, Spain. 1508[1]	1508	Explorers' charts copied from master plans. Depended upon through Age of Discovery. First effort at correction on continuing basis, with obvious legal implications. Plane surfaces with possibilities of large areas.

	5. Mercator projection	First mathematically accurate projection of earth's curvature on plane surface.	Gerardus Mercator, Flemish, 1569. Corrected by Edward Wright, 1599.	1750	Final system for convenient and accurate measurement of large and small areas. By this system, positions of jurisdictional lines could be accurately shown on any scale charts.
B. Prime Meridian	1. Ptolemy	2° Longitude west of Canary Islands	2nd Century A.D.	200 A.D. to about 1675 A.D.	Used by states and map-makers, but little by mariners, since longitude could not then be calculated.
	2. Pope Alexander VI, (Borgia)	Decreed meridian to be 300 leagues west of Azores. Changed to 370 leagues west in 1494.	1493–1494	Virtually none for navigating purposes.	Result of dispute between Spain and Portugal. Decree had some lasting political implications.
	3. Greenwich	Establishment of Greenwich observatory and correction of charts to show 0° Longitude at Greenwich	1676 A.D.	1775 A.D.	Uniformity throughout the world for East-West location on charts. Removed this element of doubt in respect of future claims, and decrees could be spelled out in latitude and longitude terms.
C. Sailing Directions	1. Periplus of Scylax	Provided mariners with information on distances, ports, aids and dangers, etc. Similar to modern sailing directions. Furnished model for centuries. Not oriented to charts.	About 5th Century B.C	5th Century B.C. to 15th Century, A.D.	Provided description for landmarks and general orientation. Written for mariners. Made it possible at very early date to describe jurisdictional limits in understood terms.

[1] Casa de Contratacion was the Government organization established to conduct the Spanish trading monopoly in America.

(*continued*)

Aid or System	Develop-ment	Description	Probable Date and Originator	Approx. Date of General Use	Sifnigicance
	2. Portolano Rizo	Similar aid, oriented to Portolan Charts.	1490, Venice	1500 A.D.	First chart-oriented sailing directions.
	3. "Waggoner"	First compendium of sailing directions for navigating in all waters. Published in volumes.	1584, Holland	1600 A.D.	Model of all modern sailing directions. This was chart-oriented and provided mariners with information on legal as well as natural obstacles and restrictions.
D. The Compass	1. Draconis, The Pole Star	Used for steering.	Origin of use is prehistoric		First direction orientation for mariners and geographers.
	2. Magnetic Compass	Direction orientation for steering. Night or day and in all weather.	Disputed, but about 1000 A.D.	13th Century, A.D.	Most important single development in maritime history. Charts and sailing directions of limited use without it. Mariners could now position themselves in pilot waters. Led to Age of Discovery. Legal implications tremendous since mariners could and did use it for positioning.
	3. Compass Card	Card or "Rose" showing directions, ultimately placed under magnetic	Very ancient, used to describe wind	14th Century, A.D.	A simple refinement to show directions other than north when used in conjunction with

		compass needle.	directions. Put under magnetic compass in 14th Century A.D.		magnetic compass needle.
	4. Variation	Change in apparent position of North-pointing by magnetic compass. Varies with geographical area and subject to secular change in earth's magnetism.	Columbus, 1493 A.D.	About 1600 A.D.	Further refinement in direction finding and ship-positioning.
	5. Deviation	Effect upon magnetic compass of ship's own magnetism.	First observed and reported in 1627	Not corrected for until about 1800.	Last refinement in navigation with magnetic compass. Without correction for deviation, ship positioning could not be completely accurate.
E. Lights and Buoys	1. Lighthouses	Usually used to warn mariners of natural obstacles.	Sigenum of Troy, 660 B.C.	About 16th Century, A.D.	Prevented shipping losses and contributed directly to increases in size of ships and volume of marine traffic. Seldom used as warning for jurisdictional purposes.
	2. Buoys	Small warning markers.	Antiquity	About 14th Century, A.D.	Further aid to prevent grounding
F. Finding(2) Latitudes	1. Meridian transit of the sun	Observing sun at highest point of daily sun, and calculation from daily declination sai sun's altitude.	Pre-Christian era.	15th Century, A.D.	Map-makers used the system before it was used by mariners. Landmarks could be easily located.

[2] For purposes of this book, it is considered unnecessary to delineate the historical development of astronomy, which in fact precedes all aids and systems for finding latitude and longitude.

(*continued*)

Aid or System	Develop-ment	Description	Probable Date and Originator	Approx. Date of General Use	Significance
	2. Polaris system	Observation of pole star and correction to obtain latitude by use of the "nocturnal" or correction tables.	15th Century, A.D.	18th Century, A.D.	Permitted greater flexibility so that latitude could be determined more than once a day.
G. Finding Longitude	1. Parallel sailing	Sailing north or south to latitude of destination and then sailing along a parallel of latitude, and estimating daily distance sailed.	Antiquity	1400 A.D.	Highly inaccurate but only system available. Prevented scientific cartography of distant areas. East-West locations were always approximations.
	2. Lunar distances	Noting position of the moon with respect to stars.	1514, John Werner	1750 A.D.	Removed necessity for parallel sailing.
	3. The Chronometer	Noting time of sun's meridian transit and comparison by table correction, with chronometer keeping prime meridian time.	1767, A.D.	About 1790, A.D.	Only reliable and accurate method until development of the Sumner line in 1837.

concepts of boundaries. Heretofore boundaries, were, in general, either vague zones or identifiable lines resulting from some natural feature of the earth's surface.[15] While harbors were undoubtedly internal waters in the antiquity,[16] there commenced to exist in the Middle Ages, adequate means for accurately delimiting larger areas of internal waters, and there arose the political impetus to do so. Now this does not mean that such steps came universally to be taken. New claims based on discovery were made by explorers and adventurers and not by professional geographers; they were made by visitors and not usually by inhabitants.[17] Expanded claims, if any, in Europe, were not usually expressed in precise terms, although there are some notable exceptions.

If one wishes to consider a claim to a bay as internal waters, allegedly based on some very old act or practice, it is the belief of this author that the limits of such a claim to a bay or other coastal waters should reflect a degree of accuracy commensurate with the degree of development in the means to honor their pretensions. During the Middle Ages and thereafter such means were continually being perfected. If a State's claim made in that era, or subsequent thereto, should become the subject of international controversy, it would appear desirable to inquire into the technical possibility of the claim's being honored as of the time it was made. If it was technically impossible to respect the claim and if actual acquiescence cannot be proved, the merits of the claim seem rather dubious.[18] Also, if a claim is made in vague terms at a time when there are available the technical means for delimiting it accurately and for navigating accurately with respect to it, it is suggested that the claimant State is under something of a handicap in arguing its case. Clearly, there is a relationship between the limits of

[15] S. Whittemore Boggs, *International Boundaries* (1940), pp. 6–9; Paul de Lapradelle, *La Frontière* (1928), pp. 25–6; Sir Thomas Holdich, *Political Frontiers and Boundary Making* (1916), p. 14.

[16] Chapter I, Section B, above.

[17] Keller, Lissitzyn, Mann, *Sovereignty through Symbolic Acts* (1938) contains numerous examples.

[18] In *United Kingdom* v. *Norway* (*1951*), Norway in her countermemorial relied upon an exclusive fishing right granted in 1688 for the establishment of an historic title. The limits of the concession were 10 leagues, or 80 marine miles from the coastal littoral. *I.C.J. Pleadings*, Fisheries Case, vol. I, p. 243. (The measurement apparently refers to an old Norwegian league of eight miles. Meyer, *The Extent of Jurisdiction in Coastal Waters* (1937), pp. 521–2). The United Kingdom reply did not point out the extreme unlikelihood of a mariner's being able to determine his position with respect to the consession's boundary ,using 17th Century navigating methods, hence the questionable character of the concession on these grounds alone. For other reasons, not pertinent to this footnote, the Court in its opinion took a qualified view of this early concession. *I.C.J. Reports*, 1951, p. 142.

claimed sovereignty and the actual means for establishing them and honoring them.

Returning now to the evolution of the ship-building art during the Age of Discovery and after, our principal interests are in the increasing size and sea-worthiness of ships, and in the measures adopted for fighting them and defending them. As techniques of navigation steadily improved, the history of changes in ship design and size is a reflection of the history of economic change during the Age of Discovery and later. The Spaniards and Portuguese commenced early to build comparatively large ships for the lucrative American and East Indies trade.[19] Not at first assured of similar financial success in overseas ventures, the British were slower to construct large ships.[20] The sudden increase in size of Spanish ships was accomplished at the expense of their sea-keeping quality. They were very slow, unwieldy and very unseaworthy in heavy weather.[21] Moreover, they were manned by prisoners and the dregs of humanity.[22] To add to their difficulties Spanish ships were constantly harrassed by British privateers and by pirates. The distinction between the two activities, privateering and piracy in this period is often quite blurred. The Spanish recourse in the face of such troubles was the organizing of convoys which were sailed on an annual or semi-annual basis. Large numbers

[19] Between 1550 and about 1628, Spanish ships increased in size from a maximum of 200 tons to 600 tons. Clarence H. Haring, *Trade and Navigation Between Spain and the Indies* (1918), pp. 212–3. A ton incidentally is derived from the word tun, meaning a barrel of wine. A ship's displacement was reckoned on imagining how many barrels of wine could be stowed below decks. Richard Hakluyt, *A Selection of the Principal Voyages, Traffiques, and Discoveries of the English Nation*, Ed., Laurance Irving (1926), p. xiv. Obviously tonnage measurement as applied in this context can only be used as some rough measure of comparison.

[20] A. L. Rowse, "The Elizabethans and America" X *American Heritage*, April 1959, p. 4f and June 1959 p. 4f. Early British overseas commercial ventures were, in general, unprofitable for the participants, chiefly because they were directed to relatively barren areas of the North American continent, and they were ill-managed. Accordingly, the early incentive for construction of large ships was absent.

[21] Sources of information concerning ship construction of this period are: John Charnock, *History of Marine Architecture*, 3 vols. (1802); Hakluyt, *The Principal Navigations of the English Nation*, 12 vols. (1904 Edition of the Hakluyt Society; W. S. Lindsay, *History of Merchant Shipping and Ancient Commerce* (1874), 4 vols.; and LCDR John Forsyth Meigs USN (RET), *The Story of the Seaman*, 2 vols. (1912); A. Du Sein, *Histoire de la Marine de Tous les Peuples* (1879). Worthy of special comment is the Charnock work whose title is something of a misnomer. Printed on quarto-size pages numbering some 450 per volume, and containing numerous finely-engraved illustrations and line drawings, this now very rare work is in reality a maritime history of Western Europe and the Ancient World. For the period of the 17th and 18th Centuries it is also a documented administrative history of the Royal Navy. The author combines unquestionable talents of a professional naval constructor with those of an historian and man of letters.

[22] Until comparatively recent times this has been a fairly common phenomenon, relieved only occasionally when sailors were guaranteed shares in the venture or shares in prizes. It was much easier to find men for a privateer for a warship.

of ships remained for protracted periods in the more sheltered bays and harbors of the mother country and her colonies. The necessity for absolute control over such bays was obvious. Sovereignty was declared and defended.[23] Over the Gulf of Fonseca sovereignty was proclaimed as early as 1552.[24] Additional factors contributing to Spanish and Portuguese policies are discussed in Sections C and D hereunder.

In a relatively short time after the commencement of large ship construction by Spain, other Western European powers found it in their interest to follow the trend.[25] The wooden shipbuilding art, insofar as it is concerned with the *assembling* of wooden ships achieved its apex of development by the middle of the Seventeenth Century.[26] Thereafter, the science of marine architecture,[27] was concerned primarily with evolving better sea-keeping characteristics, slight increases in the size of ships, and improved arrangements of sails. Ships became more expensive to build and the time under construction lengthened considerably. Maritime countries of western Europe began to experience increased difficulty and expense in obtaining suitable wood for ship construction. In short, a ship became more and more of a major investment and this could only result in greater pressure being brought to bear upon the State for protection. Conversely, the State became more conscious of the lucrative rewards that were possible through trading at sea. During this period of the 16th through the 18th Centuries, wars and conflicts at sea were virtually endemic. While there were occasional periods of peace on land, communications were such that States could exercise only the poorest of control over ships at sea. Large navies, convoys, and protected anchorages were an absolute necessity. It is small wonder then that Azuni, writing on law within a year of Charnock's work on Marine architecture, could say with ample justification:

These obligations relative to ports, are of equal force in bays and gulfs, inasmuch as they also make a part of the sovereignty of the State, within whose domain they are situated, and are equally under its safeguard and protection, Conse-

[23] Harbors and bays were defended by forts as well as by guard ships. In 1579, a rule was laid down for Spanish Indies ports that no ship might enter or leave under cover of darkness without being fired opun. Special gun signals were prescribed to indentify friendly ships. Haring, *Trade and Navigation*, p. 224.

[24] *Anales de la Corte de Justicia Centroamericano*, vol. V.

[25] W. S. Lindsay, *History of Merchant Shipping and Ancient Commerce*. (1874), vol. II, pp. 165–185.

[26] Charnock, *History of Marine Architecture* (1800), vol. III, p. 109.

[27] At the time of Charnock (1800), marine architecture was the general term, and naval architecture was the term used to indicate the science of designing war ships. Today, the term, naval architecture, is the general term used, regardless of the type of vessel considered. This is manifested even among educational institutions, for example: the Webb Institute of Naval Architecture and the Department of Naval Architecture, University of Michigan.

quently, the asylum afforded in a bay, or gulf, is no less violable, than in a port and every breach of jurisdiction, committed in the one, as well as in the other must be considered as an open violation of the law of nations.[28]

While most of the maritime powers constructed some large ships, it was those who enjoyed some military or natural protection on land as well as some capital-forming capacity who could undertake foreign commerce on a large scale. On the other hand, navigation and construction of small vessels must not be neglected. At this, the Dutch and the Scandinavians were especially adept, and they were hardy mariners as well. While the base reasons for fishing industries differed as among the western European States, it was the type of vessel and its manner of operation that contributed most toward determining which States would participate in the formulation of sovereignty rules. As something of a corollary to this, there is the suggestion that the mode of expression of the rules, and the legal argumentation in connection therewith, might be predetermined by the prevalent legal thought of the States directly concerned.

Returning momentarily to the art of navigation, strictly defined, it is of some interest to comment upon several later voyages of discovery. Those of Captain Cook and Captain Davis were of especial importance inasmuch as they were carried out by men well-trained in cartography and surveying. With respect to the law of bays and that having to do with historic bays, the author believes that the work of such scientifically minded marine explorers points up a rather material consideration. It was they who not only discovered and claimed new territories, but they also surveyed and delimited such areas and their shore lines with relative accuracy. It would seem that in present day discussion of claims to bays on the grounds of historic possession, due attention should be paid to the relative accuracy with which the original claim was delineated.

Section C THE ECONOMIC INTEREST

In western Europe, the general break-up of the Empire of Rome saw the disintegration of the expensive Roman road system, the vanishing of the camps and market centers, and the reversion to a subsistence type of economy in which the villages produced practically everything

[28] Domenico A. Azuni, *The Maritime Law of Europe* (1806), p. 234. Writing similarly at p. 206, Azuni states this to be the practice among "polished" nations.

they used and little they did not use. When Roman administration and protection disappeared, so did inter-regional trade, the use of coinage and any significant market for luxury goods.[1] In this era of decline, however, there remained flourishing one segment of western civilization while a second one came into being. Some might say that the second was a revival in a new form. The flourishing segment was the new Rome on the Bosphorus, Constantinople. Here there was an orderly central government, an adequate and standardized gold coinage and a banking system. Manufacturing and foreign trade reached their peak in the Eastern Empire at a time when the Empire of the west had completely disintegrated. During this period (about 500–800) A.D., a thriving silk industry grew up in Greece and Syria and intensive agriculture reached a high state of perfection. The empire that came into being and rapidly possessed itself of many of the lands of eastern Rome was that of the Mohammedan Arabs whose capital was Bagdad. The Greeks of Constantinople and the Arabs traded with each other and both tapped the resources of the East Indies and China.

The Arabs marched across North Africa, into Spain and on into France where they were halted by Charles Martel at Poitiers in 732 A.D.[2] The Arabs were less interested in religious fanaticism in Spain than in building an empire. Agriculture, stock-raising, mining and manufacturing developed. The Jewish merchants were allowed to emigrate to Spain, and trade with the Byzantine Empire and the Moslem East expanded on a large scale. Southern Italy and Sicily continued under the rule of Constantinople after the Lombards descended into the north of Italy in 568 A.D. Sicily was conquered by the Moslems in the Ninth Century. The two southern parts of Italy were conquered by the Normans in the Eleventh Century. Until then, and for two centuries thereafter, Amalfi, on the Gulf of Salerno was the great East-West exchange port. In the North of Italy, the German invaders were agriculturists who found an attractive civilization which they did not totally destroy. The cities of Milano and Genova continued to exist. Venezia was founded in the Fifth Century.

Britain, after the Roman departure, reverted to a Celtic society which was quite unable to continue any of the Roman institutions. It was an easy prey to the invasions of the Picts, Saxons, Frisians, Danes, and Angles. There was little readjustment to new overlords

[1] Knight, Barnes and Flügel, *Economic History of Europe* (1928), Ch. III.
[2] Bernard Lewis, *The Arabs in History*, Rev. Ed. (1958), p. 121.

required of the Celts; they were simply weaker than the invaders. The latter proceeded slowly to consolidate their possessions, but there was little in the way of outside trade and less incentive for it.

With the joining of forces to repel the Arab invader in France, there arose a Frankish king with real power. At the request of the Pope, the Franks subdued the Lombards in Northern Italy, and Charles, or Charlemagne, became Emperor in 800 A.D. After his death the Frankish Kingdom broke up into two parts: roughly, what are now France and Germany. Thereafter, too, the Pope lost much of whatever power he had, and there was a general revolt against clerical and feudal authority. The towns took the lead in the South, but in the North, the landed aristocracy formed itself into large, self-sufficient units. It should be noted that the feudalism of the North could not easily take root because there was too much town life, foreign and domestic trade and too much of money. The North was thinly populated, made little use of money, and was generally agricultural in its structure. It was also weak and fragmentized. Without substantial trade, communications decline. When communications decline, so does any semblance of binding power.

Into this power vacuum in Northwestern Europe, came the Normans or Northmen. But before discussing that phenomenon of invasion and change, one should note that there existed in miniscule degree a communications interchange between the Italian towns and the Teutonic North. A small amount of trade and the all pervasive Church organization carried North a trickle of oriental goods. Papal taxes were sent to Rome. Northern Europeans came to the center of Church Government. Bishops and great lay lords knew something of southern and eastern luxuries and wanted them. When the Frankish Empire broke up and a German King (Otto) became Emperor, there commenced a fierce struggle to determine whether the German Emperor, the Pope or the Italian Cities were to control the Peninsula. These cities and their middlemen plus Papal revenues tended to build up Italy at the expense of her neighbors.

Feudalism had not been completely established at the time of Charlemagne's death, and he apparently was not aiming toward it, but toward a strong central government. But the Church and lay lords added to their holdings and the remaining freeholders gave up the struggle, in many instances, and commended themselves to holders of estates. Since freemen and holders of property were the only ones to render military service – as revenue for their land – their declining number quickly led to a decline of military power. The trend of events was firmly decided by the Teutonic invasions. At first these caused a period of complete anarchy in the Frankish lands of the Rhine. Thereafter, the French manorial feudalism emerged, complete with its well-stratified society. With the Norman invasion of England in 1066, the system was established in England. But in England, there was devised a variation in the feudal system which was to have extraordinary consequences in succeeding history.[3]

William and the Kings in England who followed him deliberately avoided certain features of French feudalism which were contrary to their interest. They scattered the fiefs, rather than allowing centralization, thus making it more difficult for nobles to resist the crown. Whereas in France, great lay and clerical vassals purchased or wrung immunities from the crown, these immunities from tax-gatherers, and judicial and administrative officers, were not granted in England. An elaborate system of royal courts was established to forestall excessive local independence. Sub-infeudation was discouraged and finally forbade altogether; the sub-vassals were required to do homage directly to the crown, over the heads of immediate lords. Thus the crown was able to play off lesser nobles against greater, and eventually, the upper strata of commoners against both. In such a fluid system where power was divided, more or less equally, and where there was the possibility of limited but not dominating political combination and pressure, it should be obvious that a common law should evolve. By the end of the Twelfth Century, the establishment of English law was practically an established fact.[4]

Feudalism spread to Germany, but much more slowly, and its power was for some time checked by the presence of royal officials, after a series of futile wars in which German emperors sought to govern Italy. When Henry the Lion fell in 1181 A.D., disintegration set in rapidly in southern Germany and millions of free men became serfs. But northern Germany and the Netherlands resisted; here trading towns had already come into being.[5]

By the Tenth Century, towns were growing and some revival of [6]

[3] Sir Paul Vinogradoff, *Cambridge Medieval History*, vol. I, Ch. XIX, vol. II, Ch. XX.

[4] George H. Sabine, *A History of Political Theory*, Rev. Ed. (1958), p. 202. One must hasten to add, perhaps, that this development did not run the same course in Scotland, where the Clan definitely could and did oppose the crown. Edward Jenks, *Law and Politics in the Middle Ages* (1914), p. 97.

[5] Max Weber "Capitalism and Rural Society in Germany", *Max Weber's Essays in Sociology*, Tr. H. H. Gerth and C. Wright Mills (1947), pp. 363–380.

[6] Lynn Thorndike, *The History of Medieval Europe* (1917), Chs. XIII, XIV,

trade and manufacturing became evident in Western Europe. There resulted a revived interest on overland trade routes and numerous fairs where goods were exchanged. But as trade became more general, so did the avarice of petty nobles, monastaries, and brigands along the trade routes. Tolls for transit of goods became a lucrative form of unearned income, with a result that could be forecast.[7] Although seas abounded in pirates. Italian and eastern merchants soon found that by combining efforts, and by a system of marine insurance, they could enjoy greater profit and ship larger cargoes by sea. Already, there was a thriving cross-channel trade between England and the continent. Coastal towns became larger, and merchant fleets more numerous; moreover, in the northern countries, where feudalism was less rigidly developed, men had far more opportunity to become freemen. Port towns grew, in part from settlements of adventures and fugitives, as well as merchants. A special code of behavior grew in these areas and this is one of the sources of the law merchant.[8]

A by-product of the periodic efforts of the Germans to organize Italy into a part of a centrally controlled Empire was the brillant idea of Pope Urban II, conceived in 1095 A.D. to divert this menace toward the Moslems of the Holy lands, north Africa and Spain. For two centuries, the Crusaders butchered their fellow human beings, but their most permanent effect was among the lands where they originated rather than (with the exception of Spain) in the lands against which they were directed. The great commercial beneficiary was Venice [9] who sacked and ruined her rival, Constantinople. But the great effect was that northern europeans discovered the comforts of civilization, and became accustomed to fine cloths, spiced food, jewels and ornamental furnishings. Great fleets of Venetian ships commenced to sail to northern ports and to England where their goods were traded for minerals, timber, and wool. It might be added, that Venetians went to extraordinary lengths to preserve their eastern trade monopoly. They closed the Adriatic [10] to foreign commerce, established tributary city States with closed harbors, and they had a large navy to enforce their monopoly. It is hardly surprising that western europeans sought diligently some other route to the orient. Part of their problem was to be solved with the advent of the magnetic compass.

[7] Eli Heckscher, *Mercantilism*, Tr. Mendel Shapiro, (1935), pp. 45–6.
[8] William S. Holdsworth, *A History of English Law*, vol. V, (1924), p. 103.
[9] W. C. Hazlitt, *The Venetian Republic*, Vol. I, Chs. VIII, XI.
[10] Percy T. Fenn, Jr., *The Origin of the Right of Fishing in Territorial Waters* (1926), pp. 224–231.

The Venetian and Italian trade methods were highly sophisticated for their time, and the investments and dividends therefrom were exceedingly large. General use of money, money-lending and banking, insurance, and manufacturing all grew rapidly. The Church, at first opposed to all interest and lending as sinful, soon became a major investor and lent its power to the development of trade and the growth of the monopoly. There appears here, as in another development, a singular coincidence with the resurgence of Roman law in the hands of the glossators. Von Savigny writes that the period of the glosses is from about 1100 to 1260 A.D.[11] Without proceeding into the theories of Roman Law, which will be discussed as necessary at somewhat greater length below, it will suffice to observe that this revival coincided with a need for an orderly system of law that would in some part meet the needs of those exercising political and economic power at the time. Roman Law in this era was a highly exportable product, and seems to have lent itself rather nicely to the needs of a growing feudalistic society in Germany.[12]

With the revival of sea trade in the Middle Ages, a new lawlessness, smuggling, makes its real entry. As was noted above, one of the factors militating toward commerce by sea, was the succession of tolls collected by petty lords and others along the trade routes. Like the lords inland, the lords and princes on sea coasts, who were sovereign over ports, sought also an income, more or less unearned, from customs duties. In the early Middle Ages such duties were especially onerous, inasmuch as the Prince provided little in the way of protection or port services to the merchant. Smuggling began early – probably at about the time when piracy in the Mediterranean and on the west coast of Europe became rather too risky because of difficulties in disposing of stolen goods and because of the increasing armament carried by ships.[13] The

[11] F. C. von Savigny, *Geschichte des Romanischen Rechts im Mittelalter* (1834–58), vol. III, p. 83 *et seq.*

[12] Knight, Barnes, and Flügel, *Economic History of Europe*, write: "To the Roman jurist, law must be written and based upon the will of a prince. The nobility of Germany got the necessary courts into their own hands. The tendency was for the lord to invest himself legally with the arbitrary powers of the Roman dominus and for the partially free peasantry of various grades to be classified and treated as coloni or servi – serfs or slaves." p. 196. This is one view, of course, but another is simply a desire for order and organization after an era of anarchy and disunion. This desire would appear to call for a philosophy rationalizing and strengthening authority and the imposition of a legal yoke upon society." See, also, Roscoe Pound, *An Introduction To the Philosophy of Law* (1922), Yale Paperbound, p. 12.; Julius Stone, *The Province and Function of Law* (1946), pp. 424–6; Sir Hersch Lauterpacht, *Private Law Sources and Analogies of International Law*, p. 129; and Edward Jenks, *Law and Politics in the Middle Ages* (1919), Ch. V.

[13] William E. Masterson, *Jurisdiction in Marginal Seas* (1929), p. 1. Actually, charging of customs duties is a very ancient measure, and was especially well developed in the Roman Empire. W. S. Lindsay, *History of Merchant Shipping and Ancient Commerce*, vol. I, p. 109.

levying of customs and the apprehension of smugglers were quite early influences upon the growth and necessity of some understood rules for determining jurisdictional boundaries at sea.

The trading behavior of the Venetians, the capture of Constantinople by the Ottoman Turks in 1453, and the rise of commerce and manufacturing in the West furnished the impetus for discovering new trade routes. Improvement in ships, the advent of the compass, and the appearance of powder firing cannon on ships provided better protected means for searching for those routes. By the beginning of the Age of Discovery, moreover, Spain had become a united country, and the Netherlands provinces had become commercially strong. Before proceeding to discuss the age of Discovery, we should first take note of another economic by-product of the Middle Ages: the question of fisheries.

As we have observed before, fishing has been one of man's oldest sources of food. In the earliest of times fish formed a part of the diet of those near coasts and for those whose meat or protein diet was otherwise limited by the scarcity of animal food. This was a totally natural phenomenon and control of this resource by man was rather late in its appearance.[14] The Christian era and the mediaeval revival of trade brought on two man-made developments which created a permanent disturbance of the older state of things. In the more rigorous climates of the north where trade and manufacturing began to flourish, the division of labor and shift from a subsistence economy made it necessary that people engaged in the non-agricultural pursuits be fed from the produce of the remainder of the population.[15] Within the limits of cheap transportation, fish was a cheaper meat food than animal meat.[16] At an early time, the process of preservation by salting or drying was discovered. subsequently, the recovery of salt itself became an industry of

[14] The works of Cicero, Seneca, Paulus and Ovid express the belief that the sea, and the fish in it, were open or common to all men. Fenn, *Origin*, p. 5. See also, Stefan A. Riesenfeld, *Protection of Coastal Fisheries under International Law* (1942), pp. 7–8.

[15] For present purposes, the author has indicated the development of manufacturing and commerce in northern europe and elsewhere simply as facts rather than as phenomenological problems requiring further study. It is necessary, however, to note and keep in mind that the matter of where human economic activity becomes geographically located is, in itself, a complex study, generally termed as the location theory. The author has endeavored to orient his writing in accordance with general precepts of this theory as he understands it. William H. Dean, Jr., *The Theory of Economic Activities with Special Reference to Historical Change* (Unpublished Harvard University PhD dissertation, 1938). Bertil Ohlin, *Interregional and International Trade* (1931), pp. 183–229. Carl J. Friedrich, Ed., *Alfred Weber's Theory of Location of Industries* (1929), pp. 1–12, 23–36, 39.

[16] From birth to death, domesticated meat animals must be fed, somehow. See Chapter I, Section C, for a more detailed explanation. It is to be noted, also, that there is far less waste in the use of fish as food than in animals used for the same purpose.

significant size.[17] Subsequent to the general use of fish as a food came the requirements of the Church of Rome: fish came to be eaten once a week and for forty days during the lenten period. When all Christendom was subject to the rules of the Church, the business of catching and distributing fish became highly profitable.[18]

It will be recalled that the northern german and lowland towns resisted the trend toward feudalism. These towns grew into a cooperative organization which history knows as the Hanseatic League.[19] When the Holy Roman Empire was weak in authority, this League, with no visible executive, came to wield enormous power and it conducted great wars to preserve and extend that power. One of the sources of Hanseatic wealth and power was the fishing industry in the spawning area of the Sound. Repeated wars with Sweden and Denmark were fought to retain unhampered Hanseatic control. Moreover, the German traders had a practical monopoly of the Norwegian export trade in fish. With the profits earned and the generated capital, the Hansean merchants opened up stations and invested in commercial and industrial enterprizes on the Continent and in England. During this early period, fish was not only a primary source of food for the Scandinavian countries, but for Norway at least, fishing was a primary source of economic life. It is to be noted, however, that while the Norwegians were fish harvesters, their fish export trade was in other hands.[20]

In the middle of the Fifteenth Century, the herring suddenly shifted their spawning from the Baltic to the North Sea,[21] and the long feud between the Germans and Scandinavians was transferred westward to the Dutch and the English.[22] Thereafter, Dutch fishermen swarmed

[17] Huntly M. Sinclair, *A Preface to Economic History* (1934), pp. 26, 29.

[18] Sinclair, p. 101.

[19] Heckscher, *Mercantilism*, pp. 329–330.

[20] Norwegian fishing has traditionally been done by thousands of little boats, each manned by two or three men who sold their product ashore. The product was used either at home or exported by others. It seems always to have been a laborintensive, low capital operation. Mead, *Economic Geography of the Scandinavian States and Finland* (1958), Ch. VIII. By comparison, English fishing, even in early periods, was characterized by larger boats and more significant capital investment. The requirement therefor was simply explained by Adam Smith in 1776: "The fish must generally be sought tor a greater distance, larger vessels must be employed, and more expensive machinery of every kind made use of." *Wealth of Nations*, (Modern Library Edition), p. 235.

[21] This is a rather uncommon phenomenon. W. R. Mead, in his *Economic Geography of the Scandinavian States and Finland* (1958), writes, "Long experience has shown that fish are so persistently associated with certain areas that they may be mapped with fair precision", p. 176. In this excellent work, Mr. Mead has gone to some length to explore the natural causes for the presence of fish in certain geographical areas.

[22] Up to that time, it appears that English coastal fisheries did not catch enough for domestic requirements. To alleviate the condition, treaties were signed in the reign of Edward III (*circa* 1330 A.D.) guaranteeing the general liberty of fishing. In 1468 Edward IV and

into the North Sea and herein lies one of the bases for subsequent Dutch prosperity. During the latter part of the reign of Elizabeth I, the fisheries had begun to decay. The extension of general freedom to fish to the Dutch fishermen, while continued in Elizabeth's reign, was never agreed to in Scotland where fisheries were confined to firths and bays from which foreigners were excluded (or were required to pay tithes). In Scotland, fisheries were held to be of basic economic importance to the population; waters within a landkenning (14–28 miles, discernible from masthead height), were considered as exclusive waters of Scotland.[23]

The Anglo-Dutch situation is wanting of some further explanation. The suppression of Catholicism and the relaxation of ecclesiastic rules among the laity in England appears to have been detrimental to the fishing industry. Apart from the commercial and economic value, however, this industry was looked upon as indispensable for the maintenance of maritime power. For this reason, any decline in the number of men and vessels engaged in it was viewed with great concern. Fulton advises that this was the primary reason for the passages of rather drastic legislation to protect the fisheries industry.[24] Under the Tudors, the legislation did not aim at interfering with foreign fishermen; it simply compelled people to eat more fish, to restrain importtation of fish, and to encourage export of English-caught fish. The legislation was embodied in the Act of 1563, entitled: "Touching Certain Politic Constitutions for the Navy." It was the learned John Dee who first urged the claim to *mare clausum* as an additional measure.[25] We shall deal with the long fishing controversy between England and the United Provinces in *Section D*. It is sufficient to note that the aforementioned legislation and that of subsequent years, for whatever reason it was passed, served to perpetuate the British fishing industry, and at considerable capital investment.[26] At the time the

the Duchess of Burgundy signed a treaty granting Holland the right to fish without a license. In 1946, Henry VII and the Duke of Burgundy signed the *Intercursus Magnus* reaffirming the right and extending to all fisherman the use of any ports without license.

[23] Fulton, *The Sovereignty of the Sea* (1911), Ch. III. L. Larry Leonard, *International Regulation of Fisheries* (1949), pp. 12–17. Professor Raestad argues that the situations of Scotland and Norway are the same, both being lands on the North Sea and less fertile than those further to the south. *La Mer territoriale* (1913), p. 40. See also, Bustamante, *The Territorial Sea* (1930), p. 5.

[24] Fulton, *Sovereignty*, p. 87.

[25] Advanced in a book published in 1577, entitled: *Rare Memorials pertayning to the Perfecte Arte of Navigation.*

[26] It is of some interest that Adam Smith, writing two centuries after the passage of this legislation condemns the uneconomic and artificial subsidation of the English fishing industry – for defense purposes. *Wealth of Nations* (Modern Library Edition), pp. 484–8.

legislation was passed, the British fishing industry was declining and might have, except for Scotland, passed virtually out of existence since the British needs for fish were beginning to be served adequately by foreign import. In later times, however, this industry became of such economic importance as to raise doubts as to whether British requirements for fish could have been satisfied from other than British sources.

The history of Scotland, on the other hand, shows every inducation of having a fishing industry that was necessary for the subsistence of the people; it was not artificially stimulated, nor at this time does it appear to have been the source of any wealth through external trade.[27]

Fishing, as we have seen, is very often done near the shores of the sea and in bays. When the fishing is done by nationals of other than the littoral state, international questions are likely to arise. But the economic reasons for the esistence of a country's fishing industry are varied and the foregoing examples of historic beginnings of such questions serve to emphasize these reasons. To recapitulate:

(a) Fishing may be necessary as an absolute means to ensure country's supply of subsistence food.

(b) Fishing may be undertaken and developed as a primary source of a country's income through external trade. This is the likely course of events when the country concerned is situated next to a profitable market and has no product other than fish to sell.

(c) Fishing may be stimulated artificially for extraneous reasons but with the ultimate result that it becomes a fixed feature of a country's economy, subject only to some later substitution, if any.[28]

Were the real or imagined requirements of a country to be satisfied by a fishing industry entirely within a country's recognized littoral, or perhaps on the high seas, there would be a relatively low level of probability of controversy. But completely static economic behavior is rather uncommon, and more so where the ownership of the resource is neither clear cut nor agreed upon. To settle an international dispute arising in such a fluid atmosphere requires, in this author's eyes, a

[27] Fulton, *Sovereignty*, pp. 76–77. See also, James Anderson, *Observations on the Means of Exciting a Spirit of National Industry* (1775).

[28] Substitution, in this context, has to do with choice of occupations and the motivations toward change experienced by an occupation group. Economic factors, of course, are not necessarily controlling, as was evident in the fishmonger's reply to Sir William Cecil's 1528 inquiry into the declining state of English fisheries. Fulton, *Sovereignty*, p. 91. For a theoretical discussion, see, Tibor Scitov sky, *Welfare and Competition* (1951), pp. 94–5.

clear understanding of the economic equities at stake – it would seem that economic habits and real or imagined economic requirements often exhibit tenacities every bit as strong as those exhibited by legal conceptions.[29]

While one could trace, within the period considered by this chapter, the influence exercised upon the development of the law of bays by the economics of the fishing industry, the picture is more complicated than that. There seems to be a gnawing question of whether rules for bays having their origin in one segment of man's activity on the sea at a given era in time seem adequate or equitable when applied to another segment of such activity at another point in time.[30] If they are not and if a State's view of the rules is a reflection of whatever dominates its interest (could it be otherwise?), the probability of a consensus of views on the rules is severely diminished. We shall now turn to another feature of the economic consideration, the Age of Discovery.

We noted above that the Venetians came to exercise what for us might appear to be a peculiarly monopolistic stringency upon the conduct of their middle-man trade between the East and the North and West of Europe. This continued into a period when there occurred a coincidence of events calculated to break their monopoly. The Ottomans captured Constantinople in 1453 and thereafter made the eastern trade route more costly and precarious. The compass had come into use, ships had increased in size, and the powder-loaded cannon showed some promise as a defensive weapon against the galley mounted ram. In every age, there are adventurers who are willing to explore

[29] "But everyone will cling as tightly as possible to habitual economic methods and only submit to the pressure of circumstances as it becomes necessary. Thus the economic system will not change capriciously on its own initiative but will be at all times connected with the preceding state of affairs.... All the preceding periods have .... entangled him (a farmer, for example), in a net of social and economic connections which he cannot easily shake off." Joseph A. Schumpeter, *The Theory of Economic Development* (1951), pp. 6, 8–9. "Owing to the tenacity of legal concepts and principles, the past always possesses a great bearing upon the present law." Stefan A. Riesenfeld, *Protection of Coastal Fisheries Under International Law* (1941), p. 3.

[30] For purposes of comparison with the position of Northern European countries in the present era, it is of interest to note that in the mid-sixteenth century, Denmark-Norway and Sweden-Finland were very powerful States, the latter occupying an area greater than that of the German Empire of 1914. England and Scotland had about 5 million inhabitants and Denmark-Norway had about 2 million. While in these countries there was greater absolute dependence upon fish for food than there was in England and West Central Europe, there was otherwise much greater economic parity than there exists today. See, Chapter 4, below. Mead, *Economic Geography*, pp. 85–6; M. K. Bennett, *The World's Food* (1954), p. 15; A. M. Carr-Saunders, *World Population, Past Growth and Present Trends* (1936).

and take risks, and, by the Fifteenth Century, there was sufficient market incentive and capital in Western Europe to back a new trade route that might have great economic rewards. The prices of goods shipped over the caravan routes were very high. Also, there were countries like Spain and Portugal for whom new trade might make up for a paucity of other sources of wealth. In the latter two countries, the Mohammedans and Jews had been finally expelled in the Fifteenth Century; heretofore the Iberian Peninsula had, for centuries, been the home of freedom of thought and enterprize. The crusaders gradually absorbed some of this civilization and the new Spanish nation was thus not by accident a leader in exploration, colonization and overseas trade.

The various European states who undertook expeditions of discovery made extensive claims to regions touched by their navigators. In many cases the real extent of such lands remained unknown for a century or more. While some lands discovered and subsequently colonized yielded returns of a kind different from what was anticipated, the rewards were such that expeditions continued and rival commercial and colonial empires emerged. Conceptions of control and sovereignty accompanied the colonizers and traders. New ports were founded but the elements of customary social and military control were yet to develop. Private adventurers and companies could hope to maintain their positions as against rivals through the interventions of State power. The States themselves, to a greater or lesser degree, underwent metamorphoses in their economic structures, and they came to depend upon their overseas holdings for maintenance of economic standards, opulence and power.[31] Mercantilism emerged. With these developments there seemed to arise new efforts at legalistic rationalization of policies pursued – a curious admixture of previously expounded ideas and principles being recompounded to justify the points of view of States seeking empire. This occurred in an atmosphere of renewed vitality in Western Europe. The pressure for gaining and exploiting new possessions and for greater care in demarking new boundaries and preserving old ones increased. In general, States seemed to be pursuaded that they had much more at stake in their seaward and overseas territory. As the Age of Discovery proceeded, there occurred the Thirty Years War whose termination in 1648 saw the foundations of the modern State

[31] Knight, Barnes and Flügel estimate that between 1492 and 1550, Spain's revenues in gold and silver from the new world surpassed all the world's previous output of these metals. *Economic History of Europe* (1928), p. 269.

system. Finally, in about mid-18th Century there commenced the upsurge in European population which has never really abated, down tc the present time.

There are a number of characteristics of the Age of Discovery contributing to mercantilism in particular and to State attitudes toward overseas possessions in general that must be considered:

(a) Voyages became longer, more costly, and more dangerous than ever before, resulting in an increased demand for capital and a greater demand for insurance. Fitting out cost more and there was a longer period of investment from the beginning of fitting out until the business was wound up.

(b) There was an increased demand for capital for permanent uses such as setting up business establishments, defense works, military establishments, and administration.

(c) The capital thus required, generated and expended made it necessary that the source of such capital be more closely preserved against foreign encroachment and that its expenditure overseas be protected in order to ensure returning profits.

(d) The new trade, into countries where European methods of government were not in force, demanded that certain State functions be bound up with that trade. Political problems arose and the trading States were forced to found colonies.[32]

Such characteristics, binding economic activity and political functions, led to greater cooperation by the State and to ensuring State legislation that looked toward the tying of colonial trade completely with the mother State and the restricting of such trade to ships bearing the mother country's flag.

At this juncture we must note a peculiarity of State interest in colonial expansion and overseas trade. In countries long developed and populated by Western Europeans, ports grew up in small bays and natural harbors, and claims to sovereignty over the areas expanded outward under various demands and pressures. The closing of the Adriatic by Venice,[33] and subsequently the King's Chambers declaration of James I are the most extreme examples.[34] In the course of

[32] Heckscher, *Mercantilism*, pp. 340–1.

[33] Sir Geoffrey Butler and Simon Maccoby, *The Development of International Law* (1928), p. 41, citing Corpus Christi College Cambridge MS No. 370.7, written by an English Franciscan pilgrim to the Holy Land in 1344 A.D.

[34] Fulton, *Sovereignty of the Sea*, Ch. IV.

overseas exploration and colonization, something of a reserve procedure took place. Rather vague but sweeping claims were made to vast sea areas,[35] long before any real ports or colonies could be said to exist. Subsequently, attempts were made to enforce these claims[36] in order that the claiming State might monopolize the newly-developed trade.[37] The Venetian hegemony vanished with the decline of Venetian power, and the Sovereignty of the King's Chambers was attenuated for different reasons.[38] But when vast European claims abroad could no longer be defended and were left to decay, there persisted some assertions to sovereignty over quite large bays. While perhaps some of these claims have lain dormant for quite protracted periods, it appears that when they are revived, they are usually grounded in the original claims of early discoverers. It appears that the Age of Discovery and the subsequent mercantilist period planted seeds for later claims to sovereignty over arms of the sea. Sovereignty on the basis of such claims has been occasionally conceded by tribunals. This being the case, what is to prevent non-European States from asserting new claims to bays with nothing more solid or substantial than these precedents? This matter will be considered in more detail in subsequent chapters.

One could perhaps accept in its broadest implications the 1927 statement of Sir Herch Lauterpacht that "the basic function of law is protection of acquired rights," [39] and then perhaps on the basis of private law analogy argue that rights or assertions thereof to territorial sea or internal waters find their origins in economic causes. It is very difficult, moreover, to differentiate out from the many causes those which are definitely devoid of economic content. It is probably

[35] Concerning the foundation of British sovereignty claims to Hudson Bay and other bays in North America, and subsequent legislation, see Keller, Lissitzyn and Mann, *Sovereignty through Symbolic Acts* (1938), Ch. V; *The Alleganean, Stetson* v. *United States* IV *Moore's Arbitrations*, 4332. On Portuguese and Spanish claims, see Hecksher, *Mercantilism*, Ch. VII; Haring, *Trade and Navigation*, Ch. I; Fulton, *Sovereignty*, Ch. IX; Reddie, *Maritime International Law*, (1844), Ch. VI; Butler and Maccoby, *Development*, Ch. II.

[36] Fulton, *Sovereignty*, Ch. IV.

[37] Heckscher, *Mercantilism*, Ch. VII; Shepard B. Clough and Charles W. Cole, *Economic History of Europe*, 3rd Ed., (1952), Chs. VII, VIII. For our purposes here, it matters little whether the desired monopoly was under the aegis of State trading (Spain) or under the control of a chartered company (England and United Provinces).

[38] Fulton, *Sovereignty*, p. 122, argues that in any event, the King's Chambers were limited to neutrality and jurisdiction in view of the war existing between Spain and the United Provinces and the frequent depredations of privateers. Judging from the wealth of evidence in Fulton's work, it would appear that the boundaries of the areas known as the King's Chambers have been more discussed in the books than they were ever enforced in fact or even reiterated in subsequent legislation.

[39] Sir Hersch Lauterpacht, *Private Law Analogies*, p. 129.

possible to show that in the quest for territory and in the assertion of claims to absolute jurisdiction over arms of the sea there have been reasons other than economic. Of these, national ambitions appear to be rather important, but in the era in question, it seems to this author that one is unable to demonstrate that national ambitions alone led to such assertions. The nearest that one can come to the causality of national ambitions is to argue that some claims were made and defended to ensure economic support for the attempted realization of national ambitions. This is probably true in the case of the Spanish policies in the 16th and 17th centuries.

In this section, the author has endeavored to trace the economic growth of western Europe as it appears to be related to claims to sovereignty over portions of the seas and to national waters and bays. Touched upon are harbors, early trade, smuggling, piracy, fisheries, discoveries, and mercantilism. It is to be noted that in any specific claim to sovereignty over an arm of the sea, there was usually only one of these economic considerations that was probably dominant. Little attempt has been made in this section to delineate specific claims over specific bays; it appears more desireable at this juncture simply to ascertain what were some of the economic causes giving rise to the claims. It now remains to suggest the existence of a system of self generating economic and technological cycles which seem to engender a real or imagined need for territorial expansion and the concommittant need to preserve the acquired territory as against the encroachments of others experiencing the same needs. In the period from the fall of Rome to 1800, Western Europe began with a subsistence economy plus some tastes and ideas reminiscent of an earlier period. The latter served as the impetus for some small amount of trade. As the trade grew, so did incipient capitalism. With the technological developments, they grew faster. As capitalism grew and the range of tastes broadened, more trade and new avenues of trade were sought. With these phenomena came specialization and division of labor and greater particularization of the masses of society. For reasons never too clear, there was added in the 17th century the beginning of a continuous rise in population. Thereafter, build-up of capital, seeking of trade channels, and increased volume of trade proceeded at a faster pace, each factor feeding upon and contributing to the other. With each step of the process, known resources were more intensively exploited, or new resources were sought, or both. And with every step of the process, individuals, groups and States exhibited the characteristic human tendency to keep what they have and to obtain more.[40] As the process has continued, and it may be thought of as not only cyclical but also centrifugal, there has been at work a centripetal force tending to bind peoples having some similarities of economic interests, cultures and political values into States.[41] The opposing forces at work have produced political boundaries between States. These have become more perfectly defined with the passage of time and further expanded where this has been possible.[42] One of the most propitious ways of expanding boundaries has been to seaward – as far as they can be defended and to the point where they impinge upon the interests of another State or group. It appears to this author that at least until the beginning of the Nineteenth Century, the predominating drive was the economic one. It further appears that the process occasionally shows signs of achieving some sort of temporary equilibrium quality wherein the interests, needs, and strengths of the potentially opposing groups are either approximately matched or satisfactorily complementary.[43] In other words, a plateu in social integration is reached. When this occurs, there appears to be an accelerated and more mutually satisfactory effort towards the establishment of some norm of international conduct marking the boundary of allowable action. It would appear that at such a juncture, something susceptible of being called a rule of international law is likely to come into being. This author believes that throughout the eighteenth century there was developing a situation of equilibrium with respect to sovereignty over sea areas. A temporary balancing of strengths and complementarity

[40] John Charnock, writing in another field, describes this as 'avariciousness' *History of Marine Architecture.* John Stuart Mill classes the process as a "progressive state of wealth". *Principles of Political Economy*, bk. IV, Ch. I. It is not believed, however, that the present-day "economic development" should be viewed in the same light inasmuch as it does not carry with it the same connotations of movement and exploitation of the heretofore unclaimed. The present author's thoughts about the cyclical development are the result of some reflection upon Mill's *Principles* and Schumpeter's *The Theory of Economic Development.*

[41] Implicit in this statement, of course, is the tendency toward what is generically classed as nationalism, about which there is a huge literature and a plethora of theories more or less finely delineated. Hans Kohn, *Nationalism, Its Meaning and History* (1955); Karl W. Deutsch, *Nationalism and Social Communication* (1953) (One of the theories).

[42] S. Whittemore Boggs, *International Boundaries* (1940), Chs. I, X; Hans W. Weigert and others, *Principles of Political Geography* (1957), pp. 85–6.

[43] Rationalizations of untimely aspirations toward upsetting the equilibrium are usually met with attitudes ranging from an academic interest to a disdain to an apprehension. The generic term "geo-politics" covers the field. The literature is extensive but much of it reflects narrow thinking and very strong bias, for example: Sir Halford Mackinder, "The Geographic Pivot of History," 33 *Geographic Journal* (1904), pp. 434–7; Karl Haushofer, *Grenzen in ihrer geographischen und politischen Bedeutung* (1927); Andrew Gyorgy, *Geopolitics, The New German Science* (1944). For a general discussion of territorial rationalizations and irrationalities, see Norman Hill, *Claims to Territory in International Law and Relations* (1945).

of interests was in evidence, and this equilibrating climate appears to have been of sufficiently lengthy duration for some rules on bays, however rudimentary, to take shape and gain a measure of respect.[44]

Section D THE DEFENSE INTEREST

The preceding two sections can rather broadly be said to demonstrate technological and economic influences upon the development of the law of bays during the period 476–1800 A.D. As already suggested, there is a bond of interdependence between the two. The third pillar of influence is the defense interest. Within the instant context, we refer to those actions of a violent nature tending to encroach upon or to defend that maritime territory which a political group or State conceives of as being under its exclusive sovereignty. Defense of said territory must be construed to include defense by a State against the depredations of other States engaged in war. Like the preceding two sections, it is proposed that this section be concerned primarily with technical and historical facts.

In considering the defense interest in this era there are three features of over-riding importance:

(1) The introduction of and the general use of the gunpowder propellent in weapons.[1]

(2) The decline, but not quite the extinction of piracy and its more legitimate variations such as privateering.

[44] In the author's view, herein is implied the most difficult and vexing intellectual problem in the study of international law. By comparison much else is simply frosting on the cake. It occurs to the author that too much preoccupation with the sociologic aspects of international law propagates a tendency toward stalling one's contemplating machinery on dead center. Rather than argue out the problems and contradictions and views that have been considered, the author will simply cite a few of the authorities whose writings are believed to merit some reflection. To do otherwise would be to depart considerably from the scope of this thesis. Julius Stone, *Legal Controls of International Conflict* (1954), Ch. II, Sect. IX; Kenneth S. Carlston, *Law and Structures of Social Action* (1956), pp. 1–28; Edward Jenks, *Law and Politics in the Middle Ages* (1919), pp. 64–5; Carleton K. Allen, *Law in the Making*, 4th Ed., (1946), Ch. I: Julius Stone, *The Province and Function of Law* (1946), Part III; Roscoe Pound, *An Introduction to the Philosophy of Law* (1922), Ch. II.

[1] Although said to have been used by the Chinese, the man who was probably the most careful recorder on the subject, LCOL Hime, Royal Artillery, credits the original compounding of gunpowder to the English friar, Roger Bacon, who recorded for posterity his experiment of 1249 A.D. By 1300 the explosive was being used for propelling missiles. H. W. L. Hime, *Gunpowder and Ammunition, their Origin and Progress* (1904), Ch. VII; Lyn Montross, *War through the Ages* (1944), Ch. VII. Care must be exercised in differentiating between the time when any gunpowder weapon or device was invented and the time when it came into general use. For example, General Fuller writes that rifling was invented in 1520. But rifled cannon were not in general use until the time of the American Civil War.

(3) The revival of and the technical development of methods of prosecuting organized war.

Study of the historical development of the technical means for waging war demonstrates the never-ending race between weapons designed to overcome all hitherto known defenses and defenses designed to neutralize all hitherto known weapons.[2] Until the coming of the atomic bomb there never existed for long an absolute weapon or an absolute defense. But the race did have its differentiated trend: wars involved increasing expense in men, material and money. The appearance of gunpowder weapons accelerated the trend. But after a certain developmental period, the effective range of the gunpowder weapon became stabilized and remained so for about three hundred years.[3] War decision-making then came to involve much more carefully considered committent of men, materials and finances; questions of degree rather than kind. Technical means of prosecuting war had not reached the stage where it was impossible for a fair number of States to have respectable war-making capacity. At the same time, the pace of international trade and commercial interdependence increased.[4] In view of the large number of human factors concerning war-making, the number of States who could, with some hope of success, make war, and with the known possible effects of war upon the commerce of belligerents and non-belligerents, there seems to have come into being a certain atmosphere of quasi-stability favorable to the formulation of a few rules of the international game. Memory of the extraordinary destruction of the Thrity Years' War undoubtedly contributed to the stabilizing effect.

It then remains for us to look into the stabilized position of the

[2] Almost any short history of warfare will demonstrate this. An excellent and thoroughly documented example is: MGEN J. F. C. Fuller, British Army, *Armament and History* (1945).

[3] For an historical analysis of gunfire weapons and artillery, the author has relied primarily on the following works: LCOL Hime, *Gunpowder and Ammunition* (1904); *Seacoast Artillery* (1944), and Arthur Marshall, *Explosives, Their Manufacture, Properties, Tests and History* (1915). Both LCOL Hime and Mr. Marshall were professional ordnance engineers and their works may be considered most authoritative. Strictly speaking, there are three different end-ranges of guns, enumerated here in decreasing distance from the muzzle: extreme range, maximum range, and maximum effective range. Extreme range is the greatest distance which will be reached by a given gun firing a given projectile using a given powder charge. Maximum range is the greatest distance, for which the gun and its fire control equipment are designed and maximum effective range is the maximum distance at which a gun can be expected to be an effective weapon in battle.

[4] Professor Schumpeter in *Imperialism and the Social Classes* (1951), goes to great lengths to demonstrate that with the rise of commerce and early industrialization in the 18th Century, wars came less and less to be fought for the adventure of it or to divert troublesome elements at home. He argues that to an increasing extent wars had to be justified in terms of some alleged misdeed on the par t of the prospective enemy.

gunfire weapon itself. Research on this matter reveals an interesting answer. Major General Fuller points out that of the five characteristics of weapons (Range of Action, Striking Power, Accuracy of Aim, Volume of Fire, and Portibility), it is the range of action that dominates the fight.[5] But not without reason, his book, like many another, is completely silent on any influences exercised upon the outcome of pre-1800 battles by range advantage of weapons. Even in 1830, the immortal von Clausewitz is silent on this point. The reason is that weapon ranges had reached an upper limit and had gone no further. All interested parties knew what the limits were.[6]

From the time of Queen Elizabeth until well past the beginning of the Nineteenth Century, the maximum effective range of cannon did not exceed 1.000 yards.[7] The author was aware of this fact long before commencing the study of International Law. Hence he has been somewhat mystified at the more or less casual manner in which some International Law publicists have spoken of the limit of territorial waters being one league from shore or the range of a cannon shot.[8] Some publicists were more wary of this pseudo-equation, and Fulton has cited their views and discussed the matter in detail, albeit he is silent on precise gun-ranges. It would appear that the insertion of a

[5] Fuller, *Armaments*, p. 7.

[6] There were some slight increases in ranges, but their order of magnitude was too low to have any significant effect upon the tactical outcome of wars of the time. Tactical outcome was governed by numbers of weapons, their size, and their maneuverability. A most complete study and report of artillery tactics, using these fixed range weapons, appears in von Clausewitz, *On War*. By his time there had been the fullest flowering of military experience with these guns.

[7] Bernard Brodie, *Sea Power in the Machine Age* (1941), pp. 229, 181–198; I. S. Bloch, *The Future of War* (1899), p. 103; One work asserts that in Queen Elizabeth's day, the heaviest cannon had a range of three miles. Stevens and Wescott, *A History of Sea Power* (1937), p. 109. The authors offer no documentation and this author considers such a range to be very unlikely in view of the known state of the science of metallurgy at the time, as well as the absence of any method of effective fire control at that range. The muzzle velocity of any given gun was very low because the shape of the projectile and its imperfect fit in the gun tube permitted a large fraction of the propelling gases to escape. Efforts to remedy this defect resulted, usually, in gun explosions because the science of metallurgy had not advanced sufficiently to permit the construction of a gun capable of withstanding the total strain of the explosion. In theory one might conquer the problem by building the gun massively enough, but then it became too big to move. The result was that it was unfeasible to achieve greater ranges. Some military men, accustomed to this state of affairs, were given to theorizing that long ranges were undesirable because one might waste too much ammunition before the enemy closed to "decisive range!" LT A. W. Wilson, R.N., *The Story of the Gun* (1944), p. 47. The direct relationship between muzzle velocity and range can now be shown by the relatively simple empirical formulae devised in the study of exterior ballistics. LCDR E. E. Herrmann, USN, *Exterior Ballistics 1935*. See also: Brodie, *Sea Power*, p. 186.

[8] Fulton, in *Sovereignty of the Sea* at pages 681–689 mentions a great number of these, and their roster need not detain us. See also: Henry G. Crocker, *The Extent of the Marginal Sea* (1919), pp. 3–471; Butler and Maccoby, *Development*, pp. 53–57; CAPT Meyer, *Extent of Territorial Jurisdiction*, p. 48ff.

comma might have sufficed: one league, or the range of a cannon shot. On the other hand, the theory propounded by Bynkershoek and others that sovereignty should terminate with the limit of control from shore was certainly quite reasonable for its time. It is the somewhat easy but highly inaccurate equating of gun range to one league that must be criticized. One English league is equal to approximately 6,000 yards. This was the maximum effective range of a number of guns in general use during the relatively short era, 1865–1880.[9] After that era, ranges lengthened very rapidly, far outstripping the methods available to aim the guns.[10] Thus, save for about a fifteen-year period there existed little technical basis upon which to formulate the "one- league or gun range rule". Perhaps there was the vague possibility that a ship coming within one league of the shore *might be hit* by gunfire.[11] It should be added that the gunfire aiming problem of a ship is far ,more complex than that of shore batteries and it is highly doubtful that an 18th Century ship firing from a position 1000 yards from shore would constitute much more than a bothersome source of noise and smoke. Where fortresses ashore were successfully besieged in the 17th and 18th Centuries, the ranges were under 500 yards.[12]

It would perhaps be pleasantly convenient to dismiss the matter of one league and the cannon-shot rule as something born and nurtured in ignorance. It is not characteristic of human actors or decision makers in the international drama, however, to pay blind attention to such an objective fiction unless the fiction itself serves a purpose of greater usefulness than does precise knowledge of the range of artillery pieces.[13] There rises the suggestion that other factors may have been at work.

[9] RADM S. S. Robison USN (Ret). *A History of Naval Tactics, 1530–1930* (1942), pp. 695, 714, 717, 723, 730.

[10] It is well known among students of naval history that during the Nineteenth Century, technical developments in gun design and propellents brought forth guns whose ranges far outstripped any known capabilities for accurate aiming. Target practice was something virtually unknown. Captain Broke RN of HMS *Shannon*, victor over USS *Chesapeake*, did some target firings. The gunnery reforms of CAPT Sir Percy Scott RN and the then LCDR William S. Sims USN, are epics of determination and insubordination. COMO Dudley Knox USN, *A History of the U.S. Navy* (1948) p. 99; Stevens and Westcott, *History of Sea Power*, (1937), p. 307; FADM E. J. King USN and CDR Walter M. Whitehill USNR, *A Naval Record* (1952), p. 39; *Brassey's Naval Annual* 1903, p. 106.

[11] This author was unable to ascertain whether there existed in the 17th, 18th or 19th Centuries any tables designed to show dispersion at long range, or fall of shot patterns; the latter type of table is unlikely because of the relative infrequency of salvo firing.

[12] Examples are: Porto Farina, Tunis on 4 april 1655; Santa Cruz on 20 April 1657; Gibralter, 4 August 1704. CAPT Alfred T. Mahan, USN *Influence of Sea Power Upon History 1660–1783* (1890), p. 210. Stevens and Westcott, *History, pp.* 139, 141.

[13] On fictions, see Julius Stone, *Province and Function of Law* (1946), p. 678; Vilfredo Pareto, *The Mind and Society* (1916), Tr. Livingston, Sect, 242, pp. 146–170 (On English

There were other important forces at work, especially after the gun powder cannon came generally to be mounted on ships, that is from about 1500 A.D. onward. What occurred, fundamentally, was one of the first steps in the depersonalization of warfare. Ships no longer fought by boarding and sword play alone – an action wherein audacious men in small groups could indeed overpower a large ship. Sea fighting became more and more a matter of skillfull tactical maneuver for wind advantage plus the capacity to build, man and arm large ships. With this development, merchant ships became larger, and convoys for mutual protection against pirates and privateers became common. As ships grew larger, too, investment in them became greater as did marine insurance. There was an increased clamor for organized naval protection requiring not only more ships but more men. While privateering continued popular among its practitioners, it became less so with the governments of England and France. A privateer was far less under control of the State than a warship; the privateer had men that could be used on the Navy ship;[14] and the depredations of privateers were a potential source of international embarrassment.[15]

It appears that as naval wars came more and more to be fought by organized and disciplined forces, the situation of non-belligerents with respect to the organized forces and privateers of the belligerents came to achieve gretaer importance. And the non-belligerents could enforce their views. This appears to be especially true with respect to bays, ports and harbors inasmuch as convoys of a belligerent would occasionally anchor in them. In the Seventeenth and Eighteenth Centuries there

legal life), and Kelsen, *General Theory of the Law and the State* (1949) p. 225, (on contradiction to "legal reality determined by the principle of effectiveness"). Raestad does perhaps the most outstanding job of demonstrating that the range of artillery had to do only with the limits of neutral rights. He writes: "Les raisons qui ont fait adopter la portée du canon comme limite des eaux neutres, raisons non fondées sur une occupation de la mer territoriale ou des droits a exercer, mais sur le respect de la côte proprement dite, respect imposé ou volontairement observé, ne sauraient être appliquées pour déterminer les limites des eaux territoriales a d'autres égards que celui de la neutralité. Si la portée du canon, ainsi introduite, a été ensuite adoptée, par exemple, pour définir la zone réservée aux pêcheurs nationaux, c'est, encore une fois, par analogie." Arnold Raestad, *La Mer territoriale* (1913), pp. 165–6. Raestad, an advocate, argues on rather treacherous grounds here. Analogies *per se* are not necessarily to be ruled out because subsequent history deprives them of continuing objective validity. What is more important is the degree to which a rule originally based on an analogy continues to be honored.

For further views on the "cannon shor tule," see: Wyndham L, Walker, "Territorial Waters: The Cannon Shot Rule" *The British Yearbook of International Law* (1945), pp. 210–231; H.S. K. Kent, "The historical Origin of the Three-Mile Limit", 48 *American Journa of International Law*, (1954), pp. 537–553; *The Anna* (1905), 5 C. *Rec.* 373; S. Whittemore Boggs, "National Claims in Adjacent Seas", *The Geographical Review* (April 1951), p. 185.

[14] T. S. Ashton, *Economic History of England in the Eighteenth Century* (1959).

[15] Butler and Maccoby, *Development*, pp. 308–311.

grew up among neutrals a body of State practice in which complete sovereignty over ports, harbors and bays was insisted upon.[16] The next logical step was to define the limits of a bay for the purposes of a neutral's jurisdiction. Here it must be noted that there was one primary purpose for fixing the limit – prevention of encroachment by belligerents. A second purpose was the need for criteria in questions of prize.[17] Inasmuch as the width of coastal waters in which damage by ships or shore batteries was determined by the range of cannon, and this had become a relatively fixed and well-known quantity, it would appear reasonable to predict the emergence of a consensus. Toward the end of the Eighteenth Century, the prediction was in fact fulfilled. It seems clear, too, that in this era of frequent war, those powers in a position to enforce the consensus were more concerned with defense matters than with fishing interests. In any event, *coastal* fishing boats were relatively immune from the ravages of war.[18] Fulton points out the following factors of prominence: (1) Continued decay of claims to sovereignty over extensive areas, (2) the growing custom of fixing definite boundaries by international treaties or by municipal laws; (3) legal decisions by which the limit of cannon range was recognized in certain cases.[19]

But at the end of the Eighteenth Century, it is not evident that States had established the practice of clearly delimiting the seaward limits of bays. There is a clear evidence that the cannon shot rule was to be applied within bays, and this was emphasized in a number of State decrees [20] and in at least one treaty.[21] These instruments specified that acts of hostility were forbidden in ports and gulfs within the range of guns. It is conclusive, that it was the defense consideration which was paramount in the achieving of the limited consensus that did exist.

16 An excellent example is the Ordonnance of Louis XIV in 1681, Fulton, *Sovereignty*, p. 562. There was the expected corollary, of course, whereby neutral States adopted strict measures to ensure abstention from belligerency, and to impose their attitudes upon their citizens or subjects.

17 Examples with respect to prize and the cannon-shot rule are: The Italian, Casaregi, writing in 1740. Fulton, *Sovereignty*, pp. 558–9; The Spaniard, d'Ahren, writing in 1746, Reddie, *Maritime International Law* (1846), pp. 251–263; and the French Valin, *Nouveau Commentaire sur l'Ordonnance de la Marine du mois d'Aôut* (1766), pp. 687–8. See also Kunz, *Kriegsrecht und Neutralitätsrecht* (1935), pp. 212; and Hübner, *De la Saisie des Bâtiments Neutres* (1759), p. 57.

18 For a discussion of this, see the opinion of the U.S. Supreme Court in *The Paquete Habana, The Lola*, 175 U.S. 677 (1900).

19 Fulton, *Sovereignty*, p. 566.

20 The Republic of Genoa, Venice, Tuscany, American Colonies in 1777, Fulton, *Sovereignty*, pp. 564–573.

21 Franco-Russian treaty of 17 January 1787, Martens, I *Recueil* iv. p. 237.

Section E SYNTHESIS AND THE LAW

The preceding sections have dealt with those aspects of international maritime activity which exercised some influence upon the development of rules for bays during the period 476–1800 A.D. It remains to sum up the presence or absence of such rules at the turn of the Nineteenth Century.

Inasmuch as many authors of that century and later have made detailed studies of the pre-1800 development of the law of the sea, and nearly every one has had something to say about bays, there appears no sound reason to dwell once more the work already done, or even to offer detailed comment upon it. Instead, there is appended to this chapter (at pages 215–6) a summary of what are believed to be the more prominent statements of treaties, publicists, court opinions, and State practices with respect to developments up to 1800. With certain obvious exceptions, the summarized remarks demonstrate that attitudes toward rules on bays tend to reflect the general trend of events described in the preceding sections of this chapter.

It appears to this author that as of 1800 A.D., the following statements can be made about an international law of bays:

(1) That the defense and neutrality interest were the predominant considerations among the principal Powers in 1800, and that the validity of rules was dependent upon the power to make them effective.

(2) That, in general, older pretentions of soveriegnty to great sea areas had disappeared and sovereignty over bays was considered to be similar to sovereignty over ports and harbors. The writings of the time would indicate that the difference between a bay and a harbor or port was primarily one of terminology.

(3) That the limit of sovereignty over a bay was primarily a function of the range of cannon. This was the predominant view, although there were some opinions concerning limits of vision.

(4) That sovereignty over a bay implied soveriegnty for neutrality and defense purposes, for customs purposes, and for fishing purposes – in approximately that order of importance. There is evidence that, for the minimum area generally envisioned under State sovereignty, such sovereignty was absolute, with the area being, in law, assimilated to the surrounding land.

(5) That definite rules regarding a closing line for bays were in an infant state of development, being in one case in the mind of a publicist (Azuni) and otherwise a letter of instructions to American delegates in 1800. This is not surprising in view of the general understanding that bays were, for purposes of law, rather small areas of water. In such cases bays are readily indentifiable and agreement is easy to reach.

(6) That there were already being manifested some desires for an enlarged of sovereignty over bays. These appear to stem from the American conception, influenced by the geography of Delaware Bay, and Norway's economic requirements with respect to fisheries. In subsequent years, these manifestations led writers to draw a somewhat hazy distinction between bays and "wide bays."

Annex B

SUMMARY OF TREATIES, OPINIONS, WRITINGS AND PRACTICES TO 1800.

Author, Case or Treaty	Date	Publication	Publisher	Page No.	Summary
1. Domenico A. Azuni	1805	*Droit Maritime de l'Europe*	I. Riley (1806)	p. 254, Sect. 17	We draw a line from one point of the enclosing land to the other or along small islands extending beyond the headlands, and all inside is considered as territorial sea.
2. Treaty: France and Russia, Art. 28	1787	De Martens, *Recueil*, 1st Series, Tome IV, (1818)		p. 210	The strictest neutrality shall be observed in ports, harbors, gulfs, and other waters included in the term *closed waters* ...
3. Treaty: United States and Great Britain, Art. 25	1794	I *Malloy* (1910)	U. S. Government Printing Office	p. 604	Neither of the two parties shall permit that the vessels or effects belonging to subjects of the other be captured within ... any bay, river, or port of their territory by vessels of war or others having letters of marque ...
4. William E. Hall (Higgins, Ed.)	1924	*A Treatise on International Law* (8th ed.)	Oxford, Clarendon Press	p. 189	Down to beginning of the 19th Century, course of opinion and practice had developed from idea that the sea could be appropriated the the principle that maritime occupation must be effective to be valid.
5. *The Franconia*, R. V. Keyn (Opinion of Lord Chief Justice Cockburn)	1876	2. L. R. Exch. Div.		p. 63	From the earliest period of English legal history ... If an offense was committed in a bay or gulf, *inter fauces terrae*, the common law could deal with it, because the parts of the sea so circumstanced were held to be within the body of the adjacent county or counties.

6. Emmerich de Vattel	1758	*The Law of Nations* (Fenwick translation)	Carnegie Institution	p. 109	. . . those bays of small extent and not those wide stretches of water to which these names are sometimes given . . . such as Hudson Bay . . . over which sovereignty could not extend, much less ownership. A bay whose entrance may be defended may be occupied and subjected to the laws of the sovereign. This is necessary since the country could be much more easily invaded or attacked at those places than on the coasts open to the winds and impetuosity of the tides.
7. Hugo Grotius	1633	*The Freedom of the Seas* (Magoffin Translation)	Oxford Univ. Press New York	—	. . . the sea can be occupied by him who possesses the land situated on both shores, if this area is open at the mouth like a gulf, provided that part of the sea is not of such an extent to constitute a part of it.
8. *The Grange*	1793	I *Official Opinions of Attorney General of United States*	U. S. Government Printing Office	Vol. I, p. 33	U. S. Attorney General's opinion concerning U. S. sovereignty over Delaware Bay. Establishes boundary between Cape Kenlopen and Cape May. Sovereignty on grounds of neutrality and non-injury to other States.
9. Treaty: Great Britain, Denmark-Norway, and Netherlands, Art. 6	1691	Crocker, *Extent* (1919)	U. S. Government Printing Office	p. 518	No enemy of Great Britain or Netherlands permitted to capture their ships in . . . the bays or ports of the Dano-Norwegian King.
10. Regulations of the Grand Duke of Tuscany, Art. 1	1778	De Martens, *Recueil*, 2nd Series, Tome III	—	p. 25	No act of hostility between belligerent power can be committed in seas adjacent to . . . ports, bays, . . . of the Grand Duchy. Vessels must there enjoy entire security in virtue of the protection accorded.

Continued

Author, Case or Treaty	Date	Publication	Publisher	Page No.	Summary
11. Edict of Republic of Genoa, Art. 1	1779	De Martens, *Recueil*, 2nd Series, Tome III		p. 53	No act of hostility between belligerent powers can be committed in the ports, gulfs, . . . and consequently it is forbidden in that area to commit any kind of depredation, pursuit, summons, visit.
12. Treaty: Russia and Two Sicilies, Art. 19	1787	De Martens, *Recueil*, 2nd Series, Tome III		p. 237	Absolute neutrality shall also be observed in the ports, harbors, gulfs, and all waters without distinction that are comprised under the designation of cl sed waters.
13. Argument of Netherlands delegates to Great Britain	1610	Fulton, *Sovereignty of the Sea*	Blackwood, London (1911)	p. 156	2. For that it is by the law of nations, no Prince can challenge further into the sea than he can command with a *cannon* except gulfs within their land from one point to another.
14. Norway: Royal Concession for Whale Fishing	1692	Crocker, *Extent*, (1919)	U. S. Government Printing Office	p. 608	All foreigners and unprivileged persons shall be forbidden to hunt whales in or outside the fjords or in the surrounding waters within a distance of ten leagues [40 miles] from the land.
15. Treaty: Russia and Sweden	1801	De Martens, *Recueil*, 2nd Series, Tome VII		p. 329	They also agree to observe the most perfect neutrality in the ports, harbors, gulfs and other waters comprised in the term closed waters, which belong to them respectively.
16. Decree of Philip II, King of Spain	1565	Crocker, *Extent*, (1919)	U. S. Government Printing Office	p. 622	No one can come to our coasts, harbors, roadsteads or rivers, or within sight of our land to wait for or damage the ships of our allies.

17. Royal Decree of Spain	1775	Crocker, *Extent,* (1919)	U. S. Government Printing Office	p. 623	Detention of small French vessels loaded with contraband and found at distance of two leagues from coast, near ports, river mouths, bays, etc.
18. Opinion of U. S. Secretary of State	1796	Moore, *Digest of International Law* (1906) Vol. I	U. S. Government Printing Office	p. 704	Jurisdiction fixed at three miles from shore, (at least for purposes of regulating conduct with respect to European war then in progress) with exception of bays so landlocked as to be unquestionably within the jurisdiction of the United States – be their extent what they may.
19. U. S. Act of 2 March, 1799	1799	*U. S. Statutes at Large,* Vol. I	U. S. Government Printing Office	p. 627, 646	Asserts for customs purposes, jurisdiction within bays, harbors, ports, rivers, creeks and inlets.
20. U. S. Letter to Negotiators with Great Britain	1800	U. S. Naval War College, *International Law Topics and Discussions, 1913*	U. S. Government Printing Office	p. 36	Expresses opinion that there exists general agreement on restraints against war vessels' seizures or actions within a line drawn between headlands.
21. French prize case, *The Daniel Frederick*	1808	Pistoye et Duverdy, *Traites des Prise Maritime,* Vol. I	Paris: A. Durand	p. 102	Opinion of court is that roadsteads and bays do not render inviolable the ships anchored therein, except as such ships remain under the protection of the cannon or of the coast.
22. Fulton	1911	*Sovereignty of the Sea*	London: Blackwood	p. 547	"With regard to bays, straits, and arms of the Sea, the general usage from the earliest times has included them within the jurisdiction of the neighbouring State. They have always regarded as differing from the sea on an open coast, the only disputes about them referring to the size of such areas that might justly be looked upon as territorial."

Continued

Author, Case or Treaty	Date	Publication	Publisher	Page No.	Summary
23. Sir Mathew Hale	1650(?)	*History of the Foreshore*		p. 370–7	The sea is that which lies within the body of a country or without. That arm or branch of the sea which lies within the *fauces terrae*, where a man may reasonably discern between shore and shore, is or at least may be within the body of a country . . . In this sea the King of England hath a double right, a right of jurisdiction . . . and a right of propriety or ownership.

CHAPTER FOUR

DEVELOPMENT FROM 1800 TO THE PRESENT

Section A INTRODUCTION

Chapter THREE, covering a very long span of time, mirrors, we believe, the slow growth of western civilization, population, and technology during that period. Toward the end of the period, populations had begun to show marked rates of growth; the nation-State system as we know it had come into being; and weapons of war had reached a plateau in their development. War itself had become more and more an activity that had to be regulated so as not to encroach upon non-participating States. Moreover, as war and the preparation therefor became more expensive, it became less and less the whimsical sport of monarchs.[1] The decision to go to war had to be rationalized to those who were expected to fight or to pay. It is no wonder then that some serious thought and effort were being devoted to the formulation of international rules of conduct. As industrialization, technology, and populations grew, the problems of government and society became more complex and there seem to have arisen increasing tensions between nation-States. There was a need for rules. The purpose of this chapter is to review the patterns of growth in three general areas during the last century and a half in order to show how this growth influenced the development of international rules for bays.

Section B NAVIGATION

The art of navigating in 1800 was not in a rudimentary stage, but it was still a comparatively difficult matter for the mariner to know with accuracy his position after several days at sea with, perhaps,

[1] Joseph Schumpeter, *Imperialism and Social Classes* (1951), Chs. I, II.

periods of bad weather and low visibility since taking departure.[1] In 1800, it would have been unfeasible to expect a mariner to have such precise knowledge of his position that he could accurately orient himself with respect to a mythical line laid down beyond visual piloting distance of coastal landmarks. But during the nineteenth century his problems became more and more easy to solve. The path of development in navigating during the period considered by this Chapter will be briefly sketched.

In 1800, the Hydrographic Office of the British Admiralty was five years old.[2] One of the reasons for its founding was the need for standardization of marine charts. During the first half of the Nineteenth Century, the Admiralty commenced its world-wide survey work. This was closely followed and supplemented by the work of the United States Navy and its Hydrographic Office, which was founded in 1842 and placed under the command of Lieutenant Mathew F. Maury, USN.[3] With such surveys and improved charts, the sailing directions which had long been in use could be made more useful. It is also followed that coastal States could lay down on charts lines of jurisdiction that would have meaning to mariners everywhere. And the mariners were fast becoming equipped to find their positions. By 1800, the chronometer had come into use and longitude could be calculated.[4] It remained for the Harvard-educated merchant captain, Thomas H. Sumner [5] in 1843, and the French Navy Commander Marc St. Hilaire [6] in 1850, to perfect methods for calculations of ships' positions under any system of sailing. The sextant, the instrument for measuring the altitude of celestial bodies, was in common use in 1800 as was the nautical mile of 6,080 English feet.[7] More slowly in the evolution of

[1] CDR Carl H. Amme, USN, "The Not So Gentle Art of Navigation 175 Years Ago", 80 *U.S. Naval Institute Proceedings* (Sept. 1954), pp. 1023–1029.

[2] CDR J. B. Hewson, RNR (RET), *A History of the Practice of Navigation* (1951), pp. 40–42.

[3] Nathaniel Bowditch, *The Practical American Navigator*, 1958 Edition, p. 30.

[4] LCDR David C. Holly USN, "All for the Purpose of Marking Time", 79 *U.S. Naval Institute Proceedings* (Mar. 1953), pp. 303–309.

[5] Hewson, *Navigation*, p. 252; Bowditch, *Navigator*, p. 57; Thomas H. Sumner, *A New and Accurate Method of Finding a Ship's Position at Sea by projection on Mercator's Chart* (1843).

[6] Bowditch, *Navigator*, p. 56. Thereafter followed continuously refined methods for solution of the spherical triangle of celestial navigation. The cosine-haversine formula of 1850 was followed by the work of many naval officers and mathematicians, Such systems as H.O.207 (worked out by LCDR Joseph Y. Dreisonstok U.S.N.), H.O.211 (worked out by LCDR Arthur A. Ageton, U.S.N.) and the monumental H.O.214 (A 9-volume system of tables worked out as a "New Deal" relief measure) are well known to mariners of this author's vintage.

[7] LCDR Alton B. Moody USNR, "The Nautical Mile, 75 *U.S. Naval Institute Proceedings* (Nov. 1949), pp. 1257–1262.

precision navigation came improvements in the compass and the dead reckoning log. Observations of the earth's magnetic field for purposes of correction of variation [8] have continued over the years, with greater and greater accuracy being achieved. Methods for correction of deviation, first started by Mathew Flinders did not become perfected until the work of Lord Kelvin in 1873.[9] Until the perfection of the Gyro compass in the first decade of this century, however, mariners could never be entirely certain of fixing with precision their positions with respect to coastal landmarks.[10]

Another aid to navigation that proliferated in the Nineteenth Century was buoyage. Buoys had been in use for thousands of years, but commencing around 1850, countries standardized their buoyage systems.[11] One of the agreements formulated at the International Marine Conference of 1889 had to do with standardization of buoy shapes on an international scale.[12] In the latter half of the century, bell, whistle and lighted buoys came into general use. During this era, too, the lighthouse came into its own after Fresnel's invention of the concentric prism system, and the advent of the Swedish system of distinguishing lights by alternate flashing.[13] It should be clearly noted however, that there is little evidence of any effort being made to

[8] Hewson, *History*, pp. 148–151.

[9] *Ibid.*, p. 65; Bowditch, *Navigator*, p. 24.

[10] The gyro compass was perfected by the American, Sperry, and the German, H. Anschütz-Kämpfe, working simultaneously, but independently. It was first used successfully in 1911 on the east coast of the United States. Like many another device, war hastened its general use. The pay-off ot the instrument and its secure future were ensured in a single event. After the battle of Coronel, in November 1914, VADM Sir Doveton Sturdee, RN, was ordered to proceed with two battle cruisers from England to the South Atlantic. Time was extremely critical and the two ships were in Southampton unable to sail because of an inpenetrable fog. Their magnetic compasses were completely out of adjustment by reason of recent armorplate alterations. Mr. Elmer Sperry, Jr., who had been trying to sell his new compass to the Admiralty, was summoned from his hotel room to install his model compass in the flagship HMS *Invincible.* (The Admiralty had previously rejected the compass). He installed the compass and the two ships were able to get out of port. They arrived in Port Stanley, Falkland Islands, twenty-one hours before the appearance of VADM Graf von Spee IGN and his squadron. The result was the sea battle of 8 December 1914. All German ships but SMS *Dresden* were lost. John van Duyn Southworth, "The 'Yankee' Device," 85 *U.S. Naval Institute Proceedings* (Apr. 1959), pp. 97–103; H. Müller, *Cruiser Warfare in the South Pacific* (Unpublished diary, U.S. Naval War College, 1922). The Imperial German Navy commenced installing the gyro compass in submarines in about 1910. Bernard Brodie, *Sea Power in the Machine Age* (1941), p. 296. The German, H. Anschütz-Kämpfe, designed his compass after his plans to go to the north pole by submarine in 1900 were frustrated by the absence of reliable navigational equipment. T. E. Curtis and J. M. Slater, "Inertial Navigation in Submarine Polar Operations of 1958", 5 *Navigation* (Spring 1959), pp. 275–283.

[11] Bowditch, *Navigator*, p. 29; *Aids to Navigation Manual*, U.S. Coast Guard (1952), pp. 35.

[12] *Report of International Maritime Conference*, 1889, vol. III.

[13] LT. Kenneth A. Andersen USN, "Lead Kindly Light", 77 *U.S. Naval Institute Proceedings* (Apr. 1951), pp. 405–409.

station buoys or erect lighthouses for the primary purpose of marking jurisdictional boundaries. The extraordinary expense of lighthouse erection and in buoy upkeep would no doubt preclude any decisions to do so. On the other hand, coasts adjacent to fishing areas are unusually well-lighted.[14] Such a measure is necessary inasmuch as the fishing boats of those States have usually been rather small and not equipped for high seas navigation.[15]

Finally, of great importance to perfecting the art of navigation and to making life at sea somewhat less hazardous have been the international efforts among seafaring nations. From the first conference in 1889, States have undertaken many agreements in the interest of safe navigation. Of primacy interest to our study is the International Hydrographic Conference of 1919, out of which grew the International Hydrographic Bureau with headquarters in Monaco.[16] This Bureau assists States in the clearing of timely information for navigators. The interchange facilities of the Bureau are such that a mariner will not very likely be in ignorance for long concerning new navigating aids or newly made regulations concerning claimed maritime sovereignty of States. By 1919, then, it can be said that non-electronic aids had practically reached the limit of their development. During this entire period, from 1800 to 1919, however, there does not appear to the author to be any evidence that navigating aids or techniques were installed or designed for the purpose of ensuring that imaginary seaward boundaries were not transgressed. It remains to be seen whether, in the future, States will undertake to change the habits of centuries and commence installing boundary markers. The author is disposed to think that there will continue the implicit assumption that if a mariner can fix his position for purposes of safe navigation, he can also fix his position for jurisdictional reasons. In this connection, it is to be noted that charts and sailing directions issued by the United Kingdom and the United States do not generally include immediately available data on jurisdictional boundaries.[17] One of the by-products of the 1958 Geneva Convention on the Law of the Sea and the Contiguous Zone,

[14] An excellent example on the coast of Norway is shown in W. R. Mead. *An Economic Geography of the Scandinavian States and Finland* (1958), at page 175.

[15] Robert Morgan, *World Sea Fisheries* (1956), Chs. IV and V.

[16] RADM C. L. Nichols USN (RET), "The International Hydrographic Bureau", 77 *U.S. Naval Institute Proceedings* (July 1951), pp. 717–720. (An American officer is usually one of the three directors of the Bureau. At present RADM Knox USC&GS (RET) serves in this capacity. RADM Nichols is a former director).

[17] An exception is the case of the United States where Sailing Directions show the boundaries inside which mariners are to comply with Inland Rules of the Road.

(Part I, Art. 4(6)), is that such data will be required. If that provision and others similar thereto are carried out to the letter, a great deal of survey work and chart revision will probably be required.[18]

Partially in support of the author's conjecture concerning the unlikelihood of installation of boundary marking buoys and other devices, we shall turn briefly to a few of the electronic decides which have come into use within the last forty-odd years. The first of these is the sonic depthfinder, first installed in a ship in 1924.[19] Research and improvement have gone on down to the present time.[20] The sonic depthfinder or fathometer now finds much use in locating fish for deep trawling.[21] Other electronic aids, including loran, radar and decca have been discussed previously in Chapter II. For the future, and of interest in development of the law of bays, are new devices which will render position finding more accurate, and others which can be used to warn vessels when they have crossed water boundaries.

In the first category are devices for overcoming weather problems and problems of human error. These involve electronic integration of information and special data computing devices for use with radar, sonar, and depth-finders.[22] The second category has to do with a movement toward the installation of bridge radio telephones on a

[18] Article 4(6) reads: "The Coastal State must clearly indicate straight baselines on charts, to which due publicity must be given." Article 9, on roadsteads, reads in part: "The coastal State must clearly demarcate such roadsteads and indicate them on charts together with their boundaries, to which due publicity must be given." Article 12(2) reads: "The line of demarcation between the territorial seas of two States lying opposite to each other or adjacent to each other shall be marked on large-scale charts officially recognized by the coastal States." Article 7, on bays, on the other hand, includes no provision on demarcation, but the closure line of a bay is a base line of a special type. One can speculate almost endlessly upon the implementation and practical effects of these boundary-marking provisions. Chapters 5, and 10, below. Suffice it to say, this is one of the detailed and expensive technical ramifications of such an attempt to "codify and develop" the law.

[19] Hewson, *History*, pp. 218–222. Mr. R. P. Curtis of the Raytheon Company has written in that company's house magazine an excellent short article on the technical history of this equipment. R. P. Curtis, "The Fathometer." See also, Arthur H. Lynch, *Making Life Safe at Sea* (1922).

[20] Kenneth V. Curtis, Raytheon Manufacturing Company, "New Developments in Depth Sounding Equipment," a paper presented at a meeting of Radio Technical Commission for Marine Services, 13 October 1952; 11 November 1957 Report of U.S. Army Enigeer Conference on Electronic Developments as Aids to the Surveying-Dredging Computing Processes. LT Henry C. Bailey USN, "The Evolution of Deep Sea Sounding Methods," 63 *Journal of American Society of Naval Engineers* (May 1951), pp. 349–362.

[21] "Deep Mystery" 320 *Industrial Bulletin of Arthur D. Little, Inc.* (May 1955), pp. 1–2.

[22] CAPT F. J. Wylie RN (RET), "Automation in Marine Navigation," XII *The Journal of the Institute of Navigation* (Apr. 1959), pp. 163–183; Thomas J. Kelly, "Improvement in Radar Presentation," paper presented at International Meeting on the Use of Radar at Sea, Genoa, Italy, 16 May 1957; CAPT David R. Hull USN (RET) "Safe Passage," *Marine News* (Feb. 1956), pp. 18–28; K. V. Curtis, "A Discussion of 'Anti-Collision and Piloting Segment'," 25 Oct. 1956, (Paper presented at meeting of Radio Technical Commission for Marine Services).

world wide basis.[23] With this equipment, it will be possible to exchange information and give appropriate warnings.

In the electronic field, there appears to be a very wide field for future refinement and increased accuracy. Judging from the contents of trade literature and materials in the technical journals of navigation societies, the demand for such equipment exists and manufacturers are striving to develop it and provide it. But two unknown factors remain insofar as we are concerned with possible influences on the law of bays arising from the problems of navigation. The first is the extent to which ships will install new equipment. The powerful influences of insurance companies and of high initial costs of ships have been discussed in previous chapters. The other unknown factor is the extent to which States will make surveys and improve charts.[24]

During the Nineteenth Century and the first part of this century, the state of the navigating art was such that there could be established a closing line of such limit [25] as to elicit fairly general agreement among navigators, jurists, and decision makers. Recent and current changes in equipment, have placed the art in a highly unstable con-

[23] This equipment is installed to assist in collision prevention but its use for harbor traffic control and coastal warning is a natural development. Earle Porter, "The Small Boat Radio" 12 May 1959. CAPT F. J. Wylie RN (RET), "The Future of Marine Electronics – the International Viewpoint," paper delivered at New York meeting of Radio Technical Commission for Marine Services, 25 October 1956. LCDR Edward F. Oliver USCG, "Ships that Pass in the Night," 85 *U.S. Naval Institute Proceedings* (Nov. 1959), pp. 70–78.

[24] "The Admiralty Chart," *The Journal of the Institut of Navigation* (Apr. 1959), pp. 163–183. Captain Wylie has this to say on charts: "Major changes in charts in general use will, of course, be made only after trials have proved their worth. Practical experience in the use of radar brings to light new information every day." *The Use of Radar at Sea* (1953), p. 133.

[25] The perhaps classic view and explanation of the 10-mile rule is that of John Basset Moore in his letter to Mr. Barclay, quoted in 13 *Annuaire de L'Institut de Droit International*, p. 146. part of this letter is requoted.

> "Since you observe that there does not appear to be any very convincing reason to prefer the ten mile line in such a case to that of double three miles, I may say that there have been supposed to exist reasons both of convenience and of safety. The ten mile line has been adopted in the cases referred to, as I understand them, as a practical rule. The transgression of an encroachment upon territorial waters by fishing vessels is generally a grave offence, involving in many instances the forfeiture of the offending vessel and it is obvious that the harrower the space in which it is permissible to fish the more likely the offense is to be committed. In order therefore that fishing may be both practicable and safe and not constantly attended with the risk of violating territorial waters, it has been thought expedient not to allow it where the extent of free waters between the three mile line drawn on each side of the bay, is less than four miles.

This is the reason of the ten-mile line." Professor Gidel concurs in this suggestion and then adds a second reason: that a fisherman can usually see the shore five miles away and thus if he is able to dee both shores, he will know he is inside the closing line of a bay. *Le Droit international public de la Mer* (1934), vol. iii, pp. 544–546. Through the same system of reasoning. Münch arrives at the conclusion that the width of a bay should be 15 or 16 miles. *Die techischen Fragen des Küstenmeers* (1934), p. 94. Neither Gidel nor Münch takes into account the fact that, assuming good atmospheric conditions, the range of visibility is a direct function of the observer's height of eye above the waterline.

dition of progress and the plateau which it may reach is difficult to speculate upon, although there are practical limits to the size and speed of ships.[26] The limits of development and installation of new equipment are likely to be governed primarily by safety and financial considerations. When those limits are reached, shipping owners will probably look to the State for further protection of their interests should coastal State sovereignty claims and restrictions prove too onerous. At the present time, it does not appear to this author that the proposed rules on bays present problems that cannot be solved by use of equipment that is now being designed and installed in ships primarily for reasons of increased safety at sea. This opinion does not apply however to possible claims to large so-called historic bays, for which no rules have been formulated.

Turning now to the growth of ship constructuon and engineering in the period in question, we see development which, like that in many another field, proceeds faster and more fundamentally than in all of previous human history. To retell this story would be quite beyond the scope of this book, and only a few events will be mentioned:

1785–1810: Development of steam driven vessels.[27]
1819: S.S. *Savannah* crossed Atlantic Ocean.[28]
1838: S.S. *Sirius* and S.S. *Great Western*, both British, made first transatlantic crossings under steam.[29]
1842: S.S. *Great Britain* launched. This ship was the first large vessel built of iron and the first ocean going vessel to use the screw propeller.[30]
1870–1880: Commencement of steel construction in ships.[31]
1880: Introduction of mechanical refrigeration on shipboard.[32]

[26] J. D. van Manen, "Fundamentals of Ship Resistance and Propulsion," 4 *International Shipbuilding Progress* (Feb. 1957); LCDR G. C. Manning (CC) USN and LCDR T. L. Schumacher (CC) USN, *Principles of Warship Construction and Damage Control* (1935), Ch. IV.

[27] There is now ample solid research to demonstrate that Robert Fulton's "Claremont" was not the first steamboat, although his was perhaps the first practical one. Robert Taggart, "Early Developments in Marine Propulsion" 70 *Journal of the American Society of Naval Engineers* (May 1958), pp. 191–208. See also *Gibbons* v. *Ogden* 9 Wheat. 1 (1824), and Robert E. Cushman, *Leading Constitutional Decisions*, 10th Ed., (1955), pp. 316–7.

[28] Actually, she steamed for only about 100 hours, and was otherwise a failure. Frank O. Braynard, *Famous American Ships* (1956), pp. 22–3.

[29] CAPT R. T. Merrill USCG (RET) "The Decade of Transition - Our Early Steam Navy and Merchant Marine," 78 *U.S. Naval Institute Proceedings* (Sep. 1952), pp. 1005–1015.

[30] Bernard Brodie, *Sea Power in the Machine Age* (1941), p. 35.

[31] Brodie, *Sea Power*, p. 164.

[32] S. W. Brown, "Modern Practice in Marine Refrigeration." 61 *Journal of the American Society of Naval Engineers* (May 1949) pp. 442–449.

1895: Rudolph Diesel produced the first oil-burning internal combustion engine.[33]
1900–1910: Commencement of steam turbine propulsion.[34]
1912–1915: Oil fuel came into general use for steam ship propulsion.

This rather sketchy table is illustrative of a trend in marine construction. The distinguishing characteristics are stronger ships, larger and larger sizes of ships, increased speeds, greater efficiency of engineering plants (lower fuel consumption and smaller engines per unit of horsepower) and more versatile cargo carrying capacity. This trend continues, as marine architects and engineers build hundred thousand ton tankers, gas turbine engines, nuclear power plants and experiment with hydrofoil systems. Of tangential interest is the fact that as ships grew larger and more efficient, they became more expensive to construct, and there are now proportionally fewer ships.[35] Of direct interest to us, however, are the developments in steel construction, refrigeration and the diseel engine.

During the Nineteenth Century, ocean-going fishing craft grew in size, but at a somewhat slower pace than did ships constructed for other uses. Labor was still rather plentiful and demands for greater efficiency, from whatever the source, were not so clearly in evidence. The technique of otter-trawling was developed in the latter half of the century by the British fishing companies.[36] This was a major revolution

[33] Sir Claude Gibb, "Two Thousand Years of Engineering". 64 *Journal of the American Society of Naval Engineers* (Feb. 1952), pp. 95–103.

[34] CAPT (E) Edgar C. Smith, RN (RET) "The Hon. Sir Charles A. Parsons," 66 *Journal of the American Society of Naval Engineers* (Nov. 1954), pp. 823–828. Sir Charles was the designer of the first practical marine turbine propulsion system. The advantage of the steam turbine is higher speed and greater thermal efficiency at high speeds. A turbine plant requires a smaller propellor than would be required in a reciprocating engine plant of similar horsepower. For similar horsepower output, the turbine plant is smaller and weighs less the than reciprocating engine.

[35] See Chapter I, above.

[36] Robert Morgan, *World Sea Fisheries* (1956), Ch. 5. Mr. Morgan's book is outstanding for its discussion of fishing techniques and equipment. Otter trawling and its predecessor technique are vastly more efficient than long-line fishing. These methods, however, can remove so many fish that if used in coastal areas, other fisherman dependent on older methods, may be deprived of a livelihood. This conflict of methods and interests was basically what gave rise to the famous Moray Firth Case of *Mortensen* v. *Peters*. Mr. Wilberforce, Counsel for the United Kingdom in *United Kingdom* v. *Norway*, argued before the International Court of Justice that current research indicated this potential evil is not as great as feared, and, in any event is susceptible to mitigation through internal regulation. *Pleadings*, Vol. IV, pp. 153–161. For an example of the international regulation that is relevant, see *Convention fot the Regulation of Meshes of Fishing Nets and Size Limits of Fish* (1946). *British Command Paper No. 8815*. The date of entry into force of this Convention was 5 April 1954. Both Norway and the United Kingdom signed and ratified the Convention. MacChesney, *Naval War College International Law Situation and Documents* 1956, pp. 317–324.

in the industry and has presaged mass production techniques in fishing. It requires a comparatively large, mechanically-powered ship. As Mr. Morgan points out, the greater the effective market in a fishing port's economic hinterland, the larger the craft it employs and the more advanced its techniques.[37] Further discussion of the economics of the fishing industry will continue in Section C of this chapter. It is sufficient to note here, however, that the use of the diesel engine in fishing craft reduces the ship's fuel requirements and increases its fish-carrying capacity.[38] The larger steel ship with a complete refrigeration plant has tremendous capacity and fishing capability. When some coastal States are confronted with the incursions of such ships, under foreign flags and supported by large markets and heavily capitalized industries, one can readily understand their desire to widen the coastal areas under their sovereignty through establishment of new rules for bays. Although the interests of the coastal State may in time receive greater protection through the workings of the 1958 Geneva Convention on Fishing and Conservation of the Living Resources of the High Seas,[39] there can be little doubt that the coastal State would prefer to have sole jurisdiction over a fishing ground, if that is possible.

The author has previously suggested that in codification of the law of the sea and in studies made concerning that law, appropriate attention should be paid to the navigational aspects of the problem. The suggested is now made that such studies also demonstrate some understanding of the advances made in ship construction, especially in the fishing vessel field.

Section C ECONOMICS

It was the general conclusion of Chapter THREE that the international rules on bays which had evolved by the close of the 18th Century were the result, primarily, of military influences; that there had been a plateau in the development of gunpowder weapons; that the concept of neutrality had come into being; and that inordinate claims to sover-

[37] Morgan, *Fisheries*, p. 71.

[38] A remarkable discussion of this matter is that of A. C. Hardy in his article, "The Adaptability and Value of Diesel Engines for Securing Efficiency in Trawlers," *Fishing News*, 30 October 1959) p. 1. of Propulsion and Maneuver Supplement). *Fishing News* is the trade journal of the British fishing industry.

[39] UN Doc. A/Conf. 13/L.54; reprinted in 38 *Dept. of State Bulletin* (1958), p. 1118ff.; reprinted in 52 *American Journal of International Law* (Oct. 1958), pp. 851–858.

eignty over sea areas had receded, chiefly because they could not be defended.

The period from 1800 onwards presents a somewhat different picture. We shall see that during the 19th Century further developments in the International Law of Bays were primarily influenced by economic considerations. When neutrality regulations concerning bays came to be formulated, they followed a pattern clearly established in the economic sphere. In the 20th Century the picture becomes more blurred: the economic positions of States become intertwined with purely political and ideological considerations, and military considerations must again be taken into account, but for altered reasons. In the 20th Century, one doubts whether any one factor can be said to be dominant.[1]

Professor Carr has indicated that the two salutary illusions of the 19th Century were that the world economic system was truly international, and that the economic and political systems were entirely separate and operated independently of each other.[2] This is a view subject to considerable qualification,[3] but the works of a great many scholars and commentators on 19th Century political and economic history tend to support it.[4] This author does not propose to retrace the politico-economic history of the 19th Century on order to submit the Carr proposition to test since to do so would probably involve an extensive diversion from the principal objective of this book. He believes that there exists sufficient concurrence with Carr in this matter to merit the use of his proposition as an initial hypothesis, to be used or modified as the development of the law on bays would appear to dictate. With such an hypothesis in mind, we can proceed to a

[1] For obvious reasons, it would be premature to elucidate on this statement at this point. Involved, of course, are the East-West struggle, the advent of International Organization, the politicizing of economic issues, the gradual freezing of State positions with concomittant reluctance to settle disputes through judicial means, and the apparent unacceptability on military grounds of solutions based on economic considerations.

[2] Edward H. Carr, *Nationalism and After* (1945), p. 13. Professor Carr asserts that this state of affairs was the result of a general belief that the economic order was one of absolute *laissez-faire*, hence impersonal and truly international, and that it was all hinged to the financial machine in the City of London which, in itself, was free of political control or partiality.

[3] Professor Imlah, in his book *Economic Elements in the Pax Britannica* (1958) has gone into the matter with much more probity and has suggested that Britain's military strength and security as well as her great economic strength made it possible for her to act in the role of mediator. It would appear that economic growth was considered to be of primary importance and that political differences should interfere as little as possible.

[4] Examples are: Delbert A. Snider, *Introduction to International Economics* (1954), pp. 88–91; Seymour E. Harris, *International and Inter-regional Economics* (1957), p. 195; Judd Polk, *Sterling* (1956), pp. 32–8.

rather brief review of those facets of 19th Century economic history which have a bearing on the law of bays.

The 19th Century is distinguished above all else for the Industrial and Mechanical Revolution. The Revolution actually started in 18th Century England and somewhat later elsewhere. Its overall distinguishing features were: continued increase in the availability of manufactured products; the continuous invention and development of manufacturing processes and techniques; very rapid capital formation in industrial countries; rapid growth in the volume of international trade and communication; in general, rapid population growth where there was also rapid industrial growth; a definite and final division of labor as between food producers and the industrial population; and a more marked international division of labor as between industrial and primary producers.

The sudden acceleration of population growth is generally agreed to have commenced around the year 1750 A.D. Actually this turning point appears arbitrarily selected inasmuch as it can be demonstrated convincingly only in the case of England. Mr. Carr-Saunders writes that the turning point came somewhat later for most other European countries.[5] The interdependence of the beginning of great population growth and the industrial revolution is explained in the following manner by Professor Thompson in his book, *Population Problems:*

> For the first time in history, man's control over nature gradually became more and more secure so that it was possible for him to live in fairly healthful conditions and thus to avoid the high death rates which had been his usual lot.[6]

He then writes:

> ... it will be well to call attention to the fact that throughout man's life on earth prior to the industrial revolution, it had been necessary to devote its effort to production of the agricultural necessities of life.[7]

[5] T. S. Ashton, *An Economic History of England: The Eighteenth Century* (1955), Ch. I. Professor Ashton (Emeritus Professor of History at the London School of Economics), entitles Chapter I of his book, "The People of England." He explains his research into population studies and records. He concludes that between the years 1695 and 1801, the populations increased by two-thirds. Mr. Carr-Saunders in his monumental work, *The Population Problem* (1922) places the date of 1760 as the take-off point (p. 300).

[6] Warren S. Thompson, *Population Problems* (1953), p. 75.

[7] Thompson, *Population Problems*, p. 77. One is likely to note that these statements by Thompson ignore the rapid growth of populations which, seemingly, have not been affected by the industrial revolution and whose populations are for the most part in a subsistence condition. Carr-Saunders points out that from earliest recorded history on there are evidences of social customs imposing restraints on human reproduction (over and above high mortality rates), of which recognition of limits to feed the offspring is only one. But, he adds:

> That which is common to these races, where over-population is suspected, is the absence of hope and fear alike, of ambition and of a standard of living; they are content to subsist on what will just support life.... In these cases we seem always to find that

One estimate of the growth in world population during the period in question has been from 906 million in 1800 to 2, 691 million in 1955.[8]

We noted in the previous chapter that from earliest times fish formed a part of the human diet. We noted that the relative dependence upon fish for food has been in part a function of the nearness of fisheries and in part a function of the comparative scarcity of other foods. We have also noted that on occasions human consumption of fish has been artificially stimulated by government and church policies. To some degree, the effects of these policies were permanent. We should now take note of further tendencies toward an increase in fish consumption which are peculiarly the result of 19th Century industrialization:

(a) Rapidly growing industrial populations which domestic agriculture in some countries was unable to support.

(b) Occasional agricultural depression in Europe, particularly in animal husbandry. This was chiefly the result of such diseases as foot and mouth disease, pleuro-pneumonia, sheeprot and cattle plague.

(c) Lack of fodder raising land.

As Mr. Bennett points out, it is really quite difficult to establish with certainty over any period the consumption of various foods by type.[9] What is apparent in the studies of Morgan [10] and Woytinsky [11] is that prices of fish have advanced less rapidly than those of meat; the relative output of fish to meat is increasing; and that fish output

political misfortunes have overtaken these people. They have suffered from oppression in one form or another and gradually the old customs have been lost; hope and ambition have faded from the outlook. Carr-Saunders, *The Population Problem*, p. 277. This is a statement as to cause which seems to be debated by demographers, for example, see M. K. Bennett, *The World's Food* (1954), Ch. I. We shall not attempt any judgments on this question; it is sufficient for our purposes to note the rapid upsurge in world population, and to note that it has occurred in both primitive and highly industrialized countries.

[8] Kingsley Davis, "The World's Population Explosion," *Private Investment: The Key to International Development*, James Daniel, Ed., (1958), p. 18. See also: *U.S. Foreign Policy, A Study by Stanford Research Institute for U.S. Senate Committee on Foreign Relations*, 1959.

[9] M. K. Bennett, *The World's Food* (1956), Ch. I.

[10] Morgan, *World Sea Fisheries* (1956), p. 284. Dr. Morgan writes that the best and most easily applied broad criterion of the importance of a country's fisheries to it as a source of real wealth in terms of food and/or exports (and thus of imports of other goods) is in production per head of total population. Production rate for fisheries is measured in kilograms/head/year. Morgan, *Fisheries*, p. 140. Examples follow:

Year	Country	Production Rate
1951	Norway	550 kgm/head/year
1951	United Kingdom	22 ,, ,, ,,
1952	Canada	65 ,, ,, ,,
1952	United States	15.5 ,, ,, ,,

[11] W. S. Woytinsky and E. S. Woytinsky, *World Population and Production* (1953), Ch. XX.

per fisherman engaged in the industry has been rising steadily. In this connection, Dr. Morgan has written:

Expansion of meat production, however, is much less easy than that of fish on unexploited grounds. In the areas where food needs are rising fastest ... there is small likelihood of much increase of food livestock because of existing pressure on suitable land.[12]

Dr. Morgan also calls to our attention that since the Nineteenth Century, some countries must use their fisheries as a source of foreign exchange with which to purchase goods from more industrialized countries.[13]

As indicated in previous chapters, fishing on distant grounds has a long history, as does the rivalry between States having fishing industries. The rivalry and the probability of international disagreement are heightened by the fact that some of the better fishing grounds are adjacent to the coasts of some States or actually within the geographical bays of such States. It is hardly surprising that the increased demand for fish in the 19th Century resulted in a plethora of unilateral rules on coastal fisheries, the need for fishery agreements, and finally some agreements that had about them some law making qualities.[14] Along with the greater markets for fish resulting from population growth and division of labor, the Industrial Revolution has provided improved technical means for harvesting fish. The technical improvements, of course, involve an expenditure of capital in an industry which already by its very nature involves a large element of risk, a relatively low margin of profit, and requires an efficient organi-

[12] Morgan, *Fisheries*, p. 284.

[13] Morgan, *Fisheries*, p. 140. Lest one be dismayed by the seeming indulgence in generalities manifested in the foregoing statements concerning the economic implications of a country's fishing industry, the writer, having suffered many frustrations in research aimed at spelling out in more finite detail the economic implications of a country's fishing industry, takes some comfort in quoting from a recent United Nations Document:

> It is clear from these examples alone that in order to assess the effect on national economies of most of the changes likely to occur in a fishery, one would need information on what is technically known as the mobility of factors, *i.e.*, the costs involved in diverting capital, labor and other factors of production to other uses (and vice versa) and on the elasticity of demand. Hardly any such information is available and it is certain that much research would be needed to obtain it. If economic considerations were to be taken into account objectively in determining legal questions connected with the sea fisheries, there would be need for much greater knowledge of the relevant economic factors and consequently for a very great deal of economic investigations.

Secretariat of the United Nations Food and Agriculture Organization, *The Economic Importance of the Sea Fisheries of Different Countries* (Prepatory Document No. 13, United Nations Conference on the Law of the Sea) A/Conf.13/16 of 20 November 1957.

[14] It is doubtful whether anyone has described this process more effectively and succinctly than the late Professor Gidel ih his book, *Le Droit international public de la Mer* (1934), vol. iii, bk. II, Ch. iii. Despite the lapse of twenty-five years since the publication of this great work, it is still a misfortune that it has not been translated into English.

zation for distribution if profits are to be maximized. To some greater or lesser degree, amalgamation of effort, corporate organization and large capital investment may be expected in such a situation.[15]

Although for centuries States have exercised interest in their fishing industries, ir would appear that the developments of the 19th Century brought a new complexion to this interest. In a free economy large industries are likely to be politically articulate, especiallty so when the legal status of one of the factors of production is in doubt. The hiatus will be filled in some fashion, and where the doubt arises through an absence of international rules the State may be expected to intervene.[16] With respect to the fishing industry, then, the Carr proposition becomes subject to some important qualifications. It appears to this author that during the early part of the 19th Century the separation of economic and political matters in the conception of governmental responsibility was such that economic questions having an international flavor were rather easily susceptible of settlement by agreement, on the basis of mutual interest. In other words such matters were not politicized to the point of involving larger questions of national honor and sovereignty. Moreover, it would appear that tacit or formal agreement on economic matters were made by States who were in fact "Great Powers." Thus the rules they made for their own conduct were likely to exercise strong influence upon such unilateral declarations as might have international consequences. It is believed that in this way agreements on fishery matters tended to influence subsequent growth

[15] Dr. Morgan cites the example of the British industry thus:

> The great technical complexity and development of British fisheries is the maritime projection of the general industrial development of the past century and a half. Conversely, there are no large modern fishing industries based on otherwise backward countries. Growth and modernization of Asian fisheries, outside Japan, cannot take place on a large scale in the absence of an industrial base to sustain it.

World Sea Fisheries, p. 140. Dr. Morgan perhaps suggests a greater disparity between Britain and less industrialized countries than may exist in fact. Britain's industry can be said to be an outstanding example of the trend toward large enterprise in fishing. J. T. Johnson, in his book, *The Sea Fisheries* (1920), wrote:

> The industry as a whole tends toward concentration, to the use of larger boats, to the need of greater harbors, p. 34.

[16] An excellent account of the exertions of such pressure in the case of the United Kingdom is given by CAPT Christopher B. V. Meyer, RNorN, *The Extent of Jurisdiction in Coastal Waters* (1927), at pages 118–120. See also, Philip C. Jessup, "L'Exploitation des Richesses de la Mer," 29 *Recueil des Cours de la Haye* (Vol. iv, 1929), at pp. 406–9; and Fulton, *Sovereignty*, pp. 700–715. Deutsch and Eckstein write simply:

> As has been amply attested by political studies, such economic changes often are apt to become linked to political changes through the mechanism of interest groups, ...

and then proceed at length to document their statement. Karl W. Deutsch and Alexander Eckstein, *National Industrialization and the Declining Share of the International Economic Sector*, 1890–1957 (Unpublished paper, 1959).

of practices with respect to sovereignty over bays. We shall now briefly note the growth of rules on bays during the 19th Century.

Recalling the comment of Azuni at the beginning of the Nineteenth Century ("it is already established among polished nations...."), we may assume, as a point of departure, the high probability of a general understanding that a bay was, for legal purposes, the water area inside a line joining two headlands and that the area was territorial sea "even though the center may be, in some places, at a greater distance than three miles from either shore." [17] Elsewhere in his work, Azuni, assimilates the legel status of a bay to that of a port.[18] Thus at the beginning of the Nineteenth Century, a writer whose work is primarily one of reporting what he believes to be a consensus rather than one of advocating certain propositions, concludes that there exists a conception of a bay which is juridical as well as geographical; that the juridical bay has an outer boundary; and that the littoral State enjoys rather complete sovereignty over the waters inside the boundary. Where there was no indication of a consensus was with respect to the distance between headlands (although it might be greater than six miles), and the degree of concavity that the geographical bay should have in order to constitute it a juridical bay.

The views of Azuni appear to be the same as those evident in the 1793 opinion of Attorney General Randolph in the case of the *Grange*, seized in Delaware Bay.[19] This was also the British view of the Bay of Fundy when considered as a bay within the sense intended by the Anglo-American Convention of 1818.[20] Interpretations of that treaty were to be the subject of dispute for the following century, and every one of them, of course, had to do with alleged violations by American

[17] Domenico A. Azuni, *The Maritime Law of Europe* (1806), p. 206.

[18] Azuni, *Law*, p. 234.

[19] I *Am. State Pap. For. Rel.*, p. 148; 1 *Op. At. Gen.*, p. 32; I *Moore's Digest* (1906), pp. 735–9. Mr. Randolph, of course, primarily from a defense point of view, cited Grotius, Nattel, Puffindorf, Bynkershoek, Selden and Valin, and emphasized the property characteristics of Delaware Bay and bays in general which tended to constitute them possessions of the littoral States. See also David R. Deener, *The United States Attorneys General and International Law* (1957), pp. 210–211.

[20] Law Officers of the Crown letter of 9 April 1844, to Lord Aberdeen, Prime Minister. I Lord McNair, *International Law Opinions* (1956), pp. 350–1. As Professor Moore points out, the above letter made use of the headland theory in conjunction with a treaty in which the term was not used. I *Moore's Digest* (1906), p. 785. Actually, the concept of a particular *headland* theory of bays is a rather confusing one and too much, perhaps, has been said about it. The theory is that the littoral State should enjoy sovereignty over all of the water inside a line drawn from one headland of a bay to another. The important point is that the extent of this line is immaterial. Jessup, *The Law of Territorial Waters and Maritime Jurisdiction* (1927), pp. 358–9. In the headland theory there appears to be a pre-supposition that every bay has a pair of readily-identifiable headlands – something which a mariner knows is not at all a universal truth. The treaty of 1818 is quoted hereunder at Annex A.

flag fishermen.[21] That the clash was entirely one of opposing economic interests is not open to doubt. The 1818 treaty itself was an unhappy compromise between parties who were unwilling to yield very much,[22] and the ensuing difficulties might very well have been anticipated.

It should be no surprise, therefore, that the British and French Governments, after some years of disputes among the fishermen of their respective countries,[23] sought to fix rather precisely the limits of their coastal fisheries.[24] Of special interest to us, here, is the following provision

> It is equally agreed, that the distance of three miles fixed as the general limit for the exclusive right of fishery upon the coasts of the two countries shall, with respect to bays, the mouths of which do not exceed ten miles in width, be measured from a straight line drawn from headland to headland.

The British legislation implementing this treaty, Act of 1843, *6 & 7 Vict., c. 79*, contains a provision of especial importance to us, namely that the ten-mile closing line for bays was to be measued from the low-water marks of the headlands.

Of further interest in connection with this treaty is the fact that when it was signed there was an atmosphere of considerable tension in the political relations between England and France: there was a strong clash of interests between them in the Ottoman Near East.[25] On the other hand, 1839 was a year of poor harvest, high food prices, and unemployment in England.[26] Both England and France were then protectionist States and England was a net food importer.[27] But despite certain possibilities of economic advantage, France was apparently quite willing to negotiate the treaty, and to join in a mixed committee to study the matter for two years before the agreement was signed. It appears that economic and international political matters

[21] Examples are: The Schooner *Washington* and the *Argus*, sailing in the Bay of Fundy and Caw Bay, respectively. Their cases came before Umpire Bates in 1853. IV *Moore's Arbitrations*, p. 4344; I *Moore's Digest*, p. 787; The Fortune Bay case of 1878 and the Aspee Bay Case of 1881, I *Moore's Digest*, p. 807. The U.S.-Canadian disputes over the 1818 treaty finally led to the North American Fisheries Arbitration of 1910, which is discussed below.

[22] I *Moore's Digest*, p. 782; IV *Am. State Papers, For. Rel.* pp. 380–406.

[23] Fulton, *Sovereignty of the Sea* (1911), pp. 607–615.

[24] *Convention between Her Majesty and the King of the French, defining and regulating the Limits of the Exclusive Rights of the Oyster and Other Fishery on the Coasts of Great Britain and of France*, Paris, 2 August 1839; Herstlet, *Treaties*, vol. 5, p. 89. Implementation of this treaty was, in Great Britain, in the Act 6, 7 Victoria, cap 79 (Herstlet, *Treaties*, vol. 6, p. 414), entitled The Sea Fisheries Act, 1843. An excellent discussion of this treaty and the circumstances attending it is contained in L. Larry Leonard, *International Regulation of Fisheries* (1944), pp. 35–42.

[25] Seton-Watson, *Britain in Europe*, pp. 198–201; J. A. R. Marriott, *The Eastern Question, A Study in European Diplomacy*, 4th Ed., (1940), pp. 239–41.

[26] Imlah, *Pax Britannica*, p. 147.

[27] Knight, Barnes, and Flügel, *Economic History of Europe* (1928).

were, at this juncture at least, completely separate areas of consideration. Certainly economic policy was not used for leverage in the international dispute which concurrently was taking place in another sphere of activity.[28]

Inasmuch as some of the 1839 treaty provisions did not prove entirely satisfactory in practice, a second treaty in the same premises was negotiated in 1867.[29] This treaty had this provision included in it:

> The distance of three miles fixed as the general limit fot the exclusive right of fishery upon the coasts of the two countries shall with respect to bays, the mouths of which do not exceed ten miles in width, be measured from a straight line drawn from headland to headland.[30]

The French Government failed to ratify the 1867 treaty.

A very important difference between the circumstance attending the Anglo-French treaties of 1839 and 1867, and the Anglo-American treaty of 1818 was that in the former case there were fishermen on both sides committing violations against the other party's territory. In the latter case there were American fishermen in Canadian coastal waters – but no appreciable number of Canadian fishermen in American coastal waters. The imagination undergoes no great strain in perceiving that proximate mutuality of both interests and problems is more likely to lead to an agreement framed in precise terms. The 1839 situation presented fertile ground for germination of the 10-mile rule. Of further interest is the dictum of Mr. Joshua Bates, umpire in the *Washington* case of 1853, in which he expressed the view that the headlands doctrine had received a proper limit (10 miles) in the 1839 convention.[31]

In May 1870, the Canadian Minister of Marine and Fisheries issued instructions to apply the 1839 limits against American fishermen; but these were withdrawn and the limits for bays were contracted to a closing line width of six miles.[32]

The 1839 Convention was simply between Great Britain and France and thus not binding upon other powers. But as among the countries surrounding the North Sea there persisted problems of encroachment similar to those precipitating the 1839 negotiations. Finally, in 1881,

[28] Although there were numerous violations of the treaty provisions, by the fishermen of both parties, it would appear that no force other than that of fishery police was used at any time. The defense or military element were completely absent, and it does not appear that gun-fire ranges *per se* were considered in establishing the 10-mile rule. *Reports of the Commissioners for the Herring Fishing* 1839, 1840, 1841.

[29] Fulton, *Sovereignty of the Sea* (1911), p. 619.

[30] LVII *British and Foreign State Papers*, p. 8.

[31] I *Moore's Digest*, p. 786.

[32] Fulton, *Sovereignty*, p. 627.

Great Britain invited the cooperation of France, Belgium, Holland, Sweden and Norway, and Denmark to assist in devising a remedy. The Dutch Government suggested a joint convention and the Powers, with Germany now included, convened to negotiate it. While there was some objection to defining the limits of maritime jurisdiction in precise terms, agreement to do so was ultimately reached. The provision of primary interest to us reads:

As regards bays, the entrances of which do not exceed ten miles in width, the distance of three miles shall be measured from a straight line joining the two extreme points of the bay.[33]

Although the Kingdom of Sweden-Norway signed the protocol, that country did not ratify the Convention. Fulton's comment on this reads:

They believed, however that to agree to so restricted a boundary for their territorial waters in respect to fishery would be disadvantageous to them .... It is curious indeed, that the limits for exclusive fishery, both in the convention with France in 1839 and with the other North Sea Powers in 1882 were fixed as it were incidentally.[34]

What is to be noted is that the States parties to the 1882 convention bordered on the east, south, and west sides of the North Sea, and that their fishing activities were either carried out in an area common to all of them, or in areas completely outside the North Sea. While Norway borders on the North Sea, her real fishing grounds face the Atlantic and Arctic Oceans. Moreover, the economies of none of the other signataries was as fully dependent upon fisheries as was (and is) the economy of Norway. Obviously, Sweden-Norway did not join the other States in viewing the limits as a matter of common interest; her economic interests were different and far more crucial.

And here we find another qualification to the Carr proposition. Agreement on this economic issue was, even in the 19th Century, to be achieved only when the parties involved had cause to view the issue in approximately the same light. What distinguishes the United Kingdom-Norway and United States-Canada situations and made agreement less likely was the absence of reciprocal activity: British and United States fishermen fished in Norwegian and Canadian waters, respectively, but Norwegian and Canadian fishermen did not operate in British and Unites States waters. Thus while in the 19th Century

[33] Fulton, *Sovereignty*, p. 634.

[34] Fulton, *Sovereignty*, p. 634, Sir Cecil Hurst explains the "incidental" way in which this came about. He writes that the framers of the Convention thought it was the fisheries outside territorial waters they were to regulate and therefore they were to agree on a definition of the waters which were not subject to the convention. "The Territoriality of Bays," *The British Yearbook of International Law* 1922–23, pp. 42–54.

economic considerations did bring about some widely accepted refinements on the rules for bays, there were also at work economic considerations which prevented such refinements from gaining universal acceptance.[35] It appears worthwhile, however, to note in tabular form herewith (Pages 158–161) those State acts or international conventions which set out delimitations of the closing lines of bays for fishery purposes.

In the table, it is to be noted that nowhere is the bay itself defined; the primary point of interest or agreement is the mathematical limit to be placed upon the measured outer limit of the State's absolute sovereignty over the waters of the bay. When we turn to another manifestation of the State's economic interest, that having to do with customs and fiscal matters, we find a similar situation. In the table below (Page 161) are the relevant provisions of the customs laws of two States. Here, again, the States never seemed to be in doubt as to their being able to identify a bay for purposes of implementing their laws.[36] Moreover, it does not appear in any of the laws, regulations or treaties cited that the States concerned undertook to express the juridical quality of the internal waters within the bay. But, as Sir Cecil Hurst has pointed out, if the material provided by treaties, statutes, decisions in the municipal courts and awards in international arbitrations where Great Britain was a party are considered, there is little scope left to doubt as to what must be the British view as to the status

[35] One should hasten to add, however, that on 15 February 1888, there was signed in Washington a treaty providing for a mixed commission to delimit the British waters, bays, creeks, harbors and coasts described in the Convention of 1818. One of the provisions of the treaty read in part: "... but at every bay, creek, or ... harbor, not otherwise specially provided for in this treaty, such three marine miles shall be measured seaward from a straight line drawn across the bay, creek, or harbour, in the part nearest the entrance at the first point where the width does not exceed ten marine miles." The treaty failed to receive the constitutional approval of the U.S. Senate. Fulton writes, at page 629, that it was the United States who proposed the 10-mile line, and that Great Britain consented only after strong objection.

[36] On the other hand, there may have been a reluctance on the Governments to take a position of this matter, although information in these premises is extremely sparse. Lord McNair records this instance where such a position was requested:

> The Danish Government having represented to the British Government the desirability of arriving at an understanding as to the meaning of the word 'bay' occuring in the North Sea Fisheries Convention of 1882, which is scheduled to the Sea Fisheries Act, 1883, it was proposed by certain interested British Departments to define a bay as including all indentations of the coast, irrespective of size. The Law Officers ... advised (5 December 1899, General) *against this or any definition:*
>
>> Each case should be decided as it arises. It is quite clear that a bend in the coast, very shallow in proportion to its lateral extension, is not a bay, and no limit can be fixed by way of general definition. On the other hand, to define "bay" as including what are generally called gulfs might lead to difficulties of another sort, as territorial jurisdiction is, in many cases, claimed over gulfs, though more than 10 miles across, if they extend far inland. I *International Law Opinions*, p. 361.

Table of Fishery Regulations and Conventions containing Provisions Delimiting Bays

States	Date	Instrument	Provisions	Sources
Cuba	28 March 1936	Legislative Decree No. 704 of 28 March 1936: General Fisheries Statute.	Art. 5 . . . "Where the coast is indented or cut into by harbors, rivers, creeks or other features, the base line shall be deemed to follow the straight line drawn across the entrance of the indentation, provided that such entrance does not exceed six miles."	U.N. Leg. Series, *Laws and Regulations on the Territorial Seas*, (1956), p. 464. (Hereinafter referred to as "UN Laws 1956.")
Denmark	27 Feb. 1903	Order No. 29 of 27 February 1903 respecting the Supervision of Fisheries in the Sea Surrounding the Fowe Islands and Iceland outside the Danish Territorial Sea.	Art. 1 . . . "In the case of a bay, the distance of three nautical miles shall be measured from a straight line drawn across the bay at the point nearest to the entrance where the width does not exceed ten nautical miles."	*UN Laws 1956*, p. 468.
Denmark	29 June 1933	Decree No. 230 of 29 June 1933, concerning Fishing in the Waters Bordering on Denmark and Sweden.	2(1) . . . "As regards bays, the fishermen of both countries shall be entitled to fish up to a distance of three nautical miles from a straight line drawn across the bay in the part nearest the opening where the width is not greater than ten nautical miles."	*UN Laws 1956*, p. 471.
Denmark	11 Nov. 1953	Notice No. 292 of 11 November 1953 respecting Commercial Trapping, Fishing and Hunting in Greenland and Exports from Greenland.	Art. 1(2) . . . "provided that in bays and inlets the distance of three nautical miles shall be measured from a straight line drawn across the bay of inlet at the place nearest to the entrance where the width does not exceed ten nautical miles"	*UN Laws 1956*, p. 476.

France	16 April 1933	Loi ayant pour objet d'interdire la pêche aux étrangers dans les eaux territoriales de France et d'Algérie du 1er Mars 1888 comme modifiée par la loi du 30 Mars 1928 et par la loi du 16 Avril 1933.	Art. 1er . . . "Pour les baies, le rayon de trois milles est mesuré à partir d'une ligne droite en travers de la baie, dans la partie la plus rapprochée de l'entrée, au premier point où l'ouverture n'excède pas dix milles."	*UN Laws 1956*, p. 497.
Morocco	15 June 1924	Règlement du 31 Mars 1919 sur la Pêche Maritime modifié par le Danir du Juin 1924.	Titre 1e , Art. 2 . . . Pour les baies, le rayon de 5 milles est mesuré à partir d'une ligne droite, tirée en travers de la baie dans la partie la plus rapprochée de l'entrée au premier point où l'ouverture n'excède pas 12 milles.	*UN Laws 1956*, p. 528
Netherlands (New Guinea)	29 April 1927	General Regulations of 29 April 1927 for the Hunting of Whales within three nautical miles of the coasts of the Netherlands Indies, as amended	Art. 1(2) . . . "As far as bays, inlets and river mouths are concerned, the said distance of three nautical miles shall be reckoned from a straight line drawn across the bay, inlet or river mouth as near as possible to the entrance where the bay, inlet or river-mouth does not exceed ten nautical miles (each equal to one sixtieth part of a degree of latitude)".	*UN Laws 1957*, p. 535.
Sweden	2 June 1933	Royal Order No. 282 of 2 June 1933 on Fishing on the Frontier Waters of Sweden and Denmark.	Art. 2(1) . . . "In bays, the fishermen of either country are entitled to fish not nearer than 3 minutes of distance from a straight line drawn across the bay at a point nearest to its mouth where it is not wider than 10 minutes of distance."	*UN Laws 1957*, p. 565.
United Kingdom, Belgium, Netherlands, France, Germany and Denmark.	6 May 1882	North Seas Fisheries Convention.	See page 156 above.	*UN Laws 1957*, p. 695.

Continued

States	Date	Instrument	Provisions	Sources
United Kingdom, France	2 Aug. 1839	Fisheries Convention of 1839	See page 154 above.	*UN Laws 1957*, p. 739.
Spain and Portugal	27 March 1893	Treaty of Commerce and Navigation.	Appendix 6, Fisheries, Art. 2 ... "As regards bays the aperture of which is not more than 10 miles, the 6 miles may be reckoned from a straight line drawn from one point to the other."	*UN Laws 1957*,
Great Britain, Denmark	24 June 1901	Convention between Great Britain and Denmark, for regulating the fisheries outside territorial waters in the ocean surrounding the Farve Islands and Iceland.	Art. 2 ... "As regards bays, the distance of 3 miles shall be measured from a straight line drawn across the bay, in the part nearest the entrance, at the first point where the width does not exceed 10 miles."	*UN Laws 1957*, p. 771.
Great Britain, United States	20 July 1912	Agreement between the United States of America and the United Kingdom, etc., adapting with certain modifications the rules and method of procedure recommended in the Award of 7 September 1910 of the North Atlantic Coast Fisheries Arbitration, signed at Washington 20 July 1910.	Art. 2 ... "In every bay not hereinafter specifically provided for, the limits of exclusion shall be drawn three miles from a straight line across the bay in the part nearest the entrance at the first point where the width does not exceed ten miles."	*UN Laws 1057*, p. 780.
Great Britain, North German Confederation	1868	Fishery Treaty of 1868	"The exclusive fishery rights of North Germany are ... those bays which are ten sea miles or less in breadth reckoned from the extremest points of the land and the flats ..."	XIV Herstlet, *Commercial Treaties*, p. 1055.

Germany, Denmark	1880	Fisheries Agreement of 1880	A ten mile base line for bays.	Fulton, *Sovereignty of the Seas*, p. 652.

Table of Customs Regulations Delimiting Bays

State	Law	Provision	Source
Brazil	Regulations concerning Port Officers Annexed to Decree No. 5796 of 11 June 1940.	Chapt. III, *Jurisdiction Exercised by Port Authorities*. "At places where the coast, including the shore line of islands, turns in to form a bay, inlet or the like, the three mile belt of territorial water shall be reckoned from a line extending between two points not more than twelve miles apart situated opposite each other at the seaward end of the inlet."	*UN Laws 1957*, p. 79.
Iceland	Act No. 33 of 9 January 1935 governing intoxicating beverages.	Art. 5. "For the purposes of this act . . . it is provided that all parts of bays lying to landward of a straight line, twelve nautical miles in length, drawn between headlands nearest to the mouth of the bay, and the area extending seaward for four miles from that line, shall be deemed to be within territorial waters."	*UN Laws 1957*, pp. 146–7.

of the internal waters of a bay. He then proceeds to demonstrate this point and to explain the great likelihood that other States share this view.[37]

We shall now turn to certain judicial and arbitral decisions, and here the economic interest comes into full play, since from conflicting economic interests have come most of the case settled through judicial action. We shall note the economic issues bringing about some of these cases and the relevant opinions of the tribunals.[38]

THE MORAY FIRTH CASE OF 1906

(*Mortensen* v. *Peters.*) [39]

Moray Firth is on the northeast coast of Scotland (See figure 15, Chapter II). It is 73 miles wide "between headlands" and some twenty miles deep. In its waters, Scottish fishermen had operated for centuries, usually in small boats. Encroachments by larger boats using more modern equipment were feared because they would deplete the supply of fish and make the Scottish industry unviable. In 1889, Parliament passed the Herring Fisheries Act, a section of which authorized the Fishery Board of Scotland to establish regulations forbidding beam and otter trawling. The Board made an implementing by-law in 1892, and there was no doubt about its applicability as to British trawlers. But foreign trawlers appeared in large numbers, including a number registered in Norway, but actually British owned. Most of them fished outside the 3-mile coastal limit but inside the Firth. One Fisherman, Captain Mortensen, the skipper of the *Catalonia* took his ship within 3 miles of the 10-mile base line. He was brought to trial but his objection to the jurisdiction on the ground of Norway's failure to sign the 1882 Convention was sustained. On appeal it was reversed, the judge holding that the above-mentioned law was applicable to foreigners as well as British. Mortensen's ship was inside the bay, but outside the 3-mile limit, and outside the 10-mile line. He was tried and con-

[37] Sir Cecil Hurst, "The Territoriality of Bays," *BYIL 1922–3*, p. 44ff.

[38] It is tempting, of course, to undertake more or less thoroughgoing discussions of a number of these cases. In most instances this has been done repeatedly by others and there is little purpose to be served in going over the same ground. In 1956, Professor MacChesney recorded what was up to that time a fairly complete bibliography of the voluminous comment on *United Kingdom* v. *Norway;* he records twenty-three different articles. *U.S. Naval War College International Law Situation and Documents* 1956, pp. 62–65.

[39] 14 *Scots Law Times* Rep. 227 (1906); Fulton, *Sovereignty* pp. 717ff; 169 Hansard, *Parl. Debates* (4th Series), col. 979ff; 170 *Ibid.*, col. 472; 196 *Ibid.*, col. 236; Ralph Jones, *Unpublished Naval War College Manuscript* (1957).

victed, but his appeal failed, the court saying that English law applied to foreigners as well as to British subjects. The court said that it was bound to give effect to the terms of the statute and that it was not a tribunal whose purpose it was to decide whether a legislative act was *ultra vires* as in contravention to international law. This was simply an acknowledgement of the British doctrine of parliamentary supremacy.

The court nevertheless paused to examine international law in these premises, but concluded that Moray Firth, with well-marked headlands, was a bay and that the ten-mile rule was "arbitrary and artificial."

Thereafter several more masters of Norwegian-flag trawlers were arrested, tried and convicted. At their trial, a Norwegian vice-consul read a protest initiated by the Foreign Minister of Norway. The Norwegian Minister at London made representations to the British Foreign Office and ten days after the trial the men were released and their fines remitted. As part of these post-judicial consequences there ensued an interesting debate in the House of Lords. Here the Government modified their previous position by saying that in international law the extent of sovereignty in bays is an unsettled matter. Subsequently the Foreign Office stated that the Act, as interpreted by the court, was in conflict with international law and that other peoples would not readily admit that Moray Firth was within territorial waters.

What becomes apparent is the British Government's realization that claims to the Moray Firth would be met by reciprocal claims in foreign waters with resultant injury to British fishing interests. It was for these reasons that the United Kingdom chose not to claim sovereignty over Moray Firth. Absent, however, was any position on a 10-mile rule for bays – or any other expression of a mathematical limit.

The circumstances leading up to this case and the post-judicial attitude toward it were entirely of an economic nature. The Herring Fishery Act of 1889, the ultimate attitude of the Foreign Office toward the Act, and the absence of any rigidly defined position demonstrate that economic interests were dictating policy. Should, as an aftermath, the British Government have adopted a position subscribing to a 10-mile rule they would have deprived themselves of the flexibility *vis à vis* international law that their economic interests appeared to dictate. While they were willing to commit themselves to a 10-mile rule in a treaty for a particular area, as in the North Seas Convention of 1882, they were unwilling to subscribe to a rule that might have more universal effect. It is probably outside the scope of this book to attempt comment upon the long range consequences implicit in this failure of a State to attempt to exercise in the interest of a more stable international order her then great position of political and economic leadership. There is no merit in quarterbacking fifty-three years after the event, but there is a good deal of merit in noting this case as an example of the need for great wisdom on the part of statesmen in determining where their long-range interests really lie.

THE NORTH ATLANTIC COAST FISHERIES ARBITRATION OF 1910.[40]

The roots of the controversy which came to a head in the 1910 arbitration are found in the economic consequences of the settlement of the American Revolution. Prior to that revolution, American colonial fishermen had fished the Grand Banks and the coastal waters of Canada and had dried and cured their catch on the shores of Newfoundland and Canada. With American independence came the political fact that such economic activity would either stop or be continued within the territory of, and by a hoped-for agreement with, a foreign State. Professor Moore writes that the former mother country was, if possible, more anxious for a peace treaty than the newly independent country. Thus the 1783 Peace Treaty of Paris contains the fishing concession demanded by the Delegates of the United States. Of interest to us is the clause:

> ... and also that the inhabitants of the United States shall have the liberty to take fish of every kind on such part of the coast ... and also on the coasts, bays and creeks of all the other of his Britannic Majesty's dominions in America.

"Bays" were not defined further and there would have been no precedent for doing so. After the War of 1812, the British delegates at Ghent said that the fishing privileges would not be renewed "without an equivalent." The American delegates were unwilling to acquiesce and no article in these premises was included in the peace treaty. When, in 1815, an American fishing vessel was warned away from the Newfoundland coast, and the American Minister at London protested, maintaining that the 1783 treaty provisions were still in force, the

[40] *Moore's Digest*, pp. 767–874; Dana Frank Fleming, *The Treaty Veto of the American Senate* (1930), pp. 68–72; Jessup, *Law of Territorial Waters and Maritime Jurisdiction* (1927), pp. 364–382.

British Government replied that subsequent wars put an end to such treaties. The consequence was the Treaty of 1818, with this important difference:

And the United States hereby renounce forever, any liberty heretofore enjoyed or claimed by the inhabitants thereof, to take, dry, or cure fish on, or within three marine miles of any of the coasts, bays, creeks, or harbours of his Britannic Majesty's dominions in America not included within the above-mentioned limits; Provided, however, that the American fishermen shall be admitted to enter such bays or harbours for the purpose of shelter and of repairing damages therein, of purchasing wood, and of obtaining water, and for no other purpose whatever.

The Bay was left undefined and this was a continuing bone of contention. It would be a trifle tedious to recite the history of this controversy and the various attempts at negotiation. The British attempted to enforce their regulations and the American fishermen regularly violated them, there occurring some 300 seizures of American fishing boats between 1818 and 1838.[41] In general, the picture is that in repeated negotiations, the British tended to become more generous in their offers, especially with respect to bays. One might guess that policing costs must have been onerous. They proposed the 10-mile rule on bays, but in general, the United States stood on an argument of abstract right, asserting that there was no such rule of International Law, nor was there any headland rule. Finally, in 1888, a new treaty was negotiated. Article III thereof provided:

... that three marine miles is to be measured from low-water mark, and that in bays, creeks, and harbors the distance, except where otherwise provided shall be measured from a straight line drawn across the part nearest the entrance, at the first point where the width does not exceed ten marine miles.

The treaty was rejected in the United States Senate. From then until 1905, the question became more or less dormant, British and Canadian authorities refraining from vigorous measures against American ships. In 1905 it was revived. On 27 January 1909 there was signed an Agreement to submit it to an arbitral tribunal selected from the Permanent Court of Arbitration. The Agreement provided for the referral of seven questions to the tribunal, the fifth question being:

From where must be measured the 'three marine miles of any of the coasts, bays, creeks or harbors' referred to in the said Article. [Article 1 of the 1818 Treaty].

[41] Fleming, *Treaty Veto*, p. 71, citing Senator Morgan (D., Alabama) in *Congressional Record*, 1st Session, Vol. 19, Part 8, pp. 7158–60. (50th Congress).

Dispensing with the arguments of the two parties [42] we shall note those parts of the award and recommendations which are of direct interest at this point.

The United States contended that the renunciation in the 1818 treaty pertained only to bays six miles in width *inter fauces terrae*. The tribunal was unable to agree. Quoted hereunder are the most immediately relevant portions of the tribunal's opinion:

... admittedly the geographical character of a bay contains conditions which concern the interests of a territorial sovereign to a more intimate extent than do those connected with the open coast. Thus conditions of national and territorial integrity, of defense, of commerce and of industry are all vitally concerned with the control of the bays penetrating the national coast line. This interest varies, speaking generally, in proportion to the penetration inland of the bay; but as *no principle of international law recognizes any specified relation between the concavity of the bay and the requirements for control by the territorial sovereignty*, this tribunal is unable to qualify by the application of any new principle its interpretation of the treaty of 1818... nor can this tribunal take cognizance in this connection of other principles concerning the territorial sovereignty over bays such as ten-mile or twelve-mile limits of exclusion based on international acts subsequent to the treaty of 1818 and relating to coasts of a different configuration and conditions of a different character. [emphasis supplied]

... it is evident that the three-mile rule is not applied to bays strictly or systematically either by the United States or by any other Power;

the tribunal is unable to understand the term "bays" ... in other than its geographical sense, by which a bay is to be considered as an indentation of the coast, bearing a configuration of a particular character easy to determine specifically, but difficult to describe generally. [emphasis supplied]

The negotiators of the treaty of 1818 did probably not trouble themselves with subtle theories concerning the notion of "bays"; they most probably thought that everybody would know what was a bay. In this popular sense the term must be interpreted in the treaty. The interpretation must take into account all the individual circumstances which for any one of the different bays are to be appreciated, the relation of the width to the length of the penetration inland, the possibility of its being defended by the state in whose territory it is indented; the special value which it has for the industry of the inhabitants of its shores; the distance which it is secluded from the highways of nations on the open sea and other circumstances not possible to enumerate in general.

The foregoing excerpts express rather completely the complex problem confronting a tribunal called upon to arbitrate a dispute involving bays. It is the same complex problem facing a body convened to codify the law on bays. It is the problem of attempting to apply legal concepts to a geographical phenomenon in an admixed atmosphere of individual

[42] Dr. Jessup discusses in considerable detail the argument of the American agent, Mr. Elihu Root. See also, Bacon and Scott, eds. *North Atlantic Coast Fisheries Arbitration at the Hague – Argument on behalf of the United States by Elihu Root* (1917); *Proceedings in the North Atlantic Coast Fisheries Arbitration* 12 vols., U.S. Senate Doc. No. 870, 61st Cong., 3rd Sess. 1912.

economic interests, more or less crystallized state policies, and social change that is difficult to predict.

Inasmuch as the agreement to submit the matter to arbitration imposed upon the tribunal the responsibility to make appropriate recommendations, the tribunal recommended:

In every bay not hereinafter specifically provided for the limits of exclusion shall be drawn three miles seaward from a straight line across the entrance at the first point where the width does not exceed ten miles.

The tribunal was careful to indicate that the several circumstances of previous cases which influenced them in making this recommendation were not sufficient to constitute it a principle of international law.

In his cogent dissent to the opinion of his brother arbitrators, Dr. Luis Drago of Argentina pointed out the great remaining difficulty, defining a bay for juridical purposes:

The tribunal has decided that: "In case of bays the three miles" (of the treaty) "are to be measured from a straight line drawn across the body of water at the place where it ceases to have the configuration characteristic of a bay. At all other places the three miles are to be measured following the sinuosities of the coast." But no rule is laid out or general principle evolved for the parties to know what the nature of such confriguation is or by what methods the points should be ascertained from which the bay should lose the characteristics of such. There lies the whole contention and the whole difficulty, not satisfactorily solved.

The award and recommendations of the Court were substantially accepted by the two Governments in the treaty of 20 July 1912.[43] The case has been reviewed here very briefly. Its significance lies in the fact that the arbitration was the culmination of a dispute entirely economic in origin and one which had continued for over a century. It was this economic dispute and its arbitration which, for the first time, delineated in detail, the very complicated nature of bays and their position in international law. It should be noted, too, that as between the parties the dispute was for most of its history considered an isolated situation, an economic question and not one involving the vital interests of either State. The dispute was not related by either party to any concepts of national consciousness, defense, or power tensions. It was in such an atmosphere, basically economic, that there took place some growth in the law on bays.

[43] III *Malloy* 2632, 2635.

THE ANGLO-NORWEGIAN FISHERIES CASE.[44]

Captain Meyer of Norway, and before him Professor Fulton of the United Kingdom, have discussed in detail the long-standing dispute arising out of British-owned fishing boats fishing in Norwegian coastal waters. From time to time in the preceding pages of this book mention has been made of the importance of the fishing industry to the economies of the two countries. It would perhaps be inappropriate and no doubt redundant for this writer to undertake a lengthy description of the dispute that preceded its adjudication by the International Court of Justice. Our interest in this section is in the predominantly economic character of the dispute and the effects its settlement may have upon the law of bays.

We should pause, however, to observe the pattern of relationships existing between the two parties at the time their dispute was submitted to the International Court of Justice: Both States were governed by the parliamentary system and were working democracies; both States were members of the North Atlantic Alliance; the overall relationships between the two States were traditionally friendly; both States participated as Allies in World War II; the United Kingdom has a comparatively rich and relatively diversified manufacturing economy; Norway, much smaller and more poorly favored, has an economy more dependent on fishery and agricultural products. Absent from their relationships are any indications of power struggle polarity or ideological difference. The dispute, economic in its foundation, could be so looked upon by both parties, and the settlement could be expected to result, at most, in some economic realignment. The atmosphere was such that settlement under the rule of law was possible.

The dispute concerning the coastal fisheries off Norway has its

[44] International Court of Justice, *Reports of Judgments, Advisory Opinions and Orders*, 1951, pp. 116–206; International Court of Justice, *Fisheries Case, Pleadings, Oral Arguments and Documents* (1951); Jans Evensen, "The Anglo-Norwegian Fisheries Case and its Legal Consequences," 46 *American Journal of International Law* (1952), pp. 23–30; Brunson MacChesney, *U.S. Naval War College International Law Situation and Documents* 1956, pp. 59–136; J. H. W. Verzijl, "Territorial Controversies before the International Court of Justice," I *Netherlands International Law Review* (1954), pp. 234–267; R. O. Wilberforce, "Some Aspects of the Anglo-Norwegian Fisheries Case", 38 *Transactions of the Grotius Society* (1952), pp. 151–168; C. H. M. Waldock, "The Anglo-Norwegian Fisheries Case," 28 *British Yearbook of International Law* (1951), pp. 114–171; D. H. N. Johnson, "The Anglo-Norwegian Fisheries Case," I *International and Comparative Law Quarterly* (4th Series, 1952), pp. 145–179; Sir Gerald Fitzmaurice, "The Law and Procedure of the International Court of Justice, 1951–54: General Principles and Sources of Law," 30 *British Yearbook of International Law* (1953), pp. 1–70.

origin only at the beginning of this Century when British steam-driven trawlers commenced to operate in large numbers off the Norwegian coast. There were numerous violations of the waters over which Norway by various decrees had claimed sovereignty. The United Kingdom had, without great success, attempted to arrive at some agreement with Norway concerning the extent of her sovereignty. While of course there is the question of the legality of the Norwegian claims, there is also considerable evidence that Norway did not follow a clear cut policy with respect to her claims and that on occasions her fishery cruisers made arrests outside the waters she was believed to have claimed. There is also evidence in the record which might lead a mariner of another State to surmise that on some occasions the fishermen, when they were arrested, probably did not know their exact navigational positions. This latter is purely a reasoned conjecture of the author.

The specific action on the part of Norway that brought on the application to the International Court by the United Kingdom was the Decree of 12 July 1935 establishing the limits of a Norwegian fisheries zone north of Lat. 66°28.8′N. The limits were measured by perpendiculars drawn from the outer islands and rocks along the coast and from base lines drawn between these islands, or from base lines drawn between the headlands of certain bays. The Application of the United Kingdom requested the Court:

(a) to declare the principles of international law to be applied in defining base lines to which the Norwegian Government is entitled to delimit the fisheries zone, extending to seaward *four sea* miles from those lines and exclusively reserved for its own nationals, and to define the said base lines insofar as it appears necessary, in the light of the arguments of the Parties, in order to avoid further legal differences between them;

(b) to award damages to the Government of the United Kingdom in respect to all interferences with British fishing vessels outside the zone which, in accordance with the Court's decision under (a), the Norwegian Government is entitled to reserve for its nationals.

The arguments of the Parties on the matter of bays alone are quite voluminous. In essence, the British argument concerns itself first with the mounting number of disputes and arrests since the beginning of the present century, with the efforts of the British Government to come to some agreement and the allegedly intransigent and dilatory attitude of the Norwegian Government. Next, the British agent makes it clear that the "United Kingdom now finally accepts as a general rule of international law the ten-mile rule for bays and other enclosed waters...." He contends that international law does not give each State the right to choose its own base-lines and a State, in prescribing base-lines for any particular area, can do so only within the limits imposed by international law. He argues: "there is the strongest evidence that international law recognizes that apart from historic titles – bays can only be claimed as part of a State's territory within strict limits and that the limit is that of 10-miles." Finally, the United Kingdom submitted:

(e) A bay for this purpose is any well-marked indentation of the coast whose penetration inland bears a reasonable proportion to the width of its mouth (In case of dispute the geometrical test proposed by the United States at the 1930 Conference might be applied).[45]

(f) The onus of proof in the case of a claim to a bay wider than 10 miles, on historic grounds, is on the State making the claim.

The Norwegian argument, in addition to addressing itself to the strictly legalistic propositions, went into a thorough historical development of the Norwegian fishing industry and Norway's undisturbed possession, through many uncontested decrees, of the coastal waters in controversy. Then, her agent undertook a thorough discussion of custom as a source of International Law, its elements, elements of proof establishing it, and its force with respect to a State which has constantly and unequivocally refused to accept it. He then argues and seeks to prove that the 10-mile rule cannot be said to be a general rule of internationa law. Of very great importance is the Norwegian Agent's discussion of the economic importance of the fishing industry to Norway. Attached to his Counter Memorial is substantiating statistical information on this point.

It is appropriate to mention here the Norwegian agent's criticism of the British argument that the three-mile rule for the marginal belt and the ten-mile rule for bays are independent of each other. The Norwegian agent says:

Les deux règles sont en tout cas inspirées par une même tendance. Elles visent l'une et l'autre à imposer au pouvoir de l'Etat sur les eaux adjacentes des limites étroites, uniformes et rigides.[46]

To lump these two notions together is to inspire mischief wherever it is done because the attempt to do so is usually a rather transparent effort at extending sovereignty over the greatest possible amount of sea area when the justification for doing so on any other grounds cannot

[45] See Chapter FIVE, Section B.
[46] *Pleadings*, vol. I, p. 450.

be established. It appears to this writer that publicists who have married the two concepts have ignored their respective origins, which are quite different. An interesting example of the terminological problem that can occur in this respect is in the recent work of Dr. Garcia Amador, *The Exploitation and Conservation of the Resources of the Sea* (1959). At page 2 he writes that traditional international law recognized the subdivision of the sea into two areas only: "the territorial sea (together with the internal waters) and the high seas or open sea." Aside from the fact that this author's lack of comparable wisdom precludes such self-assurance with respect to identifying "traditional international law," he is struck by the fact that Dr. Garcia Amador concludes, as we have done in preceding chapters, that "territorial" waters and internal waters are different concepts with different origins.[47]

At the end of his oral reply to the Norwegian Argument, the Agent of the United Kingdom presented his conclusions, of which we shall cite the following:

> (5) That Norway is entitled to claim as Norwegian internal waters, on historic grounds, all fjords and sunds which fall within the conception of a bay and defined in international law, whether the proper closing line of the indentation is more or less than 10 sea miles long.
>
> (6) That the definition of a bay in international law is a well marked indentation, whose penetration inland is in such proportion to the width of its mouth as to constitute the indentation more than a mere curvature of the coast.
>
> (7) That, where the water is a bay, the principle which determines where the closing line should be drawn is that the closing line should be drawn between the natural geographical entrance points where the indentation ceases to have the configuartion of a bay.

The Norwegian Agent, on behalf of his Government, asserted that the Decree of 12 July 1935 is not inconsistent with International Law binding upon Norway and rejected all submissions to the contrary.

The majority of the court, noting that the claim of the United Kingdom was founded upon what that Government regarded as the general international law applicable to the delimitation of the Norwegian fisheries zone, pointed out that it could not deliver a judgment confining itself to adjudicating on the definitions, principles or rules purporting to justify the contentions of that Government. The court offered the opinion that the ten-mile rule for bays has not acquired

[47] An incidental terminological shortcoming noted in Dr. García Amador's work is his designating *inland* waters as synonymous with internal waters. (At page 52 of his *Exploitation and Conservation*). As noted in Chapter ONE, above, these terms do not mean the same thing in the domestic law of the United States.

the authority of a general rule of international law. It said, further, that the ten-mile rule would appear to be inapplicable as against Norway inasmuch as she has always opposed any attempt to apply it to the Norwegian Coast. But, on the other hand, the Court said:

Although it is true that the act of delimitation is necessarily a unilateral act, because only the coastal State is competent to undertake it, the validity of the determination with regard to other States depends upon international law.

The court then outlined certain criteria which "though not entirely precise, can provide courts with an adequate basis for their decisions, which can be adapted to the diverse facts in question." These criteria are:

(a) The close dependence of the territorial sea upon the land domain, or the degree of linkage between the sea areas and the land formations which divide or surround them. In other words, cognizance must be taken of purely geographical factors.

(b) The economic interests peculiar to a region, the reality of which are clearly evidenced by a long usage. "... these grounds were known to Norwegian fishermen and exploited by them from time immemorial.... In these barren regions the inhabitants of the coastal zone derive their livelihood essentially from fishing.... Such rights, founded on the vital needs of the population...."

There is no doubt in this writer's mind that the outcome of this case was primarily determined by economic factors, but that the Norwegian claims were of such a nature as to go no farther than could be justified by Norway's economic situation. By ten votes to two, the Court found that the delimination of the 12 July 1935 Decree was not contrary to International Law, and by eight votes to four that the base lines fixed by the Decree are not, in method, contrary to International Law.

In Section E of this Chapter we shall comment upon some possible future implications for the law of bays that grow out of this decision.

We have undertaken, in this section, to reviews the possible economic influences that have acted upon the law of bays from the beginning of the 19th Century to the present time. During this period, we have seen how the economic growth of States has been both intensive and extensive: States commenced to use more completely than ever before the resources within what they envisioned to be their sovereign competence. States also commenced to utilize more thoroughly than ever before those resources in areas where sovereignty had not yet been asserted or where the sovereignty was at least in doubt. These include marine life resources. So long as economic activities were not politicized to the point of precluding international agreement or arbitration, there existed the possibility that some generally agreed upon rules might emerge – as a sort of equilibrium between conflicting economic interests. It is this author's theory that in the development in rules for bays such an equilibrium was reached in the emergence of the 10-mile rule. It would seem that thereafter, the steadily rising nationalistic interest in economic activity and the politicizong of economic issues rather tended to prevent further growth, development, and agreement on primarily economic grounds. It would seem that international relations entered a new sphere in which economic interests became more directly enmeshed with the totallity of political interests. Populations continued to grow and technological improvements continued to appear. Thus, the 10-mile rule, economically grounded, seems an anachronism and more open to question on the merits of its continiung to represent the best compromise from an economic point of view. But the constantly accelerating aglomeration of State interests, including those patently economic, does not appear to have found its counterpart in a system of international legal development which accurately reflects the interdependence of States and peoples, modern technical improvements, and the multi-disciplined and interconnected advancements in the social and physical sciences. Therefore the law of bays, with its recently interred 10-mile rule, its 24-mile rule arrived at through a sort of legislative slight of hand, and its historic bay vagaries, remains in a rather unstable condition.

Annex A THE UNITED STATES-GREAT BRITAIN CONVENTION OF 20 OCTOBER 1818.[48]

Article 1

Whereas differences have arisen respecting the liberty claimed by the United States for the inhabitants thereof, to take, dry, and cure fish on certain coasts, bays, harbours, and creeks of His Britannic Majesty's dominions in America, it is agreed between the high contracting parties, that the inhabitants of the said United States shall have forever, in common with the subjects of His Britannic Majesty, the liberty to take fish of every kind on that part of the southern coast of Newfoundland which extends from Cape Ray to the Rameau Islands, on the western and northern coast of Newfoundland, from the said Cape Ray to the Quirpon Islands, on the shores of the Magdalen Islands, and also on the coasts, bays, harbours, and creeks from Mount Joly on the southern coast of Labrador, to and through the Streights of Belleisle and thence northwardly indefinitely along the coast, without prejudice however, to any of the exclusive rights of the Hudson Bay Company: And that the American fishermen shall also have liberty

[48] *I Moore's Digest* (1906), pp. 780–1.

forever, to dry and cure fish in any of the unsettled bays, harbours, and creeks of the southern part of the coast of Newfoundland hereabove described, and of the coast of Labrador; but so soon as the same, or any portion thereof, shall be settled, it shall not be lawful for the said fisherman to dry or cure fish at such portion so settled, without previous agreement for such purpose with the inhabitants, proprietors, or possessors of the ground. And the United States hereby renounce forever, any liberty heretofore enjoyed or claimed by the inhabitants thereof, to take, dry, or cure fish on, or within three marine miles of any of the coasts, bays, creeks, or harbours of his Britannic Majesty's dominions in America not included within the abovementioned limits; Provided, however, that the American fishermen shall be admitted to enter such bays or harbours for the purpose of shelter and of repairing damages therein, of purchasing wood, and of obtaining water, and for no other purpose whatever. But they shall be under such restrictions as may be necessary to prevent their taking, drying or curing fish therein, or in any other manner whatever abusing the privileges hereby reserved to them.

Section D DEFENSE

The Defense section of Chapter III noted, in passing, that there was little change in the range of gunfire weapons until about the middle of the 19th Century. Thereafter, the ranges of such weapons increased very rapidly, and this development was somewhat later joined by the perfection of the techniques for range-finding and fire control, including, finally, the appearance of radar. After about 1860, the suggestion that the limit of gunfire range should determine the limit of coastal waters seemed more and more to depart from what the States themselves considered necessary or even desirable. Since it was common knowledge that constantly more powerful weapons were not only possible but very likely on the drawing boards of some War Ministry or steel manufacturer, the factor that may once have been the prime determinant had taken on a highly unstable quality.[1] Even had this not been the case, and had the range of weapons settled at some new figure, say 10 miles (or 20,000 yards), it is extremely doubtful that States would have settled upon this distances as width of the marginal belt. Even more doubtful is the possibility that such new weapons would have determined the closing lines for bays. On this point we shall dwell no further.

From the defense point of view, however, a more significant factor was the 19th Century evolution of a set of recognized rules on neutrali-

[1] Nevertheless, Annex II of the French *Instructions sur L'application du Droit international en Cas de Guerre*, dated 19 December 1912, shows that as of that date the extent of Russian, Swedish and Italian territorial waters was the range of cannon. U.S. Naval War College. *International Law Topics and Discussions* (1913), p. 24.

ty.[2] As the century passed and particularly in the final years before 1914, it became fairly common for States neutral in a conflict to publish declarations to that effect, and to spell out in considerable detail their neutrality regulations. Such declarations were made even at the outbreak of World War II in 1939. Neutrality became the subject of deliberations at the Second Hague Conference in 1907 [3] and five of the Conventions issuing from that conference had to do with the condition of a State's neutrality in the event of a war. In turn, the concept of neutrality, and the Paris Declaration of 1856, brought to a high state of development the law of prize. These events, plus the Declaration of London 1909,[4] were eminently conductive to the making of neutrality declarations in very precise terms.[5] Below (Pages 176–179) is a table of excerpts from a number of such declarations, and other instruments, wherein, for the purpose for which the instrument was issued, bays are in some manner defined.

One should note that in these declarations and regulations describing the closing lines of bays, there is almost no change from the language used in connection with the agreements and regulations having to do with fisheries. It is to be noted also, that the dates of these regulations are, in general, somewhat later than those concerned with fisheries. There is reason for a strong inference, at least, that the pattern for these rules was set by the economic consideration, and that there were no over riding reasons dictating any differences in neutrality rules on bays.

A military weapon that came to be perfected at about the turn of the century must be considered in connection with bays. This weapon is the mine. By the time of the Hague Conference of 1907, the war potential of this inexpensive and relatively passive weapon had come to be appreciated. The conference, attempting to mitigate the severity of war and to ensure peaceful navigation insofar as possible, despite the existence of war, formulated a Convention Relative to the Laying of Automatic Submarine Contact Mines. The Third Commission of the Conference prepared a draft convention on this subject and included therein was an article reading as follows:

[2] Lauterpacht writes that this was due to three factors: The attitude of the United States in 1793 and 1818; the permanent neutralization of Switzerland; and the 1856 Declaration of Paris. *Oppenheim's International Law*, Vol. II, 7th Ed. (1952), pp. 631–4.

[3] U.S. Naval War College, *International Law Situations*, 1908, pp. 117–255.

[4] U.S. Naval War College, *International Law Topics*, 1909.

[5] Kleen. *Lois et usages de la Neutralité*, 1900 vol. I, p. 530; U.S. Naval War College, *Internatioanl Law Topics and Discussions*, 1913, pp. 11–35.

Table of Excerpts from Neutrality Declarations in which Bays are Delimited

State	Date	Acts	Provisions	Sources
Iran	19 July 1934	Loi du 24 Tir (19 Juillet 1934) relative à la limite des eaux territoriales et à la zone de supervision et de Contrôle.	*Article 2*. Pour les baies, l'étendue des eaux territoriales sera mesurée à partir d'une ligne droite tirée en travers de l'ouverture de la baie: si l'ouverture de la baie excède dix milles, cette ligne sera tirée en travers de la baie dans la partie la plus rapprochée de l'entrée, au premier point où l'ouverture n'excèdera pas dix milles.	UN Legislative Series, *Laws and Regulations on the Regime of the Territorial Sea* (1957), p. 24. (Hereinafter referred to as *UN Laws*.
Netherlands	3 June 1940	Decree of 3 June 1940 to promulgate prize regulations in respect of the Kingdom of the Netherlands.	Article 13. At bays, the distance of 3 nautical miles shall be measured from a straight line drawn through the mouth of the bay exceeds 10 nautical miles, the line shall be drawn as near as possible to the entrance at the first point where the width of the bay does not exceed 10 nautical miles.	*UN Laws*, p. 33.
Greece	26 March 1913	Law No. 4141 of 26 March 1913 concerning passage and sojourn of merchant vessels along the Greek shores and policing of ports and harbors in time of war.	*Article 1* . . . With regard to gulfs and bays, the entrance of which does not exceed in width twenty miles, the ten nautical miles belt shall be measured from a straight line drawn across the seaward limit of the gulf or bay.	*UN Laws*, p. 140.
Italy	30 March 1942	Navigation Code of 30 March 1942.	*Article 2. Territorial Sea.* Any gulf or bay the coasts of which form part of the territory of the Kingdom shall be subject to the sovereignty of the State if the distance between the outermost points of the opening of the gulf, inlet or bay in question does not exceed	*UN Laws*, p. 162. Note: This law is practically a repetition of the Italian Law of 16 June 1912.

			twenty nautical miles. If such distance exceeds twenty nautical miles, then the portion of the gulf, inlet or bay enclosed within a straight line drawn between the two points lying furthest to seaward which are separated by a distance of twenty nautical miles shall be subject to the sovereignty of the State.	*Gazzetta ufficiale*, 27 June 1912, No. 151,
Netherlands New Guinea	1939	Territorial Sea and Maritime Districts Ordinance 1939 (Provisions concerning the Maintenance of order and security in the territorial waters of the Netherlands Indies).	I. A . . . If the width of the said opening exceeds ten nautical miles, this line shall be drawn across the bay, arm of the sea, river or canal mouth as close as possible to the entrance at the first point at which the width of the opening is not more than ten nautical miles.	*UN Laws*, p. 194.
Yugoslavia	1 Dec. 1948	Act of 1 December 1948 concerning the coastal waters of the Federal People's Republic of Yugoslavia.	*Article 3.* The inland waters of the Federal People's Republic of Yugoslavia shall include: . . . All other bays and estuaries the width of which, measured from the shortest point of junction to the opposite shore in the direction of the mainland shore does not exceed twelve nautical miles:	*UN Laws*, p. 314.
Morocco	18 July 1917	Neutrality Regulations.	*Article 1.* "... In the roadsteads, bays, or gulfs, the openings of which measured between the most prominent points of land are less than 12 miles in width, the line etc. ..."	U.S. Naval War College, *International Law Documents 1918*, p. 116.
France	18 Oct. 1912	Décret portant fixation de certaines règles de neutralité en cas de guerre maritime du 18 Octobre 1912.	Pour les baies, le rayon de 11 kilomètres est mesuré à partir d'une ligne droite tirée de la baie, dans la partie la plus rapprochée de l'entrée, au premier point où l'ouverture n'excède pas 10 milles.	*UN Laws*, p. 639.

Continued

State	Date	Acts	Provisions	Sources
Netherlands	12 Feb. 1904	Proclamation of Neutrality in the Russo-Japanese War.	*Article VIII*. As concerns the bays this distance of three leagues is measured from a straight line drawn across the bay as near as possible to the entrance at the first point where the opening does not exceed ten nautical miles of 60 to the degree of latitude.	*UN Laws*, p. 643; Crocker, ***Extent of the Marginal Sea***, p. 607. (An obvious typographical error occurs in UN Laws.)
Netherlands	3 Oct. 1911	Proclamation in the Italo-Turkish War.	*Article XVIII*. In regard to bays, that distance of three nautical miles is measured from a straight line athwart the bay, as near as possible to the entrance at the first point where the opening of the bay does not exceed ten nautical miles of 60 to the degree of latitude.	*UN Laws*, p. 644. (An obvious typographical error occurs in this Article as quoted in *UN Laws*).
Netherlands	4 Aug. 1914	Proclamation of Neutrality in the World War.	*Article XVII*. In the case of bays, this distance of 3 nautical miles shall be measured from a straight line drawn across the bay as near as possible to the entrance, at the first point where the mouth of the bay does not exceed 10 nautical miles of 60 to the degree of latitude.	*UN Laws*, p. 646–7.
Netherlands	3 Sept. 1939	Proclamation of Neutrality	*Article 1(2)*. With respect to bays, the distance of three marine miles is measured from a straight line drawn across the mouth of the bay; in case the mouth of the bay is wider than ten	*UN Laws*,

			marine miles, the line shall be drawn in the entrance as close as possible to the first point at which the width does not exceed ten marine miles.	
United Kingdom	14 Dec. 1953	Statement of Policy on Territorial Waters.	"... or, in the case of bays and estuaries, from a closing line drawn at the first place where they narrow to 10 miles in width.	522 *Parliamentary Debates, House of Commons*, p. 36; *NWC 1956*, p. 492.
Germany	30 Sept. 1909	Naval Prize Regulations	3. The right of capture is not to be expressed within neutral territorial waters, i.e. ... any bay, the coast of which is exclusively in the possession of neutral States and which is not more than *6 nautical miles* wide at the opening.	Crocker, *Extent of the Marginal Sea* (1919), p. 533; *U.S. Naval War College International Law Documents 1926*, p. 4.
	1916	Prize Code of 1916		
Great Britain	1888	British Manual of Naval Prize Law.	2. ... The territorial waters of a State are those within 3 miles from low water mark of any part of the territory of that State, or forming bays within such territory; at any rate, in the case of bays the entrance to which is not more than 6 miles wide.	U.S. Naval War College, *International Law Topics and Discussions 1913*, p. 20.
Uruguay	7 Aug. 1914	Maritime Rules of Neutrality.	Art. 2. "... With regard to bays, the distance of 5 miles will be measured along a straight line run across the bay at the point nearest its entrance. In addition to the bays or roadsteads established as such which possess their characteristic form and also have an opening of not more than 10 miles.	U.S. Naval War College, *International Law Topics 1916*, p. 107.

Article 2

It is forbidden to lay anchored automatic contact mines beyond a distance of three nautical miles from low-water mark, throughout the length of the coast line, as well as along the islands and islets adjecant thereto.
In the case of bays, the zone of three nautical miles shall be measured, starting from a straight line drawn across the bay in its part nearest the entrance at the first point where the opening does not exceed ten miles in width.

The draft article provoked some highly interesting discussion concerning the real restrictions it would impose in coastal waters having various geographical peculiarities. The arguments for and against a specific limit for this particular purpose are not worthy of reproducing here. What is of interest to us is that for military purposes, a naval Power then as now desires as much freedom of action at sea as possible. In 1907, the 10-mile rule and the 3-mile rule were considered too restrictive for defensive mining purposes, and the rules were not included in the Convention finally accepted.[6] It is of further interest that what was then generally accepted as a good rule for economic and commercial reasons was found unsatisfactory for military reasons. Unlike the attitude of those naval officers at the Hague, the present attitude (and for other reasons) is to hold for the minimum distances in bays and in the margianl belt.

Since the Hague efforts, and the sporadic declarations of neutrality, the defense influence upon the question of bays has been largely dormant. The Hague Convention on Mines proved entirely ineffectual when put to the test of two world wars,[7] and one would have no reason to think that omission of the Article cited above would have made any difference. Hence, the matter of mines cannot be said to exercise any great influence upon the law of bays, save to observe that a neutral State wishing to defend against belligerent encroachment from the sea might plant mines in its bays or other internal waters. This can be done effectively if the water is not too deep. There are, however, many technical complications to planting mines and subsequently sweeping them after they have served their purpose.

Another military interest in the law of bays was that having to do with prize. So far as this author has been able to determine, only Great Britain and Germany had prize regulations in which, for pur-

[6] Henry G. Crocker, *Extent of the Marginal Sea* (1919), pp. 487–508; U.S. Naval War College, *International Law Situations*, 1908, pp. 98–113, 194–197.

[7] *Robert W. Tucker, U.S. Naval War College International Law Studies*, 1955, p. 303; H. A. Smith, *The Law and Custom of the Sea* 2nd Ed. (1950), p. 95. See, further, *U.S. Naval War College International Law Situations*, 1932, pp. 99–107, on the "illegal" use of mines during World War I.

poses of prize capture, the limits of bays were prescribed. It is interesting to note, however, that for such a purpose the closing line of a bay was described as being only six miles long. Prize capture involves an operation on the high seas, and a belligerent violates certain restrictions should he attempt the capture in neutral waters. Obviously, then, those naval Powers anticipatifig contraband traffic in time of future war, would want neutral waters reduced to the narrowest limits. This interest is diametrically opposite to that of naval powers who want the widest possible freedom to plant mines outward from the coast. In the Hague Conferences of 1907, the potential neutrals appeared to exercise little influence in these matters, and as we have already observed in the discard of Article 2 in Convention VIII, no agreement was reached on the limits of bays for military purposes. While there were many prize cases in World War I,[8] there were very few in World War II. The prize problem, like the matter of mining had ceased to be an influence upon the development of rules on bays. What is more important, perhaps, is the fact that all the great military Powers were engaged in these wars, and that, in contradistinction to the 18th Century, the neutrals of the 20th Century did not really have the power to enforce any rules with respect to the sanctity of their coastal waters. Under conditions of total war, the weak neutral will not enjoy respect for his status unless it appears to the opposing belligerents that there is some advantage to be gained by respecting the neutral's territory – or that there is no military advantage to be gained by violating the neutral territory. In the 20th Century, neutrality has come to thrive upon fearful hope rather than upon the intrinsic strength of those who espouse it. Under such conditions alone, it can hardly be expected that old rules on sea boundaries will grow in strength or that new ones will spring to life. Thus, during the period with which this chapter is concerned, this author concludes that the defense or military influence upon the law of bays declined and disappeared.[9]

In the introductory chapters to this book we discussed some of the current military interests in bays. We suggested that such interest would continue as long as there are navies and land-sea communications contact points. What is much more problematical is the degree of influence upon rules for bays that can be expected to arise from the military interest. There is no doubt that the 24-mile rule, if finally

[8] Hackworth, *Digest of International Law* (1943) vol. VII, pp. 232–242; Tucker, *NWC 1955*, pp. 219–26.

[9] An outstanding discussion of Neutrality and Territorial Waters is contained in U.S. Naval War College, *International Law Situations*, 1931, pp. 33–93.

adopted, together with some widening of the marginal belt will restrict naval operations to sea areas more distant from coasts. Correspondingly, it will impose a far greater burden upon neutrals who are really intent upon preventing violations of their territory should war come. On the other hand it is difficult to speculate upon the course of future naval warfare – whether it will be part of an all-out atomic conflict, a semi-nuclear war of attrition, or part of a limited war. The most that one can say here is that the trend in naval weapons development is such that in war naval forces are more likely to remain ever farther out on the high seas. On the other hand, there is a real coldwar or peace time military interest in the current efforts toward rule making. The 24-mile rule, if it is finally adopted, plus a possible acceptance of a wider marginal belt, plus more restrictive interpretations regarding innocent passage of war ships will have an additive effect in keeping operating naval forces further at sea. "Showing the flag" has always been regarded as something of a psychological policy weapon. Its effects cannot be measured with precision but, on the other hand, the post World War II effects of the mere presence of U.S. Naval Forces in some of the confined waters of the world have been regarded as considerable and sometimes crucial. For these reasons, the free world naval powers have a direct interest in restricting the sovereignty of coastal States to the smallest possible areas of internal waters and marginal belts. It does not appear at this time, however, that the military interest occupies the thinking of most coastal States to anything like the degree that the economic interest does.

Section E Some current issues

Some time ago, there appeared in the *Yale Law Review* an article entitled, "Crisis in the Law of the Sea: Community Perspectives versus National Egoism." [1] As a matter of personal choice, this author is unwilling to agree with its learned authors, Professor McDougal and Mr. Burke, that we are confronted with a crisis. Nor does he feel so gifted as to prescribe a method of solution,[2] but most certainly our

[1] Myres S. McDougal and William T. Burke, "Crisis in the Law of the Sea: Community Perspectives versus National Egoism," 67 *Yale Law Journal* (Feb. 1958), p. 551ff.

[2] The McDougal-Bufke method of solution is theoretically air tight: Through use of a systematic check-off list of research and information subjects, the matter is studied in every possible detail. In this case the topics are listed under the general headings of: The Claim to Authority Arrested, The Counterclaim, and the Modality and Degree of Interference. The authors hav e concocted a beautiful blue-print for someone else to do the work. Just how

State system is confronted with a dilemma in the presently ambiguous condition of the law of the sea.

By happenstance, the case of *United Kingdom* v. *Norway* was heard and decided during the same general time period as the undertaking by the Uited Nations International Law Commission of work on the codification of the international law of the sea. Now it does not appear that there is any provision in the Statute of the Court, or in its Rules, requiring or even suggesting that its opinions should be so couched as to reflect considerations of their possible impact upon pending "international legislation." It is elementary that this is not the purpose of the judicial process, international or municipal. Just as surely, however, is it a fact that legislators – or in the matter of codification, the International Law Commission – give careful consideration to the relevant decisions and opinions of the courts.[3] It is for this reason that we should comment upon the work of the International Court of Justice in its opinion in the Fisheries Case of *United Kingdom* v. *Norway*. Before doing so, the writer believes he should make it clear that he entertains no disagreement in the ultimate justice of the court's decision in this case. Such a conclusion, however, has been reached after independent research of the economic issues and the historic pattern of economic growth in the two countries. What is of far more concern, however, is the impact that the court's reasoning and conclusions may have upon the law of bays: whether or not the court's jurisprudence in this case will aid or retard "progressive development"

this work is to be managed is never touched upon. There is little useful purpose in commenting in detail upon this article, save to assess it broadly from three points of view:

a. The International Lawyer: The methodology indicated by the check-off lists might be excellent for formulating one's case before the International Court; it might be an excellent guide for a Judge of the International Court.

b. For the "authoritative decision-maker": It is difficult to foresee that one in such a position would read or understand the article. In other words, as a guide to action it lacks communicating qualities and is therefore nearly useless. This writer might at some future time quite possibly be required to advise a decision maker on some of the very matters discussed in the instant article. It would require a great imaginative strain and no little ingenuity to transcribe the propositions of this article into a useable blue-print for policy action.

c. For the practicing mariner and student of the law of the sea: The latter part of the article, pages 574–588, suggests that the authors may not have qualified themselves completely through technical research preparatory to constructing the framework they propose.

[3] Judge Sir Hersch Lauterpacht addresses this point with caution: "While, therefore, the codification of international law under the aegis of the United Nations must continue to be be regarded as a rational and practical object of the collective endeavor of Governments, the achievement of part of that object by other means, and in particular through the activity of the International Court itself, acquires special significance. *The Development of International Law by the International Court* (1958), p. 7.

and codification; whether States will in the future act with greater or less restrain with respect to policies on maritime sovereignty; and whether or not States will endeavor to reach agreement on the basis of objective assessment of the economic realities of a given situation.

Although the Court acknowledged that the United Kingdom has conceded Norway's entitlement "to claim as internal waters all the fjords and sunds falling within the conception of a bay as defined in international law whether the closing line is more or less than ten miles long," it took the view that the United Kingdom had not abandoned its contention that the ten-mile rule is to be regarded as a rule of international law. The court then deliberately pointed out in unequivocal terms that the 10-mile rule had not acquired the authority of a general rule of international law. In light of the concession made by the United Kingdom on this point, this author is unable to view the court's action as being anything other than gratuitous. The difficulty as Judge Lauterpacht points out is:

> it was not so much any inherent excellence of that more widely adopted rule which raises questions concerning the legislative action of the Court as the possibility that no system, fully elaborated, was put in its place.[4]

Then, by positing the principle of the "general direction of the coast," and by an absence of any further effort at clarification, the court's opinion lends itself to the interpretation that the legal conception of the bay has been abandoned. This writer is reluctant to believe that such was the intention of the Court,[5] but further guidance was certainly not offered. Judge Lauterpacht comments: "Some judicial clarification or international regulation of the subject is urgently desireable."[6] There has been effort at regulation through the work of the International Law Commission and States have not sought to abandon the concept of a bay. The length of the closing line has, however, been the subject of "see-saw" voting in a manner that suggests a lack of careful consideration of its importance within the overall complex of influences impinging upon the law of bays and the necessity of possible changes thereto. While the Court was quite willing to legislate one rule out of existence, it did not undertake to offer, even implicitly through the

[4] Judge Lauterpacht, in commenting upon this action in his *Development* (1958), pp. 190–1, is more restrained than in his 8th Edition of Oppenheim, but he is none the less pointed.

[5] Lauterpacht writes: "It is possible that, far from holding that the size of the bay is irrelevant, the intention of the court was to lay down that if the shores are very far apart then they must be considered as separate coasts to which, therefore, the principle of the general direction of the coast does not apply." *Oppenheim's International Law*, vol. I, 8th Ed., p. 507n.

[6] Lauterpacht, *Oppenheim*, p. 507.

course of careful reasoning, any but vague compensatory guidance for possible future development of another rule. The ever increasing interdependence of States is such that the Court's essentially negative action is far from helpful.[7]

In defending the Court in this action, former Judge de Visscher takes pains to point out that the Court rejected technical formulas in deference to an exceptional set of facts. In this one must agree. But then, this writer believes, it is quite incumbent upon the Court to ensure that its opinion reflects the most careful evaluation of those facts. If one relates the opinion to the actual contentions and arguments of the parties and to the voluminous evidence in the record, there is room to doubt whether the court did make such an evaluation: the language of the opinion would hardly suggest it. A charitable view, perhaps, might be that the ten-man majority were simply unable to express with sufficient clarity the reasoning behind their decision; and this is understandable.[8]

It is almost trite to say that conflicting economic interests brought this case before the International Court of Justice. The controversy had been underway for some forty years, and the multiple, interdependent and cumulative economic factors gave the controversy a quality of gathering intensity over that time. It is apparent that the relative economic positions of the Parties litigant loomed large in the Court's decision. Just how large, however, and in what proportion to factors of geography and of historical record are not clearly spelled out.[9] Admittedly an opinion of the type envisioned above might be lengthy, complicated, and demanding of special expertise on the part of the members (or expert opinion as permitted by Article 50 of the Statute). But to do less would seem to ignore a challenging responsibility for judicial statesmanship. It is this author's belief that a more carefully written evaluation of the relevant factors influencing its decision would have, by reason of the stature of the Court and the inherent wisdom of such an approach, furnished tha States with

[7] Charles de Visscher in *Theory and Reality in Public International Law* (1957), at pp. 154–5, defends this action as does former Judge Manley O. Hudson in "The Thirtieth Year of the World Court," 46 *American Journal of International Law*, (1952), pp. 609–630.

[8] See Shabtai Rosenne, *The International Court of Justice* (1957), Ch. XIII. Mr. R. O. Wilberforce suggests that language differences and the diverse backgrounds of the members may contribute to the difficulties. "Some Aspects of the Anglo-Norwegian Fisheries Case," 38 *Transcations of the Grotius Society* (1952), pp. 151–168.

[9] It is to be noted that Judge Hackworth (U.S.), in his terse concurring opinion, indicated that he agreed with operative part of the judgment solely because the Norwegian Government had proved the existence of an historic title to the disputed water areas. It would have more helpful had he seen fit to share with the world the breath and depth of his probity.

objective guidance which can emanate from no other source; it might have aided more materially both the International Law Commission and the 1958 Geneva Conference.

The economic issue appears currently to be the most prominent one in the law on bays. It serves no useful purpose to ignore it by resort to abstract or irrelevant legal concepts when States are fully aware of the root cause of controversy. What is desireable, however, is that all Parties concerned in future international legislation on the law of bays exercise restraint both in their unilateral claims and in the positions they take at international conferences where the law of the sea is to be considered.

While there are certain technical and drafting problems connected with establishing a system for determining when a bay should be deemed to exist, the real issue is the length of the closing line. Since the International Court of Justice saw fit to sweep away any mystique inherent in the 10-mile rule, the length of the closing line has become something of a legislative football in which various views and arguments on it have been expressed. Emerging from the arena is a 24-mile rule. Whether or not this rule represents a true equilibrium as among conflicting interests in the Community of States remains to be seen. The need for it has not, in this writer's eyes, been demonstrated. Its birth came through a cleverly conceived legislative artifice in the which closing line for the internal waters in a bay was made a mathematical function of a not yet agreed upon width of the marginal belt. Perhaps an agreement on this width is better than no agreement at all. This writer's concern, however, is that in its formulation, the influences of defense, navigation and economics seem not to have been convincingly argued or considered. For the development of the law of the future, it is suggested that the International Court come very firmly to grips with the economic issues involved, and that international bodies, either on the technical or the political level, do likewise.

CHAPTER FIVE

EFFORTS AT CODIFICATION

Section A UNOFFICIAL BODIES

Shortly after the Hague Codification Conference of 1930, the late Professor Brierly observed that the ideal of codification is that law should be embodied in a systematic written form. He observed further:

> It is an ideal never completely realizable, because law that is living contains an element of growth and cannot be finally or exhaustively imprisoned in a series of propositions however detailed and numerous.[1]

Professor Brierly thus states, in the briefest possible way, the principal motivation for codifying international law as well as the principal stumbling block of codification. Hackworth and others [2] have cited the two generally held views on codification: (a) "that it should consist of restating existing international law, and (b) that it should consist of stating what international law should be." Without at this moment entering into further discussion of these views, we shall endeavor to trace some of the earlier efforts at codification of the law of bays.

[1] J. L. Brierly, "The Future of Codification," 12 *British Yearbook of International Law* (1931), pp. 1–12. With respect to the law of territorial waters, the late Professor John Basset Moore had some not very encouraging remarks concerning the prospect of codification: "Concerning territorial waters, the best that could be done was to incorporate various points of view in a report. On the strength of an early and long familiarity with this subject, as a student, as an administrator and as a participant in the interpretation and making of treaties, I do not hesitate to say that the subject of territorial waters is mong those that are least susceptible of codification. The physical conditions affecting the questions are of almost infinite variety." 50 *Harvard Law Review* (1937), pp. 395, 403, cited by Marjorie M. Whiteman, "The Territorial Sea," 49 *Proceedings of the American Society of International Law* (1956), pp. 116–124.

[2] *Digest of International Law* (1940), vol. I, p. 44; Sir Hersch Lauterpacht expands upon this short statement in the following fashion:

> Codification has at least two distinct meanings: (1) The process of translating into statutes or conventions customary law and the rules arising from the decisions of tribunals with little or no alteration of the law, and (2) the process of securing, by means of general conventions, agreement among the states upon certain topics of International Law, those conventions based upon existing law, both customary and conventional, but modified so as to reconcile conflicting views and render agreement possible.

Oppenheim's International Law, vol. I, 8th Ed., p. 57n.

Table of Brief Statements on Bays, as quoted from the works representative of publicists in the period 1800–1910

Scholar	Country	Date	Work	Statements	Sources
Azuni	Italian	1805	*Droit Maritime de l'Europe.*	Previously cited, see pp. 134, above.	(See col. 4)
Emmerich de Vattel	Swiss	1758	*Droit des Gens*, etc.	"A bay, entrance into which can be prevented, may be possessed and made subject to the laws of the sovereign."	*The Law of Nations*, etc.; Fenwick Translation, 1916, p. 111.
Johann K. Bluntschli	Germany	1895	*Le Droit International Codifié*, 5th rev.	"Certain parts of the sea are so closely united to the land that they ought, in a certain measure at least, be considered as a part of the territory of the adjacent State. ... We can only invoke an exception to the general rule of the liberty of the seas on serious grounds and when the extent of the bay is small." (Excepts Hudson Bay and King's Chambers).	Sect. 309; Crocker, *Extent of the Marginal Sea,* (1919), pp. 9–10.
Carlos Calvo	Argentina	1896	*Le Droit International théorétique et pratique.*	"Harbors and roadsteads belong of right to the nation which inhabits the adjacent coasts." Gulfs and bays regulated by same principles. Asserts protection principle of islands, sand bars, rocks, or cross-fire of guns.	Sections 366, 367 of Volume I. (See col. 4)
Ferdinand Baron de Cussy	French	1856	*Phares et Causes Célèbres du Droit Maritime des Nations.*	"Sovereignty extends over maritime regions, such as roadsteads, bays, gulfs and straits whose entrance and exit may be defended by cannon."	Section 40, p. 95. (See col. 4)
Frantz C. R. Despagnet	French	1910	*Cours de Droit International Public* 1910.	Asserts cannon shot rule. On 10-mile rule, he writes: "... reasonable account has been taken of the results	p. 620. (See col. 4)

				of experience, which permit the assertion that the bay may be effectively controlled from the two shores so long as the space between them does not exceed 10 miles.	
Laurent Hautefeuille	French	1868	*Des Droits et des Devoirs des Nations Neutres en Temps de Guerre Maritime.*	"... Seacoasts do not present a straight and regular line. If the maritime domain were always to be measured from every point of the coast, great inconveniences would result. Thus, it is agreed by usage to draw an imaginary line from one headland to another and to take this line as the point of departure for the range of cannon shot."	p. 53, vol. 1. (See col. 4)
James Kent	American	1896 (14th Ed.)	*Commentaries on American Law.*	"Considering the great extent of the line of the American coasts, we have a right to claim, for fiscal and defensive regulations, a liberal extension of maritime jurisdiction; and it would not be unreasonable, as I apprehend, to assume, for domestic purposes connected with our safety and welfare, the control of the waters on our coasts, though included within lines stretching from quite distant headlands, as, for instance, from Cape Ann to Cape Cod, and from Nantucket to Montauk Point, etc."	p. 29. (See col. 4)
Johan L. Kleber	German	1874 (2nd Ed.)	*Droit des Gens Moderne de l'Europe.*	"Within the maritime territory of a State are included those maritime districts or regions susceptible of exclusive possession over which the State has acquired ... and retained sovereignty. To these districts belong	Section 130, p. 180. (See col. 4)

Continued

Scholar	Country	Date	Work	Statements	Sources
				those parts of the ocean ... if they can be commanded by cannon from the two shores, or the entrance of which may be forbidden to vessels; that is gulfs, bays, and creeks."	
Albert G. De Lapradelle	French	1898	"The Right of the State over the Territorial Sea."	"Harbors, roadsteads and bays are a matter apart. They form part of what may be called the national sea, in order to express the idea that the waters that penetrate thus closely into the land form a body within the territory and are associated with it in forming the country ... The notion of the territorial sea was formed on the basis of cannon at an epoch when coasts were provided with guns for defense. *Today* [1898] the defense of our coasts rests on utterly different ideas ... Territorial Sea in its precise sense does not include harbors, roadsteads and indentations whose opening upon the open sea is less than 10 or 12 marine miles wide.	5 *Revue Générale de Droit International Public* (1898), p. 264. Crocker, *Extent*, pp. 183–236.
Joseph Latour	French	1889	*La Mer territoriale au point de vue théorétique et Pratique.*	"In regard to gulfs and bays we will note that when the openings do not exceed double cannon range their waters are territorial ... this delimitation only concerns the bays whose openings do not exceed 10 miles.	Crocker, *Extent*, p. 255.

Rev. Thomas J. Lawrence	English	1913	*The Principles of International Law.* 5th Ed.	"The claims of States to large tracts of marginal waters – claims which are themselves relics of yet wider claims to dominion over oceans and seas – increase the difficulty of the question. Some of them are dead or dormant; but when a valuable fishery is retained for native fishermen by the assertion of sovereignty over a bay of considerable size, or when considerations of self-protection or political advantages are prominent, we find that States insist upon and often obtain recognition of their demands, some of which are based on very ancient precedent."	p. 143. (See col. 4)
Franz von Liszt	Germany	1907	*Das Völkerrecht,* 5th Ed.	"The border of the inner portion of bays and inlets is determined by drawing an imaginary straight line from headland to headland at the width of the bay where the middle point of the line can be reached by the cannons placed upon both headlands of the shore. From this line landward lies the enclosed bay, and on the other side toward the open sea the coastal waters begin."	p. 88 (see col. 4). Crocker, *Extent,* p. 294.
Ernest Nys	Belgian	1904	*Le Droit International.*	"When the distance between the two shores is less than one of the distances just indicated [10, 12 miles or twice cannon range] . . . the gulf or bay is assimilated to ports, coves, closed roadsteads, and harbors."	p. 442. (See col. 4)
Marquis de Olivart	Spanish	1903	*Tratado de Derecho Internacional Publico,* 4th Ed.	"If the mainland, through explosive mines and batteries under its control can completely command the en-	p. 205. (See col. 4). Crocker, *Extent,* p. 335.

Continued

Scholar	Country	Date	Work	Statements	Sources
				trance into a gulf or bay, it is evident that all that portion of the sea should be considered territorial."	
H. B. Oppenheim	Germany	1866	*System des Völkerrechts*, 2nd Ed.	"It is ... self-evident that inland seas form a part of the State or territory, since they are actually surrounded by the same ... The actual maritime sovereignty of the State is therefore limited to the ports, mouths of rivers, etc."	p. 128. (See col. 4)
Jean F. Ortolan (Naval Officer)	French	1853	*Règles Internationales et Diplomatie de la Mer*, 2nd Ed.	"We must classify under the same heading as roadsteads and ports, gulfs and bays ... when these indentations made in a single State do not exceed in width the double range of cannon or when the entrance may be controlled by artillery or when it is naturally defended by islands, banks, or rocks."	p. 156. (See col. 4)
Sir Robert Phillimore	British	1879	*Commentaries Upon International Law*, 3rd Ed.	"Maritime territorial rights extend as a general rule, over arms of the sea, bays, gulfs, estuaries which are enclosed, but not entirely surrounded by lands belonging to one and the same State.	Vol. I–CC. Crocker, *Extent*, p. 381. (See col. 4)
P. Pradier-Fodère	French	1885	*Traité de Droit International Public.*	"Gulfs are parts of the sea which encroach upon the land. Bays are like gulfs in which ships are sheltered from certain winds. Gulfs of smaller extent and more specifically bays	p. 157. (See co. 14)

				whose extent is generally restricted are within the sovereignty of the State into which the part of the sea which forms them encroaches. . . ."	
Raestad	Norwegian	1913	*La Mer territoriale.*	"Quant aux baies, y compris les embouchures des grands fleuves, et aux fjords ainsi qu'aux parties de la mer enfermées par des îles et des îlots, c'est une question d'histoires de savoir jusqu'à quelle mesure ils auront été occupés par l'Etat riverain: car il s'agit là vraiment de parcelles de la mer faisant partie intégrante du corps de l'Etat."	p. 171 (See col. 4)
Alphonse Rivier	Swiss	1896	*Principes du Droit des Gens.*	"A gulf, even though surrounded by a single State, is a free sea if its entrance is too wide to be dominated from the shore. It is generally admitted that this is the case where the distance between the shores is more than 10 marine miles."	p. 153 (See col. 4)
Walter M. A. Schücking	German	1897	*Das Küstenmeer im Internationalen Rechte.*	". . . .it is only logical to infer that if the entrance of a bay does not exceed 10 sea miles the bay as such is property of the State. . . ."	p. 22. (See col. 4)
CDR Carlos Testa, RPortN	Portuguese	1886	*Le Droit Public International*	"We can not doubt, therefore, that ports and creeks belong, under the title of *property* to the nation which is mistress of the shore, and that the right of property gives rise to a right of domain. . . . The considerations above apply equally to gulfs and bays whose shores belong to the same Power, when the entrance or mouth is not so wide as to be unable to be	p. 68. (See col. 4) Crocker, *Extent*, p. 448.

Continued

Scholar	Country	Date	Work	Statements	Sources
				commanded by the crossfire of artillery or when they are naturally defended by island, banks, or reefs which render their permanent or effective possession possible."	
John Westlake	British	1910	*International Law, Part I,* 2nd Ed.	"It is enough on *terra firma th*at the sovereign's police should be adequate to render breach of his laws exceptional."	p. 187. (See col. 4)

(1) *The Institute of International Law*

The title of this section is Unofficial Bodies, and by this is meant groups of international legal scholars who have from time to time assembled for the purpose of codifying the law with a view toward assisting Governments and individuals in achieving a clearer understanding of what the law appears to be, or, in light of objectively studied circumstances, what the law should be. It appears that the first such organization was the Institute of International Law, founded in 1873.[3] This group first addressed itself to the subject of the definition and regime of territorial waters at its Lausanne session in 1888. Certainly the time was ripe for an international body of scholars to attempt to reconcile their views on this subject and to formulate a code reflecting those views as well as the latest practices of States. Before and during the protracted period in which the institute worked in this field, individual scholars drew up general international law codes or special codes relating to the law of the sea. Such individual efforts no doubt influenced the work of both unofficial and official bodies that followed. Space does not permit discussion of the writings of these individual publicists. In the table attached hereto, however, are such excerpts from the works of a number of them as have to do with bays (Pages 188–194, above). The table lists only writers whose works appeared before or during the work of the Institute of International Law and the International Law Association. The selection of writers has been based partly upon nationality and partly upon whether the work cited contained something significant prescient or unusual. Thus, certain writers, such as Creasy, Wheaton and Twiss have not been mentioned.

Mr. Crocker writes that the value of the conclusions of this unofficial but highly authoritative international society of publicists is very great.[4] Many of the writers listed in the accompanying table were members of the Institute and participated in its deliberations. As we read and cogitate over their writings in the mid-twentieth century, however, we are apt to be struck by the fact that many of these scholars wrote in a manner which failed to reflect the economic, military and political changes taking place in the world about them. De Lapradelle, however, is a very distinguished exception to this statement.

[3] Alberic Rolin, *Les Origines de l'Institut de Droit International* (1923).

[4] *Extent of the Marginal Sea*, p. 107.

The rules adopted at the Paris meeting of 1894 gave a width of 6 miles to the territorial sea. The article on bays reads:

Article 3

Pour les baies, la mer territoriale suit les sinuosités de la côte, sauf qu'elle est mesurée à partir d'une ligne droite tirée en travers de la baie dans la partie la plus rapprochée de l'ouverture vers la mer, où l'écart entre les deux côtes de la baie est douze milles marins de largeur, à moins qu'un usage continu et séculaire n'ait consacré une largeur plus grande.[5]

It would be erroneous to jump to the conclusion that the 12-mile rule was simply enacted to effect a whole-number function of the width of the territorial sea. It represents a compromise, although the predominating factor considered was a 6-mile or 12,000 yard cannon range. On the other hand, the members were apparently in agreement that there was a well-understood difference between sovereignty in a bay and sovereignty over the marginal belt.

(2) *The International Law Association*

Subsequently, at a meeting of the International Law Association [6] in Brussels in 1895, the bay rule was altered, perhaps by reason of the cogently argued plea of the British international lawyer Thomas (later, Sir Thomas) Barclay. Mr. Barclay pointed out that the varying and uncertain cannon-shot limit might be satisfactory as a juridical basis in respect of the rights of neutrals, but that for other purposes, especially fishery rights, such a juridical basis lacked too much in the way of desired certainty. Mr. Barclay carried his point, and the International Law Association, in adopting the articles of the Institute, substituted 10 marine miles for the width of the juridical bay.[7]

[5] XIII *Annuaire de l'Institut de droit international* (1894–95), p. 329.

[6] The International Law Association is an organization of much wider membership than the Institute, and it is open to individuals who are not specialists. Founded in 1873, its former name was: The Association for the Reform and Codification of the Law of Nations.

[7] The International Law Association, *Report of the Seventeenth Conference held at Brussels* (1895), p. 102. In subsequent years, the Association has concerned itself with bays or with territorial waters in general: A. H. Charteris, "Territorial Jurisdiction in Wide Bays," Report of the Twenty-Third Conference held at Berlin (1906), p. 103; Dr. Deszo Dorday, "Notes upon the Question of the Delimitation of Territorial Waters," *Report of the Twenty-Fifth Conference held at Budapest* (1908), p. 547; Draft Rules submitted by Professor Alejandro Alvarez, *Report of the Thirty-Third Conference held at Stockholm* (1924), p. 267. (In this draft, Professor Alvarez recommended a 12-mile closing line for bays). Amended Draft Rules, *Report of the Thirty-Fourth Conference of the International Law Association held at Vienna* (1926), p. 387. (In this draft a 10-mile closing line is recommended.

(3) *U. S. Naval War College* [8]

The naval offiver students at the War College during the school year of 1912–13 were assigned, among others, the following topic for study and solution:

What regulations should be made in regard to the use in time of war of the marginal sea and other waters?[9]

Solution of this problem involved a codification of the applicable international law as then conceived. It is to be emphasized, however, that the regulations were to apply in time of war. For the most part, then, the regulations had to do with relationships between belligerents and neutrals, as is suggested by Article 1 of the student-formulated regulations:

1. Acts of war are prohibited in neutral waters and in waters neutralized by convention.

In arriving at their regulation concerning bays, there was a reasonably thorough explanation of the writings of publicists, the then recent work of the Institute of International Law, and the practice of various States. The general conclusions reached by the Naval War College upon completion of its codification study are believed worthy of quotation in this volume, written nearly fifty years later:

General conclusion. – It is evident that there is wide diversity in the ideas as to maritime jurisdiction. This diversity has led to an increasing number of complications in recent years because of the development of closer international relations and the more general use of the area under maritime jurisdiction. The ancient rules do not seem adapted to modern conditions. The policies and practices of the leading maritime states have often been inconsistent. The maritime states

[8] At one time, the Naval War College, located at Newport, Rhode Island undertook rather extensive studies in those aspects of International Law that impinge upon the practice of the Naval Officers' profession. The fruits of these studies were embodied in a series of publications, called 'blue books' which, starting in 1901, were issued annually. The primary reason for these publications was to keep responsible operating naval officers informed of solutions to problems which might very possibly confront them. As naval warfare has become increasingly complex, the War College has had to reduce the time and scope of its International Law studies in deference to other urgent requirements. The 'Blue Book' series has been continued. RADM Thomas H. Robbins, Jr., USN, "The Study of International Law at the Naval War College," 50 *American Journal of International Law* (1956), pp. 659–663. The reference for the instant study is *Naval War College International Law Topics and Discussions*, 1913, pp. 11–53. The 1960 Naval War College Blue Book, being written by Professor Carl W. Franklin of the University of Southern California, is concerned with the 1958 Geneva Conference on the Law of the Sea.

[9] The "codification" undertaken by the War College has been referred to with some frequency by publicists. For that reason it is included in this book. It is to be emphasized, however, that although the work was done in a U.S. Government institution, this codification was definitely in the "unofficial" category.

are beginning to seek for a sound basis for exercise of jurisdiction over neighboring waters. This basis may be limited in some degree by the changing range of cannon, but ultimately must have a more substantial basis in the reciprocal well being of the shore state and of the states which use the waters. This latter idea has more and more entered into the recent propositions in regard to defining maritime jurisdiction. While belligerents have rights upon the open sea and in their own waters, these rights are conditioned by the rights of neutrals, and the reverse may be equally true. It is necessary that regulations recognize this reciprocity of rights as well as the practice and precedents. The following regulations seem to embody the broad principles coming to be generally recognized in regard to maritime jurisdiction in time of war.[10]

It was the year 1913. The following regulations are arrived at by the U.S. Naval War College, pertinent to our study:

3. The area of maritime war:
 (a) The sea outside of neutral jurisdiction.
 (b) Gulfs, bays, roadsteads, ports, and other waters of the belligerents.

4. Limitations:
 (a)
 (b)
 (c) Gulfs and bays. – The jurisdiction of an adjacent state over the sea extends outward 6 miles from a line drawn between the opposite shores of the entrance to the waters of gulfs or bays where the distance first narrows to 12 miles.

(4) *Other unofficial codifications between 1913 and 1929.*

These are included primarily as a matter of record rather than by reason of their having any great value or observable influence.

(a) Projet de règlement relatif à la Mer territoriale en Temps de Paix, L'Institut de Droit International, Stockholm, 1928.[11]

Article 3

L'étendue de la Mer Territoriale se compte, des côtes, à partir de la limite de la basse marée; des ports, à partir de l'extrémité vers le large de leur ouvrage fixe le plus avancé; pour les baies et les golfes appartenant au même Etat, à partir d'une droite tirée en travers de la partie la plus rapprochée de l'ouverture de la mer où l'écart entre les deux côtes n'excède pas dix milles marins, à moins qu'un usage international n'ait consacré une largeur plus grande.

Pour les baies dont les eaux baignent des territoires appartenant à deux ou plusieurs Etats, la Mer Territoriale suit les sinuosités des côtes.

(b) Project No. 10 on "National Domain," submitted to the International Commission of Jurists at Rio de Janeiro, April 1927, by the American Institute of International Law.[12]

[10] The preface to *NWC 1913* indicated that the notes, of which this general conclusion is a part, were drawn up by Professor George Grafton Wilson of Harvard University, long-time Associate in International Law at the Naval War College.

[11] 23 *American Journal of International Law* (April 1929), Special Supplement, p. 368.

[12] *Ibid.*, p. 370.

Article 6

For bays extending into the territory of a single American Republic the territorial sea follows the sinuosities of the coast, except that it is measured from a straight line drawn across the bay at the point nearest the opening into the sea where the two coasts of the bay are separated by a distance of... marine miles, unless a greater width shall have been sanctioned by continued and well established usage.

In the case of an international bay whose coasts belong to two or more different countries, the territorial sea follows the sinuosities of the coast, unless there exists a convention to the contrary.

(c) Draft Convention on Law of Maritime Jurisdiction in Time of Peace. The International Law Association, 1926.[13]

Article 7

With regard to bays and gulfs, territorial waters shall follow the sinuosities of the coast, unless an occupation or an established usage generally recognized by Nations has sanctioned a greater limit.

Article 8

Where a territorial jurisdiction for a special purpose over bays, gulfs or other arms or parts of the sea is conceded to a State by international agreement, whether express or implied, the jurisdiction so exercised shall be limited strictly to the purpose for which it is conceded.

(d) Draft rules prepared by the Kokusaibo-Gakkwai (Japanese International Law Association) in connection with the Japanese branch of the International Law Association, 1926.[14]

Rules concerning the Extent of Littoral Waters and of Powers Exercised Therein by the Littoral State

Article 2

In the case of bays and gulfs, the coasts of which belong to the same State, the littoral waters extend seawards at right angles from a straight line drawn across the bay or gulf at the first point nearest the open sea where the width does not exceed ten marine miles, unless a greater width had been established by immemorial usage.

In the case of bays and gulfs the coasts of which belong to two or more States, the littoral waters follow the trend of the coasts according to the general rule. In those portions of such bays and gulfs where the distance between the two coasts does not amount to six marine miles, the dividing line between the respective littoral waters shall in principle be the middle line measured from the two coasts.

(5) *The Harvard Law School Research in International Law, 1929.*[15]

The Harvard Law School Research was organized for the purpose of preparing drafts of international conventions on each of three subjects

[13] *Ibid.*, p. 373; Report of Thirty-Fourth Conference of International Law Association (1926), p. 101.

[14] 23 *American Journal of International Law* (April 1929), Special Supplement, p. 376; 25 *Revue de Droit International et Diplomatie* (Tokyo), July 1926.

[15] 23 *American Journal of International Law* (April 1929), Special Supplement.

selected by the Eighth Assembly of the Leauge of Nations to be dealt with at the First Conference on the Codification of International Law. The League Assembly Resolution, dated 27 September 1927, contemplated the holding of such a conference in 1929. One of the three subjects to be examined was territorial waters. Noteworthy in the Assembly resolution is the recommendation contained in sub-paragraph (6) (d):

The spirit of the codification, which should not confine itself to the mere registration of the existing rules, but should aim at adapting them as far as possible to contemporary conditions of international life.[16]

The General Introduction to the Research Report reads that "forty-four scholars and jurists were invited to become members of an Advisory Committee under the direction of which the Research was to be conducted." The individuals who accepted the invitations could hardly have been a more distinguished group of American scholars and jurists. They included, among a host of others, Judge Learned Hand, Professor Hyde, the then Judge Charles Evans Hughes, and Professor Philip C. Jessup. For the Research on the Law of Territorial Waters, the reporter was Professor George Grafton Wilson. His advisors numbered six professors and four members of the bar, and included one former Attorney General of the United States. The group dealing with territorial waters is indicated as having met fourteen times over a period of eleven months. There is no evidence in the record that this group of distinguished scholars and lawyers took the opportunity during their deliberations to hear or consult with experts in any of a number of other fields, such as geopgraphers, mariners, naval

[16] Professor Jesse M. Reeves wrote that this Resolution resulted from the position taken by M. Politis, *rapporteur* of the first assembly committee on codification. Sub-paragraph (d) of the Resolution reads:

(d) *Rule of the Spirit of the Codification.* Codification of international law can be imagined in several forms. It might be a mere registration of the law in force. It might be something more if, instead of merely recording the rules already in existence, an attempt were made to adapt them to practical needs. Lastly, it might be an entirely original work designed to make good the present deficiencies in the law or to repalce the old rules by new. Although it is very difficult to lay down strictly beforehand in what spirit the work of the First Codification Conference should be conducted, it can be stated that while, in order to lead to useful results, the conference must refrain from making too many innovations, it cannot limit itself to the mere registration of the existing law. It must, as far as possible, adapt the rules to contemporary conditions of international life. It is in order to avoid any misunderstanding on this matter that the states which are to take part in the conference should be apprised of the spirit in which the work of codification is to be undertaken. Jesse S. Reeves. "The Hague Conference on the Codification of International Law," 24 *American Journal of International Law* (1930), p. 55; see also, L. of N. V. Legal. 1927. V. 28 (C. 548, M. 196, 1927, V), p. 48.

officers, marine biologists, and various specialized engineers. Nor were representatives of such interest groups as fishery associations or merchant shipping groups consulted. While it is an all too easy matter to criticize some thirty years after the event, one should nonetheless note the wise and perhaps troubled tenor of Professor Wilson's 1913 War College General Conclusions [17] as well as the League Assembly's recommendation in its Resolution of 27 September 1927, noted above.[18] But, judging from the content of other drafts prepared before and at the time of the Harvard effort, one can perhaps safely conclude that the Harvard work was simply representative of the then prevailing temper of international legal scholarship.[19] Moreover, one must keep in mind that the League had decided on codification and the Harvard Research had been conceived as a private undertaking to assist in the effort. While a thorough exploration of all the causal factors at work might have brought forth some cogent warnings, it would probably not have affected the action looking toward codification within the then generally agreed upon framework.

The Research on territorial waters is introduced by noting the misleading quality of the words themselves, and by advising that no provision is made for special problems arising between neutrals and belligerents in time of war. The draft divides territorial waters into the marginal sea and inland waters (called in this book, respectively, the marginal belt and internal waters). Use of the term, inland waters, was perhaps unfortunate inasmuch as it is primarily an American term associated with special rule of navigation. Although the Research cited the somewhat ponderously written opinion of Judge Hough in *United States* v. *Newark Meadows Improvement Co.* (1909),[20] they did nothing to remove the confusion in terms brought about by this uniquely United States usage.

The article of the Harvard Research draft of particular interest to us is this:

[17] Page 197, above.

[18] Page 200, above.

[19] That there were some articulate persons not altogether smitten by the then seemingly great confidence in the purely legalistic approach is evident in the article by Richard W. Hale, "Territorial Waters as a Test of Codification," 24 *American Journal of International Law* (1930), pp. 65–8, in which he complains against the attempt at codification expressed in spatial rather than in causal terms.

[20] 173 Fed. 426, 428; see p. 4, above.

Article 5

The seaward limit of a bay or river-mouth the entrance to which does not exceed ten miles in width is a line drawn across the entrance. The seaward limit of a bay or river-mouth the entrance to which exceeds ten miles in width is a line drawn across the bay or river mouth first narrows to ten miles.

In the somewhat lengthy comment that follows this Article, it is acknowledged that the word bay has been variously used. The Opinion, Recommendation and The Dissent of Dr. Drago in the North Atlantic Fisheries Arbitration are mentioned, as are a number of other decisions, but the Research did not undertake to define a bay, or to distinguish between base-line situations and bays.

Little is to be accomplished in pointing out further the shortcomings of the Harvard Research save to note that its members, however devoted they may have been, seem to have been quite unable to proceed further than to the limit established for them by past decision and practice. If the published record of their accomplishement accurately reflects the range of their contemplation, then the following quotation from that record appears accurately to describe the limit of that rather unimaginative contemplation:

There seems to be no established practice with reference to special measurement of the marginal sea in front of roadsteads or ports, apart from the usage with reference to bays.

Section B THE HAGUE CODIFICATION CONFERENCE OF 1930.[1]

The International Conference for the Codification of International Law met at The Hague from 13 March until 12 April 1930, and it was the first international conference specificallly called for that purpose. While this experiment in the creation of a sort of International Legislature is extremely interesting as a subject for general study, others have undertaken such a study, adequately and repeatedly. For that reason, we shall discuss only so much of the background and workings of the conference as appears to contribute to our subject, the law of

[1] Besides the League of Nations documents relating to the Conference, discussions of the procedures before and during the Conference are to be found, among others, in: Antonio Sanchez de Bustamente y Sirven, *The Territorial Sea* (1930), at pp. 63–77; Gilbert Gidel, *Le Droit International public de la Mer* (1934), Tome III, at various pages; J. S. Reeves, "Hague Conference on Codification of International Law," 24 *American Journal of International Law* (1930) pp. 52–57; Manley O. Hudson, "First Conference for Codification of International Law," *Ibid.*, pp. 447–466; Jesse S. Reeves, "Codification of the Law of Territorial Waters," *Ibid.*, pp. 486–499; S. Whittemore Boggs, "Delimitation of the Territorial Sea," *Ibid.*, pp. 541–555; Hunter Miller, "The Hague Codification Conference," *Ibid.*, pp. 674–693.

bays. The background to this conference will be noted in a step-by-step chronicle of events:

(1) On 22 September 1924, the Fifth Assembly of the League of Nations adopted a resolution requesting the Council of the League to convoke a committee of experts for the purpose of preparing a list of subjects of international law the regulation of which would seem most desirable and realizable, and after soliciting advice from the various Governments, to report on the questions which are sufficiently ripe for codification.[2]

(2) The Committee of Experts was duly appointed,[3] and after two meetings, they sent to the Governments questionnaires concerning seven subjects. Upon receipt of replies the Committee reported to the Council that seven subjects were ripe for codification. This report was submitted to the League Assembly. With respect to the question of territorial waters, the Committee of experts communicated to the various Governments under date of 29 January 1926 an amended draft Convention.[4] The Article in that draft relating to bays reads:

Article 4

Bays

In the case of bays which are bordered by the territory of a single State, the territorial sea shall follow the sinuosities of the coast, except that it shall be measured from a straight line drawn across the bay at the part nearest to the opening towards the sea where the distance between the two shores of the bay is ten marine miles, unless a greater distance has been established by continuous and immemorial usage. The waters of such bays are to be assimilated to internal waters.

In the case of bays which are bordered by the territory of two or more States, the territorial sea shall follow the sinuosities of the coast.

League of Nations Document C. 196, M. 70, 1927V. contains the detailed replies to the questionnaire and specific comments on this draft. Three States (France, Italy and Poland) took a negative attitude toward the possibility of success in the project. Five States

[2] 23 *American Journal of International Law* (1929), Special Supplmeent, p. 1.

[3] There was appointed a sub-committee on territorial waters: Dr. Walther Schücking (Germany), Dr. Barbosa de Magalbaes, (Portugal) and Mr. George Wickersham (U.S.A.). Bustamente, *Territorial Sea*, p. 63.

[4] The original draft, called a Project of Agreement, provided for a rather interesting innovation called an International Waters Office and Register which was to be an administrative registry for all the then present and future claims to sovereignty over sea areas. The original draft article on bays provided for a 12-mile closing line, and further provided that the article on the Waters Office shall apply to all present historic bay claims, and, further, that no such rights could be acquired in the future. After debates in the Subcommittee, the Waters Office project was abandoned, and the article on bays was changed to read as it is quoted here. Bustamente, *Territorial Sea*, pp. 64–6.

abstained from offering an opinion, and twenty-eight indicated more or less optimistic views with respect to a codification.

(3) On 27 September 1927, the Eight Assembly adopted a resolution to submit for examination to a Conference three questions for Codification. One of these was the question of territorial waters. The resolution entrusted the Council with the task of appointing a Preparatory Committee of five persons who were to prepare a report comprising detailed bases of discussion on each of the three codification questions, including that of territorial waters.[5]

(4) The Preparatory Committee prepared an elaborate questionnaire in respect of the three codification subjects and transmitted it to the Governments. This was called a schedule of points.[6] With respect to bays, the points read:

B. Territorial Waters

IV. Determination of the base line for calculation of the breadth of territorial waters.

a. Along the coasts....
b. In front of bays. Breadth of the bay to be taken into account. Historic bays. Bays whose costs belong to two or more States.
c. In front of ports.

(5) With the replies before them, the Preparatory Committee drew up what were called "Bases" on each point that had been raised in the three subjects. These were bases of discussion at the Conference. They were printed, together with the questionnaire and the replies of the various Governments, in booklets called "Brown Books." Twenty-two Governments replied on the point having to do with bays.

Pausing to reflect upon this elaborate pre-conference preparation, one must concede that the system was a model of ingenuity, and in the absence of any previous experience in the conduct of a conference convened primarily for the purpose of codifying international law, one could hardly devise a system of preparation which might have appeared more mechanically sound.[7] What was not and perhaps could

[5] 23 *American Journal of International Law* (1929), Special Supplement, p. 2. The Counci appointed to this committee: M. Jules Basdevant (France), Sen. Carlos Castro Ruiz (Colombia), Mr. J. P. A. Francois (Netherlands), Mr. Cecil Hurst (Great Britain), Sig. Massimo Pilatti (Italy). Bustamente, *Territorial Sea*, p. 70.

[6] Leaugue of Nations Document C. 44.M.21.1928.V.

[7] For critical views of the preparation of the Conference, see: Mamley O. Hudson, "The First Conference for the Codification of International Law," 24 *American Journal of International Law* (1930), pp. 447–466; Hunter Miller, "The Hague Codification Conference," *Ibid.*, pp. 674–693; and James L. Brierly, "The Future of Codification," 12 *British Year Book of International Law* (1931), pp. 1–12. Professor Hudson wrote that preparation should

not be appreciated were the deeply rooted causal factors that produced such obstinately diverse views. This myriad of factors proved to be far stronger than any cluster of factors driving in the opposite direction, that is, toward achieving agreement. The Conference did, however, clarify issues and it did bring forth a more refined and scientific analysis of the problems.

The Preparatory Committee purportedly summarized the replies to the point dealing with the breadth of the bay [8] in an observation which reads as follows:

> It is agreed that the base line constituted by the sinuosities of the coast should not be maintained for every bay. The suggested exception, however, contemplates, not a mere curvature of the shore line, but an indentation presenting the characteristic features of a bay, showing in particular a well-marked entrance and a certain proportion (which it will be for the Conference to fix) between the breadth of such entrance and the depth of the indentation. Furthermore, it is necessary that the bay should not be too wide at its entrance. Divergent views exist as to the maximum size at the entrance. It seems nevertheless, from examination of the replies, that agreement could be reached in regard to bays of which the entrance is not more than ten miles wide. An imaginary line would be drawn across the bay and would serve as the basis for measurement of the breadth of territorial waters. If the opening of the bay is wider than ten miles, the line must be drawn at the nearest point to the entrance at which the breadth does not exceed ten miles. This is the system adopted in the Convention of May 6th, 1882, on the North Sea fisheries, on which the formula proposed as the basis of discussion is founded.
>
> The provisions with regard to islands set out below have the consequence that, where islands belonging to the coastal State lie at the entrance of a bay, the breadth of the opening of the bay is to be measured from the coast to the island or from one island to another.[8]

In these observations, we should note first that the matter of definition of the bay would have to be considered by the Conference. Although the matter had been raised as early as 1910, in the North Atlantic Coast Fisheries Arbitration, the various codifications by private bodies had ignored it. Likewise the preparatory questionnaires had omitted any mention of this thorny problem of geogrphical calculation. It now had to be faced. Secondly, the observations indicate that the basis of discussion is actually founded upon the North Sea fisheries formula of 1882. In this author's temerity in offerring criticism, it would

have been carried one step farther by submitting to the Governments for comment the bases of discussion, notwithstanding the previous responses to the questionnaire. While such a step might have done no harm and *might* hace crystalized positions further, it is doubtful whether the additional step would really have altered materially the discussion at the Conference or its outcome.

[8] League of Nations, *Conference for the Codification of International Law, Bases of Discussion*, vol. II, Territorial Waters, 1929.

seem that to mention such a foundation might have been a trifle obtuse inasmuch as Sweden-Norway had refused to sign that Convention. Moreover the work of Captain Meyer, appearing in 1927 [9] and arguing the Norwegian position, would hardly lend encouragement to the view that the 1882 Convention was a universally regarded landmark in the growth of a rule of international law.

The basis of discussion reads as follows:

Basis of Discussion No. 7

In the case of bays the coasts of which belong to a single State, the belt of territorial waters shall be measured from a straight line drawn across the opening of the bay. If the opening of the bay is more than ten miles wide, the line shall be drawn at the nearest point to the entrance at which the opening does not exceed ten miles.

There was no proposed Basis of Discussion on the definition of a bay.

A review of the minutes of the Second Committee (Territorial Waters) [10] and its work on bays is a rather disappointing experience. Basis of Discussion No. 7 was never on the agenda, but was assigned to the second sub-committee which had also to do with the breadth of territorial waters. Basis No. 8, having to do with historic bays, was placed on the agenda and was debated during one morning's session. A number of delegations rightly objected to such a procedure on the ground that historic bays should not be taken up without first discussing bays in general, or Basis No. 7. Much of the committee's time was taken up with this procedural difficulty, and one delegate took up more of the committee's time in what might be described as obstructive buffoonery, which may have been purposeful or even grounded in ignorance. The second sub-committee could arrive at no decision on bays, being obviously stuck hard aground on the territorial waters question. The sub-committee's observations on bays, which was included in the Final Act of the Conference, are quoted hereunder:

It is admitted that the base line provided by the sinuosities of the coast should not be maintained under all circumstances. In the case of an indentation which is not very broad at its opening, such a bay should be regarded as forming part of the inland waters. Opinions were divided as to the breadth at which this opening should be fixed. Several Delegations were of the opinion that bays, the opening of which did not exceed ten miles, should be regarded as inland waters; an imaginary line should be traced across the bay between the two points jutting out furthest, and this line would serve as a basis for determining the breadth of the territorial waters. If the opening of the bay exceeds ten miles, this imaginary

[9] CAPT Christopher B. V. Meyer RNorN, *The Extent of Jurisdiction in Territorial Waters* (1927).

[10] League of Nations Document C. 351(b) M.145(b) 1930.V. of August 1930.

line will have to be drawn at the first place, starting from the opening, at which the width of the bay does not exceed ten miles. This is the system adopted, *inter alia*, in the North Sea Fisheries Convention of May 6, 1882. Other Delegations were only prepared to regard the waters of a bay as inland waters if the two zones of territorial sea met at the opening of the bay, in other words, if the opening did not exceed twice the breadth of the territorial sea. States which were in favor of a territorial belt of three miles held that the opening should therefore not exceed six miles. Those who supported this opinion were afraid that the adoption of a greater width for the imaginary lines traced across bays might undermine the principle enunciated in the preceding article [on base lines] so long as the conditions which an indentation has to fulfill in order to be regarded as a bay remain undefined. Most Delegations agreed to a width of ten miles, provided a system were simultaneously adopted under which slight indentations were not be [sic] treated as bays.

However, these systems could only be applied in practice if the Coastal States enabled sailors to know how they should treat the various indentations of the coast.

Two systems were proposed; these having been set out as annexes to the observations on this article. The Sub-Committee gave no opinion regarding these systems, desiring to reserve the possibility of considering other systems or modifications of either of the above systems.

Although the matter of bays cannot be said to have received detailed treatment at the Conference, it can at least be said that some of the problems and difficulties were ventilated, and some solutions were proposed. One of the most frutiful contributions, though never acted upon, was the attempt to come to grips with definition of a bay. A proposal in this respect was made by the Delegation of the United States and another was made by the Delegation of France.[11] The two proposals are quoted hereunder in their entirety:

Appendix A Proposal of the United States Delegation

In the case of a bay or estuary the coasts of which belong to a single State, or to two or more States which have agreed upon a division of the waters thereof, the determination of the status of the waters of the bay or estuary shall be made in the following manner:

(1) On a chart or map a straight line not to exceed ten nautical miles in length shall be drawn across the bay or estuary as follows: The line shall be drawn between two headlands or pronounced convexities on the coast which embrace the pronounced indentiation or concavity comprising the bay or estuary if the distance between the two headlands does not exceed ten nautical miles; otherwise

[11] League of Nations Document C.351(b).M.145(b) 1930.V., pp. 197, 219. These proposale are described in: S. Whittemore Boggs, "Delimitation of the Territorial Sea," 24 *American Journal of International Law* (1930), pp. 546–7; Gilbert Gidel, *Le Droit international public de la Mer* (1934), Tome III, pp. 583–593, as well as in other articles. The American proposal was presented at the 1930 Conference by Mr. Boggs, Geographer of the U.S. State Department and member of the United States Delegation. According to a letter of 8 December 1958 from RADM Karo, Director U.S. Coast and Geodetic Survey, to this author, the proposed American system had its origin with a former Director of the U.S. Coast and Geodetic Survey, RADM R. S. Patton, USC&GS.

the line shall be drawn through the point nearest to the entrance at which the width does not exceed ten nautical miles;

(2) The envelope of all arcs of circles having a radius equal to one-fourth the length of the straight line across the bay or estuary shall be drawn from all points on the coast of the mainland (at whatever line of sea level is adopted on the charts of the coastal State) but such arcs of circles shall not be drawn around islands in connection with the process which is next described;

(3) If the area enclosed within the straight line and the envelope of the arcs of circles exceeds the area of a semi-circle whose diameter is equal to one-half the length of the straight line across the bay or estuary, the waters of the bay or estuary inside of the straight line shall be regarded, for the purposes of this convention, as interior waters; otherwise they shall not be so regarded.

When the determination of the status of the waters of a bay or estuary has been determined in the manner described above, the delimitation of the territorial waters shall be made as follows:

(1) If the waters of the bay or estuary are found to be interior waters, the straight line across the entrance or across the bay or estuary shall be regarded as the boundary between interior waters and territorial waters, and the three mile-belt of territorial waters shall be measured outward from that line in the same manner as if it were a portion of the coast;

(2) Otherwise the belt of territorial waters shall be measured outward from all points on the coast line;

(3) In either case arcs of circles of three mile radius shall be drawn around the coasts of islands (if there be any) in accordance with provisions for delimiting territorial waters around islands.

Appendix B
Compromise-Proposal of the French Delegation

In the case of indentiations where there is only one Coastal State, the breadth of the territorial sea may be measured from a straight drawn across the opening of the indentation provided that the length of this line does not exceed ten miles and that the indentation may properly be termed a bay.

In order that an indentation may be properly termed a bay, the area comprised between the curve of the coast and its chord must be equal to or greater than the area of the segment of the circle the centre of which is situated on the perpendicular to the chord in its middle, at a distance from the chord equal to one half the length of this chord and of which the radius is equal to the distance which separates this point from one end of the curve.

The figures below (Annexes A and B, pp. 212–213) illustrate the two systems.

Before commenting on the merits of the American and French proposals, we shall note two others advanced at the Hague Conference.

The German Delegation made the following proposal in the form of an amendment to Basis of Discussion No. 7:

This rule shall apply only to bays the length of which is not less than five marine miles, reckoned from the above-mentioned line.[12]

[12] League of Nations Document C.351(b).M.145(b) 1930.V., p. 186.

The British proposal, not formally submitted to the Second Subcommittee, and thus not a matter of official record, was that account should be taken of the ratio between average depth and breadth by measuring the area.[13] Gidel describes the British proposal thus:

La suggestion britannique ne fit pas l'objet d'une rédaction formelle soumise à la Sous-Commission n° II. Il ne semble pas qu'on dénature les vues énoncées par les représentants britanniques en exprimant dans la formule ci-après qui aurait été ajoutée à la proposition allemande ci-dessus rapportée: "... pourvu que la surface de la baie ainsi délimitée ne soit pas inférieure à la surface du segment déterminé par un arc de cercle ayant pour corde la ligne susmentionnée et tracée à partir d'un point distant du milieu corde d'une longeur égale au quart de cette corde."[14]

A British proposal that was formally submitted as an amendment, albeit to Basis of Discussion No. 8 (Historic Bays), was this:

2. For the purpose of determining whether the waters of any particular bay are or are not part of the national waters of the coastal State, regard shall always be had to the configuration of the bay, that is to say, the shape and degree of enclosure of the area of water therein, with special reference to the extent to which it penetrates into the land.[15]

Both the German and the British recommendations were withdrawn in favor of the United States Proposal. In arguing the merits of the American proposal in the *American Journal of International Law*, Mr. Broggs makes an interesting comment in his introduction, with which this author is in emphatic agreement:

If the territorial sea is to be delimited in a manner to occasion the least possible interference with navigation, it will be necessary to *assume the viewpoint of one who is on the sea* and who wishes to know where territorial waters begin. The viewpoint of a man on land who wishes to know where territorial waters end is of no more than theoretical importance except as it may be said to coincide with the fisherman's interest in those limited areas in which fishing is profitable. The difficulties hitherto encountered in delimiting portions of the territorial sea have arisen, however, largely from the fact that the problem has generally been considered from the viewpoint of a man on the land rather than the viewpoint of the navigator. This is particularly true with reference to bays.[16]

[13] Boggs, *op. cit.*, p. 550.

[14] Gidel, *op. cit.*, p. 584.

[15] League Document C.351(b).M.145(b) 1930.V., p. 188; we should perhaps as a matter of foot-noted record, note other methods. One is a publicists' proposal and the other is a provision of a bilateral agreement.

Münch in his book, *Die technischen Fragen des Küstenmeers* (1934), at pages 97–100, suggests a method whereby the relationship between the perimeter of the concavity behind the closing line and the length of the closing line is examined. There would exist a bay when the length of the perimeter is equal to or greater than twice the length of the closing line. In the fisheries treaty between Russia and Japan dated 28 July 1907, the provisions of the treaty were agreed as not having application in bays whose depth was three times greater (or more) than their breadth. I *Martens Recueil*, 3rd Series, p. 861; II *American Journal of International Law* (1908), p. 274.

[16] Boggs, "Delimitation," p. 543.

In commenting upon the American proposal after it was presented at the Conference, Mr. Raestad, a jurist in the Norwegian Delegation said:

> Moreover, when I examine the proposal of our American friends, with their vast geometrical and mathematical system, I am somewhat afraid that we may get into very deep water, and that the technical experts will have a good deal more to say than we jurists.[17]

The answer is simple in thought but often very difficult of realization: The experts should not be on top, but should be very much on tap. Perhaps more liberal utilization of expert assistance might have rendered the opinion in *United Kingdom* v. *Norway* a more valuable document.

Mr. Boggs argues that the system proposed in the American amendment is an attempt to apply to all coasts of whatever character, in a scientific and impartial manner, the method of drawing the envelopes of the arcs of circles.[18] But, as Professor Gidel rightly points out, it was impossible to conceal the great difficulties in application of the proposal as it was offered at the Conference. Actually, in comparing the writings of both Professor Gidel and Mr. Boggs with an article by Mr. A. L. Schalowitz of the United States Coast and Geodetic Survey, the organization in which the idea originated, we are forced to conclude that in 1930, the explanation tended to overcomplicate the basic idea with which we are already quite familiar.[19] This idea was embodied in a memorandum sent by Rear Admiral Patton to the United States Delegation at the Hague. The pertinent part of this memorandum is quoted hereunder:

> In theory, the question whether a bay is intra-territorial or extra-territorial would seem to depend upon the extent to which the waters penetrated into the land, or, more precisely, upon the ratio of that penetration to the dimension of the entrance.
>
> Can that ratio be expressed satisfactorily in mathematical terms? To state briefly the conclusion, without discussing all the considerations by which it was reached, a semicircular bay having its diameter along the line joining the headlands is the theoretical, ideal bay which lies on the borderline between intra- and extra-territorial bays. It is not a perfect rule, but probably as satisfactory a one as can be derived. To assume with respect to such a theroretical, ideal bay, that if more than half the full circle lies inside the line joining the headlands, the bay is intra-territorial, while if less than half lies inside that line, the bay is extra-territorial.

[17] League of Nations Document C.351(b).M.145(b), p. 110.
[18] Boggs, "Delimitation," p. 553.
[19] A. L. Shalowitz, U.S. Coast and Geodetic Survey, "The Concept of a bay as Inland Waters," XIII *Surveying and Mapping* (October-December 1953), pp. 432–440.

Bays in nature are never exactly semicircular, and we must therefore resort to the theory of equivalence. A possible rule would be "*If the area of the natural bay, included within the low-water line and a line joining the headlands, exceeds the area of a semicircle whose diameter is equal to that part of the line joining the headlands which lies outside the low-water line, the bay is intra-territorial.*" (italics supplied).[20]

The statement of the rule assumes, of course, that the line joining the headlands is given. The proposal of the United States Delegation stated that this line was ten miles long, a limit that not all States were prepared to accept. Then, of course, the United States Delegation embellished the basic idea by the envelope-of-arcs system, which in reality is simply a convenient technique for making a comparison between the two areas with which the rule is concerned.

The Hague Codification Conference of 1930 was a very significant milepost in the development in the law of bays, not because of any agreement reached (and none was reached on bays), but for these reasons:

(a) The need for a definition of a bay was brought out clearly.

(b) The semi-circular rule was originated, albeit within a context that in itself was confusing and politically unworkable.

(c) The complexities of the bay problem came more clearly to be appreciated. No doubt implicit in such appreciation was the germ of the idea that codification of a law of bays was not a task to be entrusted to jurists alone – or, for the matter, to technical experts alone.

[20] *Ibid.*, p. 433. Lest one conclude that the semi-circular rule was entirely an American invention, Mr. Shalowitz quotes from a letter sent to RADM Patton by the U.S. Delegation advising this principle had been independently arrived at by the British Delegation.

Annex A THE AMERICAN PROPOSAL REGARDING BAYS AND ESTUARIES SUBMITTED TO THE HAGUE CODIFICATION CONFERENCE, 1930

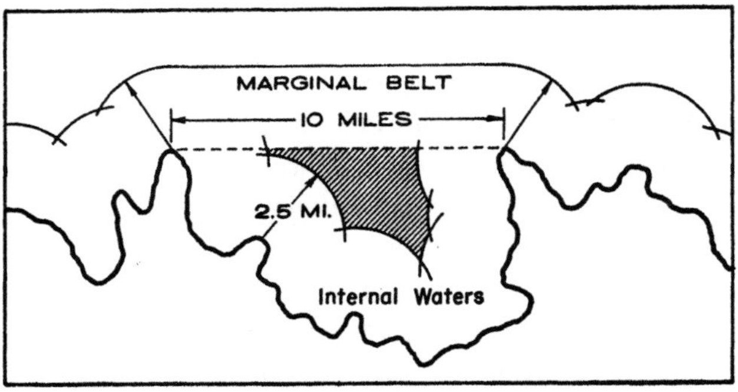

THE AMERICAN PROPOSAL-1930 [1]

Fig. 22

(1) On a chart or map a straight line not to exceed ten nautical miles in length shall be drawn across the bay or estuary as follows: The line shall be drawn between two headlands or pronounced convexities on the coast which embrace the pronounced indentation or concavity comprising the bay or estuary if the distance between the two headlands does not exceed ten nautical miles; otherwise the line shall be drawn through the point nearest to the entrance at which the width does not exceed ten nautical miles;

(2) The envelope of all arcs of circles having a radius equal to one-fourth the length of the straight line across the bay or estuary shall then be drawn from all points on the coast of the mainland (at whatever line of sea leve lis adopted on the charts of the coastal State) but such arcs of circles shall not be drawn around islands in connection with the process which is next described;

(3) If the area enclosed within the straight line and the envelope of the arcs of circles exceeds the area of a semi-circle whose diameter is equal to one-half the length of the straight line across the bay or estuary, the waters of the bay or estuary inside of the straight line shall be regarded, for the purpose of this convention, as interior waters; otherwise they shall not be so regarded.

When the determination of the status of the waters of a bay or estuary has been made in the manner described above, the delimitation of the territorial waters shall be made as follows:

(1) If the waters of the bay or estuary are found to be interior waters, the straight line across the bay or estuary shall be regarded as the boundary between interior waters and territorial waters, and the three-mile belt of territorial waters shall be measured outward from that line in the same manner as if it were a portion of the coast;

(2) Otherwise the belt of territorial waters shall be measured outward from all points on the coast line;

[1] S. Whittemore Boggs, "Delimitation of the Territorial Sea," 24 *American Journal of International Law* (1930), p. 547.

(3) In either case arcs of circles of three mile radius shall be drawn around the coasts of islands (if there be any) in accordance with provisions for delimiting territorial waters around islands.[2]

Annex B THE FRENCH COMPROMISE PROPOSAL REGARDING BAYS AND ESTUARIES SUBMITTED TO THE HAGUE CODIFICATION CONFERENCE, 1930

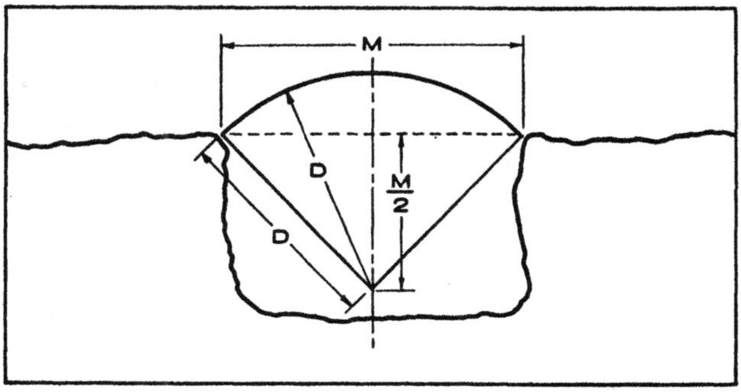

THE FRENCH COMPROMISE PROPOSAL–1930

Fig. 23

In the case of indentations where there is only one Coastal State, the breadth of the territorial sea may be measured from a straight line drawn across the opening of the indentation provided that the length of this line does not exceed ten miles and that the indentation may be properly termed a bay.

In order that an indentation may be properly termed a bay, the area comprised between the curve of the coast and its chord must equal to or greater than the area of the segment of the circle the centre of which is situated on the perpendicular to the chord in its middle, at a distance from the chord equal to one half of the length of this chord and of which the radius is equal to the distance which separates this point from one end of the curve.[3]

Section C THE UNITED NATIONS INTERNATIONAL LAW COMMISSION.

Article 13 of the United Nations Charter provides, *inter alia*, that the General Assembly shall initiate studies and make recommendations for the purpose of encouraging the progressive development of international law and its codification.[1] In a resolution of 11 December 1946, the General Assembly established a committee to study methods

[2] League of Nations Publication V. Legal. V. 14., p. 132.

[3] *Ibid.*

[1] For a brief discussion of the genesis of this article, see Yuan-li Liang, "The General Assembly and the Progressive Development and Codification of International Law," 42 *American Journal of International Law* (1948), at pages 66–68.

by which the Assembly "shall encourage the progressive development of international law and its eventual codification." [2] After consideration of the committee's report and recommendations,[3] the Assembly by a resolution of 21 November 1947 set up a permanent International Law Commission for the purpose and adopted a Statute of the Commission.[4] The Commission, according to its Statute, is to be composed of fifteen members of recognized competence in international law, representing the chief forms of civilization and the basic legal systems of the world. Members are nominated by the Governments and are elected by the General Assembly. The Statute defines the procedures to be followed both in the progressive development and in the codification of international law. The Statute, in Article 15, defines the terms:

(a) "Progressive development of international law" is used for convenience as meaning the preparation of draft conventions on subjects which have not yet been regulated by international law or in regard to which the law has not been sufficiently developed in the practice of States.

(b) "Codification of international law" is used for convenience as meaning the more precise formulation and systematization of rules of international law in fields where there already has been extensive state practice, precedent and doctrine."

As an abstract idea, the difference between the two functions appears easy to comprehend. In practice, at least insofar as the matter of territorial waters is concerned, the differentiation has been unworkable and has been disregarded.[5] In this respect there has been little change from the attitude prevailing in the 1930 Conference at the Hague, where similar procedures were to be observed, but which could

[2] UN Document A/64/Add. 1, p. 187.

[3] UN Document A/504.

[4] UN Document A/519, p. 105.

[5] Sir Hersch Lauterpacht, *Oppenheim's International Law*, vol. I, 8th Ed. (1955), p. 69. Former Judge De Visscher writes that codification is never a mere declaration or restatement of rules said to be already in existence: it always aims to replace divergent views and practices with some unity in the interpretation and application of the Law; *Theory and Reality in Public International Law* (1957), p. 144.

In its report to the General Assembly upon the completion of its work at the Eighth (1956) Session, the International Law Commission made this comment: "In preparing its rules on the law of the sea, the Commission has become convinced that, in this domain at any rate, the distinction established in the statute between two activities can hardly be maintained. Not only may there be wide differences of opinion as to whether a subject is already "sufficiently developed in practice," but also several of the provisions adopted by the Commission, based on a "recognized principle of international law," have been framed in such a way as to place them in the "progressive development" category. Although it tried at first to specify which articles fell into one and which into the other category, the Commission has had to abandon the attempt, as several do not wholly belong to either.

not be enforced.[6] In short, for our purposes the distinctions can be dropped and it may be assumed that so much of the Commission's work as we shall discuss falls into the category of progressive development.

This is a highly important problem in the development of International Law in general, as well as in the development of rules for bays. Professor Corbett, writing in 1951, predicted that the Commission would indulge in the harmless activity of elaborating and refining abstract rules for the government of States. He suggested that if the Commission were to make any durable contribution to a world legal order, it might do well to transform itself into a body studying conditions of such development. He noted that a merely analytical jurisprudence, coupled with a drafting technique, would do no more than scratch the surface.[7] What Professor Corbett seemed to suggest was that a group of legal scholars would detach themselves from their countries and the political realities of life and commence to formulate rules. He seems to ascribe to them the function of what Professor Stone calls summing up of the past rather than working on projects for the future.[8] Now, were Professor Corbett to limit his comment to the work of private efforts at codification, then such comment might have an element of soundness, if our brief look at the work of the Institute, the Association and the Harvard Research offer samples of the probity of those bodies. On the other hand, if he includes the Hague Conference of 1930 in the background to his comment, he may perhaps have misread the record of that conference. It appears to this author that the jurists who gathered in 1930 had no illusions as to their responsibilities for doing more than simply agreeing upon the law as it stood. They were really attempting to argue for agreement on rules that reflected their respective countries' conception of the law. And

[6] Manley O. Hudson "First Conference for Codification of International Law," 24 *American Journal of International Law* (1930), at pp. 448–9. Former Judge Hudson writes: "The Preparatory Committee ... drafted rules of procedure ... which distinguished between declarations establishing agreed principles of existing law and conventions dealing with matters not clearly covered by previously existing law ... The Conference was reluctant to commit itself to these distinctions .... Sentiment grew quite rapidly against any attempt to state what was the existing law as distinguished from new legislation, and after two weeks it became clear that even the use of the term *declaration* was stoutly opposed."

[7] P. E. Corbett, *Law and Society in the Relations of States* (1951), p. 278.

[8] Julius Stone, *Legal Controls of International Conflict* (1954), p. 22. Liang notes the view of Professor Brierly which holds that codification is a necessary "scientific" task. "General Assembly and Codification," p. 71. This writer has the greatest respect for the works of the late Professor Brierly and has no wish to appear frivolous, but he is compelled to ask whether Brierly and a host of others, really think that there can be such a thing as a scientific codification of international law.

this was from the standpoint of past practice and what, for the future, would most likely support their countries' policies. In other words, they were trying to legislate for the future,[9] but the basis for the legislation was past practice as interpreted by the States they represented. The breakdown, of course, resulted from an absence of harmonization of goals. Short of this, however, as has often been pointed out, the 1930 Conference failed more totally by not formulating a convention on those features of the law of territorial waters where there was prospect of agreement. We shall see whether the International Law Commission enjoyed any greater success.

At its first session, held in 1949, the International Law Commission made up a provisional list of fourteen topics selected for codification.[10] One of these topics was called the Regime of Territorial Waters. Pursuant to a recommendation contained in General Assembly resolution 374 (IV), the Commission decided at its 1951 meeting to initiate work on this topic. Professor J. P. A. Francois of the Netherlands, and rapporteur of the Second Committee of the 1930 Conference, was appointed Special Rapporteur for the work on the Regime of the Territorial Sea.

At the fourth (1952) session of the Commission certain aspects of the regime of the territorial sea were considered. This was done on the basis of an initial report by the Special Rapporteur.[11]

In introducing his report to the Commission, Professor Francois pointed out that inasmuch as at the Hague Conference there had been virtual agreement on all points except the breadth of the territorial sea, he was taking the Hague work as a basis for the draft regulations submitted in his first report. With respect to bays, as we shall see, he chose to ignore the American proposal at the Hague. He then recommended that the Commission concern itself, *inter alia*, with the question as to whether it should consider itself bound by the decision of the International Court of Justice in *United Kingdom* v. *Norway*.[12]

[9] Lauterpacht makes the following well-taken points: "... the experience of codification under the United Nations fully confirms the past attempts to the effect that there is very little to codify if by that term is meant no more giving, in the language of Article 15 of the Statute of the International Law Commission, precision and systematic order to rules of international law in fields where there already has been extensive State practice, precedent and doctrine ... the task of codification ... calls for a combination of legislative activity with measured adherence to a legal rule sactioned by tradition and by considerations of unimpaired validity." "Codification and Development of International Law," 49 *American Journal of International Law* (1955), pp. 16–43.

[10] Clyde Eagleton, "First Session of the International Law Commission," 43 *American Journal of International Law* (1949), pp. 758–762.

[11] U.N. Document A/CN.4/53.

[12] *Yearbook of the United Nations International Law Commission* 1952, vol. I, p. 143.

As the then Professor Lauterpacht pointed out to his brother members of the Commission, it was possible to argue that the Court had abolished altogether the legal concept of a bay. Paradoxically, Mr. Kozjevnikov, the Soviet Union member, argued strongly for taking into account the judge-made law in the Fisheries case.[13]

The Commission never actually came to a vote on the binding effect upon them of the Court's decision in the Fisheries Case. Instead, the Commission concerned itself with the substance of the article on bays as submitted by Professor Francois in his report. This article, consisting of a single paragraph, reads:

> In the case of the bays the coasts of which belong to a single State, the belt of the territorial sea shall be measured from a straight line drawn across the opening of the bay. If the opening of the bay is more than ten miles wide, the line shall be drawn at the nearest point to the entrance at which the opening does not exceed ten miles.[14]

In his commentary on the Article, Professor Francois expressed the opinion that inherent in the question of bays were problems of a nature so technical as to warrant the advice of experts before proceeding further. The consensus of the Commission was that they could not accept the ten mile closing line, that they could not at that point replace the ten miles with another figure, and that they could not simply wash their hands of the whole question. It was relatively easy, therefore, for the Commission to ask the Special Rapporteur to study the matter further. The record of the discussion on the 10-mile rule would suggest that the Commission was not prepared to consider the Court's decision in the Fisheries Case as either final or even very authoritative guidance. While this writer certainly agrees that the Commission should adopt this attitude, he is nevertheless distressed by the fact that the opinion of this highest international tribunal, written only twelve months before, should not have been composed in a manner that would truly invite the Commission to use it for guidance.

In the course of the discussion on bays, the matter of a relationship between the length of the closing line and the breadth of the terri-

[13] It is to be observed that his position does not reflect the usual Soviet attitude toward courts and the development of law, but it does reflect the Soviet policy with respect to sovereignty over coastal waters. In other words, here is an example where the participation of a jurist, schooled in a particular legal system, ignored the precepts of his system in a situation where they might clash with policy. Marek St. Korowicz, *An Introduction to International Law* (1959), p. 145f.

[14] *Yearbook of the United Nations International Law Commission*, 1952, vol. II, p. 35; English translation taken from UN Document A/C.6/L.378.

torial sea was debated. While the members took sides with respect tc the existence of such a relationship, no one demonstrated wherein it really exists. Mr. Cordova brought to light a unique and hithertc unheard of rule to the effect that the breadth across the opening of a bay should be three and one-third times the breadth of the margina belt. The foregoing summary reflects all of the discussion on bays at the Fourth (1952) Session of the Commission.

Pursuant to the approved suggestion of the Special Rapporteur, a group of experts met at the Hague from 14 to 16 April 1953 for the purpose of examining questions of a technical nature raised during the Commission's meeting of the previous year. The membership of this committee was:

1. Prof. J. P. A. Francois, Chairman,
2. Prof. L. E. G. Asplund (Geographic Survey Department, Stockholm), member,
3. Mr. S. Whittemore Boggs (Special Adviser on Geography, U. S. Department of State), member,
4. Mr. P. R. V. Couillault (Ingenieur en Chef du Service central hydrographique, Paris), member,
5. CDR R. E. Kennedy, RN (RET), (Hydrographic Department Admiralty, London), member,
6. VADM A. S. Pinke, RNN (RET), (The Hague), member.

The report of the committee indicates that the members were acting in their personal capacity. It emphasizes that the replies given by it to the technical questions submitted by the special rapporteur stem from the technical point of view, "bearing in mind in particular the practical difficulties of the navigator." [15]

Part II of the committee's report is quoted hereunder in its entirety:

Questions: Accepting the low-water line system as a general rule for measuring the territorial sea, while in bays a straight line across the bay should circumscribe the "inland waters," what technical observations can be made as to:

A. the definition of a bay as opposed to a mere curvature in the coastline?

B. any relation between the maximum length (B miles) of the above-mentioned straight line and the width of the territorial sea?

C. the points which the said straight line should be drawn?

D. the direction of or the points betwwen which this line should be drawn in case different lines of B miles are conceivable?

[15] UN Document A/CN.4/61/Add. 1.

Answers:

A(1) A bay is a bay in the juridical sense, if its area is as large as, or larger than that of a semi-circle drawn on the entrance of that bay. Historical bays are excepted; they should be indicated as such on the maps.

A(2) If a bay has more than one entrance ... this semi-circle should be drawn on a line as long as the sum-total of the length of the differet entrances.

A(3) Islands within a bay should be included as if they were part of the waters of the bay.

B(1) The closing line across a (juridical) bay should not exceed 10 miles in width, this being twice the range of vision to the horizon in clear weather, from the eye of a mariner at a height of 5 meters (which is the internationally accepted height for hydrographical purposes). In cases of considerable tidal differences the low-water lines should be taken as the shore lines between which the width of the bay is computed.[16]

B(2) If the entrance of a (juridical) bay is split up into a number of smaller openings by various islands, closing lines across these openings may be drawn provided that none of these lines exceeds five miles in length – except one which may extend up to a maximum of 10 miles.

C(1) In case the entrance of the bay exceeds 10 miles, a closing line of this length should be drawn within the bay. When different lines of this length can be drawn, that line should be chosen which encloses the maximum water area within the bay.

D(1) D has become redundant by the answer to the foregoing question.

In connection with questions relating to straight base lines, the Committee coined the term "fictitious bay" for special cases involving islands in a group or string or a string taken together with a portion of the mainland coastline.[17] The report by the Committee indicates that it met for two or possibly three days. That is a remarkably short time considering the range and technical difficulty of the subject matter with which it had to deal. On the other hand, from the point of view of the navigator or hydrographer, the answers of the committee are simple and easy to understand. The late Mr. Boggs was on the Committee and we see that the American proposal of 1930, somewhat simplified, has found its way into the Committee's report. [18]

For the Fifth (1953) Session of the International Law Commission,

[16] If the height of the observer's eye is 5 meters or 16.3 above the surface of the sea, he will hav a horizon distance of visibility of 4.63 miles. This is called the visible horizon. Twice this distance is 9.26 miles. Bowditch, *American Practical Navigator*, 1959 Edition, Table 8.

[17] See sketch of Buzzard's Bay, figure 19, page 77.

[18] S. Whittemore Boggs was a geographer by profession and author of the still standard work, *International Boundaries: A Study of Boundary Functions and Problems* (1940). He once wrote: "Problems on delimiting territorial waters should be studied objectively from every practical aspect and especially that of the navigator, with a view to simplicity, impartiality of results, and economy in publication." His own prescription for the solution of our problem is contained in "Delimitation of Seaward Areas under National Jurisdiction," 45 *American Journal of International Law* (1951), pp. 240–266.

the special rapporteur submitted a new article on bays,[19] which was almost exactly a reproduction of the statements contained in the Committee of Experts' report. The matter, however, was passed over at the Fifth Session.

At the Sixth (1954) Session of the Commission, the special rapporteur submitted a new draft. In addition to the report of the committee of experts, he had also before him the observations of several Governments.[20] The article on bays in the 1954 draft, in which the rapporteur said he had adopted the suggestions of the committee of experts, is quoted hereunder:

Article 7

1. The waters within a bay shall be considered inland waters if the line drawn across the opening does not exceed ten miles.

2. The term "bay," for the purposes of the preceding paragraph, means an indentation of an area as large as or larger than that of the semicircle drawn on the entrance of that indentation. If a bay has more than one entrance, this semicircle shall be drawn on a line as long as the sum total of the length of the different entrances. Islands within a bay shall be included as if they were part of the water area of the bay.

3. If the entrance of a bay is split up into a number of smaller openings by various islands, closing lines across these openings may be drawn provided that none of these exceeds five miles in length, except one such line which may extend up to a maximum of ten miles.

4. Where the entrance of a bay exceeds ten miles, a closing line of such length shall be drawn within the bay. When different lines of such length can be drawn, the line shall be chosen which encloses the maximum water area within the bay.[21]

Discussion of bays was not undertaken at the 1954 session, although other aspects of the territorial sea were considered.[22] Nevertheless the United Kingdom Government, in its *note verbale* of 1 February, indicated approval of the above article, subject to the addition of the phrase "measured from low water mark" after the words "ten miles."[23]

The draft article quoted above is interesting in that it is the one article of the series that approaches the problem entirely from a

[19] The specific wording of this draft contained in Document A/6N.4/61/Add 1, is quoted in Annex A to this section.

[20] UN Documents A/CN.4/71 and Add. 1 and Add 2. Actually these documents recorded obeservations and information regarding the question of the delimitation of the territorial sea of two adjacent States, but some strong claims and counter-claims were made by Netherlands and Belgium in connection with the mouth of the River Schelt. The United Kingdom stressed adherence to "first principles," one of which is freedom of the seas, and pointed out that if disputes arise, they should be settled according to international law and not *ex aequo et bono*.

[21] UN Document A/CN.4/77, p. 10.

[22] UN Document A/CN.4/88, pp. 35–58.

[23] UN Document A/CN.4/90, p. 25.

mathematical standpoint. Even reference to the historic bay has been omitted. Several Governments were not slow to protest that the ten mile rule was without basis in international law. Sweden, in particular, criticized the efforts of the "cartographic experts," as her Government's letter of 12 April 1955 termed them.[24] These comments of the several Governments indicate that each has the view that the International Law Commission should do its work in such a way as to harmonize with the views of the Government concerned. If a commission draft provides for a 10-mile rule and the particular Government has bays of greater width in the littoral of its State, then the Commission's draft is attacked as being contrary to prevailing international law. If another Government finds that the 10-mile rule does not conflict with its views, the rule is not criticized. What becomes quite evident is that the International Law Commission had to become a drafting board for the reconciling of sovereign State policy objectives into generally agreed upon "rules" rather than a commission of jurists aided by experts and charged with objective and progressive development of rules of international law. This is not meant as a criticism of any particular State or the Commission, but to note what has been demonstrated many times: However sound they be, rules formulated by technical experts may find little acceptance in a political atmosphere unless there is present some outside force (or catalyst) of such strength as to cause the parties to decide that adherence to the technical rules is more advantageous than is adherence to divergent points of view and policies.

At the Seventh (1955) Session, the Commission adopted a new draft article for bays. In this article, the limit of the length of the closing line is extended to twenty-five miles. This 25-mile rule is explained thus:

> Although not prepared to establish a direct ratio between the length of the closing line and the width of the territorial sea – such a relationship was formally denied by certain members of the Commission – it felt bound to take some account of the tendencies to extend the width of the territorial sea by prolonging the closing line in bays.[25]

It appears that the twenty-five mile rule was justified on the basis that the closing line across bays would be slightly more than twice the permissible maximum width of the territorial sea (12 miles) which the Commission was also considering.[26] At this session a proposal

[24] UN Document A/CN,4/90, Add 2, pp. 6–7.
[25] UN Document A/2984, p. 18.
[26] *Ibid.*

was made that the length of the closing line should simply be designated as twice the breadth of the marginal belt. This was rejected on the grounds that for countries favoring a 3-mile marginal belt, such a rule would permit only a six-mile bay. The Commission regarded it essential to specify a definite length. The 1955 draft article is quoted hereunder:

1. For the purpose of these regulaitons, a bay is a well-marked indentation whose penetration inland is in such proportion to the width of its mouth as to contain landlocked waters and constitute more than a mere curvature of the coast. An indentation shall not, however, be regarded as a bay unless its area is as large as or larger than that of the semicircle drawn at the entrance of that indentation.

2. If a bay has more than one entrance, this semicircle shall be drawn on a line as long as the sum total of the length of the different entrances. Islands within a bay shall be included as if they were part of the water area of the bay.

3. The waters within a bay the coasts of which belong to a single State shall be considered internal waters if the line drawn across the opening does not exceed twenty-five miles measured from the low water line.

4. Where the entrance of a bay exceeds twenty-five miles, a closing line of such length shall be drawn within the bay. When different lines of such length can be drawn, that line shall be chosen which encloses the maximum water area within the bay.

5. The provision laid down in paragraph 4 shall not apply to so-called "historical Bay" or in cases where the straight base-line system provided for in Article 5 is applicable.

In the Government comments that followed adoption of this draft article, five States indicated that they considered the twenty-five mile limit to be excessive.[27] Only China indicated complete approval of the new draft afticle. The special rapporteur noted that the twenty-five mile limit met with little support. The comment of the Brazilian Government criticized the definition of the bay, arguing that it seemed unnecessary and complicated, and asserted further:

If, however, a definition is desired it would be preferable to adopt that proposed by the United Kingdom Government ... for the 1930 Conference, namely, that for the purpose of definition of the baseline a bay "must be a distinct and well-defined inlet, moderate in size, and long in proportion to its width."

To this Rapporteur pointed out that the Committee of Experts mentioned above were unanimous in considering the definition proposed by the United Kingdom in 1930 to be inadequate. The Union of South Africa Government suggested that the article should leave no doubt that "historical bays" were to be treated as *sui generis*, and

[27] UN Document A/CN.4/99. The States were Brazil, Turkey, Israel, United Ki ngdom and United States.

excluded not only from the operation of the rule in paragraph 4, but also from the criteria laid down in the rest of the article. At the Eighth (1956) Session, the Special Rapporteur suggested that this was worthy of the Commission's attention. Norway raised an objection similar in tenor to that of the Union of South Africa.

The Eighth (1956) Session's consideration of bays opened with a review of the various objections. This was followed by a review of the several proposals on the length of the closing line.

The debate on both the definition of the bay and of the closing line exhibited a continued divergence of views and a rather weak series of efforts to invoke past judicial decisions and other authorities in support of the views propounded. Two members suggested that the questions should be referred to an international conference. Mr. Zourek of Czechoslovakia proposed an amendment which would have caused paragraph 3 of the draft article to read as follows:

> 3. The waters within a bay the coasts of which belong to a single State shall be considered internal waters if they are linked to the land domain by reason of the configuration of the bay, the width of its entrance, its economic value to the people of the State or by reason of the distance separating the bay from international shipping lanes on the high seas.

Sir Gerald Fitzmaurice criticized this proposal for its tautology, and it must be agreed that he was correct in doing so if one reads the amended paragraph as part of the whole and otherwise unchanged draft article. Were Mr. Zourek's amendment to have been accepted, the content of the entire article would have had to be altered. Contained in his amendment are elements which all the members must have recognized as being those which cause States to exercise an interest in their bays – or not to exercise such an interest. But they are elements which the State itself is usually unwilling to permit an international institution to assess. To have accepted Mr. Zourek's amendment would have really resulted in no codification at all; it would have resulted in the absence of any rule designed to operate as an equiliberating standard as between the interests of one State and the interests of all States.

Fortunately, Mr. Zourek's amendment was rejected. The length of the closing line was a compromise solution in which amendments for 10 miles and 12 miles were rejected and an amendment for 15 miles was accepted, seven votes to five.[28] No changes were made to the system of defining bays. The draft article, as adopted by the Eighth (1956) Session of the International Law Commission reads:

[28] United Nations, *Yearbook of the International Law Commission*, 1956, vol. I, p. 197.

Article 7

1. For the purpose of these articles, a bay is a well-marked indentation whose penetration is in such proportion to the width of its mouth as to contain land-locked waters and constitute more than a mere curvature of the coast. An indentation shall not, however, be regarded as a bay unless its area is as large as or larger than, that of a semi-circle drawn on the mouth of that indentation. If a bay has more than one mouth, this semi-circle shall be drawn on a line as long as the sum total of the length of the different mouths. Islands within a bay shall be included as if they were part of the water area of the bay.

2. The waters within a bay, the coasts of which belong to a single State, shall be considered internal waters if the line drawn across the mouth does not exceed fifteen miles measured from the low water line.

3. Where the mouth of the bay exceeds fifteen miles, a closing line of such length shall be drawn within the bay, When different lines of such length can be drawn that line shall be chosen which encloses the maximum water area within the bay.

4. The foregoing provisions shall not apply to so-called historic bays or in any cases where the straight baseline system provided for in Article 5 is applied.

Save for the change in the length of the closing line, the wording in this article is almost identical to that contained in the draft article of the 1955 Session.

In its report upon the completion of the Eight Session, the International Law Commission recommended that the General Assembly summon an international conference of plenipotentiaries to examine the law of the sea, taking into account not only the legal but also the technical, biological, economic and political aspects of the problem. It recommended that the conference embody the results of its work in one or more international conventions or such other instruments as it might deem appropriate.[29]

Annex A DRAFT ARTICLE ON BAYS SUBMITTED TO THE FIFTH (1953) SESSION AFTER CONSULTATION WITH THE COMMITTEE OF EXPERTS [30]

1. A bay is a bay in the juridical sense, if its area is as large as, or larger than that of the semi-circle drawn on the entrance of that bay. Historical bays are excepted; they shall be indicated as such on the maps.

2. If a bay has more than one entrance, this semi-circle shall be drawn on a line as long as the sum-total of the length of the different entrances.

3. Islands within a bay shall be included as if they were part of the water area of the bay.

[29] UN Document A/3159, p. 3.

[30] U.N. Document A/CN.4/61/Add. 1.

4. The closing line across a (juridical) bay shall not exceed 10 miles in width, this being twice the range of vision to the horizon in clear weather, from the eye of a mariner at a height of 5 metres. In cases of considerable tidal differences the low-water lines shall be taken as the shorelines between which the width of the bay shall be computed.

5. If the entrance of a (juridical) bay is split into a number of smaller openings by various islands, closing lines across these openings may be drawn, provided that none of these lines exceeds 5 miles in length, except one which may extend up to a maximum of 10 miles.

6. In case the entrance of the bay does not exceed 10 miles in width, the line *inter fauces terrarum* shall constitute the delimitation between inland waters and the territorial sea.

7. In case the entrance of the bay exceeds 10 miles, a closing line of this length shall be drawn within the bay. When different lines of this length can be drawn that line shall be chosen which encloses the maximum water area within the bay.

Section D THE GENEVA CONFERENCE OF 1958

The Eleventh General Assembly of the United Nations passed a resolution on 21 February 1957 [1] accepting the report of the International Law Commission [2] on the work of its Eighth (1956) Session, and, in accordance with the recommendation contained therein, decided to convoke an international conference to examine the law of the sea, "taking into account not only the legal, but also of the technical, biological, economic and political aspects of the problem, and to embody the results of its work in one or more international conventions or such other instruments" as it might deem appropriate. The Resolution contained the following additional provisions considered especially relevant to our book:

a. Invited all States Members of the United Nations and all States members of the specialized agencies to participate and to include among their representatives experts competent in the field to be considered.

b. Requested the Secretary General to, *inter alia:*

(1) Invite appropriate experts to advise and assist the Secretariat in preparing the conference.

(2) Obtain from the Governments any further provisiona lcomments that they might wish to make on the Commission's report and related matters.

c. Referred to the Conference the report of the International Law Commission as the basis for its consideration of the various problems involved in the development and codification of the law of the sea.

d. Called upon the Governments invited to the Conference and groups thereof to utilize the time remaining before the Conference for exchanges of views on controversial questions relative to the law of the sea.

[1] Resolution 1105(XI), reproduced in A/Conf.13/30 at p. xi.
[2] Document A/3159.

It is to be noted that this Conference was convened to examine the problem of the law of the sea from all points of view, technical, biological, economic and political – as well as legal. The Secretary General was requested to invite appropriate experts to assist in preparing for the Conference, and to prepare or arrange for the preparation of working documents of a legal, technical, or economic nature in order to facilitate the work of the Conference. This was to be the first world political conference on the law of the sea to be held since 1930,[3] and the Charter therefor was framed so as to ensure that preparation would be as thorough as possible in the time available. As Professor Jessup writes, "one gets from the outside the impression that this was a conference ready and able to address itself to the practical maritime problems which confront the world seafaring community...."[4] A review of the preparatory documents[5] submitted by the United Nations Secretariat would suggest that abundant and well-digested technical information was made available from that source.[6] Whether or not the individual delegations chose to inform themselves thoroughly and objectively on the facts relevant to the positions taken by them, one cannot very easily determine. It is possible, however, that most of the positions were formulated long before the distribution of the preparatory documents, and that such positions were little influenced by the contents of the documents. This appears particularly true with respect to the rules for bays. Despite the availability of well-ordered information concerning the factors which tend to impinge on sovereignty over bays, it is not apparent that States took positions sub-

[3] Since the end of World War II, however, there had been a number of Inter-American Conferences dealing with the same subject matter on a regional basis. A review of that activity is contained in McChesney, U.S. Naval War College *International Law Situation and Documents*, 1956, at pages 237–294. The article on bays drafted by the Inter-American Council of Jurists is reproduced in Annex A to this Section.

[4] 52 *American Journal of International Law* (Oct. 1958), p. 731.

[5] UN Document A/Conf.13/7.

[6] One commentator on the Geneva Conference made the comment: "Frankly, I think it should be recognized that knowledge of fisheries biology, and equally importantly, of the economic aspects of fisheries, is not particularly far advanced and certainly that available information is very unevenly distributed." William T. Burke, "Some Comments on the 1958 Conventions," *Proceedings of the American Society of International Law*, 1959, p. 204. This, of course, is a value judgment, but it is one that is difficult to reconcile with the rather voluminous literature available on marine biology, fisheries and fishery economics. Much of the more important literature was expertly digested in preparatory documents for the Conference. It is somewhat surprising that Mr. Burke did not distinguish more clearly between ignorance of facts and ignoring of facts when State decision makers take or maintain policy decisions in the "world arena." It is observed that Mr. Burke, in his learned comment, omitted any mention of the excellently done paper, "The Economic Importance of the Sea Fisheries in Different Countries," A/Conf.13/16, a preparatory document for the 1958 Geneva Conference submitted by the UN Food and Agriculture Organization.

stantially different from those evidenced by the utterances of corresponding members of the International Law Commission or by previous Government comments upon work of that Commission.

The written record would indicate that the work of the Geneva Conference on the subject of bays was very brief. The closing line was debated for a short time during one meeting of the First Committee and a length of 24 miles was proposed, jointly, by Bulgaria, Poland, and the Soviet Union. The proposal was adopted by a vote of 31 to 27, with 13 abstentions.[7] While dealing with bays, the First Committee concentrated most of its attention on historic bays, a matter with which we will deal in another chapter.

At the Conference, the defenders of the 10-mile limit of bays urged the visibility argument. Superficially, this appears to have merit (ignoring the fact it is actually a 9.26 limit at 5 meters height of eye above the surface), but, as we have indicated in the introduction to this book,[8] there are a host of arguments to demonstrate that at the present time a 10-mile limit is not essential to accurate navigation. Only Mr. Dean of the United States and Mr. Pheiffer of Germany [9] touched upon the real reasons why certain States desired the widest possible length of closing line: that, together with a 12-mile limit of marginal belt, the subterfuge of the 24-mile closing line would allow the littoral State the greatest possible amount of sovereignty over what had previously been high seas - and the greatest derogation of the principle of freedom of the seas since the day of the King's Chambers. Despite the fact that this Conference was convoked for the purpose of reviewing all aspects of the problem, the record fails to show that the advocates of the 12-mile limit plus the 24-mile closing line were effectively challenged to demonstrate the economic necessity for each sovereignty. Nor does the record show that while the First Committee was addressing itself to this problem, the Third Committee (High Seas: Fishing: the Conservation of Living Resources) was busy hammering

[7] A/Conf. 13/39, p. 146.

[8] Chapter ONE, Section D.

[9] Both of these gentlemen touched on the matter in a somewhat oblique fashion: Mr. Dean (U.S.) is reported to have: "... cited a recent case in the Far East, in which a State, by drawing an arbitrary line 115 miles long across a bay, had enclosed thousands of square miles of open sea and had claimed a territorial sea of twelve miles *in addition to that.*" (italics mine). The State was the Soviet Union. The bay was the Bay of Peter the Great off Vladivostock. The Rapporteur of the First Committee was Mr. Koretzky of the Ukrainian Soviet Socialist Republic. A/Conf.13/39, p. 26. Mr. Pheiffer is reported to have said that "there was [is] a close link between articles 5 and 7; any undue extension of straight baselines or the closing lines of bays, as envisaged in article 7, paragraph 2, would bring parts of the territorial sea under the regime of internal waters." A/Conf. 13/39, p. 45.

out a Convention which has good prospects of preventing abuses of coastal fisheries by the fishermen of foreign coastal States.[10] What the record does show is that the 24-mile rule was urged because the maximum breadth asserted over the marginal belt was twelve miles; that it would "correspond to an established international practice, and would protect the vital interests of the States concerned." [11] No one rose to challenge this statement by demonstrating how these vital interests would be jeopardized by a 10-mile for bays, nor did anyone rise to demonstrate that the mathematical relationship between the width of the marginal belt and the length of a bay's closing line is extremely tenuous and is based upon a proposition that is basically fallacious, and is really no more than a rule-of-thumb that through usage has acquired some modicum of stature.

It appears to this author that the proponents of the 3-mile limit for the marginal belt may have been so pre-occupied with that issue, that they probably failed to analyze thoroughly the problem of the closing line for bays. It would appear, too, that they failed to attack the problem on the economic ground – the ground upon which the proponents of the 24-mile rule established their position. That is, all proponents except the Soviet Bloc who have military reasons for wanting wide sea sovereignty and who, by clever manipulation, were able to maneuver other States into voting with them.

We have previously quoted the article on bays adopted by the 1958 Geneva Conference, and we have attempted to analyze it in detail.[12] The quotation will not be repeated here.

[10] The convention is "Convention on Fishing and Conservation of the Living Resources of the High Seas." It is this author's belief that if States ratify and abide by this Convention, there will be little ground for assertion that exclusive sovereignty over extended coastal waters is necessary for economic reasons. The convention does not remove the economic incentive for making such claims, but it appears to rob the economic argument of any validity it may previously have had.

[11] A/Conf.13/39, p. 145.

[12] Chapter TWO, Section A.

Annex A DRAFT OF THE INTER-AMERICAN COUNCIL OF JURISTS

Resolution xiii
Principles of Mexico on the Juridical
Regime of the Sea[13]

E

Bays

1. A bay is a well-marked indentation whose penetration inland in proportion to the width of its mouth is such that its waters are *inter fauces terrae*, constituting more than a mere curvature of the coast.

2. The line that encloses a bay shall be drawn between its natural geographica entrance points where the indentation begins to have the configuration of a bay

3. Waters comprised within a bay shall be subject to the juridical regime of internal waters if the surface thereof is equal to or greater than that of a semicircle drawn by using the mouth of the bay as a diameter.

4. If a bay has more than one entrance, this semicircle shall be drawn on a line as long as the sum total of the length of the different entrances. The area of the islands located within a bay shall be included in the total area of the bay.

5. So-called "historical bays" shall be subject to the regime of internal-waters of the coastal State or States.

(Approved at the Fourth Plenary Session, February 3, 1956)

Section E SUMMARY

The work of the Geneva Conference of 1958 is the terminal point of our discussion of codification of the law of bays. The historic bay has, of course, been omitted and will be dealt with in a subsequent chapter. At the end of the Geneva Conference, the Cuban delegation submitted a resolution requesting the General Assembly to study the advisability of convening a second international conference for further consideration of the questions left unsettled by the 1958 Conference. It appears that the article on bays, except for the matter of historic bays can probably be considered settled, although, as discussed in Chapter Two, the drafting of the article could be improved upon.

This Chapter has undertaken to sketch out the various efforts at codification of the law of bays. The author wishes it could be his conclusion that all of the rules proposed for bays were the result of

[13] MacChesney, *op. cit.*, p. 246; Pan American Union Document CIJ-29 (English), p. 38.

thorough going analyses of past precedent, current State practice, and future need as might become evident through study of the complex of factors – geographic, economic, and technical – that might exert an influence upon future development. Unfortunately such has not always been the case. In the codifications framed by individuals and private bodies, the author's research has left him with the distinct impression that many of the draft articles on bays were written because their authors simply felt bound to place something on record with respect to bays. There was a repetition of the same wording and the same concept of a relationship with the width of the marginal belt. Only the official bodies to probe more deeply, and final product, even product, even with its imperfections in drafting and its inconclusiveness on historic bays, is not unacceptable.

There are no doubt many who view with alarm the 24-mile rule for bays on the ground that it is an excessive derrogation of the freedom of the seas, that it is economically harmful to foreign States, and that it inhibits accurate coastal navigation. While this author does not believe that most States who want a 24-mile closing line have proved, on any objective grounds, a real economic or other necessity for it, neither does he believe that other States whose ships may sail along coasts of such countries have an intolerable burden placed upon them. Navigation becomes more difficult but it can almost always be accomplished. Fisheries are at sea as well as close to the shore and improved locating and harvesting techniques tend to reduce the necessity for fishing only in areas adjacent to foreign coasts. On the other hand, the author would find it most difficult to envision any sympathetic international reception for a move toward amending the rule for bays to provide closing lines greater than 24 miles in length. If the Geneva Convention on Fisheries is ratified, it would be most difficult to argue the need for such an increase on economic grounds or for conservation reasons.

Thus, it is believed, that on balance the codification process has served a useful purpose in connection with the law of bays.

PART TWO

THE BAYS WITHIN THE LITTORAL OF A SINGLE STATE

B. The historic bay

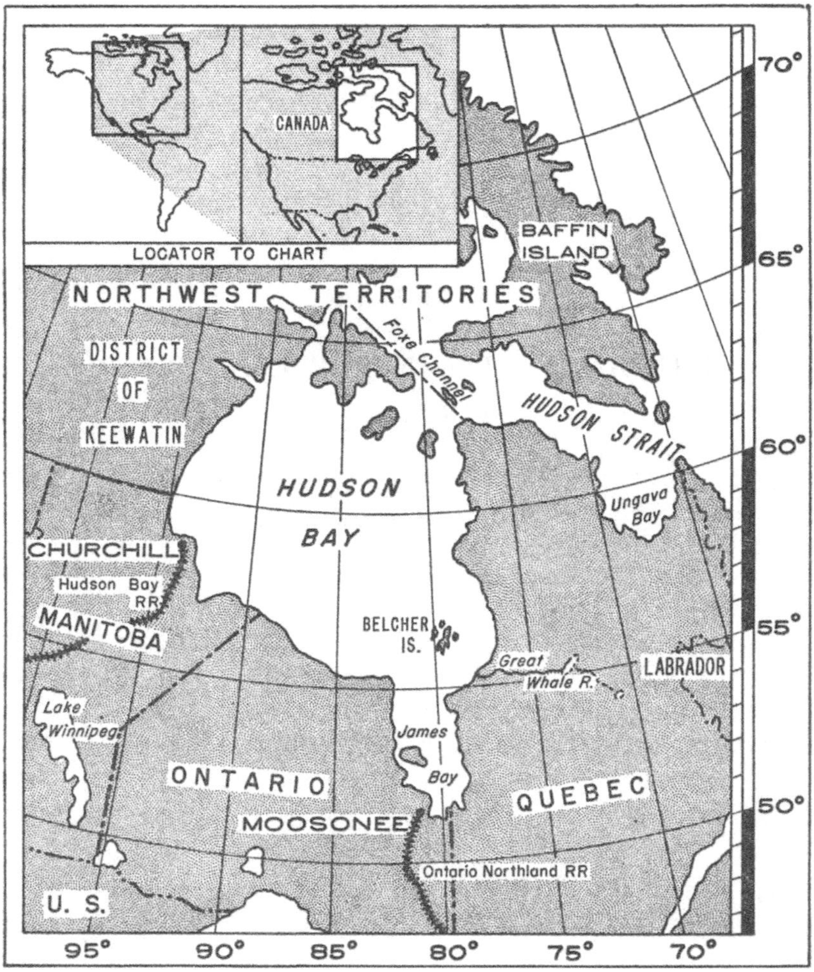

HUDSON BAY

Fig. 24

CHAPTER SIX

HUDSON BAY, A CASE STUDY

Section A GEOGRAPHICAL DESCRIPTION [1]

It is generally understood that the Canadian claim to title over Hudson Bay includes also Hudson Strait, the bay's connecting link with the Atlantic Ocean. Hudson Bay, in northeastern Canada, has a length of about 900 miles between extremes of latitude,[2] and its greatest width is 520 miles. Nearly one quarter of the total area of Hudson Bay is accounted for by James Bay which leads southward from the perimeter of Hudson Bay for a distance of 200 miles. James. Bay has a width of 80 to 100 miles throughout most of its course.

The only channel to Hudson Bay suitable for navigation is Hudson Strait which is about 430 miles long. The Atlantic entrance to Hudson Strait is 38 miles wide between Goodwin Island on the south and Hilton Headland on Resolution Island to the north. If one adds the water distances between the islands forming a rough chain at the entrance to Hudson Strait, the distance is 59 miles. The western end of Hudson Strait, at the entrance to the Bay proper, has a water distance of 74 miles across the island chain at that location. Immediately inside the entrance to Hudson Strait is located Ungava Bay, a

[1] Sources consulted for the geographical description of Hudson Bay are: U.S. Navy Hydrographic Offive, *Sailing Directions Northern Canada* (H. O. Publication No. 77), pp. 6a-8, Ch. 4; U.S. Navy Hydrographic Office Chart No. 5797 (reproduced from a Canadian Chart of 1957); *Funk and Wagnall's Standard Reference Encyclopaedia*, vol. 13, pp. 4704–5; V. Kenneth Johnson, "Canada's Title to Hudson Bay and Hudson Strait," 15 *British Yearbook of International Law* (1934), p. 1; F. Murray Greenwood and E. N. Smith, "Diesels To Desolation," 20 *Trains* (Dec. 1959); various political and geophysical maps; Henry B. Collins, jr., "Vanished Mystery Men of Hudson Bay," CX *National Geographic Magazine* (Nov. 1956), pp. 669–687; Henry B. Collins, Jr., "Exploring Frozen Fragments of American History," *Ibid.*, May 1939; U.S. Navy Publication, *Canadian North*, Prepared April 1956 by Technical Assistant to The Chief of Naval Operations for Polar Projects (OP-O3A3), p. 235ff.

[2] Great care must be exercised in taking map or chart measurements of the Hudson Bay-Hudson Strait area because of its northerly latitude. This is especially true when working with charts drawn on the Mercator projection, the projection generally used.

body of water which is roughly triangular in shape and which is 128 miles wide *inter fauces terrarum* and 130 miles deep at its greatest extremity. Hudson Bay is connected to the Arctic Ocean by Foxe Channel and Ne Ultra Strait.

The navigation seasons in Hudson Bay and Hudson Strait is from about 25 July to 1 November. The central part of the Strait and Bay never freezes over but is rendered practically impassable during other than the navigation season by great ice floes carried back and forth by strong tidal currents. Ice conditions are well plotted and broadcast by Canadian Government facilities. The Strait and the Bay are remarkably free of schoals and one can steam from the Atlantic entrance to Churchill Harbor, a distance of about 933 miles using only four course changes. By reason of the proximity of the north magnetic pole, the magnetic compass is practically useless in much of this area. The water depth averages from 150 to 350 fathoms in Hudson Strait and from 70 to 100 fathoms in Hudson Bay. Tidal ranges in Hudson Strait are from 31 feet at springs to $14^3/_4$ feet at neaps, with extremely large semi-monthly variations. Tidal currents in the Strait are strong and definite. In the bay there is a generally counter clockwise current and the tidal ranges at Churchill are $15^1/_2$ feet at springs. During the navigation season winds and weather are reasonably satisfactory. During the summer months, temperatures of 90°F. have been recorded at the southern part of James Bay. Winter temperatures of −50°F. are recorded. They decrease about 5°F. with every 4° increase in latitude.

Hudson Bay is surrounded by a great plateau which is rough, rocky, and hilly and is drained by numerous rivers and lakes. So many rivers drain into Hudson Bay that its water is merely brackish rather than salty ocean water. The northern forest limit is near Churchill on the west side and somewhat further south on the east side of the bay.

Until recently there have been few Caucasians to enter the Hudson Bay area to live, but prospectors are now being attracted in great numbers. Within this region are large stands of commercially valuable timber, potential farm and grazing land, and considerable iron ore in the Belcher Islands [3] and on the Ungava Peninsula. There is no

[3] The Belcher Islands in Southeastern Hudson Bay are reported to contain a solid iron ore of 35 to 40 per cent iron. On the Ungava Mainland to the east, along the Great Whale River, is another such deposit. It is planned to commence active extraction of this ore in 1965. Discussion with Mr. O. H. Daly, General Freight Agent, Canadian National Railways, Boston, Mass.

commercial sea fishing in the bay, although whales and walrus are hunted by the Indians and Eskimos in season.[4]

The principal ports of the region are Churchill, at the railhead of the Hudson Bay Railway in Manitoba, and Moosonee, at the railhead of the Ontario Northland Railway on James Bay. Churchill is an important grain shipping port on a route from western Canada to Europe. It is an administrative center for the national and provincial governments and for the Hudson's Bay Company. Moosonee is, at present, hampered by shallow water off its entrance, but extensive harbor development is planned.

There are no overland roads from the south to any point on James Bay, Hudson Bay, or Hudson Strait.

Of strategic importance to our study is the fact that from a point in the southern part of James Bay where there is a depth of water from 20 to 36 fathoms. The air distance to Montreal is 500 miles, to Toronto about 550 miles, to Detroit about 700 miles, to Chicago 725 miles, and to New York about 800 miles. From the nearest point of similar depth in Hudson Bay, the distance is 550 miles to Montreal.

Section B Discovery and claim to possession

What appears to be the first claim to possession over Hudson Bay appears in a document entitled, "Memorial Presented to the French Commissioners as to the King of England's Right to Hudson Bay." This paper reads, in part,

> 1. The northern part of America, where Hudson's Bay lies, was discovered by Sebastian Cabot, holding commissions from King Henry VII, in 1497.[1]

In another early document, dated 4 March 1699 and addressed by the Hudson's Bay Company to the Lord Commissioners, one reads:

> Hudson Bay, with all that belongs thereto within Hudson's Straits, was first discovered by Sir Sebastian Cabot, Grand Pilot to King Hen. VII, who gave English names to several places in the Bay, 1497.[2]

[4] Letter of 17 March 1959, from Canadian Consulate General, Boston in response to this writer's inquiry, and quoting information received from the Canadian Department of Transport. Mr. F. H. Kitts, in his book, *The Hudson Bay Region*, published in 1929 for the Canadian Department of the Interior, wrote (pp. 24–6) that there are cod in Ungava Bay, and some rock cod on the eastern shores of Hudson and James Bays. There are salmon in Hudson Bay. The commercially valuable species of whale are very rare and there are limited numbers of seal and walrus.

[1] Great Britain, *Calender of State Papers, Colonial Series*, 1685–1688, p. 309.

[2] Great Britain, *Calendar of State Papers, Colonial Series*, 1699, p. 89.

According to the research of James A. Williamson, it would appear that the Cabots were given credit for more in the way of discovery than their own record lays claim. Mr. Williamson quotes this from the inscriptions on the Mapamundi, the so-called Paris Map of 1544:

The 8th legend: This land [the northeastern coastal region of North America] was discovered by John Cabot the Venetian, and Sebastian Cabot, his son, in the year of the birth of our Saviour Jesus Christ 1494 [this of course should read 1497], on the 24th day of June in the morning, to which they gave the name Land First Seen, and to a large island which is near the said land they gave the name Saint John, because it had been discovered on the same day. (Words in brackets are Mr. Williamson's)[3]

Mr. Williamson then quotes the following from the legend on the back of Dr. John Dee's 1578 Map of the North Atlantic:

Circa An. 1497.4. Sebastian Cabote, sent by King Henry the Seventh, did discover from Newfoundland so far long and abowt the Coaste next to Labrador tyll he came to the Latitude of 67½. And styll fownd the Seas open before him.[4]

It would appear from the Williamson research that Sebastian Cabot saw the entrance to Hudson Strait but did not enter the Strait or the Bay. We next turn to the monumental work of Richard Hakluyt who reports that the Elizabethan explorer, Martin Frobisher, anchored in Jackman Sound [5] on 20 July 1577 in order to explore and take formal possession of the region in the vicinity of Hudson Bay.[6]

In the year 1610, Henry Hudson under the patronage of an English company explored much of the eastern side of Hudson Bay and made his way down to the southern limit of James Bay.[7] This voyage of exploration was followed by that of Sir Thomas Button in 1612.[8] In May 1631, Luke Foxe entered Hudson Bay and sailed for a mile up the Nelson River, on the southwest side of the bay, and anchored on August 10. There, in a formal ceremony, he took possession of an indefinite area for his sovereign, Charles I, and named it New Wales.[9] On 24 June 1632, Captain Thomas James, formally took possession of

[3] James A. Williamson, *The Voyages of the Cabots and the English Discover of North America under Henry VII and Henry VIII* (1929), p. 28.

[4] Williamson, *Voyages of the Cabots*, p. 23.

[5] Jackman Sound is against Baffin Island, on the north side of Hudson Strait, about 110 miles from the entrance.

[6] Richard Hakluyt, "The Second Voyage of Master Martin Frobisher ... 1577 ...," *The Principal Navigations, Voyages, Traffiques & Discoveries of the English Nation*, vol. VII, p. 217.

[7] Sir John Barrow, *A Chronological History of Voyages into the Arctic Regions* (1818), pp. 187–195.

[8] Thomas Rundall, Ed., *Narratives of Voyages towards the North-West, in Search of a Passage to Cathay and India*, 1496–1631, Series I, vol. V, (1849), p. 178.

[9] Rundall, Ed., *Narratives*, p. 153; also, 89 *Publications of the Hakluyt Society*, Ser. I, p. 348.

the regions around Charlton Island in James Bay, in the name of King Charles I.[10]

It appears, however, that the French were also busy during this era. In 1656, Captain Jean Bourdon took possession of several regions bordering of Hudson Bay in the name of his employers, the Canada Company, a trading corporation.[11] From then until 1713 possession of Hudson Bay and its shoreline was in dispute as between England and France.[12]

In 1668, Gillam and Grosseliez, leading a British expedition into Hudson Bay, entered the Rupert River on James Bay, and there erected a stone fort naming it Fort Charles.[13] Finally, on 2 May 1670, the English Government made their famous grant to the Hudson's Bay Company. It appears, from the terms of this Charter, that the English Government had assumed possession of, and title to, Hudson Bay and the territories surrounding it.

By the terms of its Charter, the Hudson's Bay Company was granted by the English Crown "all waters, lands & c., within the entrance to Hudson Strait, not possessed by any other British company or colony." [14] This territory, later named Rupert's Land, was described by the Company as including all the territory in North America and the Arctic Islands, drained by rivers flowing into Hudson Bay.[15] The special legal position of the Hudson's Bay Company from 1670 until 1870 when Rupert's Land was purchased by Canada from the Hudson's Bay Company should be noted. According to Moore's view, the Hudson's Bay Company was one of a number of English companies to which the Crown delegated powers which are usually possessed only by a State.[16] Judging from a review of two histories of the Hudson's

[10] Thomas James, *The Dangerous Voyage of Captain Thomas James, in His intended Discovery of a North-West Passage into the South Sea.* (1740, reprint of 1635 edition), p. 95.

[11] Gabriel Marcel, "La Cartographie de la Nouvelle France, supplément à l'ouvrage de M. Henry Harrisse sur le même sujet," *Revue de Géographie* (Mar.-April 1885) pp. 186–194. 282–289, 359–365. 442–447.

[12] In 1670, France claimed, through New France, title to the whole. Marcel, *op. cit.*

[13] Barrow, *Voyages*, pp. 254–61.

[14] The major portion of this Charter is reproduced in the opinion of John Rose, Q. C., of 1 December 1848, on "The Nature of the Rights of the Hudson's Bay Company over its Territories," reprinted in William R. Manning, *Diplomatic Correspondence of the United States-Canadian Relations* (1945), vol. IV, 1849–1860, at pages 402–8. A portion of this charter is reproduced at Annex A.

[15] Mr. V. Kenneth Johnston in his article "Canada's Title to Hudson Bay" 15 BYIL (1934), at p. 5, cites as authority for this statement *Report from the Select Committee on the Hudson's Bay Company*, Minutes of Evidence, Examination of Sir G. Simpson, 26 February 1857, Question nos. 737–742, p. 46. Mr. Johnston writes that so far as can be discovered, the above citation contains the only official description of Rupert's Land that has ever been given.

[16] *Moore's Digest* (1906), vol. I, p. 16.

Bay Company, this analysis would appear descriptive of the state of affairs in Rupert's Land from 1670 to 1870.[17] Moreover, a reading of the Company's charter will resolve any doubt concerning the very wide degree of sovereignty that was granted. It should also be clear, from the terms of the charter, that full and unequivocal possession of Hudson's Bay was asserted to lie with England.

In 1713 the disputatious claim of France was terminated in Article 10 of the Treaty of Utrecht. By that article the King of France ceded to Great Britain "The Hudson Bay and the Hudson Strait with all the Land." [18]

During the period 1713 to 1870, it does not appear that any protest or objection was made by any State to the asserted jurisdiction (or sovereignty) over Hudson's Bay.

In 1870, the Hudson's Bay Company surrendered to the Crown "all the lands and territories within Rupert's Land granted or purported to be granted to the Company by the Charter of 1670. Then, under the authority of the "Rupert's Land Act of 1868," an Imperial Order in Council was issued admitting Rupert's Land into the Dominion of Canada.[19]

By an Order in Council of 1897, the northern territories of Canada were split up into administrative units whose boundaries run through the middle of Hudson Bay and Strait rather than along the sinuosities of the coast of either body of water.[20] At the present time, however, the official maps of Canada consulted by this author show that all boundaries except one terminate at the shores of Hudson Strait or Hudson Bay. The exception is the boundary between the District of Keewatin and the District of Franklin. This is a water boundary drawn in a NW-SE direction through Foxe Channel.

Finally, in 1906, the Canadian Parliament passed an Act imposing an annual license fee for the privilege of whaling in Hudson Bay. This Act reads in part as follows:

> 14 Notwithstanding anything in this section, the license fee payable for any vessel or boat engaged in the whale fishery or hunting whales within the waters of Hudson Bay, or the territorial waters of Canada north of the 55th parallel of north latitude, if not so engaged or hunting in connection with a factory established in Canada, shall be fifty dollars for each year; and, *inasmuch as*

[17] Sir William Schucking, *The Hudson's Bay Company* (1911), J. Mackay, *The Honourable Company* (1938).

[18] J. Almon, *Collection of Treaties, &c. between Great Britain and other Powers* (1772), vol. I, p. 136.

[19] *Statutes of Canada*, 1869, p. iii; 1872, p. lxiii, lxxvii-lxxxiii.

[20] *Statutes of Canada*, 1898, p. xxxvi; XXXI *Canada Gazette* (14 May 1898), pp. 2613–14.

Hudson Bay is wholly territorial water of Canada, the requirements of this section as to licensing, and as to the fee payable therefor, shall apply to every vessel or boat engaged in the whale fishery of hunting whales in any part of the waters of Hudson Bay, whether such vessel or boat belongs to Canada, or is registered and outfitted in, or commences her voyage from, any other British or foreign country. (Italics mine).[21]

The Canadian Government performs the following administrative functions in Hudson Bay at this time:

(a) During the navigation season, the Canadian ice-breaking patrol vessel, *N. B. McLean,* equipped with salvage apparatus, acts as a depot ship in Hudson Strait.[22] Masters of commercial vessels are required by the terms of their insurance coverage to consult with the Commanding Officer concerning ice conditions near the beginning and end of the navigation season.[23]

(b) Foreign ships have been asked to report when passing Cape Chidley, on the south side of the entrance to Hudson Strait, "but they do not always do so."[24]

(c) An Eastern Arctic Patrol visits sea coastal points where Eskimos congregate in the summer.[25]

(d) There is a patrol by the Royal Canadian Mounted Police for the enforcement of criminal and civil law.[26]

(e) Maintenance of aids to navigation.

Information received by the writer from the Department of Transport, Ottawa, in a letter, dated 17 March 1959, is quoted:

1. Insofar as this department is concerned there are no regulations in force in Hudson Bay and Hudson Strait for foreign shipping.

2. This Department maintains no enforcement agency in Hudson Bay and Hudson Strait.

3. Ships bound for Hudson Bay are not required by this Department to obtain clearance.

A review of a number of histories of Canada published in the last thirty years fails to disclose any mention of sovereignty over Hudson Bay. *Canada Year Book* 1957–58, a very large and complete work published by the Government and described as the "official statistical annual of the resources, history, institutions, and social and economic conditions of Canada," gives no hint concerning the Government's current attitude in this question. The book mentions the mileage of the coastlines of Hudson Strait and Hudson Bay along with those of

[21] *Revised Statutes of Canada 1906*, cap 45, sec. 9(12) and included in *Revised Statutes of Canada 1927*, cap. 73, sec. 9(10).

[22] U.S. Navy Hydrographic Office Publication, H.O. 77, pp. 8, 227–8.

[23] *Ibid.;* Canadian Consul General, Boston, Letter of 17 March 1959 to author.

[24] *Ibid.*

[25] Letter from Deputy Minister of Northern Affairs and National Resources, Ottawa, dated 5 February 1959.

[26] *Ibid.*

the Atlantic and Pacific coasts.[27] In describing the extent of the Northwest territories, the Year Book has this to say:

1. All that part of Canada north of the Sixtieth Parallel of North Latitude, except the portions thereof within the Yukon Territory and the Provinces of Quebec and Newfoundland, and

2. the islands in Hudson Bay, James Bay and Ungava Bay, except those islands within the Provinces of Manitoba, Ontario and Quebec.[28]

The book appears to be without any other incidental reference to the status of Hudson Bay.

Judging from the above-mentioned writings as well as from the information this writer was able to obtain from the Canadian Goovernment, it does not appear that sovereignty over this huge inland sea has been any recent source of pre-occupation among Canadian authorities.

Annex A Excerpt from the Charter of the Hudson's Bay Company [29]

And to the end the said Governor and Company of adventurers, of England, trading into Hudson's Bay, may be encouraged to undertake and effectually to prosecute the said design of our more especial grace, certain knowledge and mere motion, we have given, granted, and confirmed, and, by these presents, for us, our heirs and successors, do give, grant, and confirm unto the said Governor and Company, and their successors, the sole trade and commerce of all those seas, straits, bays, rivers, lakes, creeks, and sounds, in whatsoever latitude they shall be, that lie within the entrance of the straits commonly called Hudson's Straits, together with all the lands and territories upon the Countries, Coasts, and confines of the seas, bays, lakes, rivers, creeks, and sounds aforesaid, that are not already actually possessed by, or granted to, any of our subjects, or possessed by the subjects of any other Christian prince or state, with the fishing of all sorts of fish, whales, sturgeons, and all other royal fishes in the seas, bays, inlets, and rivers within the premises, and the fish therein taken, together with the royalty of the sea upon the coasts within the limits aforesaid; and all mines royal, as well discovered as not discovered, of gold, silver, gems, and precious stones to be found or discovered within the territories. limits and places aforesaid; and that the said land be, from henceforth, reckoned and reputed as one of our plantations or colonies in America, called Rupert's Land. And, further, we do, by these presents, for us, our heirs and successors, make, create, and constitute the said Governor and Company, for the time being, and, and their successors, the true and absolute lords and proprietors of the same territory, limits, and places aforesaid, and of all other the premises, saving always the faith, allegiance, and

[27] *Canada Year Book*, 1957–58, p. 13.
[28] *Ibid.*, p. 72.
[29] William R. Manning, *Diplomatic Correspondence of the United States-Canadian Relations* 1945), vol. iv, 1849–1860, pp. 402–408.

sovereign dominion due to us, our heirs and successors; for the same to have, hold, possess, and enjoy the said territory, limits, and places, and all and singular other the premises hereby granted as aforesaid, with their and every of their rights, members, jurisdictions, prerogatives, royalties, and appurtenances whatsoever to them the said Governor and Company, and their successors, forever to be holden of us, our heirs and successors, as of our manor of East Greenwich, in our Country of Kent, in free and common soccage, and not in capite, or by knights' service, yielding and paying yearly to us, our heirs and successors, for the same, two elks and two black beavers, whensoever, and as often as we, our heirs and successors, shall happen to enter into the said countries, territories, and regions hereby granted.

And further, our will and pleasure is, and by these presents, for us, our heirs and successors, we do grant unto the said Governor and Company, and to their successors, that it shall and may be lawful to and for the said Governor and Company, and their successors, from time to time to assemble themselves for or about any the matters, causes, affairs, or business of the said trade, in any place or places for the same, convenient within our dominions or elsewhwere, and there to hold court for the said Company and the affairs thereof. And also it shall and may be lawful to and for them, and the greater part of them, being so assembled, and that shall then and there be present, in any such place or places, whereof the Governor or his deputy, for the time being, to be one, to make, ordain, and constitute such and so many reasonable laws, constitutions, orders and ordinances, as to them, or the greater part of them, being then & there present, shall seem necessary and convenient for the good government of the said Company, and of all governors of Colonies, forts and plantations, factors, masters, mariners, and other officers employed, or to be employed, in any of the territories and lands aforesaid, and in any of their voyages, and for the better advancement and continuance of the said trade, or traffic and plantations, and the same laws, constitutions, orders and ordinances, so made, to put in use and execute accordingly, and at their pleasure to revoke and alter the same, or any of them, as the occasion shall require. And that the said Governor and Company, so often as they shall make, ordain, or establish any such laws, constitutions, orders and ordinances, in such forms as aforesaid, shall and may lawfully impose, ordain, limit and provide, such pains, penalties, and punishments upon all offenders, contrary to such laws, constitutions orders and ordinances, or any of them, as to the said Governor or Company, for the time being, or the greater part of them, then and there being present, the said Governor or his deputy being always one, shall seem necessary, requisite, or convenient for the observation of the same laws, constitutions, orders and ordinances, and the same fines and amerciaments shall and may, by their officers and servants, from time to time to be appointed for that purpose, levy, take and have, to the use of the said Governor and Company, and their successors, without the impediment of us, our heirs and successors, or of any the Officers or ministers of us, our heirs or successors, and without any account therefore to us, our heirs and successors, to be made. All and singular which laws, constitutions, orders and ordinances so as aforesaid to be made, we will to be duly observed and kept under the pains and penalties therein to be contained, so, always, as the said laws, constitutions orders and ordinances, fines and americaments, be reasonable, and not contrary or repugnant, or customs of this our realm.

After the mentiou of sundry other minor privileges, there is a further grant, as follows:

And further of our special grace, certain knowledge, and mere motion, we do, for us, our heirs, and successors, grant to and with the said Governor and Company of adventurers of England, trading into Hudson's Bay, that all lands, islands, territories, plantations, forts, fortifications, factories, or colonies, where the said Company's factories, and trade are, or shall be, within any the ports or places afore limited, shall be immediately and from henceforth under the power and Command of the said Governor and Company, their successors and assigns, saving the faith and allegiance due to be performed to us, our heirs and successors and assigns, as aforesaid. And that the said Governor and Company shall have liberty, full power, and authority to appoint and establish governors and all other officers to govern them; and that the governor and his council of the several and respective places where the said Company shall have plantations, forts, factories, colonies or places of trade, within the countries, lands, or territories hereby granted, may have power to judge all persons belonging to the said Governor and Company, or that shall live under them in all causes, whether civil or criminal, according to the laws of this Kingdom and to execute justice accordingly.

The territories mentioned in this charter are:

All those seas, straits, bays, rivers, lakes, creeks, and sounds, in whatever latitude they shall be, that lie within the entrance of the straits commonly called Hudson's straits, together with all the lands, countries, and territories upon the coasts and confines of the seas, straits, bays, lakes, rivers, creeks, and sounds aforesaid, which are not now actually possessed by any of our subjects, or by the subjects of any other Christian prince, or state.

Section C RECOGNITION OF THE CLAIM

The two sides of the 17th Century controversy concerning coastal waters were argued by the young Dutch lawyer Hugo de Groot, or Grotius who wrote *Mare Liberum* and by the English advocate John Selden, who wrote *Mare Clausum.* Professor Jessup has rather aptly called this controversy the "battle of the books." [1] In the twentieth century, Hudson Bay furnished us the issue over which there has been something of a miniaturized parallel which might be called the "skirmish of the articles." It really cannot be seen as more than a skirmish inasmuch as the possession of Hudson Bay appears never to have attained much stature as an international question.

The first of the skirmishing articles was written in 1912 by an American international lawyer, Thomas Willing Balch, and is entitled "Is Hudson Bay a Closed or Open Sea?" The article appeared in the *American Journal of International Law,* and in shortened form, in

[1] Philip C. Jessup, *The Law of Territorial Waters and Maritime Jurisdiction* (1927), p. 4.

French, in *Revue de Droit International et de Législation Comparée.*[2] Mr. Balch exhaustively analyzed what he considered to be analogous cases and arrived at the conclusion that an exclusive claim to Hudson Bay would not be reasonable.

The second of the articles was written in 1934 by a Canadian lawyer, V. Kenneth Johnston, and is entitled "Canada's Title to Hudson Bay and Hudson Strait." The article appeared in the *British Yearbook of International Law.*[3] Mr. Johnson addresses himself more directly to the problem instead of resorting to analogies. He seeks to demonstrate that through specific Canadian or British acts of sovereignty, as well as acts of American acquiescence, Canada has indisputable title to Hudson Bay. He also writes:

> By the rule of international law, which Sir Cecil Hurst deduces from British authorities, Canada has title to Hudson Bay and Hudson Strait.

Apparently Mr. Johnson has reference to Sir Cecil Hurst's article. "There Territoriality of Bays,[4] although he does not so indicate. This author's review of all the writings of Sir Cecil Hurst which he was able to locate has failed to disclose anything but that jurist's silence with respect to Hudson Bay.

Neither Mr. Balch nor Mr. Johnston makes any effort to discuss Hudson Bay from an economic, military, or geographical point of view. Nor does either author attempt to relate the Canadian-American controversy to the political climate of the time in which it occurred. In other words, those factors of economic and political life which tend to produce a linkage between a bay and the surrounding land, and thus to produce a state of mind or political position which may sharpen into a legalistically conceptualized position are not touched upon by either writer. Both writers have submitted richly annotated arguments, and they are both worthy of study, but neither author has referred to the excellent summary of the issue by the Australian jurist Pitt Cobbet,[5] or to the excellent discussion of the controversy and its multi-faceted background by Mr. P. T. McGrath, "The Hudson Bay Dispute," published in *The Fortnigthly Review* in 1908.[6]

[2] 6 *American Journal of International Law* (1912), pp. 409–459. The title of the article in French is "La Baie d'Hudson, est-elle une mer libre ou une mer fermée," and the citation thereof is XIII *Revue de Droit International et de Législation Comparée* (2ième Série), pp. 539–586.

[3] 15 *British Yearbook of International Law* (1934). pp, 1–20.

[4] *The British Yearbook of International Law*, 1922–23, pp. 42–54.

[5] Pitt Cobbett, *Cases and Opinions on International Law*, Part I, 3rd Ed. (1909), pp. 145–6.

[6] P. T. McGrath, "The Hudson Bay Dispute," *The Fortnightly Review*, 1 Jan. 1908, pp. 125–136.

We shall now examine the manifestations of recognition of a Canadian title to Hudson Bay, or a denial of it, and some further Acts of sovereignty on the part of Canada.

In the 20 October 1818 Convention between Great Britain and the United States, the parties agreed that the inhabitants of the United States should have, in common with British subjects, the liberty to take fish along the coasts of a number of parts of northeastern Canada and Newfoundland, which are specifically described, but "without prejudice to the exclusive rights of the Hudson of Bay Company." [7] This clause is explained by the American negotiators as follows:

> To the exception of the exclusive rights of the Hudson's Bay Company, we did not object as it was virtually implied in the treaty of 1783 and we had never, any more than British subjects, enjoyed any right there, the Charter of that Company having been granted in the year 1670. The exception applies only to the coasts and their harbours and does not affect the right of fishing in Hudson's Bay beyond three miles from the shores, a right which could not exclusively belong to or be granted by any nation.[8]

Mr. Johnston writes that in some quarters this dispatch has been accepted and treated as a caveat against any British claim to jurisdiction in and over all of Hudson Bay and Strait. He offers three reasons why a caveat is non-existent in the circumstances: (a) It was not communicated to the other party; (b) That the Hudson's Bay Company had exclusive possessions and jurisdiction over these areas from the British Crown; and (c) That British subjects, like Americans, were prohibited from fishing and whaling in those waters, hence there was no right of British subjects which Americans might enjoy "in common." [9]

Mr. Johnston offers no explanation of whom the "some quarters" might be, and save for the Balch article and one reference in Hackworth's Digest, (mentioned hereunder) this writer has been unable to find any material tending to substantiate Mr. Johnston's statement. Moreover, his statement that British subjects, like Americans, were prohibited from fishing and whaling in Hudson Bay and Hudson Strait, is at least open to debate inasmuch as Newfoundland fishermen were known to fish in Hudson Strait and Ungava Bay, without fear of arrest, during the years that the area was subject to the rule of the Hudson's Bay Company.[10]

It is highly doubtful whether any genuine economic interests were

[7] John Bassett Moore, *Digest of International Law* (1906), vol. I, p. 781.
[8] VII *U.S. State Papers* (1818–19), p. 167.
[9] Johnston, *op. cit.*
[10] McGrath, *op. cit.*

at stake at the time that the controversy reached its height at the turn of the present century. By then, the American whaling industry from Atlantic Coast ports was in a decline. Although American whalers had hunted in Hudson Bay for some seventy years, relatively few were doing so by 1900. Mr. J. T. Jenkins, in his book, *A History of Whale Fisheries*, tells us that American whale fishing in Davis Strait and Hudson Bay from 1890 to 1897 consisted of the following expeditions: 1890, 1 ship; 1892, 2 ships; 1895, 5 ships; 1896–7, 1 ship; and 1897, 2 ships both of which were money losing ventures.[11] Research in the vast Fearing Collection on Fisheries at Harvard University would indicate that at no time were the Hudosn Bay whaling grounds of even minor economic prominence.[12] On the Canadian side of this issue, we have the statement of Mr. McGrath: "The Canadians are not conspicuous for maritime enterprize." [13] Judging from the absence of any mention of a Canadian whaling industry in works having to do with that subject, it appears that Mr. McGrath was on solid ground, at least as far as Canadian whaling enterprize is concerned.

This author has been unable to ascertain that any commercial fishing, other than whaling, has ever been undertaken in Hudson Bay. The Canadian Government authorities advised the author that there is none at the present time.[14]

In view of this absence of opposing economic pressures, we must look further for reasons which might have given rise to a re-assertion of the British/Canadian claim and the ensuing controversy. Writing in 1908, Mr. McGrath offers a clue:

> In Canada there is a far-reaching and deep-rooted fear that her best interests are always in danger of being sacrificed to the desire of conciliating the American Republic, and this probably accounts for her vigorous and independent action in the present instance.[15]

Mr. McGrath then goes on to cite instances wherein Canadians felt that they were the losers in the 19th Century relationships between the United States and Great Britain. He ends his dispassionate article by hopefully suggesting that this (1908) is no time for the Imperial

[11] J. T. Jenkins, *A History of the Whale Fisheries* (1921), p. 350.

[12] This collection has a most impressive number of volumes on whaling. One of these, Walter S. Tower, *A History of the American Whale Industry* (1906), is a work of obvious academic merit. Whaling in Hudson's Bay is mentioned in the Tower book as being a rather unprofitable venture.

[13] McGrath, *op. cit.*

[14] Section A, above.

[15] McGrath, *op. cit.*

Government to leave outstanding Canadian-American disputes unresolved.

It should be recalled that a the beginning of this century there was afoot an American imperialist movement – an imperialist conception of national self interest. The United States had defeated a fifth rate military power in 1898. It was the age of Theodore Roosevelt and Rear Admiral Mahan. At the same time, there was the ambitious ascendancy of the German Empire. In this power situation, it was Great Britain's policy to cultivate American good will by a variety of official acts and private assurances.[16] In Canadian-American relations it was the time of Alaska boundary dispute, a matter settled by an arbitration commission who made their award lon 20 October 1903.[17] Although the tribunal did not accept the line advocated by the United States, nor that claimed by Great Britain, rhe Canadian reaction was anything but a happy one. It was the British member of the Commission who voted with the three American members and against the two Canadian members.[18] It would appear that independent Canadian action might very well be expected in any other controversies.

In August 1903, the Canadian Government sent the ship, "Neptune" to Hudson Bay to reassert Canadian sovereignty over the area and to expel or subject to Canadian authority any United States whalers.[19] It does not appear that any were found, although Mr. Johnston ascertained that in 1908, a private fishing and hunting expedition from the United States was met, license fees were demanded, and they were paid.[20] In 1904 the Canadian Government ship, "Arctic" was sent to Hudson Bay. On board was a Major Moodie, North-West Mounted Police, who had been commissioned Governor of Hudson Bay and directed to establish a number of posts on the shores of the bay. The "Arctic" was also directed to explore Hudson Bay and Hudson Strait in order to advise upon the feasibility of establishing a

[16] Lionel M. Gelber, *The Rise of Anglo-American Friendship* (1938), pp. 30–32; A. L. P. Dennis, *Adventures in American Diplomacy, 1896–1906* (1928), p. 98.

[17] An excellent summary of the background is contained in I *Moore's Digest* (1906), pp. 462–475; For the record of the tribunal's proceedings see *Alaska Boundary Tribunal, Proceedings*, Senate Document No. 162, 58th Congress, 2nd Session, Washington, 1904.

[18] Gelber, *op. cit.*, pp. 140–165.

[19] McGrath, *op. cit.;* Johnston, *op. cit.*

[20] It was reported in *Cruise of the Arctic*, 1908–9, that licenses for fishing were issued, and whalers and others were informed that regulations in regard to fishing and Canadian customs duties upon imported goods to be disposed of in trading with the natives were to be collected. Johnston, *op. cit.* These actions were in implementation of the 1904–06 legislation which applied to Canadians and foreigners alike. This writer has been unable to uncover evidence as to the amount of fishing actually done in Hudosn Bay during the period, where it was done (with respect to the 3-mile limit), or what nationalities were doing the fishing.

northern sea route, to connect with a proposed railroad to Churchill.[21]

During the period that these voyages were being undertaken, the Canadian legislation of 1904 and amendment of 1906 were passed. It is to be observed that these moves were entirely Canadian in origin.

In October 1906, four months after the passage of the Canadian legislation asserting that Hudson Bay is wholly territorial water of Canada, there was addressed to the U.S. Department of State an inquiry "whether any treaty exists with Canada under which United States vessels are permitted to fish in the waters of Hudson Bay, or whether the waters of Hudson Bay proper, as well as Ungava Bay and James Bay are international waters outside the three-mile limit." In reply, Assistant Secretary of State Adee replied that the rights of American citizens to fish in Hudson Bay are limited by the provisions of the treaty of 1818, by article I of which it was agreed that the inhabitants of the United States shall have liberty to take fish on certain clearly defined parts of the coast of Newfoundland and Labrador, and on the southern shores of the Magdalen Islands, and the United States renounced forever any liberty theretofore enjoyed or claimed by its inhabitants to take, dry or cure fish on or within three marine miles of "His Britannic Majesty's dominions in America so defined," and that under this treaty stipulation "citizens of the United States have no right to whale or fish in the waters of Hudson Bay within three marine miles of the shore." Mr. Adee continued:

> In any event, with respect to Hudson Bay, which is a body of water 900 miles long by 600 miles wide, and connected with the Atlantic Ocean by a strait about 400 miles in length and varying from 60 to 100 miles in width, the United States will take the position that citizens of the United States have the right to whale and fish within its waters outside the three mile limit.[22]

It is not known that the United States Government has had any subsequent occasion to express a position in that matter. Nor does it appear that the United States availed itself of the privilege of protest at the time the 1906 Amendment was passed. That the matter was discussed by either the British or the American representatives at the North Atlantic Sea Coast Fisheries Arbitration in 1910 is not a matter of record, although Mr. Root in his oral argument did mention it in passing as an example of a large body of water which might more properly be called a gulf.[23] The treaty of 20 July 1912 for

[21] The first surveyors reported unfavorably on the project.

[22] *Hackworth's Digest* (1940), vol. I, pp. 700–1.

[23] Elihu Root, *Argument on Behalf of the United States, North Atlantic Coast Fisheries Arbitration*, Bacon-Scott Ed. (1917), p. 46.

carrying out the award of the arbitral tribunal reads, in Article II,

It is understood that the award does not cover Hudson Bay.[24]

Since the Canadian legislation of 1906 and the State Department correspondence of the same year, there is an absence of officially published views on the subject either in Canada or the United States. The Canadian Government seems to maintain an attitude of scrupulous silence [25] and there appear to have been within the last fifty years no incidents to revive the issue. At present, then, the legal status of Hudson Bay appears to be about as follows:

(a) An item of Canadian legislation in 1906 posits that Hudson Bay is a part of Canadian territorial waters. What is probably meant here, of course, is internal waters.

(b) There appears to have been no official protest to this assertion either on the part of the United States, or on the part of any other government.

(c) There appear to have been a number of acts on the part of the United States, prior to 1906, which can be construed as recognizing a certain proprietary right either of the Hudson's Bay Company, or its successor, the Government of Canada, to the whole of Hudson Bay and Hudson Strait.

(d) Since 1906, there has been no official protest by the United States against the licensing and customs activities in Hudson Bay in those apparently isolated cases where Americans or their ships were involved.

(e) There does not appear to have been any specific act since 1906 which might be construed as implying recognition of the Canadian claim, by the United States or any other State.

(f) Since 1906, the Canadian Government has never reiterated its claim, although it has been presented with periodic opportunities to do so. That Government has taken some elementary measures which can be construed as acts of sovereignty but they are primarily aimed at safe navigation of the waters of the bay and the maintenance of

[24] III *Malloy's Treaties* 2632, 2636.

[25] Neither at the 1930 Conference nor at the 1958 Conference, nor in the preparatory phases for either, does the matter seem to arise. Mr. George Drew, Chairman of the Canadian Delegation at the 1958 Conference, addressed the First Committee in a lengthy and comprehensive manner concerning the Canadian view on territorial water. A/Conf.13/39, pp. 51–3. Hudson Bay was not mentioned. For a verbatim transcript of the main portion of this address see *Canadian Weekly Bulletin* No. 13 (26 Mar. 1958), Department of External Affairs, Information Division, Ottawa.

law and order among the few inhabitants of its shores. There has been no provocation for the Canadian Government to do more.

What can be derived from the story of Canadian sovereignty over Hudson Bay is that where there is an absence of any real conflict of economic interest, as between States, with respect to a bay over which one State claims sovereignty. Any other grounds for conflict are likely to have a low level of reality in the public eye and are unlikely to enlist any continuous policy interest of the parties concerned. This would appear especially true when the Governments of the States concerned are, fundamentally, not motivated by aggressive or aggrandizing ideologies. The lesson to be learned from the Johnston article is that, despite its display of an advocate's rather cavalier handling of materials, a rather convincing case can be made for exclusive sovereignty over a bay on historic grounds alone. The lesson to be learned from the Balch article is that with respect to bays, argument by analogy has a certain air of abstractness. Each bay is a different problem and the use of analogies in an argument seeking to demonstrate the illegality of a State's asserting sovereignty over a bay on historic grounds has a heavy burden if is to be convincing. Finally, as one ponders the two articles, one has the feeling that argument over sovereignty of a bay whose economic value is miniscule partakes of vacuous futility.

Section D THE CHANGING ECONOMIC AND DEFENSE SITUATION

Within the past few years there has been a growing amount of economic activity in the Canadian North. This has to do primarily with the discovery and extraction of minerals, especially iron ore. There appears to be no new interest in the waters of Hudson Bay either for commercial fishing or by reason of oil or other mineral deposits in the sea-bed or sub-soil of the bay. The most likely increase in economic activity on the waters of Hudson Bay is in the realm of communications because sea transportation is required for ores, either to railheads at Churchill or Moosonee or through Hudson Strait to the Atlantic Ocean. On the other hand the opening of the St. Lawrence Seaway, permitting the passage of ocean-borne shipping to the western end of the Great Lakes can present a serious challenge to the Hudson Bay route. The ice free navigation season for the Seaway route is, normally, from mid-April to mid-December, while on the Hudson Bay route the season is from July to November.[1]

[1] *Canada Yeat Book*, 1957–58. p. 868.

In Section A, above, we noted the distances from the center of deep water in James Bay to a number of large metropolitan areas in the United States and Cabada. These distances are within the range o missiles that can be carried by submarines. While open navigation in Hudson Bay is seasonal and submarine navigation amid sea ice is a hazardous undertaking, year around navigation in the Arctic is not impossible, as the United States Navy has recently demonstrated. From a strategic standpoint there are military advantages to the missile-carrying submarine and there might be some further advantages to firing from a position in James Bay. The submarine carried missile has value as a strategic weapon, a surprise weapon and as a tactical weapon. It is believed, for this reason, that Hudson Bay is a potential operating area for such submarines. With its tremendous area and location it constitutes a real problem for anti-submarine defense. For this reason Canada may be expected to see Hudson Bay as being more intimately connected with her national security than in times past If Hudson Bay remains a part of Canadian internal waters, then Canada can, by international law, forbid the entry of foreign warships including submarines. This does not make an intruding submarine any easier to find, but it does permit Canada to take forceful and positive measures such craft if their presence is detected.

Hudson Bay does not have the characteristics of a sheltered naval base or harbor, and thus does not have the intimate connection with the land that one usually associates with the bays in connection with defense.

In sum, it is problematical whether possession of Hudson Bay as inland waters can be regarded as especially essential to the national security of Canada. In the short term, a fairly good argument for such a thesis is possible. In the long term, the prosposition becomes more doubtful.[2]

In the 1906 era, there seemed to exist in Canadian eyes some commanding reasons for claiming title to Hudson Bay as internal waters. Today, on military or economic grounds, the necessity for such title is debatable. But on those same grounds, there is little legitimate and material reason for any other State to wish Hudson Bay were a part of the high seas. That being so, it is doubtful whether the legal status of Hudson Bay will be the subject of international controversy in the immediate future.

[2] To undertake an analysis of the East-West race in missile development is quite beyond the scope of this thesis. The conclusions reached here are based primarily upon U.S. Senate Document No. 8, 86th Congress, 1st Session, *Developments in Military Technology and their Impact on United States Strategy and Foreign Policy*, dated 6 December 1959, and prepared by the Washington Center of Foreign Policy Research, The Johns Hopkins University.

CHAPTER SEVEN

THE CONCEPT OF THE HISTORIC BAY

Section A Origin of the term

The first five chapters dealt with the growth of a general set of rules to accommodate this peculiarity of the earth's crust called a bay. We have seen that, for purposes of ascertaining when in international law a bay exists, and when the littoral State has the right to claim as her internal waters some or all of the area of the bay, certain criteria have been formulated and generally agreed upon. But in Chapter Six, we have examined an exception to some of these criteria. Earlier, we have noted the sixth and final paragraph of Article 7 of the 1958 Geneva Convention on the Territorial Sea and the Contiguous Zone. To repeat, this paragraph reads:

> 6. The foregoing provisions shall not apply to the so-called "historic bays," or in any case where the straight base-line system provided for in article 4 is applied.

It is, of course, only with the first, the historic bay clause, that this chapter deals. The bay whose entrance breadth is greater than that contemplated by the general rules, or whose configuration is such that it fails to fulfill the requirements of the evolved rules, but which is held to be in the national territory of the littoral State, falls into the perhaps inaccurately named category of "historic bays." It is an exception to the rules,[1] or as Professor Gidel called it, the safety valve that accompanies the general rule.[2]

The term, historic bay, appears to be a comparatively recent one in the lexicon of international law. A review of the publicists' writings on territorial waters and bays or a review of judicial decisions along these

[1] On the matter of exceptions, see Georg Schwarzenberger, *International Law*, vol. I, 3rd Ed., (1957), p. 328.

[2] Gilbert Gidel, *Le Droit international public de la Mer*, Tome III (1934), p. 621.

lines would appear to disclose that the term crept in only after the mathematical criteria for delimiting the internal waters of a bay came into some general usage.[3] There was an obvious need for a term to be used for bays where the mathematical criterion, by reason of its being exceeded by the breadth of a specific bay to which a State made exclusive claim, was considered inapplicable. Such bays seem to have come to be called historic bays because the littoral States claiming title to them have been generally considered to enjoy the title through long, uninterrupted and peaceful possession, and sometimes by reason of some relatively ancient symbolic act of claim which has gone uncontested.

Now, whether or not one agrees with the propriety of the term, *historic* bay, one should be loathe to conclude that the "safety valve" exception for the historic bay has no merit, if it is based upon the objectively assessed needs of the inhabitants of the surrounding land. Although the 1958 Geneva Convention prescribes a maximum closing line of twenty-four miles, it can probably be demonstrated that universal application of this rule, as well as that of the semi-circular area rule, might be repugnant to the interests of the littoral State in the case of a particular bay, without significantly benefiting the whole aggregate of States. On the other hand, since the agreed upon criteria are not being met in the claim to the historic bay, there follows the very natural question as to why such an exceptional claim should be recognized. It would appear logical and natural to conclude that there should lie with the State making the claim the onus to prove such an exceptional title. But in a world of legally equal and sovereign States, there appears no orderly or simple machinery for establishing such proof and no agreed upon criteria against which the proof can be measured.

We have discussed the efforts at codification for bays, and we have noted the exception to the general rules. The question is whether there should not be a codification of criteria for the exceptional situation of historic bays. We have explained the factors that motivate States to make claims to bays as internal waters. We can be certain that the reasons for a State's assertion to a bay that does not meet the requirements of the general rules are identical with those that have prompted a great many States to agree to reciprocally recognize that bays meeting the general rules are inland waters of the States concerned.

[3] See Section C, below, on publicists' writings. See also, Secretariat of the United Nations, *Memorandum Concerning Historic Bays* (1957), document A/Conf.13/1, pp. 47–58.

But with the historic bay we are confronted with the additional problem in that the State concerned pleads exception to the rules in the case of a specific bay on the grounds of historic claim or possession. In order to keep such claims within reasonable bounds there would appear to exist the necessity for some agreed upon criteria. This chapter proposes to examine this gap in the existing rules with a view toward ascertaining whether such criteria can be established.

Section B STATE PRACTICE AND CLAIMS TO SPECIFIC BAYS

Although the Geneva Convention of 1958 on Territorial Waters and the Contiguous Zone extends the length of a bay's closing line from 10 to 24 miles, that fact will be disregarded in the following discussion wherein are mentioned specific bays over which States have made exclusive claims to sovereignty. These claims, whether made on historical grounds or for other exceptional reasons, were made before the time of the United Nations International Law Commission's consideration of the subject. Omitted also from this section are bays whose status has been the subject of judicial decision.[1]

As Professor Bourquin has so aptly observed, it is often difficult to know what the practice of States on this question may be. Most governments abstain from declaring a formal delimitation of their maritime territory unless some particular circumstances push them to do so, and therefore it is only occasionally that one is informed on this point.[2] This writer's own research with respect to Hudson Bay seems to bear out Professor Bourquin's observation: Only once, and then in 1906, has the Canadian Government given a positive indication of its position concerning sovereignty over Hudson Bay.

(1) *Australia*

The United Nations *Memorandum Concerning Historic Bays* advises that Australia claims or regards as historic 15 different bays in the littoral of that country.[3] The citation offered is A. H. Charteris,

[1] These are considered in Section D.

[2] Maurice Bourquin, "Les Baies historiques," *Mélanges Georges Sauser-Hall* (1952), pp. 37–51. Professor Bourquin's article is of especial interest by reason of his having written it after the proceedings in *United Kingdom* v. *Norway*, but before the court had rendered its decision, *ibid.*, p. 40n. Professor Bourquin, of the faculty at the Graduate Institute of International Studies, University of Geneva, was counsel to the Norwegian Agent in the above-mentioned case.

[3] A/Conf.13/1, at p. 23.

Chapters on International Law (1940), page 99. The Memorandum notes that this citation is quoted in the Norwegian Counter-Memorial in *United Kingdom* v. *Norway*.[4] As the Norwegian Counter Memorial indicates, Professor Charteris' authority is a letter from the Secretary of the Navy Office, Melbourne, addressed to him, and dated 26 April 1936. Mr. Charteris' footnote to his writing on this matter is quoted verbatim:

(1) According to a letter from the Secretary of the Navy Office, Melbourne to Professor Charteris, of 26 April 1936, the following is "a list of Australian Bays whose width between heads exceeds 6 miles."

Northern Australia	*South Australia*
*Van Diemen Gulf	Coffin Bay
Buckingham Bay	Streaky Bay
Blue Mud Bay	Spencer Gulf
	Investigator Strait with St. Vincent's Gulf
Western Australia	*Queensland*
*Exmouth Bay	Broad Sound
Roebuck Bay	Upstart Bay
*Shark Bay	*Moreton Bay
	Hervey Bay
Tasmania	
Oyster Bay	
Storm Bay	

The bays marked with an asterisk "were claimed as 'Historic Bays' for the various reasons." (sic)
(Navy Office letter, *supra*.)

Professor Charteris offers no further interpretation of this letter, but he does quote a portion of the Commonwealth Memorandum of 9 July 1929 in reply to the Committee of Experts on Codification of International Law, then engaging in the preparatory work for the 1930 Conference. An except from that memorandum reads:

There are certain Historical Bays whose width exceeds 6 or even 10 miles which are regarded by general acquiescence as territorial waters.[5]

The Australian memorandum makes no mention of bays in this category claimed by Australia, nor does the United Nations publication *Laws and Regulations on the Regime of the Territorial Sea* (1956). Records of the Hague Conference, the International Law Commission, and the 1958 Geneva Conference all fail to indicate any Australian position on the matter. Referring, then, only to the Charteris work, this writer feels constrained to interpret it differently from the way

[4] Judgment of 18 December 1951, vol. 1, pp. 445.
[5] Also found in League of Nations Document ii C.73.M.39, 1929 V., at p. 117.

it has been interpreted by the authors of the UN Memorandum and the Norwegian Counter-Memorial: It is believed that only those bays marked by asterisks in the above quotation are claimed by Australia as historic bays. The bays so marked, and their dimensions in nautical miles are:

	Breadth at Mouth	Penetration
1. Van Diemen Gulf	34.4	95.5
2. Exmouth Bay	26	42.5
3. Shark Bay	46	70.4
4. Moreton Bay	8.7	8.7 [6]

(2) *Bulgaria*

Article 2 of the decree of 10 October 1951 concerning the territorial and inland waters of the People's Republic of Bulgaria provides:

2. The Sea between the coast and a straight line drawn, in the case of Stalin Bay, from Cape Saint Constatine to Cape Slandzhik and, in the case of Burgas Bay, from Cape Emine to the Cape of Olives (Zeytin Burun) is deemed to be part of the inland waters of the People's Republic of Bulgaria.[7]

(3) *Canada*

Hudson Bay. See Chapter SIX, above.

(4) *Dominican Republic*

Article 2 of Act No. 3343 of 13 July 1952 concerning the extent of the territorial waters of the Republic reads as follows:

The bays of Samaná, Ocoa and Neyba are declared to be historical waters or bays and as such to be subject to the full sovereignty of the State, within the following boundaries:

(a) In the case of Samaná Bay: a transverse line plotted between Cape Samaná and Cape San Raphael.

[6] The recent article by Dr. D. P. O'Connell of the University of Adelaide, discloses no new information with respect to Australian claims. He writes that there are other possible claims about which no final judgment has been made. e.g. Buckingham Bay (20 miles), Blue Mud Bay (15 miles), Coffin Bay (12 miles), Streaky Bay (14 miles), Roebuck Bay (14 miles), Upstart Bay (10 miles), Hervey Bay (38 miles), Oyster Bay (15 miles), and Storm Bay (13 miles). He then makes this interesting comment: "In Australia the Navy Department is anxious to restrict the national boundary as far as possible because of the difficulty of policing a long and complicated coastline, and because it does not want to encourage Indonesia to make excessive claims in its Archipelago, while the States [Australia] are anxious for economic reasons to expand it." D. P. O'Connell, "Problems of Australian Coastal Jurisdiction," 34 *British Year Book of International Law* (1959), pp. 199–259, at p. 242.

[7] United Nations, *Laws and Regulations on the Regime of the Territorial Sea* (1956), p. 80. See also, Marin Pundeff, "Bulgarian Decree on Territorial Waters," 46 *American Journal of International Law* (1952), pp. 330–2. Mr. Pundeff notes that the regulations on Stalin Bay (formerly Varna Bay) and Burgas Bay are similar to those contained in the Decree-Law of 1935. He points out that in the instant Decree, emphasis is upon security against foreign observation and penetration by way of the sea.

(b) In the case of Ocoa Bay: a transverse line plotted between Salinas Point and Martin Garcia Point.

(c) In the case of Neiba Bay (*sic*): a transverse line plotted between Martin Garcia Point and Avarena Point.
The transverse lines referred to in sub-paragraphs (a), (b) and (c) serve to demarcate the boundaries of the internal waters and the base line of the territorial waters of the bays aforesaid.[8]

(5) *France*

The United Nations *Memorandum Concerning Historic Bays* mentions five bays in Equatorial Africa and one in "East Africa" which are either regarded as historic bays or claimed as such by France[9] The reference cited is Gidel, *Le Droit international public de la Mer*, at page 657. We shall discuss first the case of Tadjura Gulf in French Somaliland ("French East Africa").

Gidel, without offering any authority, writes that this bay is a historic bay in its entirety, and he states its dimensions which, he says, embrace the roadsteads of Djibouti and Obok. This writer has been unable to discover any evidence to substantiate Professor Gidel's contention, although the configuration of Tadjourah Bay would certainly suggest the probability of such a claim. There were three separate treaties between France and local native rulers in which the latter ceded their land to France.[10] While the Gubbed Khrab or inner bay (with an opening about one mile wide), is actually ceded, in the treaty of 1884,[11] the larger bay of Tadjoura is never specified. Moreover, in the Anglo-French exchange of notes of 2–9 February 1888, wherein the two Powers recognized each other's rights in the Somaliland area, it is specifically set out that Grat Britain recognized France's authority on the coasts of the Gulf of Tadjoura and in the islands of the Gulf.[12] Great Britain chose to ignore the 1840 purchase of the island of Mussah in the Persian Gulf by the East India Company.[13]

The United Nations Memorandum indicates that, in what was formerly French Equatorial Africa, the following bays are regarded

[8] United Nations, *Laws and Regulations*, p. 11–12.

[9] *Ibid*, 23–4.

[10] By the treaty of 11 March 1862, Obok was ceded to France. The treaty spells out that Obok harbor, coast, roadstead and anchorage are ceded. No dimensions are specified. II Hertslet, *The Map of Africa by Treaty* (1909), p. 628. On 21 September the Sultan of Tadjurah gave his land to France. *Ibid.*, 630–1; Article 2 of the treaty reads "Le Sultan Hamed donne son pays à la France pour qu'elle le protège contre tout étranger." XIV De Clercqu, *Recueil des Traités de la France* (1884), p. 418. No mention is made of any water area.

[11] On 18 October 1884, the Sultan "gave" the Gubbed Khrab to France, Hertslet, *op. cit.*, p. 632.

[12] II *Hertslet*, pp. 726–8.

[13] The sale was made on 19 August 1840 for ten bags of rice. I *Hertslet*, p. 408.

as historic bays (the writer has included the dimensions of these bays):

	Width at Entrance	Penetration
Bay of Mondah	6.6 miles	13.8 miles
Cape Lopez Bay	33 ,,	18 ,,
Loango Bay	24 ,,	9 ,,
Pointe Noire and Carisco Bay	34.8 ,,	16.2 ,,
Estuary of the Gabon	10,8 ,,	55.8 ,,

The Memorandum cites Gidel's work (at page 657) as the authority for the proposition. We shall take these citations in turn.

(1) The Bay of Mondah. Gidel writes:

La baie de la Mondah (ou Munda ou de Corisco) s'étend des bancs de sable du Cap Esterias à ceux de la pointe Dumbo, sur une distance de 28 milles marins. Nos droits historiques sur cette baie remontent au traité du 4/18 septembre 1852 (De Clercq, VI, 217) passe par le commandant du comptoir Vignon, avec les chefs du Cap Esterias.

It is difficult to reconcile the statement of Gidel with the text of the treaty as published in De Clercq's collection. The treaty has to do primarily with the rights of missionaries and makes no mention whatsoever of the Bay of Mondah or any coastal waters.

(2) Cape Lopez Bay, Gidel writes:

La baie du Cap Lopez est délimitée par une droite joignant le Cap Lopez à la pointe Fétiche. Elle comporte des bancs de sable. Son ouverture est de 18 milles. Cette délimitation a fait l'objet du traité conclu le 1er juin 1862 par le Baron Didelot et M. d'Aulnois, Commandant supérieur et Commandant particulier du Gabon avec les rois et chefs du Cap Lopez (De Clercq, VII...) Ce traité important a été le point de départ des explorations de l'Ogoué.

Gidel's citation of Volume VII of *De Clercq* is in error. The treaty appears in Volume VIII of De Clercq's collection, at page 413. There is no delimentation of the Bay mentioned in the treaty. The pertinent article is quoted:

Article 5

La souveraineté des pays concédés s'étend depuis le Cap Lopez dans le sud jusqu'à la pointe Liame dans le nord. Cette dernière limite borne les Etats du Roi Denis dans le sud.

(3) Estuary of the Gabon. Here Gidel cites the treaties of 9 February 1839 (IV *De Clercq* 445) and 9 March 1843 (V *De Clercq* 6). The text of the 1839 treaty discusses cession of land down to the shore line on either side of the estuary, but makes no mention of the estuary itself. The 1843 treaty is given only a three-line summary in De Clercq's collection, and possession of the Estuary is not mentioned.[14]

[14] Of passing interest, perhaps, is that at V *De Clercq* 6, there is printed the summary of a French treaty of 25 March 1843, concluded with one Okunao, "Chief of the Bay of Pua" in the Marquesas Islands.

Following the Estuary of the Gabon, Professor Gidel mentions the following which he classes as historic bays:

> 2° la baie de Loango; 3° la baie de Pointe Noire;
> 4° la baie du Rio Muni; 5° du Cap Lopez.

It is to be noted that Gidel mentions Cap Lopez bay a second time. For the others, he offers no authority, reference or reasoning for his calling them historic bays. Unlike the case of the Bay of Tadjourah, the writer was unable to probe the matter independently. This writer is most reluctant to criticize the author of the United Nations Memorandum on Historic Bays or the eminent work of Professor Gidel, but he is perplexed at the way in which these two scholars have arrived at their conclusions. It is also, perhaps, in order to note at this point that if France had announced claims to the bays in question (and this writer was unable to find that she had), and these claims were based on cessions made by native chiefs in treaties with France, there would still appear to be ground in international law for another State to protest the claim until France had discharged the onus of showing that the native chief knew and understood what he was granting, and that he was in fact up to the time of the cession, recognized in the customary law of his habitat as empowered to make such a conveyance.[15] But it is not evident that France or the new successor States have published any claims to these bays, although they may very well exercise exclusive sovereignty over some or all of them. To inquire into such exercise, or the lack of it, for each bay, might turn into an extraordinarily time-consuming process, although we have attempted to do so in the case of Hudson Bay, In the absence of such inquiry, one must await some challenge to the exercise, if any, of this jurisdiction.

(6) *Egypt*

In its reply to Questionnaire No. 2 (1926) of the Committee of Experts on the Progressive Codification of International Law, the

[15] This is not to say rhat a treaty with a Native Chief should always be open to question by reason of differing conceptions of territorial rights and title to land, although the original abuses are numerous. Lord Hailey, *An African Survey*, Rev. 1956 (1957), pp. 544ff, 744, 746. But it should be understood that he is recognized as having both the power and the possession to convey what the instrument purports. Arnold D. McNair, *The Law of Treaties* (1938), pp. 133–4; Kenneth S. Carlston, *Law and Structures of Social Action* (1956), p. 35. A treaty ceding an arm of the sea, and negotiated by a native chief, would appear especially suspect until proven otherwise, inasmuch as aboriginal conceptions of territory, if any, did not usually extend to large bodies of water. Chapter ONE, Section B, above. Even at this late date the descendants of the Gabon chiefs are of the opinion that their ancestors were not in fact aware of the import of the agreements they made with France. "Le Gabon Reclaime ses Terres," 37 *Interafrique Presse*, 28 July 1955, pp. 9–11.

Egyptian Government indicated that the extent of Egyptian territorial waters was fixed at three miles by the Decree-Laws of 21 April 1926 on Fishing and Sponge-fishing, except for the Bay of El-Arab, all of which, by the terms of the aforesaid law, is included in the territorial sea.[16] On 15 January 1951, there was issued the Royal Decree Concerning the Territorial Waters of the Kingdom of Egypt.[17] This Decree reads, in pertinent part, as follows:

Article 1

For the purpose of this decree,

(b) The term "bay" includes any inlet, lagoon or other arm of the sea;

Article 4

The inland waters of the Kingdom include:

(a) The waters of the bays along the cosats of the Kingdom of Egypt;

Article 6

The following are established as the base-lines from which the coastal sea of the Kingdom of Egypt is measured:

(b) where a bay confronts the open sea, lines drawn from headland to headland across the mouth of the bay;

On 28 May 1951, the Government of the United Kingdom addressed to the Government of Egypt a note indicating that they were unable to accept the decree as being in conformity with the rules of international law.[18] The note urges the 10-mile rule except in cases of historic bays. The note finds the Egyptian definition of a bay unacceptable. The note also reads, in part:

Apart from certain historic bays (none of which is situated in Egypt), where a greater distance has been established by continuous and immemorial usage...

On 4 June 1951, the Government of the United States addressed the Egyptian Government a note taking exception to certain provisions of the decree,[19] and reading in part as follows:

1. All provisions which purport to extend the inland waters of the Kingdom seaward from the waters of ports and harbors and such bays and other enclosed arms of the sea as are recognized as inland waters by international law.

[16] League of Nations Publication V. Legal, 1927, V. 1 (document C.196.M.70. 1927.V. p. 257. See also UN *Memorandum on Historic Bays*, p. 17.

[17] Text of the translation of this Decree is printed in 6 *Revue Egyptienne de Droit International* (1950), at page 175ff. It is reprinted in MacChesney, *U.S. Naval War College International Law Situation and Documents* 1956, pages 458–460.

[18] The note is reprinted in *I. C. J. Pleadings, 1951, UK-Norway IV*, pp. 578–580, and in 7 *Revue Egyptienne de Droit International* (1951), p. 91.

[19] The note is reprinted in *I. C. J. Pleadings 1951, UK-Norway IV*, p. 603, and in 7 *Revue Egyptienne de Droit International* (1951), p. 94.

In the issue of *Revue Egyptienne de Droit International* in which reprints of these notes (Vol. 7, pp. 91ff) appear, there is a series of maps showing, on the Egyptian coast, the locations of what are considered to be bays within the meaning of the 1951 decree. These bays and their dimensions [20] are:

Bay	Distance between Headlands	Greatest distance from closing line to inner shore
1. Gulf of Salum	45.4 miles	19.9 miles
2. Abu Hashaifa Bay	31.6 miles	7.9 miles
3. Arabs Gulf (El-Arab)	94.7 miles	25.7 miles
4. Bay of Pelusium	49.3 miles	13.3 miles
5. Bay of El Arish	65 miles	11.8 miles

The Judgement of the International Court of Justice in *United Kingdom* v. *Norway* is dated 18 December 1951. In this connection, it is of particular interest that the gently undulating coast line of Egypt has little in common with the deeply-indented coast line of Norway.

In its letter of 4 May 1955 to the United Nations the Permanent Delegation of Egypt [21] expressed the view that the Draft Articles of the Sixth Session (1954) were in accordance with the Egyptian internal law. The Article on Bays (actually that of the 1951 Draft) allowed a 10-mile closing line. In its comment on bays, the letter said there was no unanimity on the question but suggested the convenience of a 12-mile width, subject to a greater extent of jurisdiction established by long-continued usage.

The subesequent comment by*Revue Egyptienne de Droit International.*[22] on the 1955 report of the International Law Commission compares rather strikingly with the mild tone of the above-mentioned letter. The article indicates Egypt's position to be that the Anglo-Norwegian Fishereis case judgment permits a rather liberal interpretation concerning economic interests, general direction of the coasts and a sufficiently close land link. The difficulties of proof of historic or long-continued usage are commented upon and it is the tenor of the article that the Judgment in the Fisheries Case opens avenues where such proof is unnecessary. Of interest is this quote from the article:

As to the method of asserting claims, it is obviously for the country, in the first instance, to make the decision. In the words of the International Court, it is

[20] Measurements are those stated in *Egyptian Review*. The maps are again produced in 11 *Revue Egyptienne de Droit International* (1955), at page 206.

[21] Reprinted in UN Document A/2934, at pages 26–7.

[22] Vol. 11, p. 190ff.

"in the best position to appraise local conditions dictating a selection...." Its decision must conform to the principles of international law which the highest world tribunal has been at pains to define in a decision which contributes one of the few fixed beacons in a sea of controversy.

While this polemic in the Egyptian International Law Review does apply a rather loose interpretation of the Fisheries Case Judgment, it is unfortunately a fact that the Judgment is so written as to invite unilateral and very generous interpretation. The tenor of a 1957 article in the Egyptian International Law Review would indicate that the Egyptian attitude has not changed. In that Article, entitled "The Law of the Sea, Progress toward International Agreement – The Egyptian Position," the author comments upon Article 7 (Bays) of the International Law Commission's Draft Convention on the Territorial Sea. His comment is that the Article is of limited value inasmuch as itcannot be made to apply to the bays in Egypt.[23]

(7) *Iceland* [24]

This country is mentioned only by reason of the fact that her legislation concerning fishery limits is such that the concept of the bay is done away with altogether. Thus, what might otherwise have come under the category of historic bays are entirely within the system of straight base-lines. A novel basis for these limits is offered in the published reasons for the present law. Although passage of the law was prompted by a desire to preserve coastal fishery grounds for the use of Icelandic fishermen, the Government reasoned that the limit of coastal fisheries should be determined by the limit of the continental shelf (normally the 100-fathom curve). This is not altogether beyond the realm of future tendency and if States should try to ground their claims to marginal seas on the limits of the 100-fathom curve, much of the controversy over bays and historic bays in particular might become academic.

(8) *Portugal*

In 1929, Portugal advised the Preparatory Committee for the Hague Codification Conference that she regarded as part of her territory the following two areas:

(a) The Tagus River Estuary within a line drawn from Cape Rozo to Cape Espichel. This line marks off an area of sea which is not an

[23] 13 *Revue Egyptienne de Droit International* (1957), pp. 70–71.

[24] MacChesney, *U.S. Naval War College International Law Situation and Documents* 1956, pp. 466–472.

estuary at all but which is outside the entrance to the Tagus River and Lisbon. The line is 24 miles long and the area has a maximum indentation of 8 miles.

(b) The Sado River Estuary within a line drawn from Cape Espichel to Cape Sines. Also not an estuary, this area is bounded by a line 36.5 miles long and its maximum indentation is 18 miles.[25]

(9) *Norway*

Aside from the "system" of base lines applied to the north coast of Norway by virtue of the royal decree of 12 July 1935, as amended 10 December 1937, and upheld as against the United Kingdom by the International Court of Justice in 1951, we should consider two specific bays in Norway which, by State practice, were long considered Historic Bays.

The first of these is Vestfjord whose line of closure is about 50 miles long and whose indentation is about 110 miles. Professor Fulton advises that these dimensions were stated in an 1868 letter of the Minister of Foreign Affairs of Sweden Norway.[26] Although the Government did not promulgate any law or regulation concerning this bay until the present era, the waters have been considered Norwegian internal waters for centuries.[27] The primary reason for this attitude has been the economic well-being of the inhabitants of the area, nearly all of whom depend upon fishing for their livelihood.

Varangerfjord, about 32 miles wide at the entrance and about 50 miles long falls into the historic category by reason of a series of Government laws, but primarily for reasons similar to those applying in the case of Vestfjord. Varangerfjord's status has been subject to considerably greater scrutiny by reason of the 1911 case of the British trawler, *Lord Roberts* [28] and the 1934 case of the German trawler, *Deutschland*.[29]

Both Vestfjord and Varangerfjord are discussed at great length in the pleadings in *United Kingdom* v. *Norway*, and rather briefly by Gidel [30] and Fulton.[31] It serves no great purpose to repeat what has already been said, but in the cases of these two bays there are a number

[25] League of Nations Publication V, Legal, 1929, V.2 (document C.74, M.39. 1929 V., p. 117.

[26] Fulton, *Sovereignty of the Sea* (1906), pp. 672–3.

[27] *Ibid.*

[28] I *Pleadings, U.K.* v. *Norway*, 1951, pp. 290–6.

[29] *Ibid.*, pp. 162–70.

[30] *Op. cit.*, pp. 661–2.

[31] *Op. cit.*, pp. 672–8.

of factors which should be emphasized when one considers them as examples of historic bays:

(a) They truly are bays in any literary or geographical sense of the word, and one's ordinary reasoning need not be strained to accommodate some special rationalization as in the Egyptian example.[32] They are bays in the sense of Article 7, paragraph 2, of the 1958 Geneva Convention if we are willing not to pursue the term land-locked to a logical absurdity.

(b) The two bays have a very old history of linkage to the surrounding land, both as sheltered seas and as sources of economic livelihood. This linkage appears to ante-date any regulation by the State. In other words there is a clearly identifiable historic quality to their status. Moreover, it appears quite difficult to demonstrate that peoples of any other State or area have had, historically, any continuing claim upon the shelter of those bays or upon the sea-products that are extracted therefrom.

(c) Exclusive possession of these bays by Norway cannot very successfully be shown to be inequitable to the interests of any other State or the community of States.

(d) It cannot be shown that in any recent times Norway has used these bays for such military purposes as might threaten the tranquility of surrounding States.

(10) *Tunisia*

Professor Gidel writes that the Gulf of Tunis and the Gulf of Gabes constitute historic waters.[33] He offers no authority for his statement but points out that foreign States have never protested the various rules laid down for these waters, and especially those which have been implemented against foreign sponge fishermen in the Gulf of Gabes. The Gulf of Tunis has a closing line of about 23 miles and an indentation of 22 miles. The Gulf of Gabes has a closing line of about 50 miles and an indentation of about the same magnitude. Both can be considered bays within the meaning of Article 7, paragraph 2 of the 1958 Geneva Convention.

[32] Having navigated along the coasts of both States. and speaking only as a mariner, the writer would be willing to say that the bays in Norway are really bays and those in Egypt are not.

[33] *Op. cit.*, p. 663.

(11) *Thailand*

On 7 March 1958, at the Eighth Meeting of the First Committee of the 1958 Geneva Conference on the Law of the Sea, Mr. Luang Chakrapani, Chairman of the Thai delegation advised that the Bight of Bangkok is a historic bay and that Thailand regards the waters therein as internal waters. He gave the dimensions of these waters as 53 miles across and a penetration inland of 50 miles.[34]

(12) *United States*

The classic case of State practice concerning a historic bay in the United States is that having to do with Delaware Bay. The status of the bay was established by the Executive Branch of the Government in 1793 in connection with the capture of the British vessel *Grange* in Delaware Bay by the French frigate *L'Embuscade*. The United States was neutral in the war that was then going on between Great Britain and France.

In his opinion for the Executive, Attorney General Randolph,[35] reasoned that from the time of the establishment of British colonies on either side of the bay, its waters were considered peculiar navigation of the British Empire; that Britain had relinquished sovereignty over the colonies; that no other State could be injured by appropriation of the bay to the United States; that in the absence of such appropriation, the United States would, to its own possible injury, lose control of these waters; and that this was a principle unshaken by any other usage.

The argument used here would seem to find equal application in the case of Varangerfjord in Norway.

What appears to be of permanent interest in this early action of the United States is the attention focused upon the possible future consequences of the decision.

(13) *Sweden*

The Swedish Government, in its reply to Questionnaire No. 2 (1926) of the Committee of Experts on the Progressive Codification of International Law, advised that the Bays of Laholm and Skelderviken were entirely Swedish territorial waters.[36] It was explained that in accor-

[34] UN Document A/Conf. 13/39, p. 17.

[35] John Bassett Moore, *Digest of International Law*, vol. I, (1906), pp. 735–9; David Deener, *U.S. Attorneys General and International Law* (1958), pp. 210–211; 1 *Official Opinions of the Attorneys General of the United States* (1793), p. 32.

[36] League of Nations Publication V. Legal, 1927. V.1 (document C.196, M.70. 1927, V. at p. 232.

dance with Swedish Law, the whole area of any bay indenting the coast "to an appreciable extent" is to be regarded as "territorial" water and exterior territorial waters are measured from a line drawn across the bay between two extreme points where the bay merges into the general coast-line. This is simply the headland theory.

Actually, the Bay of Skelderviken is only about eight miles wide at the mouth. The Bay of Laholm, however, is about 12 miles wide between headlands and, although it has an indentation of but 8 miles from the closing line to the opposite shore, its configuration is such as would constitute it a bay under the semi-circle rule. The two bays open on the Kattegat, and actions within their waters during World War I gave rise to Swedish protests concerning alleged German and British violations of Swedish neutrality. Germany refused to concede Swedish sovereignty over the Bay, and the British matter was settled by arbitration in connection with the general prize right agreement with Great Britain, without specific reference to the Bay of Laholm.[37] The reply also reads:

In the case of the bay of Laholm the Swedish argument was singularly strengthened by the provisions of a fisheries convention concluded between Sweden and Denmark.

The Convention referred to is "Convention pour régler la pêche dans les eaux avoisinant la Suède et la Danemark"; signed in Stockholm on 14 July 1899. Article One of the treaty provides, *inter alia*, that Danish fishermen are allowed to fish as close as 3/4 mile from a straight line drawn from Halland's Väderö lighthouse to the Tylö lighthouse.[38]

The Convention of 1899 was abrogated by a new treaty of 31 December 1932 which in pertinent part reads as follows:

Article 2

... As regards bays, the fishermen of both countries shall be entitled to fish up to a distance of three minutes latitude from a straight line drawn across the bay in the part nearest the opening where the width is not greater than 10

[37] Opinion of Mr. Eliel Lofgren, Swedish Foreign Office, dated February 11, 1925, and addressed to Swedish Minister of Foreign Affairs in Connection with the *Heinrich Agustin* (discussed below). Mr. Lofgren's opinion is reprinted, in full in Jessup, *Law of Territorial Waters and Maritime Jurisdiction* (1927), pp. 413–424.

[38] 6 Martens, *Nouveau recueil général de traités*, 3rd series, p. 577. The treaty is published only in Danish and Swedish. It uses the words *rat linie* which are believed to mean straight line rather than base line as translated in Jessup, *op. cit.*, at page 422. The Swedish language version of this treaty reads in pertinent part:
"Art. 1... Dock skall det vara medgifnet att drifva fiska: för svenska fiskare vid ön Anholt pa ett aftånd af intill 3/4 geografisk mil från kusterna af denna ö, och för danska fiskara på enahanda avstånd ustanför en rät linie, drogen från Hallands Väderös fyr till Tylö fyr." The pertinent part of the 1932 treaty reads: "Art. 2... Utanför Laholmsbukten skall dock nämnda afstand räknas frän en rät linie, dragen från Tylö fyr till Hallands Väderö fyr."

minutes latitude. Off Laholm bay, however, this distance shall be calculated from a straight line drawn from the Tylö lighthouse to Halland's Väderö lighthouse.[39]

This matter will be discussed further in the section on Judicial Decisions, Section D, below.

(14) *Union of Soviet Socialist Republics*

The present practice of the Soviet Union Government with respect to claiming sovereignty over large areas of the sea appears but a continuum of the practice of its predecessor government, that of the Russian Empire. This practice seems to have had its modern inception with the Imperial ukase of 1821 wherein the Emperor declared that in all ports and gulfs and in the whole sea area from Bering Strait to Latitude 51 degrees North there were comprehended all the conditions of closed seas and that Russia judged itself authorized to exercise all rights of sovereignty and especially so the right of preventing entrance.[40] The claim was opposed by Great Britain and the United States, and the controversy was finally set at rest by the Behring Sea Arbitration of 1893. Fulton advises that in 1853, Russia declared the Sea of Okhotsk to be a Russian inland sea.[41] Apparently, in 1893, Russia declared the entire White Sea to be a closed sea within a line eighty miles long. The area of water so enclosed is 30,000 square miles.[42] Captain Christopher Meyer, RNorN, undertakes in his work a rather lengthy discussion of the White Sea case [43] which was rendered rather problematical by protests of other States and by Russia's delay in formally asserting sovereignty.

On 24 May 1921, the Government of the Russian Soviet Federative Socialist Republic issued regulations prohibiting alien fishing in the White Sea within a straight line drawn from Sviatoi Noss to Kanin Noss, a line 80 miles long, and in a bay called Cheshkaia Guba south of a line between Mikulkin Point and Sviatoi Noss, a line 45 miles long. (Note: Sviatoi Noss is a name given to two different landmarks).[44]

[39] 139 *League of Nations Treaty Series*, p. 205. English translation at p. 214.

[40] Martens, 5 *Nouveau Recueil*, 2nd series, p. 358.

[41] Fulton, *Sovereignty of the Sea* (1911), p. 585. He cites 1 *Parliamentary Papers, United States*, p. 87.

[42] Fulton, *op. cit.*, p. 657; Captain Meyer, *The Extent of Jurisdiction in Coastal Waters* (1927), p. 249, writes that the regulations were actually introduced in the form of instructions issued to the Russian cruiser *Najesdnik* which was sent on an Arctic inspection tour. Captain Meyer cites a memorandum the Swedish-Norwegian Naval Attache in St. Petersburg.

[43] Meyer, *op. cit.*, pp. 248–260. See also: Viktor Böhmert, "Die russische Fischereigrenze," 21 *Zeitschrift für Völkerrecht* (1937), pp. 441–496. Dr. Böhmert furnishes a comprehensive historical account of Russian practices along the Arctic littoral.

[44] Meyer, *op. cit.*, p. 425.

Great Britain, Norway and Germany protested, inasmuch as the primary issue involved was the prohibition against fur seal hunting in the area. After much negotiating, agreements between the Soviet Union and the three Governments [45] were reached. All of these permitted the fishing north of Latitude 60°40′ North. In the treaties, the last of which was concluded in 1930, there were special stipulations concerning fishing in the White Sea, or up to the entrance of the White Sea, thus recognizing Soviet possession of that body as internal waters.

Up to this point, in the discussion of the White Sea, there has been no evidence of a claim to it on the basis of historic grounds. The exclusion decree and the subsequent agreements arise out of economic considerations pure and simple. According to a passage from *International Law* (1957), published by the Institute of Law of the Academy of Sciences of the USSR, the Soviet Union now holds the Sea of Azov, the Gulf of Riga and the White Sea as interior waters by virtue of immemorial practice.[46] This latter view appears now to be adhered to rather exclusively and especially so in connection with the Soviet claim to Peter the Great Bay which we shall discuss in detail in Chapter EIGHT.

(15) *The United Kingdom*

In recent times there has been little evidence that the United Kingdom has actively maintained a right of sovereignty over large bays on the grounds of historic possession. There are a number of reasons for this, but one should not conclude that it is the practice of the United Kingdom to refuse to concede that such a right can still exist. At the end of his oral reply the Agent of the United Kingdom Government in *United Kingdom* v. *Norway* stated:

> Norway is entitled to claim as Norwegian internal waters, on historic grounds, all fjords and sunds which fall within the conception of a bay ... whether the proper closing line of the indentation is more or less than ten sea miles long.[47]

Actually, as Fulton points out, the concept of jurisdiction over

[45] The Norwegian Treaty is of 15 December 1925. 26 Martens *Recueil*, Series III, p. 460. It grants Norway most favored nation treatment in the White Sea. With Germany there was an exchange of notes of 12 October 1925. Böhmert *op. cit.*, pp. 493–4. With Great Britain, agreement was reached on 22 May 1930. This agreement reads in part: "3. As regards the White Sea, fishing operations by fishing boats registered at the ports of the United Kingdom may be carried on to the north of Latitude 68°10′ North, outside a distance of three miles from the land..." 25 Martens *Recueil*, Series III, p. 143.

[46] France de Hartingh, *Les Conceptions Soviétiques du Droit international de la Mer* (1960), p. 30.

[47] *I.C.J. Reports* 1951, p. 121.

waters *inter fauces terrae* is a very ancient one in England, traceable at least to the early fourteenth century. It is interesting, moreover, to note that this jurisdiction is one having to do with offenses triable at common law. In the Sixteenth and Seventeenth Centuries, it was the practice, culminating in the King's Chambers proclamation, to define such areas for purposes of neutrality.[48] On the other hand, it was in Scotland that the practice grew to define such areas for purposes of fishing.

Fulton remains the unequalled authority on the legal history of the British territorial sea. In this span of history, the following general features are in evidence:

(a) The United Kingdom has not had, in the modern era such economic pressures placed upon her as to precipitate claims to wide bays on historic grounds. When such claims have been asserted, there have been over-riding considerations which by reason of the British international position, have made it expedient not to maintain such claims in the face of discontent on the part of her neighbors. Such was the post-judicial consequence of *Mortensen* v. *Peters*.

(b) There are certain bays which have closing lines greater than 10 miles in length, which are probably considered by Governments of the United Kingdom to enclose internal waters, but whose status has never been challenged either in the Courts or on the diplomatic level. These include: The Thames Estuary, The Wash, The Firth of Clyde,[49] Solway Firth, Morecumbe Bay, and Caernarvon Bay. In this connection, one should note that the King's Chambers Proclamation of 1604 has never been repealed.

(c) That the United Kingdom attitude on this subject, while regarding the 3-mile limit and the 10-mile rule of bays as legal landmarks, is otherwise rather pragmatic and seldom given to the expounding of legalistic abstractions for the purpose of justifying an otherwise unprofitable or politically useless position.

Section C WRITINGS OF PUBLICISTS

There appear to be three classifications of publicists' comments on historic bays: those which deal with the historic bay in general or conceptual terms, those in which the scholar on his own initiative

[48] Fulton, *op. cit.*, p. 548.
[49] *Ibid.*, pp. 719–20.

advises that a certain bay should be regarded as a historic bay, and those in which the author's writing is really an official vehicle for publishing a Government position. The latter category of writings on this subject seems primarily confined to totalitarian States.[1]

Other authors and works have undertaken to excerpt from publicists' writings the comments on historic bays and allied subjects,[2] and there appears little useful purpose in covering this same ground. This is especially true when one contemplates the simple fact that not a few publicists have done little more than quote or cite others and have relatively little in the way of original thought or research to add. For this reason, the author will attempt to cite only those writings to which for one reason or another, some importance can be attached by reason of the valuable advice or insight evident in the writing.[3] Finally, it should be noted that the term, historic bay, descriptive of an exceptional situation, is a relatively modern one, probably dating back no further than Dr. Drago's dissent in the North Atlantic Coast Fisheries Arbitration of 1910.

We shall not review the writings of publicists in any chronological order, but rather, in accordance with the manner in which their writing may have contributed to an understanding of the concept of the historic bay.

(1) *Lawrence*

The claims of States to large tracts of marginal waters – claims which are themselves relics of yet wider dominion over oceans and seas – increase the difficulty

[1] Somewhat akin to this type of writing is the work of CAPT Christopher B. V. Meyer, RNorN, whose book *The Extent of Jurisdiction in Territorial Waters* (1927) is described as a report to the Norwegian Storting, but which is in fact an extended argument in support of the Norwegian point of view. One should not, however, regard the Meyer work as one of limited usefulness by reason of its rather channeled arguments. In many pages it records original research which might not otherwise be available.

[2] UN *Memorandum on Historic Bays* (1957); Meyer, *op. cit.;* Crocker, *Extent of the Marginal Sea* (1919). In *United Kingdom* v. *Norway*, the four volumes of pleadings, oral arguments, and documents contain references to a great number of publicists.

[3] The ideal dividing line would be one which separates those authors' writings which influence State policy from those which do not. But there seems, unfortunately, little possibility of making such a differentiation with any great hope of achieving accuracy or of being able to defend the choice with convincing proof. This writer is quite unwilling to accept the statement contained in the United Nations publication: *Ways and Means of Making the Evidence of Customary International Law more Readily Available* (1949), at page 85: "The creative contribution of writers of different nations and different schools to the defelopment of international law and to its systematization is too well known to require further discussion here." But the statement leaves much unanswered: Which authors? On what subjects? In what way? When? Perhaps the best guide is that of Lauterpacht: "But inasmuch as a source of law is conceived as a factor influencing the judge in rendering his decision, the work of writers may continue to play a part in proportion to its intrinsic scientific value, its impartiality and its determination to scrutinize critically the practice of States by reference to legal principle." *Oppenheim's International Law,* vol. I, 8th Ed. (1955), p. 33.

of the question. Some of them are dead or dormant; but when a valuable fishery is retained for native fishermen by the assertion of sovereignty over a bay of considerable size, or when considerations of self-protection or political advantage are prominent, we find that States insist upon and often obtain recognition of their demands, some of which are based upon very ancient precedent.[4]

Although with respect to bays we take exception to the clause "claims which are themselves relics of yet wider dominion over oceans and seas," as being historically questionable,[5] the Reverend Mr. Lawrence shows us rather clearly the cause of the claim and the argument that can be used to defend it.

(2) *Gidel*

La théorie des "eaux historiques," de quelque nom qu'on la désigne est une théorie nécessaire; elle joue en quelque sorte le rôle de soupape de sûreté en matière de délimitation des espaces maritimes; la repousser serait ruiner la possibilité d'aboutir à des règles générales sur cette matière du droit international maritime ... Mais si la théorie des eaux historiques est une théorie nécessaire c'est une théorie exceptionnelle; son application est rigoureusement liée à des conditions physique données ...[6]

Here we see that Gidel has in mind the desirability of enacting some general rules, but that to do so, allowance for exceptions must be made. In his typically dogmatic way, he points out what we are more inclined to view as an optimistic hope, that applications of the theory is rigorously tied to governing physical conditions.

(3) *Westlake*

But although this [6 mile closing line] is the general rule, it often meets with an exception in the case of bays which penetrate deep into the land and are called gulfs. Many of these are recognized by immemorial usage as territorial sea of the States into which they penetrate, notwithstanding that their entrance is wider than the general rule for bays would give as a limit for such appropriation ... it is only in the case of a true gulf that the possiblity of occupation can be so real as to furnish a valid ground for the assumption of sovereignty, and even in that case the geographical features which may warrant the assumption are too incapable of exact definition to allow of the claim being brought to any other test than that of accepted usage.[7]

Here we see that Westlake, first noting the exception to the general rule, tries to establish a geographical guide post in order to explain the necessary linkage to the land if a claim to sovereignty over a large bay is to be valid. Mindful of the variation of geographical forms that

[4] Thomas J. Lawrence, *The principles of International Law*, 5th Ed. (1913), p. 143. This passage is reprinted in Crocker, *op. cit.*, p. 282.

[5] Chapter ONE, Section B, above.

[6] Gilbert Gidel, *Le Droit international public de la Mer*, (1934), Tome III, p. 651.

[7] John Westlake, *International Law*, Part I, 2 Ed. (1910), p. 191.

exist, however, he concludes that "accepted" usage is the only test. Elsewhere he uses the phrase "recognized by immemorial usage," a phrase which is semantically obstinate. What appears to be meant is that such usage, tacitly accepted, confers upon the littoral State the right of exclusive sovereignty over a particular bay by a process similar to the ripening of a usage into a rule of customary international law.

(4) *Fauchille*

... there exist certain gulfs or bays which despite their great width, must be declared under the sovereignty of the State which surrounds them. These gulfs and bays are what are called *historic* or *vital* bays, as distinct from others which are referred to as *common* or *ordinary* bays. What exactly is the correct definition of a historic or vital bay? It is one of the large gulfs or bays the territorial character of which has been recognized by long-established usage and undisputed custom.[8]

(5) *Jessup*

It is believed that ... no established rule of International Law exists as to bays except to the effect that bays not more than six miles wide are deemed territorial waters as well as those to which a nation has established a prescriptive claim. Such a prescriptive claim may be established over bays of great extent; the legality of the claim to be measured, not by the size of the area affected, but by the definiteness and duration of the assertion and the acquiescence of foreign powers. The evidence of international practice and usage does not indicate that a claim to a large bay is illegal.[9]

This quotation is entered because it introduces the notion of prescription and because of the author's emphasis upon the "definiteness and duration of the assertion and the acquiescence of foreign powers." The theory of prescription will be discudess in more detail in a succeeding section of this chapter.

(6) *Jessup*

Where the mouth of a bay is not of very great extent but the bay itself opens up widely well within the body of the country, – as in the case with the Chesapeake and Delaware Bays of the United States, – it seems highly proper that the littoral State should have complete authority over the water so lying within its territory. To make such a principle generally useful for universal application, it would be practically necessary for the nations of the world to meet in conference with the assistance of geographic experts and to make a list of all the bays of the world which were to be considered entirely the property of a single country. There seems to be little chance that such a conference could be arranged or that its labors would be successful if it were to be convoked.[10]

[8] Fauchille, *Traité de droit international public*, vol. I, (1925), p. 380.
[9] Philip C. Jessup, *Law of Territorial Waters and Maritime Jurisdiction* (1927), p. 382.
[10] *Ibid.*, p. 363.

In this passage, Jessup discusses the proposition of making a list of historic bays, an idea to which attention is invited from time to time. This will be discussed in a subsequent section of this chapter.

(7) *Bustamente*

A solution is required for the problem of historic bays, by virtue of which the coastal State is recognized the right over them, whatever the extent of their openings. There are many in this case, both great Powers and countries less strong or materially not very great. As is natural, there is a tendency to convert into a *de jure* rule this *de facto* situation. But when attempt is made to determine what is to be understood by the word "historic," some Governments maintain that to the traditional possession of the bay there must be added the consent of other States.

It is a very dangerous, because this last condition lends itself to notable abuses. No one specifies from how many and from which States this conformity must proceed, or what is the legal value of one or more divergent opinions. In respect to a certain bay, the continuous possession of which is claimed by a coastal State by right of sovereignty, no controversies or difficulties have ever arisen, either on account of its distance from the great maritime or commercial currents of the Globe, or because the opportunity of expounding and solving doubtful questions has not presented itself. It is inadmissable that such circumstances should suffice to deprive the bay of its historic character. ... The permanent right of the coastal State may be proved, both by the provisions of its internal legislation, if it has such, and by acts of jurisdiction and of government, as well as by declarations ... by the competent authorities.

Some means must, however, exist so as to avoid future abuses, as well as discussions and conflicts. With this aim, the Project of Convention establishes that every country having historic bays, within the definition that it contains, shall specifically state this on depositing its ratification. And as the claims from third parties may arise, the opportunity to try them and the jurisdiction to try them must not be passed over in silence.[11]

Bustamente proposes elsewhere a procedure for adjudicating contested claims: diplomatic negotiation, third party decision, the permanent Court of International Justice, or arbitration.

Unfortunately, this writer is not conversant in the Spanish language, and he suspects that some quality of meaning may have become lost in this official translation of the American Institute of International Law. Nevertheless, the Bustamente proposition is interesting in that it calls our attention to the practical difficulties of satisfactorily establishing that consent has been obtained. Thus he recommends a system of listing as well as resolving the inevitable disputes that a listing scheme would precipitate. Apparently he proposes that consent would not be one of the recognized elements of proof in the event of a dispute.

[11] Antonio Sanchez de Bustamente y Sirven, *The Territorial Sea* (1930), pp. 99–100.

(8) *Hyde*

All of that part of Professor Hyde's great work that has to do with bays is worthy of careful study. In his writing, one should note the emphasis placed upon the geographical factor.

> Numerous instances where general acquiescence has long rewarded the assertion of dominion over certain broad expanses have begotten the term "historic bays" by way of explanation. The phrase signifies that in each case where it is applied the interested coastal State at some earlier time began to endeavor to possess itself as it were of the waters of the particular bay, regardless of its magnitude, and to assert a right to control them as a part of its territory; and it suggests also that the geographical relationship of those waters to that State were generally deemed to be such as to justify assertion and to discourage foreign opposition to it. Thus, the situation, that made a bay geographically a part of its territory, was the decisive factor. It is believed that the term "historic bays" is illustrative of the full effect of a habit of maritime States, rather than a token of an exceptation to an accepted rule ... It reveals the fact that maritime States have not acted on the theory that international law as such yielded water indentations of defined limits or calculated width to the sovereign of the adjacent land, and withheld others of greater extent from its grasp.
>
> The present state of the law appears to be at variance with what a majority of maritime powers would welcome as the basis of a multi-partite arrangement. Possibly this circumstance is prophetic of the ultimate conclusion of a general agreement that shall serve to amend the customary law. Such an achievement must however, depend upon and await the growth of an opinion that the latitude now asserted and enjoyed by the individual maritime State is sufficiently detrimental to the welfare of international society to demand the imposition of a fresh restraint. What, however, still weighs the scale in favor of the freedom of the individual State is the circumstance that its assertions of dominion do not necessarily extend over areas that in a geographical sense constitute a part of the high sea, and are chiefly confined to acts which in their application are primarily local and involve little interference between foreign States generally.[12]

If the problem were primarily one of navigation between States, then we could agree with Professor Hyde. And if it were primarily a question of free navigation, then the latitude asserted by the individual State might seldom be viewed as so detrimental to the welfare of international society as to demand a fresh restraint. Mr. Hyde assumes, it appears, that a claim to a bay on historic grounds is unlikely if there does not exist a very obvious geographical relationship. Furthermore, his writing is suggestive of the difficulty that must ensue when agreement is reached on a given maximum width for a juridical bay but which also contains the Gidel safety valve. Mr. Hyde, it is feared, was overly optimistic when he wrote the foregoing because he seems to assume that States are unlikely to assert claims to bays for purposes

[12] Charles C. Hyde, *International Law Chiefly as Interpreted and Applied by the United States*, 2nd Ed. (1947), pp. 469–470, 482.

of defense, for purposes of economic self-help, or even for purposes of economic warfare.

We shall not undertake to discuss the writings of publicists which are primarily concerned with positing that certain bays are historic bays. If there does not exist some evidence of a positive State action or judicial decision with respect to a given bay, then the writing concerning its status as a historic bay has limited value to us since, fortunately or otherwise, text writers do not make law.

An exception to the above statement must be made in the case where a publicist's writing can with reasonable certainty be depended upon as officially voicing the policy of the Government of the State from which it emanates.

(9) *Nikolaev*

Into this classification falls the writing of Mr. A. N. Nikolaev of the Soviet Union. The statement hereunder is one taken directly from the United Nations *Memorandum on Historic Bays*, in which an English translation of an excerpt appears. The Statement is included because in all probability it reflects a State policy, at least as of the time it was written, and also because it proposes that sovereignty over a bay should belong to the State who does some special work in rendering it navigable:

> In areas containing internal maritime waters or other national waters, the territorial sea is measured from the outer limit of those waters. The internal waters of the USSR include the Sea of Azov, the Gulf of Riga, the White Sea (to the south of a straight line drawn from Cape Svyatoy Nos to Cape Kanin Nos) and Cheskaya Bay (south of a line going from Cape Mikulino to Cape Svyatoy Nos).
>
> The author of this work is in full agreement with the Soviet scholars who regard as "historic" and subject to the regime of the internal waters of the USSR the seas which form bays in the Siberian Coast: the Sea of Kara, the Laptev Sea, the East Siberian Sea and the Chukchi Sea. Many centuries were required by Russian navigators to establish mastery over these seas, which by now constitute a national waterway of the Soviet State. Through these seas passes the northern maritime route from Murmansk and Archangel to Vladivostok, which was only opened through the prodigious efforts of our heroic Soviet people. In this connexion, we should also recall the judgement delivered on 18 December 1951 by the International Court of Justice in the dispute between the United Kingdom and Norway: this judgement recognizes the maritime route of Indrelaia, which follows the Norwegian coast and was only rendered navigable by special work executed by Norway, forms part of Norwegian internal waters.[13]

The analogy here is somewhat strained and wanting of further explanation. Perhaps the very work of rendering a given arm of the

[13] A. N. Nikolaev, *Problems territorialnykh vod v mezhdunarodnom prave* (1954), pp. 207–208. Translation in UN *Memorandum on Historic Bays* at page 56.

sea navigable is representative of an occupation of it, but this is a question of fact which is dependent upon a sufficiency of evidence. Without any intention of appearing facetious, the United States might raise a similar claim to the Gulf of Alaska, Bristol Bay and Norton Sound on the basis of having rendered these areas more navigable. The efforts expended were not without some heroic feats on the part of the U.S. Coast Guard and the U.S. Coast and Geodetic Survey. The difficulty with the Soviet argument is that it endeavors to establish a claim to exclusive sovereignty over a bay on the basis of erected navigational facilities, hydrographic surveys, or both. It is not believed that such criteria will find ready acceptance among other maritime States.

(10) *Coenen*

In his rather brief thesis *Das Küstenmeer im Frieden*, Doctor Coenen dismisses the matter of historic bays rather quickly by observing that they are much more of a political problem than a legal one. He recommends that international codification conferences should not become bogged down with this problem, but that a special conference should be convened solely for the purpose of preparing a convention establishing which of the world's bays are of a nature so exceptional as to warrant classification as historic bays and the exclusive sovereignty of the littoral State.[14]

(11) *Florio* [15]

The Italian government official Franco Florio proposed a rather novel solution which would probably render the concept of the Historic Bay obsolete. He would group the coastal areas of the world into three types with territorial waters as follows:

(a) Type A (Ocean Coasts) – 30 miles. Into this group would fall the coasts of States facing open oceans. Among States so included are: United States, Norway, and India.

(b) Type B (Coasts of open waters) – 12 miles. Such waters would include the North Sea, Mediterranean, Sea of Japan, Gulf of Mexico, etc.

(c) Type C (Coasts of interior waters (Coste di mari interni)) – 6 miles.

[14] Hanns-Wolf Coenen, *Das Küstenmeer im Frieden* (1933), pp. 64, 109–110. Dr. Coenen's work was *not* written to reflect the views of the German Government of the time.

[15] Franco Florio, *Il Mare territoriale e la sua Delimitazione* (1947), pp. 103–105. Dr. Franco's work was *not* written to reflect the views of the Italian Government of the time.

Bays with openings of 60, 24, or 12 miles, respectively, depending upon the coasts in which they are located, would be within the domain of the States concerned.

The projected convention in which the foregoing proposals appear contains provision for a Special Commission for the Territorial Sea which would be under the Transport and Communications Commission of the United Nations. (Note: the Florio book was written in 1947). This Commission would interpret the convention.

This writer does not deem it necessary to offer any comment upon the radical suggestion of Signor Florio. As a blue print for the future, it might not be too unrealistic.

Section D JUDICIAL DECISIONS

It is our purpose in reviewing the case law on historic bays to emphasize the bases upon which the courts arrived at their conclusions. Many of these cases have been commented upon elsewhere and therefore this discussion of them is intentionally brief.

(1) *United States* v. *Morel* [1]

In this early case, heard by the Circuit Court for the Eastern District of Pennsylvania, the question to be settled was whether a crime committed on board a vessel in Great Harbor, Long Island, Bahamas, was a crime committed on the high seas, within the meaning of 4 Stat. 115. In arriving at its decision the court found it necessary to distinguish clearly between high seas on the one hand and bays or harbors on the other. In doing so, the court laid stress on the aspect of shelter as a function of the geographical formation of a bay. They concluded that the distinguishing feature of a bay is that it is "an opening into the land where the water is shut in on all sides except the entrance."

(2) *Chesapeake Bay* [2]

The status of Chesapeake Bay was raised in 1882 in a case arising out of claims resulting from damage done on the high seas by Confeder-

[1] *U.S.* v. *Morel* (1834) 26 Fed. Cas. 1310.

[2] *The Alleganean, Stetson* v. *United States*, No. 3993, Class I, Second Court of Commissioners of Alabama Claims, IV Moore's *Arbitrations*, 4332, 4335, 4338; I Moore's *Digest* (1906), p. 741; Philip C. Jessup, *The Law of Territorial Waters and Maritime Jurisdiction* (1927), pp. 388–391.

ate cruisers during the Civil War. The claims are generally known as the Alabama Claims. The instant case involved a claim concerning destruction of a ship in Chesapeake Bay, claimant contending that the act took place on the high seas. The United States maintained that the waters of the bay "are territorial waters of the United States and subject to the exclusive control and jurisdiction thereof."

Chesapeake Bay has a closing line of about twelve miles. Inside the bay there is a maximum width of twenty miles and a length of 200 miles. The general orientation of the bay is in the North-South direction, and is thus at right angles to the entrance. Most of the bay is truly land-locked. The court, in holding that the bay was entirely under the jurisdiction of the United States applied these criteria:

(a) Geographical:

"To call it a bay is almost a misnomer. It is more like a might river than an arm or inlet of the ocean. It is entirely encompassed by our own territory... It can not become an international commercial highway ... its headlands are well marked."

(b) Defense:

"Other nations, by common consent of all, have well recognized peaceable rights even in our territorial waters. Ought we to admit that they have any rights hostile to the United States [as on the high seas], or can we permit belligerent operations between foreign nations within the shores of this bay? *What injustice can be done to any other nation by the United States exercising sovereign control over these waters? What annoyance and what injury may not come to the United States through a failure to do so?*"

Herein there was the consideration of belligerent action while the United States was neutral. Of great importance, this author believes, is whether exclusive sovereignty over a bay can be shown to be harmful to the interests of other States.

(c) Long and undisturbed possession

Here the court traced the status of the bay from the time of the 1609 charter granted by James I to the Virginia Company granting the land which happened to encompass Chesapeake Bay, "together with all the soils, grounds, havens, ports, rivers, waters, fishings, etc." The states of Maryland and Virginia were shown to have claimed jurisdiction over the waters and that they continued to do so. United States legislation was shown to have assumed the bay as being within the territorial limits of the United States.

(d) Analogy with Delaware Bay whose status as an exclusive inland body of water was acknowledged by France and England in connection with the *Grange*.[3]

(3) *Conception Bay* [4]

The status of this bay came to be considered in 1877 by the Judicial Committee of the Privy Council of Great Britain in a case involving two competing cable companies, one of whom had been granted by Newfoundland a monopoly of trans-Atlantic cable privileges in all places subject to its jurisdiction. The appellants in the case had anchored a buoy in Conception Bay, but had taken care to keep it well outside the 3-mile limit.[5] Respondents had sought an injunction to prevent the other party from using the bay for its cable laying scheme. If all of Conception Bay were held to be in Newfoundland, then respondents' monopoly entitled them to enjoin the competitor's activity.

The Privy Council considered itself bound by a British statute of 1819 which, in giving effect to the Anglo-American Convention of 1818, imposed on all those who were not British subjects entrance restrictions with respect to all bays in Newfoundland; no exception was made in the case of Conception Bay.

With respect to the specific issue at bar, the Privy Council might very well have said no more. But they chose to consider the status of Conception Bay against the background of bays in general under international law. In light of the endemic Canadian-American fishery controversies of the time there would appear to have been considerable foresight wisdom in so doing. The Council addressed themselves primarily to two factors: geography of a bay, and general acquiescence in a State's exercise of sovereignty over it.

The Council found universal agreement that harbors, land-locked bays and estuaries belonged to the territory of the nation possessing the surrounding shores, but that there was no agreement on a rule for determining what, for this purpose is a bay. Having used the ad-

[3] See Section B, above.

[4] *The Direct United States Cable Company* v. *the Anglo-American Telegraph Company*, Privy Council, 1877. L.R. 2 Appl, Cas. 394. See also: Jessup, *op. cit.*, pp. 392–5; Charles C. Hyde, *International Law Chiefly as Interpreted and Applied by the United States* (1947); Higgins and Columbos, *International Law of the Sea*, 2nd Rev. Ed. (1950), pp. 120–1; Moore's *Digest* (1906), p. 740.

[5] The Buoy was anchored about 30 miles from the mouth of the bay. There are some discrepancies in publicists' descriptions of the measurements of this bay. Hyde, Moore, and Jessup differ from each other. In the published opinion the measurements are: average width, 15 miles; penetration, 40 to 50 miles. The author's measurements on U.S. Navy Hydrographic Office Chart H.O. 1102 are: width, 16.7 miles; penetration, 51.2 miles.

jective "land-locked" once, they ignored the temptation to apply it literally. The history of bays to that time certainly furnished no precedent for such a strict applicaion. The Council found it generally agreed that "where the configuration and dimensions of a bay are such as to shew that the nation occupying the adjoining coasts also occupies the bay, it is part of the territory." They noted that the usual test for occupation, according to publicists, was either twice cannon shot distance or an arbitrary 10 miles. But, they observed that in the Bristol Channel case of *Regina* v. *Cunningham* the Court had found that these rules would have excluded Bristol Channel from British Territory. Concluding, then, that jurists and textwriters were not in agreement as to a rule, and also concluding that such a rule had never been ground for any judicial interpretation, the Council now felt themselves confronted with the question of whether or not they were obliged to lay down such a rule. They decided that this was unnecessary. And rightly so, because very early in the opinion they had issued their decision. The subsequent discussion about a rule served the purpose of planting the seed of doubt as to the existence of such a rule; really, it would be difficult to envision a Privy Council of 1877 finding otherwise. With such seed planted, the ground was better prepared for the next finding: that through long, acquiesced-in occupation, "this bay is by *prescription* part of the territory of *Great Britain.*" It does not appear that the United States, the State of incorporation of the losing firm in this case, availed itself of the privilege of diplomatic protest following on this decision.

The decision and opinion in this case are important because they are illustrative of the difficulties inherent in the establishment of any rule in these premises – primarily by reason of the consequences flowing from any decision embodying such rule. A mathematical rule, when recognized by the Court of a common law country might tend to set a somewhat rigid precedent. On the other hand, the workings of the international community are such that when title is found to exist through long and unchallenged occupation, challenge by another international person poses great difficulty.

Jessup has noted that text writers have not been unanimous in supporting this decision.[6] Moreover, the opinion fails to cite the obvious economic interest of the population of the adjoining land area as well as the fact that there would be no interest in the bay from the point of view of international shipping. The shape of the bay is such as to

[6] Jessup, *op. cit.*, p. 395.

constitute it a bay within the meaning of the present mathematical definition. There is little doubt in this writer's mind that today, in light of *United Kingdom* v. *Norway*, an international tribunal would find Conception Bay to be exclusively under the sovereignty of Canada.

(4) *The Senator Schröder* [7]

This case, tried in the Hamburg Maritime Court, Germany, in 1932, concerns an alleged violation of an Icelandic fishery decree. The so-called bay was 8 miles wide, but its indentation from the closing line to shore was only one mile. The trawler, *Senator Schröder*, was apprehended at a point more than three miles but less than four miles from shore. The court decided neither in a geographical sense nor in a legal sense was the indentation a bay. This case is mentioned here as illustrating a most extreme attempt at use of the bay concept.

(5) *Monterey Bay* [8]

In Chesapeake Bay and Conception Bay, we have cases of historic bays which,, by current legal definition or by any geographical lexicon, may be considered bays. The case of the *Senator Schröder* illustrates an indentation which could hardly by conceived of as a bay even under the most strained interpretation. In Section B, above, we have taken note of the Egyptian policy with respect to some indentations having long closing lines but with relatively shallow penetration into the land. In the United States we have had judicial decisions on two bays of similar configuration.

The first of these cases involves Monterey Bay. According to the opinion of the Court, Monterey Bay is about 18 miles between headlands "with receding shores, giving a total width of 22 miles inside the headlands," and has an indentation of 9 miles. This writer finds the dimensions to be 20.8 and 9.6 nautical miles respectively.

The case involved the seeking of an injunction against members of the California Fish and Game Commission for preventing operations which were alleged to be unlawful and destructive of fisheries. Plaintiff, relying on a *6-mile rule* for bays, contended that Monterey Bay was open sea.

The Court, observing that normal territorial jurisdiction of California ends at the three-mile limit, and noting that the Federal Govern-

[7] *Annual Digest and Reports of Public International Law Cases*, 1931–32, pp. 124–126.

[8] *Ocean Industries, Inc.* v. *Green et al.* (1926) 15 F. 2nd 862.; *Annual Digest*, 1927–1928, pp. 135–136; 200 Calif. 235.

ment had never assumed to regulate or control fishing in Monterey Bay, found that by suitable legislation, the state had assumed such jurisdiction. The Court declared Monterey Bay to be within the boundaries of Califiorna as defined by the Constitution of that state. It used the following areas of reasoning:

(a) Analogy: It was noted that other bays having closing lines greater than 6 miles had been found by the courts to be within the territorial limits of the states concerned.

(b) That the state government had passed fisheries legislation, which in accordance with the state constitution it was empowered to do, dividing the state into districts, and that one of these districts included Monterey Bay.

(c) Lexicographer's definition: "a body of water around which the land forms a curve; or a recess or inlet between capes or headlands."

(6) *Santa Monica Bay*

Like the Bay of Monterey, Santa Monica Bay has a shallow indentation in proportion to the length of its closing line. In the case considered here[9], the Court's opinion described the bay as being located between the headlands of Point Vicente and Point Dume, 25 nautical miles apart and curving inward to a distance of 10 miles from the line joining the two headlands. The case arose in 1939 out of the arrest of the proprietors of a non-powered gambling ship, *Rex*, which was anchored six miles to landward of the closing line and four miles to seaward of the Santa Monica municipal pier. Convicted, thede fendants appealed on the single question of whether the jurisdiction of the State of California extends over the area of Santa Monica Bay.

Inasmuch as Article XII, Section 1 of the California constitution fixed the ocean boundaries of the state to include "all the islands, harbors, and bays along and adjacent to the coasts," the problem for the Court was to determine whether this body of water was a bay within the meaning of the article – and in the language of the Court: "Is the body of water a bay geographically? Is it a bay historically? Is it a bay legally?"

The case holds a considerable element of interest because its rather well-developed and well-written opinion is uncomplicated by any economic interest or any interest on the part of another State. The Court was

[9] *The People* v. *Stralla and Adams*, 96 Pac. (2nd) 941. See also 34 *American Journal of International Law* (1940), pp. 143–153, and *Annual Digest*, 1938–1940, pp. 133–140.

both willing and able to give extensive scope to a narrow set of issues.

The Court, in the absence of any controlling legislation, executive act or judicial decision, followed the doctrine of the *Pacquete Habana*,[10] and looked to international law – the customs and usages of civilized nations, and, finding that there was no agreed definition of a bay, considered that they were bound to determine whether this body of water could in fact be recognized as a bay. They explored the following areas of reasoning:

(a) Comparison with authoritative literal definitions and what men have come to think of as bays.

(b) Early historical assertions to jurisdiction of the bay by the predecessor sovereigns of Spain and Mexico.

(c) Early geographical designation as a bay.

(d) Evidence of the use of the bay as a shelter as contemplated in *U.S.* v. *Morel*, noted above.

(e) Analogy with other bays of large mouth.

(f) Positive acts of assertion to jurisdiction, namely fishery legislation by the state of California.

(g) That there is not, and there cannot become, a pathway between nations, in the case of Santa Monica Bay.

In this case we see the clear need for an exception to the mathematical definition of a bay. It was a matter of removal of a public nuisance which could operate with impunity in sheltered waters if such waters were high seas. Neither by the semi-circular area rule nor by the then more commonly accepted 10-mile rule could Santa Monica Bay be classed as a juridical bay. Santa Monica Bay is no less of a shelter today than in 1939. The Court's opinion has shown us a number of criteria which, in its eyes, justified classing as a bay this arm of the sea. Much emphasis was placed upon common usage in the past.

(7) *San Pedro Bay*

In the case of *United States* v. *Carrillo et al.*, the United States District Court, Southern District of California, determined that San Pedro Bay, another shallow bay having a closing line distance of 14 miles and a 3 mile indentation, was within the United States. The case was in connection with a piracy indictment wherein the defendants

[10] 175 U.S. 677, 700.

were alleged to have joined in a conspiracy to rob a gambling ship in San Pedro Bay.[11] Even more than in the case of Santa Monica Bay, the Court's reasoning centered on the work of map-makers and geographers.[12]

Reverting for a moment to the overall conceptual framework of this book, these cases of California bays invite our attention to the navigation interest. As we have noted from time to time bays have been associated with harbors and shelter. Other things being equal, greater shelter is provided where the arm of the sea has a penetration proportionally greater than the width of the entrance. But to generalize on this relationship with a view toward arriving at an overall definition of a bay would tend to exclude certain arms of the sea where by reason of generally good weather or shelter from certain prevailing winds, the rather open configuration of the body of water does not at all preclude its being thought of in a very real sense as a bay by the inhabitants and Government of the littoral State. Thus exceptions, on historical grounds, should not necessarily be thought of as confined to bays whose openings happen to exceed in breadth the agreed upon maximum. As in the case of the Senator Schröder there can be a threshhold of logical absurdity in denoting some vague concavity a bay, but where this threshhold may be seems difficult to ascertain and certainly a relationship in dimensions the inverse of what appear to be generally considered in bays, is not an unreasonable possibility.

(8) *The Bay of Fundy* [13]

We pass now to a bay wherein the geographical principle was applied to the reasoning and wherein it was found that in accordance with that principle sovereignty could not be said to rest with the possessor of the surrounding shores. The status of the Bay of Fundy was considered in 1853 as a result of a claim against Great Britain for siezure of an American fishing schooner in the Bay. The question was whether this

[11] *United States* v. *Carrillo et al.* 13 Fed. Supp. 121, 122 (S. D. Cal. 1935); *Annual Digest*, 1935–1937, pp. 169–170; I *Hackworth's Digest*, p. 694.

[12] In its opnion the Court wrote: "Such three miles was not a line following the exact contour of the coast, which would seem impracticable, but was three miles from the line joining headlands or points between which lie indentations or bays... The practice of governments, explorers, geographers, etc., has generally confined such formula to bays which are not in fact open sea, and so the coasts of the continents have been mapped, the points between which the sea curves inward have been designated, and the waters between such points have been designated as bays."

[13] I. *Moore's Digest* (1906), p. 785; John Basset Moore, *International Arbitrations* (1898), vol. IV, p. 4342.

body of water was a bay within the meaning of the Anglo-American treaty of 1818. By the terms of a bi-partite Claims Convention of 8 February 1853,[14] an umpire, one Bates, was appointed to settle this and other claims.

Mr. Bates noted that the Bay of Fundy was 65 to 75 miles wide and 130 to 140 miles long and had several bays on its coasts. Thus, he decided, the word bay, as applied to this body of water had the same meaning as that applied to the Bay of Bengal and the Bay of Biscay where no nation could have the right to assume sovereignty. He also noted that the headlands were each in a different country and thus ruled out the possibility of this bay being classed as a British Bay, were it a bay at all.

Although the case is an old one and it is interesting to speculate on how it might be adjudicated today, the Bay of Fundy is still the largest, in terms of closing line length, of any whose status has been the subject of judicial decision. While the writer would hesitate to conclude that the Bates ruling can furnish something of a guide as to the limit in the size of a bay over which a State can, for exceptional reasons, urge claim to exclusive sovereignty, the case of the Bay of Fundy does suggest the probability that even for historic bays there is some undetermined upper limit in size beyond which the case for exclusive possession becomes increasingly difficult to justify.

(9) *The Bay of Chaleurs*

This bay lies between the Canadian provinces of New Brunswick and Quebec and opens into the Gulf of St. Lawrence. It has a penetration of about 100 miles and a closing line 16 miles long. Within the bay there is a maximum width of 20 miles. In the 1880 trespass action of *Mowat* v. *McFee*.[15] plaintiff's fishing boats and nets were seized within the bay but more than three miles from shore. In ordering a verdict for the defendant, the Supreme Court of Canada relied upon an Imperial Statute of 1851 which provides that the boundary between the provinces of Canada and New Brunswick runs down the center of the bay.[16] Canadian statutes, moreover, assume jurisdiction over the entire bay.[17] Inasmuch as the Court concerned itself with no more than giving effect to the statutes, their action is of less interest to us

[14] I *Malloy*, 664.
[15] *Mowat* v. *McFee* (1880), 5 Sup. Ct. R. 66.
[16] Imp. 14 and 15 Vict., c.63.
[17] 47 Geo. III, c.12, s.15, 4 Geo. IV, c.1, s.25.

than the consideration given the bay in the North Atlantic Coast Fisheries Arbitration of 1910, and in the implementing treaty of 1912.[18]

In finding the British claim to this bay to be justified, the Tribunal stressed the fact that Great Britain not only had asserted the claim but had enforced it "in statutes and otherwise." The Tribunal went further by recognizing the navigation problem confronting fishermen in respect of this bay and proposed a closing line between the headlands of Birch Point and Macquereau Point, both of which are identifiable by lighthouses.[19] Dr. Drago, in his dissenting opinion, included this bay as one of those properly claimed by a State.[20]

(10) *Miramichi Bay*

This bay, having a closing line length of about 15 miles and a penetration of 20 miles is located in New Brunswick. Its treatment in the North Atlantic Coast Fisheries Arbitration was almost identical to that accorded the Bay of Chaleurs. Similarly provided for by the Tribunal and the subsequent treaty were the following bays whose locations and general dimensions are as indicated.

(a) Edgmont Bay, Prince Edward Island. Closing line 15.6 miles long; indentiation 11.3 miles.

(b) St. Ann's Bay, Nova Scotia. Closing line 5.1 miles long; indentation, 10.2 miles.

(c) Fortune Bay, Newfoundland. Closing line 25.6 miles long; indentation, 68.1 miles.

(d) Barrington Bay, Nova Scotia. Dimensions of this bay are insignificant for our purposes.

(e) Chedabucto Bay, Nova Scotia. Closing line 9.3 miles long; indentation 20.8 miles.

(f) St. Peter's Bay, Nova Scotia. Closing line 9.2 miles long; indentation 8.5 miles.

(g) Mira Bay, Nova Scotia. Closing line 7.9 miles long; indentation, 10.4 miles.

(h) Placentia Bay, Newfoundland. (The U. S. Naval Base at Argentia is located in this Bay). Closing line 41 miles long; indentation, 74.25 miles.

[18] The closing line proposed by the Tribunal was accepted by the United States in the Treaty of 1912. III *Malloy* 2635.

[19] I *Proceedings, North Atlantic Coast Fisheries Arbitration*, p. 98.

[20] *Ibid.*, p. 106.

(i) St. Mary's Bay, Newfoundland. Closing line 20.5 miles long; indentation, 25.7 miles.[21]

As we have mentioned before, the assertion to sovereignty over the above mentioned bays is almost entirely a function of the economic interest. Correspondingly, the economic interest was the prime factor in the continuing controversy concerning the sovereignty. The exceptional status of these bays was considered by the Tribunal to be rooted in the prolonged assertion of the sovereignty and its active enforcement. The quality of shelter is evident in most of these bays, as a study of the charts will disclose. In the case of the mentioned bays in Newfoundland, the element of shelter becomes more difficult to argue as one nears their entrances and keeps in mind the prevailing weather conditions. The Bay of Placentia is now a special case in view of its having become the site of a defense installation. This installation did not exist in 1910, however. Of primary importance in considering these as historic bays is that the two parties in controversy over them submitted their dispute to arbitration, accepted the award, and finally settled the status of the bays to their mutual satisfaction through the signing of a treaty. Although the treaty in international law is only binding upon the parties signatory, the exceptional status of these bodies of water as historic bays seems further to have matured by reason of the continued exercise of sovereignty over them and the tacit acquiescence of other States.

(11) *Laholm Bay* [22]

In Section B, above, we mentioned this Bay in connection with our discussion of the practice of Sweden. The case which brought this bay to international attention is known as *The Heinrich Agustin*, which was the name of a German trawler seized near the entrance of the bay on 19 January 1925.

The *Heinrich Agustin* was seized for illegal trawling at a point 1.4

[21] Measurements taken from appropriate U.S. Navy Hydrographic Office charts.

[22] This case is discussed at length by Eric C. Bellquist in 24 *American Journal of International Law* (1930), pp. 776–783. In his note, Mr. Bellquist presents the rather brief opinion of the Court of first instance, which opinion was sustained by the Supreme Court of Sweden. Professor Jessup quotes in entirety, the opinion of Mr. Lofgren, legal advisor of the Swedish Foreign Office, *op. cit.*, pp. 413–424. Captain Meyer, in his work, has rather sharply criticized the argument of Doctor Schücking, the defendant's counsel, *op. cit.*, pp. 415–418. See, also, *Pleadings United Kingdom* v. *Norway*, vol. I, p. 441 and vol. II, pp. 490–1. (Mr. Bellquist's note contains a reference error at page 778; The Naval War College International Law Documents volume to which he refers is 1918 vice 1919 as he has stated.) It is unfortunate that this writer is unable to read Swedish inasmuch as Mr. Bellquist's note raises some doubt as to the precise wording and intent of the arguments.

miles *outside* the line drawn from Halland's Väderö lighthouse to Tylö lighthouse. It will be recalled that this was the closing line described in the Dano-Swedish treaty of 1899. The complainant maintained that the point of seizure was in Swedish outer territorial waters, the base line of which was, at this point the closing line of Laholm Bay. This raised the question of the legal status of the waters of Laholm Bay.

The arguments before the lower court were devoid of any economic content and they attempted no reasoning as to why this particular bay should or should not enjoy an exceptional status on grounds of necessity. The argument turned entirely on what the international law of bays was thought to be, whether or not Sweden complied with the law, whether or not Swedish decrees in the premises were acquiesced in by other States, and whether or not Sweden consistently maintained and defended her claim to sovereignty over the waters of Laholm Bay. Complainant's brief maintained, *inter alia*, that tradition, according to international law, permits bays or gulfs of more than the usually accepted breadth to be included in the area of marginal jurisdiction. He then sought to demonstrate that the above-mentioned base-line is traditional and that it had been so respected. Defendant argued that no such long traditions existed in the case of Laholm Bay and that during World War I, Sweden had practically accepted the 10-mile rule.

Mr. Lofgren's argument for complainant is not especially impressive insofar as it is concerned with Sweden's *traditionally* regarding Laholm Bay to be within its territory. But perhaps it is rather instructive; just how does one show that a State traditionally, or through long usage, regards the waters of a bay as being entirely its own? This seems to be a highly relative matter which may involve a multiplicity of different factors and positive acts, all of which a court must carefully assess. The decision of the court in this case does not indicate such weighing of the factors as may have taken place during its deliberation on the case. The decision, as apparently translated by Mr. Bellquist, was as follows:

The exposition of both sides has not given any definite guidance for deciding how the limit of Swedish territorial waters at Laholm Bay was determined in former days according to Swedish law.

However, in the convention between Sweden and Denmark, July 14, 1899, regarding fishing rights in the waters of these countries, the contracting parties proceeded on the basis that unless agreement was made to the contrary the fishing privileges in the whole Bay of Laholm should be reserved for Swedish citizens for a distance of one geographical mile outside of a straight line drawn from Halland's Väderö lighthouse to Tylö lighthouse. By the convention a special concession was made to Danish fishermen who were permitted to fish ¼ geographical mile within the outer limit. The fact that Denmark, who is Sweden's closest neighbor in regard to the fishing waters in question and at the time of the convention was undoubtedly more than any other foreign Power interested in keeping Laholm Bay open for fishing, accepted the above stipulations, without doubt gives strong support to the assumptions that the Swedish Crown even before the convention maintained the conception in regard to the extension of Swedish territorial waters which was embodied in the concention.

Furthermore, inasmuch as it has not been proven that the Crown at any later date has failed to uphold the same view, it may be considered as clearly demonstrated that the Crown for a considerable period has treated as Swedish fishing waters the whole Bay of Laholm within a line drawn between Halland's Vadero lighthouse and Tylo lighthouse and in addition a region situated within one geographical mile outside of this boundary.

Under such circumstances and inasmuch as the Crown must be considered as having the power to determine as it has the extent of Swedish fishing waters, the region in question must be considered as Swedish waters, and as it is indisputable that the defendant on the 19th of January, 1925, with his ship was trawling within said region, and that the ship was apprehended within the same region.

The Magistrate's Court finds the defendant guilty.[23]

Before the Court of Appeal at Gota, the Swedish jurist Baron von Holstein argued that in accordance with more recent Swedish practice, the closing line should have a 10-mile limit and should be drawn within Laholm Bay. The Court, however, upheld the decision of the court below.

The Defendant then appealed to the Swedish Supreme Court and submitted a brief prepared by the famous German jurist, Doctor Walter Schücking. His argument centered on the territoriality of bays and in the course of its development maintained that international law imposes limitations on the extent of such territoriality. It was his contention that the closing line established by Sweden is of an origin much too recent (1899) to justify a conclusion that Laholm bay is a historic bay, and that status as such had not been recognized by any other State except Denmark. In fact, he pointed out, Germany had disagreed with this contention in 1917. He then argued that in the absence of such evidence, only the 10-mile rule had any stature in International Law. Captain Meyer has written rather caustically about Doctor Schücking's argument,[24] and in light of the complainant's argument perhaps unfairly so. The advocates of the Swedish Crown argued thus:

[23] Bellquist, *op. cit.*, p. 780.
[24] Meyer, *op. cit.*, pp. 414–419.

(a) Conventions, laws and long-established usage are to be sure, good grounds for declaring a bay territorial; but on the other hand, the absence of such facts should not mean that a bay should be regarded as subject to the three-mile limit, or to a ten or twelve-mile limit.

(b) Neither the ten nor the twelve-mile limits can be considered as constituting universally accepted rules of international law.

(c) Inasmuch as there are no generally accepted rules of international law giving a maximum measure for the line in bays separating "inner and outer" territorial waters, it follows that it is the right of each State within reasonable limits, to say which of its bays are to be considered territorial, a right which is more strongly grounded in regard to bays than in questions concerning territorial waters as a whole.

(d) In light of the practice of States elsewhere, as emphasized by the Hague Tribunal in the North Atlantic Coast Fisheries Case of 1910, the Swedish delimitation in Laholm Bay is in full accord with international practice.

The Supreme Court sustained the decision of the court of first instance on the grounds established by that court.[25]

The arguments and decision in the *Heinrich Agustin* or Laholm Bay case are interesting largely by reason of what they do not say. It is inconceivable, moreover, that the matters omitted were absent from the minds of the complainant's counsel or the Swedish court. First, it does not appear that any mention was made either of the geographical configuration or the geographical location of Laholm Bay. The Bay, as defined by the closing line maintained by Sweden meets the requirements of the semi-circle rule. (Although this rule had not yet been devised, the bay is a definite indentation having a landward dimension greater than the length of the closing line.) Moreover, it is located in the Kattegat, not very far distant from Denmark and Germany, but it is not part of an international highway. That there was a continuing defense interest on the part of Sweden might well be concluded in light of belligerent actions occurring in the bay during World War I, Sweden being neutral during that war. That there was Swedish economic interest is obvious or the 1899 treaty would probably not have been concluded. Yet none of these circumstances were considered during the proceedings, despite the fact that these are the circumstances that really brought about such development in the law as there was. The lessons that may be derived from the case seem to be these:

(a) That when a State acts to convert the waters of a bay into internal waters, the burden upon an opposing State to argue the case in terms of general international law becomes heavy indeed.

[25] Bellquist, *op. cit.*, p. 783.

(b) That the municipal tribunals of the former State are not likely to find for the opposing State. Hence recourse to an international tribunal may lead to a more balanced adjudication of the issues.

(c) That while abstract and imperfectly formulated rules of international law may furnish some guidance in a case involving a particular bay, each bay is a decidedly separate situation which is governed first of all by geography, and each bay raises issues which in degree or kind are likely to be different from those of every other case.

(12) *Bristol Channel*

Bristol Channel, on the west coast of England, is a wide bay leading to the ports of Cardiff and Bristol. In actual usage it is difficult to say just where its western extremity might be. Originally, all of the area enclosed by a line from Land's End to Milford was one of the "King's Chambers."[26] This line was nearly 100 miles long. From this line to what might be considered an inner limit of the bay, there is a penetration of about 110 miles.

In 1859, the American ship *Gleaner* was at anchor in Penarth Roads in Bristol Channel.[27] Penarth Roads is near Cardiff and actually near the inner extremity of the bay, or as the opinion of the Court reads, about ninety miles from the mouth of the Channel. The ship was anchored about one mile off shore. Here the Channel is about 7.7 miles wide. While the ship was at anchor, one Cunningham and others were alleged to have wounded a seaman of the ship, and they were convicted of that offense. On appeal there arose the question whether the prisoners were properly convicted of an offence in the county of Glamorgan. Chief Justice Cockburne in rendering the opinion wrote:

> The Sea in question is part of *Bristol Channel*, both shores of which form part of *England* and *Wales*, of the county of Somerset on the one side and the county of Glamorgan on the other. We are of the opinion that, lookingat the local situation of the sea, it must be taken to belong to the counties respectively by the shores of which it is bounded; and the fact of the *Holms* [two small islands in the channel nearby] between which and the shore of the county of *Glamorgan* the place in question is situated, having always been treated as part of the parish of *Cardiff*, and as part of the county of *Glamorgan*, is a strong illustration of the principle on which we proceed, namely, that the whole of this inland sea between the counties of *Somerset* and *Glamorgan* is to be considered as within the counties by the shores of which its several parts are respectively bounded. We are therefore of the opinion that the place in question is within the body of the county of *Glamorgan*.

[26] Thomas W. Fulton, *Sovereignty of the Sea* (1911), pp. 120, 588, 754. Professor Fulton includes in his book, at Appendix E, page 754, a reproduction of the Trinity House declaration as to the limits of the King's Chambers.

[27] *Reg.* v. *Cunningham* (1859), Bell. Crown Cases Reserved, 72.

Now all the court really concerned itself with was the extent of criminal jurisdiction over a foreign ship. The year was 1859 when seagoing life could still be one of the more brutal of human experiences, and anti-social behavior on board ships in port was annoyingly common. England was indeed mistress of the seas and had little to be concerned about encroachments into her maritime territory. It is not apparent that Bristol Channel was a fishing area frequented by foreign ships in 1859. The court, therefore, might understandably confine itself to geographical considerations, as well as to considerations of rather general prior usage in the area. It is not evident in the record that they did anything more. They offered no opinion concerning what might be the entrance to Bristol Channel.

Nevertheless it appears to this writer that in subsequent years there was expanded interpretation of the opinion beyond any reasonable justification therefor.[28] Jessup quite rightly concluded that neither this court decision nor the court's comment in the Conception Bay case implied a claim to the whole Bristol Bay area, and it is doubtful whether the British Government would press such a claim.[29] As a matter of fact the British Government has been remarkable reticent in defining the limits of its maritime jurisdiction.[30] Fulton quotes Lord Hokesbury who had charge of the Territorial Waters Jurisdiction Act of 1878 as saying:

[28] Fulton attempted to speculate upon the seaward limit of internal waters of Bristol Channel. *op. cit.*, p. 588. In the Privy Council opinion in the Conception Bay Case (*Direct United States Cable Co.* v. *Anglo-American Telegraph Co.*), Lord Blackburn wrote": It was not, however, necessary for the decision of *Cunningham's Case* to determine what was the entrance of the Bristol Channel, further than that it was below the place where the crime was committed, and though the language used in the judgment is such as to shew that the impression of the Court was that at least the whole of the Channel between the counties of *Somerset* and *Glamorgan* was within those counties perhaps that was not determined. But this much was determined, that a place in the sea, out of any river, and where the sea was *more than ten miles wide* (italics here are mine) was within the county of *Glamorgan*, and consequently, in every sense of the words within the territory of *Great Britain*. It also shews that usage and the manner in which that portion of the sea had been treated as being part of the county was material..." *Law Reports, Appeal Cases*, ii, p. 419. With the latter sentence one must certainly agree. Otherwise this writer is quite unable to plumb the reasoning by which Lord Blackburn arrived at his interpretation of the other court's opinion. In *Regina* v. *Cunningham*, the court did not mention the 10-mile rule, and in 1859 that rule was a rather novel idea. Finally, if one is to take literally what the court actually said: "The whole of this inland sea between the counties of *Somerset* and *Glamorgan*," a map should be used. This will disclose that the western boundary of the County of Somerset terminates on the Bristol Channel. Here the bay is 14.8 nautical miles in width. It is quite disillusioning to read the comments of various publicists concerning British sovereignty over Bristol Channel. For example, Klüber says that Bristol Channel is a closed sea recognized by other Powers. *Droit des Gens Moderne de l'Europe*, 2nd Ed. (1874), sec. 130.

[29] Jessup, *op. cit.*, p. 385.

[30] The Foreign Enlistment Act of 1870 was declared to extend to all dominions of Her Majesty, including the adjacent territorial waters, but the term was not interpreted further. The Territorial Waters Jurisdiction Act of 1878 makes no provisions for bays.

... in that act they took care specially to avoid any measurements. The distance was left at such limit as was necessary for the defence of the Realm; then the exact limit was given for the particular purpose in view.[31]

This was done with respect to smuggling, slave ships and the Herring Fishery Act of 1885.

Whatever sovereignty Britain may have been assumed to have over Bristol Channel was not brought to question until the 17 March 1926 collision between the British steamer *Cornish Coast* and the Italian steamer *Fagernes*.[32] The collision occurred at a spot in the Channel 10.5 miles from Ilfracombe on the English coast and 9.5 miles from Oxwich Head on the coast of Wales. This position is inside a line between Worms Head and Boggy Point, which, geographically speaking, might very well be thought of as the *fauces terrae*. The *Fagerness* was sunk and the *Cornish Coast* was damaged. The owners of the latter ship sought damages on the grounds that the negligence of the *Fagernes* caused the collision. If proceedings were brought in England, the plaintiffs had the possibility of recovering damages up to a limit of eight pounds sterling per ton. If they were brought in Italy, damages were limited to the value of the *Fagernes*, a value that had ceased to exist. Plaintiffs obtained leave to serve a writ for an action *in personam* against the Italian owners of the *Fagernes*. Defendants appeared conditionally and applied to set aside the writ on the ground that the collision took place outside the jurisdiction of the Admiralty Division of the High Court. The court of first instance, basing its decision on the dicta of *Regina* v. *Cunningham*, held that the place of collision was within the jurisdiction of the court.[33] On an appeal to the Court of Appeal, that court decided that there were raised issues of public interest on which the Crown might desire to be represented. The Attorney General appeared and argued, *inter alia*:

There is no recognized rule of international law on the question, and it is not desirable that the Court should lay down any principles unless bound so to do. The high seas, however, should be as wide as possible. It is clear that at least so much as is within a six-mile line drawn from shore to shore is *inter fauces terrae*,

[31] Fulton, *op. cit.*, p. 592. *Law Reports* (1927), *Probate*. 311.

[32] *Law Reports* (1927) *Probate*, 311; For further comment see: W. E. Beckett and Hugh H. L. Bellott, "Territorial Limits in the Bristol Channel," 9 *British Yearbook of International Law* (1928), pp. 120–126; H. A. Smith, *The Law and Custom of the Sea*, 2nd Ed. (1950), pp. 13–14; U.S. Naval War College, *International Law Situations*, 1928, pp. 35–37; *Hackworth's Digest* (1940), vol. I, pp. 707–8; Charles G. Fenwick, *Cases on International Law*, 2nd Ed. (1951), pp. 569–572.

[33] Hill, J., held that the waters of Bristol Channel, at any rate above a line drawn from Ball Point in Devonshire to Port Eynon in Glamorganshire were *inter fauces terrae*. The distance between these two points is 21.2 miles. The line so drawn would lie about 1.5 miles to seaward of the scene of the collision.

and such waters are national as distinct drom territorial. It is conceded also that whenever a country has possessed itself of a gulf or bay over which it has effectively asserted dominion, such waters, although considerably wider, may become the territory of that country...

In the present case there is no evidence of appropriation, and if the Court wishes information as to whether the Crown claims this part of Bristol Channel as being within the territorial jurisdiction of His Majesty it can be given.

In reply to a direct question by the Court, the Attorney General replied that the Home Secretary had instructed him to say that:

... the spot where this collision is alleged to have occured is not within the limits to which the territorial sovereignty of His Majesty extends.

The Court of Appeal reversed the decision of the Court below and held that this spot was not within the jurisdiction of the Court. Two of the three judges, however, stated that in the absence of this statement by a proper representative of the Crown, which had to be treated as conclusive, they would have arrived at the same conclusion as the lower Court.

Aside from settling the status of the Bristol Channel, the *Fagernes* case is important in that the British Government took a positive position repudiating a claim to one of the King's Chambers. This is in contrast to the statement of the British Agent, Sir William Robson, at the North Atlantic Coast Fisheies Arbitration of 1910:

They have never been abandoned. The claims of Great Britain to the King's Chambers stand perfectly good.[34]

In his critical comment upon this case in 9 *British Yearbook of International Law* (1928), at page 123, Mr. Hugh H. L. Bellot notes that the whole of Bristol Channel east of Fundy Island (twenty miles to seaward of the scene of the collision) is a pilotage district and in part remains so. He writes that compulsory pilotage is usually only compulsory within territorial waters. While compulsory pilotage regulations make for an interesting theoretical question on the extent of maritime jurisdiction, it is not known by this writer that an international case of such a particular nature has come to bar, although some variations thereof have been so subject.[35]

[34] James B. Scott. Ed., *Argument of Elihu Root before the North Atlantic Coast Fisheries Arbitration Tribunal*, 1910 (1922), p. 291.

[35] There have been numerous international cases having to do with compulsory pilotage, but they all seem to turn on discriminatory practices with respect to dues charged or with collision liability in waters where the pilotage requirement is common ground. Jessup, *op. cit.*, pp. 133–144; Hyde, *op. cit.*, pp. 701–2; Hackworth, *op. cit.*, vol. II, pp. 263–272; *Moore's Digest* (1906), vol. II, pp. 160–1. As a practical matter, there appears little reason for such a case to arise inasmuch as the need for pilotage is unlikely to be questioned if it has been prescribed for a port. While this matter could be explored further there appears little profit in doing so save to note that extension by a State of the area in which compulsory pilotage is required could be a means of demonstrating that sovereignty was being exercised.

(13) *Long Island Sound*

This body of water is about 100 miles long and has a maximum width of about 20 miles. It has a maximum opening, counting distances between islands at the mouth of about 8.7 nautical miles. Its status was considered by the New York Court of Appeals in the case of *Mahler* v. *Transportation Co.*[36] This was a collision case involving two U.S. flag vessels wherein one Mahler was killed and his administratrix sued to recover damages for his death. The status of these waters was determined on these two bases:

(a) Inclusion of the Sound's waters as territory granted by King Charles II to the Duke of York.

(b) Reference to publicists' writings concerning jurisdiction over bays the entrances to which are between headlands sufficiently contiguous so that command of the entrance can be maintained by cannon from either side.

(14) *Palk Bay*

This bay is actually part of the strait separating India and Ceylon. Its inner boundary is considered to be Adams Bridge, a string of islets crossing the strait. It is 30 miles wide at the entrance and has a penetration distance of 70 miles.[37] The case in which the status of this bay was considered is *Annakumaru Pillai* v. *Muthupayal* (1904).[38] It appears that chank beds [39] are located about five miles off shore and that these were leased by the Rajah of Ramnad to the complainant in the case. Defendant was accused of stealing chanks from the beds. The court of first instance dismissed the case on the ground, *inter alia*, that the chank beds in question were in the open sea. The Appellate Criminal Division of the Indian High Court of Madras reversed the decision, finding that Palk Bay was an integral part of His Majesty's Dominions. Reasoning was based on these factors:

(a) That the bay is land-locked for eight-ninths of its circumference, and cannot be regarded as open sea.

(b) That historical evidence showed the bay to have been effectively occupied for centuries by the inhabitants of adjacent districts of India and Ceylon.

(c) That British occupation of the bay had been enjoyed with the acquiescence of other States.

[36] (1866) 35 N.Y. 352.
[37] UN Document A/Conf.13/37, pp. 125, 152.
[38] XXVIII *Indian Law Reports, Madras Series*, 551, 553.
[39] A chank is a type of mollusc.

The shape of Palk Bay, approximately circular with an interior of far greater breadth than the entrance, is such as to invite a claim to exclusive possession of its waters. The chank fisheries, the dense littoral population, and the relatively mild climate all contribute toward a tendency upon the part of the inhabitants to regard the bay as their own. The Court found that the Rajah of Ramnad claimed the chank beds by immemorial privilege and that he had a property right in them.

The bay appears to be an outstanding example of one where immemorial possession can be demonstrated and where State control of its waters is highly necessary from an economic standpoiút.

(15) *Penobscot Bay*

The Supreme Judicial Court of the State of Maine in *State* v. *Ruvido* [40] reviewed the case of a non-resident apprehended for fishing without a license in Penobscot Bay. While the decision dd not ultimately turn on the limits of the bay, the Court's opinion contains an interesting passage in connection with their view concerning the State's jurisdiction over the bay:

It is difficult to conceive of a body of water more clearly defined than this, or more easily patrolled and protected by the State which controls its shores. All the islands which surround it are in the State of Maine. The mariner who passes through any of the channels almost instinctively feels himself to be within our domain.

(16) *North Atlantic Coast Fisheries Arbitration*

This case has been referred to rather frequently during the course of this book and in some detail in Chapter FOUR. With respect to historic bays, only so much of the arguments, award, and dissent as relate directly to this category of bays will be considered here. Pertinent passages are quoted.

(a) Argument of the United States

There is no such sovereignty accorded over any bay, or creek, or inlet, or harbor that does not come within that normal zone, [three-mile limit] unless the nation has affirmatively elected to take the Bay, creek, or harbor into its jurisdiction, and asserted its right to take it into its jurisdiction, upon facts which, when analyzed, will be found always to go back to the same doctrine of protection.

The United States had no rights over Delaware Bay unless she elected to appropriate Delaware Bay, as she did. Great Britain had no rights over the Bay

[40] (1940) Rept. 15A (2nd) 293 Maine; *Annual Digest*, 1938–40, pp. 128–132.

of Fundy, over Chaleur, Miramichi, Conception, Placentia, White Bay, unless she elected to appropriate them. The writers say these bays, more than double the width of the territorial zone, may be prescribed for.[41]

It is to be seen that the contention of the United States is quite narrow here and one that would be unlikely to enjoy the concurrence of many other States at the time it was voiced. The logical conclusion to be drawn is that exceptional rights to what have come to be called historic bays can only exist after the States concerned have made unilateral declarations in the premises. In this present day of speedy communications and strongly nationalistic tendencies, however, such claims may very likely be asserted with increasing frequency and States who might prefer, in the interest of continuing friendly relationships with other States, not to make such positive declarations, may consider themselves forced by outside pressures to do so. In such event, the agreed listing of such bays, the codification of criteria, or the conference suggested by Dr. Coenen will be of increasing utility. Codification will be discussed in the next section.

(b) Argument of Great Britain

The United States and Great Britain have both continuously insisted on claims which would have been tenable if there had been any such limit as in now suggested by the former Power, and other States have exercised sovereignty over territorial waters equally extensive.[42]

This is simply a statement of quite objective fact and requires no explanation save to note that the State asserting sovereignty over a historic bay has, morally at least, an even greater than usual burden in attempting to dislodge the claim of another State to another bay on similar grounds.

(c) The Award of the Tribunal

... the geographical character of a bay contains conditions which concern the interests of the territorial sovereign to a more intimate and important extent than do those connected with the open coast. Thus conditions of national and territorial integrity, of defence, of commerce, and of industry are all vitally concerned with the control of the bays penetrating the national coast line. This interest varies, speaking generally, in proportion to the penetration inland of the bay;[43]

As in other judicial decisions, we note a continuing concern with the geographical factor. Moreover, there is little doubt that for most

[41] Scott, *op. cit.*, p. 275.

[42] IV *Proceedings in the North Atlantic Coast Fisheries Arbitration*, U.S. Senate Document No. 870, 61st Congress, 3rd Sess. 1912, p. 96.

[43] Scott, *op. cit.*, p. 509.

ports of the world the final sentence of this passage truly reflects the existing state of affairs.

It has been recognized by the United States that bays stand apart, and that in respect of them territorial jurisdiction may be exercised farther than the marginal belt in the case of Delaware Bay by the report of the Unites States Attorney General of May 19th 1793; and the letter of Mr. Jefferson to Mr. Genet of November 8th, 1793, declares the bays of the United States generally to be "as landlocked, within the body of the United States".

(5) In this latter regard it is further contended by the United States that such exceptions only should be made from the applications of the three mile rule to bays as are sanctioned by conventions and established usage; that all exceptions for which the United States of America were responsible are so sanctioned; and that His Majesty's Government are unable to provide evidence to show that the bays concerned by the treaty of 1818 could be claimed as exceptions on these grounds either generally, or, except possibly in one or two cases, specifically.

But the tribunal, while recognising that conventions and established usage might be considered as the basis for claiming as territorial those bays which on this ground might be called historic bays, and that such claim should be held valid in the absence of any principle of international law on the subject, nevertheless is unable to apply this, *a contrario*, so as to subject the bays in question to the three mile rule as desired by the United States;

(a) Because Great Britain has during this controversy asserted a claim to these bays generally, and has enforced such claims specifically in statutes and otherwise...

(b) Because neither should such relaxations of this claim as are in evidence be construed as renunciations of it; nor should omissions to enforce the claim in regard to bays as to which no controversy arose be so construed. Such a construction by this Tribunal would not only be intrinsically inequitable, but internationally injurious, in that it would discourage conciliatory diplomatic transactions and encourage the assertion of extreme claims to their fullest extent.[44]

In the first part of this passage we note the adjective, "land-locked" and that it is closely associated with Delaware Bay. At that early date the term was apparently given a construction more liberal than what common reasoning might suggest. The remainder of the passage is a judgment upon the contention of the United States. It implies that with respect to bays the tribunal was not satisfied as to the existence of governing principles of international law. The final sub-paragraph of the passage, however, is one of considerable importance. Here there is implied a distinction between the *possibility* of enforcing of a claim and actively maintaining it (and, presumably, publicizing its existence). The tribunal appeared to consider that omission of enforcement should not necessarily justify the conclusion that no claim exists. In a world where land areas are usually quite unmistakably bounded and under

[44] *Ibid.*, p. 510.

the jurisdiction of some State, this dictum seems to acknowledge not only that the status of waters in some bays is not similarly delimited but that a decision tending to bring about such an effect might lead to some undesirable consequences. It is believed that even to this day the dictum has considerable merit. On the one hand it can be condemned as being founded upon a philosophy which encourages postponement of problems that will eventually arise anyway. On the other hand it can be praised as being founded upon the philosophy that counsels the empirical settlement of specific questions when and if they arise.

(d) The dissent of Doctor Luis Drago

...it may safely be asserted that a certain class of bays, which might properly be called the historical bays, such as Chesapeake Bay and Delaware Bay, in North America, and the great estuary of the River Plata, in South America, form a class distinct and apart, and undoubtedly belong to the littoral country, whatever depth or penetration and the width of their mouths, when such country has asserted its sovereignty over them, and particular circumstances, such as geographical configuration, immemorial usage, and, above all, the requirements of self defense, justify such a pretension. The right of Great Britain over the bays of Conception. Chaleur, and Miramichi are of this description.[45]

This view of Doctor Drago is an eminently sound one for describing the criteria that should be applied in questions on historic bays, and it probably can stand the test of time. The difficulty, of course, is in the perfecting of machinery for its universal application.

(17) *Moray Firth*

This bay has been discussed in Chapter FOUR, Section C. Strictly speaking, a British claim to exclusive sovereignty over the Bay was never really pressed. The judgment in *Mortensen* v. *Peters* [46] was based on a by-law made by the Fishery Board under The Herring Fishery (Scotland) Act, 1889,[47] which the High Court of Justiciary of Scotland construed as applying not only to British subjects for whom it was obviously designed, but also to foreigners. Most of the so-called foreign subjects were British trawler owners who employed foreign flags to escape the provisions of the Act. When the Norwegion Government protested, the British Government decided not to enforce the Act as against foreign vessels,[48] and today they do not claim the Firth as being wholly within British waters. Under the Trawling in Prohibited

[45] *Ibid.*, p. 519.
[46] (1906) *14 Scots Law Times Rep.* 227.
[47] 52 & 53 Vict. c.23.
[48] *Hansard* (Lords) 4th Series, vol. 169, col. 989; *Hansard* (Commons) 4th Series, vol. 169 col. 979.

Areas Prevention Act of 1909, no prosecution can take place for the exercise of prohibited fishing methods beyond three miles from the coast, although fish so caught may not be landed or sold in the United Kingdom.[49]

(18) *United Kingdom* v. *Norway*. (The Anglo-Norwegian Fisheries Case)

The arguments, opinion of the Court, and the concurring and dissenting opinions of individual judges contain a body of material that is uniquely instructive and thorough in its coverage. One cannot but agree with the comment of Major Richard R. Baxter, U.S. Army Reserve, and member of the Faculty of Harvard Law School, to this writer, that in this case almost the whole field of international law is touched upon. By the same token, however, the vast materials in the case are susceptible of a variety of interpretations some of which do violence both to the probable intentions of the Court who were confronted with an isolated but difficult problem in a shrinking world, and to the interests of the body of States in the world community. As previously expressed in this book, it is this writer's view that the court's opinion falls short in its failure of forthright precision. For the present era, it is believed that such precision would have been most timely. It is quite appreciated that there are many who would hardly share this view.

Hereunder, the author quotes from the several opinions passages concerned more or less directly with historic bays.

(a) Judgment (Opinion of the Court)

By "historic waters" are usually meant waters which are treated as internal waters but which would not have that character were it not for the existence of an historic title.[50]

While this is indeed correct, it is to be noted elsewhere in the Court's opinion, and in the separate opinions that there are some material differences as to the weight to be given to evidence based upon historical fact.

It does not at all follow that, in the absence of riules having the technically precise character alleged by the United Kingdom Government, the delimitation undertaken by the Norwegian Government in 1935 is not subject to certain principles which make it possible to judge validity under international law. The

[49] 9 Edw. VII, c.8.
[50] International Court of Justice, *Reports*, 1951, p. 130.

delimitation of sea areas always has an international aspect; it cannot be dependent merely upon the will of the coastal State as expressed in municipal law, although it is true that the act of delimitation is necessarily a unilateral act. Because only the coastal State is competent to undertake it, the validity of the delimitation with regard to other States depends upon international law.[51]

This is the beginning paragraph of a section of the opinion wherein the court endeavors to establish criteria for determining the validity of a State's claim to areas of what might otherwise be considered as high seas and so contested by other States.

Among these considerations, some reference must be made to the close dependence of the territorial sea upon the land domain. It is the land which confers upon the coastal State a right to the waters off its coasts.[52]

This is the geographical factor, which in one form or another, has been a recurrent theme in most judicial decisions on bays. Here it is stated with great clarity.

Finally, there is one consideration not to be overlooked, the scope of which extends beyond purely geographical factors: that of certain economic interests peculiar to a region, the reality and importance of which are clearly evidenced by a long usage.[53]

In the present era and phase of international relations, one cannot but agree with the Court. To ignore the economic factor is to act in a manner out of keeping with the increasing interdependence of world society. But this places a heavy burden upon the Court and one which they did not discharge adequately in the writing of their opinion. If the Court marks out such a criterion, then it would seem incumbent upon them to show that they have weighed the economic merits of the positions of both parties litigant. Perhaps to do so may be viewed as premature, but in this writer's eyes, it is an inevitable development. This writer does not believe that the long run consequences would be other than salutary.

"The Norwegian Government does not rely upon history to justify exceptional rights, to claim areas of the sea which the general law would deny; it invokes history together with other factors, to justify the way in which it applies the general law." This conception of an historic title is in consonance with the Norwegian Government's understanding of the general rules of international law.[54]

It is believed that this is really the only tenable position to be taken with respect to historic claims. While it is conceivable that there could arise a dispute over a bay which would parallel the Palmas

[51] *Ibid.*, p. 132.
[52] *Ibid.*, p. 133.
[53] *Ibid.*
[54] *Ibid.*

Islands dispute,[55] this writer thinks this is an unlikely eventuality.

The notoriety of the facts, the general toleration of the international community, Great Britain's position in the North Sea, her own interest in the question, and prolonged abstention would in any case warrant Norway's enforcement of her system against the United Kingdom.[56]

The Court found that the "prolonged abstention" was for a period of over sixty years. They gave weight to the absence of protest, thus reiterating a lesson on the desirability of timely expressions of disagreement.

Such rights, founded on the vital needs of the population and attested by very ancient and peaceful usage, may legitimately be taken into account in drawing a line which, moreover, appears to the Court to have been kept within the bounds of what is moderate and reasonable.[57]

One must agree, but it is believed that the Court should have issued a more detailed expression of its reasoning.

(b) Separate statement of Judge Hackworth (United States)

Judge Hackworth declares that he concurs in the operative part of the Judgment but desires to emphasize that he does so for the reason that he considers that the Norwegian Government has proved the existence of an historic title to the disputed areas of water.[58]

In the present era, such a terse statement by the American member of the Court is something less than a significant contribution to the cause of international jurisprudence.

(c) Individual Opinion of Judge Alvarez

It is not enough to stress the general principles of law recognized by civilized nations; regard must also be had, as I have said, to the modifications which these principles may have undergone as a result of the great changes which have occurred in international life, and the principles must be *adapted* to the new conditions of international life; indeed, if no principles exist covering a given question, principles must be *created* to conform to those conditions. [59] ... It follows that the traditional distinction between *legal* and *political* questions, and between the domain of law and the domain of politics is considerably modified at the present time.[60]

This is an expression of the general concept of what one writer has

[55] Tribunal of the Permanent Court of Arbitration, 1928. J. B. Scott, *Hague Court Reports*, Second Series, 84.

[57] *Ibid.*, p. 139.

[53] *Ibid.*, p. 142.

[58] *Ibid.*, p. 144.

[59] *Ibid.*, pp. 147–8.

[60] *Ibid.*, pp. 149.

called "The New International Law of Alejandro Alvarez." [61] It is beyond the scope of this book to comment further upon the Alvarez philosophy. The principles with respect to wide bays which he says the Court must "bring to light, adapt if necessary, or even create" seem to be these:

1. The great variety of geographical and economic conditions of States render it impossible to lay down general or uniform rules.

2. The international status of every great bay must determined by the coastal States directly concerned, having regard for the general interest.

3. If a State appears to adopt base-lines arbitrarily, that will constitute an *abus de droit*.

4. Any State directly concerned may raise an objection if it alleges that the above conditions have been violated. "Disputes arising out of such objections must be resolved in accordance with the provisions of the Charter of the United Nations."

These are the words of an idealist written into an opinion of a World Court serving a World which, to borrow from the special vocabulary of the Deutsch school of behavioral political scientists, has probably arrived at the condition of "mutual interdependence" but not the necessary "mutual responsiveness" [62] which would have to be a precondition for general acceptability of the Alvarez idea.

(d) Separate Opinion of Judge Hsu Mo

In support of her historic title, Norway has relied on habitual fishing by the local people and prohibition of fishing by foreigners. As far as the fishing activities are concerned, I need only point out that individuals, by undertaking enterprises on their own initiative, for their own benefit and without any delegation of authority by their Government, cannot confer sovereignty on the State, and this despite the passage of time and the absence of molestation by the people of other countries.[63]

This is an arguable proposition, at least. It would seem to vitiate any concepts of possession "from time immemorial." Certainly the status of Palk Bay, referred to above, was settled on this basis.

With regard to the licenses for fishing granted on three occasions by the King of Denmark and Norway to Erich Lorch, Lieutenant-Commander in the Dano-Norwegian Navy towards the close of the 17th century, I do not think that this is sufficient to confer historic title on Norway to Lopphavet. In the first place, the granting by the Danish-Norwegian Sovereign to one of his own subjects of what was at the time believed to be a special privilege can hardly be considered as conclusive evidence of the acquisition of historic title to Lopphavet *vis-à-vis* all foreign States. In the second place, the concessions were limited to waters

[61] William Samore, "The New International Law of Alejandro Alvarez," 52 *American Journal of International Law* (1958), pp. 41–54.

[62] Karl W. Deutsch, *Political Community at the International Level* (1954), pp. 37–8

[63] *Ibid.*, p. 157.

near certain rocks and did not cover the whole area of Lopphavet. Lastly, there is no evidence to show that the concessions were exploited to the exclusion of participation by all foreigners for a period sufficiently long to enable the Norwegian Government to derive prescriptive rights to Lopphavet.[64]

Should one choose to generalize from this particular opinion, then one would have to question a number of the rights to possession that seem to derive from charters granted to individuals during the Age of Discovery. Perhaps these are susceptible of attack, but one can hardly ignore a fairly substantial body of case law in which courts heve seen fit to trace title to such concessions.

(e) Dissenting Opinion of Judge Sir Arnold McNair

The other category of bay whose headlands may be joined for the purpose of fencing off the waters on the landward side as internal waters is the historic bay, and to constitute an historic bay it does not suffice merely to claim a bay as such, though such claims are not uncommon.[65]

Claims to fence off and appropriate areas of the high seas by joining up headlands have been made from time to time, but usually in the case of particular pieces of water and not on the thorough-going scale of the Decree of 1935.[66]

Judge McNair writes that there is required the evidence of long and consistent assertion of dominion over the bay and he cites the specific instance of the Conception Bay case, noted above. In the next passage, it is his purpose to condemn the headland theory, and rightly so, because there is almost no limit to how that can be applied.

In my opinion the manipulation of the limits of territorial waters for the purpose of protecting economic and other social interests has no justification in law; moreover, the approbation of such a practice would have a dangerous tendency in that it would encourage States to adopt a subjective appreciation of their rights instead of conforming to an international standard.[67]

Here Judge McNair touches at the very heart of the difficulty of applying general international law in the settlement of present-day disputes. Most of these disputes have their bases in clashes of economic interest. We have tried to show in Chapter FOUR that from 1800 on, the development of the law of bays has been grounded chiefly in the economic interest. It is doubtful that anything the Court could do in the present era would mitigate the "subjective appreciation," unless there were an undertaking to assess the economic and other social interests; these are simply unavoidable.

[64] *Ibid.*
[65] *Ibid.*, p. 164.
[66] *Ibid.*, p. 165.
[67] *Ibid.*, p. 169.

"But the general presumption certainly bears strongly against such exclusive rights, and the title is a matter to be established, on the part of those claiming under it, in the same manner as all other legal demands are to be substantiated, by clear and competent evidence" (Quotation from Lord Stowell in *The Twee Gebroeders* (1801), 3 *Christopher Robinson's Admiralty Report* 339).

Another rule of law that appears to me to be relevant to the question of historic title is that some proof is usually required of the exercise of State Jurisdiction, and that the independent activity of private individuals is of little value unless it can be shown that they have acted in pursuance of a license or some other authority received from their Governments or that in some other way their Governments have asserted jurisdiction through them.[68]

Here, again, as in Judge Hsu Mo's Separate Opinion, the proposition of title through ancient usage comes under attack. It is the belief of this author that such usage is really the manifestation of a continuing necessity on the part of the peoples concerned. There would seem to be a close tie between the ancient or historic usage and the economic necessity therefor. And it would seem to be a continuing responsibility of the State to protect what its citizens have thought to be their exclusive right through the centuries, so long as that right is not demonstrably abused. It is probable that the very social fabric of some peoples was in a high and identifiable condition of development long before the existence of this corporate entity called a State.

(f) Dissenting Opinion of Judge Read

... it was recognized [historically] that, regardless of breadth, the coastal State could treat as internal waters those bays over which they had exercised sovereignty, without challenge for a long time... The rights of the coastal State are, in this case, fully supported by customary law.[69]

This is quoted only to show Judge Read's general view of the historic bay.

No question of *res nullius* or annexation arises in the case of the sea. All nations enjoy all rights and all privileges in and over all of the sea beyond the limit of territorial waters. It follows that the power of the coastal State to mark out its maritime domain cannot be used so as to encroach on the high seas and impair these rights and privileges. Its power is limited to the marking out of areas already subject to its sovereignty.[70]

Here, again, we have the view that, when carried to what this writer believes to be a logical conclusion, title can never be acquired through of discovery, subsequent legislation, and absence of protest.

[68] *Ibid.*, pp. 183–4.
[69] *Ibid.*, p. 188.
[70] *Ibid.*, p. 190.

Customary international law is the generalization of the practice of States. This cannot be established by citing cases where coastal States have made extensive claims, but have not maintained their claims by the actual assertion of sovereignty over trespassing foreign ships. Such claims may be important as starting points, which, if not challenged, may ripen into historic title in the course of time.

The only convincing evidence of State practice is to be found in seizures, where the coastal State asserts its sovereignty over the waters in question by arresting a foreign ship and by maintaining its position in the course of diplomatic negotiation and international arbitration.[71]

Here Judge Read applies what is really the doctrine of effectiveness. As a purely practical matter, there is great merit in the above-stated proposition, so long as the arrests of foreign ships involve no more than the exercise of ordinary domestic police power.

... I must explain that I do not regard the older historical data as important.[72]

Here, again, there is a jurist who is inclined not to apply such data to present day cases.

Section E EFFORTS AT CODIFICATION

An oddity in the history of the law of bays is that while most of the case law on bays and nearly all of the controversies with respect to specific bays has been concerned with those that fall into the historic category, the efforts at codification of rules for bays usually mention the historic bay rather incidentally, as a sort of exception to the general rule. The codifications proceed no further and do not concern themselves with any limiting criteria other than vague phrases about "usage."

(1) *Institute of International Law* [1]

The 1894 Paris meeting of the Institute appears to have been the first to take up the matter of the historic bay.[2] In the draft prepared for the meeting by Mr. Barclay, the article on bays provided no exception from the mathematical rule for the closing line (double the width of the territorial sea in this case). Mr. Aubert, a member from

[71] *Ibid.*, p. 191.

[72] *Ibid.*, p. 197.

[1] Although the work of the Institute is mentioned here rather briefly, it was mentioned frequently, and much importance was attached thereto, by both sides in *United Kingdom* v. *Norway*.

[2] Most of the material on this meeting is to be found in 20 *Annuaire de l'Institut de Droit international* (1894).

Norway, had previously advised Mr. Barclay concerning this matter in the following terms:

> It is undoubtedly impossible to submit geographical relations of this nature [fjords in Norway] to general rules of an absolute character. It is necessary to leave the detailed application of them to custom and the regulation of each State, provided that it is done in good faith or is dictated by plausible reasons. The general international rule to be established ought consequently to be elastic enough to permit such local anomalies.[3]

Subsequently, at the 1894 meeting, Mr. Aubert expressed the matter in more clearly understood economic terms:

> It is within the role of the Institute to leave to poor and small countries the means of struggling against other States.[4]

Mr. Aubert also pointed out the existence of some wide bays in Western Australia over which territoriality had been claimed.

The draft article adopted by the Meeting reads:

> Article 3.
>
> For bays, the territorial sea follows the sinuosities of the coast, except that it is measured from a straight line, drawn across the bay at the place nearest the opening toward the sea where the distance between the two sides of the bay is 12 marine miles in width *unless a continued usage of long standing has sanctioned a greater breadth.* (Italics mine)[5]

The matter was not debated again by the Institute until 1928 when, at its meeting in Stockholm, the qualifying phrase adopted was:

> unless international usage has sanctioned a greater width.[6]

The original draft of the clause contained the words: "uncontested international usage." It was proposed to drop the word "uncontested" and this proposal received a favorable vote. The meeting found no fault with the words "international usage," and a reading of the record discloses no clue as to what is meant by them in the instant context.[7]

(2) *International Law Association*

In 1895, the Association adopted an article (No. 3) on bays in which there was a modifying clause reading as follows:

> Unless a continued usage of long standing has sanctioned a greater width.[8]

[3] *Ibid.*, vol. 11, p. 141.
[4] *Ibid.*, vol. 13, p. 287.
[5] *Ibid.*, p. 328.
[6] *Ibid.*, vol. 34, p. 755.
[7] *Ibid.*, pp. 640–645.
[8] International Law Association, *Report of 17th Conference* (1895), p. 115.

At the 1926 Conference, the Association adopted an article (No. 7) which reads:

Article 7

With regard to bays and gulfs, territorial waters shall follow the sinuosities of the coast, unless an occupation or an established usage generally recognizes by Nations has sanctioned a greater limit.[9]

In the Association's 1926 draft, there was no closing line limit established for bays. Thus, by virtue of the 3-mile limit of territorial waters prescribed in Article 5, all bays having closing lines over 6 miles in length would fall under the historic bay category if the State concerned were so to claim them.

(3) *International Law Association of Japan*

The Association adopted a draft in 1926. In its article on bays (No. 2), the saving clause for historic bays reads:

unless a greater width has been established by immemorial usage.[10]

(4) *American Institute of International Law*

In a draft submitted by this Institute to the Pan American Union in 1925, Article 6 on bays has the following saving clause:

unless a greater width shall have been sanctioned by continued and well-established usage.[11]

In a subsequent draft prepared in 1933 for the Seventh International Conference of American States, the Institute submitted the following article:

Article 11

There are excepted from the provisions of the two foregoing articles, in regard to limits and distance, those bays or estuaries called historic, *viz.*, those over which the coastal State or States, or their constituents have traditionally exercised and maintained their sovereign ownership, either by provisions of internal legislation and jurisdiction, or by deeds or writs of the authorities.[12]

This article is identical with that contained in Judge Bustamente's "Project Convention" submitted by The American Institute of International Law to the Hague Codification Conference of 1930. In his study, *Territorial Sea*, Bustamente proposes that each State having historic bays will declare them at the time of depositing its ratification

[9] *Ibid.*, *Report of 34th Conference* (1927), p. 102.

[10] 20 *American Journal of International Law* (1926) (Special Supplement), p. 376.

[11] Antonio Sanchez de Bustamente y Sirven, *The Territorial Sea* (1930), p. 57.

[12] *Pleadings*, (*United Kingdom* v. *Norway*), p. 455.

of the Convention.[13] The Article of the "Project Convention" designed to bring this about reads:

Article 19

The contracting States which maintain, for all purposes of for some, a greater extent which has been fixed previous to the signing of the present Convention, shall declare this extent when depositing their respective ratification or when adhering to same.[14]

(5) *The Harvard Research* [15]

This project, undertaken in 1929 in anticipation of the Hague Codification conference, provided one article (Art. 5) for bays in which the closing line was spelled out in mathematical terms and a different article for waters upon which States attached historic claim. The comment on Article 5 reads, in part:

It is to be recognized, however, that certain bays ate considered as wholly territorial waters of certain States because of Claims long maintained, though the entrance to such bays exceeds ten miles in width. Such bodies of water are frequently called "historic bays"; Delaware, Chesapeake and Conception bays are good examples. The text of the convention does not interfere with claims based on established usage since such cases are provided for in Article 12.[16]

Article 12 reads:

The provisions of this convention relating to the extent of territorial waters do not preclude the delimitation of territorial waters in particular araes in accordance with established usage.[17]

With respect to historic bays the Harvard Research comment on this general article is:

This article seems necessary because of historic claims made by certain States and acquiesced in by other States with reference to certain bodies or with reference to particular areas of water. The simplest case is that of an historic bay such as Chesapeake Bay or Conception Bay. It seems desirable that the convention should not interfere with historic claims of this kind based upon usage which has been established before this convention comes into force. Such claims may enlarge or diminish the extent of territorial waters. Similarly it seems desirable that it should be recognized that usages with respect to other areas may become established in the future and that well founded claims may be based upon such established usage.

It is to be observed that no mention is made of the feasibility of States' declaring their historic bays. The possibility that such a pro-

[13] Section C, above.

[14] Bustamente, *op. cit.*, p. 143.

[15] 23 *American Journal of International Law* (Apr. 1929 Special Supplement), pp. 243–380.

[16] *Ibid.*, p. 266.

[17] *Ibid.*, p. 288.

cedure might tend to inhibit any future claims seems indirectly to be reflected in the final sentence of the Harvard Research comment. Mr. George W. Wickersham, one of the original Leaugue of Nations Committee of Experts was an adviser for the Harvard Research on Territorial Waters, and it may be presumed that the Harvard Research had the benefit of his pre-Conference experience on the Committee of Experts. The comments on the bay article are too terse to really reflect whatever degree of consideration may have been given the question of historic bays.

(6) *Hague Conference for the Codification of International Law*

Doctor Schücking, in his first draft convention, submitted the following Article on bays:

Article 4

In the case of bays which are bordered by the territory of a single State, the territorial sea shall follow the sinuosities of the coast, except that it shall be measured from a straight line drawn across the bay at the part nearest to the opening towards the sea, where the distance between the two shores of the bay is 12 marine miles, *unless a greater distance has been established by continuous and immemorial usage.* (Italics mine)

In the case of bays which are bordered by the territory of two or more States, the territorial sea shall follow the sinuosities of the coast.

As regards the recognition of rights which are in contradiction with the tenor of the general rules, the provisions of Article 3 concerning presentation and registration in the International Waters Register shall be applicable. It shall not be possible to acquire such rights in the future.[18]

Dr. Schücking's comment on historic bays, immediately preceding the draft article are worthy of recording:

There remains to be considered the legal status of bays which are only bordered by a single State and which are subject for historical reasions to claims of exclusive right of user. As we have already observed, such a right must be recognized on principle. The position is an anomalous one, and for that reason such rights must be dealt with in the same way as the rights to be exercised outside the fixed zone of the territorial sea by particular States. At the same time, it must not be forgotten that in case of bays such rights might lead to the recognition of a general right of dominion over the waters in question (the internal waters of the bay) and not merely to the exercise of certain special rights of dominion (such as, for example, the right of sanitary or Customs control).

As these historical rights restrict in a special manner the common use of the sea, it is necessary that they should be definitely formulated in an international convention, as was proposed in respect of the riparian rights outside the terri-

[18] 20 *American Journal of International Law* (Special Supplement July-October, 1926), p. 85.

torial sea. This should be done under the same conditions as in the case of the rights enumerated in Article 3, *i.e.*, the rights in question should be registered in the International Waters Register. It should be made impossible for such rights to be acquired in the future.[19]

What Dr. Schücking had in mind, of course, was that all States would declare and register those bays of exceptional size to which they laid claim on the basis of historic ("immemorial") usage, and that thereafter no such claims would be permitted to arise. Now theoretically this makes good sense: The world in 1926 (and in 1960) is a closed politico-geographical system [20] and States either have what they believe to be "historic" bays or they do not. The emphasis is on the historic and immemorial usage and this would in logic exclude future claims to exclusive sovereignty over bays of exceptional size. It will be noted, on the contrary, that the Harvard draft makes a point of providing for future claims on the basis of "established usage."

In view of the importance that this author attaches to the concept of an international water register as a possible solution to the problem of historic bays, Dr. Schücking's note and his proposed article for the establishment of it are quoted here in their entirety:

If the rules proposed by us be put into operation by Convention, there will still be very varied forms of legal rights in the parts of the sea near the coast, for, apart from the fundamental rights of common user in respect of the territorial sea, to which we shall return later, third States will be able to exercise various rights in respect of the territorial sea solely by virtue of the fact that they exercised such rights before the conclusion of the Convention in consequence of the common usage of the high seas or of special treaties. Again, riparian States could exercise special rights in waters which do not, strictly speaking form part of the territorial sea. The legal position in this respect cannot be changed. The present state of affairs will continue. It is therefore necessary to prevent, at any rate in the future, the possibility of conflicts arising as a result of this confused legal position. This is not, we think, in any way impossible. All the questions which may arise can be reduced to this one question: To what point does the common right of user of the sea extend, and to what point do the rights of particular States extend? This question of the limitations of the common use of waters is not new to jurists. It arises also in the interior of States, and civilized States have endeavored to solve it by establishing registers of special waters, sometimes in connection with the establishment of land registers and sometimes separately. These documents, which are published and controlled by State authorities, contain a record of all special rights restricting common use; and these records create the law of the future. *All that is necessary is to transplant this institution*

[19] *Ibid.*

[20] A. E. Moodie, *Geography behind Politics* (1947), p. 26. The geographers generally make this statement for varied and different purposes, including that of counter-argument against some of the more aggressive geo-political theories. See further: Whittlesey, *The Earth and the State* (1944); Weigert, et al, *Principles of Political Geography* (1957); and Gyorgy, *Geopolitics: The New German Science* (1944).

to the domain of legal rights which restrict the common use of waters in the neighborhood of riparian States. (Italics mine).

International unions with special offices were established for many administrative purposes even before the formation of the League of Nations. The duty of an International Waters Office would be to compile a register of the rights which particular States consider they possess in the fixed zone of foreign riparian States, or which such riparian States consider that they possess outside their own fixed zone.

In the case of rights arising out of the traditional common use of waters not hitherto included in the fixed zone, the registration of such rights in favor of any State will suffice to ensure their enjoyment in the future by all other States.

In the case, however, of rights arising from special treaties, such rights can, naturally, only be claimed by the States signatory to these treaties, and only provided that they register them within a fixed time-limit. A time-limit must also be fixed for the registration of rights which the riparian State claims to exercise outside the fixed zone of the territorial sea. The legal instruments concerned must be presented and registered. The onus of proof will be upon the State applying for the registration of a right in its favor. Applications must be communicated to all the States signatory to the Convention; they may be opposed within a time-limit to be fixed. If an application is opposed, the question will be decided, in the first instance, by a mixed commission of experts and jurists. Appeal lies from decisions of this commission to the Permanent Court of International Justice. All States will be informed of the registration of a right. The register will be published.

The same procedure would apply in cases in which a State claims to have an urgent and new need outside the sphere of its dominion over the territorial sea. It must apply to the International Waters Office, which may only grant a right after publication of the application and provided it is not opposed. In the event of opposition, the question goes before a mixed commission, before which the State claiming the right must prove that it cannot otherwise protect the interests affected. In this case also, both parties have a right of appeal to the Permanent Court of International Justice.

The International Waters Office will also be responsible for publishing maritime charts showing the zones of the territorial sea.[21]

The Schücking draft article providing for the International Waters Office reads as follows:

Article 3

The States signatory to the Convention undertake to establish an International Waters Office.

The duty of this Office is to compile a register of rights possessed by the different States in the fixed zone of foreign riparian States, or by riparian States themselve outside the fixed zone.

The registration of a right in the International Waters Register kept by the International Waters Office in favor of any State in a foreign territorial sea shall be in favor of all States, if such right is founded upon common usage.

[21] 20 *American Journal of International Law* (Special Supplement, July–October 1926), pp. 80–81.

A time limit of shall be fixed by the International Waters Office for the submission of all applications for such rights, as also for rights claimed by a riparian State outside its fixed zone by virtue of usage.

The relevant legal instruments must be presented and registered. The onus of proof shall be upon the State applying for registration of a right in its favor. Applications must be communicated to all the States parties to the Convention.

Applications may be opposed within a time-limit to be fixed. If an application is opposed, the question is decided, in the first instance, by a mixed commission of experts and jurists. Appeal lies from decisions of this commission to the Permanent Court of International Justice. All States shall be informed of the registration of a right. The register shall be published.

The same procedure shall apply in cases in which a State claims to have an urgent need outside the sphere of its dominion over the territorial sea. It must apply to the International Waters Office, which may only grant a right after publication, and provided that it is not opposed. In the event of opposition, the question shall go before a mixed commission, before which the State claiming the right must prove that it cannot otherwise protect the interests affected. In this case also, appeal lies to the Permanent Court of International Justice.

The International Waters Office shall also be responsible for publishing maritime charts showing the zones of the territorial sea.[22]

The proposal of Dr. Schücking [23] possesses a great deal of surface charm and it might very well be the most satisfactory system for regulating the historic bay problem. It has the added feature of probably ensuring the development by the International Court of a considerable body of jurisprudence on the subject.[24] It pre-supposes, however,

[22] *Ibid.*, pp. 116–117

[23] A similar proposal was made by Professor Strupp at the 1928 Meeting of the Institute of International Law. The proposition was made in the form of an amendment to Article 12 (Contiguous Zones) of the Institute's Draft Code on Territorial Waters. The President of the Institute declared that such a novel proposition could not be examined at the meeting. Subsequently, Dr. Alvarez demanded a committee to examine the proposal. This was accepted. 34 *Annuaire de L'Institut de Droit international* (1928), pp. 673–5, 733. A committee was subsequently appointed with members, among others: Sir Thomas Barclay, Messrs Gidel, Alvarez, Marshall Brown (U.S.), Unden (Sweden), and Strupp. A committee report, supplemented by lengthy observations, was presented at the 1929 Meeting. Should such a project be contemplated for the future, the report, which cannot be reproduced here, would be useful for reference purposes. Professor Gidel felt (quite rightly) that the Commission as proposed would be clothed with an unacceptable amount of power. Instead, he proposed an International Bureau of the Sea which would be primarily an information and technical organization. See: 35 *Annuaire* (1929), vol. I, pp. 155–228; Gidel, *op. cit.*, Tome I, pp. 23–38; Walter Schücking, "Le Dévelopment du Pact de la Société des Nations," 20 *Recueil des Cours de l'Académie de Droit international de la Haye* (1927), pp. 353–456, at p. 448. For subsequent discussion of the International Waters Office, See 36 *Annuaire* (1931), vol. I, pp. 6ff; 37 *Annuaire* (1932), pp. 65ff; and Stefan Riesenfeld, *Protection of Coastal Fisheries under International Law* (1942), p. 109.

[24] In this connection, the Committee of Experts originally selected a total of twenty-one topics more or less suitable for codification. Topic No. 8 in this list was the application of the conception of prescription in international law. *Ibid.*, p. 20. This subject was never actively considered by the committee. Roger Pinto, "La Prescription en Droit International" 87 *Recueil des Cours de l'Académie de Droit international* (1955), pp. 391–449.

certain pre-conditions of international political life that were rather uncertain in 1926 and appear more so today.

In his comment on the Schücking draft, Professor Magalhaes appeared to favor the International Waters Office.[25] The third member of the Committee of Experts, Mr. Wickersham, omitted any mention of it in his published comment.[26] At the end of his report, Dr. Schücking has this to say about the stillborn International Waters Office:

> After discussion with various members of the Committee, I convinced myself that the moment had not yet come to propose the establishment of an International Waters Office. My colleagues on the Sub-Committee felt, however, that this proposal might be taken into account as a simple suggestion.[27]

It is perhaps important to note that in the Amended Draft Convention which was communicated to various Governments by the League Committee of Experts, Article 3, *International Waters Office* was marked "(suppressed)." [28] In the Amended Draft so communicated, the article on bays reads:

> Article 4
>
> *Bays*
>
> In the case of bays which are bordered by the territory of a single State, the territorial sea shall follow the sinuosities of the coast, except that it shall be measured from a straight line drawn across the bay at the part nearest to the opening towards the sea where the distance between the two shores of the bay is ten marine miles, unless a greater distance has been established by continuous and immemorial usage. The waters of such bays are to be assimilated to internal waters.
>
> In the case of bays which are bordered by the territory of two or more States, the territorial sea shall follow the sinuosities of the coast.[29]

The maximum width of a bay has been reduced to ten miles, as compared with twelve miles in the Schücking draft, and the paragraph on the International Waters Register has been removed. Added is the provision positively assimilating the waters of bays to internal waters.

The Preparatory Committee appointed to succeed the Committee of Experts drew up a "schedule of points" to be submitted to the Governments for comment. Point IV, "Determination of the base line for calculation of the breadth of territorial waters," contained the

[25] 20 *American Journal of International Law* (Special Supplement, July-October 1926), p. 130.

[26] *Ibid.*, pp. 134–141. Mr. Wickersham's contribution on bays is limited to stressing the sovereignty of the United States over Chesapeake and Delaware Bays.

[27] *Ibid.*, p. 146.

[28] *Ibid.*, Vol. 23 (Special Supplement, 1929), p. 366.

[29] *Ibid.*

single word "Historic bays." After receiving the Governments' replies, the Preparatory Committee made the following Observation:

The Government replies appear to indicate that agreement can easily be reached to extend the same method of calculation to bays of a greater breadth than ten miles where the coastal State is in a position to prove the existence of a usage to that effect. (historic bays).[30]

Following on this Observation, the Preparatory Committee set out the following basis of discussion for the Conference:

The belt of territorial waters shall be measured from a straight line drawn across the entrance of a bay, whatever its breadth may be, if by usage the bay is subject to the exclusive authority of the Coastal State: the onus of proving such usage is upon the coastal State.[31]

The Observation of the Preparatory Committee was considerably wide of the mark in its prediction and as it developed, the debate in the Second Committee of the Conference was rather lengthy and inconclusive. During the course of the debate, the Chief of the British delegation brought up the idea of a small body "which might examine the claims of the various nations to historic bays with a view to making a report and possible recommendations on the subject at a later date, to Geneva or elsewhere." He stated further:

The subject is one which has caused much dispute in the past and this seems to be a golden opportunity first of all to settle the principles on which the classification is to be based, and then, having settled the principles, to agree upon some list which is to be binding in the future.[32]

The proposal was concurred in by a number of delegations and roundly condemned by others. During the debate Professor Magalhaes of Portugal revived the idea of the International Waters Office. Professor Spiropoulous of Greece made these sound observations:

Everything depends on the meaning we attach to the word historic... The reasons which make a bay historic are diverse ... The reasons may be military, economic, connected with national defense, or even archaeological...[33]

The Swedish and American delegations rejected the thesis of the historic bay altogether.[34] It was the United States delegation, however, that probably stalled any real progress on basis of discussion Number 8. Most of the statement of the American delegation is quoted hereunder:

[30] League of Nations publication V. Legal, 1929, V.2 (document c.74 M.39, 1929.V.), p. 45.
[31] *Ibid.*
[32] League of Nations publication C.351(b.) 1930.V., p. 105.
[33] *Ibid.*, p. 108.
[34] *Ibid.*, pp. 107–109.

The delegation of the United States is not in accord with Basis of Discussion No. 8 as at present drafted, but for reasons which are quite different from, and even opposed to, some that have already been expressed.

I would mention in passing that the delegation of the United States has this morning laid on the table certain amendments of a technical nature [35] and which I do not propose to discuss; this question is not, in my opinion, one of historic bays. Both words are inaccurate – both "historic" and "bays." It is a question, so far as the latter word is concerned, of waters, not merely waters that either from habit or some technical definition are called bays, but waters by whatever name they may be generally called. Furthermore, the word "historic" is an inaccurate word, because it is not only a question of history, it is also a question of the national jurisdiction of the coastal State.[?] That, I submit, is the question involved in regard to these waters, and the continual use of the expression "historic bays," with mention of one or two bays here and there in different parts of the world, has led to a great deal of confusion of thought as to the principles involved.

I wish to call attention to the amendment proposed by the delegation of the United States as an additional article, in Document 19, paragraph (c). I desire to read the first paragraph:

> "Waters, whether called bays, sounds, straits, or by some other name, which have been under the jurisdiction of the coastal State as part of its interior waters, are deemd to continue a part thereof."

I consider, therefore, that Basis of Discussion No. 8, which reads: "If by usage the bay is subject to the exclusive authority of the coastal State," is totally inadequate in its use of the word "bay." I shall comment in a moment or two on the remainder of that Basis, which deals with the question of proof.

I quite agree with the view that it is nor possible at this conference, either in a Committee or in a Sub-Committee, to frame a list of these waters or to establish a line which would indicate where these waters are. No one could propose that, but in Basis of Discussion No. 8, and in various amendments that have been put forward, reference is made to the question of proof.

The last sentence of Basis No. 8 reads, "The onus of proving such usage is upon the coastal State." In certain of the amendments, and during the discussion, use has been made of the expression that a claim shall be established or that a claim shall be proved. The view has been put forward that a Committee should be set up. What powers is that Committee to have? Is it a Committee for purposes of examination? In that case, I cannot see its utility. *If it is to have power to take a decision I am bound to say that we could never agree to it.*

Any question in regard to these matters is, in my opinion, a question which could only arise between Governments and could only be discussed by them. Nothing can be done until that discussion has taken place. The point cannot be settled in this Convention. We have agreed that all these meticulous questions of detail cannot be settled by this Convention or by any Committee of this Conference. So far, therefore, as there may be a difference of view between the Governments, they must exchange opinions on the subject. The point cannot be settled by any tribunal to be set up by the Convention we are to prepare here.

[35] This was the "arcs of circles" proposal.

Accordingly, the second sentence of (c) of the United States proposal provides that "charts indicating the line drawn in such cases shall be communicated to the other parties hereto." (Italics mine).[36]

While the writer considers it necessary to have quoted the above statement, little purpose would be served in attempting any analysis of it. The statement is no doubt a product of a number of complex factors and attitudes prevalent at the time. The debate thereafter was inconclusive but decidedly frustrated and disappointed in tone. As Professor Raestad of Norway said, the principle of the American proposal was to support the *status quo*.[37] In its report to the Conference, prepared by the rapporteur, Professor Francois of the Netherlands, the Second Committee reported, in part:

One difficulty which the Committee encountered in the course of its examination of several points of its agenda was that the establishment of general rules with regard to the belt of the territorial sea would, in theory at any rate, effect an inevitable change in the existing status of certain areas of water. In this conversation, it is almost unnecessary to mention the bays known as "historic bays"; and the problem is besides by no means confined to bays, but arises in the case of other areas of water also. The work of codification could not affect any rights which States may possess over certain parts of their coastal sea, and nothing, therefore, either in this report or in its appendices, can be open to interpretation. On the other hand, it must be recognized that no definite or concrete results can be obtained without determining and defining those rights.[38]

The end result of the Hague Conference work on this problem was was that there was no codification of the law of bays and therefore none on historic bays. In commenting on the lack of achievement of the Conference in this respect, Mr. Jesse S. Reeves wrote:

To endeavor to clothe the geographical definitions with scientific exactitude and to impute to them legal validity is the way of hindrance and not of aid to the progressive development of international law.[39]

While there is maybe some truth in Mr. Reeves' comment, it must be observed that the world is getting smaller and as it does, such an attitude may partake more of a rationalization of a position with respect to a problem than a conclusion reached after real efforts

[36] *Ibid.*, p. 107.

[37] *Ibid.*, p. 110. Subsequently Mr. Miller, the head of the U.S. delegation agreed with this observation. Hunter Miller, "The Hague Codification Conference," 24 *American Journal of International Law* (1930), at page 691. Mr. Raestad also remarked: "Our United States colleague not only destroys the theory of bays, but he destroys history as well by saying that we need take no account of it."

[38] League Publication, *loc. cit.*, p. 211.

[39] Jesse S. Reeves, "The Codification of the Law of Territorial Waters," 24 *American Journal of International Law* (1930), pp. 486–499; see also S. Whittemore Boggs, "Delimitation of the Territorial Sea," *ibid.*, pp. 541–555.

have been made, not only to solve it, but in the exercise of leadership toward effecting a solution. In 1930 the United States seemed unprepared to lead or even to state its case convincingly.

(7) *United Nations International Law Commission and the Geneva Conference of 1958*

In the International Law Commission's first draft on the law of the territorial sea, the historic bay went unmentioned.[40] The report of the Special Rapporteur, Professor Francois, after his consultation with the specially appointed Committee of Experts, was likewise silent on the matter. This Committee, which met for two days in April 1953, was not requested to comment on historic bays.[41] The Third (1954) Report of the Commission is again silent on this subject.[42] In the 1955 draft of the International Law Commission, Article 7, on the law of the bays, contains the following relevant provisions:

4. Where the entrance of a bay exceeds twenty-five miles, a closing line of such length shall be drawn within the bay. When different lines of such length can be drawn, that line shall be chosen which encloses the maximum area of the bay.

5. The provision laid down in paragraph 4 shall not apply to so-called "historical" bays or in cases where the straight base-line system provided for in Article 5 is applicable.[43]

Article 7 of the 1956 draft of the Commission provides the following paragraph on historic bays:

6. The foregoing provisions shall not apply to so-called "historic" bays or in any cases where the straight base-line system provided for in Article 5, is aplied.[44]

This paragraph was adopted without change by the United Nations Conference on the International Law of the Sea, meeting in 1958 at Geneva.[45] If taken literally, the first clause of paragraph 6 means that *all* provisions regarding bays would be disregarded in any consideration of historic bays, including the first sentence of paragraph 2, embodying a geographical concept:

For the purposes of these articles, a bay is a well-marked indentation whose penetration is in such proportion to the width of its mouth as to contain land-locked waters and constitute more than a mere curvature of the coast,

[40] United Nations Publication A/C N.4/53;

[41] A/C N.4/61 Add 1.

[42] A/C N.4/77.

[43] A/2934; A/c.6L.378, p. 40.

[44] A/2934; A/3159, p. 5; p. 36; reprinted in U.S. Naval War College, *International Law Situation and Documents*, 1956, p. 166.

[45] It became Article 7, paragraph 6, Annex I of the Final Act. Within the paragraph, the words "article 5" were changed to read "article 4." A/Conf. 13/L.52; reprinted in 38 *Department of State Bulletin* (1958), p. 1111; reprinted in 52 *American Journal of International Law* (1958), pp. 834–842.

and the final clause of paragraph 4, embodying what appears to be a well agreed upon legal concept:

and the waters enclosed thereby shall be considered as internal waters.

One might raise the question whether there was not some oversight in the drafting of this paragraph, but judging from the documentation this writer has found, it would appear that the drafting was knowingly so accomplished and later by implication, at least, admitted to be imperfect. The Union of South Africa Coment on the 1955 Draft, reads *inter alia:*

Article 7 would be acceptable to the Union Government only if it were amended in such a way as to leave no doubt, the the so-called "historical bays" were to be treated as *sui generis* and excluded not only from the operation of the rule contained in paragraph 4, but also from the application of the criteria laid down in the rest of the article.[46]

In his reply to this comment, the special Rapporteur wrote:

The Rapporteur believes that the Union Government could be satisfied by replacing the words, "the provision" laid down in paragraph 4 [now paragraph 5] by the words "the foregoing provisions shall not apply" which already appears in the comment.[47]

Thus the whole article was excluded from governing any consideration of historic bays.

In preparation for the Geneva Conference, and apparently mindful of the incomplete status of the International Law Commission's work on the historic bay, the United Nations Secretariat prepared and distributed a study on the subject, *Memorandum Concerning Historic Bays*, Preparatory Document No. 1.[48]

The delegates at Geneva were not unanimously satisfied with the drafting in question, and differences of opinion were much in evidence. Some careful parliamentary management seems to have been required in order to retire the complex and only partially pre-digested matter from debate. At the third meeting of the First Committee, the Panamanian delegate, Mr. Rubio proposed the establishment of a subcommittee to examine the problem of bays, and in pasticular the question of the legal status of historic bays. He is recorded as saying, *inter alia*, that:

It was therefore indispensable that the international instruments to be drafted should deal with such questions as the definitions of historic bays, the rights of

[46] A/CN.4/Ser A/1956/Add. 1., p. 27.
[47] A (CN.4/99).
[48] A/Conf.13/1 of 20 September 1957.

coastal state or states, the procedure for declaring a bay "historic", the conditions concerning their recognition by other states, and the peaceful settlement of the disputes arising from objections by other states.[49]

He then went on to cite the great importance attributed to this question by eminent writers such as Gidel, Bustamente, and to mention Gidel's "safety valve" analogy.

Mr. Carmona of Venezuela, speaking at the Ninth Meeting of the First Committee, is recorded as having made this remark:

Venezuela could never accept the thesis that rights could be acquired through immemorial usage. There could be no acquisition of a prescriptive title to the detriment of new countries now in the full process of development.[50]

Mr. Pfeiffer, the German delegate, made this apt observation several days later, at the fifteenth Meeting:

With regard to Article 7, paragraph 4 [now paragraph 6], historic title should of course be respected as in other cases, but it would be difficult to establish general rules applicable to historic bays.[51]

Finally, at the Twenty-First Meeting, Professor Francois, Special Rapporteur of the International Law Commission's Eight Session in 1956, and now serving as expert to the Secretariat of the Geneva Conference made a statement, paragraphs 13 and 14 of which are quoted in their entirety in Annex A to this paper.[52] He stated:

In my opinion, the Conference might merely use the term "historic bays" and leave it to be construed, in case of dispute, by the Court, with due regard for all the features of the special case, which could not possibly be provided for in a general rule.

Although the subject was gasping, it was not quite dead for the Geneva Conference. At the Fifty-Seventh Meeting, Mr. Mukatra of Japan is recorded as remarking:

The definition of historic bays could not be left to the arbitral tribunals or courts which would deal with disputes. The definition of such bays was part of the codification and could not be left to the courts. The intention of his delegation's amendment was to introduce such a definition into the text of paragraph 4 [paragraph 6]; the definition had been prepared with the aid of A/Conf.13/1.[53]

According to a recent article by Professor Oda, the Japanese com-

49 A/Conf.13/39, p. 2.
50 A/Conf.13/39, p. 23.
51 A/Conf.13/39, p. 45.
52 The full statement, summarizing the Commission's work on the International Law of the Sea is published in A/Conf.13/39, at pp. 68–70.
53 A/Conf.13/39, p. 145.

ment is considerably longer on this point. He writes that Japan was much concerned with clarification of the concept of the historic bay especially because of the recent Soviet proclamation placing Peter the Great Bay under the regime of its internal waters, "under the pretext of the historic bay concept." He further writes that when Professor Francois proposed to refer to the court all conflicts arising from the definition of the historic bay, the Japanese delegate explained his country's view as follows:

The function of the court... is to determine whether a given bay falls under the definition of historic bays, such definition having been formulated beforehand. Formulation of a definition is a part of the function of codification; it surely is not a function of the court... [M] ere mention of "so-called historic bays" without stipulating their definition would lead to confusion and possible abuse of the term. In the past, there have actually been a number of cases where a State has claimed vast sea areas as territorial, on the pretext of historic bays, without the slightest historic elements whatsoever. Unfortunately, similar claims have been made in recent years as well. In order to avoid recurrence of such claims, it is essential that a definition of historic bays should be provided for in the article.[54]

This writer will make no attempt to conceal his annoyance at the apparent discrepancy between the above quotation and recorded tenor of the same remarks, as entered in the record by Mr. Koretsky of the Ukrainian Soviet Socialist Republic, Special Rapporteur for the first committee. It would probably be more in the general interest to have all remarks entered *verbatim* on the record.

The Japanese definition reads:

4. The foregoing provisions shall not apply to historic bays. The term "historic bays" means those bays over which the coastal state or states have effectively exercised sovereign rights continuously for a period long standing, with explicit or implicit recognition of such practice by foreign states.[55]

At the same meeting the following remark of Mr. Chakrapani of Thailand is recorded:

The definition of such bays in the Japanese amendment was, however, not precise enough and should be referred to the drafting committee.[56]

While there was manifestly present a subsidiary question of

[54] Shigeru Oda, "Japan and the U.N. Conference on the Law of the Sea." 3 *The Japanese Annual of International Law* (1959), pp. 65–86, at p. 72. Mr. Oda, Assistent Professor of International Law, Tohoku University, was an advisor to the Japanese Delegation at the 1958 Geneva Conference on the Law of the Sea.

[55] A/Conf.13/C.1/L104 of 1 April 1948; reproduced in A/Conf. 13/39 at page 241.

[56] *Ibid.*

drafting[57] it is quite apparent that such referral would have simply retained the complicated question within the Conference framework, and might well have re-opened it in a forum which was obviously unprepared to deal with it. In any event, the colloqui ended in the adoption of a recommendation that the Conference refer the matter to the General Assembly of the United Nations with the request that the General Assembly make appropriate arrangements for the juridical regime of historic waters, including historic bays, and that the result of these studies be sent to all members of the United Nations.[58]

The 1958 Conference was no doubt an advance over the work of 1930: There was an agreed-upon Convention on territorial waters; the Convention has an article on bays; and the article mentions and makes an exception for the historic bay. It is quite evident from the above review of the work, that no more than the mention and exception could be expected. The idea of a Commission or "International Waters Office" was not even raised, and the Convention was unprepared to discuss criteria or conditions which claims to historic bays should satisfy. In connection with the latter, Professor Francois said the following in his 19 March 1958 statement to the Geneva Conference:

> If ... however, it is desired to go farther and state the conditions which bays must satisfy in order to be considered historic bays, the matter becomes much more complicated. It raises the whole problem of acquisition by prescription, and several uncertain points will have to be cleared up. ... The Secretariat's excellent memorandum [A/Conf.13/1] does not provide us with the material needed for a thorough study of this question.[59]

[57] While it is beyond the scope of this paper to comment on the technical quality of the drafting done at the Geneva Conference, there is some evidence that this work might have been accomplished with greater nicety. In our own Government, we appear to be well aware of the problems encountered in drafting treaties and domestic legislation. Although there are marked diferences in the two activities, there appear also to exist some similarities. We appear to have gone to great lengths to solve them, and so apparently has the United Kingdom. We know that after all political debate has been concluded, and the decision has been taken, there remains the task of reducing the decision to the written word in a legal instrument, in a manner that will reflect the decision accurately. The instrument should be understandable to those who are required to interpret it and to act upon it in the future. That there is an upper limit to the precision that can be attained is shown by the accepted reference to "legislative history" or *travaux préparatoires*. Can it be that an *ad hoc* operation such as the Geneva Conference does not lend itself to such technical proficiency? Julius Stone, *The Province and Function of Law* (1946), pp. 149–158; Bertram Gross, *The Legislative Struggle* (1952), pp. 185–192; 205–216; *Legislative Reorganization Act of 1946;* Public Law 601, 79th Congress, 2nd Session; Herman Finer, *Governments of Greater European Powers* (1956), p. 119; *U.S. Foreign Service Manual* vol. 4, Sec 200; Department of State Circular No. 175; U.S. Naval War College, *A Few Things the Naval Officer Should Know about Treaties and Other International Agreements* (1958), written by this author. UN International Law Commission, *8th Session Report on Law of Treaties*, A/CN.4/101 of 14 March 1956.

[58] A/Conf.13/C.1/L158, Rev. 1 of 17 April 1958, A/Conf. 13/39, p. 253.

[59] See Annex A to this Section.

In the summary to this Chapter, Section G, some comments will be made with respect to further codification of the law on historic bays.

Annex A EXCERPT FROM STATEMENT BY PROFESSOR FRANCOIS, EXPERT TO THE SECRETARIAT OF THE UNITED NATIONS CONFERENCE ON THE LAW OF THE SEA, 1958.

13. As regards historic bays, the International Law Commission has given no definition, for it thought that the concept was familiar to everyone concerned with international law. Moreover, historic bays could be defined very satisfactorily in the words of the Internatioanl Court of Justice: "By 'historic waters' are usually meant waters which are treated as internal waters but which would not have that character were it not for the existence of an historic title."[2] That definition is a very innocuous one. If, however, it is desired to go farther and state the conditions which bays must satisfy in order to be considered historic bays, the matter becomes much more complicated. It raises the whole problem of acquisition by prescription, and several uncertain points will then have to be cleared up. Is this "continued and well-established" usage, as the Institute of International Law called it in 1894, or "international" usage, as the Institute called it in 1920? Or is it "uncontested" international usage, the word used in the 1928 draft? Must there be "established" usage, as the International Law Association's draft of 1926 requires, or established usage "generally recognized by nations," as required by the wording finally adopted? Can the vital interests of the coastal State be the sole root of a right? The 1930 Conference thought that, before beginning to study historic bays, it should have before it information from all the States on the bays which they claimed to be historic and the reasons for their claims.

14. The Secretariat's excellent memorandum (A/Conf.13/1) does not provide us with the material needed for a thorough study of this question. I therefore do not think it would be of any use to set up a sub-committee for that purpose, as proposed by the delegation of Panama (3rd meeting). In my opinion, the Conference might merely use the term "historic bays" and leave it to be construed, in case of dispute, by the Court, with due regard for all the features of the special case, which could not possibly be provided for in a general rule. If necessary the International Law Commission could be instructed to study acquisition by prescription with special reference to historic bays.

15. The Commission was criticized for not having drafted some of the articles as precisely as might be desired. Such expressions as "where circumstances necessitate," "to any appreciable extent," "sufficiently closely linked," "adequate grounds," "reasonable measures," "unjustifiable interference" and others are, it is said, out of place. The Commission cannot regard the objections as fully justified. It is true that the articles ought to be drafted in the clearest possible language. Perhaps the Commission's texts can still be improved in this respect. Nevertheless, it should be remembered that these expressions all occur in national legislation. In the opinion of the International Law Commission, a codification of international law can no more do without these expressions than can national law. Any attempt to codify international law without using

[2] *Fisheries case, Judgment of 18 December 1951: I.C.J. Reports*, p. 130.

such expressions will prove vain. I entirely agree with the views expressed on this subject in another committee by the representative of India. In contentious cases, the meaning will have to be decided by an impartial authority, to which disputes regarding the interpretation of these expressions in specific cases will have to be submitted.

Section F ON THE THEORY OF PRESCRIPTION

Although it was the economic issue thet brought the dispute between the United Kingdom and Norway before the International Court of Justice and it was an economic consideration that played a large part in the formulation of the Court's opinion, it is certain that the question of both economics and historic possession were thoroughly interwined in that case. If the Court intends to settle any future bay cases by weighing the economic factors, and I think it should do so, there is little to be said by the student of the bay problem other than to suggest that the Court view the problem with great probity and avail itself of technical experts in a number of relevant fields. If, however, a dispute involves questions of historic rights and most cases seem to have this quality also, there can be invoked some purely legal concepts. That being so, there arises the question whether such purely legal concepts are susceptible of incorporation into a codification of the law. The purpose of the codification in this case would be, of course, to provide agreed upon criteria which must be complied with should a State contemplate making a claim to exclusive possession of a bay of exceptional size or configuration.

This writer believes that the making of such claims for other than clearly economic reasons is altogether possible in this era. Nationalism, defense in depth and neutralism would appear also to be underlying motives for making new claims to bays or for enlarging old ones.For the foregoing reasons, it is believed desirable to explore the theory of prescription, a word which, it seems to this author, has been used with some imprecision in connection with bays.

Professor Jessup has pointed out that applying the doctrine of prescription to historic bays has been extremely useful and that insofar as established, it can not be disregarded.[1] In arguments before international tribunals, claims by prescriptive right to large bodies of water have been admitted.[2] The proposition is not, however, without challenge. Hyde writes:

[1] Philip C. Jessup, *The Law of Territorial Waters and Maritime Jurisdiction* (1927), p. 363.

[2] Bacon and Scott, *Fisheries Arbitration Argument of Elihu Root* (1912), pp. 292–327.

The frequent suggestion that a "historic bay" marks the acquisition or perfecting of a right of dominion by way of prescription is not believed to be in complete harmony with the theory on which maritime states have acted. A prescriptive right is one which grows out of conduct which in its initial stages might have been deemed wrongful ... No prescriptive claim ... begins to run that may not be lawfully opposed ... That the claim or assertion ripens into something worthy of respect is due to the failure of the possessor to make objection for a prolonged period. ... A bay regarded as "historic" doubtless betokens a common acquiescence in the assertion of dominion by the coastal state; but it does not necessarily signify that the original assertion of that dominion constituted a violation of any legal obligation towards any State or the society of States. When nature made a bay geographically a part of the domain of the littoral State, that State when first asserting dominion did not in fact assume that in occupying the water area as a part of its territory it failed in any international obligation because of the width of the entrance. In a word, the absence in every quarter of a sense that the assertion of dominion amounted to wrongful conduct, distinguished the acquisition of the right from one that might have been said to have a prescriptive character.[3]

Professor Hyde emphasizes that in his belief "prescription is not a mode by which rights of property and control come into being, and therefore, no instance of it is apparent when dominion is asserted over an area to be regarded at the time as *res nullius*." [4]

Prescription, as we shall note below, is first of all a private law conception. Judge Lauterpacht wrote that it is generally regarded as a principle common to all branches of law, but denounced by others as purely a private law notion. On this latter point, he writes:

Arbitral tribunals resort to private law because international relations demand such recourse to analogy, and because international law is not always developed enough to supply a solution itself.[5]

Professor Scwarzenberger, on the other hand, argues that reliance upon private law analogies is unsatisfactory in international law because in so doing the operative rules are not apparent. This he illustrates in the matter of title to territory which, he says, may rest on consent, recognition and acquiescence in a historical process of consolidation.[6] But, returning to Lauterpacht, we are reminded by him that the analogy to private law with regard to original acquisition of territory...

[3] Charles C. Hyde, *International Law Chiefly as Interpreted and Applied by the United States*, 2nd Edition (1946), p. 469n.

[4] *Ibid.*, p. 386.

[5] H. Lauterpacht, *Private Law Sources and Analogise of International Law* (1927), pp. ix, 36.

[6] Georg Schwarzenberger, "Title to Territory: Response to a Challenge," 51 *American Journal of International Law* (1957), pp. 308–324, at pp. 311–312.

has been called into life by the necessities of international intercourse, and it is owing to these necessities and to the identity of the legal relations that a close analogy of rules has been established.[7]

It is the belief of this writer that the arguments of both writers have merit. Certainly title to territory would appear to rest more securely in international law on the basis of consent, recognition, and acquiescence. Preponderance of evidence of these may very well be sufficient for an unchallengeable title. But is it not possible that consent, recognition and acquiescence could be more readily realized when the claimant's title could also be defended in terms of a private law principle? Scholars such as Hyde and more recently, Professor Roger Pinto,[8] may argue quite convincingly that prescription has little usefulness in public international law. But the obstinate fact remains that Courts have seen fit to make use of the concept and its operating factors.

In the case of historic bays it is doubtful whether codification of criteria such as consent, recognition and acquiescence is possible unless there is established some institutional machinery such as that associated with the long ago proposed International Waters Register. Since there seems no disposition toward reviving that idea, there remains the question whether a codification turning on a private law concept is possible. The private law concept that has been occasionally referred to by writers, and sometines relied upon in cases, is that of prescription.

It appears that to define prescription in its relationship to international law is not without some difficulty. Sir Hersch Lauterpacht offers us this:

... the acquisition of sovereignty over a territory through continuous and undisturbed exercise of sovereignty over it during such a period as is necassary to create under the influence of historic development the general connection that the present condition of things is in conformity with international order.[9]

Perhaps it might be more satisfactory for us to discuss prescription from the point of view of its operating components, as they might be related to historic bays, and therefore to dispense with any advance attempt at special definition.

There are two meanings of the word prescription: extinctive pres-

[7] Lauterpacht, *Private Law Sources*, p. 103.

[8] Roger Pinto, "La Prescription en droit international" 87 *Recueil des Cours de l'Académie de Droit international de la Haye* (1955), pp. 391–449.

[9] Sir Hersch Lauterpacht, *Oppenheim's International Law*, vol. I, 8th Ed. (1955), p. 576.

scription and acquisitive prescription.[10] The principle of extinctive or negative prescription is the bar of claims by lapse of time.[11] While this is recognized and applied in International Law,[12] it does not appear germane to this discussion. On the other hand acquisitive or positive prescription is the creation of a right through lapse of time.[13] Our attention is invited by Salmond to this distinction: "Custom is long practice operating as a source of law; prescription is long practice operating as a source of rights."[14]

For convenience, and for our purposes, the term, prescription, where used hereinafter refers to acquisitive prescription.

It appears that the rational basis for prescription is consideration for stability and order, and legalization of the *status quo*. Lauterpacht explains that some publicists have argued that in public international law, force and possession confer title, and for this reason prescription is unnecessary.[15] While it can no doubt be demonstrated that a piece of land twenty-four miles wide can be seized by force and permanently so held, use of force as conferring good title is seldom likely to be applicable in the case of a bay. Would there be a case in which a State seized by force a bay in its own littoral? When a state seizes by force the land territory of another and such territory happens to embrace a bay, it is believed that rules extraneous to this discussion would apply.

One form of acquisitive prescription is said to be based on immemorial possession, postulated on the idea that a state of affairs exists, the origin of which is uncertain. In a case between Austria and Hungary in 1902, immemorial possession was described as one that lasted for so long that it is impossible to furnish proof of a different situation and which no person can remember having spoken of.[16] It appears that the Court decided the status of Palk Bay entirely upon this basis.[17] Judge

[10] D. H. N. Johnson, "Acquisitive Prescription in International Law," 27 *British Yearbook of International Law* (1950), pp. 332–354.

[11] B. E. King, "Prescription of Claims in International Law," *ibid.*, vol. 15 (1934), pp. 82–97; Sir John Salmond, *Jurisprudence*, 8th Ed. (1930), p. 466.

[12] The Williams Case, Moore, IV *International Arbitrations* (*1898*), pp. 4179–4203; *Sarropoulos* v. *Bulgarian State* (Decision of Graeco-Bulgarian Mixed Tribunal of 14 Feb. 1927, partially based on this principle) 7 *Recueil Tribunaux Arbitraux Mixtes* (1927), p. 47; *Russian Indemnity Case of 1912*, Scott, *The Hague Court Reports* (1916), pp. 532–555; Briggs, *The Law of Nations: Cases, Documents, Notes*, 2nd Ed. (1952), pp. 37–42.

[13] Salmond, *op. cit.*

[14] *Ibid.*, p. 221.

[15] Lauterpacht, *Private Law Sources*, p. 116.

[16] 13 September 1902, 8 *Revue de droit international et legislative comparée* (1906), p. 207. Also cited in Stuyt, *The General Principles of Law as applied by International Tribunals to Disputes on Attribution and Exercise of State Jurisdiction* (1946), p. 20.

[17] Section D, above.

Alvarez, however, in his separate opinion in the Anglo-Norwegian Fisheries Case, wrote:

International Law does not lay down any specific duration of time necessary for prescription to have effect. A comparatively recent usage relating to the territorial sea may be of greater effect than an ancient usage insufficiently proved.[18]

While immemorial possession might indeed be difficult to establish to the satisfaction of a court in a case involving disagreement over a "historic" bay, and the larger such bay must be in order to qualify for historic status (perhaps, over 24 miles in breadth at the entrance), the more remote would appear the reasonableness of such argument for most of the world's bays. The criterion of immemorial possession would appear to be susceptible of codification for the historic bay, but the value of the codification has probably not been advanced very far by so doing.

Another form of acquisitive prescription is somewhat akin to the *usucapio* in Roman Law.[19] The theory is that although the title may be defective originally, continued possession cures the fault. In the interests of the stability of society the law must draw a line somewhere and under reasonable conditions lend its authority to a state of affairs which observably exists in fact. This principle, *quieta non movere*, has been applied in judgments in international tribunals, as former Judge De Visscher has pointed out,[20] citing the *Grisdabarna* case of 1909 between Norway and Sweden.[21] In an overall view, it is believed that this principle is more readily applicable to a question of land territory, where normally the contesting interests of only two States may be expected to be involved, than to a question of historic bays where the contest is between one State on the landward side and the whole community of States on the high seas. Since some of the factors called to our attention by Dr. Drago in the North Atlantic Coast Fisheries Arbitration are variable in relation to time and development, and definitely

[18] *I.C.J. Reports*, 1951, p. 152.

[19] As understood by this author, *usucapio* involves a thing capable of ownership (*res habilis*), a title though perhaps a defective one (*justus titulus*), good faith (*fides*), possession implying physical control (*possessio*), intention of the owner (*animus*), and uninterrupted possession for a period defined by law (*tempus*). Interruption defeated acquisition of title by *usucapio*. In calculating the term of possession, one could reckon the possession of the predecessor from whom the *titulus justus* was acquired. Sohm, *The Institutes: A Textbook of the History and System of Roman and Private Law*, 3rd Ed. (1907), pp. 318–22; Radin, *Handbook of Roman Law* (1927), pp. 361–8.

[20] De Visscher, *Theory and Reality in Public International Law* (1957), p. 200.

[21] In this case, the Court's judgment reads, *inter alia:* "Whereas . . . it is a settled principle of the law of nations that a state of things which actually exists and has existed for a long time should be changed as little as possible." Scott, *op. cit.*, p. 130.

cannot be ignored, the criterion of stability becomes somewhat equivocal. Perhaps, viewed in this light, the rationale of Mr. Carmona's statement can be more readily appreciated.[22] But stability in relationships in the present era is more than ever required.[23]

In adapting prescription to international law there should be evidence of the possession through physical control. This obviously operates through the exercise of official acts on the part of the sovereign. In the case of a bay – a body of water and an arm of the sea – the acts are physically more limited than on land. But that fact of life is universal hence it should be understood.[24] On the other hand, where there is the uncertainty that still exists in the case of historic bays, the sovereign acts manifesting ownership in good faith are susceptible of challenge, commencing from the first symbolic act of laying claim, if there has been one. There should be "continuous and peaceful display of State authority" wrote Judge Huber in his judgment in the Island of Palmas case.[25] Moreover, there must be shown to exist the will and intention to act as sovereign, as the Permanent Court of International Justice wrote in its judgment in *The Legal Status of Eastern Greenland*.[26] Thus, in the case of a bay, there should quite reasonably be, in order to establish "historic" title by prescription, the will and intention to act as sovereign and the peaceful and continued display of such sovereignty.

As suggested above, an operating factor of prescription, is the matter of intention (*animus*). Evidence of this in the case of a bay would be, *inter alia*, occupation and usage.[27] In the case of a land territory,

[22] Section E, above.

[23] Obviously, this is a postulate, but it is one upon which codification of international law seems to rest.

[24] We are not unmindful, of course, of the extreme view taken by Nicholl, J., in *Regina* v. *Forty-Nine Casks of Brandy*, 2 Hagg, Adm. 259: "No one ever heard of the body of a county extending three miles into the sea.", or Savigny: "La mer n'est pas susceptible de tomber dans la propriété des hommes, parce que la mer ne peut pas être possédée." – quoted in Lauterpacht, *Private Law Sources*, p. 110.

[25] II *Reports of International Arbitral Awards*, 879; 22 *American Journal of International Law* (1928), p. 110.

[26] Permanent Court of International Justice Series A/B. No. 53, pp. 45–6.

[27] This is a quite complex matter in case law. Johnson, *op. cit.*, pp. 348–9, endeavors to show the technical difference between occupation and prescription, citing *Legal Status of Eastern Greenland* (Series A/B. No. 53 (1953), and Judge Huber's award in *Island of Palmas* case (1929), demonstrating the difference in *ratio decidendi* in the two cases. It appears that in claiming title by prescription one must show stricter proof of possession and a longer period of possession than in the case of occupation. If this were to be pursued to a logical conclusion, alone, it might be argued that title to a bay by prescription would be very difficult to establish. Title by occupation, an act more sensible to the imagination would be difficult, too. The analogy to land in case law presents the problem that geographical propinquity has not been held a strong argument in land cases. *The Palmas Case.*

occupation and usage can be established by objective criteria. The nature of a large water body makes occupation much more a matter of judgement upon individual sets of facts: How much use? For what reasons? For how long? By how many people? Here the proponents of the claim can advance selected facts of practice and history [28] and they must then be judged against other selected facts. This is a matter for judicial determination. Again we are confronted with a component of prescription that is probably unsusceptible of codification if applied to historic bays.

In the matter of uninterrupted and peaceful possession, this component would forecast little in the way of a problem. Possession maintained by force in the teeth of forceful opposition would be contrary to the purpose of the doctrine of prescription.

In the matter of uninterrupted and peaceful possession, this component of prescription with respect to bays would appaer to offer little in the way of a codification problem. But when does possession cease to be peaceful? Since resort to aggressive war is now ruled out as a means of redress, the term peaceful, if it is to have any further usefulness, could perhaps refer to the degree of police protection required to maintain exclusive possession of a bay as against encrochment by non-nationals. But this too seems a matter fit only for judicial determination.

As Hyde has suggested, the application of the doctrine of acquisitive prescription to historic bays is strained. The long jurisdiction can be seen as proof of adverse interest, perhaps. But against whom is it adverse? When the sea is characterized as being *res communis*, this is not community property in which a particular interest may harden after a time, but it is really community property which is put beyond appropriation altogether. Thus, strictly speaking, the concept of acquisitive prescription can be theoretically argued as having no relevance to the historic bay.

It appears, that some of the operating factors of the theory of acquisitive prescription do find some limited applicability, but it seems unlikely that States would be willing to agree upon codification of prescriptive criteria at this time.

Section G SUMMARY

For a book pretending to cover the general subject of the law of bays, this chapter on The Concept of the Historic Bay has no doubt

[28] Norman Hill, *Claims to Territory in International Law and Relations* (1945), p. 81.

been overly long. Yet it has certainly not exhausted the subject and especially is this true with respect to acquisition by prescription.

This writer is fairly well convinced that any attempt at codification of general rules for historic bays would really be futile at this time, although he has endeavored to incorporate some rules into the suggested codification for bays set out in Chapter TEN. It is believed that any codification efforts by a public international body will yield little more than unfruitful and heavily politicized debate. It is even doubtful that a private international body would arrive at a clearer understanding of the problem, although the debate might ventilate the positions of some States. It appears to this writer that three possible courses of action are open:

(1) Leave the matter of historic bays exactly as it stands, that is, simply mentioned as part of a saving clause to the presently codified rules on bays, and in case of dispute leave the term to be construed by the Court. This is the suggestion of Professor Francois. To do this, of course, signifies little progress toward a greater rationalization of the international law of the sea and prolongs the present situation in which, truly, we do not know of all the large bays whose waters are considered by the riparian States to be internal waters.

(2) Revival of the idea of an International Waters Office and Register, with all claims to Historic Bays declared and registered, and allowing for the contesting of such claims and their referral to the International Court for settlement. Admittedly, this course of action involves compulsory submission to the jurisdiction of the Court, by way of the back door. While this course of action would probably prove unacceptable to many States at the present time, it is really believed to be the ultimate solution to the problem if we are to progress toward a more integrated World Society. Short of this step, but in the same general direction is a proposal that the United Nations International Law Commission to address the States a questionnaire inquiring about bays, which do not meet the criteria of Article 7 but which are nevertheless claimed as internal waters on the basis of historic usage. With either of these proposals there is the unhappy possibility that the States may suddenly declare as historic waters bays to which no such pretension had ever previously been contemplated. Moreover, such claims might possibly be rather extensive.

(3) Establishment of a body of technical experts to explore the problem further. Such a body should be composed of international lawyers, geographers, hydrographers and historians and it should be

in a position to consult with other experts such as marine biologists, geologists, economists, military officers, etc. Such a body might be more productive if it were established outside the public aegis. They would attempt to ascertain all claims to Historic Bays, and then to proceed to study all of the circumstances surroundig each such claim. They would prepare detailed written reports and they would attempt some general conclusions. The difficulty about this proposal is that the results of such study might find only limited use and thus not justify the expense and effort that would be involved in it. The prospect of information compiled by relatively unbiased experts always has a charming quality about it, and in the instant situation it would no doubt do much toward unraveling some of the complexities of historic bays. But we would be quite remiss were we not to acknowledge that for any particular situation in dispute there are likely to be available other and equally qualified experts to dispute the "impartial" findings and conclusions already compiled. Nevertheless, this course of action, the writer believes, is likely to be the only one reasonably feasible at this time.

CHAPTER EIGHT

PETER THE GREAT BAY, A CURRENT ISSUE

Section A GEOGRAPHICAL DESCRIPTION OF THE SOVIET CLAIM [1]

On 21 July 1957, Moscow Radio announced that the Soviet Council of Ministers had discussed matters concerning the border question of the Bay of Peter the Great and had proclaimed it an inland sea. The council of Ministers were said to have ascertained that the line between Tuman Ula and Cape Povorotni is the border line of the Soviet Inland Sea. The Soviet territorial sea should be measured from this basic line as a starting point.[2] Only Nakhodka port in America Bay,[3] at the extreme east side of the delineated area, is to be open to foreign ships under specified navigation conditions.

The closing line is 108 miles in length and it encloses a water area roughly triangular in shape. Using this line as a diameter, the enclosed water area, would not meet the requirements of the semi-circle rule. The area so enclosed contains 32 arms of water called bays, one called a gulf, and one called a road. The main part of the enclosure is divided into two bays, Ussuri Bay and Amur Bay, by the Muraviev Amurski Peninsula on which Vladivostok is located, and by the Eugenie Archipelago. The closing line is just inside the 100 fathom curve for about five-eighths of its length. For the eastern three-eighths of the line, the 100 fathom curve averages about six miles to seaward. From the mariner's point of view, the natural limits of Peter the Great Bay would be between Askold Island on the east and Cape Gamov on the west. These two points are 51 miles apart. The line connecting them is about eleven

[1] See Figure 23.

[2] *The New York Times*, 21 July 1957, p. 1, col. 7. Published also in *Isvestia*, 21 July 1957.

[3] All navigation terminology and calculation for this discussion utilizes U.S. Navy Hydrographic Office Chart No. 1780 and Publication No. 122B, *Sailing Directions for the Southeast Coast of Siberia and Korea.*

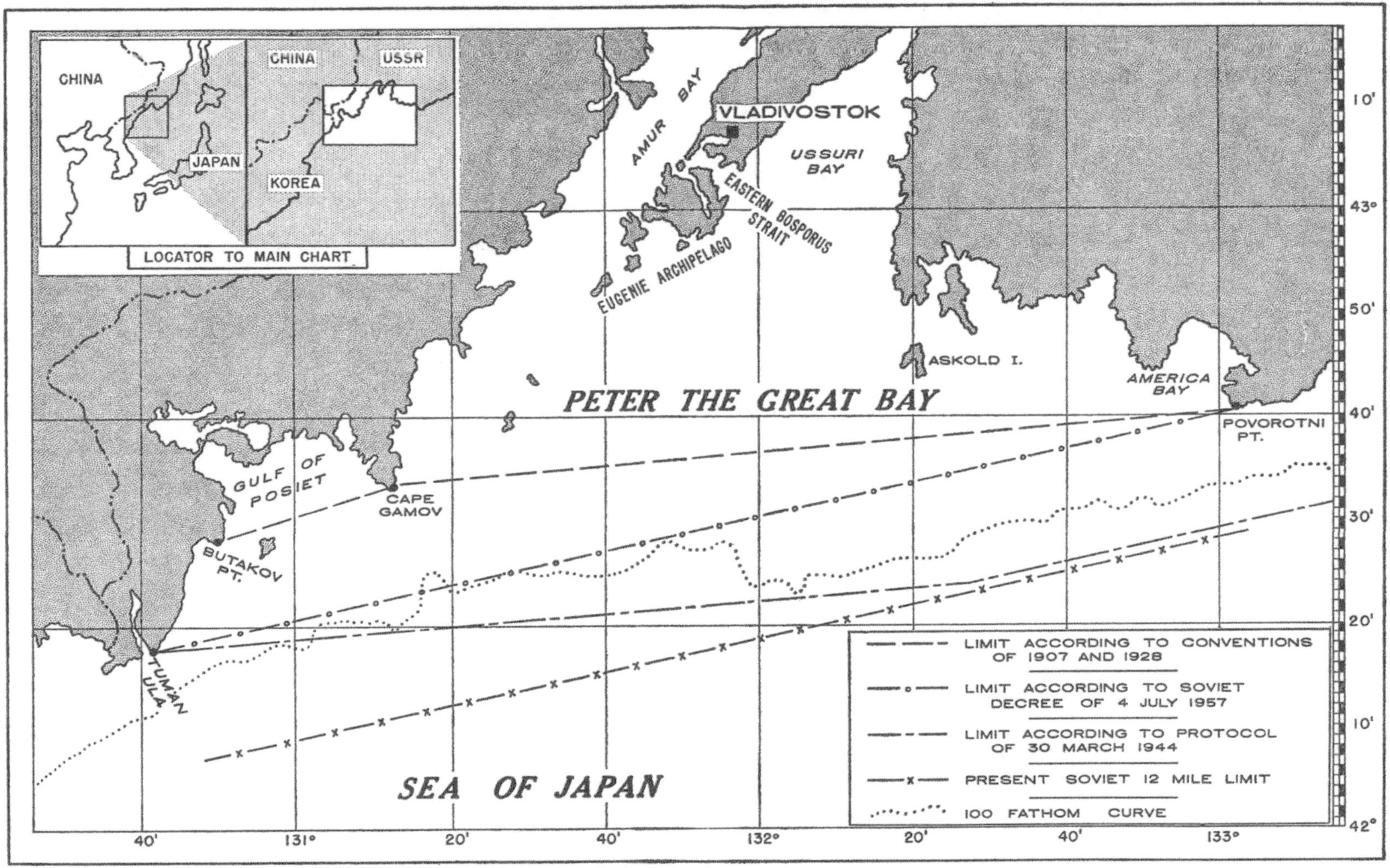
CHINA
CHINA
USSR
JAPAN
KOREA
LOCATOR TO MAIN CHART
AMUR BAY
VLADIVOSTOK
USSURI BAY
EASTERN BOSPORUS STRAIT
EUGENIE ARCHIPELAGO
ASKOLD I.
AMERICA BAY
PETER THE GREAT BAY
POVOROTNI PT.
GULF OF POSIET
CAPE GAMOV
BUTAKOV PT.
TUMAN ULA
SEA OF JAPAN
LIMIT ACCORDING TO CONVENTIONS OF 1907 AND 1928
LIMIT ACCORDING TO SOVIET DECREE OF 4 JULY 1957
LIMIT ACCORDING TO PROTOCOL OF 30 MARCH 1944
PRESENT SOVIET 12 MILE LIMIT
100 FATHOM CURVE
10'
43°
50'
40'
30'
20'
10'
42°
40'
131°
20'
40'
132°
20'
40'
133°

Fig. 25

miles to landward of the decreed closing line. The area enclosed by the inner line would satisfy the semi-circle rule. From the decreed closing line, Ussuri Bay has a landward penetration of about fifty-one miles and Amur Bay has a penetration of about sixty-seven miles.

If Peter the Great Bay is approached from the east during darkness on a clear night there should be no navigating difficulty despite the non-recognized 12-mile width of the Soviet marginal belt. There is a 21-mile light on Povorotni Point and a 24-mile light on Askold Island. On the west side, the light at Tuman Ula has only 12-mile visibility. The 21 mile light on Cape Gamov cannot be seen until one is inside the 12-mile marginal belt. A ship can approach Peter the Great Bay directly from the south and be well inside Soviet internal waters without ever seeing any lights. For daytime navigation, one could probably fix his position on a clear day with the help of several high mountain peaks on the east side. There are no such natural landmarks on the west side and none, of course, in the center. For purposes of celestial navigation, the area has an average of 110 cloudy (8 tenths to overcast) days per year, averaged over an 18-year period. The highest number of cloudy days is in July with an average of 20.4.[4] The area is blanketed by loran coverage from transmitting stations located in Japan.[5] The harbor at Vladivostok if frozen on an average of 86 days per year, from December to March. Approximately the same conditions obtain in Nakhodka. Both ports kept open by ice breakers. Vladivostok is fogbound on an average of 85 days per year. Other ports in eastern Siberia are Nikolayevsk and Sovetskaya Gavan. But, the Vladivostok area contains the best and most important ports. This area has the shortest and most complete means of communications egress to the Asiatic interior including the Soviet Union.[6]

Cape Povorotny, the eastern end of the delimited area of Peter the Great Bay, is about 290 miles almost due west across the Sea of Japan from the Japanese island of Hokkaido. The Tuman Ula river, whose mouth marks the delimited area, is also the border line between Korea and Siberia. At this southern extremity of Soviet territory, the Chinese border is only about ten miles inland from the bay. Vladivostok is the terminus of the Trans-Siberian Railway as well as railways from

[4] U. S. Navy Hydrographic Publication 122B, p. 19.

[5] CDR John C. Hill II, USN, LCDR Thomas F. Utegaard USN and Gerard Riordan, *Dutton's Navigation and Piloting* (1958), p. 255.

[6] Geographical data taken from: Thodore Shabad, *Geography of the USSR, A Regionale Survey* (1951), pp. 326–329;and Erich Thiel, *The Soviet Far East* (1953), pp. 314–326.

China and Korea. It is connected by a 45-mile rail line with Nakhodka. Since about 1872,[7] Vladivostok has been a Russian naval base,[8] though often neglected. The entire Maritime Province in the general area of Vladivostok is a rather heavily garrisoned military district.[9]

Vladivostok is the shipping center for the entire area and it is the administrative center of the Maritime District which is bounded by the Amur and Ussuri Rivers. The district had an estimated population of 1.5 million in 1951,[10] of which ninety per cent are of European Russian stock. The population has undoubtedly increased a great deal since that time. Coal, iron, tin, lead and zinc are mined in the area. Cement is produced in large quantity. There are now ample crops, and the main food processing area is at Voroshilov. It is believed that this area is now self-supporting in food, but for a great many years it was dependent upon imports of food. Until well into the 1930's, also, the Maritime province was heavily dependent upon Chinese and Korean labor and upon Japanese merchants.

Vladivostok is the principal fish packing center of the Soviet Far East and is the center of a growing fleet of trawlwers. The fish which are frozen or canned are sent west across Siberia by rail.[11] Doctor Morgan classes the mid latitude Far East, including the Sea of Japan and Peter the Great Bay as the most important single fishing region in the world,[12] and this is borne out by the statistics of the United Nations Food and Agricultural Organization.[13] The number of edible species of fish, shell fish, molluscs and bêche-de-mere (sea slugs) that are harvested annually is quite large.[14] It is the opinion of Doctor Morgan that the area is over-fished. Partly, at least, for this reason there came into force on 12 December 1956 a Treaty between Japan and the Soviet Union concerning fisheries on the High Seas in the Pacific Ocean. The treaty, not applicable in territorial waters, provides

[7] Admiralty Naval Staff, *A Handbook of Siberia and Arctic Russia* (*circa* 1920), p. 363.

[8] The entire Peter the Great Bay area is included in a "military danger zone" which extends for 160 miles along the coast from a point five miles to the west of Tuman Ula. Foreign ships headed for ports in the bay are boarded by military pilots prior to entering the zone. Navigation *along the coast* is permitted without a pilot provided ships obtain instructions from the Chief Military pilot in Vladivostok or in Bukhta Valentina. H.O. Publication 122B, p. 191.

[9] Unofficially estimated to include: 3 cruisers, 26 destroyers, 80 submarines, 9 Army divisions (strength 129,000) and 2700 aircraft. U.S. Senate, *Review of Foreign Policy* 1958, pp. 469–488.

[10] Shabod, *op. cit.*, p. 327.

[11] Robert Morgan, *World Sea Fisheries* (1955), pp. 164–5.

[12] *Ibid.*, p. 166.

[13] A/Conf.13/37, p. 263.

[14] Morgan, *op. cit.*, p. 167.

for a Commission which has, among other duties, the determination of the annual catch of certain species, Studied from a technical point of view, Article III of this treaty raises a lot of questions concerning political intervention into the function of the Commission.[15]

The species of greatest importance in the waters of Peter the Great Bay is the herring. Generally, this fish enters the bay about the middle of November, comes again from the end of December to the middle of February and pays a final visit in April. Another important product found on the rocky bottom of Peter the Great Bay area is the bêche-de-mer or sea slug for which there are two seasons: end of March to June and mid-September to October.[16] During the principal fishing season there is the minimum number of cloudy days in this area. The outer bay is not iced over during the fishing season.[17]

It appears with within the last fifteen years, the Maritime Province and surrounding area has changed from a rather neglected military back door to an industrialized and newly populated complex.[18] There appears little doubt that whatever fish products can be harvested from the surrounding seas are highly desired for this newly expanding economy. Professor Ohira writes:

> It is generally observed that the recent Soviet action in declaring Peter the Great Bay as internal waters was intended to protect the fortress area surrounding Vladivostok.[19]

While there is undoubtedly good reason to justify this conclusion, there is probably a strong economic motive behind the Soviet action.

A final note on the geographical features of the bay. For a well-equipped vessel, navigation should present no great difficulty. A small fishing craft, however, might encounter considerable trouble in staying outside the Soviet 12-mile limit if she fished fairly close to that line.

Section B HISTORICAL BACKGROUND

Russian interests in Eastern Siberia commenced in the Seventeenth Century, but they were successfully checked in the Amur region until

[15] The text of the treaty is to be found in MacChesney, *U.S. Naval War College International Law Situations and Documents*, 1956, at pp. 361–368. See also: Zengo Ohira, "Fishery Problems between Soviet Russia and Japan," 2 *The Japanese Annual of International Law* (1958), pp. 1–18, and M.I., "A Map Analysis of Japan's Fishery Problems," 3 *Ibid.*, (1959), pp. 103–108.

[16] Admiralty Naval Staff, *op. cit.*, p. 85; G. Baievsky, *The Fisheries of Siberia* (1926), p. 35.

[17] H. O. Publication 122B, p. 19.

[18] Erich Thiel, *op. cit.*

[19] Ohira, *op. cit.*, p. 15.

the era 1840–1860.[1] It was not until 1846, that thorough exploration of the Amur region commenced. In 1847, the Czar appointed the young Nicholas Muraviev as Governor-General of East Siberia. He was an ambitious empire builder who held office until 1861, during which time Russia acquired the Maritime Province. It was a fortunate period for him because the Chinese Empire was embattled in a series of wars with Great Britain and France as well as with the remnants of the Taiping Rebellion.[2] On 16/28 May 1858, Muraviev concluded with Prince Yishan, military commander of the Amur, the treaty of Aigun. This treaty was not ratified by the Chinese Government who are said to have dismissed Yishan for his stupidity.[3] This treaty gave to Russia all territory on the left bank of the Amur as far as the Ussuri River while the area between the Ussuri and the sea was to be held in common between China and Russia.[4] At almost the same time, Admiral Putiatin, the Russian Minister to China. concluded with the Chinese, the Treaty of Tientsin, whereby Russia was given access to five ports on equal terms with Great Britain and France. Admiral Putiatin is also said to have asked for a settlement of the Maritime Province frontier question.[5]

The Soviet writer, A. N. Nikolaiev, is cited by Mme France de Hartingh as having written that in 1854 Admiral Putiatin (also spelled Poutiatine), while on board the frigate *Pallada,* traveled over Possieta Bay, now claimed as a part of Peter the great Bay. Possieta Bay is about ten miles from the present Chinese frontier. He is further quoted as writing that in 1859, the now Count Muravieff-Amurski[6] discovered America Bay and the port of Nakhodka.[7] The Soviet writer V. A. Romanov writes that in the 1850's French and English ships sailed in different areas of the bay.[8]

[1] F. A. Golder, *Russian Expansion to the Pacific 1641–1850* (1914), esp. Ch. VI; Harold M. Vinacke, *A History of the Far East in Modern Times*, 5th Ed., (1950), pp. 393ff; Victor A. Yakhontoff, *Russia and the Soviet Union in the Fae East* (1931).

[2] Hosea Ballou Morse, *The International Relations of the Chinese Empire, The Period of Conflict 1834–1860* (1910), p. 609ff.

[3] Aitchen K. Wu, *China and the Soviet Union* (1950), p. 66. This book is a somewhat emotional and colorful account which other authorities say must be read with caution.

[4] I *de Martens Recueil* XVII (1861), pp. 1–2; An English translation of this appears in Yakhontoff, *op. cit.*, at pp. 352–3.

[5] Yakhontoff, *op. cit.*, pp. 353–7.

[6] Rewarded by the Czar for his concluding of the Treaty of Aigun. Vinacke, *op. cit.*, p. 395.

[7] France de Hartingh, *Les Conceptions Soviétiques du Droit de la Mer* (1960), pp. 35–7. Mme de Hartingh quotes ,in translation from A. Nikolaiev "The Bay of Peter the Great," 2 *Mezhdunasodnaia Zhizu* (International Life) (Feb. 1958), pp. 50–57.

[8] V. A. Romanov, "The Gulf of Peter the Great-Internal Waters of the Soviet Union," 5 *Sovetskoe Gasudarstov i Pravo* (*Soviet State and Law*) (May 1958), pp. 47–55. Translations furnished the writer by Office of the Chief of Naval Operations (OP61) and Robert Muller, Russian Research Center, Harvard University.

He repeats the statements of Mr. Nikolaiev and offers two citations.[9] Mr. Romanov writes further:

Further detailed study of the bay was conducted in 1862–63 by the Russian expedition of LTCOL Babkin. Results of the work of these expeditions were reflected in the complete chart of the Bay of Peter the Great issued in 1865 by the Maritime Minister of Russia. The Chart was significantly fuller than the English chart of 1857, and the next English chart copied the Russian chart of 1865. M. Klykov, *Hydrographic Survey of the Shores of the Bay of Peter the Great in the Japanese Sea* 22. Later foreign charts (in particular, English) [10] in which originally separate sections of the bay were not given only one name, use the name which was given to the bay by the Russians, Peter the Great. According to the facts at hand, all later explorations of the Bay of Peter the Great were done by Russian sailors and scientists. At the same time, particularly after the founding of Vladivostok in 1858, an intensive study by Russia of the coasts of the bay, its shores and the islands located in the bay was undertaken.

This writer has been unable to confirm these statements by reference to independent or other contemporary sources.[11] It will be observed, immediately below, that if the Russians founded Vladivostok in 1858, they did so while the area was legally a part of the Chinese Empire.

In 1860, China was again at war with England and France.[12] Major General Ignatieff, a 28-year old soldier-diplomat who was to achieve fame elsewhere,[13] had succeeded Admiral Putiatin as Russian Minister at Peking. Doctor Morse writes that the General first offered the Chinese some small arms and cannon for the Maritime Province, and subsequently served as "honest broker" between the Chinese and Anglo/French, extracting as his fee the treaty of Peking 2/14 November 1860.[14] Mr. Wu asserts that the General threatened to send the Russian fleet against the Chinese port of Peitang if the Maritime Province was not

[9] M. Klykov, *Hydrographic Survey of the Shores of the Bay of Peter the Great in the Japanese Sea* (St. Petersburg: 1872), p. 10; P. V. Vittenburg, "Geological Description of Cape Muraviev Amursky and the Archipelago Empress Evgeniya," XV *Zapsky of the Society for the study of the Amur Region*, Petrograd, 1916, p. 17.

[10] The U.S. Navy Hydrographic Office Chart of the whole area, No. 1780, is indicated as having been compiled from various sources and cites as authorities British Admiralty, Japanese and USSR Charts.

[11] MGEN Constantin von Zepelin, Imperial German Army, *Russland in Asien*, vol. XI (1909), Section III, and Yakhontoff, *op. cit.*, who uses as one of his primary authorities B. A. Romanov, *Rossiia v. Mandzhurii* (1928). Mr. Yakhontoff writes that Soviet authorities have found it necessary to suppress the 1928 of the Romanov work and that it has now been re-written. Major General von Zepelin's work, *Der Ferne Osten*, volume XI of the series *Russland in Asien*, is a first class work of area military intelligence reporting. Written in meticulous detail, this book would no doubt find some use even at the present time. Many passages of the British Admiralty *Handbook on Siberia and Arctic Regions* appear to be direct translations from von Zepelin.

[12] Morse, *op. cit.*, pp. 613–614.

[13] General Ignatieff was Ambassador at the Porte from 1864 to 1877. It was he who negotiated the short-lived treaty of San Stefano after the Russo-Turkish War of 1878. A. J. P Taylor, *The Struggle for Mastery in Europe 1848–1918* (1954), pp. 246–9.

[14] Morse, *op. cit.*, pp. 613–614.

ceded to Russia.[15] Mr. Clyde writes that Count Muraviev occupied what is now the Vladivostok area on 20 July 1860, before the treaty was signed.[16] Russian colonization of the province had actually begun in 1859.[17] It is generally agreed that Vladivostok was founded in 1860.

The Treaty of Peking is a rather long and detailed document [18] ceding, of course, the Maritime Province to Russia. No mention was made of any sea areas although it is mentioned that Chinese were permitted to continue to fish in the Maritime Province. It is certain that upon cession of the territory by China to Russia, the latter State did not succeed to any previous conception of ownership or exclusive possession over any of the waters of Peter the Great Bay except such parts of Ussuri Bay, Amur Bay, or America Bay as might fall into the category of exclusive possession as understood in the law of Nations of the time. At the time of the 1858–1860 treaties, the Peter the Great Bay area was inhabited by a mixture of Chinese, Koreans and tribal natives. There is no evidence that the Imperial Government of China exercised any but a very loose colonial administration in the area. There were no towns, and most of the littoral and many of the islands were covered by thick forest.[19]

Vladivostok was declared a free port.[20] The Japanese, however, did not commence to appear in the area as fishermen until about 1885.[21] Until then most of the fishing done in Peter the Great Bay was

[15] Wu, *op. cit.*, p. 68.

[16] Paul H. Clyde, *International Rivalries in Manchuria* (1928), p. 20. This date is confirmed by Zeppelin, *op. cit.*, p. 30.

[17] Admiralty Naval Staff, *A Handbook of Siberia and Arctic Russia* (*circa* 1920), p. 204.

[18] II *de Martens Recueil* XVII pt. 2, p. 2; Yakhontoff, *op. cit.* pp. 357–365.

[19] The pre-westernized Chinese Empire had nothing comparable to the western legal concept of territorial waters or internal waters. The Maritime Province became an extension of the Empire in 1644 when the Manchus, originally from that general area, arose and took possession of the Chinese Throne. Until its cession to Russia in 1860, it was ruled as a distant family fiefdom of the Empire – almost completely undeveloped and without any of the usually understood administrative and legal trappings of State government. Franz Michael, *The Origins of Manchu Rule in China* (1942); Erich Hauer, *Die Grundung des Mandschurischen Kaiserreiches* (1927); Henry Landsdell ,*Through Siberia* (1882), chs. XLIV, LII; George F. Wright. *Asiatic Russia* (1901), pp. 213–4; Yuri Semyonov, *The Conquest of Siberia* (1944); von Zepelin, *op. cit.*, pp. 25, 43, 96–7; Consultation with Professor Albert Feurwerker, Harvard University Center for East Asian Studies, 23 February 1960.

[20] von Zepelin, *op. cit.*, p. 99.

[21] This point is difficult to establish. It would appear however, that Japanese fishermen did not operate outside Japanese coastal waters until after the Meiji restoration of 1868. Japanese Bureau of Maritime and River Products, *Histoire de L'Industrie de la Pêche Maritime et Fluviale au Japon* (1900), pp. 98–101; Marinori Okoshi, *A Sketch of the Fisheries of Japan* (1883); Imperial Fisheries Bureau, *Japanese Special Catalog of Sea Fisheries* (1915); Hansjulius Schepers, *Japans Seefischerei* (1935), pp. 58–63, 153–5. Mr. Scheper's monograph relates the fishing industry to the overall economy of Japan. It appears that after the Meiji restoration, overseas fishing had to await the construction of larger craft. The industry

done by Koreans, Chinese, and local tribes who sold their catch in Vladivostok. When the Japanese entered the trade, they sold some of their catch in the Maritime Province and also took over a good share of the retail food trade ashore. According to General von Zepelin, the Japanese so controlled the market by 1892, that they were dictating the prices.[22]

In 1898, an interdepartmental committee was appointed by the Foreign Ministry in St. Petersburg to report on the question of the right of foreigners to fish near the Russian coasts in the Sea of Okhotsk, the Sea of Japan, and the Kamchatkan Sea. The Chairman was the famous Russian International Lawyer Fedor F. de Martens, privy councillor. The committee decided that they should consider also the economic interests of the realm and the strategic and fiscal interests. The committee urged a minimum breadth of 6 miles (10.5 verst) for the marginal belt. They reported that, in their opinion, Russian law and Russian authority were absolute in this zone, that fishing in this zone shall only be under Russian license, and that within this zone Russian and foreign vessels might be examined by Russian customs authorities. No mention, apparently, was made of any bays. The recommended regulations were not carried into any legislation.[23]

In 1900 the Russian Government, anxious to obtain for itself and for Russians some of the profits from fishing in the Bay, established revenue regulations. Until then, the only regulation on fishing was one forbidding it in Ussuri Bay, in the Eastern Bosphorus, and in the anchorage areas.[24] The writer has been unable to ascertain what were the limits of the prohibited area. Actually, as of 1900, it appears that the only Russian legislation on territorial waters was that of 1/13 July 1868 stipulating a marine customs belt of three miles along Russian coasts.[25] It appears, however, that commencing in about 1900, local regulations were enforced in Peter the Great Bay. In these regulations, fishing "lots" were sold to foreigners by an annual auction held by the

achieved rapid industrialization under government aegis. The impetus was a fast-growing population, occupational substitution and the need for capital formation. On this latter point: Ragnar Nurkse, *Problems of Capital Formation in Underdeveloped Countries* (1957), pp. 143, 146, 148–9.

[22] von Zepelin, *op. cit.*, p. 183.

[23] The only account of this study known to this writer is in CAPT Gustave B. V. Meyer RNorN, *The Extent of Jurisdiction in Coastal Waters* (1927), pp. 237–9.

[24] *Histoire* etc. (1900), p. 99.

[25] Meyer, *op. cit.*, p. 237. Captain Meyer cites the legislation as being in *Laws of Russia*, No. 46071.

Department of Domains in Vladivostok.[26] In addition, a special ta: based on weight was charges foreigners for the fishing catch.[27]

The Soviet *note verbale* of 7 January 1958 to the Japanese Embassy in Moscow in reply to notes protesting the closing of Peter the Grea' Bay reads, in part, as follows:

The historical right of Russia concerning Peter the Great Bay was confirmed by the Regulations governing fisheries in the territorial waters of the Office of the Governor-General of Amur River Province, Promulgated in 1901. According to these Regulations, the line connecting the mouth of the Tuman-Ula and Cape Povorotnoy was established as the limit of the Russian internal waters of the said Bay.[28]

In its reply of 17 January 1958, the Japanese Embassy replied, in part:

... The Government of Japan has no knowledge of the existence of such regulations,[29]

Madame France de Hartingh shows this line in her recent work.[30] Professor Keishiro Irie of Aichi University was able to uncover the regulation which was referred to in the Soviet *note verbale:*

... fishing in the territorial waters of the Trans-Heilungkiang [31] is authorized to Russians, especially from Tuman Ula River to Povorotni Cape and the southern region of the Russian maritime province of Siberia.[32]

According to the Soviet writer, V. A. Romanov,[33] this regulation reads as follows:

Temporary Laws for the Regulation of the Maritime Fishing Industry in Territorial Waters of the Priamur Governor Generalship, approved 29 November 1901. ... Paragraph 4... the right to the produce of the fishing industry in the territorial waters of the Priamur region is only granted to Russian subjects...

[26] A fishing lot permits the user to catch a specified amount of fish of a specified species in a specific area and permits the use of a specified section of the shore for factories and storage. L. Larry Leonard, *International Regulation of Fisheries* (1944), p. 29.

[27] von Zepelin, *op. cit.*, p. 187.

[28] An unofficial translation of this note appears in 2 *Japanese Annual of International Law* (1958), at pp. 215–217.

[29] *Ibid.*, p. 217.

[30] de Hartingh, *op. cit.*, carte No, 6.

[31] Heilungkiang is the Chinese word for Amur. Kenneth S. Latourette, *The Chinese, Their History and Culture* (1934), vol. I, p. 375; From 1884 to 1918, the Government General of Amur included the Maritime Province. David Threadgold, *The Great Siberian Migration* (1957), Appendix III.

[32] Keishiro Irie, "Bay of Peter the Great," *Territories and Military Bases* (1959), Part 2, Ch. 1, Sect. 3. The writer is indebted to Professor Irie who sent this article from Japan. Translation of it was done by the Office of Naval Intelligence.

[33] V. A. Romanov, *op. cit.*

Mr. Romanov writes further:

However, as one of the exceptions to the fore-mentioned regulations it was provided that "in the southern area of the Primorsky Oblost [Maritime of Primorsk Province] from the mouth of the Tyuman–Ula to Cape Povorotny, foreign subjects are permitted to conduct a fishing business from boats under the regulations in paragraph 28." Paragraph 28 of the Regulations of 1901 speaks of the concession of a right to fishing in the waters of Russia to be certified by the issuance of a license from the Russian Government to those in the fishing industry.

This writer has attempted without success to find the above regulation in other sources, in order to arrive at some judgment of its notoriety. Although the regulation itself appears not to have received wide publication, its provisions appear in some greater or lesser degree to have been enforced. In the Peter the Great Bay area, and elsewhere along the coast of the maritime province, Japanese fishermen were subject to Russian regulation and to the purchase of lots. In Peter the Great Bay and elsewhere, the exact outer limits of Russian jurisdiction seem not to have been made clear. It is apparent that the working arrangement was satisfactory to both parties, probably because the Russian colonization of the Maritime Province was not so extensive as to include much in the way of Russian fishing activity in the Bay.[34] Then came the war between Russia and Japan.

Vladivostok was a rear base for this war and home port of a small squadron. Russia laid mines well inside the line of the 1957 delimitation. Her mines were laid to the west of Kasakewitsch Island closing Amur Bay and from Skryplev Island to Askuld Island, closing Ussuri Bay.[35] The Japanese laid 715 mines "right across Peter the Great Bay, from Askold Island to Kurakoff Island, a distance of forty miles," as the Japanese admiralty later stated.[36] There would appear to be no evidence in that war of any prize situation or blockade situation in which the legal status of the waters of Peter the Great Bay was brought into question.[37]

[34] Through a review of all materials available to him and deduction therefrom, it is the writer's conclusion that the Russians exercised jurisdiction in the approximate area to landward of a boundary line drawn three miles to seaward of a closure line drawn from Askold Island to Cape Gamov. This conclusion is arrived at after study of the species harvested, the lots purchased, the mine barrier, and the 1900 account of the Japanese Fisheries Bureau. This writer has been unable to ascertain that there was any commonly recognized closing line drawn across the bay.

[35] von Zepelin, *op. cit.*, p. 105.

[36] U.S. Naval War College. *International Law Situations*, 1908, pp. 102–3.

[37] F. A. Smith and N. W. Sibley, *International Law as Interpreted during the Russo-Japanese War* (1905), p. 360; Amos S. Hershey, *The International Law and Diplomacy of the Russo-Japanese War* (1906); Sakuye Takahashi, *International Law Applied to the Russo-Japanese War* (1908).

As the war was drawing to an exhausting close and the Parties were contemplating peace, the Japanese Government submitted a Statement of Terms of Peace which included the following:

Art. XIII

Russia to grant to Japanese subjects full fishery rights along the coast and in the bays, harbours inlets and rivers of her possessions in the Japan, Okhotsk and Bering Seas.[38]

The demand for fishing rights was quite over-shadowed by other topics at the Portsmouth Conference and the provision of the Peace Treaty having to do with such rights seems to have been almost an afterthought.[39] That provision reads:

Art. XI

Russia engages to arrange with Japan for granting to Japanese subjects rights of fishing along the coasts of the Russian possessions in the Japan, Okhotsk, and Behring Seas.

It is agreed that the foregoing engagement shall not affect rights already belonging to Russians or foreign subjects in those regions.[40]

It will be observed that the Treaty article omits the word bays altogether. Thus the Russians, at this point conceded nothing concerning sovereignty over Peter the Great Bay – or any other. They merely agreed, in general terms, to negotiate the matter at a later date.

The Fisheries Convention so contemplated was signed at St. Petersburg on 28 July 1907, and was to run for 12 years.[41]

A Protocol to the treaty contains *inter alia* the following provisions:

Art. I

... Fishing shall, moreover, be prohibited for strategical reasons, within limits of the territorial waters of the following:

3. Peter the Great Bay, from Cape Povorotny to Cape Gamov, incluidng islands within.
4. Possiet Bay, from Cape Jamov [sic] to Cape Boutakov.[42]

[38] Tyler Dennett, *Roosevelt and the Russo-Japanese War* (1925), pp. 231–2.

[39] On the Peace Conference see Dennett, *op. cit.*, chs. VIII-X; Count Sergius Witte, *Memoirs* (1921), ch. V; Melville S. Stone, *Fifty Years a Journalist* (1922), ch. VI. The large number of contemporary books and articles on the Peace Conference are conspicuously silent on the demand for fishery rights. Actually the Portsmouth Treaty was a negotiated and not an imposed treaty. Other demands made by the Japanese were such that the demand on fishery rights stood little chance of fulfillment.

[40] I *American Journal of International Law* (1907), Supplement, p. 20.

[41] *Ibid.*, II, (1908), Supp, 274–285; 101 *British and Foreign State Papers* (1912), pp. 453–462.

[42] In her book, *Soviet Trade from the Pacific to the Levant* (1935), Violet Connolly includes at page 35 a Map, which she writes, was annexed to the 1907 Convention. This excellent map shows the locations of all bays closed to Japanese fishermen.

It will be observed that Possiet Bay, now included in the 1957 delimitation, was considered as a separate bay in 1907. This would appear to emphasize the fact that both Parties were in agreement as to the extent of Peter the Great Bay.

At the time this agreement was made, the three-mile limit of the law of 1868 was still in force.[43] But this limit seems not to have affected fishery rights up to the line of demarcation in Peter the Great Bay. On 29 May 1911, the Russian Duma passed a bill which, when enacted into law, stipulated:

In those places where the coastal belt has not been fixed by special international rules or conventions these regulations shall apply to a coastal belt of 3 geographical leagues to be reckoned from the lowest low-water mark, or from the edge of the ice along the coast.[44]

Unlicensed fishing was forbidden in the areas defined.[45] The law was vigorously protested by the Japanese who were now bound to pay taxes for fishing in a much broader belt of waters. It does not appear, however, that the new law was very vigorously enforced.[46]

Immediately following the Russian Revolution the Japanese are reported to have exploited the fishery waters vigorously.[47] Provisional arrangements were made with the new Soviet Government in 1924. In the Peking Convention of 20 January 1925, the Parties concluded a new convention of friendship and economic cooperation, which provided, among other matters, for early negotiations with respect to the 1907 Convention.[48] During the period of the provisional arrangements, the 1907 closing line of Peter the Great Bay remained in force. A new fisheries convention was signed on 23 January 1928.[49] Protocol (A) of this Convention reads, in part:

[43] Page 339 above.

[44] This is cited by CAPT Meyer, (*op. cit.*, p. 240), as Code of Laws I, No. 115 of 14 June (old style).

[45] U.S. Ambassador St. Petersburg disp. 3 Feb. 1912 to SEC STATE, 1912 *For. Rel. U.S.* 1303.

[46] U.S. Chargé St. Petersburg disp. 19 July 1912 to SECSTATE, 1912 *For. Rel. U.S.* 1309. The Soviet Union seemed to take a rather flexible attitude toward the 12-mile limit as is evidenced by the Anglo-Soviet temporary agreement of 22 May 1930, Article 1(2) of which provides for a 10-mile rule for bays and a 3-mile marginal belt to seaward of the closing line U.S. Naval War College, *International Law Situations 1930*, p. 100.

[47] Edward W. Allen, *North Pacific Fisheries* (1936), ch. XXV; Special Delegation of the Far Eastern Republic to the U.S., *Fisheries of the Far Eastern Republic* (1922); Barbara Wertheim, "The Russo-Japanese Fisheries Controversy," VIII *Pacific Affairs* (1935), pp. 185–198.

[48] Allen, *op. cit.*

[49] III *de Martens Recueil*, vol. XXV, pp. 425–443.

Fishing shall, moreover, be barred to Japanese subjects, as well as to others, within the following bays, not, as a matter of course, including high seas:

3. Peter the Great Bay, from Cape Povorotni to Cape Gamova [sic], including islands situated in that bay.

4. Posiette Bay, from Cape Gamova to Cape Boutakov.

The dimensions of Peter the Great Bay show no change from the 1907 Convention and Posiette Bay remains a separate Bay.

The Convention was to have expired in 1936. It was modified by a protocol (not pertinent to our discussion) in 1932. The Convention itself, despite many fisheries disputes and difficulties was renewed on annual bases until 1944. The disputes were concerned with Japanese fishing up to three miles from Siberian coasts, the system of auctioning for fishing grounds, and the yen/ruble exchange rate. There is an extensive literature on these disputes and it would be almost impossible and not very profitable at this late date to attempt to weigh the merits or even to discuss the charges and counter charges.[50] What appears to sum up the situation is that the Japanese came into Siberian waters as industrious and aggressive entrepreneurs in the fishing industry at a time when the Russians had little interest in the waters. The Japanese, with their rapidly rising population, acquired self-conceived but very real vested interests in the fisheries exploitation of the Siberian coast. When the Soviet industrial expansion reached the area, and the coastal fisheries became to the Soviet authorities something more than a source of revenue and local food supply, there was bound to be a clash. The Japanese came and remained as rather aggressive and hungry guests. The Soviet Union was rather blunt and equally aggressive in its policies with regard to the area. On the Government levels, this situation seems to have had a series of uneasy truces.

On 30 March 1944, the Soviet Union and Japan concluded several agreements including one which provides that Japanese subjects and other foreigners are prohibited from certain fishing areas.[51] The fishing

[50] Among other sources, these disputes are discussed in the following: Leonard, *op. cit.*, pp. 27–34; Gordon Ireland, "The North Pacific Fisheries" 36 *Ameican Journal of International Law* (1942), pp. 400–424; Stefan Riesenfeld, *Protec'ion of Coastal Fisheries Under International Law* (1942), pp. 194–203; R. Levine, "La Pêche japonaise dans les eaux russes," 2 *L'Asie Française* (1937), pp. 46–48; V. Böhmert, "Die russische Fischereigrenze," 21 *Zeitschrift für Völkerrecht* (1937), pp. 441–470; Barbara Wertheim, *op. cit.*, Kathleen Barnes, "Fisheries, Mainstay of Soviet-Japanese Friction," 9 *Far Eastern Survey* (1940), p. 75f.

[51] *The New York Times*, 1 April 1944, pp. 1, cols. 6–7, 4 cols. 2–6; *Ibid.*, 2 April 1944, p. 8, col. 1, p. 28, col. 1. The fisheries matter was quite secondary to the principal issue in the negotiations: the Japanese oil and coal concessions in Northern Sakhalin. By an agreement of 13 April 1941, the Japanese had agreed to give these up during the following six months. When Germany attacked the Soviet Union in June 1941, the latter's power position became

agreement is in the form of an exchange of notes in which the Soviet Government transmitted to the Japanese Ambassador at Moscow a protocol extending for five years (running from 1 January 1944), the Convention of 1928, subject to certain modifications.[52] The change which is of specific relevance to our study is quoted:

(A) the provisions of the final paragraph of Article One Protocol (A) [of the 1928 Convention] are altered and are replaced by the following provisions: "fishing shall be moreover forbidden to Japanese subjects as well as to the Gulf of Peter the Great including Possiet Gulf the area bounded by a line drawn from Oposny Island [53] to the mouth of the river Tyumen Ula.

Exact boundaries of the above-designated five areas prohibited for fishing are defined in Note Number Two supplementary to the present Protocol which were exchanged by the Plenipotentiaries of the USSR and Japan simultaneous with the signature of the present Protocol.[54]

The Japanese note in connection with this protocol brought to the notice of the Soviet Union Government the following:

(a) That the Japanese Government agreed to prohibit its subjects from fishing in their leased areas on the coast of Kamchatka and in Obyntorsk area *until the conclusion of the war*. (Italics mine)

(b) That such abstention will not serve as reason for cancellation of treaties for exploitation of any fishing areas and factories in the above districts.[55]

The U.S. State Department telegram (Ambassador, Moscow to Department 1123, of 31 March 1944), reads, in this connection, as follows:

greatly altered, and the Japanese chose to retain the concessions. The agreement of 30 March 1944 was one obviously forced upon Japan. *The New York Times* of 2 April 1944 cites an editorial in *Pravda* in which it is stated that with the new agreement the USSR "had successfully forced Tokyo to accept vital and essential changes."

[52] Inasmuch as this Protocol has received rather ambiguous mention in the 1957 Exchanges of Notes between the Soviet Union and other States, it is reproduced as Annex A to this section. The author is indebted to Mr. Raymund T. Yingling, Assistant Legal Advisor, U.S. Department of State for furnishing him with a copy of this Protocol. Apparently, there are at least two rather important supplementary notes to this Protocol. Search of Department of State files failed to disclose them. Author's consultation at State Department, 6 April 1960. The rather extensive coverage given the pertinent set of negotiations by *The New York Times* of 1–2 April 1944, does not include a reprint of this Protocol. To the best of this writer's belief it has not been reprinted elsewhere.

[53] Oposny Island is along the coast to the eastward of Povorotny Point and 160 miles from the Tumen River. U.S. Navy Hydrographic Office Publication No. 122B reads as follows in connection with this island: "A zone dangerous for navigation exists between Ostrov [Island] Oposny and the mouth of the Tumen (Tynmen Ula) River 160 miles west-southwestward. Vessels approaching the danger zone from northward or eastward meet their military pilots within Bukhta Valentina..."

[54] The Supplementary Note numbered Two was not included with the text of the Protocol supplied to this writer.

[55] See Annex A to this section.

In a note confirming the receipt of the note of the Plenipotentiary of Japan the Plenipotentiary of the USSR stated that he is taking note of the above statement.[56]

No mention is made in the Protocol of any understanding of a post-war relaxation of the prohibition of fishing in the Peter the Great Bay area. The Soviet Government did not mention any post-war termination of the prohibition in its note and merely "took note" of the Japanese reservation. Mr. Romanov writes, however:

In addenda to the protocol, which were agreed to by the Soviet and Japanese ambassadors, it was pointed out that the borders forbidden for fishing in the region "are established until the end of the present war." [57]

After World War II, the Japanese appear to have been rather slow to approach the Siberian coast. This resulted from the establishment of the "MacArthur Line" by the occupation authorities, the establishment of the "Bulganin Line" off the Kamchatka Coast by the Soviet Union, and the technical state of war that existed between the Soviet Union and Japan until the re-stablishment of normal relations after the Soviet-Japanese Joint Declaration of 19 October 1956. The 1928 Convention, as amended by the 1944 Protocol, terminated on 1 January 1949 when the Parties were still, technically, in a state of war. The Convention has not been revived nor has it been superceded by any other similar agreement. These handicaps, however, have not prevented Japanese fishing vessels from venturing knowingly or otherwise into Soviet controlled areas. Many of these Japanese vessels are not e-quipped with modern navigating devices,[58] and navigation near some of the forbidden areas is rather difficult because of weather conditions. Soviet maritime control has been vigilant and many arrests have ensued.[59]

The Order of the Council of Ministers of the USSR of 10 August 1954 provides in part:

Art. 1

Para. 2. Marine fishery waters comprise the internal maritime waters (inland seas, gulfs, bays, and creeks of open seas) and territorial waters of the U.S.S.R. (maritime frontier zone) to a width of twelve nautical miles measured from the low water mark (both on the mainland and on islands) or, in the case of internal waters, from their outer edge.

[56] *Ibid.*

[57] Romanov, *op. cit.*, p. 559, fn. 52.

[58] Asia Kyokai, *Japanese Fisheries, Their Development and Present Status* (1957). This is strictly a trade and technical publication.

[59] Alvin D. Coox, "Japanese Attitudes toward the Soviet Union," 26 *World Affairs Quarterly* (Jan. 1956), pp. 338–357, at pp. 340–2.

Art. 6

Foreign nationals and bodies corporate of foreign States may not engage in commercial fishing or the commercial catching or gathering of other aquatic animals or plants in the waters of the U.S.S.R., except as provided in international agreements concluded by the U.S.S.R.[60]

In the treaties in which Peter the Great Bay was concerned, no special reference was made to the 12-mile belt of territorial waters. When the unilateral declaration on the limits of internal waters for Peter the Great Bay was made in 1957, the 12-mile belt was, by the terms of the above order, also a zone in which fishing was prohibited.

The first Japanese fishing operations in the Peter the Great Bay area, after the 1956 Joint Declaration, were carried out from 10 to 19 April, 1957. This operation was described as a test. During the second such test on 24 August 1957, a Soviet patrol boat ordered the Japanese trawlers to suspend operations and withdraw from the area. When the Japanese Ambassador in Moscow protested the Soviet action, he was advised that the waters included a former mine-laying area, that trawling operations were still dangerous, and that it was hoped that Japanese fishing vessels would suspend operations in the area in order to avoid any unfortunate incidents. On 20 July 1957, the Soviet Council of Ministers announced the closure of Peter the Great Bay, declaring its internal waters to be bounded by a line joining Cape Povorotny and the Tuman-Ula Estuary.

Annex A JAPAN-SOVIET UNION EXCHANGE OF NOTES, 30 MARCH 1944 [61]

–5– 1123, thirty-first, from Moscow
USSR S. A. Lozovski.
Japanese Ambassador in Moscow, N. Sato.

PROTOCOL concerning the remaining in force for a period of five years of the Fisheries Convention between the Union of Soviet Socialist Republics and Japan.

The Government of the U.S.S.R. and the Imperial Government of Japan as a result of the negotiations which have taken place between them recently regarding the fisheries question have agreed on the following article on the Fisheries Convention bteween the USSR and Japan as well as all the documents supplementary to it signed on January 23, 1928 the term of effectiveness of which after annual extensions beginning in 1936 expired on December 31, 1943, shall remain in force for a period of five years beginning January 1, 1944 according to the conditions established in the present protocol.

[60] Brunson MacChesney ,U.S. Naval War College *International Law Situation and Documents, 1956*, p. 493.

[61] Copy furnished the writer by U.S. Department of State. This reprint is exactly as it eppears in Departmental files,

Article Two.* All questions relating to the fishery activity of the fishing industry organizations and citizens of the USSR are not regulated by articles of the Fisheries Convention and the documents supplementary thereto as they are considered to be subject to the exclusive jurisdiction of the USSR.

In conformity with the provisions of the preceding paragraph all the provisions contained in the Fisheries Convention and in the documents supplementary thereto which relate to the fishery industry activity of fishery industry organization and citizens of the USSR lost their force and in the future will not be effective.

Article Three. The following changes and supplements are embodied in Article One Protocol (A) supplementary to the Fisheries Convention: (A) the provisions of the final paragraph of Article One Protocol (A) are altered and are replaced by the following provisions "fishing shall be moreover frobidden to Japanese subjects as well as to other foreigners in the following bays (one) Avachinski Gulf the area bounded by a line drawn from Cape Kruty to Bechevinski Bay (inclusive) (two) De Castrie Bay the area bounded by a line drawn rom South Cape to St. Croix[61a] Bay (inclusive) (three) Sovetskaya Gavan the area bounded by a line drawn from the points longitude 49 degrees 26 minutes east to the point longitude 4840 north latitude 140 degrees 11 minutes east (four) the bay of St. Olga and the Bay of St. Vladimir the area bounded by a linə drawn from the mouth of the River Lafule to Cape Nakhvalny (five) the Gulf of Peter the Great including Possiet Gulf the area bounded by a line drawn from Opasny Island to the mouth of the river Tyumen Ula."

The Bays designated in Article One Protocol (A). By the numbers 16, 27, 30, and 32 shall not be referred to henceforth by these numbers of reason of their being included in the above designated five arcas.

Exact boundaries of the above-designated five areas prohibited for fishing are defined in note Numbered Two supplementary to the present Protocol which were exchanged by the Plenipotentiaries of the USSR and Japan simultaneous with the signature of the present Protocol.[62]

(B) The list of bays cited in Article One Protocol (A) which are the subject of the exception referred to in Article One of the Fisheries Convention are supplemented by the following two designations (one) Ossora Bay (two) the northwestern part of Tauiski Gulf.

Article Four. The total sum of taxes and imposts provided for in notes Numbered One attached to the Fisheries Convention the exchange of which took place on January 23, 1928 is increased and is fixed at the rate of 30% of the payment for the rent of the corresponding fishery lots.

Article Five. The rates of special fees (part payment) established by Section Six of Paragraph (B) Protocol (TS) for the operation of canneries is increased and is fixed in accordance with the following schedule (one) for red fish 25 kopecks per box (two) for Siberian salmon, Kizhuck and Chavych 20 kopecks per box (three) for humpback salmon 13 kopecks per box (four) for crabs 50 kopecks per box.

Article Six. The present Prtocol takes effect from the day of its signature.

The present Protocol is done in the Russian and Japanese languages both texts have equal force.

[61a] Probably intended to read: "latitude 49 degrees 26 minutes north." Corresponding longitude coordinate not given.

[62] This supplementary note has not been seen by the writer. Footnote 52, above. The boundary indicated on the large chart (enclosed in the back cover) as being that stipulated by the 30 March Protocol was taken from de Hartingh, *op. cit.*, Chart No. 6. Mme de Hartingh does not indicate her authority for the line in question, and it is unverified.

* No Article One labeled as such

In witness thereof the undersigned duly authorized by their Governments have signed the present Protocol and have affixed their seals thereto.

Done in two copies in the city of Moscow on the 30th day of March 1944 which corresponds to the 30th day of the 3rd month of the 19th year of Siova.

Plenipotentiary of the USSR Vice Commissar of Foreign Affairs of the USSR S/A Lozovski.

Plenipotentiary of Japan Ambassador Extraordinary and Plenipotentiary of Japan in the USSR Naotake Sato.

Note of the Plenipotentiary of the USSR to the Plenipotentiary of Japan Moscow 30th March 1944 Mr. Plenipotentiary in connection with the signature on this day of the Protocol for renewing for a period of five years the Fisheries Convention between the USSR and Japan and the attached documents signed on 23rd January 1928 I have the honor to bring the following to your knowledge.

One. The Government of the USSR agrees to renew on the former terms for a period of five years beginning from the 1st January 1944 provided other stipulations are not laid down in the Protocol and the documents attached to it the validity of the special treaties concluded on 2rd November 1928 for the utilization by Japanese subjects of the canning factories and fishing lots attached to them together with the documents relating to these treaties and the subsequent supplementary agreements.

Two. The 24 fishing lots enumerated below which were leased to Japanese subjects but not exploited by them for two consecutive years in 1939 and 1940 are closed and will not in the future be subject to auction independently of the expiration of the periods of their lease.

The numbers of the fishing areas – 41, 42, 269, 271, 273, 367, 497, 498, 543, 555, 556, 561, 638, 641, 1002, 1003, 1004, 1082, 1104, 1190, 1265, 1266, 1267, and 95 (crab catching).

The leasing agreements for those of the lots enumerated above the period of which has not yet expired are subject to cancellation.

Three. The fishing areas which were under lease to Japanese subjects at the end of 1943 with the exception of the areas enumerated in points one and two above will at the expiration of the periods of their lease be put up for auction on lease for the appropriate period laid down in the first part of Article Six of Protocol (A) attached to the Fisheries Convention.

In this Connection it should be borne in mind that the number of the fishing lots which will be acquired by bidding by the fishing organizations and citizens of the USSR at the auctions mentioned in the preceeding paragraphs and which are to be held annually for five years beginning with 1944 shall not exceed 10% of the total number of lots auctioned in the respective year and that the fishing organizations and citizens of the USSR have no intention of bidding for those fishing lots on which canning factories are located.

I take this opportunity, Mr. Plenipotentiary, to renew the assurances of my highest esteem.

Plenipotentiary of the USSR Vice Peoples Commissar for Foreign Affairs of the USSR S/A Lozovsky.

The Plenipotentiary of Japan in a note confirming the receipt of the note of the Plenipotentiary of the USSR stated that he is taking note of the announcement indicated above.

Note of the Plenipotentiary of Japan to the Plenipotentiary of the USSR Moscow 30th March 1944:

Mr. Plenipotentiary in the name of my Government I have the honor to bring the following to your notice.

One. In accordance with the wish of the Government of the USSR the Government of Japan agrees to guarantee that all the fishing areas leased to Japanese subjects lying on the eastern coast of Kamchatka and in the Olyutorsk area will not be exploited by the lease holders until the conclusion of the war in the Pacific.

Two. In this connection it is understood that the abstention from exploitation by Japanese subjects of the above-mentiloned fishing areas will not serve as a reason for the cancellation of treaties for the exploitation of any fishing areas and factories in the above-mentioned districts.

I take this opportunity, Mr. Plenipotentiary to renew the assurances of my highest esteem.

Plenipotentiary of Japan Ambassador Extraordinary and Plenipotentiary of Japan in the USSR Naotake Sato.

In a note confirming the receipt of the note of the Plenipotentiary of Japan the Plenipotentiary of the USSR stated that he is taking note of the above statement.

PRE HARRIMAN

Section C THE SOVIET CLAIM AND EXCHANGES OF NOTES

The Soviet decision on Peter the Great Bay, as we have noted at the beginning of this Chapter, was communicated to the world and to interested parties by means of the Moscow Radio, a device used by by the Soviet Government from time to time in lieu of more conventional diplomatic methods. What is believed to be an exact quotation of the statement is:

The Council of Minister has discussed matters concerning the border question of the Bay of Peter the Great, proclaiming it as a Soviet inland sea. The Council of Ministers ascertained that the line between the embouchures of Tuman Ula and the Cape of Povorotni is the border line of Soviet inland sea. The Soviet territorial sea should be measured from this basic line as a starting point. The sailing of foreign ships and flight of aircraft are not allowed in or over the area of the Bay of Peter the Great unless they get permission from Soviet authority to do so. But foreign vessels may freely enter or leave the Soviet open harbor, Nakhodka. However, they must obey Soviet instructions and limit their navigation route (two nautical miles for entering or leaving the harbor).[1]

The reaction of the Japanese Government was prompt, and on 26 July 1957, the Japanese Ambassador in Moscow was instructed to make the following oral protest to the Soviet Government.

It is evident that the sea area thus designated falls short of necessary conditions for an inland sea in the light of international law, and as such, runs counter to the accepted principle of international law. The Japanese Government cannot therefore recognize the decision of the USSR Council of Ministers.

The area in question has traditionally been a fishing ground for Japanese nationals. The decision illegally infringes the fishery rights and freedom of navigation long enjoyed by the nationals of Japan. The Government of Japan hereby declares that it shall not be bound by the present measures taken by the Soviet Government, and reserves all its rights involved in this issue.[2]

[1] *The New York Times*, 21 July 1957, p. 1, col. 7.

[2] Announcement of Public Information and Cultural Affairs Bureau, Ministry of Foreign Affairs, Tokyo, Japan, 27 July 1957, reprinted in 2 *The Japanese Annual of International Law* (1958), p. 214.

According to the 27 July 1957 news release of the Japanese Government, Soviet Deputy Foreign Minister Semenov replied to the Japanese Ambassador that Peter the Great Bay is a traditional bay of the Soviet Union.[3]

In a second *Note Verbale*, dated 7 August 1957, the Japanese Ambassador in Moscow is reported to have made the following observations:

1. The Soviet Government has never in the past claimed it as a historic bay. The only reason given by the Soviet Government for its demand that Japanese fishing vessels be kept away from the waters of Peter the Great Bay was the existence of dangers that the mines on the sea-bed might still explode and did not refer to the Bay as a historic bay.

2. The Protocol of the Japan-USSR Fisheries Treaty of 1928 designated Peter the Great Bay as one of the Bays in which fishing was prohibited. But the area of the bay as designated in that treaty was narrower than that which was recently announced by the Soviet Government and which includes as the bay area a part of the high seas.

3. Prior to the war, Japanese trawlers had long carried on fishing operations freely without any protest from the Soviet Government.

4. By the exchange of notes dated 30 March 1944, fishing by Japanese vessels in the bay was prohibited by mutual agreement. Nevertheless, it was expressly provided therein that the prohibition was a provisional measure during wartime.

5. The Bay does not satisfy the necessary conditions for a historic bay under the law of nations, namely, the long-established international recognitions as a historic bay.[4]

The Ambassador is reported as receiving from Soviet Deputy Foreign Minister Kuznetsov the reply that he would refer the protest to the Soviet Government and that the Bay is a historic bay of the Soviet Union.[5]

On August 12, 1957, the United States Embassy at Moscow delivered to the Soviet Foreign Ministry a note advising that "The Government of the United States most strongly protests the reported action of the Council of Ministers, which it regards as contrary to international law." In part the note reads as follows:

Under international law, the body of water enclosed by the line drawn between the estuary of the River Tyumen-Ula and the Povorotny promontory cannot either geographically or historically, be regarded as part of the internal waters of the U.S.S.R. The Government of the United States views the action of the Council of Ministers as constituting an attempt by the Government of the U.S.S.R. unlawfully to appropriate a large area of the high seas by unilateral

[3] *Ibid.*

[4] *Ibid.*, pp. 214–5.

[5] *Ibid.*

action. Such an attempt has no foundation in international law and encroaches upon the established principle of freedom of the case.

The Government of the United States must, therefore, regard the enforcement of this decree as violative of the fundamental principles of international law and reserves its right to take such action as it deems necessary to protect each and all of its rights in the area of Peter the Great Bay. The Government of the United States requests that the Government of the U.S.S.R. reconsider the reported action of the Council of Ministers and conform it to the requirements of international law.[6]

The Government of the United Kingdom addressed a note of protest to the Soviet Union on 17 September 1957. The British note pointed out that there was no evidence that the area claimed by the U.S.S.R. had been recognized historically as an actual bay or that Moscow had ever before made any claim that it formed internal waters.[7] In addition, the following Governments have addressed protests in these premises to the Soviet Government: France, 11 November 1957; Italy, 16 October 1957; Greece, 9 November 1957; Sweden, 6 December 1957; Federal Republic of Germany, 14 February 1959.[8]

The Government of the Soviet Union addressed simultaneous notes to the Japanese, United States and United Kingdom Governments on 7 January 1958. The note to the Japanese Government is quoted hereunder in its entirety:

The Ministry of Foreign Affairs of the USSR presents its compliments to the Embassy of Japan and in reference to the said Embassy's Notes Vervale [sic] Nos. 00094–57 and 00103–57, dated 26 July and 6 August 1957 respectively, has the honour to state, as follows:

The Area of the waters of Peter the Great Bay historically belongs to the Soviet internal waters, owing to the special geographical conditions of the Bay and to its significance in economy and national defense. The historical right of Russia concerning Peter the Great Bay was confirmed by the Regulations governing fisheries in the territorial waters of the Office of the Governor-General of Amur River Province, Promulgated in 1901. According to these Regulations, the line connecting the mouth of the Tumen-Ula and Cape Povorotny was established as the limit of the Russian internal waters in the area of the said Bay.

The decision of the Council of Ministers of the USSR concerning Peter the Great Bay does not add anything new to the status of the Bay from the point of view that the Bay belongs to the USSR. It only confirms the status and the limit of the internal waters in the Bay established over half a century ago. It is well known that the entire coast of the Bay that penetrates deeply into the mainland, is part of the territory of the USSR, and that the shape of the Bay itself shows that it forms an inseparable part of the land territory of the USSR. It is from this point that the Decision of the Council of Ministers concerning Peter the Great Bay as well as the Regulations promulgated in 1901 have originated.

[6] 37 *Department of State Bulletin* (2 Sept. 1957), p. 388.

[7] *The New York Times*, 19 Sept. 1957, p. 7, col. 3.

[8] Keishiro Irie, "Bay of Peter the Great.'

The fact that Peter the Great Bay is internal waters of the USSR has been recognized by the neighboring countries of the USSR, for instance, by the Chinese People's Republic.

The fishery conventions concluded between Russia and Japan in 1907, and between the USSR and Japan in 1928, and also the Soviet-Japan Protocol of 1944 extending for five years the validity of the Convention of 1928, are based upon the principle that Peter the Great Bay belongs to the Soviet Union. By these conventions, the Japanese subjects as well as other foreigners were prohibited from fishing in the greater part of the said Bay, and by the Protocol of 1944 the prohibited area was expanded to all of the Bay.

The fact that on the basis of the Convention of 1928, as well as the Convention of 1907, right of fishery in some parts of the Bay for some years was given to the Japanese subjects, does not change the status that the Bay belongs to the Soviet Union. On the contrary, it confirms the right of the USSR to the Bay, since it is self-evident that the right of fishery naturally could not be granted in connection with the waters of the high seas, but was granted in connection with the waters belonging to the USSR. It is necessary to point out that the Japanese Government explicitly agreed in 1907 and 1928 that the right of fishery of the Japanese subjects was given and granted by the USSR side, as clearly provided in the above conventions. The temporary character of the right was confirmed by the Protocol of 1944, which was agreed upon by Japan, providing that the fishery by the Japanese subjects in all the area of the Bay was prohibited. The said prohibition also was effected in connection with the principle that the waters of the Bay belong to the Soviet Union. In this connection, it is necessary to draw the attention to the fact that the limit of the prohibited area of fishery was set for "during the period until the termination of the present war," by Exchange of Notes between the Plenipotentiaries of the USSR and Japan, effected at the same time with the signing of the Protocol, but there was no stipulation in the Notes or the Protocol providing for the removal of the limit after the termination of the war to that established in 1928.

In consideration of the frequent voyages in or flying over the area of the waters of Peter the Great Bay recently on the part of foreign fishing boats and airplanes, the Government of the USSR was obliged to remind the foreign countries that the Bay belongs to the Soviet Union, indicating the limit of the internal waters of the USSR in the area of the said Bay.

The assertion that the decision by the Government of the USSR concerning Peter the Great Bay is an infringement on freedom of navigation and fishery, is groundless, in so far as freedom of navigation and fishery concerns the high seas only, and Peter the Great Bay constitutes internal waters of the USSR.

In view of these facts, representation by the Japanese Government to the Government of the USSR on its decision concerning the limit of the Soviet interal waters in Peter the Great Bay has no foundation, and the Government of the USSR sees no cause for further deliberation on this question.

Concerning the statement in the Embassy's Notes Verbale that the Japanese Government does not consider the said Decision binding, and reserves all rights involved in this issue, the Government of Japan itself must bear all responsibility for any possible consequences of such position.[9]

The note of the Soviet Ministry of Foreign Affairs to the United States Embassy is similar in tenor though somewhat shorter. The only matter peculiar to this note is the following paragraph:

[9] 2 *The Japanese Annual of International Law*, pp. 215–6.

As for the announcement in the note of the Embassy that the Government of the U.S.A. reserves to itself the right to take the necessary measures for the defense of its rights in the region of Bay of Peter the Great, this announcement is deprived of any bases whatsoever, inasmuch as there can be no question of any rights whatever of the Government of the U,S.A. in Soviet internal and territorial waters in the region of the indicated bay, which is located may thousands of kilometers from the U.S.A.[10]

The Japanese Embassy in Moscow replied to the Soviet Government in a note dated 17 January 1958. This note is quoted hereunder in its entirety:

The Japanese Embassy presents its compliments to the Ministry of Foreign Affairs of the USSR and in reference to the Note Verbale, D.V. No. 5 of the said Ministry, dated 7 January 1958, has the honour to state, under instructions from the Government of Japan, as follows:

1. The Government of the USSR asserts that its claims concerning Peter the Great Bay are evidenced in the Regulations governing Fisheries in the Territorial Waters of the Office of the Governor-General of Amur River Province, promulgated by the Russian Government in 1901.

However, the Government of Japan has no knowledge of the existence of such regulations, nor has it at any time ever recognized the validity of any such regulations, unilaterally declaring a part of the high seas as internal waters.

2. The Government of the USSR states further that Peter the Great Bay penetrates deeply into the land and that its entire land boundary is part of the territory of the USSR, and also that the said Bay forms an inseparable part of the land-territory of the Soviet Union.

However, the distance across the entrance of the sea area claimed to be internal waters of the Soviet Union exceeds one hundred miles, and moreover, contrary to the assertion of the Government of the USSR, the indentation is by no means deep. It is beyond dispute that such an indentation as in the present case can not ge recognized under international law as a bay, the waters within which are to be considered internal waters, even though its entire coast may belong to one State.

3. Further, the Government of the USSR asserts that the area of the waters has been recognized by the various neighbouring States to be internal waters of the Soviet Union.

In this connection, the Government of Japan is bound to point out the fact that many States including the leading maritime countries of the world have lodged protests against the decision of the USSR Council of Ministers.

4. The Government of the USSR claims that, by virtue of the Japan-Russia Fishery Convention of 1907, the Japan-USSR Fishery Convention of 1928, and the Protocol extending for five years the Japan-USSR Fishery Convention of 1944, the Government of Japan too has recognized the waters concerned to be internal waters of the Soviet Union.

It is the view of the Government of Japan that such claims of the Government of the USSR are entirely groundlesss for the following reasons:

(1) With respect to prohibition of fishing by nationals of Japan in Peter the Great Bay, it is provided in the Protocol to the Convention of 1907 that such fishing shall be prohibited "within the limits of territorial waters," and it is stipulated in the Protocol (A) to the Convention of 1928 that the waters where

[10] 38 *The Department of State Bulletin* (24 March 1958), pp. 461–2.

such fishing is prohibited do "not, as a matter of course, include high seas." Thus, it is made clear that the provisions prohibiting fishing in each of these Conventions are not applicable in the high seas portion of the said Bay. In other words, the Government of the USSR recognized in these Conventions the existence within the said Bay of waters belonging to the high seas.

(2) The Protocol of 1944 does not mean that the Government of Japan has in any way recognized the area of waters in question to be internal waters of the Soviet Union. The fact that prohibition of fishing under this Protocol was a provisional war time measure, as has already been pointed out in the Note Verbale of the Japanese Embassy of 6 August 1957, is clearly borne out by the term "during the period until the termination of the present war" in the Exchange of Notes between the Plenipotentiaries of the two countries, dated 30 March 1944, which was quoted in the Note Verbale of the Ministry of Foreign Affairs of the USSR. Moreover, the fact that the two countries thus agreed to prohibit fishing for a limited period is a proof that the USSR does not have any "historical rights" with respect to the area of waters in question.

5. In view of the facts stated above, the Government of Japan considers entirely groundless the points newly raised in the above-mentioned Note Verbale of the Ministry of Foreign Affairs of the USSR, dated 7 January 1958. Therefore, the Government of Japan wishes to reaffirm its position as clarified in the Japanese Embassy's Notes Verbale, Nos. 0094–57 and 00103–57, dated 26 July and 6 August 1957 respectively.[11]

The United States Embassy replied in a note dated 6 March 1958. The note is rather short; a part of it is quoted:

The configuration of the coast in the area of Peter the Great Bay is not such that that body of water could in any way be regarded as being comprised of landlocked waters which could properly be considered internal waters of the Soviet Union. Encroachments on the high seas are of concern to the entire world and neither internal regulations of the Russian Government, which were not communicated to the Governments of other States, nor fishing agreements between the Union of Soviet Socialist Republics and Japan could be sufficient to establish the degree of acceptance on the part of the rest of the world that would be necessary to justify the Government of the Union of Soviet Socialist Republics in claiming that the body of water referred to above constitutes internal waters of the Soviet Union either as an historic bay or under any other prinicple of international law. Moreover, the Government of the United States notes that the Government of Japan does not agree with the interpretation of the Government of the Union of Soviet Socialist Republics of the fishing agreements of 1928 and 1944...

The Government of the United States ... reserves its right to take such action as it deems necessary to protect each and all of its rights in the area.[12]

Subsequent to the Soviet announcement of 21 July 1957, articles concerning Peter the Great Bay appeared in legal journals both in Japan and the Soviet Union. Save for some light shed on the 30 March 1944 Soviet-Japanese Agreement, the Japanese articles add little to what is set out in the Japanese notes. One Soviet Union writer, Mr.

[11] 2 *Japanese Annual of International Law*, pp. 217–8.

[12] 38 *Department of State Bulletin* (24 March 1958), p. 461.

A. N. Nikolaiev, however, has endeavored to bring forth evidence to substantiate the Soviet contention that Peter the Great Bay is a historic bay.[13] Mr. Nikolaiev makes the following statements in this regard:

1. Admiral Poutiatin, in 1854, on board the frigate *Pallada* surveyed the area now known as Posiett Bay.
2. Count Mouraviev-Amourski, in 1859, discovered America Bay and the port of Nakhodka.
3. Count Mouraviev-Amourski gave the area the name, Peter the Great Bay
4. In 1860, the commanding officer of the Russian transport *Manchuria* founded on the shore of the Golden Horn the military post which in 1862 became officially the port of Vladivostok.

Mr. Nikolaiev then goes on to say that on the occasion of the 30 March 1944 treaty, the temporary closing of the Bay was not agreed to with a view toward returning to the 1928 provisions after the war. He says that recognition of historic right, contrary to the statements of the United States and Japan, need not be obtained from other States despite Mr. Hyde. He cites the fact that Canadian historic rights over Hudson Bay are not recognized by the United States and that the claim of England to Moray Firth is not recognized by all the States He ends his arguments by showing examples of bays which are classed as historic bays and which have entrances greater than ten miles in width.

Japanese sources have said that "investigations" disclose the presence of guided missible installations on the shores of Peter the Great Bay.[14] Professor Ohira writes:

> It is generally observed that the recent Soviet action in declaring Peter the Great Bay as internal waters was intended to protect the fortress area surrounding Vladivostok.[15]

Section D SUMMARY

It now remains for us to summarize and assess the arguments propounded by the disputants in the Peter the Great Bay controversy. As a preliminary observation of the controversy, we should note that the Parties have assumed an "all or nothing" attitude with respect to Soviet possession of the Bay as internal waters.

[13] France de Hartingh, *Les Conceptions Soviétiques du Droit de la Mer* (1960), pp. 35–38.

[14] *The New York Times*, 9 January 1958, p. 37, col. 5.

[15] Zengo Ohira, "Fishery Problems between Soviet Russia and Japan," 2 *The Japanese Annual of International Law* (1958), pp. 1–18, at p. 15.

(1) *The Japanese Position on the Facts*

(a) "The Area in question has traditionally been a fishing ground for Japanese nationals, and the decision illegally infringes the fishery rights and freedom of navigation long enjoyed by the nationals of Japan." *Comment.* From about 1890 to 1944 the area in question was a Japanese fishing ground, and Japanese fishing firms enjoyed a very favorable position in the area. However, except for the revolutionary phase of the Soviet Union, Japanese fishing was nearly always conducted in compliance with some administrative arrangement, such as the lot auctions held by Russian authorities, or according to the terms of Russo-Japanese treaties. *Traditionally,* Japanese fishermen operated in Peter the Great Bay, but it is difficult to argue that the usage ever hardened into a Japanese right or servitude. Moreover, there are areas within Peter the Great Bay where it can be shown that neither Japanese nor other foreign nationals ever enjoyed fishing rights or freedom of navigation. Such areas, generally speaking, are those to landward of the line established by the treaties of 1907 and 1928.

(b) "The Soviet Government has never in the past claimed it as a historic bay." This is most certainly correct and there are on record a number of occasions and writings in which such a claim might quite easily have been made. Some of these are relatively recent.[1]

(c) The area designated in the treaty of 1928 as being prohibited to Japanese fishermen was narrower than that recently announced by the Soviet Government. That is correct, and here as elsewhere in the Japanese and United States positions, one must keep in mind that whereas these two States mention Peter the Great Bay in general terms, there is really very little doubt about the exercise of exclusive Russian and Soviet sovereignty over the inner reaches of the bay, or that such exercise seems tacitly to have been acquiesced in by the Japanese Government.

[1] Examples of these are the following: (a) Order of the Council of People's Commissars, No. 2157, for the regulation of fishing and the conservation of fisheries resources, 25 September 1935. (b) Article 625, Regulation concerning protection of State Borders of the Union of S.S.R., "Collection of laws and Decrees of the Workers' and Peasants' Government of the Union of Soviet Socialist Republics," No. 62 of 19 November 1927. (c) The Law of 29 May/11 June 1911 concerning the maritime fisheries in the Trans-Amur Government. (d) Regulation of 10 August 1954 Concerning the Conservation of Fishery Resources and of the Regulation of Fishing in the Waters of the U.S.S.R. (e) *Memorandum on the Soviet Doctrine and Practice with respect to the Regime of the High Seas,* submitted to the United Nations International Law Commission on 21 November 1950. (A/CN.4/38). (f) The Treaty of 1928. This treaty, but not the 1907 treaty, is considered relevant because it was concluded subsequent to the inception of the use of the term "historic bays" by the tribunal in the North Atlantic Coast Fisheries Arbitration of 1910.

(d) "Prior to the war, Japanese trawlers had long carried on fishing operations freely without protest from the Soviet Government." True, but the observations in sub-paragraphs b and c, above, apply.

(e) The 30 March 1944 exchange of notes expressly provided that the fishing prohibition was a provisional measure during wartime. There seems little doubt that such is the only interpretation that one can reasonably impute to that agreement.

(2) *The Soviet Position on the Facts*

(a) "The historical right of Russia concerning Peter the Great Bay was confirmed by the Regulations governing fisheries in the territorial waters of the Office of the Governor General of Amur River Province, promulgated in 1901." There is no reason to dispute that such regulations were probably issued. There is no evidence whatsoever that the regulations received even limited publication. Major General von Zepelin's quite complete monograph makes no mention of them. The Capital of Trans-Amur General Government in 1901 was Khabarosk, situated in the Maritime Province about 400 miles from Vladivistok, and not so remote as to preclude publication and enforcement. But it appears doubtful that publication or complete enforcement ever took place. The Japanese Government maintains that it has no knowledge of such regulations and that at no time has it recognized their validity. It will be recalled that regulations, their notoriety, and failure of the British Government to acknowledge their existence, were points at issue in *United Kingdom* v. *Norway*. In the case here, however, the Japanese position appears at this time to be far more solidly established than was that of the United Kingdom.

(b) "It is well known that the entire coast of the Bay penetrates deeply into the mainland, is part af ɟhe territory of the U.S.S.R., and that the shape of the Bay itself shows that it forms an inseparable part of the land territory of the USSR." A study of the map will indicate that in part this statement is reasonably correct. From a geographical point of view there are two deep indentations into the littoral. These are Ussuri Bay and Amur Bay. A closing line from Maidel Point on the East to Clarke Point on the West would, geographically speaking, mark the outer limits of these indentations. From a mariner's point of view, the reasonable conclusion as to the limits of the indentation would be that of a ˡine drawn between Askold Island and Cape Gamov. These are the two landmarks that navigators might be expected to use in entering the bay.[2] Outside the, line Askold-Gamov, neither the navigator nor the geographer would be likely to view the sea area as being a part of the penetration.

The degree to which this penetration has become an inseparable part of the land territory of the USSR is a matter that is difficult to assess and is certainly changeable with the times. It is highly doubtful that there exists the same degree of economic inseparability that exists in the case of the fjords of northern Norway or some of the bays of Iceland, where the population depends for its existence on the waters of the bays. On the other hand, Vladivostok and the Soviet Far East in general, have become a large economic and manufacturing complex and, although statistics are absent, it is reasonable to believe that the general commercial traffic in the bay and the marine products harvested from its waters are highly important to the general economic pattern of the area. Such being the case, and given the traditional Russian fear of attack and secretiveness, it might be reasonable to conclude that from a Soviet point of view the waters of Peter the Great Bay, as currently delimited, are an inseparable part of the land territory in the matter of area defense. Were this writer to be charged with maritime defense of the area in question, he too would probably conclude that it would be most desirable to close Peter the Great Bay up to the limits that the Soviet Government has chosen. Such a hypothesis should be viewed as a distinctly *military* one and no more. Along the same line of reasoning, this author would want to revive the King's Chambers of England and Chancellor Kent's view of the Gulf of Mexico. So long as the Soviet Government continues to foster the belief that there is a likelihood of war, the waters of Peter the Great Bay, as presently delimited, will be regarded by them as an inseparable part of the land territory for defense purposes.

(c) "The fact that Peter the Great Bay has been recognized by the neighboring countries of the USSR, for instance by the Chinese People's Republic." The Soviet Government does not indicate any other instances of recognition although it could probably secure such recognition from North Korea, North Vietnam, and other members of the Soviet Bloc. On the other hand, the Japanese Government points out that many States, including the leading maritime countries of the

[2] A useful rule of thumb here is that in planning an entrance to Peter the Great Bay, the navigator, after rounding either Askold Island or Cape Gamov, would instinctively desire to use large scale charts for purposes of steaming into the interior waters of the bay. Actually, the U.S. Navy Hydrographic Office Charts are so arranged as to provide for this requirement, which to the mariner is an obvious one.

world have lodged protests against the decision for the present delimitation.

(3) *The Japanese Position on the Law*

(a) "The decision illegally infringes the fishery rights and navigation long enjoyed by the nationals of Japan." Assuming, for the moment, that some part of Peter the Great Bay is inland waters, then it must be pointed out that under international law, the littoral State has the complete right to control the shipping within such waters, or to exclude altogether shipping in internal waters. Outside internal waters, but within the marginal belt, foreign shipping continues to have the right of innocent passage. Fishing, of course, does not necessarily come within the meaning of innocent passage if the foreign fishing vessels

> do not observe such laws and regulations as the coastal State may make and publish in order to prevent these vessels from fishing in the territorial sea.[3]

Inasmuch as there is no agreement upon the width of the territorial sea, this writer will hypothesize that the universally agreed minimum width is three nautical miles and that any greater limit is at least not universally recognized and at the most is actively disputed. In the instant case the width of twelve miles claimed by the Soviet Union is not common ground as between the parties. This being posited, we can further consider the alleged infringement of navigation rights. The Soviet Union has the Port of Nakhodka open to foreign shipping, subject to certain regulations. Article 16(2) of the 1958 Geneva Convention provides:

> In the case of ships proceeding to internal waters, the coastal state shall also have the right to take the necessary steps to prevent any breach of the conditions to which admission of those ships to those waters is subject.

It would appear then that in connection with the approach to Nakhodka port, there is no illegal infringement of navigation rights.

Now with respect to navigation otherwise in the marginal belt, our attention may be directed to the following provisions of the 1958 Geneva Convention:

> Art. 16(3). Subject to the provisions of paragraph 4 [straits], the coastal state may without discrimination amongst foreign ships, suspend *temporarily in specified areas* of the territorial sea the innocent passage of foreign ships if such suspension is essential for the protection of security. Such suspension shall take effect only after having been duly published. (Italics supplied.)

[3] Art. 14(5) of 1958 Genva Convention on the Territorial Sea and the Contiguous Zone.

Article 17 provides:

> Foreign ships exercising the right of innocent passage shall comply with the laws and regulations enacted by the coastal state in conformity with these articles and other rules of international law and, in particular, with such laws and regulations relating to transport and navigation.

It is not evident at this time that the Soviet Union has issued any regulations generally prohibiting the passage of foreign ships in its marginal belt. On the other hand, the present limits of the inland waters, as decreed by the Soviet Union, do constitute an infringement upon previous rights of innocent passage simply by reason of pushing the area of Soviet jurisdiction, actual or potential, further to seaward. Moreover, the above-cited provisions allow for considerable latitude on the part of the Soviet Union for imposing restrictions on innocent passage of foreign vessels. We shall consider below the alleged illegality of the overall Soviet decision.

> b. "... the distance across the entrance of the sea area... exceeds one hundred miles, and moreover, contrary to the assertion of the Government of the USSR, the indentation is by no means deep. It is beyond dispute that such an indentation as in the present case can not be recognized under international law as a bay, the waters within which are to be considered internal waters, even though its entire coast may belong to one States."

As we have indicated above, the indentation is a fairly deep one if it is in relation to a closing line that is shorter and closer inshore. But, in comparison with the Soviet-selected closing line it is not very deep. But argument about such comparison is not calculated to be very profitable, inasmuch as the present wording of Article 7, Paragraph 6 of the 1958 Geneva Convention removes all restrictions as to what constitutes a bay in cases where the so-called "historic" bays are concerned. In its Judgment in *United Kingdom* v. *Norway*, the Court would not entertain the suggestion of the United Kingdom that it rule upon a definition of a bay. Unfortunately, the International Law Commission and the 1958 Geneva Convention provided no more guidance with respect to historic bays than did the Court. In view of the negative positions taken by these bodies, it becomes very difficult to overcome the presumption that at this juncture there is little within the framework of international law to provide any sort of geographical limit upon what a State may declare to be a historic bay. It must be concluded therefore that this particular contention by Japan has little to substantiate it at this time.

c. "... the Government of the USSR recognized in these Conventions [1907 and 1928] the existence within the said Bay of waters belonging to the High Seas."

The 1907 treaty provides that fishing shall be prohibited in the territorial waters of Peter the Great Bay from Cape Povorotny to Cape Gamov. At that time (before the 1910 Arbitration), there very often occurred a rather unclear use of terms and we believe that at the time of the treaty, the word territorial, when applied to bays, meant internal waters, inside the closing line. It is therefore believed that, as of 1907, Russia tacitly acknowledged that waters outside the closing line and the 3-mile limit were high seas. There appears to be nothing that would warrant a contradiction of this inference.

The 1928 treaty provides that fishing shall be prohibited in Peter the Great Bay inside the Povorotni-Gamov line, but "not, as a matter of course, including high seas." Does this mean that it was agreed that there were some high seas areas inside the line? If it does not, then it would have been unnecessary to place the high seas proviso in the article. The Convention contains no protocol explaining the location of the boundaries of Soviet internal waters or marginal belt in this area. Without intending to second-guess what the negotiators may have had in mind, we may note in passing that Japan was in a very strong bargaining position, power-wise, in 1928, and that her negotiators may have insisted that fishing must be permitted in so much of the area inside the line as was high seas. Even if wedouble the unilaterally proclaimed 12 mile rule of the Soviet Union and thus obtain a 24-mile rule of bays, there would be some high seas area inside the line. Marginal belt or territorial waters are not mentioned withrespect to this part of the Convention. It is believed that a definite conclusion as to the intentions of the parties can only be made by study of the following:

(1) The *Travaux Préparatoires of the Convention.*

(2) Post-Treaty orders to Soviet Fishery patrol boats.

(3) Records of arrests for alleged violations and action taken thereon.

We do not have access to such information and thus will confine our conclusions to these points:

(1) Japan did acknowledge exclusive Soviet jurisdiction to *some* area of the waters inside the line, for fishing purposes.

(2) Japan did not concede that Peter the Great Bay in its entirety was Soviet internal waters and cannot be interpreted as having done so. It is highly doubtful that in 1928 she would have bargained that far.

It is more likely, but by no means positive, that the Soviet Union conceded the existence of *some* area of high seas inside the Povorotni-Gamov line.

(4) *Soviet Position on the Law*

(a) The Soviet Union argues that the bay historically belongs to Soviet internal waters by reason of special geographical, economic and defense conditions, as well as by a predecessor provincial Government's assertion of administrative control over all of the bay's waters from Povorotni Point to Tuman-Ula. First, we might note that the length of time (or history) in which exclusive possession may have existed is highly flexible. Judge Alvarez wrote:

> A comparatively recent usage relating to the territorial sea may be of greater effect than an ancient usage unsufficiently proved.[4]

The notion of "time immemorial" has no application to Peter the Great Bay nor can it have to any bay whose possession commenced during the age of discovery or colonization. The "history" can be short, but when we admit this, we come very close to suggesting the likely presence of a dynamic quality about a State's interest in a particular bay. This, in turn, suggests that the claim to exclusive possession may be an expanding one. Here the case is quite different from *United Kingdom* v. *Norway*. In that dispute we had an expanding foreign fishing industry entering an area which had been used, within some identifiable limits by the people of another State for a great many years. And it was an area upon whose waters the littoral inhabitants were greatly dependent for their livelihood. In Peter the Great Bay, we have the situation where the littoral States interest is *expanding outward* and where the foreign State, very dependent economically upon sea products is attempting to continue to hold the line on the sources of these products. It would appear that the problem can best be solved by endeavoring to establish what part, if any, of the bay has been historically tied to the land domain. Obviously there must be an outer limit to the expansion process. This seems all the more important when the claim being propounded by the littoral State exceeds the true geographical limits of a bay, the *inter fauces terrae* of nature. Such is the case we have before us. Now, in assessing the degree of this tie to the land domain, and the history of it, it would appear necessary to refrain from according equal weight to all of the items of

[4] *I.C.J. Reports, 1951*, p. 152.

evidence submitted. The fact that Poutiatin surveyed a part of the area and that Muraviev-Amursky named the Bay and settled Vladivostok might be very significant were there no other factors of greater significance. What seems of greater moment is the continuous Russian prohibition of fishing in the inner reaches of the bay which have been, since 1872, a military area. What also seems of greater moment is that more or less continuously from 1907 to 1944 there was an inner area in the bay where fishing by foreigners was prohibited, and so acknowledged by Japan. The limits of this area are such as not to do violence to the geographical conception of a bay, *inter fauces terrae*, although admittedly they are generous. It is within this area, also that mine barrages were laid. The Provincial Government's decree might be of much moment in the consideration, if it had been enforced during the period of its existence, known to those to whom it was adverse, and acquiesced in by the foreign States. It meets none of these elementary criteria.

(b) The Soviet Union takes the position that the Conventions of 1907 and 1928 granted only a temporary right, and that by those Conventions Japan acknowledged the status of the Bay as internal waters since the Soviet Union could not grant fishery rights on the high seas. But the articles in question read: "within the limits of the territorial waters of the following ... Peter the Great Bay, from Cape Povorotny to Cape Gamov, including the islands within." There seems little doubt that the Japanese Government in 1907 and 1928 were willing only to concede that this line was the *limit of the bay's "territorial waters."* Moreover, both treaties mentioned, as a separate bay, Possiet bay, which by the terms of the present decree is not mentioned and is evidently considered as being entirely within the Peter the Great Bay area. It is believed that the Soviet Government reads into these two treaties a conception that is not supported by their wording, and one that was probably not in the minds of the negotiators on either side.

(c) A part of the Soviet Union *Note Verbale* of 7 January 1958 reads:

> ... and by the protocol of 1944 the prohibited area was expanded to all of the bay.

As has been observed above, the Japanese Government maintains that the prohibition of 1944 was for the duration of the war only. We do not have the addendum to the Protocol showing that such a termination of the prohibition was agreed to by the Soviet Union. Such agreement does not exist in the body of the Protocol, but we have the word of Mr. Romanov that it is included in addenda thereto.[5] It is to be observed that the Protocol does not contain an agreement on the part of the Japanese Government to the effect that they will restrain or prohibit Japanese fishermen from operating beyond the line. Rather, the Protocol contains the agreement by the Japanese Government that her fishermen as well as other foreigners are prohibited from fishing beyond the line in question. The present Japanese argument is that it was not their intention to recognize that the waters in question were internal to the Soviet Union. Whether or not Japan's bargaining position in the Far East on 30 March 1944 was less favorable than that of the Soviet Union is debatable, and raising the issue of duress would involve some highly awkward questions at the present time. In any event, the tenor of the Protocol seems clearly to indicate that Japanese fishermen were being forcibly ousted. Nevertheless, the fact that Japan alone conceded to the Soviet Union the right of prohibition as against herself and other foreigners does not serve to constitute the waters internal waters as against other maritime States who do not recognize the right of this prohibition. Apparently no other State save the Chinese Peoples Republic does recognize the Soviet claim.

(d) The Soviet *note verbale,* in another passage, reads:

> The fishery conventions concluded between Russia and Japan in 1907, and between the USSR and Japan in 1928, and also the Soviet-Japan Protocol of 1944 extending for five years the validity of the Convention of 1928, are based upon the principle that Peter the Great Bay belongs to the Soviet Union.

Viewed as a whole, the Conventions of 1907 and 1928 appear to be designed to grant to Japan fishing concessions in the territorial waters of Russia or the Soviet Union. They prohibit fishing in particular waters: Peter the Great Bay inside a specified line and Posiett Bay. It appears that by these arguments Japan conceded that the waters inside these lines belonged to Russia-Soviet Union, no more and no less. The phrase concerning the 1944 extension of the 1928 Convention for five years requires some mention. The Protocol provides that the five year extension shall be:

> according to the conditions established in the present protocol.

One of the "conditions" was a prohibition, the change to limits of Peter the Great Bay inside which fishing was prohibited. But apparent-

[5] V. A. Romanov, "The Gulf of Peter the Great – Internal Waters of the Soviet Union," 5 *Sovetskoe Gosudarstvoi Pravo* (Soviet State and Law) (May 1958), pp. 47–55.

ly this prohibition was only for the duration of the war. The amended treaty expired on 1 January 1949 at which time Japan and the Soviet Union were still in a technical state of war.

There is no question in this writer's mind but what the 1907 and 1928 Conventions were based upon the principle that Peter the Great Bay belongs to the Soviet Union. The limits of the Bay, as defined in those Conventions were recognized by Japan and apparently acquiesced in by other States. Certainly we know of no protest against them. The intimation by the Soviet Union that these limits were merely representative of a concession to Japan whereby Japanese fishermen were permitted to operate in Russian/Soviet waters up to those limits appears highly tenuous. Neither in 1907 nor in 1928 was Japan in a position of poor bargaining *vis à vis* the other Party. Accordingly, all the Soviet Union has to support her right to the present limit is a well-hidden regulation of 1901 and the expired 1944 Protocol in which Japan certainly did get the worst of the bargain.

(5) *Conclusion*

It appears to this writer that an excellent argument can be made to show that the inner reaches of Ussuri and Amur Bays, to landward of Kozarevich Island, have been closely tied to the surrounding land since about 1872. It is nor evident that at any time since then have they been regarded as high seas by any other State. It appears that an almost equally good case can be made for an further extension of internal waters to the Cape Povorotny-Cape Gamov line. By the terms of the 1907 and 1928 Conventions, fishing beyond this line was prohibited *for strategic reasons*. As we have indicated immediately above, however, the Soviet case for claiming all the waters inside a line Cape Povorotny-Tuman Ula is on much more tenuous grounds, despite the wording of the 1944 Protocol wherein Japan agreed to the prohibition both for herself and other foreigners.

The difficulty with the instant situation is the attitude taken by Japan, the United States, the United Kingdom and others who protested the Soviet action of 21 July 1957. The Soviet Union proclaimed all of Peter the Great Bay, up to the Cape Povorotny-Tumen Ula line as an inland sea. The Japanese and other protests refuse to recognize that *any part of the Bay* can justifiably be accorded such status. In assuming such an attitude, the protesting States weaken their case. Before an International tribunal, it would not be difficult for the Soviet Union to argue convincingly on the historic character of the

Bay, within the limits Cape Povorotny-Cape Gamov. Before such a tribunal, an almost equally good case agaainst the present enlargement could be made by Japan. As the matter now stands, with inflexibility evidenced by both parties, a relatively simple compromise solution, quite tenable on an objective review of the facts, is stalled by the intransigent positions taken by both sides.[6]

[6] The writer is not unmindful of the rather extensive literature on the Soviet attitude toward international law that has accumulated during the last forty years. A discussion of it, however, would appear to add little to an understanding of the instant case save, perhaps, that most writers are agreed that the Soviet Union regards the treaty as the most important and perhaps only valid source of international law. As of the time it was written, Emanuel Margolis presents in his unpublished doctoral thesis, what is perhaps the best synthesis of views on this point. Emanuel Margolis, *Certain Aspects of the Impact of Communism on International Law* (Harvard PhD thesis, 1951), pp. 49–52. See also: Timothy A. Taracouzio, *The Soviet Union and International Law* (1935), pp. 13, 63–66; Rudolf Schlesinger, *Soviet Legal Theory*, 2nd Ed. (1951), p. 286; and the excellent recent paper of Oliver J. Lissitzyn, "Western and Soviet Perspectives on International Law – A Comparison," *Proceedings of the American Society of International Law*, 1959, pp. 21–30.

PART THREE

THE BAY WITHIN THE LITTORAL OF TWO OR MORE STATES

CHAPTER NINE

THE BAY WITHIN THE LITTORAL OF TWO OR MORE STATES

Section A Introduction

Sir Hersch Lauterpacht in his Eighth Edition of *Oppenheim's International Law* (volume I) writes:

Gulfs and bays surrounded by the land of one and the same littoral State whose entrance is so wide that it cannot be commanded by coast batteries, and, further, as a rule, *all gulfs and bays enclosed by the land of more than one littoral State, however narrow their entrance may be are non-territorial.* They are parts of the open sea, the marginal belt inside the gulfs and bays excepted. (Italics mine).[1]

In his footnote to this statement, the distinguished English jurist writes:

This is not uncontested. A few writers – see, for instance, Twiss, i, Sect. 181 – assert that narrow gulfs and bays surrounded by the land of two different States are territorial, the central line dividing the territorial portions. However, the majority of writers do not accept this opinion, and it would seem that the practice of States likewise rejects it, except in the case of such bays as possess the characteristics of a closed sea.[2]

Professor Leo Gross writes:

... for if there is a rule of international law regarding which there is practically no controversy, it is the rule that bays and gulfs with several littoral states, "however narrow their entrance may be, are non-territorial..."[3]

Professor Gross cites Lauterpacht and Gidel.[4] Professor Gidel cites numerous authorities.

The question that rises in the mind of the ocean mariner, and perhaps in the mind of the geographer, is what makes a bay having two or more

[1] Lauterpacht, *Oppenheim's International Law*, vol. I, 8th Ed., (1955), p. 508.

[2] *Ibid.*

[3] Leo Gross, "The Geneva Conference on the Law of the Sea and the right of Innocent Passage through the Gulf of Aqaba," 53 *American Journal of International Law* (1959), pp. 564–594.

[4] Gilbert Gidel, III *Le Droit International Public de la Mer* (1934), pp. 593–608.

States bordering upon it so much different from any other bay? Surely since Lauterpacht, Gross, and Gidel are so positive on this point, there must be very strong ground for their taking the position they do. The problem of navigating into a bay within the littoral of two or more States presents no special problems. Despite the fact that the inhabitants of the shores of such a bay may be separated by national boundaries, their dependence upon the natural resources of the bay, if any, is likely to be the same for all, unless whatever normal dependence that would exist has been artificially affected by the policies of one or another of the littoral States. The utility of the bay as a shelter is likely to be the same for all the inhabitants of the shores unless the policies or economy of one or more of the hinterland States is different from that of the others.

But there *are* important differences brought about by the existence of State boundaries terminating at the shore of the bay. By reason of the differences in geography, natural resources, economy, and political structure, the bay in question *may* be of greater importance to one of the littoral States than to another: one might have a port elsewhere and the other State might have its only port on the bay in question. One State may be sovereign over most of the shore line while another is sovereign over very little. One State may have a rich hinterland and the other a very poor one. The two or more States may, respectively, pursue policies that are antithetical. The fundamental difference is this: in the case of a bay in single State's littoral, that State exercises sovereignty *ergo omnes*, while in the instant case two adjacent neighbors are, by their geographical proximity, *forced to share* the shores of the bay. If the States have a significant community of interest, at least with respect to the bay, they will no doubt arrive at some agreement as to the exercise of sovereignty over it, or failing that they will allow their differences to be settled through judicial proceedings. On the other hand, they may perceive of no useful purpose in *sharing* sovereignty over the waters of the bay, and thus by default permit the waters to be regarded as high seas. Or, they may be unable to agree on water boundaries, with the same end result. Or they may choose to exercise collective sovereignty over some or all of the bay's waters. It appears, then, that when two or more States border on a single bay, their geographical propinquity raises a host of problems not encountered when the bay is entirely in the littoral of one State. Commander R. H. Kennedy, RN (RET), in his document, *A brief Geographical and Hydrographical Study of Bays and Estuaries the Coasts of which belong to different States,*[5] lists a total of fifty such arms of the sea. Of these, thirty are actually estuaries through which run boundaries which are actually the continuations of river boundaries originating in the hinterland. It is quite natural that the boundaries in the estuaries should be continuations, unless, as in the Grisdebarna case [6] there is evident an ancient usage that brings about some different rule. In the cases of estuaries, where there is waterborne traffic, the waters are likely to be used in common, if for no other reason than simple rules of the road convenience. Since they are so used, and often by ships of ocean going commerce, they may simply never have been subject to formal sovereignty declarations. This writer has sailed in several of these estuaries and they are subject to the same number of sailing and administrative rules as any other bays or harbors. The rules are formulated by reason of the obvious community of interest that exists. As a practical matter the size of the entrance is quite important and no mariner would, for one moment, consider himself authorized to enjoy the same freedom of action in, say, Lough Foyle as he would on the high seas. Now at what point in comparative sizes, the littoral State practice might more likely lean toward considering such bays or estuaries as high seas is difficult to determine. But it is doubted that the limit is marked by twice the width of a 3-mile marginal belt.

In his somewhat perfunctory way of lumping together wide bays and (as a rule) bays enclosed by the land belonging to more than one State, Lauterpacht writes that foreign fishing-vessels cannot be compelled to comply with municipal regulations of the littoral State concerning the mode of fishing. Noting the adjective qualifier, "however narrow their entrance may be," we should question whether this is, "as a rule," true. Here we must, perforce, enter upon some speculation. We shall take the case of Flensburg Bay which is shared by Germany and Denmark. Commander Kennedy, quoting from the British Admiralty's *Baltic Sea Pilot*,[7] writes that intensive fishing is carried out throughout the year in the whole bay.[8] Both for conservation reasons as well as for control of traffic and obstructions to navigation, there are likely to be local regulations which local fishermen are required to obey. If we take the high seas argument and Lauterpacht's statement concerning fishing regulations, then any fisherman, German, Danish, or other would be under no compulsion to obey the regulations. Such

[5] UN Document A/Conf.13/15.
[6] J. B. Scott. *The Hague Court Reports* (1916), p. 130.
[7] British Admiralty Publication, I *Baltic Sea Pilot*, 7th Ed., 1944.
[8] UN Document A/Conf.13/1, p. 217.

a state of affairs would doubtless find a rather low level of tolerance among Danish and German officials.

We are led from here to a return to the idea of community of interest and, it is believed a fairly important factor of consideration. Many bays and estuaries bordered by two or more States were at one time and sometimes fairly recently, within the littoral of a single country Flensburg Fjord was in the Duchy of Schleswig until 1864, within Prussia/Germany from 1864 to 1918, and since 1918 divided between Germany and Denmark. Before one can generalize upon the status of such a bay in international law, it would appear prudent to inquire whether it is the arbitrarily drawn boundary which will govern the State practice with respect to such a bay, or whether it will be the continuing community of interest which will do so. Is there not some probability that the practice of States in certain of such cases may really find its origin in the necessary local arrangements worked out in an effort to disturb as little as possible the continuing local order of things? It is for these reasons, that this author is unable to agree that the rule propounded by Lauterpacht is either as general or as certain as he intimates. It is doubted that the State practice is as well understood or even known, as he seems to suggest. It is not considered feasible to set about, in this book, to determine what the actual State practice is with respect to every one of the bays in Commander Kennedy's document, nor is it even feasible to inspect a representative number of them.[9] What can be suggested, however, is the rather strong likelihood that every bay having more than one State on its littoral has its own peculiar set of factors: Size, configuration, needs of the inhabitants on the littoral, traditional usage, relations of the neighboring States, sea traffic in the bay, and fisheries in the bay. While these are the same factors at work in any other bay, the difference in attitude toward sovereignty probably lies in the fact that where two States occupy the littoral, the factors militating toward exclusive possession must be of a very high order of importance in the eyes of local inhabitants and decision makers. They must be of such an order as to outweigh the advantages that the two or more States might have in arriving at agreement on water boundaries, fishing rules, pilot regulations, and so forth. It is suggested, too, that where two or more States are forced by geography to live side by side on one bay there is diminished prestige value to owning only part of it. It would seem that

[9] Moreover, as we have indicated by the example in Section D, below, there may be reason to believe that Commander Kennedy has not included all bays of the type in question.

only where there are obvious requirements for jurisdictional rules will there be agreement as among the States with regard to the status of the bay as internal waters. In the case of some bays, such as Flensburg, it is suggested that an intolerable and chaotic state of affairs might result if the States concerned would regard such bays as high seas. The persistent entertaining of such an attitude would probably diminish seriously the usefulness of the bay to the inhabitants on its littoral.

In practice, it is not believed that a general rule on such bays exists at the present time. In fact, both Professor Hyde and the Harvard Research suggest that there is no requirement of international law which prevents the riparian States from jointly claiming the bay and agreeing upon a division of its waters as inland waters.

Professor Francois, the *Special Rapporteur* of the International Law Commission at its 8th Session, expressed the view that the situation of the Gulf of Aqaba was exceptional – possibly unique.[10] A study of the world's bays and internal waters discloses that the situation wherein a State has a port in the bay or estuary but does not have possession of the shores at the point where the bay connects with the open sea is exceptional – but by no means unique. A study of Commander Kennedy's document discloses that such is the situation with respect to the following bays:

a. The Tana Lagoon, shared by Ghana and The Ivory Coast. Here The Ivory Coast controls the headlands. (On Commander Kennedy's Chart, it is called French West Africa).[11]

b. The Gulf of Fonseca. The headlands are, respectively, in El Salvador and Nicaraugua.[12]

c. Chetumal Bay in Central America. The only navigable entrance to the bay, hence the headlands of it, are in British Honduras. The head of the bay is in Mexico.[13]

We have another case where there is a blurring between what can be regarded as an estuary and what is generally regarded as an international river. This is the estuary of the River Schelde, both shores of which are in the Netherlands. The highly important Belgian port of Antwerp is just above the point where the Schelde widens into an estuary.

This book has to do with the law of bays, of which the bays lying

[10] *Yearbook of the International Law Commission*, 1956, p. 202, par. 89.

[11] UN Document A/Conf.13/1, p. 223.

[12] *Ibid.*, p. 226.

[13] *Ibid.*, p. 227.

within the littoral of two or more States represent a special case. It is not believed that one can, within the limits of this work, be definitive with respect to this special case. Each bay of this type is in itself a special situation wherein the practices of the States concerned have usually evolved through the mutual recognition of their combined needs. Four special situations are discussed hereunder. In two cases, the Bays of Fonseca and Fundy, differences were submitted to judicial decision. In a third case, The Bay of Gibraltar, the littoral States are silent on their differences and seem to conduct their affairs in the Bay in studied disregard of such differences and of each other. In the fourth case, The Gulf of Aqaba, there are differences that are highly complicated and well publicized.

Section B The gulf of fonseca

The Gulf of Fonseca, bordered by the Pacific coast territories of El Salvador, Honduras, and Nicaraugua, is about fifty miles long and has a mean width of thirty miles.[1] The distance between the headlands at the entrance is nineteen and one-third miles. The headlands are in El Salvador and Nicaraugua, respectively. Honduras has a coast line of about forty miles inside the Gulf and this is the only frontage of Honduras on the Pacific coast. The land boundaries separating the countries bordering the Gulf are marked by the rivers Rio Goascorau and Rio Negro. There are a number of islands within the Gulf. The principal port of El Salvador, La Union, is on the Gulf and is connected to the interior of the country by a branch of International Railways of Central America, a United States corporation. The principal port of Honduras, Amapola, is also located on the Gulf. The port of Honduras nearest the capital and chief city of the country, Amapola, is connected with the interior by motor road. A port of Nicaraugua, El Viejo, is on the river Estero Real about twenty miles from the Gulf. El Viejo, though connected to the interior of the country by rail is of minor importance. The Gulf has well-sheltered anchorages in a number of places.

The international case involving the Gulf of Fonseca arose after the conclusion on 5 august 1914 of a treaty between Nicaraugua and the United States – commonly known as the Bryan-Chamorro

[1] Descriptive material concerning the Gulf of Fonseca is taken from the following sources: Report of *Salvador* v. *Nicaraugua*, (1916), 11 *American Journal of International Law* (1917), p. 674; UN Document A/Conf.13/15, p. 203; U.S. Navy Hydrographic Office Publication No. 84; *Encyclopeadia Britannica* World Atlas (1951).

Convention.[2] This convention provided, *inter alia,* the granting of a ninety-nine year right "to establish, operate and maintain a naval base at such place on the territory of Nicaraugua bordering on the Gulf of Fonseca as the Government of the United States may select".[3] El Salvador protested the Convention [4] and in 1916 brought an action against Nicaraugua in the Central American Court of Justice.[5] El Salvador alleged, *inter alia:* (1) that the establishment of a naval base in the immediate vicinity of El Salvador constituted a "serious menace to its free and independent life"; and (2) that the Bryan-Chamorro Convention "ignores and violates the rights of dominion [co-ownership] which Salvador has in the Gulf of Fonseca. El Salvador urged that she, Honduras and Nicaraugua had co-ownership of the Gulf, which, she maintained, was a historic bay. She petitioned the Court, *inter alia,* to compel Nicaraugua to abstain from fulfilling the Bryan-Chamorro treaty.

In its reply, the Government of Nicauraugua stipulated that the Gulf of Fonseca was a closed bay, but only because of its smallness and not because of any communal ownership stemming from a time when the three countries were one political entity – the former Federal Republic of Central America.[6] It was maintained that absolute juris-

[2] This was really the third attempt to conclude such a convention, and apparently much of the initiative for it came from Nicaraugua, to whom the initial payment of three million dollars was a major consideration. For the diplomatic background of the treaty see George A. Finch, "The Treaty with Nicaraugua granting Canal and other rights to the United States," 10 *American Journal of International Law* (1916), pp. 344–351.

[3] III *Redmond,* pp. 2740–2. The text of the treaty, and U.S. ratification is also reprinted in U.S. Naval War College, *International Law Documents,* 1924, at pages 31–34. In consenting to ratification of this treaty, the Senate of the United States inserted the following proviso:

> "whereas, Costa Rica, Salvador and Honduras have protested against the ratification of said Convention in the fear or belief that said Convention might in some respect impair existing rights of said States; therefore, it is declared by the Senate that in advising and consenting to the ratification of the said Convention as amended such advice and consent are given with the understanding, to be expressed as a part of the instrument of ratification, that nothing in said Convention is intended to affect any existing right of any of the said named States."

Nicaraugua accepted this understanding and ratifications were exchanged on 22 June 1916. I *Hackworth's Digest* (1940). p. 702.

[4] El Salvador, Costa Rica, and Honduras protested at nearly all stages of the negotiations. The second attempted treaty was reported to contain provisions similar to those in the Platt Amendment to the U.S.-Cuban Treaty of 22 May 1903. I *Malloy* p. 632. The general tenor of protests was to the effect that U.S. presence in Nicaraugua would dominate the entire country. Finch, *op. cit.* See also Salvador R. Gonzales, "The Neutrality of Honduras and the Question of the Gulf of Fonseca," 10 *American Journal of International Law* (1916), pp. 509–542.

[5] Established 20 December 1907 at the Central American Peace Conference at Washington. II *Malloy,* p. 2399; Hyde, *op. cit.,* p. 1599.

[6] This point seems to be taken up in most subsequent discussions of the case. e.g. I *Hackworth's Digest* at page 704. In light of the current situation in the Gulf of Aqaba, it would appear desirable to emphasize this point.

diction could only be coextensive with the coast line of each State concerned. The Court's problem, therefore, insofar as it bears upon the instant discussion, was three-fold:

(a) To determine the basis upon which the Gulf of Fonseca should be denominated a closed or "territorial bay," and

(b) Whether there existed among the three States a community or co-ownership of the waters of the bay.

(c) The juridical nature of the co-ownership, if it was found to exist.

The majority of the Court found that the Gulf of Fonseca was a closed bay for the following reasons:

(a) That it was incorporated into the patrimony of the Crown of Castile from the time of its discovery in 1522 until 1821.

(b) That this exclusive possession continued during the existence of the successor State, the Federal Republic of Central America, until its dissolution in 1839.

(c) That the three State successors to the Federal Republic incorporated into their respective territories, as a necessary dependency thereof for geographical reason and purposes of common defense, both the Gulf and its archipelago.

(d) That the ownership and possession of the Gulf was notoriously affirmed.

(e) That ownership was enjoyed and maintained without protest or contradiction by any other State.

(f) That "representative authorities" have performed acts and enacted laws having to do with the national security, the observance of health and with fiscal regulations.

(g) That possession has been peaceful and continuous.

(h) That the special geographical configuration safeguards many interests of vital importance to the economic, commercial, agricultural and industrial life of the riparian States. In its judgment, the Court went to great lengths to stress this aspect of the Bay, citing authoritative charts and the opinions of hydrographic surveyors. The measurements of the bay are set out in precise detail.

(i) That it fulfills the characteristics of a closed sea as enunciated by the tribunal in the North Atlantic Coast Fisheries Arbitration of 1910, and in Dr. Drago's dissent.

(j) That the closed status was specifically recognized by the Government of the United States.[7]

[7] The judgment quotes from a United States note to El Salvador, dated 18 February 1914: "In your protest the position is taken that the Gulf of Fonseca is a territorial bay whose waters are within the jurisdiction of the bordering States. This position the Department is not disposed to controvert."

The Court then found that there existed a real co-ownership of the bay, as among the States whose territories form its littoral. The Court's judgment on this question suggests an intertemporal approach:

> ... in regard to the co-ownership in the Gulf of Fonseca claimed by the high party complainant, and in view of what is alleged on that point by the high party defendant, the question of division, demarcation or delimitation of jurisdictions between the provinces that constituted the patrimony of the Spanish Crown must be examined in the light of historical truth in order to harmonize their conclusions with the legal relations that now govern among the riparian States.

The Court then went on to cite the facts which would seem to contribute to the conclusion noted above:

(a) That during the Spanish Empire period, there were provisional boundaries and disputes concerning them, but there were many errors in mapping, and little Royal concern about provincial jurisdictions. This resulted in much confusion and general absence of detail.

(b) That inasmuch as the successor States bordering on the Gulf lived in relative harmony, with respect to the use and benefits of its waters, the Governments concerned themselves only with fixing upon those portions thereof where the exercise of rights of neighboring countries might involve them in conflict. The Court noted that mixed boundary commissions had established division lines extending into the Gulf but terminating short of points where the waters were entirely divided. In short, no complete division was ever made.

(c) That in accordance with a text-writer's view, things which belong privately to no one, but are actually owned, must necessarily be possessed in common. Obviously since the Court concluded that the Gulf was a closed bay, and yet concluded that its waters were not divided by complete boundaries, then such ownership must, in part, at least, be a common one.

In ruling upon the juridical nature of the co-ownership, the Court observed that "community is not common in the relations among nations, but it is not inconceivable or an isolated fact." The Court then cited the textbook writer, Heffter [8] and the Austro-Prussian joint sovereignty over Schleswig-Holstein in 1864, as well as certain areas of Chile-Bolivia joint sovereignty.[9] The Court then went on to a private

[8] Although not specifically cited in the opinion, the Court probably had reference to August W. Heffter, *Das Europäische Völkerrecht der Gegenwart* (1888), pp. 148–160, in which the author repeatedly mentions possibility of joint possession.

[9] It was not pointed out that the Austro-Prussian arrangement lasted only from 22 August 1864 until the Bad Gastein Agreement of 14 August 1865. A. J. P. Taylor, *The Struggle for the Mastery of Europe 1848–1918* (1954), pp. 154–7. The Chile-Bolivia arrangement endured

law principle and to a reference to certain common ownership provisions in the civil code of the defendant State, Nicaraugua. In stating and applying the principle, the judgment reads:

> ... none of them could properly dispose of its rights independently without affecting those of other sovereigns, in view of the status of community in which the Gulf has been and is held, thanks to the universal principle handed down by Roman law and faithfully observed in modern law, that copartners may not perform any act disposing of a thing possessed in common except jointly or with the consent of all. The absence of that *joint will* is equivalent to the omission of an empowering formality, since the Government of Nicaraugua lacks the legal capacity to alter by itself the *status jure* existing in the Gulf, and hence is born the right of the high party complainant to hold that the Bryan-Chamorro treaty violates its rights.

Although weighty and overly long,[10] the Court's decision in this case is well argued, and much is to be gained by careful study of it. There was a proven mutuality of interest in the Gulf of Fonseca, as among the littoral States. There was in force a series of treaties of relatively recent vintage which gave legal expression to this interest. The States were sovereign and there was never any question of mutual recognition of that fact. Finally, there was a willingness to submit the dispute to a court of law. It is unfortunate that Nicaraugua, the high party defendant, in its circular note of 24 November 1917 rejected the decision.[11]

Section C THE BAY OF FUNDY

Nearly the entire area of the Bay of Fundy is bordered by one State, Canada, and only a limited part of its coast line belongs to the United States. We shall consider this bay as an example of one being bordered by two or more States, because the dispute concerning its status was settled almost entirely on the basis of geographical factors.

from 1876 to 1884, but under highly unstable conditions. Mary W. Williams, *The People and Politics of Latin America* (1938), pp. 574–6. It would appear that joint sovereignty has had, in general, an unhappy history, save perhaps for the Anglo-French Condominion of the New Hebrides. In coastal waters, and in certain border zones, there is as a practical matter often a good bit of *de facto* joint sovereignty despite the presence of an actual boundary. Hans W. Weigert, *et al*, *Principles of Political Geography* (1956), shows a number of examples at pages 87–89. Such local working arrangements will inevitably come into being whenever there is an undisturbed community of interest.

[10] This writer is inclined to agree with Sir Hersch Lauterpacht that the translation of the judgment published in 11 *American Journal of International Law* does not appear to be satisfactory. Lauterpacht, *Private Law Sources and Analogies of International Law* (1927), p. 288n.

[11] I *Hackworth's Digest* (1940), p. 705.

The specific situation giving rise to the arbitration in which the status of the Bay of Fundy was ruled upon was really only an incident in the prolonged disagreement between the United States and Canada over fishing rights along the Canadian coast. This lengthy dispute which has been discussed elsewhere in this book,[1] was in general laid to rest by the 1910 North Atlantic Coast Fisheries Arbitration.[2]

The schooner *Washington* was seized by a Canadian revenue schooner on 10 May 1843 while fishing ten miles off the Canadian shore in the Bay of Fundy.[3] The vice-Admiralty Court in Yarmouth, Nova Scotia decreed her forfeited to the Crown and ordered her, together with her stores, sold. Her owners claimed damages to the amount of $ 4,121. The case was brought before a Claims Commission provided for under the Anglo-American Claims Convention of 8 February 1853.[4] The Commissioners differing on the case, it was referred to Mr. Joshua Bates, umpire.

Mr. Bates decided that the case turned on the meaning to be given to the word "bays" in the treaty of 1783 between Great Britain and the United States. The British Government had urged that by "bay" it was meant the water to landward of an imaginary line drawn between headlands. Mr. Bates, finding that the doctrine of headlands was new and that headlands were not mentioned in the treaty of 1783, proceeded to decide whether the Bay of Fundy was a bay (hence Canadian territorial water) within the meaning of the treaty. In deciding that it was not a bay within this meaning, Mr. Bates relied upon these points of reasoning:

(a) Being of great size and having several smaller bays on its coasts, the Bay of Fundy must needs have the same meaning as applied to the Bay of Biscay aud the Bay of Bengal over which no nation could assume the right of sovereignty. Comment: While the Bay of Fundy in no wise approximates the Bay of Bengal or the Bay of Biscay either in size or configuration, Mr. Bates was obviously seeking, by analogy, to restrict the size of the body of water to which a State could claim sovereignty under the bay concept. Here one should pause to observe that in 1843–1853, fishing vessels were small, wind-driven and equipped with rather limited capabilities for catching and storing fish. Thus, it is

[1] Chapter FOUR, Section D, above.

[2] *Ibid.*

[3] This case is cited frequently in the literature on the law of the sea: Moore, *International Arbitrations* (1898) IV, pp. 4342–3; I *Moore's Digest* (1906), pp. 785–7; Jessup, *Law of Territorial Waters and Maritime Jurisdiction* (1927), pp. 365–6; U.S. Naval War College, *International Law Situations*, 1904, p. 137.

[4] I *Malloy* 664.

conceivable that a body of water "65 to 75 miles wide and 130 to 140 miles long" would likely loom as a much larger body of water in his eyes than would a similar body extensively fished by foreigners today.

(b) One of the headlands in in the United States, and ships bound to the Passamaquoddy must sail through a large space of the Bay of Fundy.

Comment: Here he pointed out that part of the coast line of the bay belonged to another State. The Passamaquoddy is itself a bay having both Canadian and United States soil on its littoral. (It is to be noted that the exact boundary in Passamaquoddy Bay and in the Bay of Fundy was not settled until 1891.[5] While renouncing the headland theory as a doctrine for bays, Mr. Bates appears to have made use of the term here simply to indentify a geographical phenomenon.

(c) The Islands of Grand Menan (British) and Little Menan (American) are situated on a line from headland to headland, and these islands, declared Mr. Bates, are represented in all geographies as being situated in the Atlantic Ocean.

Comment: Here Mr. Bates relied upon the usage of geographers who, presumably, were to be regarded as being pre-eminently authoritative in determining when an island should or should not be classed as lying in a bay or in the ocean. The implication seems to be that inasmuch as the islands were thus located and labeled by geographers, the Bay of Fundy must be a branch of the high sea. While the services of a professional geographer may be indispensable in the study of problems involving territorial jurisdiction, one should be careful in placing reliance upon how the geographer applies his pen to the page in the process of labeling controversial bodies of water. Accordingly, this writer is unwilling to accord much weight to this pillar of Mr. Bates' reasoning.

Discounting, then, the geographer's assignment of labels, we see that the Bay of Fundy was found to be high seas on two grounds: its large size and the presence of the territory of a second State along a part of the shore of the bay, albeit a relatively small section of the toal shore line. Mr. Bates did not indicate that the points of his reasoning were listed in descending order of importance (or any other order), and in the absence of such indication, we must assume that each appeared of equal weight in his appraisal.

[5] A chartlet of Passamaquoddy Bay is shown in UN Document A/Conf.13/15, at p. 225. For the boundary settlement, see Moore, *International Arbitrations*, I, pp. 65–83.

This writer would hesitate to use the 1853 case of the Bay of Fundy as a point of argument by analogy in respect of the status of any other bay bordered by two or more States.[6] The case is important, however, in that it was settled by reference to geographic factors alone.

Section D THE BAY OF GIBRALTAR [1]

The Bay of Gibraltar has been selected for discussion because, despite its small size, it is rather unique. Controversy over its waters has raged periodically since the British seizure of the Rock from Spain in 1704, and the question, although dormant, remains unsettled down to the present day. The Bay of Gibraltar is of minor commercial value at present, but it has been of great political and military significance for centuries. There is little doubt that today the Rock and the Bay are very real symbols of sentiment in British public opinion, whatever their actual value may be. The Bay is not one of the forty-eight bays mentioned by Commander Kennedy in his United Nations study of bays having coasts belonging to two or more States.[2]

The Bay of Gibraltar is about five miles wide at its entrance between Europa Point and Carnero Point. From the center of its closure line, it has a maximum depth of slightly over six miles. The two ports on the bay are Algeciras in Spain and the British port of Gibraltar. Both of these have man-made harbors.[3] The former has rail egress to other ports of Spain and a limited amount of commercial traffic, chiefly with Moroccan ports on the Strait of Gibraltar. The British Crown Colony of Gibraltar contains a free-port area, dating from about 1716,[4] but it has served primarily as a military and naval base. Aside

[6] Professor Hyde goes so far as to write: "The suggestion may be offered that the Bay of Fundy, by reason of its geographical relationship to the land into which it is projected might be fairly dealt with by the Unitde States and Canada, should they so agree, as a closed bay." *International Law Chiefly as Interpreted and Applied by the United States*, 2nd Edition, vol. I, p. 476.

[1] Despite the failure to mention the Bay of Gibraltar in UN Document A/Conf.13/15, Gibraltar and Gibraltar Bay have been the subjects of an enormous litterature through the years, and it is believed that there is no aspect – economic, military, political, legal, geographic or hydrographic – that has not been discussed on numerous occasions and with great scholarly care. Wilbur C. Abbott, *An Introduction to the Documents Relating to the International Status of Gibraltar 1704–1934* (1934), lists 572 items. For typical histories, see: G. T. Garratt, *Gibraltar and the Mediterranean* (1939); H. W. Howes, *The Story of Gibraltar* (1946); and Allen Andrews, *Proud Fortress* (1959).

[2] UN Document A/Conf.13/15.

[3] U.S. Navy Hydrographic Office Publication No. 151 (1952), Ch. 2. U.S. Navy Hydrographic Office Charts 2430 and 2429. This writer has visited the British port of Gibraltar many times within the past thirteen years. He has had occasion to discuss the Rock and the surrounding area with a number of local officials and residents.

[4] Colonial Office, *Report on Gibraltar 1937* (1958), Ch. VI.

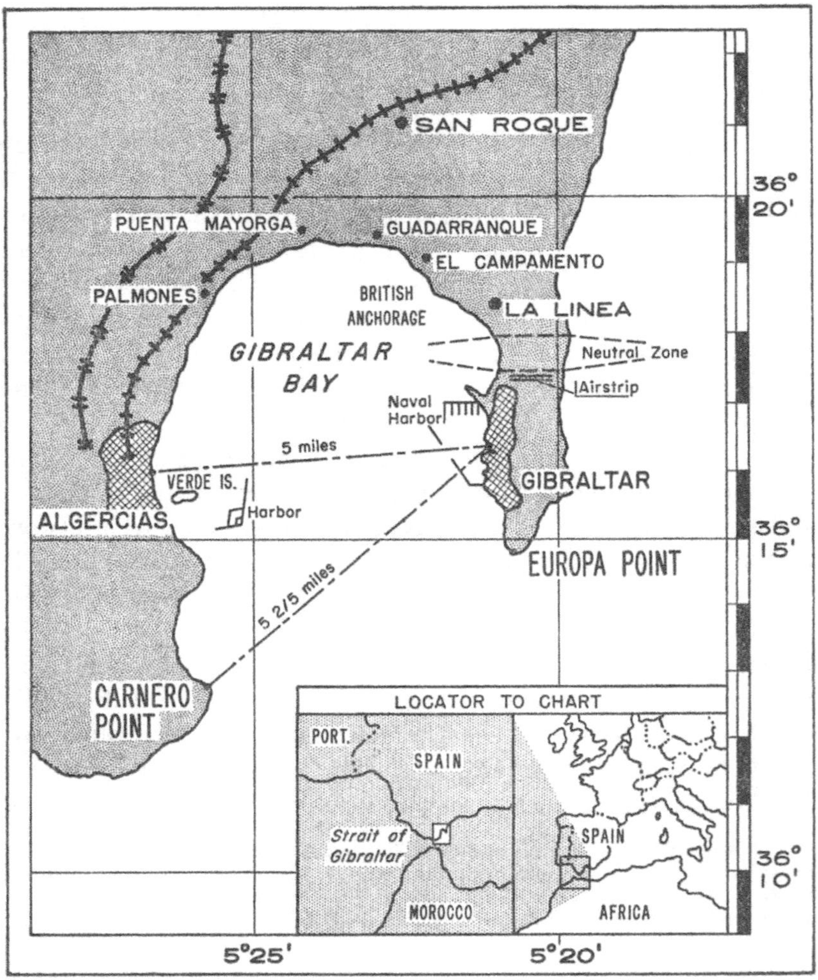

GIBRALTAR BAY

Fig.26

from being something of a tourist attraction, and thus a port of call for passenger liners, Gibraltar's primary commercial importance has been as a coaling and fuel depot for merchant ships.[5]

While even today, Gibraltar might be of some use as a naval base guarding the entrance to the Mediterranean, its military usefulness is likely to be marginal.[6] It was very important as a base in World Wars I and II,[7] although the equivocal neutrality of Spain in both wars was a constant security problem to the Allies and a source of friction between the United Kingdom and Spain. Today, although the Governor of the Crown Colony continues to be a general officer in the British Army[7a] and Gibraltar is the headquarters of a NATO Command,[8] the garrison is of limited strength and the Her Majesty's Dockyard is virtually in a caretaker status· Constant frictions at the border have severely reduced commercial traffic with Spain,[9] and are a source of labor difficulties in Gibraltar where thousands of Spaniards were employed as day laborers.

British Gibraltar is separated by an isthmus about 1/4 mile wide and 1/2 mile long called "neutral ground." It is truly neutral; no one inhabits it; and it is traversed by a two-lane road. The Rock is the object of Spanish irredentism which is revived at intervals through the years. The British possession is about three miles long and 3/4 miles wide. Gibraltar Bay is subject to occasional swift currents and peculiarly strong winds. Large ships usually anchor in the bay and conduct loading from lighters. There is little if any fishing.

The British title to Gibraltar is grounded in Article X of the Treaty of Peace and Friendship concluded on 2/13 July 1713 between Spain and England. This treaty is one of a number of instruments loosely described as the Treaty of Utrecht. The original treaty is in Latin. An English translation of Article X reads:

> The Catholic King does hereby, for himself, his heirs and successors, yield to the Crown of Great Britain the full and entire propriety of the town and castle of

[5] *Ibid.*

[6] Richard A. Preston, "Don't Sell Gibraltar Short," 76 *U.S. Naval Institute Proceedings* (Dec. 1950), pp. 1329–1336; Wyatt E. Barnes, "Changing Trends in the Mediterranean Balance of Power," *Ibid.*, vol. 84 (March 1958), pp. 53–62.

[7] Howes, *op. cit.*, Ch. ix; VADM Giuseppe Fioravanzo, IN, "Italian Strategy in the Mediterranean, 1940–43," 84 *U.S. Naval Institute Proceedings* (Sept. 1958), pp. 65–83; VADM Friedrich Ruge, GFN, *Der Seekrieg*, Tr. CDR M. G. Saunders RN (1957); CDR Marc Antonio Bragodin RIN (Ret), *The Italian Navy in World War II* (1957).

[8] Flag Officer Gibraltar, an officer of the Royal Navy, is also a NATO Commander under Allied Forces Mediterranean.

[9] By reason of these difficulties, American Export Lines shifted its local port of call from Gibraltar to Algericas in 1956. The U.S. Consulate General in Gibraltar, a very old American post, was closed in 1954.

[7a] War Office, *The Army List*, Sept. 1962, p. 113

Gibraltar, together with the port, fortifications, and forts thereunto belonging; and he gives to the said propriety to be held and enjoyed absolutely with all manner of right for ever, without any exception or impediment whatsoever.[10]

The cession was hedged with a number of conditions, none of which are believed directly pertinent to the present discussion. The Article ceding Gibraltar was confirmed in successive treaties between England and Spain: Seville 1729, Aix-La-Chapelle 1748, Paris 1763 and Paris 1783.[11] The cession article and the confirmations thereof are indefinite as respects boundaries and the land boundary has been a matter of occasional dispute. The seaward boundaries, within the Bay of Gibraltar appear never to have been discussed until 1826 when a British merchant ship ran aground in the Neutral Ground area and Spanish coast guards refused access to the ship. The ensuing British note of protest, addressed by the then Foreign Minister, Canning, reads in part:

In the absence of all mention by the Treaty of Utrecht of any boundary, real or imaginary, of the Port of Gibraltar... it becomes necessary in the first place to look for a boundary in the trending of the coast. That boundary is to be found in the curvature of the Coast terminating in the Punta Mala, the whole of which space is within the range of the guns of the garrison. Accordingly that point of land has invariably been considered as the limit of the Port to northward; and from the time of the Fortress coming into possession of Great Britain, Port Charges have... invariably been levied on all vessels anchoring within that limit.[12]

Punta Mala is about $2^1/_2$ miles from the location of the nearest gun emplacements at Gibraltar. Accepting with some misgiving the Canning note's crediting British batteries of 1826 with a range of 5,000 yards, this note meant that all of the water, up to land itself, within the range of the guns was British. The land at this point was (and is) of course Spanish. Inasmuch as the Bay and British land run in a North-South direction, and assuming the same cannon-shot basis for a British claim through the length of the Bay, the British jurisdiction would have extended over slightly less than one half of the surface of the Bay. The waters adjacent to the Spanish soil terminating at neutral ground were claimed as British for good reason. It is in this area that ships calling at Gibraltar customarily anchored and do so to this day.[13]

[10] Carrington, *op. cit.*, p. 8.

[11] *Ibid.*, p. 22.

[12] *Foreign Office Papers*, 97/377, 30 November 1826.

[13] In this anchorage are located several fuel hulks of the Shell Oil Co., Ltd. The writer believes, from his own experience, that this area is the most desirable anchorage by reason of the peculiarly strong wind effects in evidence further to the south along the Bay side of the Rock.

Thus, the Note's reference to the area in which Port Charges were "invariably" levied seems well taken. Obviously, this is a prescriptive basis for the claim.

The following decades, however, saw incessant smuggling from ships in this area adjacent to the Spanish held land. It would appear that the positive attitude shown by the British Government with respect to their claim to the waters was not paralleled by any great zeal in harbor policing. Nevertheless, in 1851, Lord Palmerston re-asserted British rights in strong terms.[14] In 1858, the Spanish Minister in London addressed to the Foreign Office a note, reading in part:

> To put a stop to this perennial source of disputes and difficulties which arise from the maritime boundaries of Gibraltar not having been settled... the Spanish Government is ready to admit the principle that fortresses may extend their jurisdictions as far as the range of the direct shot of their cannons; but at the same time it maintains that the sovereign of the territory whose coasts are washed by the waters in which that jurisdiction is to be exercised [has sovereign rights over such waters].

He then proposed that these problems should be referred to a Commission of two Spaniards and two Englishmen whose terms of reference should be confined to interpreting the Treaty of Utrecht.[15] Lord Derby's Government merely referred back to the Canning Note on which it was prepared to stand firm.[16] A desultory bickering continued. The Spanish Government maintained that the whole of the isthmus was theirs *de jure*. The British stood on their *de facto* right to the field of fire from the fortress.

The dispute flared up again in the eighteen seventies. The Spanish Government proposed a boundary commission. The British Government advised that they would look with favor upon such a commission, subject to the following conditions:

(a) That any arrangement arrived at would be temporary, a *modus vivendi*.

(b) That any arrangement arrived at would be effective only so long as both Parties were at peace.

(c) That no question would be raised as to Great Britain's *right* to a 3-mile jurisdiction around Gibraltar, although she might, as a *modus vivendi* be willing to compromise upon a lesser limit.

The Spanish Government found these conditions much too restrictive and refused to agree to the establishment of a Boundary Commission

[14] *Foreign Office Papers* 185/246, 16 December 1851.
[15] *Ibid.*, 72/948, 10 October 1858.
[16] *Ibid.*, 72/1094, 15 March 1859.

on such bases. There was an interchange of correspondence in these premises between the two Governments until 1883 but no agreement was reached.[17]

When, in the latter part of the Nineteenth Century, rifled breech-loading coast artillery attained a range of 10,000 yards and beyond, the point was reached where all of the waters of Gibraltar Bay could be brought under fire from either the Spanish or the British side. In the United Kingdom there ensued official and unofficial discussion concerning the advisability of abandoning Gibraltar and exchanging it for Ceuta on the African side of the Strait. The matter generally met with little favor in Spain and little official favor in the United Kingdom whose defense investment in the Rock had become very large. This discussion continued from 1883 to 1939. In 1925, the Spanish caudillo, Primo de Rivera, suggested an exchange of Gibraltar for Ceuta, but this was rejected by the United Kingdom.[18] In 1937, the Spanish Government addressed to the British Government a note expressing the desire to maintain the territorial *status quo*.[19]

From 1938 down to the present there have been heard expressions of official Spanish opinion challenging the legality of British possession and asserting the Spanish right to the Rock. In recent years Spanish policy has been to make positive efforts to weaken the Gibraltar economy. Finally in January 1956, General Franco was reported to have said the return of Gibraltar was a matter of honor for every Spaniard and that the present status of Gibraltar is contrary to the whole spirit of post-war Europe. He then suggested retro-cession to Spain and leasing of the port and naval installation under an agreement similar to that governing United States bases in Spain.[20] In a subsequent debate in Commons, the Government stated they were not prepared to consider any alteration in the status of the Rock.[21] There is no evidence that the positions of the two Governments have altered since that time.

Since the interchange of notes in 1879–83, there appears to have been no effort to draw water boundaries in Gibraltar Bay. On the other hand, neither Party to the dispute appears to have attempted to enforce actively any maximum claims it may have. Currently there is no evi-

[17] 74 *British and Foreign State Papers*, pp. 1319–52.

[18] C. E. Carrington, *Gibraltar*, pamphlet of the Royal Institute of International Affairs, pp. 27–31.

[19] 100 *British and Foreign State Papers*, pp. 570–1.

[20] *London Daily Mail*, 27 January 1956, cited by Carrington, *op. cit.*, at p. 36.

[21] Carrington, *op. cit.*, p. 36.

dence that the Europa-Carnero closing line has any practical significance for shipping. Neither State appears to exercise any administrative control over shipping save within the immediate vicinity of each of the two ports, Algeciras and Gibraltar. On the other hand there is not in evidence any attempy at agreement on jurisdictional boundaries or even coordination of harbor services and regulations. As a result, one would have a difficult problem in deciding what, on the basis of perceivable practice, the legal status of the waters of the Bay might be. And, in view of the present atmosphere of Anglo-Spanish relations on the possession of Gibraltar, there would appear little hope of reaching any agreement on boundaries. But, while the relationship is officially cold, and distinctly unfriendly ashore, there appears to be little in the way of friction with respect to the waters of the Bay. Each Party appears to conduct his own business in studied disregard of the other and without infringing on the other Party's preserves. In this political climate, it would appear that any efforts to arrive at a water boundary in the Bay, or to apply any internationally agreed upon rules if such were to be devised for bays belonging to more than one State, would serve only to present one more source of friction between the United Kingdom and Spain in the Gibraltar area. This is a situation having political overtones too unstable for the application of any general rules or for specific agreement in a framework of international law. But, as a practical matter, neither Party can be said to be under any perceivable handicap arising out of the activities of the other at the present time.

Section E THE GULF OF AQABA

The Central American Court of Justice found that the Gulf of Fonseca was a closed bay whose status rested upon historic title and that there was a co-ownership of its waters save for a marginal belt adjacent to the coast of each of these bordering States.[1] The Bay of Gibralter presents a case where there is probably a co-ownership, where the boundaries appear never to have been established, and where the two littoral States have settled into a sort of *modus vivendi* in which the bay is probably internal waters but in which no claims have been voiced for many years.[2] The Gulf of Aqaba presents the interesting case in which the international controversy regarding its waters arises out of a host of circumstances quite extraneous to the

[1] Section B, above.
[2] Section D, above.

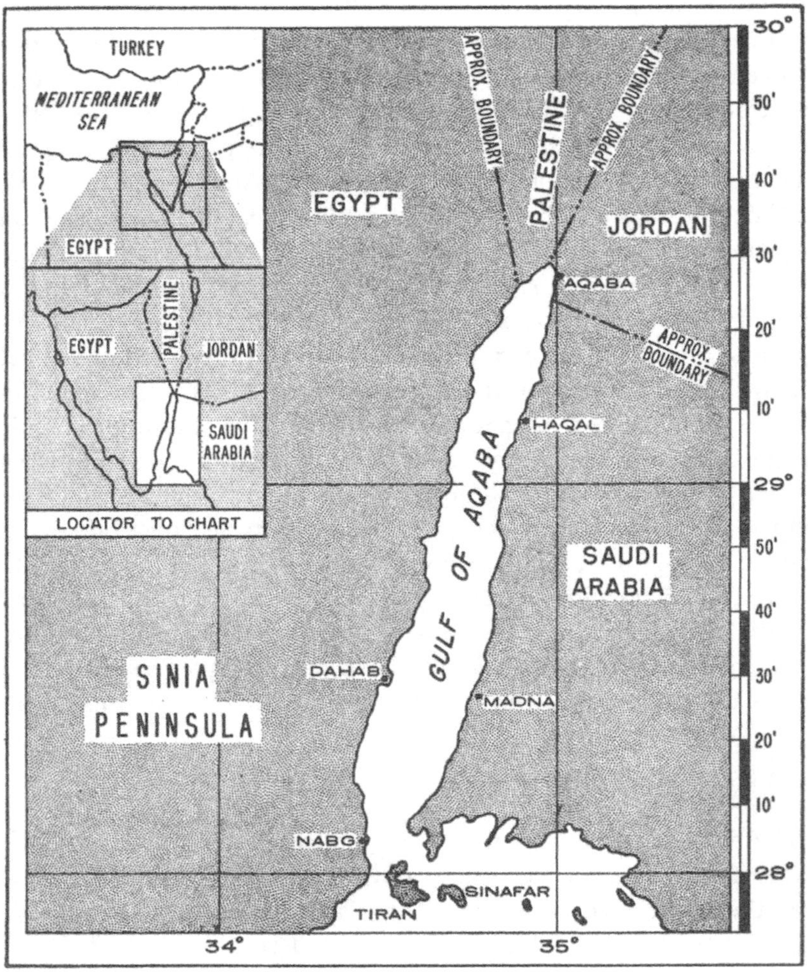

GULF OF AQABA

Fig. 27

Gulf and its surrounding littoral. One need only contemplate that if the following events were to transpire, the Gulf of Aqaba would probably lapse into the condition of relative economic worthlessness that has been its lot throughout most of history:

(a) Recognition of Israel by the surrounding Arab States, and the commencement of normal political relationships.

(b) Opening of the Suez Canal to Israeli ships and ships bound for Israel. Were this to occur, it is unlikely that many ships would proceed to the poorly equipped port of Elath in preference to Israel's Mediterranean ports which are tied to the country by adequate lines of communication. By comparison, Elath has no railroad connection to the rest of the country, although there are roads and an eight-inch oil pipeline to Beersheba, 135 miles away.[3]

(c) Resumption of oil pumping through the Iraq-Haifa line.[4] This would no doubt terminate the usefulness of the Elath-Beersheba line.

(d) Establishment of transit rights through Israel ports to Jordan. Such an arrangement is an obvious necessity. It would largely terminate the usefulness of the Jordanian port of Aqaba save as a port for pilgrims en route to and from the Muslim Holy Places. Jordan has poor road connections to Aqaba, and the port has never had a connection with the Hedjaz Railway, a railway which in the Aqaba area has been inoperative since World War I.

The foregoing matters are mentioned in order to emphasize the fact that political questions of sovereignty over the surrounding territory, and recognition of it, largely control this situation.[5] They emphazise, too, perhaps more strongly than in any other case that where a bay is bounded by the territory of more than one State, the geographical propinquity of the land territories of such States can bring about legal problems with respect to the bay which are substantially different

[3] George Lenczowski, *Oil and State in the Middle East* (1960), p. 345.

[4] *Ibid.*, p. 26. This line has been inoperative since the establishment of the State of Israel.

[5] The economic factors in evidence are largely a result of the political problems. The legal situation in the Gulf of Aqaba and its entrance, the Strait of Tiran, has been written upon in quite thorough and careful detail and this writer can see no useful purpose in a detailed review of the same materials so recently discussed by very able scholars: Charles B. Selak, Jr., "A Consideration of the Legal Status of the Gulf of Aqaba," 52 *American Journal of International Law* (1958), pp. 660–698; Alexander Melamid, "Political Geography of the Gulf of Aqaba," 47 *Annals of the Association of American Geographers* (1957), pp. 231–240; Alexander Melamid, "Legal Status of the Gulf of Aqaba," 53 *American Journal of International Law* (1959), pp. 412–3; Leo Gross, "The Geneva Conference on the Law of the Sea and the Right of Innocent Passage through the Gulf of Aqaba," 53 *American Journal of International Law* (1959) pp. 564–594; L. M. Bloomfield, *Egypt, Israel and the Gulf of Aqaba in International Law* (1957).

in degree, if not in kind, from those encountered where there is only one littoral State.

The political controversies causing the emergence of the Gulf of Aqaba from obscurity are closely followed by statements concerning sovereignty over its waters. This Section will be confined to a discussion of the arguments used to advance the proposition that the Gulf is a historic bay under the collective sovereignty of the surrounding Arab States.

Professor Gross writes:

> ... the burden of proof with respect to the elements of a historic title rests with the government or governments which claim it.[6]

He offers authoritative opinion to support his observation.[7] In a footnote, Professor Gross, after citing a geographer, concludes:

> there would seem to be no basis whatever for any historic or exclusive title to the Gulf in any of the riparian States.[8]

Turning now to the argument of Mr. Ahmad Shukairy of Saudi Arabia, we see the opposite point of view.[9] In support of his contention that the Gulf of Aqaba is a historic bay, Mr. Shukairy presents the points set out hereunder. On these points this author offers occasional comment.

(a) "Yet for a body of water to be historic, the origins need not be ancient."

Comment: Our discussion in this book of several other bays, notably the inner reaches of Peter the Great Bay, would tend to confirm this point of view. Certainly there is no writer or official body who has ever pretended to lay down any finite period of time that must elapse before a historic title can be said to be consolidated. This is a relative matter. On the other hand, there appears to exist a requirement that historic title must be grounded in usage of sufficient duration to enlist the respect of other States and such non-nationals as against whom it

[6] Gross, *op. cit.*, p. 571.

[7] Memorandum concerning Historic Bays, UN Doc. A/Conf.13/1, and UN Doc.A/Conf. 13/C.1/L.104, Conference on the Law of the Sea, *Official Records*, vol. III, First Committee, p. 241 (The Japanese proposal on defining historic bays, submitted at the 1958 Geneva on Conference on the Law of the Sea.)

[8] The geographer is Alexander Melamid, note 5, above. Mr. Melamid does not actually voice an opinion, but his factual description of the Gulf would tend to support Professor Gross's conclusion. Mr. Melamid's article in the *Annals of the Association of American Geographers* is a careful and unbiased appraisal of the politico-geographic features of the gulf.

[9] Ahmad Shukairy, Chairman of the Saudi Arabian Delegation to the United Nations, "On the Question of the Regime of Historuc Waters, Including Historic Bays," an address before the United Nations Sixth Committee, 30 November 1959.

may operate. The very term "historic" suggests some rather long period of time. It is believed that the inner reaches of Peter the Great Bay represent a possession grounded in historic title which dates no earlier thna 1872. This possession is believed to be the shortest one time-wise, that can be said to rest on historic title.

(b) "In our region, the Gulf of Aqaba, as an Arab *mare clausum* is at least thirteen centuries old.

Comment: If the advocate can prove this, he would establish a rather strong claim to historic title.

(c) "There is a special reciprocal relationship between historic waters and the adjacent land."

This view is confirmed by the Judgment in United Kingdom v. Norway, and it is eminently sound. However, in the cases we have considered in this book it should be observed that the reciprocal relationship was usually one which developed through a historical process in which a genuine link came to be forged. Mr. Shukairy eloquently embroiders upon this view.

(d) "... historic waters have never been part of the high seas – nor are they a rival category."

Here Mr. Shukairy, arguing that these waters were originally *res nullius* rather than *res communis*, seems to imply that the existence of historic waters is a self-evident truth – "It is a rule of law by itself." He cites Baldoni on this point. While this writer might be inclined to agree with the learned representative of Saudi Arabia, he is willing to do so only up to a certain not-too-well established point. There is a limit in the size of the body of water so claimed beyond which the claimant is likely to incur the opposition of other States, or of individuals in actions at law, and hence to be called upon to prove the title. In this connection, we should note that the Gulf of Aqaba is somewhat over one hundred miles in length, and varies in width from three to seventeen miles. Whenever issues have arisen with respect to bays of comparable size, the claimant has been called upon either to prove or explain the basis of the claim; the claim seems never to be regarded as self-evident.

(e) "If the claim is well-grounded, amply proven, and meets satisfactorily all the legal requirements, then a finding in favor of historic waters can be pronounced without hesitation whether the claim is one or many."

Comment: There is no reason to dispute this as Professor Hyde has pointed out,[10] and as was adjudged in the case of the Gulf of Fonseca. The joint claim is a rarity, first because it has seldom been expressed although there are numerous bays in the instant category,[11] and second, because even where the need for such an expression as against non-littoral States is evident, the mutuality of interest among the littoral States is seldom so complete as to bring about a joint agreement leading to the voicing of the claim. If the littoral States are, jointly, the successors of a larger entity which once occupied the entire shore, there might be sufficient reason to view the sovereignty over the bay as a joint one, but in the absence of published agreement in these premises, there must inevitably arise the question whether all the successor States concerned speak with one voice. While Mr. Shukairy argues that the Gulf of Aqaba is an "Arab" historic bay, the political and legal relations of what have come to be called Arab States have not been distinguished for their unity of thought or action at any time in recent history.[12] Thus, while mutuality of interest in the Gulf of Fonseca found expression in the 1907 treaties of the riparian States, comparable agreement with respect to the Gulf of Aqaba is not in evidence.

(f) "At present, the bordering States on Aqaba are Saudi Arabia, United Arab Republic and Jordan... the Gulf of Aqaba had been previously under a common predecessor. It was exclusively under Arab dominion, and the predecessor is virtually a common ancestor."

Comment: This is a purely argumentative and implies that there once existed an Arab State. The common ancestor, of course, was the Ottoman Empire but the difficulty arises in applying the precepts of a relatively modern State system to the rather loose and autonomous system of provinces that comprised much of the Ottoman Empire, and then to fix with objective precision the territorial holdings of the successor States on the Gulf of Aqaba. The evidences of predecessor sovereignty, of clear demarcation of the territorial rights of the successor States, and of Acts of Sovereignty of successor States are not altogether convincing or free of dispute, even as among the successor States. The Saudi Arabian Government, through Mr. Shukairy, says:

... the States of the area do not recognize Israel, be it the existence, territory or the boundary, if any. This is their right, in International Law, which none can

[10] Charles C. Hyde, *International Law Chiefly as Interpreted and Applied by the United States*, 2nd Ed., (1947), p. 475.

[11] UN Document A/Conf.13/15 lists forty-eight such bays.

[12] The writer deems it quite unnecessary to elucidate upon this point. One need only peruse the pages of such standard works as Bernard Lewis, *The Arabs in History* (1958), or George Lenszowski, *The Middle East in World Affairs* (1956), to arrive at this conclusion.

challenge. Secondly, Israel's foothold on the Aqaba Gulf apart from its illegal origin, is based on Armistice Agreements, which by their character and express provisions vest no sovereignty whatsoever, and leave the territory including Aqaba, subject to all rights, claims and reservations.

Now, if we grant all of these arguments, some of which partake of a concept of International Law which may be passing into obsolescence, we are confronted with the fact that there is no agreement among Saudi Arabia, Jordan, and the United Arab Republic as to what the status of the Israeli-occupied territory should be and who, in their view, is the legal sovereign over that territory. It would appear that this question must necessaruly be settled if the argument of these States is to graduate from the political polemic into argument that achieves a standard of legal precision. The term "Arab," when used in the instant context, is defectively amorphous.

(g) "Its [the Gulf of Aqaba] historical character, is a matter of law, to be decided only by a judicial authority and through judicial processes."

In this the author agrees whole-heartedly and if the Saudi Government agrees with its representative, then it should seek its remedy before the International Court of Justice. But, to do so would in and of itself require a degree of agreement among the States that now appears to be lacking. Should such agreement be achieved, this author believes that the controversy over possession of this desolate and objectively worthless arm of the sea would evaporate. Mr. Shukairy does not seem to envision settlement by the International Court in any event. It would appear that in his view judicial processes involve the International Law Commission and a conference of plenipotentiaries.[13]

Disregarding for the moment the adjective, Arab, in the claim that the Gulf of Aqaba comprises historic waters, and also ignoring insofar as possible the problem of succession ashore, we should consider briefly the evidence which is advanced in support of this claim. We should also consider the evidence tending toward a contrary view. On either side, the evidence is sparse; Mr. Shukairy submits the following as evidence that the waters of the Gulf are historic waters:

[13] In 1957 the Saudi Arabian delegate to the United Nations said: "But the matter is not to be decided on judicial grounds. The question involves matters of the highest order pertaining to pilgrimage and other national and political considerations." General Assembly, Official Records, A/P.V.697, p. 233. In this connection, it may be noted that precise knowledge of the volume of traffic along the several pilgrim routes does not appear readily available. Melamid, "Political Geography of the Gulf of Aqaba"; Houtsma, *et al*, II *The Encyclopaedia of Islam* (1927), pp. 196–201; H. A. R. Gibb and J. H. Kramers, *Shorter Encyclopaedia of Islam* (1953), pp. 121–125.

(a) The contents of Sublime Porte Ministry of Foreign Affairs Circular *Note Verbale* J. No. 54917/99 of 1 October 1914,[14] wherein omission of the Gulf of Aqaba, it is argued, is a clear indication that the Gulf was considered to be under Ottoman Sovereignty. A study of the content of the Ottoman note suggests that the Saudi interpretation is probably correct. While the west shore of the Gulf was in Egyptian territory even then,[15] the nominal Ottoman sovereignty over Egypt continued until the 18 December 1914, when Great Britain deposed the reigning Khedive, *in absentia*, and declared Egypt to be a British protectorate.[16]

(b) Omission of the Gulf of Aqaba in the International Sanitary Convention of 1912. The Saudi argument is that by such omission, the signatories of this Convention, having to do with pilgrimage traffic, recognized the Gulf as national waters. This argument appears to place an unduly strained interpretation of that treaty.[17]

(c) Article 10, Paragraph 3 of the Constantinople Convention of 1888.[18] Mr. Shukairy and others have argued:

> ... it appears from the record of the negotiations which resulted in the conclusion of the Convention, that the inclusion of that provision aimed at leaving the Gulf of Aqaba and its straits outside the scope of the order of the free passage defined for the Suez Canal ... is an asserted recognition that the Gulf of Aqaba is a locked Arab Gulf without any international character.[19]

This appears to place a rather dubious construction on the provision cited. Professor Gross writes:

> The Suez Canal Convention provides no judicial basis for the asserted "territorial" character of the Gulf.[20]

This writer is unable to disagree in any way with Professor Gross's reasoning in support of his statement.

[14] III *Martens Recueil*, vol. X, pp. 700–701. This circular note, on Turkish neutrality is an amplification of an earlier note on the same subject, No. 54676/98 of 28 September 1914. The latter note is found at *Ibid.*, pp. 698–700, and is reprinted in English in U.S. Naval War College *International Law Documents*, 1917, pp. 217–9.

[15] The territorial status of the Sinai peninsula is discussed in detail in Bloomfield, *op. cit.*, chs. 14, 15.

[16] Lenczowski, *op. rit.*, p. 394; 109 *British and Foreign State Papers*, pp. 436–439.

[17] III *Redmond* (1923), 2972.

This rather long and detailed treaty has a great many provisions dealing with the pilgrim traffic to the Muslim Holy Places. Careful study of it by the writer failed to disclose any basis for the conclusion reached by Mr. Shukairy.

[18] III *Moore's Digest* (1906), pp. 264–6.

[19] Saudi Arabian Note of 31 March 1957, cited by Selack, *op. cit.*, p. 677.

[20] Gross, *op. cit.*, p. 568.

(d) The Saudi Arabian Royal Decree of May 1949 has prescribed the Gulf of Aqaba as falling under Arab sovereignty.[21]

Actually, the decree does not spell out the legal status of the Gulf in such terms. The only mention of the Gulf in that decree is in Article 1(e):

The term "coast" refers to coasts of the Red Sea, the Gulf of Aqaba, and the Persian Gulf.

In any event, the term "Arab" must be viewed as devoid of any proper juridical content at this time.

(e) ... not a single international authority makes any mention of the Gulf as an international waterway open for international navigation.[22]

It is not clear that this statement reflects any juridical value. To do so, it is believed that there must be shown a corresponding record of shipping practice in the Gulf. In fact, through most of history, there was so little traffic in the Gulf that its legal status in the eyes of the riparian States, or other States, was of no moment.

We shall dwell no further on the Gulf of Aqaba. The case for its being classed as a historic bay is very weak. The littoral States, even the so-called Arab States, are not known to have fixed upon any water boundaries within the Gulf. Even should they do so, and should they persist in non-recognition of Israel as one of the riparian States, they will more than likely be confronted with the political fact that a number of other States will actively refuse to recognize such a partition of the waters of the Gulf.

[21] *I UN Legislative Series* (1951), p. 22; U.S. *Naval War College International Law Documents*, 1948–49, 196–8.

[22] Statement of Saudi Arabian representative in UN General Assembly, 12th Session, 2 Oct. 1957, *Official Records*, p. 233.

PART FOUR

CONCLUSIONS

CHAPTER X

CONCLUSIONS

This writer was originally attracted to the subject of this book by his rather tentative conclusion that the codification of international rules for bays neither met the requirements of the person against whom they most directly apply, the mariner, nor did it appear to reflect an understanding of the mariner's problems in coastal waters. The primary purpose of this writing, therefore, has been to conduct an inquiry into the development of the rules for bays and the factors that have influenced such development. In the course of this inquiry the writer has endeavored to probe as deeply as the rather broad scope of the study might permit, and also as deeply as his own knowledge of the theory of law as a normative discipline might permit. An attempt has been made, throughout this writing, to make it useful both for students concerned with the law of the sea as seen through the eyes of a naval officer, and for naval officers who may require some explanation of the rules on bays.

In the course of preparation of this book, the writer has become increasingly concerned with several demonstrable facts which seem to render the codification of rules on bays at best only a partially successful venture. These facts, probably not a complete list, are as follows:

(a) It is by no means apparent that States have expressed fully their views on bays in general, or on their requirements concerning bays in their own littorals. An excellent example is the somewhat confused picture we have of the bays in Australia.

(b) It is evident that the preparatory work done by the United Nations Secretariat, and its corps of experts, is not as complete as one might hope for. It is not clear whether the fault lies with fhet rame of reference set for these individuals or is a matter of other handicaps under which they have had to work. It is this writer's view that while the Memorandum on Historic Bays,[1] the 1953 Report by the Committee

[1] UN Document A/Conf.13/1.

of Experts,[2] and the study of Bays which belong to Different States,[3] are helpful, they all contain omissions which detract from their usefulness.

(c) The codification of rules on bays appears to have been conceived of as an essentially technical matter, which this writer believes it must be, but it, perhaps unavoidably, became intermixed with larger political issues. A technical example is the more or less continuous attempt at fixing a mathematical relationship between the length of the closing line and the breatdh of the territorial sea. The most productive relationship among the maritime specialist, the international lawyer, the diplomat, and the national politician, is probably one that is impossible to prescribe. Yet it is from this relationship that the rules emerge. The establishment of appropriate norms amid an ever-rising level of social communication and economic interdependence, both international and domestic, poses rather difficult problems.

However imperfectly and incompletely the writer has analyzed the International Law of Bays, he feels duty-bound to suggest his own codification of the rules. In attempting to do so, there is a strong temptation to detach one's self from the present conditions of international relations (and who can state with any precision what these conditions are?) and to do for bays what Professor Jessup has done in a more general way: to propose rules which would operate in a world that has achieved "some form of international government in which a collective will takes precedence over the individual will of the sovereign State. . . . "[4] Were he to do this, the core of the codification would probably be an institution having many of the characteristics of Professor Schücking's quickly-suppressed proposal for an International Waters Office. Inasmuch as the pre-conditions for the adoption of rules cast in such terms appear rather remote of achievement at this time, it is doubtful whether any very useful purpose can be served in proposing them. One can assume the general pre-conditions as Professor Jessup has done, but it appears to be more difficult to forecast the technological, economic and demographic developments which might be in evidence in the era for which the pre-conditions have been assumed. Without an accurate forecast of such specific knowledge, the proposing of rules applicable to the era becomes an exercise of dubious worth. For this reason, the writer shall propose rules which may pose

[2] UN Document A/CN.4/61/Add. 1.
[3] UN Document A/Conf.13/15.
[4] Philip C. Jessup, *A Modern Law of Nations* (1947), p. 2.

some difficulties in enlisting agreement, but which, he believes, contain a measure of improvement and which are reasonably synchronized with the times.

Article 7

Bays

1. For the purposes of these rules, a bay is a well marked indentation whose penetration is in such proportion to the width of its mouth as to constitute more than a mere curvature of the coast. Except for specific bays coming under the rules for historic bays, an indentation shall not be regarded as a bay unless its area is as large as, or larger than, that of the semi-circle whose diameter is a line drawn across the mouth of that indentation.

2. For the purpose of measurement the following rules shall apply:

(a) Measurement will be on the largest-scale chart encompassing the entire bay. The chart must be one drawn from surveys ensuring complete accuracy of navigation under all meteorological conditions.

(b) The area of indentation is that lying between the low-water mark around the shore of the indentation and a line joining the low water marks of its natural entrance points, at their narrowest dimension.

(c) The reference plane for the low water mark will be that which has been adopted as standard for all of the nautical charts officially authorized by the State concerned.

(d) Where, because of the presence of islands, an indentation has more than one mouth, the semi-circle shall be drawn on a line as long as the sum of the lengths of the lines across the different mouths.

(e) Islands within an indentation shall be included as if they were part of the water aera of the indentation. Where islands are located in the mouth, so much of the islands as lie to landward of the line drawn across the mouth and extended across the islands, shall be regarded as part of the water area.

(f) The water areas of all harbor systems of an indentation shall be considered as part of the total area for measurement purposes. For such purposes, harbor systems shall be construed as including roadsteads.

3(a) If the distance between the low-water marks at their narrowest dimension does not exceed twenty miles,[5] the State concerned is authorized to draw a closing line between these two points and to classify the waters as internal waters.

(b) Should the line so drawn measure twenty miles or less, and should the State concerned determine that its needs do not require that the waters so enclosed be classed as internal waters, the line enclosing internal waters may be drawn at any location within the bay, or not drawn at all. In the latter case, the bay will contain no internal waters.

(c) Where the distance between the low-water marks at the natural entrance points, at their narrowest dimension, exceeds twenty miles, a straight base line of twenty miles may be drawn within the bay in such a manner as to enclose the maximum area of water that is possible with a line of that length. Any line of lesser length may be drawn, or the drawing of any line may be foregone. In the latter case, the bay will contain no internal waters.

(d) The coastal State must clearly demarcate lines enclosing internal waters of bays by appropriate navigational aids.

(e) The coastal State must indicate on charts the boundaries of internal waters of bays and must report such boundaries to the International Hydrographic Bureau for dissemination of the pertinent information to other maritime States. In the absence of receipt of such information by the International Hydrographic Bureau, no bay shall be considered as containing internal waters.[6]

4(a) The foregoing provisions shall not, except as noted below, apply to historic bays, or in any case where the straight baseline system provided in Article ... is applicable.

(b) A historic bay is an indentation whose waters are considered, in whole or in part, to be internal waters. The indentation is one having a genuine and long-standing economic link with the surrounding coast. The historic bay contains waters over which

[5] Section D of Chapter ONE discusses the problems of navigation, including radar navigation. Although it is believed that most radar sets have the optimum capability of permitting accurate navigation at maximum ranges of twelve miles, it is believed that for the foreseeable future, a maximum effective range of ten miles is more realistic for the sets likely to be installed in medium and small-sized ships and for the overall conditions under which such ships will operate.

[6] Not all maritime States are members of the International Hydrographic Bureau. This rule pre-supposes that the member States will agree on the Bureau's processing of the information for members and non-members alike. Inasmuch as this is entirely an administrative problem, it is not considered appropriate to embody the matter within the proposed rules.

the coastal State or States have exercised a regime of internal waters for a period of long standing, with explicit or implicit recognition of such practice by foreign States.

(c) The provisions of sub-paragraph 3d and 3e, above, shall be applicable to historic bays.

5(a) An indentation whose shores belong to two or more States may be classed as a bay by reason of its fulfilling the requirements of Paragraphs 1 through 3, above, or by reason of fulfilling the requirements of paragraph 4, above.

(b) Should an indentation whose shores belong to two or more States be classed as a bay in accordance with the foregoing requirements, its waters may become subject to the regime of internal waters upon formal agreement of all of the riparian States. Such an agreement shall include provisions delimiting water boundaries both within the bay and of the bay itself.

(c) Nothing in the foregoing sub-paragraphs shall prohibit the riparian States from formally agreeing upon the joint exercise of a regime of internal waters in a bay, or any part thereof, provided that the boundaries of the joint and separate regimes, as the case may be, are delimited in the agreement, and provided that all riparian States are signatories to the agreement.

(d) The riparian States must report the agreed-upon boundaries of such bays to the International Hydrographic Bureau. In the absence of formal agreement or in the absence of receipt of such information by the International Hydrographic Bureau, no part of such bay shall be considered as internal waters.

(e) No single riparian State and no combination of such States shall, within the agreed-upon areas of their competence, enact rules calculated to deny the innocent passage of ships to the ports of any other riparian State or States.

BIBLIOGRAPHY

Adams, K. T., *Hydrographic Manual, Special Publication No, 143* (Washington: U.S. Government Printing Office, 1942).

"The Admiralty Chart" XII *The Journal of the Institute of Navigation* (April 1954), pp. 163–183.

Admiralty Naval Staff, Intelligence Division, *A Dictionary of Naval Equivalents*, Vol I (London: H.M. Stationary Office, 1924).

Admiralty Naval Staff, Intelligence Division, *A Handbook of Siberia and Arctic Russia* (London: His Majesty's Stationary Office, 1920).

Ago, Roberto "Positive Law and International Law," 51 *AJIL* (Oct. 1957), p. 691.

Ali, Abdullah Yusuf, *The Holy Qur-an, Text, Translation and Commentary*, 2 vols, (New York: Hafner, 1946).

Allen, Carleton, *Law in the making* (Oxford: Clarendon Press, 1946).

Allen, Edward W. "Fish Can Be International" 82 *U.S. Naval Institute Proceedings* (October 1956), pp. 1066–1072.

Amme, CDR Carl H., U.S. Navy "The Not-So-Gentle Art of Navigation, 175 Years Ago," 80 *U.S. Naval Institute Proceedings* (September 1954), pp. 1023–1029.

Anderson, RADM Bern, U.S. Navy (Ret.), "The Impact of Rapid Communications on the Employment of Naval Forces," 77 *U.S. Naval Institute Proceedings* (November 1951), pp. 1157–1167.

—, "The Protection of Commerce in War," 78 *U.S. Naval Institute Proc eedings* (August 1952), pp. 881–888.

Anderson, James, *Observations on the Means of Exciting a Spirit of National Industry*, (Edinburgh: I. Cadell, 1775).

Andersen, LT. Kenneth A., U.S. Navy, "Lead Kindly Light," 77 *U.S. Naval Institute Proceedings* (April 1951), pp. 405–409.

Andrews, Allen, *Proud Fortress* (New York: Dutton, 1959).

Aronsseau, L., "The Distribution of Population: A Constructive Problem," XI *Geographical Review* (1921), pp. 579, ff.

Ashton, T. S., *An Economic History of England: The 18th Century* (London: Methuen & Co., Ltd., 1955).

Asia Kyokai, *Japanese Fisheries, Their Development and Present Status* (Tokyo: Asia Kyokai, 1957).

Azuni, Domenico, A., *The Maritime Law of Europe*, 2 vols., Tr. from French, (New York: I Riley & Co., 1806).

Bacon, Robert, and Scott, James Brown, Eds., *North Atlantic Fisheries Arbitration at the Hague – Argument on Behalf of the United States by Elihu Root* (Cambridge: Harvard University Press, 1917),

Bagrow, Leo, *Die Geschichte der Kartographie* (Berlin: Safari-Verlag, 1951).
Bailey, LT Henry C., U.S.N., "The Evolution of Deep Sea Sounding Methods," 63 *Journal of the American Society of Naval Engineers* (May 1951), pp. 349–362.
Balch, Thomas W., "Is Hudson Bay a Closed or an Open Sea?," 6 *American Journal of International Law* (1912), pp. 409–459.
Baldoni, C., *Il Mare territoriale nel diritto internazionale commune* (Padova: 1934).
Ball, F. W., *Intellectual Calculus*, (London: Thames Bank Publishing Co., 1957).
Barnes, Kathleen, "Fisheries, Mainstay of Soviet-Japanese Friction," IX *Far Eastern Survey* (1940) pp. 75–80.
Barnes, Wyatt E., "Emerging Trends in the Mediterranean Balance of Power," 84 *U.S. Naval Institute Proceedings*, (March 1959), pp. 53–62.
Barton, William, *A Dissertation on the Freedom of Navigation and Maritime Commerce* (Philadelphia: John Conrad & Co., 1802).
Bates, E. S., *Soviet Asia*, (London: Jonathan Cape, 1924).
Baty, Thomas, "The Three-Mile Limit," 22 *American Journal of International Law* (1928), pp. 503–537.
Baty, T., *The Canons of International Law*, (London: John Murray, 1930).
Baty, Thomas, "The Free Sea – Produce the Evidence," 35 *American Journal of International Law* (1941), pp. 227–242.
Baxter, Richard R., "The Territorial Sea," 49 *Proceedings of the American Society of International Law* (1956), pp. 116–124.
Bayitch, S. A., *Interamerican Law of Fisheries* (New York: Ocean Publishing, Inc., 1957).
Bellquist, Eric C., "The Heinrich Augustin," 24 *American Journal of International Law* (1930), pp. 776–783.
Bencker, Capitaine de Fregate (CDR) Henri, French Navy, "Maritime Terminology Relating to various Subdivisions of the Globe," XIX *International Hydrographic Review* (August, 1942), pp. 60–74.
Bennett, M. K., *The World's Food* (New York: Harper & Brothers, 1954).
Bingham, Joseph Walter, *Report on the International Law of Pacific Coastal Fisheries* (Palo Alto: Stanford University Press, 1938).
Blanchard, W. O., and Visser, B. S., *Economic Geography of Europe*, (New York: McGraw Hill, 1931).
Bloch, I. S., *The Future of War* (New York: Doubleday & McClure, 1899).
Bloomfield, L. M., *Egypt, Israel and the Gulf of Aqaba in International Law*, (Toronto: Carswell, 1957).
Boasson, Charles, *Sociological Aspects of Law and International Adjustment* (Amsterdam: North-Holland Publishing Co., 1950).
Boggs, S. Whittemore, "Delimitation of the Territorial Sea," 24 *American Journal of International Law* (1930), pp. 541–555.
—, *International Boundaries* (New York: Columbia University Press, 1940).
—, "National Claims in Adjacent Seas," 41 *Geographical Review* (1951), p. 185.
—, "Delimitation of Seaward Areas under National Jurisdiction," 45 *American Journal of International Law* (1951), p. 243 ff.
Böhmert, Viktor, "Die russische Fischereigrenze," 21 *Zeitschrift für Völkerrecht* (1937) p. 493.
Bourquin, Maurice "Les Baies Historiques," *Mélanges Georges Sauser-Hall* (Geneva: Facultés de Droit des Universités de Genève et Neuchatel, 1952).
Bowditch, Nathaniel, *The Practical American Navigator*, U.S. Navy Hydrographic Office Publication No. 9, 1958 Ed. (Washington: U.S. Government Printing Office, 1958).

Bowen, Frank O., *The Sea, Its History and Romance,* (London: B. F. Stevens & Brown, 1924).
Bragadin, CDR Marc'Antonio, RIN (Ret), *The Italian Navy in World War II* (Annapolis: U.S. Naval Institute, 1957).
Braynard, Frank O., *Famous American Ships,* (New York: Cornell Maritime Press, 1956).
Brierly, J. L., "The Future of Codification," 12 *British Yearbook of International Law* (1931), pp. 1–12.
—, *The Law of Nations, An Introduction to the International Law of Peace,* 4th Ed. (Oxford: The Clarendon Press, 1949),
Brittin, CDR Burdick H., USN, *International Law for Seagoing Officers,* (Annapolis: U.S. Naval Institute, 1956).
Brodie, Bernard, *Sea Power in the Machine Age* (Princeton: Princeton University Press, 1941).
Brown, Harrison; Bonner, James; Weir, John; *The Next Hundred Years* (London: Weidenfeld and Nicholson, 1957).
Brown, Lloyd A., *The Story of Maps* (Boston: Little, Brown & Co., 1949).
Brown, Philip Marshall, "The Marginal Sea," 17 *American Journal of International Law* (1923) pp. 39–95.
—, "Protective Jurisdiction over Marginal Waters," *Proceedings of American Society of International Law 1923,* p. 15.
—, "Law of Territorial Waters," 21 *American Journal of International Law* (1927) pp. 101–105.
Brown, S. W., "Modern Practice in Marine Refrigeration," 61 *Journal of the American Society of Naval Engineers* (May 1949), pp. 442–449.
Bureau des Produits Maritimes et Fluviaux du Ministère d'Agriculture et Commerce, *Histoire de l'Industrie de la Pêche Maritime et Fluviale au Japon* (Paris: 1900).
de Burgh, William, *The Elements of Maritime International Law* (London: Longmans Green, 1868).
Burke, William T., "Some Comments on the 1958 Conventions," *Proceedings of the American Society of International Law,* 1958, p. 204.
Bustamente y Sirven, Antonio Sanchez de, *The Territorial Sea,* (New York: Oxford University Press, 1930).
Butler, Sir Geoffrey and Simon Maccoby, *The Development of Internatiocal Law* (London: Longmans, Green & Co., 1928).
Bynkershoek, Cornelius van, "De Dominio Maris Dissertatis," Tr. R. V. Maoffin, *The Classics of International Law,* James B. Scott, Ed., (New York: Oxford University Press, 1916).
Calahan, E. A., *The Sky and the Sailor, A History of Celestial Navigation* (New York: Harper & Bro., 1952).
Canada Yearbook, 1957–58.
Cardozo, Benjamin N., *The Growth of the Law* (New Haven: Yale University Press, 1924).
Carr, Edward H., *Nationalism and After* (London: Macmillan and Company, 1945).
Carr-Saunders, Alexander M., *The Population Problem* (Oxford: Clarendon Press, 1922).
—, *World Population, Past Growth and Present Trends* (Oxford: Clarendon Press, 1936).
Carson, Rachel, *The Sea Around Us* (New York: Simon and Schuster, 1950).
Chamberlain, Eugene T., "The Geneva Conference and Ocean Shipping," U.S. Bureau of Foreign Domestic and Commerce, *Trade Info Bulletin* No. 202 af, 3 March 1924.

Chambers, 1LT J. H. L., U.S.M.C., "The Discovery of North America," 79 *U.S. Naval Institute Proceedings* (Jan. 1953) pp. 65–72.
Channing, C. G., Fairfax, *Siberia's Untouched Treasure* (New York: Putnam, 1923).
Charnock, John, *History of Marine Architecture*, 3 vols. (London: R. Faulder, 1801).
Charteris, A. H., "Territorial Jurisdiction in Wide Bays," XVI *Yale Law Journal* (1907), 471.
—, "Territorial Jurisdiction in Wide Bays," International Law Association, *Report of the Twenty-Third Conference, Berlin*, (1906), p. 103.
—, *Chapters on International Law* (Sydney: Law School of the University of Sydney, 1940).
Clairac, Étienne, *Les Us et Coutumes de la Mer* (Rouen: Chez Jean Berthelin, 1671).
Clough, Shepard B. and Coles, Charles W., *Economic History of Europe* 3rd Ed. (Boston: D. C. Heath, 1952).
Cobbett, Pitt, *Cases and Opinions on International Law*, Part I, 3rd Ed., (London: Stevens and Haynes, 1909).
Coenen, Hanns-Wolf, *Das Küstenmeer in Frieden*, (Leipzig: Universitätsverlag von Robert Noske, 1933).
Cohn, Georg, *Neo-Neutrality*, Tr. Keller and Jensen (New York: Columbia University Press, 1939).
Colombos, C. John, "The Unification of Maritime International Law," 21 *British Yearbook of International Law* (1944) pp. 96–110.
—, *Higgins and Colombos on the International Law of the Sea*, 2nd Rev. Ed. (London: Longmans, Green, 1951).
Collinder, Per, *A History of Marine Navigation* (T. M. Michael: London: Batsford, 1954).
Colonial Office, *Report on Gibraltar* 1957 (London: Her Majesty's Stationery Office, 1958).
Conolly, Violet, *Soviet Trade from the Pacific to the Levant* (London: Oxford University Press, 1935).
Consacci, Giorgio, *L'Occupazione dei Mari Costieri*, (Torino: G. Giappichelli, 1936).
Coox, Alvin D., "Japanese Attitudes Toward the Soviet Union," 26 *World Affairs Quarterly* (1956), pp. 338–357).
Corbett, Percy E., *Law and Society in the Relations of States* (New York: Harcourt, Brace & Co., 1951).
—, *Law in Diplomacy* (Princeton: Princeton University Press, 1959).
Cox, George W., *The Tale of the Great Persian War* (London: Longmans, Green, 1861).
Creasy, Sir Edward, *First Platform of International Law* (London: John van Voorst, 1876).
Crenshaw, CDR. R. S., Jr., U.S. Navy, *Naval Shiphandling* (Annapolis: U.S. Naval Institute, 1955).
Crocker, Henry G., *The Extent of the Marginal Sea* (Washingtom: U.S. Government Printing Office, 1919).
Curtis, Kenneth V., "A Discussion of 'Anti-Collision and Piloting Segment'," A paper presented at 25 October 1956 meeting of Radio Technical Commission for Marine Service.
Curtis, R. P., "The Fathometer" (undated) Raytheon Manufacturing Company Technical Paper.
Curtis, T. E. and Slater, J. M., "Inertial Navigation in Submarine Polar Operations of 1958," 5 *Navigation* (Spring 1959), pp. 275–283.

Curtius, Ernest, *The History of Greece*, vols. II, III, Tr. Adolphus Ward (New York: Scribner's, 1883).
Cushing, Sumner W., "The Boundaries of the New England States," *Annals of the Association of American Geographers*, (Jan. 1928), pp. 17–40.
Cushman, Robert E., *Leading Constitutional Decisions*, 10th Ed. (New York: Appleton-Century-Crofts, 1955).
Custance, ADM. Sir Reginald, Royal Navy, *War at Sea, Modern Theory and Practice* (London: Blackwood, 1919).
Davies, Robert W., *Development of the Soviet Budgetary System* (Cambridge: University Press, 1958).
Daggett, A. P., "The Regulation of Maritime Fisheries by Treaty," 28 *American Journal of International Law* (1934) pp. 693–717.
Davis, Kingsley, "The World's Population Explosion," *Private Investment: The Key to International Industrial Development*, James Daniel, Ed, (New York: 1958).
Dean, William H., Jr., *The Theory of Economic Activities with Special Reference to Historical Change* (Unpublished Harvard University Ph.D. thesis, 1938).
Deener, David R., *The United States Attorneys General and International Law* (The Hague: Martinus Nijhoff, 1957).
"Deep Mystery," 320 *Industrial Bulletin of Arthur D. Little, Inc.* (May 1955), pp. 1–2.
de Hartingh, France, *Les Conceptions Soviétiques du droit de la Mer* (Paris: Librairie Générale de Droit et de Jurisprudence, 1960).
de Kerchove, René, *International Maritime Dictionary* (New York: Van Nostrand, 1948).
Dennett, Tyler, *Roosevelt and the Russo-Japanese War* (New York: Doubleday, Page 1925).
Dennis, A. L. P., *Adventures in American Diplomacy* (New York: E, P. Dutton, 1928).
Deutsch, Karl W., *Nationalism and Social Communication* (New York: John Wiley & Sons, Inc., 1953).
— and Eckstein, Alexander, *National Industrialization and the Declining Share of the International Economic Sector*, 1890–1957 (Unpublished paper, 1959).
Dickinson, E. D., "Jurisdiction at the Maritime Frontier," 40 *Harvard Law Review* (1926), pl.
Dictionnaire Diplomatique (Paris: Académie Diplomatique Internationale, 1933).
Diplomate, ("Un Ancien"), *Le Régime des Capitulations, son Application, ses Modifications* (1717).
Dizionario Enciclopedico Italiano (Roma: Istituto della Enciclopedia Italiana, 1956).
Dorday, Dezso, "Notes upon the Question of the Delimitation of Territorial Waters," International Law Association, *Report of the Twenty-Fifth Conference, Budapest*, (1908), p. 547.
Dunlap, Orrin E., Jr., *Radar*, Rev. Ed., (New York: Harper & Bros., 1948).
Durant, Will, *The Story of Philosophy*, 2nd Ed., (New York, Pocket Library (1958), (1933).
Du Sein, A., *Histoire de la Marine de Tous les Peuples*, (Paris: Librairie de Fermin-Didot et Cie., 1879).
Eagleton, Clyde, "First Session of the International Law Commission," 43 *American Journal of International Law* (1949), pp. 758–762.
East, W. Gordon and Moodie, A. E., *The Changing World* (Yonkers: World Book Co., 1956).

Easterbrook, W. T., *Canadian Economic History* (Toronto: MacMillan Co. 1956).
Ellison, John W., *Nelson's Complete Concordance of the Revised Standard Version Bible* (New York: Thomas Nelson and Sons, 1956).
Enciclopedia Universal Ilustrada, Europeo-Americano Tomo VII, (Barcelona: José Espasa e Hijos, Ed., 1912).
Evensen, Jens, "The Anglo-Norwegian Fisheries Case and its Legal Consequences," 46 *American Journal of International Law* (1952), pp. 609–630.
Farrell, ENS. Lawrence J., U.S.N.R. "Motor Ships for a stronger and More Secure American Merchant Marine," 68 *Journal of the American Society of Naval Engineers* (Feb. 1956), pp. 143–146.
Farwell, CAPT. Raymond F., U.S. Naval Reserve, *The Rules of the Nautical Road, Rev. Ed. by Alfred Prunski, LT., U.S. Coast Guard* (Annapolis: U.S. Naval Institute, 1954).
Fauchille, Paul, *Traité de droit international public*, vol. I, (Paris: Rousseau et cie, 1925).
Fawcett, Charles B., *Frontiers; a Study in Political Geography* (Oxford: University Press, 1918).
Fenn, Percy T., Jr., "Justinian and the Freedom of the Sea," 19 *American Journal of International Law* (1925) pp. 716–727.
—, "Origins of the Theory of Territorial Waters," 20 *American Journal of International Law* (1926), pp. 465–482.
Field, David Dudley, *Outlines of an International Code*, (New York: Baker, Voorhis & Co., 1876).
Field, James A., Jr., "Sea Power and Military Strategy Today," VIII *U.S. Naval War College Review* (April 1956), pp. 21–39.
Finch, George A., "The Treaty with Nicaragua granting Canal and other Rights to the United States," 10 *American Journal of International Law* (1916), pp. 344–351.
Fioravanzo, VADM Giuseppe, IN, "Italian Strategy in the Mediteranean," 84 *U.S. Naval Institute Proceedings* (Sept. 1958), pp. 65–83.
Fitzmaurice, Sir Gerald "The Law and Procedure of the International Court of Justice, 1951–54; General Principles, and Sourcest of the Law," *British Yearbook of International Law* (1953) pp. 1–70.
Fleming, Dana Frank, *The Treaty Veto of the American Senate* (New York: G. P. Putnam's Sons, 1930).
Florio, Franco, *Il Mare Territoriale e la sua Delimitazione* (Milano: Giuffre, 1947).
François, J. P. A., "La Conférence Diplomatique sur le Droit de la Mer," 4 *Netherlands International Law Review* (October 1957) pp. 338–361.
Friedrich, Carl J., *Alfred Weber's Theory of Location of Industries*, (Chicago: University of Chicago Press, 1929).
Fuller, Maj. Gen. J. F. C., British Army, *Armament and History* (New York: Charles Scribner's Sons, 1945).
Fulton, Thomas W., *The Sovereignty of the Sea* (Edinburgh: William Blackwood & Sons, 1911).
"Le Gabon Réclame ses Terres," 37 *Interafrique Presse* 28 July 1955, pp. 9–11 (Paris: Agence Parisienne de Presse, 1955).
Garcia-Amador, F. V., *The Exploitation and Conservation of the Resources of the Sea*, 2nd Ed. (Leyden: A. W. Sijthoff, 1959).
Garratt, G. T., *Gibraltar and the Mediterranean* (New York:Coward- McCann, 1939).
Gelber, Lionel M., *The Rise of Anglo-American Friendship* (London, Oxford University Press, 1938).

Gibb, Sir Claude, "Two Thousand Years of Engineering," 64 *Journal of the American Society of Naval Engineers* (Feb. 1952), pp. 95–103. (Reprint of Address to British Association for the Advancement of Science, 10 August 1951).

Gibb, H. A. R. and Kramers, J. H., *Shorter Encyclopaedia of Islam* (Ithaca: Cornell University Press, 1953).

Gidel, Gilbert, *Le Droit International Public de la Mer*, 3 vols. (Paris: Librairie du Recueil Sirey, 1934).

Gilmore, Grant and Black, Charles L., Jr., *The Law of Admiralty* (Brooklyn: Foundation Press, 1957).

Glass, CDR, Henry. U.S.N., *Maritime International Law* (Annapolis: U.S. Naval Institute, 1885).

Glazebrook, George P., *A History of Transportation in Canada*, (New Haven: Ryerson Press, 1938).

Golder, F. A., *Russian Expansion on the Pacific, 1641–1850*, (Cleveland: Arthur H. Clark, Co,. 1914).

Gonzales, Salvador R., "The Neutrality of Honduras and the Question of the Gulf of Fonseca," 10 *American Journal of International Law*, (1916), pp. 509–542.

Goldschmidt, Levin "Universalgeschichte des Handelsrechts," Tr. John H. Wigmore, *Primitive and Ancient Legal Institutions* Albert Kocourek and John H. Wigmore, Eds., (Boston: Little, Brown & Co., 1915).

Gooch, G. P., *Nationalism;* London: (Swarthmore Press, 1920).

Grant-Bailey, Samuel N., *The Law of Neutrality*, (London: Stevens & Son, 1944).

Gregory, H. E., and Barnes, K., *North Pacific Fisheries* (New York: Institute of Pacific Relations, 1939).

Gross, Leo, "The Geneva Conference on the Law of the Sea and the right of innocent Passage through the Gulf of Aqaba," 53 *American Journal of International Law* (1959), pp. 564–594.

Grosser Historischer Welt Atlas München: (Bayerischer-Schulbuch Verlag, 1954).

Guill. LT. James H., U.S.N., "The Regimen of the Seas," 83 *U.S. Naval Institute Proceedings* (December 1957), pp. 1308–1319.

Gutteridge, Harold C., *Comparative Law, An Introduction to the Comparative Method of Legal Study and Research* (Cambridge: University Press, 1946).

Gyorgy, Andrew, *Geopolitics, The New German Science* (Berkeley: University of California Press, 1944).

Haberler, Gottfried, *A Survey of International Trade Theory* (Princeton: International Finance Section of Department of Economics and Sociology, 1955).

Hackworth, Green H., *Digest of International Law*, 7 vols, (Washington: U.S. Government Printing Office, 1940–4).

Hakluyt, Richard, *A Selection of the Principal Voyages, Traffiques, and Discoveries of the English Nation* (London: J. M. Dent & Co., 1907).

Hale, Richard W., "Territorial Waters as a Test of Codification," 24 *American Journal of International Law* (1930) pp. 65–68.

Hall, John S., Jr., *Radar Aids to Navigation* (New York: McGraw-Hill, 1947).

Hall, William E., *A Treatise on International Law*, 8th Ed. by A Pearce Higgins, (Oxford: Clarendon Press, 1924).

Halm, George N., *Economic Systems, A Comparative Analysis* (New York, Rinehart, 1951).

Hardy, A. C., "The Adaptability and Value of Diesel Engines for Securing Efficiency in Trawlers," *Fishing News*, 30 October 1959, p. 1 of Propulsion and Maneuver Supplement.

Haring, Clarence H., *Trade and Navigation between Spain and the Indies* (Cambridge: Harvard University Press, 1918).

Harris, Seymour E., *International and Interregional Economics* (New York: McGraw-Hill, 1957).

Harrison, CDR., Charles W., Jr., U.S. Navy and Blower, James E., "Electronics – Your Future," 62 *Journal of the American Society of Naval Engineers*, (Feb. 1950) pp. 99–137.

Harvard Law School "Research in International Law: Territorial Waters," 23 *American Journal of International Law* (April 1929) Special Supplement.

Haushofer, MGEN. Karl, German Army, *Grenzen in ihrer geographischen und politischen Bedeutung*, (Berlin-Grünewald: K. Vorwinckel, 1927).

Hautefeuille, L. B., *Histoire des Origines, des Progrès et des Variations du Droit Maritime International* (Paris: Guillaume et Cie, 1858).

Hazlitt, W. C., *The Venetian Republic*, (London: A. and C. Black, 1900).

Heaton, Herbert, *Economic History of Europe* (New York: Harper & Bros., Rev. Ed. 1948).

Hecksher, Eli, *Mercantilism*, 2 vols. Tr. Mendel Shapiro (London: George Allen & Unwin Ltd., 1934).

Headaway, LCDR. Richard B., U.S. Naval Reserve, "Course Zero Nine Five," 83 *U.S. Naval Institute Proceedings* (Jan. 1957) pp. 40–48.

Hells, Lyman M.; Kern, Willis F.; and Bland, James R., *Piloting and Maneuvering of Ships* (New York; McGraw Hill, 1943).

Herodotus "History," *Great Books of the Western World*, Vol. 6 (Chicago: Encyclopaedia Britannica, 1952).

Herrmann, LCDR. E. E., USN, *Exterior Ballistics 1935* (Annapolis: U.S. Naval Institute, 1935).

Hershey, Amos S., *The International Law and Diplomacy of the Russo-Japanese War* (New York: Macmillan Co,. 1906).

Hewitt, James Francis, *Ruling Races in Prehistoric Times in India, Southwestern Asia and Southern Europe*, 2 vols. (Westminster: Constable & Co., 1894–5).

Hewson, J. B., *A History of the Practice of Navigation* (Glasgow: Brown, Son & Ferguson, Ltd., 1951).

Higgins, Pearce, *Hall's International Law*, 8th Edition (Oxford: Clarendon Press, 1924).

Hill, CDR., John C. II, U.S. Navy; Utegaard, LCDR. Thomas F., U.S. Navy and Riordan, Gerard, U.S. Naval Hydrographic Office, *Dutton's Navigation and Piloting* (Annapolis: U.S. Naval Institute, 1958).

Hill, Norman, *Claims to Territory in International Law and Relations* (New York: Oxford University Press, 1945).

Hime, LCOL. H. W. L , Royal Artillery, *Gunpowder and Ammunition, Their Origin and Progress* (London: Longmans Green, 1904)

Hitti, Philip K., *Lebanon in History* (New York: St. Martin's Press, 1957).

Hjort, Johann, *Report of Norwegian Fishery and Marine Investigation*, Vol I, (Kristiania: 1900).

Hoehl, E. Adamson, *The Law of Primitive Man* (Cambridge: Harvard University Press, 1954).

Holdich, Sir Thomas, *Political Frontiers and Boundary Making* (London: Macmillan & Co., 1916).

Holdsworth, William S., *A History of English Law* (Vol V.) (Boston: Little, Brown & Co., 1926).

Holly, LCDR David C., U.S.N., "All for the Purpose of Marking Time," 79 *U.S. Naval Institute Proceedings* (March 1953), pp. 303–9.
Houtsma, S. A., et al, *The Encyclopaedia of Islam*, (Leyden: E. J. Brill, 1927).
Howes, H. W., *The Story of Gibraltar* (London: Philip & Tracey, Ltd., 1946).
Hübner, *De la Saisie des bâtiments Neutres* (La Haye: 1759).
Hudson, Manley O., "First Conference for Codification of International Law, 24 *American Journal of International Law* (1930) pp. 447–466.
—, "Language Used in Treaties," 26 *American Journal of International Law* (1932) pp. 368–372.
—, "The Thirtieth Year of the World Court," 46 *American Journal of International Law* (1952), pp. 609–630.
Huet, M., *Histoire du Commerce et de la Navigation des Anciens* (Paris: Chez Coustelier, 1716).
Hull, CAPT. Daniel R., USN (Ret.), "Safe Passage," *Marine News* (February 1956), pp. 18–28.
Hunter, Holland, *Soviet Transportation Policy* (Cambridge: Harvard University Press, 1957).
Huntington, Ellsworth, *Civilization and Climate* (New Haven: Yale University Press, 1915).
Hurst, Sir Cecil, "The Territoriality of Bays," *British Yearbook of International Law* 1922–23, p. 42.
Hyde, Charles C., *International Law Chiefly as Interpreted and Applied by the United States* 2nd Rev. Ed. (Boston: Little Brown & Co., 1947).
Hydrographic Dictionary, Special Publication No. 32, 2nd Ed., (Monaco: International Hydrographic Bureau, 1951).
Imlah, Albert H., *Economic Elements in the Pax Britannica* (Cambridge: Harvard University Press, 1958).
Imperial Fisheries Bureau, *Japanese Special Catalog of Sea Fisheries*, (Tokyo: 1915).
International Court of Justice, Reports 1951 (Leyden: A. W. Sijthoff's Co., 1952).
International Maritime Conference – 1889, Report, 3 vols. (Washington: 1889).
Ireland, Gordon, "The North Pacific Fisheries," 36 *American Journal of International Law* (1942), pp. 416–22.
Irie, Keishiro, *Modern Problems in International Relations* (Tokyo: Kobun Do, 1958).
—, *Territories and Military Bases*, (Kyoto; Sanichi Shobo, 1959).
Jackson, Sir Robert, "Freedom of the Seas," 37 *Foreign Affairs* (October 1958) pp. 83–94.
Jacobsen, Friederich Johann, *Seerecht des Friedens und des Krieges* (Altona: Hammerick, 1814).
James, Thomas, *The Dangerous Voyage of Captain Thomas James, in his intended Discovery of a North-West Passage into the South Sea* (London: I. Legatt, 1633).
Jenks, Edward, *Law and Politics in the Middle Ages* (London: Longmans Green, 1918).
Jenkins, J. T., *A History of the Whale Fisheries*, (London: Witherby, 1921).
Jessup, Philip C., *The Law of Territorial Waters and Maritime Jurisdiction* (New York: G. A. Jennings Co. 1927).
—, "L'Exploitation des Richesses de la Mer," 29 *Recueil des Cours de la Haye*, Vol. IV (1929).
Johnson, D. H. N., "The Anglo-Norwegian Fisheries Case," *International and Comparative Law Quarterly.*

Johnson, V. Kenneth, "Canada's Title to Hudson Bay and Hudson Strait," 15 *British Yearbook of International Law* (1934), pp. 1–20.

Jones, Ralph H., *The Context of International Law* (Unpublished U.S. Naval War College Manuscript, 1957).

Justice, Alexander, *A General Treatise of the Dominion of the Sea* (London: J. Nicholson, 1710).

Kalijarvi, Thorsten, "Scandinavian Claims to Jurisdiction over Territorial Waters," 26 *American Journal of International Law* (1932) pp. 57–69.

Katzenbach, Nicholas "Conflicts on an Unruly Horse: Reciprocal Claims and Tolerances in Interstate and International Law," 65 *Yale Law Journal* (July 1956).

Keller, Arthur S.; Lissitzyn; Oliver J.; Mann, Frederick J., *Creation of Rights through Symbolic Acts 1400–1800* (New York: Columbia University Press, 1938).

Kelly, Thomas J. "Improvement in Radar Presentation," Paper presented at International Meeting on the Use of Radar at Sea, Genoa, Italy, 16 May 1957.

Kelsen, Hans, *General Theory of the Law and the State* (Cambridge: Harvard University Press, 1949).

Kennedy, William P. M., *Statutes, Treaties, and Documents of the Canadian Constitution 1713–1929*, 2nd Edition (New York: Oxford University Press, 1930).

Kent, H. S. K., "The Historical Origins of the Three-Mile Limit," 48 *American Journal of International Law* (1954), pp. 537–553.

Khadduri, Majid and Liebesney, Herbert J., *Law in the Middle East*, Vol. I, *Origin and Development of Islamic Law* (Washington: The Middle East Institute).

—, *War and Peace in the Law of Islam* (Baltimore: Johns Hopkins Press, 1955).

Kindleberger, Charles P., "Statement on Imports, the Tariff, and the Need for Adjustment," *Compendium of Papers on U.S. Foreign Trade Policy, U.S. House of Representatives Committee on Ways and Means* (Washington: U.S. Government Printing Office, 1957) pp. 73–87.

—, *Economic Development* (New York: McGraw Hill, 1958).

King, B. E., "Prescription of Claims in International Law," 15 *British Yearbook of International Law* (1934), pp. 82–97.

King, FADM Ernest J., U.S.N. & Whitehill, CDR., Walter M., U.S.N.R., *A Naval Record* (New York: W. W. Norton, 1952).

Kitto, F. H., *The Hudson Bay Region* (Ottawa: Department of the Interior, 1929).

Kleen, Richard, *Lois et Usages de la Neutralité*, 2 vols, (Paris: Chevalier-Marescq, 1898–1900).

Klimm, Lester E.; Starkey, Otis P.; and Hall, Norman F., *Introductory Economic Geography* (New York: Harcourt, Brace, 1937).

Klüber, Johann L., *Droit des Gens Moderne de l'Europe*, 2nd Ed. (Paris: Guillaumin et Cie, 1874).

Knight, Melvin M., Barnes, Harry E. and Flügel, Felix, *Economic History of Europe* (Boston: Houghton Mifflin Co., 1928).

Knox, COMO Dudley, U.S.N., *A History of the United States Navy*, Rev. Ed. (New York: G. P. Putnam's Sons, 1948).

Kocourek, Albert, and Wigmore, John H., *Sources of Ancient and Primitive Law* (Boston: Little, Brown & Co., 1915).

Kohn, Hans, *Nationalism, Its Meaning and History* (New York: D. Van Nostrand 1955).

The Koran, Tr. by Dawood (London: Penguin Books, 1956).

Korowicz, Marek St., "Modern Doctrines of the Sovereignty of States," 5 *Netherlands Journal of International Law* (1958) pp. 32–56, 150–164.

—, *An Introduction to International Law* (The Hague: Martinus Nijhoff, 1959).

Kunz, Josef L., *Kriegsrecht und Neutralitätsrecht* (Wien: Verlag Julius Springer, 1935).

Krypton, Constantine, *The Northern Sea Route and the Economy of the Soviet North* (New York: Praeger, 1956).

La Grande Encyclopédie (Paris: Librairie Larousse, 1912).

Lalarbe, Jules, *La Loi Navale de Themistocle* (Paris: Societé d'Edition "Les Belles Lettres," 1957).

Lansdell, Henry, *Through Siberia*, (Boston: Houghton Mifflin, 1882).

Lansing, Robert, "The North Atlantic Fisheries Arbitration," 5 *American Journal of International Law* (1911), pp. 19–25.

de Lapradelle, Paul Geouffre, *La Frontière* (Doctoral Thesis) (Paris: Les Editions Internationales, 1928).

Larousse, Pierre, *Grand Dictionnaire Universel du XIX Siècle* (Paris: Administration du Grand Dictionnaire Universel, 1867).

Latour, Joseph Imbort, *La Mer territoriale au Point de Vue théorique et pratique* (Paris: Pedone Lariel, 1889).

Latourette, Kenneth S., *The Chinese, their History and Culture* (New York, Macmillan, 1934).

Lattimore, Owen, *Manchuria Cradle of Conflict* (New York: Macmillan, 1932).

Lauterpacht, Sir Hersch, *Private Law Sources and Analogies of International Law* (London: Longmans, Green, 1927).

—, *The Development of International Law by the International Court* (New York: Praeger, 1958).

—, *The Function of Law in the International Community* (Oxford: Clarendon Press, 1933).

—, *Oppenheim's International Law*, Vol. I, 8th Ed. (London: Longmans, Green, 1955).

"The Law of the Sea, Progress towards International Agreement – The Egyptian Position," 13 *Revue Égyptienne de droit international* (1957), pp. 70–1.

Lawrence, Thomas J., *The Principles of International Law*, 5th Ed., (London, Macmillan, 1913).

League of Nations, *Acts of the Conference for the Codification of International Law*, vols. I, III, Documents V. Legal 1930. V. 14, 16.

Le Main, A. Captaine de Frégate (CDR.) F.N., *Précis de droit Maritime International et de Diplomatie* (Paris: Berger-Leurault, 1888).

Lenczowski, George, *Oil and State in the Middle East*, (Ithaca: Cornell University Press, 1960).

—, *The Middle East in World Affairs*, 2nd Ed. (Ithaca: Cornell University Press, 1956).

Leonard, L. Larry, *International Regulation of Fisheries* (Washington: Institute of Pacific Relations, 1944).

Le Roy, *La Marine des Anciens Peuples* (Paris: Chez Nyon, 1777).

Lewis, Bernard, *The Arabs in History*, Rev. Ed. (London: Hutchinson University Library, 1958).

Liang, Yuan-li, "The General Assembly and the Progressive Development and Codification on International Law," 42 *American Journal of International Law* (1948), pp. 66–68.

Lindsay, W. S., *History of Merchant Shipping and Ancient Commerce*, 4 vols. (London: Sampson Low, Marston, Low and Searle, 1874).
Lippman, Walter, *The Good Society* (Boston: Little Brown & Co., 1937).
Lipson, Leslie, *Great Issues of Politics* (New York: Prentice-Hall, 1954).
Lissitzyn, Oliver J., "Western and Soviet Perspectives on International Law – A comparison," *Proceedings of the American Society of International Law* 1959, pp. 21–30.
Littré, Émile, *Dictionnaire de la Langue Française* (Paris: Librairie Hachette et Cie., 1885).
Lombardo, Giuseppina, *Cimone, Ricostruzione della Biographica e Discussioni Storographice* (Roma: Instituto Poligraphica dello Stato, 1934).
Luhbert, H. L., and Ehrenbaum, *Handbuch der Seefischerei Nordeuropas*, 10 Vols., (Stuttgart: 1936–8).
Lynch, Arthur H., "Making Life Safe at Sea" (1922), Raytheon Manufacturing Co.
M. I. "A Map Analysis of Japan's Fishery-Problems," 3 *The Japanese Annual of International Law* (1959), pp. 103–108.
Mac Chesney, Brunson, *U.S. Naval War College International Law Situation and Documents* 1956 (Washington: U.S. Government Printing Office, 1957).
Mackay, John A., *The Honourable Company*, (New York: Macmillan, 1938).
Mahan, CAPT Alfred T., USN, *The Influence of Seapower upon History, 1660–1783*, (Boston: Little, Brown & Co., 1890).
Malek, Chafic, "La Théorie Dite des Baies Historiques," 6 *Revue de Droit International pour le Moyen-Orient* December 1957 (No. 2) pp. 100–173.
Marcel, Gabriel, "La Cartographie de la Nouvelle France, supplément à l'ouvrage de M. Henry Harrisse sur le même sujet," *Revue de Géographie* (Mar-Apr. 1885) pp. 62–85.
Martens, *Recueil des Traités*, various series and volumes.
Masterson, William E., *Jurisdiction in Marginal Seas*, (New York: The Macmillan Co., 1929).
McIness, Edgar, *Canada: A Political and Social History* (New York: Rinehart, 1947).
Mackinder, Sir Halford, "The Geographic Pivot of History," 33 *Geographic Journal* (1904), pp. 434–7.
Mahan, RADM Alfred T., U.S. Navy, (Ret), *The Interest of America in Sea Power, Present and Future* (Boston: Little, Brown & Co., 1897).
Maine, Sir Henry, *Ancient Law* (New York: Henry Holt & Co., 1888).
—, *Early History of Institutions* (New York: Henry Holt & Co., 1888).
—, *International Law* (New York: Henry Holt & Co., 1888).
Malinowski, Bronislaw, *Crime and Custom in Savage Society* (New York: Harcourt, Brace & Co., 1926).
Malloy, Charles, *A treatise of Affairs Maritime and Commerce*, 3rd Ed., (London: 1682).
Malouet, Baron, *Considérations Historiques sur l'Empire de la Mer Chez les Anciens et les Modernes* (Paris: Chez le Poittevie Delacroix, 1810).
Malozemoff, Andrew, *Russian Far Eastern Policy 1881–1904* (Berkeley: University of California Press, 1958).
van Manen, J. D., "Fundamentals of Ship Resistance and Propulsion," 4 *International Shipbuilding Progress*, Feb. 1957.
Manncy, Albert, *Artillery through the Ages* (Washington: U.S. Government Printing Office, 1949).
Mannheim, Karl, *Man and Society in an Age of Reconstruction* (London: Paul, Trench, Trubner, 1940).

Manning, LCDR., G. C., CC, U.S.N. and Schumacher, LCDR T. L., CC, U.S.N., *Principles of Warship Construction and Damage Control* (Annapolis: U.S. Naval Institute, 1935).

Margolis, Emanuel, *Certain Aspects of the Impact of Communism on International Law* (Unpublished Ph. D. thesis, Harvard University, 1951).

Marris, MID. O. R., U.S.N., "Homer Clark Poundstone and the All Big-Gun Ship," 74 *U.S. Naval Institute Proceedings* (June 1948), pp. 707–721.

Marsden, R. G., *Documents Relating to the Law and Custom of the Sea* 2 vols. (London: Navy Records Society, 1915–1916).

Marshall, Albert, *Explosives, Their Manufacture, Properties, Tests and History* (London: J. & A. Churchill, 1915).

Martineau, Harriette, *The Positive Philosophy of Auguste Comte*, 2 vols. (London: J. Chapman, 1853).

Mason, Edward S., *Economic Planning in Undeveloped Areas* (New York: Fordham University Press, 1958).

May, LCDR Robert, U.S. Maritime Service and Pearson, LT Leland, U.S. Maritime Service, "Landfall, The Navigator's Tensest Moment," 15 *Sperryscope* (2nd Qtr. 1959), pp. 12–16.

McDougal, Myers S. and Burke, William T., "Crisis in the Law of the Sea: Community Perspectives versus National Egoism," 67 *Yale Law Journal* (Feb. 1958), p. 551.

McGrath, P. T., "The Hudson Bay Dispute," *The Fortnightly Review*, 1 Jan. 1908, pp. 125–136.

McNair, Arnold D., *The Law of Treaties* (Oxford: Clarendon Press, 1938).

McNair, Lord, *International Law Opinions*, 3 vols. (Cambridge: University Press, 1956).

Mead, W. R., *An Economic Geography of the Scandinavian States and Finland*, (London: University of London Press, 1958).

Meigs, LCDR John Forsyth, U.S. Navy (Ret.), *The Story of the Seaman*, 2 vols. (Philadelphia: J. B. Lippincott Co., 1912).

Melamid, Alexander, "Legal Status of the Gulf of Aqaba," 53 *American Journal of International Law* (1959), pp. 412–3.

—, "Political Geography of the Gulf of Aqaba," 47 *Annals of the Association of American Geographers* (1967), pp. 231–240.

Menken, Henry L., *The American Language*, 4th Ed., (New York: Alfred A. Knopf, 1949).

Merrill, CAPT R. T., USCGR (Ret.), "Uniform Tonnage Measurement," 77 *U.S. Naval Institute Proceedings* (December 1951) pp. 1297–1304.

—, "The Decade of Transition – Our Early Steam Navy and Merchant Marine," 78 *U.S. Naval Institute Proceedings* (Sept. 1952) pp. 1005–1015.

Meyer, CAPT Christopher B. V., Royal Norwegian Navy, *The Extent of Jurisdiction in Coastal Waters* (Leyden: A. W. Sijthoff, 1937).

Meyers Konversationslexikon (Leipzig: Bibliographisches Institut, 1924).

Michael, Franz, *The Origins of Manchu Rule in China* (Baltimore: Johns Hopkins Press, 1942).

Mill, John Stuart, *Principles of Political Economy* (London: George Routledge and Sons, 1891).

Miller, LT Arthur P., USNR "Loran Comes of Age," 81 *U.S. Naval Institute Proceedings* (July 1955), pp. 764–770.

Miller, Hunter, "The Hague Codification Conference," 24 *American Journal of International Law* (1930), 674.

Mitchell, George S., *Russian-English Dictionary-Glossary in Geomorphology and Related Sciences*, Unpublished M.A. thesis.

Mochot, Jean, *Le Régime des Baies et des Golfes en Droit International* (Paris: Librairie Niget et Bastard, 1933).

du Mont, Jean, *Corps Universel diplomatique du Droit des Gens Contenant un Recueil des Traités*, 3 vols. (Amsterdam: Chez P. Brunel, 1726–1731).

de Montesquieu, Charles Louis, Baron, *The Spirit of Laws*, Tr. Thomas Nugent, 2vols. (London: The Colonial Press, 1900).

Montross, Lynn, *War through the Ages* (New York: Harper and Brothers, 1944).

Moodie, A. E., *Geography behind Politics* (London: Hutchinson's University Library, 1957).

Moody, LCDR Alton B., USNR, "The Nautical Mile," 75 *U.S. Naval Institute Proceedings* (Nov. 1949) pp. 1257–1262.

Moore, Harriet L., *Soviet Far Eastern Policy 1931–1945* (Princeton: Princeton University Press, 1945).

Moore, John Bassett, *A Digest of International Law*, 6 vols., (Washington: U.S. Government Printing Office, 1906).

—, *History and Digest of the Arbitrations to which the United States have been a party* (Washington: U.S. Government Printing Office, 1898).

—, Letter quoted in 13 *Annuaire de l'Institut de Droit International* (1894–95), p. 146.

Morgan, Robert, *World Sea Fisheries* (London: Methuen & Co., 1956).

Morse, Hosea Ballou, *The International Relations of the Chinese Empire, The Period of Conflict 1834–1860* (London: Longmans, Green, 1910).

Moscow, Alvin, *Collision Course* (New York: Putnam, 1959).

Müller-Jockmus, Mauritius, *Geschichte des Völkerrechts im Altertum* (Leipzig, Ernst Keil, 1848).

Münch, Fritz, *Die Technischen Fragen des Küstenmeers*, (Kiel: Verlag des Instituts für Internationales Recht, 1934).

A Naval Encyclopaedia (Philadelphia: L. R. Hammersly & Co., 1881).

Neblett, CDR William R. USNR (Ret.), "Freedom of the Seas – For Fishing," 85 *U.S. Naval Institute Proceedings* (Feb. 1959) pp. 85–87.

Nichols, RADM C. L., U.S.N. (Ret.), "The International Hydrographic Bureau," 77 *U.S. Naval Institute Proceedings* (July 1951), pp. 717–722.

Nunn, RADM Ira H., U.S. Navy, "Admiralty Law and Its Relation to Command at Sea," VI *U.S. Naval War College* Review (Dec. 1953), pp. 1–29.

Nurkse, Ragnar, *Problems of Capital Formation in Underdeveloped Countries* (Oxford: Blackwell, 1957).

Nussbaum, Arthur, "The Significance of Roman Law in the History of International Law," 100 *University of Pennsylvania Law Review* (March 1952) pp. 678–687.

—, *A Concise History of the Law of Nations*, Rev. Ed. (New York: Macmillan, 1959).

Nys, Ernest, *Les Origines du Droit International* (Haarlem: Erven F. Bohn, 1894).

O'Connell, D. P., "Problems of Australian Coastal Jurisdiction," 34 *British Yearbook of International Law* (1959), p. 199 ff.

Oda, Shigeru, "New Trends in the Regime of the Seas," 18 *Zeitschrift für Ausländisches Recht und Völkerrecht* (1957), pp. 61–87.

—, "Japan and the United Nations Conference on the Law of the Sea," 3 *The Japanese Annual of International Law* (1959), pp. 65–86.

Official Documents, Conference for the Codification of International Law, 24 *American Journal of International Law* (1930) Supplement.

Ohlin, Bertil, *Interregional and International Trade*, (Cambridge: Harvard University Press, 1957).

Okoshi, Narinori, *A Sketch of the Fisheries of Japan* (London: Clowes, 1883).

Oliver, LCDR. Edward F. USCG, "Ships that Pass in the Night" 85 *U.S. Naval Institute Proceedings* (Nov. 1959), pp. 70–78.

Organ, CAPT William H., USN., "Inshore Navigation with Radar and VPR," 75 *U.S. Naval Institute Proceedings* (Aug. 1949), pp. 925–930.

Ormerod, Henry A., *Piracy in the Ancient World* (London: Hodder and Stoughton, Ltd., 1924).

Oudet, Capitaine de Frégate (CDR) L., FN, "Radar and Collision Regulations" XII *The Journal of the Institute of Navigation* (Apr. 1958) pp. 58–65.

Pardessus, Jean Marie, *Us et Coutumes de la Mer*, 2 vols. (Paris: Imprimerie Royale, 1847).

Pareto, Vilfredo, *The Mind and Society*, 4 vols., Tr. Livingston, (New York: Harcourt, Brace, 1935).

Pearcy, G. Etzel, "*Measurement of the U.S. Territorial Sea*," (Washington: U.S. Government Printing Office, 1959).

Perry, CAPT E. B., U.S. Navy, (Ret.), "The U.S. Merchant Marine and Obsolescence," 70 *Journal of the American Society of Naval Engineers* (May 1958), pp. 354–8.

Phillipson, Coleman, *The International Law of Ancient Greece and Rome* (London: Macmillan & Co., Ltd., 1911).

Phleger, Herman, "Recent Developments Affecting the Regime of the High Seas," 32 *Department of State Bulletin* (1955), p. 934.

Pierantoni, Augusto, *Storia del Diritto Internazionale nel secolo XIX* (Napoli: Giuseppe Marghieri, 1876).

Pinto, Roger, "La prescription en droit international," 87 *Recueil des Cours de l'Académie de Droit international* (1955) vol. I, pp. 411–26.

Plutarch, *Lives* (New York: Modern Library).

Pohl, Frederick J. and Loeb, CAPT Leonard B., U.S. Naval Reserve (Ret.) "Americo Vespucci – Pioneer of Celo-Navigation," 83 *U.S. Naval Institute Proceedings* (Apr. 1957) p. 399 ff.

Politis, Nicolas, *Neutrality and Peace*, (Washington: Carnegie Endowment, 1935).

Polk, Judd, *Sterling: Its Meaning in World Finance* (New York: Harper & Bro., 1956).

Popper, Karl R., *The Poverty of Historicism* (Boston: The Beacon Press, 1957).

Porter, Earle, "The Small Boat Radio," 12 May 1959, Raytheon Manufacturing Company Technical Paper.

Pound, Roscoe, *An Introduction to the Philosophy of Law* (New Haven: Yale University Press, 1922).

Pounder, C. C., "Some Factors in the Comparison of Propelling Machinery Types," 61 *Journal of the American Society of Naval Engineers* (May 1949), pp. 450–460.

Potter, Pitman B., *The Freedom of the Seas in History, Law and Politics* (New York: Longmans, Green & Co., 1924).

Preston, Richard A., "Don't sell Gibraltar Short," 76 *U.S. Naval Institute Proceedings* (Dec. 1950), pp. 1329–1336).

Puleston, CAPT W. D., U.S.N. (Ret.), "Ancient and Modern Aspects of Sea Power," 74 *U.S. Naval Institute Proceedings* (Nov. 1948), pp. 1351–1365.

Pundeft, Marin, "Bulgarian Decree on Territorial Waters," 46 *American Journal of International Law* (April 1952).

Radar Beacons, Vol. 3 of Massachusetts Institute of Technology Radiation Laboratory Series (New York: McGraw Hill, 1949).

Radin, Max, *Handbook of Roman Law*, (St. Paul: West Publishing Co., 1927).

Raestad, Arnold, *La Mer Territoriale* (Paris: Librairie de la Cour d'Appel et de l'Ordre des Avocats, 1913).
Ratzel, Friedrich, *Das Meer als Quelle der Völker-grösse. Eine politisch-geographische Studie* (München: R. Oldenburg, 1923).
—, *Politische Geographie* (München: R. Oldenburg, 1923).
Reddie, James, *Researches Historical and Critical in Maritime International Law*, 2 vols. (Edinburgh: Thomas Clark, 1844).
Reeves, Jesse S., "Hague Conference on Codification of International Law," 24 *American Journal of International Law* (1930), pp. 52–57.
Reeves, Jesse S. "Codification of the Law of Territorial Waters" 24 *American Journal of International Law* (1930) pp. 486–499.
Reichenbach, Hans, *The Rise of Scientific Philosophy* (Berkeley: University of California Press, 1958).
Reiff, Henry, *The United States and the Treaty Law of the Sea* (Minneapolis: University of Minnesota Press, 1959).
Reinotjes, J. Francis and Coste, Godfrey T., *Principles of Radar* (New York: McGraw-Hill, 1952).
Riesenfeld, Stefan A., *Protection of Coastal Fisheries under International Law* (Washington: Carnegie Endowment for International Peace, 1942).
Rivier, Alphonse, *Principes du Droit des Gens* (Paris: Librairie Nouvelle de droit et de Jurisprudence, 1896).
Robbins, RADM Thomas H., Jr., "The Study of International Law at the Naval War College," 50 *American Journal of International Law* (1956), pp. 659–663.
Robinett, CHBOSN C. M., U.S.N. (Ret.) "Ship Technology and the Defeat of the Armada," 78 *U.S. Naval Institute Proceedings* (Feb. 1952) pp. 171–180.
Robison, RADM S. S., USN (Ret.) *A History of Naval Tactics from 1530 to 1930* (Annapolis: U.S. Naval Institute, 1942).
Rodgers, RADM William L., U.S. Navy, "What Parts of International Law May be Codified," 20 *American Journal of International Law* (1926) pp. 437–443.
—, VADM William L., U.S.N. (Ret), *Naval Warface under Oars, 4th to 16th Centuries* (Annapolis: U.S. Naval Institute, 1939).
Raested, Arnold, *La Mer Territoriale* (Paris: Librairie de la Cour d'Appel et de l'Ordre des Avocats, 1913).
Roget, Samuel R., *Roget's Thesaurus of Words and Phrases*, Rev. and Auth. American Edition (New York: Grosset and Dunlap, 1941).
Rolin, Alberic, *Les Origines de l'Institut de Droit International*, (Bruxelles: 1923).
Romanov, V. A., "The Gulf of Peter the Great," 5 *Sovetskoe Gosudarstvo i Pravo* (May 1958), pp. 47–55.
Rosenne, Shabtai, *The International Court of Justice* (Leyden: A. W. Sijthoff, 1957).
Ross, Alf, *On Law and Justice* (Berkeley: University of California Press, 1959).
Rowse, A. L., "The Elizabethans and America," X *American Heritage*, April 1959, p. 4 f. and June 1959, p. 4 f.
Roxley, Percy M., "What is a Natural Region?," IV *Geographical Review* (1908), p. 126 ff.
Rundall, Thomas, Ed., *Narratives of Voyages towards the North-West, in Search of a Passage to Cathay and India, 1496–1631* (London: Hakluyt Society, 1849).
Russell, Sir E. John, *World Population and World Food Supplies* (London: George Allen and Unwin Ltd., 1954).

Sabine, George H., *A History of Political Theory*, Rev. Ed. (New York: Henry Holt & Co., 1958).

Samore, William, "The New International Law of Alejandro Alvarez," 52 *American Journal of International Law* (1958), pp. 41–54.

Samuelson, Paul A., *Economics*, 4th Ed. (New York: McGraw-Hill, 1958).

Sapir, Edward, "Language" IX *Encyclopaedia of the Social Sciences* (New York: MacMillan, 1935) pp. 155–168.

von Savigny, F. C., *Geschichte des Romanischen Rechts im Mittelalter* (Heidelberg: J. C. B. Mohr, 1834–38).

von Scala, Rudolph, *Die Staatsverträge des Altertums* (Leipzig: B. G. Taubner, 1898).

Schepers, Hansjulius, *Japans See-Fischerei* (Breslau: Ferdinand Hirt, 1935).

Schlesinger, James R., "The Perspective of Economics," *National Security Studies 1957* (Newport: U.S. Naval War College, 1958).

Schucking, Sir William, *The Hudson's Bay Company* (London: MacMillan, 1911).

Schlesinger, Rudolph, *Soviet Legal Theory* (London: Routledge & Kegan Paul, 1951).

Schücking, Walter, "Le Développement du Pacte de la Société des Nations," 20 *Recueil des Cours de l'Académie de Droit international de la Haye* (1927), pp. 353–456.

Schumpeter, Joseph, *Imperialism and Social Classes* (New York: A. H. Kelly, 1951).

—, *The Theory of Economic Development* (Cambridge: Harvard University Press, 1951).

Schwarzenberger, Georg, "Title to Territory: Response to a Challenge," 51 *American Journal of International Law* (April 1957) pp. 308–324.

Schweizer Lexikon, (Zürich, Encyclios-Verlag, A. v., 1945).

Scitovsky, Tibor, *Welfare and Competition* (Chicago: Richard D. Irwin, Inc., 1951).

Seacoast Artillery, Basic Tactics and Technique (Harrisburg: Military Service Publishing Co., 1944).

Selak, Charles B., Jr., "A Consideration of the Legal Status of the Gulf of Aqaba," 52 *American Journal of International Law* (1958), pp. 660–698.

Selden, John, *Mare Clausum: the Right and Dominion of the Sea*, Tr. by J. H., Gent. (London: Kembe and Thomas, 1663).

Semyonov, Yuri, *The Conquest of Siberia*, (London: George Routledge, 1944).

Sereni, Anglo Piero, *The Italian Conception of International Law* (New York: Columbia University Press, 1943).

Shabad, Theodore, *Geography of the USSR, A Regional Survey* (New York: Columbia University Press, 1951).

Shalowitz, Aaron L., "Boundary Problems Raised by the Submerged Lands Act," 54 *Columbia Law Review* (Nov. 1954) pp. 1021–43.

—, U.S. Coast and Geodetic Survey, "The Concept of the Bay as Inland Waters," 13 *Surveying and Mapping* (Oct.-Dec. 1933), pp. 432–440.

—, U.S. Coast and Geodetic Survey "Where are our Seaward Boundaries?," 83 *U.S. Naval Institute Proceedings* (June 1957) pp. 616–627.

Shapera, I., *Government and Politics in Tribal Societies* (London: Watts, 1956).

Shenton, Herbert N., *Cosmopolitan Conversation: The Problems of International Conferences* (New York: Columbia University Press, 1933).

Shepard, Arthur MacCartney, *Sea Power in Ancient History* (Boston: Little Brown & Co., 1924).

Shukairy, Ahmad, Saudi Arabian Mission to the United Nations. "On the Question of the Regime of Historic Waters, Including Historic Bays," an address before the United Nations Sixth Committee, 30 November 1959.

Sinclair, Huntley M., *A Preface to Economic History* (New York: Harper, 1934).

Slack, Robert N. "Speed in Fog," 85 *U.S. Naval Institute Proceedings* (July 1959) pp. 77–85.

Smith, Adam, *An Inquiry into the Nature and Causes of the Wealth of Nations*, 1776 (New York: Modern Library Edition; Random House, 1937).

Smith, CAPT (E) Edgar C., R.N. (Ret.), "The Hon. Sir Charles A. Parsons," 66 *Journal of the American Society of Naval Engineers* (Nov. 1954), pp. 823–828.

Smith, H. A., *Great Britain and the Law of Nations*, 2 vols., (London: P. S. King & Son, 1932).

Smith, F. A. and Sibley, N. W., *International Law as Interpreted during the Russo-Japanese War* (Boston: Boston Book Co., 1905).

Smith, William, *A Dictionary of Greek and Roman Geography*, vol. I (London: John Murray, 1818).

Smythe, ADM W. H., Royal Navy, *The Sailor's Word Book*, Rev. by V. Adm. Sir E. Belcher, R. N. (London: Blackie and Son, 1867).

Snider, Delbert A., *Introduction to International Economics* (Homewood, Illinois: Richard D. Irwin, Inc., 1954).

Sohn, Rudolf, *The Institutes: A Textbook of the History and System of Roman and Private Law* (3rd Ed., (Oxford: Clarendon Press, 1907).

Solow, Herbert, "Those Resourceful Greek Shipping Men," 48 *Fortune* (Oct. 1953) p. 142 ff.

Sørenson, Max, "Law of the Sea," 520 *International Conciliation* (November 1958).

Southworth, John van Duyn, "The 'Yankee' Device," 85 *U.S. Naval Institute Proceedings* (April 1959), pp. 97–103.

Special Delegation of the Far Eastern Republic, *Fisheries of the Far Eastern Republic* (Washington: 1922).

Spykman, Nicholas J., *America's Strategy in World Politics* (New York: Harcourt Brace, 1942).

Stanford Research Institute, *U.S. Foreign Policy, A Study for the Senate Committee on Foreign Relations* (Washington: U.S. Government Printing Office, 1959).

Stevens, William O. and Westcott, Allan, *A History of Sea Power* (New York: Doubleday, Doran & Co., 1937).

Stockton, RADM Charles H., U.S.N. (Ret.). *Outlines of International Law* (New York: Scribner's, 1914).

Stone, Julius, "On the Vocation of the International Law Commission," 57 *Columbia Law Review* (Jan. 1957) pp. 16–51.

—, *Legal Controls of International Conflict* (New York: (New York: Rinehart, 1954).

—, *The Province and Function of Law* (Sydney: Associated Central Publications Ptg. Ltd., 1946).

Stuyt, A. M., *The General Principles of Law as applied by international tribunals to disputes on attribution and exercise of State Jurisdiction* (The Hague: Martinus Nijhoff, 1947).

Summer, Thomas H., *A New and Accurate Method of Finding a Ship's Position at Sea by Projection on Mercator's Chart* (Boston: T. Groone & Co., 1843).

Suy, Eric, "Les Golfes et les Baies en Droit International Public," 54 *Die Friedenswarte* (Nov. 2, 1957), pp. 101–116.

Taggart, Robert, "Early Developments in Marine Propulsion," 70 *Journal of the American Society of Naval Engineers* (May 1958), pp. 191–208.

Takahashi, Sakuye, *International Law applied to the Russo-Japanese War* (New York: The Banks Law Publishing Co., 1908).

Takano, Yuichi, "Territorial Problems between Japan and the USSR," 3 *The Japanese Annual of International Law* (1959) pp. 52–64.

Taracouzio, Timothy A., *The Soviet Union and International Law* (New York: Macmillan, 1935).

Tarshis, Lorie, *Introduction to International Trade and Finance* (New York: Wiley, 1955).

Taussig, LCDR Joseph K. Jr., U.S.N., "Radar, Collisions and the Rules of the Road," 75 *U.S. Naval Institute Proceedings* (Sept. 1949) pp. 1029–1040.

Testa, Carlos, Capitaine de Vaisseau (CAPT.), Royal Portuguese Navy, *Le Droit Public International Maritime* (Paris: G. Pedone-Lauriel, 1886).

Thiel, Erich, *The Soviet Far East*, (New York: Praeger, 1953).

Thompson, Warren S., *Population Problems* (New York: McGraw-Hill Book Co., 1953).

Thorndike, Lynn, *The History of Medieval Europe* (Boston: Houghton Mifflin Co., 1917).

Threadgold, Donald W., *The Great Siberian Migration* (Princeton: Princeton University Press, 1957).

Thucydides, "The History of the Peloponnesian War," *Great Books of the Western World*, Vol. 6 (Chicago: Encyclopaedia, 1952).

Tomasevich, Joso, *International Agreements on Conservation of Resources* (Stanford: Food Resources Institute, 1943).

Torr, J. L., *Ancient Ships* (Cambridge: University Press, 1898).

Toucie-Sarinj, Lujo, "Der Kampf um den Persischen Golf," 11 *Europa Archiv* (No. 20 – 20 October 1956) pp. 9239–49.

de Tourtelon, Pierre, *Philosophy in the Development of Law* Tr. Martha McC. Read (New York: Macmillan, 1922).

Tower, Walter S., *A History of the American Whale Industry*, (Philadelphia University of Pennsylvania Press, 1906).

Treaties and Other International Acts Series, TIAS.

Tucker, Robert W., *U.S. Naval War College International Law Studies* 1955 (Washington: U.S. Government Printing Office, 1957).

Tung, L., *China and Some Phases of International Law* (New York: Oxford University Press, 1940).

United Nations, Various Documents.

United Nations, *Report of Committee of Experts on the Law of the Sea* April 1953, A/CN.4/61/Add. 4.

—, *Committee of Experts Report on the Law of the Sea* A/CN.4/61/Add. 1 of 1953.

—, *The Determinants and Consequences of Population Trends* ST/SOA/Ser. A/17 (1953).

—, *3rd Report on the Regime of the Territorial Sea*, submitted to International Law Commission at 6th Session (1954), A.CN/4/77.

—, *Reference Guide to the Article concerning the Law of the Sea adapted by the International Law Commission at its Eighth Session* A/C.6/L.378 of 25 October 1956.

—, Food and Agriculture Organization, *The Economic Importance of Sea Fisheries of Different Countries* (Preparatory Document No. 13, United Nations Conference on the Law of the Sea) A/Conf. 13/16 of 20 November 1957.

U.S. Coast Guard, *Aids to Navigation Manual*, Rev. 1951 (Washington: U.S. Government Printing Office, 1951).

U.S. Congress, Senate, *Proceedings in the North Atlantic Coast Fisheries Arbitration,* 12 vols., 61st Cong., 3rd Session, Senate Document No. 870 (Washington, 1912).

U.S. Navy Department, *The Law of Naval Warfare,* NWIP 10–2, (1956).

U.S. Navy Hydrographic Office, *Navigation Dictionary,* Publication N. 220 (Washington: U.S. Government Printing Office, 1956).

—, Radio Aids to Navigation, Publication No. 205.

United States Navy Hydrographic Office, various charts and publications, (Washington: U.S. Government Printing Office).

U.S. Naval War College, *A Review of the Naval History of the Eighteenth Century,* 10 parts (Newport: 1941).

United States Naval War College, various volumes of the series of *International Law Documents, Situations, and Studies,* (Washington: U.S. Government Printing Office, 1901 through 1956).

Usher, A. P., "The History of Population and Settlement in Eurasia," XX *Geographical Review* (1930), pp. 110–132.

Vali, F. A., *Servitudes of International Law,* 2nd Ed. (New York: Praeger, 1958).

Verzijl, J. H. W., "Territorial Controversies before the International Court of Justice," I *Netherlands International Law Review* (1954), pp. 234–267.

de Villeneuve, Romée, *De la Détermination de la Ligne Séparative des Eaux nationales de la Mer territoriale, spécialement dans les Baies* (Paris: Thèse, 1914).

Vinacke, Harold M., *A History of the Far East in Modern Times,* 5th Ed. (New York: Appleton-Century-Crofts, 1950).

Vinogradoff, Sir Paul, *Custom and Right* (Oslo: Aschehoug & Co., 1925).

—, "English Society in the 11th Century," *Cambridge Medieval History.*

de Visscher, Charles, *Theory and Reality in Public International Law* Tr. by P. E. Corbett (Princeton: Princeton University Press, 1957).

Voltaire, *A Philosophical Dictionary,* Tr., vol. V, (London: J. and H. L. Hunt, 1824).

von Martens, G. F., *A compendium of the Law of Nations,* Tr. William Cobbett (London: Cobbett and Morgan, 1802).

Waldock, C. H. M., "The Anglo-Norwegian Fisheries Case," 28 *British Yearbook of International Law* (1951), pp. 114–171.

Walker, Thomas A., *A History of the Law of Nations,* Vol. I, *From the Earliest Times to the Peace of Westphalia* (Cambridge: University Press, 1899).

Walker, Wynham L., "Territorial Waters: The Cannon Shot Rule," 22 *British Yearbook of International Law* (1945) pp. 210–231.

Washington Center of Foreign Policy Research, The Johns Hopkins University, *Developments in Military Technology and their Impact on United States Strategy and Foreign Policy* (Washington: U.S. Government Printing Offices, 1959).

Weber, Max, "Capitalism and Rural Society in Germany," *Max Weber's Essays in Sociology,* Tr. H. H. Gerth and C. Wright Mills (New York: Oxford University Press, 1946).

Wentworth, COMO Ralph S., U.S. Navy (Ret.) and Noel, CDR John V., Jr., U.S. Navy, *Knight's Modern Seamanship,* 12th Ed., (New York: Van Nostrand, 1953).

Wertheim, Barbara, "The Russo-Japanese Fisheries Controversy" VIII *Pacific Affairs 1935,* pp. 185–198.

Westlake, John, *International Law,* Part I, 2nd Ed., (Cambridge, University Press, 1910).

Wheaton, Henry, *History of the Law of Nations in Europe and America* (New York: Gould, Banks & Co., 1845).
White, ENS J. F., Jr., USN., "Admiral Sir Percy Scott and British Naval Gunnery," 75 *U.S. Naval Institute Proceedings* (April 1949), pp. 449–455.
White, Morton, *The Age of Analysis* (New York: Mentor Banks, 1955).
Whiteman, Marjorie M., "The Territorial Sea," *Proceedings of the American Society of International Law 1956*, pp. 125–135.
Whittlesey, Derwent, *The Earth and the State* (Washington: War Department Education Manual EM234 (reprint), (1944).
Wilberforce, R. O., "Some Aspects of the Anglo-Norwegian Fisheries Case" 38 *Transactions of the Grotius Society*.
Williams, Mary W., *The People and Politics of Latin America*, (Washington: U.S. Armed Forces Institute, 1943).
Williamson, James A., *The Voyages of the Cabots and the English Discovery of North America under Henry VII and Henry VIII* (London: The Argonaut Press, 1929).
Wilson, LT Andrew W., RN, *The Story of the Gun* (London: W. Kimber, 1944).
Wilson, George G., "Les Eaux adjacentes des Etats," I *Recueil des Cours de l'Académie de droit international de la Haye* (1923), pp. 127–175.
Woerkof, A., La Géographie de l'Alimentation humaine," XX *La Géographie* (1909), pp. 224–286.
Woytinsky, W. S. and Woytinsky, F. S., *World Population and Production* (New York: Twentieth Century Fund, 1953).
Wright, George F., *Asiatic Russia*, (New York: McClure Phillips, 1901).
Wright, Quincy, *The Study of International Relations* (New York: Appleton, Century Crofts, 1955).
Wu, Aitchen K., *China and the Soviet Union* (New York: The John Day Co., 1950).
Wylie, CAPT F. J., R.N. (Ret.), *The Use of Radar at Sea*, foreword by Sir Robert Watson-Watt (New York: Van Nostrand, 1953).
—, "The Future of Marine Electronics – the International Viewpoint, "Paper presented at New York Meeting of Radio Technical for Marine Service, 25 October 1956.
—, "Automation in Marine Navigation," XII *The Journal of the Institute of Navigation* (April 1959), pp. 163–183.
Yakhontoff, Victor A., *Russia and the Soviet Union in the Far East* (New York: McCann, 1931).
Zepelin, MGEN Constantin von, IGA, *Der Ferne Osten* (Berlin, Verlag von Zuckschwerdt & Co., 1911).

MARTINUS NIJHOFF — PUBLISHER — THE HAGUE

The recent era has seen a strong surge on the part of a large number of states to increase the breadth of their legal jurisdiction over the seas bordering their coasts. Ordinarily the outer limits of such marginal seas follow the natural curvatures of the coast lines. Where such a curvature forms a noticeable indentation in the coast line, it may be argued that a bay exists. If the argument is well founded in International Law, the area of coastal sea coming into national jurisdiction may be very substantially increased. Bay boundaries have been the subject of clashing interests over a long period. It has been a task in International Law to formulate generally inclusive rules for the establishment of such boundaries. A further task has been to provide some rationale for the inevitable exceptions to such rules. The exceptions have come to be called "historic bays".

In his book the author has examined the history of the several interests that have influenced the development of rules on bays. He demonstrates the practical effects of such rules upon the mariners who must ultimately abide by them. He traces the efforts at codification of the rules, and finally he suggests a further refinement of the rules.

After examining the formulation of general rules on bays, the author analyzes the position of the exception, the "historic bay". In so doing, he singles out Hudson Bay and Peter the Great Bay for detailed study. He then proceeds to discuss the bay whose shores belong to two or more states, a situation which introduces some operating factors rather different from those observed in the bay whose littoral is entirely within one country.

The author does not suggest an ideal codification designed to operate under the all-encompassing collective will of some form of international government. He proposes no more than a set of rules which he believes offer some measure of improvement in the present era.

About the author: Born 13 July 1920 in Allentown, Pennsylvania. Education: The Citadel (1938-39); U.S. Naval Academy (B.S., 1942); U.S. Naval War College (1953); Boston University (M.A., 1958); Fletcher School of Law and Diplomacy (M.A., 1959; M.A.L.D., 1959; Ph. D., 1960).

1963. VIII and 426 pages. With 25 figs. roy. 8vo.

Cloth Guilders 45.—

GPSR Compliance

The European Union's (EU) General Product Safety Regulation (GPSR) is a set of rules that requires consumer products to be safe and our obligations to ensure this.

If you have any concerns about our products, you can contact us on ProductSafety@springernature.com

In case Publisher is established outside the EU, the EU authorized representative is:

Springer Nature Customer Service Center GmbH
Europaplatz 3
69115 Heidelberg, Germany

Batch number: 10830943

Printed by Printforce, the Netherlands